ALSO BY JAY WINIK

April 1865: The Month That Saved America

The Great Upheaval: America and the Birth of the Modern World, 1788–1800

1944

FDR AND THE YEAR THAT CHANGED HISTORY

JAY WINIK

SIMON & SCHUSTER

NEW YORK LONDON TORONTO SYDNEY NEW DELHI

Simon & Schuster
1230 Avenue of the Americas
New York, NY 10020

First Simon & Schuster hardcover edition September 2015

Interior design by Ruth Lee-Mui

Manufactured in the United States of America

1 3 5 7 9 10 8 6 4 2

Library of Congress Cataloging-in-Publication Data
Winik, Jay, 1957–
1944: FDR and the year that changed history / Jay Winik.—
First Simon & Schuster hardcover edition.
pages cm
Includes bibliographical references and index.
1. World War, 1939–1945—United States. 2. Roosevelt, Franklin D.
(Franklin Delano), 1882–1945—Influence. 3. Political leadership—
United States—History—20th century. 4. Holocaust, Jewish (1939–1945).
I. Title. II. Title: FDR and the year that changed history.
D769.W57 2015
940.53'73—dc23 2015013912

ISBN 978-1-4391-1408-7
ISBN 978-1-4391-3647-8 (ebook)

Frontispiece: Roosevelt at Casablanca.

To Nathaniel and Evan "BC"
My treasures—and the future

CONTENTS

Part Three
THE FATEFUL DECISION

Part Four
1945

ILLUSTRATION CREDITS

INTERIOR

p. iv: Courtesy of the Franklin D. Roosevelt Presidential Library

p. xiv: Courtesy of the Franklin D. Roosevelt Presidential Library

p. 13: Courtesy of the Eisenhower Presidential Library

p. 77: Courtesy of American Heritage

p. 79: Courtesy of American Heritage

p. 207: Courtesy of the United States Holocaust Memorial Museum

p. 250: Courtesy of American Heritage

p. 336: Courtesy of American Heritage

p. 356: Courtesy of American Heritage

p. 431: Courtesy of the United States Holocaust Memorial Museum

p. 493: Courtesy of American Heritage

p. 501: Courtesy of American Heritage

p. 505: Courtesy of the United States Holocaust Memorial Museum

PHOTO INSERT

1. Courtesy of the United States Holocaust Memorial Museum
2. Courtesy of the United States Holocaust Memorial Museum
3. Courtesy of the United States Holocaust Memorial Museum
4. Courtesy of the United States Holocaust Memorial Museum
5. Courtesy of the United States Holocaust Memorial Museum
6. Courtesy of the United States Holocaust Memorial Museum
7. Courtesy of the United States Holocaust Memorial Museum
8. Courtesy of the United States Holocaust Memorial Museum
9. Courtesy of the United States Holocaust Memorial Museum
10. Courtesy of the United States Holocaust Memorial Museum
11. Courtesy of the United States Holocaust Memorial Museum
12. Courtesy of the United States Holocaust Memorial Museum
13. Courtesy of the United States Holocaust Memorial Museum
14. Courtesy of the United States Holocaust Memorial Museum
15. Courtesy of the Franklin D. Roosevelt Presidential Library
16. Courtesy of the Franklin D. Roosevelt Presidential Library
17. Courtesy of the Dwight D. Eisenhower Presidential Library
18. Courtesy of the Dwight D. Eisenhower Presidential Library
19. Courtesy of the Dwight D. Eisenhower Presidential Library
20. Courtesy of the Dwight D. Eisenhower Presidential Library
21. Courtesy of the Dwight D. Eisenhower Presidential Library

22. Courtesy of the Dwight D. Eisenhower Presidential Library

23. Courtesy of the Franklin D. Roosevelt Presidential Library

24. Courtesy of the Dwight D. Eisenhower Presidential Library

25. Courtesy of the Dwight D. Eisenhower Presidential Library

26. Courtesy of the Franklin D. Roosevelt Presidential Library

At the Cairo conference en route to Tehran, Franklin Delano Roosevelt and Winston Churchill view the Pyramids and the Sphinx. As it turned out, Roosevelt was often as inscrutable in 1944 as the Sphinx itself.

PRELUDE

The Sphinx

November 22–23, 1943

STRETCHING TO THE HORIZON, it was among the most serene and sublime plots of land on the face of the earth. As the last cliff bordering the Sahara desert, it was also one of the most dangerous. During the summer, the sun-soaked grounds around the Sphinx shimmered and swelled, while the temperature perilously rose to above 110 degrees. Unknowing travelers grew disoriented, having never before encountered such pitiless heat, such enervating thirst, such relentless quiet, or such a trackless desert. So blazing was the light, reflected up from the sand, that the eye could not bear its dazzling glare. Even the weather itself played odd tricks with space and time. Then in late March came the dreaded khamsin, a torrential storm of great winds and grainy dust that often rendered the Giza plateau nearly uninhabitable for as long as fifty days. Over the years, whole flocks of sheep had been consumed in these hellacious blizzards, as had countless people, simply swallowed by the sand. For a millennium, the Sphinx itself, one of the world's oldest and most storied of monuments, had lain hidden beneath a mountain of shifting desert.

Here, under the vast blue skies, was one of the most intriguing intersections of cultures ever recorded, marrying the allure of antiquity with the romance of history. The pharaohs had once walked these lands; so had Queen Cleopatra and mighty Caesar. Ancient Roman senators in flowing white robes were showered with an abundance of gold, silver, and numerous other riches, while in later centuries, holy men supplicated themselves in prayer and crowds lined the Nile to cheer for their leaders or marvel at their conquerors. Spreading out around the Nile's banks, medieval Cairo was one of the largest cities in the world. It became a trophy for the Arab caliphate and later a dominion for the Ottoman sultans. Napoleon, too, came here, seeking to subjugate this magical, mystical region, but ultimately to no avail. Like so many other empires, this one, stretching over the desert and along the riverbanks, had ebbed and flowed, and eventually it largely faded away. Even the digging of the Suez Canal was not enough to completely reverse Egypt's fortunes. In the twentieth century, it remained a pawn of larger powers: this time, a strategic prize in the global tussle between England and France.

Yet if the glory of the Egyptian empire had long since disappeared, in the wartime fall of 1943, its breathtaking mystery had not. It was still a land of color, of dazzling sunsets and gorgeous tropical gardens, of golden fields and a profusion of flowers. Palm trees swayed in the wind; donkeys hauled carts and packs. Mosques and minarets were filled with believers, and bustling streets were a hodgepodge of coffee kiosks and sumptuous spice bazaars, buzzing with the short peals of commerce and talk of politics. Cairo itself was a densely packed warren, alive with the sights of snake charmers and fakirs, not to mention the overwhelming scent of communal Egypt. And in its environs, the past was always present.

To the southwest, the fabled Pyramids rose like ancient skyscrapers or man-made mountains that ruled the horizon. For centuries, Muslims, Christians, and Jews had forgotten the history of these massive stone peaks, and had instead largely settled on one common explanation:

these were the ancient granaries of the biblical patriarch Joseph. But not everyone agreed. More than one ruler believed that the Pyramids covered stores of ancient gold. Once, a caliph from Baghdad had commanded his forces to attack the Great Pyramid. Another time, a ruler issued a decree to demolish the Pyramids. Drillers and stonecutters spent eight months laboring to remove one or two of the mammoth stones each day, but then, simply gave up, remaining, as one chronicler wrote, very "far from accomplishing what they had set out to do." So the Pyramids were largely left alone, but not so the Sphinx. When the Ottomans bequeathed their Egyptian empire to the care of the Mamelukes, these ruling custodians used its venerable face for target practice.

Ironically, when the Pyramids were opened in the nineteenth century, it was primarily western adventurers who made off with the remaining spoils. Statues, mummies, paintings, and ancient stones were crated and bundled out of Egyptian ports, bound for the capitals of Europe. By the time a young Winston Churchill arrived to paint the Pyramids, their secrets had been largely unlocked and their treasures were displayed at the British Museum.

Only the harsh terrain of shifting sands and the vast sky remained constant in this part of the world. At night, the huge stars shone brightly as they had for millennia. According to legend, the Milky Way glimmering overhead had been crafted to form "the river Nile in the sky." Ancient priests believed it contained signposts to help the dead pharaohs navigate their way to the afterlife.

But in 1943, to look up and see this pathway of stars was perhaps to be reminded not of the ancient legend but of something else altogether. With World War II raging, the pathways to the afterlife were crowded. At a rate of one every three seconds, another human life on earth was being snuffed out.

In Cairo, meanwhile, westerners had arrived en masse once more.

Just over a year before, German forces under General Erwin Rommel had reached El Alamein, 150 miles from Cairo, from where they planned to capture the Suez Canal and move north through British Palestine, until they could link up with Nazi forces heading south from the Soviet Union. Instead, in a brutal battle, England's General Bernard Montgomery had forced them to retreat to the relative safety of Libya and Tunisia. It was the Allies' first major victory over the Germans, and the first turning point of the war. Now the war had come to Egypt again.

This afternoon, it came with a terrific roar: a caravan of dark cars, winding its way to the Pyramids and the Sphinx. Inside were the key leaders of the Allied war effort: admirals, generals, doctors, and the two men in whose hands lay the fate of western democracy—Winston Churchill and Franklin Roosevelt.

It was November 23, and a cool wind was blowing over the faint ripples in the sand. Taking a break from their Cairo summit—for the Allies, this was to be the first of three separate rounds of discussions, and among the most important of the war—the leaders of the United States and Great Britain were sightseeing. The trip was Churchill's idea. His eyes flashing, his husky voice filled with warmth and humor—he was suffering from a cold—he was seized with his customary enthusiasm. When the prime minister had first proposed the idea earlier in the day over tea at the president's villa, Roosevelt was so taken by it that he tried to rise out of his chair—a rare lapse—only to painfully realize as he gripped the handles and his knuckles whitened that he couldn't. "Mr. President," an insistent Churchill boomed, "you simply must come and see the Sphinx and Pyramids. I've arranged it all."

They drove over at sunset, as the temperature dropped and the night shadows lengthened. To the east were the three Pyramids on the plateau, and to the west was a royal cemetery containing over four thousand mummies. A local guide was procured at the last moment to help them find their way around. But it was the riddle of the Sphinx, with its body of a lion and the head of a king, that most captivated Roosevelt and Churchill. Modern Egyptians had dubbed the Sphinx *Abu al-Hol*, or "Father of Terror," but to those who built it, the Sphinx was an enduring symbol of good, embodying humor and awe. Now, examining the Sphinx from "every angle," the two men pondered its inscrutable smile, its missing nose, and its mysterious eagle-shaped wings. Their eyes turned to follow its confident gaze over the desolate Giza plain and far beyond. Churchill wondered to himself: what did she have to say?

As the sun dipped behind the Pyramids, Roosevelt and Churchill, normally the wittiest of conversationalists, fell strangely quiet. Coptic monks had once called this stirring plateau wind the "voice of eternity." It was as though, in the midst of this terrible war, far away from the killing fields of Europe, North Africa, and the Pacific, Roosevelt and Churchill had found a place of respite, a place suspended in time. And fittingly, they had done it together.

As the minutes passed, the sky was bathed in a comforting afterglow, a thin pink line pulled across the horizon, signaling the end of this day and the slow arrival of the next. Looking over at Roosevelt, Churchill was jubilant. With tears in his eyes, he announced softly, "I love that man."

But the ever-charming Roosevelt, squinting in the fading light, gave nothing away. He was in many ways as inscrutable as the Sphinx; at his core, he remained shrouded, unknowable, dispassionate. Fittingly, history would call this summit the "Sphinx Conference." And when it was over, in the days and months that followed, Roosevelt would make some of the most profound and painful decisions of the entire war.

THAT SAME LATE-NOVEMBER SUN was also setting over Adolf Hitler's *Festung Europa*. As dusk approached, at air bases in England some six hundred miles northeast of Berlin, there began a distant, deep hum in the sky. For hours, planes lined up and wave after wave of Allied aircraft took off. The voices of hundreds of pilots crackled over their interphones, while hundreds more airmen positioned themselves in their cockpits and checked their tachometers. Some crewmembers hastily reviewed crash procedures, while others examined maps. Ground crews stood outside and looked up at the semidark sky, marveling at how many planes there were. Tonight's raid was a follow-up of the previous evening, when eventually 764 had converged in the air, flying tightly in formation.

As the planes rose aloft, clouds pressed around them—an armada of 469 Lancaster heavy bombers, 234 Halifaxes, and 50 Stirlings, all escorted by a jewel of the RAF, 11 stunningly fast Mosquitos, made almost entirely of lightweight wood. After crossing the English Channel, they flew low to evade German radar. Within thirty minutes they had sliced across the upper regions of the Netherlands before going over the terraced plateaus of the Harz Mountains on their way deep into German airspace. They already knew what awaited them. November 22–23 had been the second mission and the fourth night of the Battle of Berlin, a concerted air campaign of sixteen raids against the nerve center of the Nazi state. In conjunction with the evening before, these would soon prove to be the most devastating raids of the war on the German capital.

Berlin itself was like an impenetrable fortress, the most heavily defended city in the Third Reich. It had a state-of-the-art network of air defenses, including three concrete flak towers—the deadly flak burst into razor-sharp shrapnel that shredded planes open, cutting through their aluminum underbellies like a hot knife through butter. Berlin also had a ring of highly accurate 88-millimeter guns, and a command center located in, of all places, the zoo. Searchlights combed the skies around the capital, and noisy smoke generators sent up foul, billowing puffs to obscure the city during times of attack. There was even camouflage netting strung between buildings, making it difficult for pilots, gunners, and bombardiers to identify individual streets.

Yet any calm that the German people may have felt within these meticulous defenses had been rudely shattered since July, when the city of Hamburg had been hit by a series of concentrated American and British raids. An ensuing firestorm had raced through the ancient Hanseatic port, Hitler's gateway to the world, where most of the homes were made of timber. The fire soon became insatiable. The flames scaled walls and rooftops, and quickly spread block by block, consuming everything in their path. One woman reported that entire districts had been "engulfed in a sea of flames"; she did not overstate. Within four days the Allies had killed some forty-three thousand civilians and half of Hamburg had been laid waste. The result was chaos. Traumatized refugees were sent through Berlin to the relative safety of the east. It was a futile gesture. Soon Berliners themselves were desperate to get out of the city before the Allied bombers arrived.

On November 18, the bombers had appeared with a vengeance.

This time the Allied forces, in a convoy stretching miles across the sky, prepared to concentrate their attacks in the western districts of the city. Passing south of the northern European plains, they swung northeast across the forests along the Elbe. When they were fifty miles away from Berlin, the bombers, as usual, observed radio silence to preserve the element of surprise, and quietly began picking their targets. Flying at an altitude of ten thousand feet, where the oxygen noticeably thinned and the air became icy, the Lancasters approached the city's outskirts, preparing to drop seven thousand pounds of bombs. The bomb bays were opened; there was a high-pitched whistle as the missiles fell, then a series of thunderous booms as they hit their targets, followed by a cascade of mushroom clouds spiking up into the sky. As one bombardier later jubilantly recounted, he cheered when his plane released its explosive cargo. "This," he noted, "was Hitler's town!"

On the ground below, the city itself shook. All across the capital, walls began to crack and break. Streets were abruptly filled with flying bricks and broken glass. The air was split with the sounds of doors being ripped off their hinges, windows shattering, and whole structures collapsing, crushed like paper bags. Above, the flashes from the explosions were so intense that the cockpits of the bombers were filled with a vivid, almost blinding yellow-orange light, as if the pilots were flying directly into the sun. Then, just as rapidly, they were plunged back into darkness. As the antiaircraft defenses launched their counterattacks, the Allied pilots had to fly through enemy artillery fire, ubiquitous flak, explosions from the ground, and dense black smoke. Each minute that the raid continued, Allied losses escalated. A number of crewmembers, including pilots, were hit by flak or by German machine-gun fire, or were disabled by frostbite—some had urinated in their jumpsuits during the stress of combat, and at the high altitudes in unheated cockpits the liquid froze. Eventually, the German flak crisscrossing the sky seemed thick enough to walk on; with nowhere to escape, some planes simply became balls of fire.

But in the city beneath, Berliners were stunned by the sheer vehemence of the raids. On many streets, the fires were so bright that one could have mistaken night for day. As the bluish smoke curled upward from the windows of stricken buildings, people began to fear that they would be buried alive or killed by the falling bombs, and to wonder if their corpses would even be recovered. Those who could do so hastily made their way to the public bunkers. Many, however, couldn't. With sirens wailing and the sky lit up with showers of antiaircraft fire, people began to scramble for safety, and in their desperation they were soon pushing and shoving and trampling one another to death.

For the Berliners, there would be no respite. The planes kept coming; the raids and the ensuing carnage lasted for hours. Residents could hear the ominous forward march of aircraft and bombs as the explosions crossed the city, each seeming a bit louder, a bit closer, and a bit more intense than the one before. "Everywhere it is still burning," one Berliner wrote in desperation. "Ruins are constantly collapsing." The inferno was indiscriminate. Even the Nazi propagandist Joseph Goebbels confessed, "What I saw was truly shattering." Terrified residents staggered through the streets, faces wrapped in scarves, coughing as they wound their way through collapsed walls and shattered glass and clouds of dust. Everywhere, there were mounds of smoking rubble, leaking water pipes, and wrecked trams. Everywhere, the atmosphere was thick with heated air and the odor of smoke and charred brick.

Everywhere, the Allied planes were overhead.

Entire streets ceased to exist. The diplomatic quarter was burned out. The railway stations were badly hit. So were the arsenal and the Academy of Music. The whole Tiergarten quarter, with its elegant mansions, a 630-acre park, and the German War Ministry, was destroyed. As the smoke rose skyward, the list of devastated targets included the State

Opera, the German Theater, the National Gallery, the Hotel Bristol, the Charity Hospital, the City Hospital, the Maternity Hospital, and the historic Kaiser Wilhelm Memorial Church. It also included the Iranian, Italian, French, and Slovak embassies, and the Potsdam train station. Most humiliating of all to the Germans was the fact that the Ministry of Weapons and Munitions was severely damaged, as were the Waffen SS administrative college and the barracks of the Imperial Guard. Some residents watched in dumb horror as others hysterically pushed and shoved and squeezed themselves into the bunker inside the zoo. Meanwhile, at the S-Bahn, more people were screaming on the railway platforms or inside the trains or simply wandering aimlessly in shock. It was the suburbs, however, that were hit worst. They lost electricity and telephone service. And there were the ghastly sights of people being buried alive, and of charred, crackling bodies, shrunken to the size of small children, and of corpses littering the roads.

"The streets," one Gestapo officer observed, "look like a battlefield." Even the famed zoo was left in ruins.

The bombing became an ongoing torture for those on the ground, a maddening chorus of nighttime explosions matched only by the crackling of the fires. All the while, a strange "rain" began to fall, glinting bits of aluminum foil drifting slowly to the streets from the sky. The Allies were dropping it to confuse German radar. Even the shelters did not always provide a safe haven. One horrified young resident watched as the ceiling of his bunker began to shake, swaying and tottering in slow motion for some minutes, until it collapsed. He was one of only a few people brought out alive from the ruins.

The explosions continued to thunder across the city, often in series of eights, and the Berliners came to realize that each plane's bomb cradle carried eight explosives. And as the Allied planes turned westward for the journey home, their crews could see the fiery red glow from Berlin for a full twenty minutes in the sky.

When the sun rose the next morning, the sights were devastating. People could hardly breathe, because of the clouds of smoke rising from still-burning houses. Terrified residents stumbled through the streets, tripping over fragments and debris. "Everywhere," one diarist grimly noted, "glass fragments crunched beneath our feet." The wreckage of hundreds of thousands of lives was now revealed in vivid details: in smashed chandeliers, in the remains of vases and crystal bowls, and in piles of crushed porcelain. Meanwhile, the fires continued to burn, and the sky itself had turned a dirty yellow. Surveying the smoking remains, Goebbels said, "You see nothing but remnants of walls and debris."

By the week's end, life in Berlin had become a hell on earth; nearly half a million Germans had been left homeless, and some ten thousand were injured. The dead were laid out in school halls and gymnasiums, awaiting identification. Almost four thousand had been killed in that one week alone. Still, Hitler's staunchest patriots were undeterred; throughout their city, the Nazi faithful planted little flags and swastikas on top of the rubble.

But for the millions of subjects in an occupied Europe now tormented by the ruthless Nazi regime, the Allied bombing of the Reich capital gave them a chance to hope. Among ordinary Germans, it did something else: it profoundly shattered their faith in the ability of the state to protect them. Hermann Göring, Hitler's designated successor and at one time the Luftwaffe commander, had pledged that not a single enemy bomb would drop on the sacred soil of the German capital; but as an American general had boasted, "In sixty seconds, the cumulative effort of 100 years can be destroyed." With a sense of foreboding, one Berliner summed up the mood of the city after the relentless air offensive: "We are," he muttered, "at the mercy of our enemies."

As the Allied planes returned to the relative safety of British airspace, this, of course, was precisely what Roosevelt and Churchill had in mind.

~

YET THERE WERE STILL those whom the bombers had not yet reached, however desperately they awaited and pleaded for their arrival.

Longingly they looked up into the skies and wondered: when will the Allies come?

~

FAR AWAY FROM THE battlefields and from the diplomacy at Cairo, just one day before the Allies launched their air assault on Berlin, more than five hundred Dutch citizens shuffled past a small grove of now barren fruit trees, and made their way down a ramp toward a room encased by earthen mounds. A few were sobbing, but mostly there were only the sounds of low murmurs, of feet wearily plodding forward. Small children were hoisted on hips or gripped by the hand of an older child. The aged and the infirm moved slowly, their bones already bent more closely toward the ground. As they walked, nearly 165 Poles joined them. Most were scared, but exactly of what, few were sure.

The room that awaited them was uncommonly cold. The heavy doors slammed shut behind them.

On the scrubbed walls were signs of faint scratches.

A young Polish woman began to shout: "The German nation shall . . . dearly pay for our blood. Down with savagery in the guise of Hitler's Germany!" Almost simultaneously, the Poles knelt on the ground, clasped their hands, and began to pray. Then came another sound, of singing. It was *Hatikvah* ("The Hope"), the informal national anthem of the Jewish people—"Our hope is not yet lost / to be a free people in our land," sung by the Dutch. Then the Poles joined them, matching chorus with chorus. "Poland is not yet lost," they sang, the words of their own national anthem. Hundreds of voices swelled inside that single room: "Then our hope . . . will not be lost."

Just beyond the walls, there was the rumble of vans arriving. They were marked with the symbol of the Red Cross, the universal sign of help for the sick, the injured, the displaced, and the dispossessed. But it was not to be. As children shivered—there were 166 of them now locked in the room, stripped naked—the singing reached a crescendo of emotion. Standing on the hard ground outside, guards hurriedly began unloading the tins from the Red Cross vans. At the same time, SS men calmly flipped open a peephole.

There was a clink on the roof above.

The gas started to flow downward, and the screaming began.

THIS WAS THE WESTERN world at war in 1943 on the precipice of 1944, the year that would change history. It was the world that Franklin Roosevelt and the Allies were trying to save when the three great powers—America, the Soviet Union, and Britain—were about to gather for the first time over three and a half tense days at Tehran.

Part One

Spring 1944
Everything All at Once

After the success of D-Day, General Dwight D. Eisenhower, the Supreme Allied Commander, observes air activity from the deck of a warship on his way to Normandy from southern England on June 7, 1944. President Roosevelt chose him to command Operation Overlord because he was "a natural leader."

1

Tehran

FRANKLIN ROOSEVELT HAD NEVER wanted to travel to Tehran. Throughout the fall of 1943, the president used his vaunted charm and charisma to push for the three Allied leaders—himself, Winston Churchill, and Joseph Stalin—to meet almost anywhere else. The conference, their first ever, had been a year in the making, and now, before it even commenced, it seemed on the brink of failure over the thorny question of where it would take place.

Dispatched on a visit to Moscow, Secretary of State Cordell Hull had proposed the Iraqi port city of Basra, to which Roosevelt could easily travel by ship. Roosevelt himself suggested Cairo, Baghdad, or Asmara, Italy's former Eritrean capital on Africa's east coast; all these were locations, the president pointed out, where he could easily remain in constant contact with Washington, D.C. as was necessary for his wartime stewardship. But the Soviet leader, Joseph Stalin, was unmoved. He countered that as commander of the Soviet armed forces *he* could not be out of contact with his deputies in Moscow. He maintained that Tehran, at the foot of the Elburz Mountains, had telegraph and telephone links with Moscow. "My colleagues insist on Teheran," he bluntly cabled to Roosevelt in reply, adding that he would however accept a late-November date for the meeting and that he also agreed with the American and British decision to exclude all members of the press.

Roosevelt, still hoping to sway the man he referred to as "Uncle Joe," cabled again about Basra, saying, "I am begging you to remember that I also have a great obligation to the American government and to maintain the full American war effort." The answer from Moscow was brief and direct: no. Stalin was adamant, and he now hinted that he might back out of the entire arrangement for a tripartite conference. Not until Roosevelt was preparing to set sail across the Atlantic en route to the Mediterranean did Stalin, having gotten his way on Tehran, finally acquiesce. Roosevelt promptly cabled to Winston Churchill, "I have just heard that Uncle J will come to Teheran. . . . I was in some doubt as to whether he would go through with his former offer . . . but I think that now there is no question that you and I can meet him."

So it was that at the Cairo West Airport a little past 6:30 a.m. on Saturday, November 27, Roosevelt boarded the *Sacred Cow*, a gleaming silver Douglas C54 Skymaster that could carry forty-nine passengers and a three-man crew, for the final leg of his momentous journey; in total, he would travel 17,442 miles, crossing and recrossing nearly eight time zones. For his part, Joseph Stalin simply had to travel due south from Moscow; his round-trip would be only 3,000 miles. But all this seemed forgotten as, for the first time in over four years of war, the leaders of the three great powers were at last to meet, face-to-face, to establish policies designed to bring the carnage to a close. This would be the most important conference of the conflict. As Churchill later wrote, "The difficulties of the American Constitution, Roosevelt's health, and Stalin's obduracy . . . were all swept away by the inexorable need of a triple meeting and the failure of every other alternative but a flight to Tehran. So we sailed off into the air from Cairo at the crack of dawn."

It is difficult, in retrospect, to appreciate the magnitude of this trip, or even how bold it was. The wheelchair-bound president of the United States was flying across the Middle East in wartime, unaccompanied by military aircraft and not even in his own plane. The first official presidential airplane, nicknamed *Guess Where II*, was nothing more than a reconfigured B24 bomber, designated a C87A Liberator; and in any case Roosevelt never used it. After another C87A crashed and the design was found to have an alarming risk of fire—which Roosevelt dreaded—*Guess Where II* was quietly pulled from the presidential service. Eleanor Roosevelt took the plane on a goodwill tour of Latin America, and the senior White House staff flew on it, but not the president.

Furthermore, Franklin Roosevelt hated to fly.

The paraplegic president preferred almost any mode of travel on solid ground, but even here, he had qualms: for one thing, he could not bear to ride in a train that traveled faster than thirty miles an hour. His presidential train made him feel especially secure: it had a special suspension to support his lower body, its walls were armored, and the glass was bulletproof. An accomplished sailor, he also felt comfortable on the water, where he could master the pitch and swell of the waves. But flying was an entirely different matter, and one not without considerable personal risk. Even simple turbulence was problematic because the president "could never brace himself against the bumps and jolts with his legs as we could," recalled Mike Reilly, head of Roosevelt's Secret Service detail. And Roosevelt knew better than anyone else how he was limited by his useless legs—he would have no chance of crawling away from even a minor plane wreck.

Before the Cairo-to-Tehran flight, Roosevelt had made only two other airplane journeys. One was a 1932 flight to Chicago to accept the Democratic nomination for the presidency, during which all the passengers except Roosevelt and his grown son, Elliott, succumbed to airsickness. Before takeoff, mechanics had helpfully removed one of the seats to provide more room, but none of the passengers had seatbelts, so they had to cling to the upholstered arms of their aluminum chairs or risk being tossed about when the plane hit turbulence. The interior noise from the engines was deafening, and the plane's top speed was just over a hundred miles per hour. Two military aircraft providing an escort as well as a chartered plane carrying reporters turned back in the face of thunderstorms and heavy headwinds, while the plane carrying Roosevelt soldiered on. Then, in January 1943, Roosevelt again took to the skies to meet with Churchill in Casablanca. His party of eight departed from Miami in a forty-passenger plane, the *Dixie Clipper*, which leapfrogged south across the Caribbean to Brazil and then spent nineteen hours making the 2,500-mile Atlantic crossing from South America to West Africa. The clipper planes, although they had spacious cabins and sleeping quarters including a double bed for Roosevelt, were unpressurized, and at the higher altitudes the president would turn pale, sometimes needing to inhale supplemental oxygen. Indeed, the flight to Casablanca, the first airplane trip by an incumbent president, did not make him any more of a convert to flying. As Roosevelt wrote to his wife, Eleanor, who was by contrast an enthusiastic flier, "You can have your clouds. They bore me."

But here he was, only ten months later, aloft again, this time in the *Sacred Cow.*

The 1,300-mile journey that morning took Roosevelt east, roaring through the brilliant sunshine across the Suez Canal and the vast expanses of the Sinai desert; the pilot then dipped down to circle low over the holy cities of Jerusalem and Bethlehem, glistening in the morning's rays. Next, the plane soared over chains of ancient wadis, followed by the hallowed ground of Masada, the rugged fortress in the Judaean hills where a small band of Jews chose death rather than slavery, outlasting an entire Roman legion for nearly three months in the spring of A.D. 73. When the plane reached Baghdad, it turned northeast, where the pilot raced along the Abadan–Tehran highway, guiding the plane through a tricky series of jagged mountain passes. There was no alternative: the plane needed to stay below six thousand feet to keep the oxygen level stable for the president. As Roosevelt peered out the plane's window, the land below was a chain of mountains rising from a rocky desert, resembling a brown, faded moonscape. It was isolated and empty, except for the exhilarating sight of trains and truck convoys loaded with American-made war matériel, all headed north to the eastern front.

SIX AND A HALF hours later, the president's plane landed at 3 p.m. at a Red Army airfield in Tehran. Stalin was already waiting. He had arrived in the city twenty-four hours before the British and the Americans and was ensconced at the Russian legation, where he had personally overseen the bugging of a suite of private rooms where the American president would eventually stay.

"Shabby" was how Elliott Roosevelt, the president's son, described Tehran in late November 1943. The Iranian capital was almost literally a cesspool. Except at the American, Soviet, and British legations, running water was practically nonexistent. Residents and visitors alike scooped their drinking water from a stream that ran along the street gutter, the same stream that also served as the city's sewage disposal system. Downtown, much of the public drinking water was contaminated with refuse and offal; each sip risked typhus or dysentery, and outbreaks of typhoid fever were common. The city was unappealing in other ways as well. It was occupied by Allied forces, and even the most basic goods were in short supply; a year's salary might be spent on a sack of flour.

Nor was the city a glamorous place, able to recall a storied past. Among world capitals, Tehran was—surprisingly—almost as much of a newcomer as the young Washington, D.C., had been at its inception, when it was little more than a charming semirural landscape derided as a city of "magnificent distances." By contrast, in 1800, Tehran's total population of about twenty thousand had lived inside twenty-foot-high mud walls, which were bounded by a forty-foot-wide moat as deep as thirty feet.

The entire city itself was accessible by a total of four gates. By 1943, the gates had been pulled down, and a newer city had sprung up beyond the original walls. Gone were many of the quaint old houses that had faced an intricate series of elaborate courtyards and fabled Persian gardens; gone were the donkey carts laden with dates and figs and honey and henna en route to the bustling markets. Instead, newer homes looked outward toward wide main streets designed to accommodate automobiles, trucks, and the occasional horse or wheelbarrow. And beyond its modern boulevards, the city emptied out into a vast, barren space with little more than grazing land and oil fields.

The drive from the airfield to downtown Tehran was far from tranquil. The route took the leaders and the accompanying aides through long stretches of curious onlookers and many miles of unprotected road. Before arriving forty-five minutes after the Americans, Winston Churchill, like Roosevelt before him, had endured a potentially deadly journey not unlike that of Archduke Franz Ferdinand in 1914 through the streets of Sarajevo. Churchill's daughter, Sarah, who was with him, thought the drive "spine-chilling." The roads were rough, the crowds were ubiquitous, and there was only the barest security. Churchill himself drily remarked, "If it had been planned out beforehand to run the greatest risks . . . the problem could not have been solved more perfectly." The prime minister and his daughter were traveling in an unsecured car, while their British security detail followed in a closed jeep, too far behind to be of much use should trouble arise.

The route into the city was lined with magnificent white horses of the Persian cavalry—in Tehran itself, crowds four or five people deep thronged in between the gleaming animals. Meanwhile, the Allied security details constantly feared a well-lobbed grenade or a pistol shot, and for good reason: near the end of the drive, the British car came to a halt in traffic and curious Iranians swarmed the vehicle. Undaunted, Churchill kept smiling at the crowd until the traffic parted and he was under way again. Once he reached his embassy, tightly guarded by a regiment of Indian Sikhs, he brushed off any meetings and went directly to bed, with a fifth of scotch whisky and a mound of hot-water bottles.

As Churchill took to his bed, Roosevelt was spending his first and only night at the residence of the American minister on the outskirts of Tehran. The residence was about four miles from the Soviet and British embassies, which were nearly adjoining in the center of the city. The American embassy itself was a mile away, so either Roosevelt or Stalin and Churchill would have to travel through Tehran's unpredictable streets just to meet. Whether because of paranoia, fear of assassination, or perfidy, Stalin seemed particularly unwilling to make the trip to the American residence. In fact, on the day of Roosevelt's arrival, he turned down the president's invitation to dinner, pleading exhaustion.

Instead, as Roosevelt was settling in, the Soviets anxiously reported to the Americans that their intelligence services had discovered an assassination plot against some or all of the leaders at the conference. The Soviet NKVD, forerunner of the KGB (state security committee), claimed that thirty-eight Nazi paratroopers had been dropped inside Russian territory around Tehran; only thirty-two were now accounted for, yet six remained missing, and these had a radio transmitter. Was this a genuine concern, or was it fabricated by the Soviets? That was unclear. In any event, to prevent a problem, Stalin offered Roosevelt a suite of rooms at the heavily guarded Soviet complex for the remainder of the time in Tehran. This was actually Stalin's second such invitation. The first Roosevelt had politely declined through an envoy. This time the president accepted. The following day he moved his personal staff to the large Soviet complex. Outwardly, Roosevelt displayed little concern; not so his Secret Service. Very much worried about the apparent German threat, the Secret Service agents lined the entire main route with soldiers and then sent out a heavily armed decoy convoy of cars and jeeps. As soon as this cavalcade had departed and was slowly making its way through Tehran's central streets, Roosevelt was hustled into another car with a single jeep escort and was sent "tearing" through the ancient side streets of Tehran to the Soviet legation. Roosevelt was highly amused by what he called the "cops and robbers stuff," but his protection agents, who knew better, were terrified.

Once inside the Soviet compound, the American Secret Service agents quickly discovered that they were very much outnumbered. Across Tehran, some three thousand NKVD agents had already been deployed for Stalin's personal protection. And nowhere was this more apparent than inside the Soviet residence. "Everywhere you went," agent Mike Reilly noted, "you would see a brute of a man in a lackey's white coat busily polishing immaculate glass or dusting dustless furniture. As their arms swung to dust or polish, the clear, cold outline of a Luger automatic could be seen on every hip." Actually, even Scotland Yard had sent far more protection for Churchill than the Americans had sent for Roosevelt.

~

FINALLY, THE TEHRAN CONFERENCE of the Allied powers could open. In the next few days, the three leaders and their military men would do no less than chart the Allied course for the remainder of the war, as well as begin to define the outlines of the peace. Yet like the Americans' security arrangements, the summit was to be almost entirely improvised. The Americans had arrived without even a provision for keeping the minutes of the high-level meetings. To address this glaring oversight, four soldiers with stenographic skills were hastily plucked from the nearby American military camp and assigned to take dictation after each session. But there were still no schedules, and there was no one who had been told to organize the meetings or handle the logistics. As a result, the head of the American Joint Chiefs, General George Marshall, actually missed the first meeting; he had misunderstood the start time and had instead gone sightseeing around the city.

The president had also arrived in Tehran without any position papers, the bureaucratic lifeblood of Washington. In short, the conference was vintage FDR. As always, he had no use for rules or regulations when they did not suit him. His plans were simple: improvise, follow his own instincts, and pursue his own agenda. He had come to Tehran in large part to work his legendary, Prospero-like magic on Stalin. His overarching goal was to make a friend and ally of the Soviet leader, to bring him, as he had brought so many others, into the fold.

It was what Roosevelt had been doing for a lifetime.

~

FEW MEN IN AMERICAN history brought to the presidency such a combination of prodigious political talents and formidable leadership skills as Franklin Roosevelt. By nature he was a dissembler, a schemer, a deceiver. But he also had an unconquerable will and an ingrained sense of immortality. Too easily forgotten is that when Roosevelt was first elected to the White House, there was sober talk of a revolution, and the American political system seemed to be on the verge of dissolution from within, so great were the strains of the Great Depression. But through improvisation and adjustment, buoyed by his legendary oratory and constant experimentation, Roosevelt managed to uplift a dispirited nation.

Now, as the Allies' fortunes on the far-off battlefields were changing, the world was looking to him to do the same in the war.

How does one even begin to describe him? No one on the global stage was neutral about him, and he was sui generis in every sense of the word. An astonishing blend of political genius and inspired ambition, he was an aristocrat like Thomas Jefferson, a populist like Andrew Jackson, a crafty politician like Abraham Lincoln, and a beloved figure like George Washington. He was as extravagant as he was original, as formidable as he was cosmopolitan, as mercurial as he was flamboyant, and as provocative as he could be puzzling. And he was tall, a fact obscured when polio cut him down: he was six foot two, the nation's fourth-tallest president, taller than either Ronald Reagan or Barack Obama. Actually, when he had walked, his gait was bowlegged.

Were there any inklings that he would rise to historic greatness? He was born late in the evening on January 30, 1882, "a beautiful little fellow," to enormous wealth and privilege; and he was an only child. With impressive foresight, one relative described him as "fair, sweet, cunning." His doting mother, Sara Delano, became the dominant influence in his life; still, Franklin worshipped his father, James, a lawyer, already in his mid-fifties when Franklin arrived. Reared on the family estate in Hyde Park, New York, he was, in effect, the center of the universe. Roosevelt was homeschooled by tutors and governesses, and fussed over by all sorts of domestic help, all under the watchful eye of Sara. From an early age he was drilled in the finer points of penmanship, the dreary particulars of arithmetic, and the searing lessons of history. And with the benefit of a Swiss teacher, he became fluent in German, French, and

Latin. He also absorbed a sense of social responsibility—that the more fortunate should help the less fortunate.

His mother read to him every day—including his favorites, *Robinson Crusoe* and *The Swiss Family Robinson*—while his father took him riding, sailing, and hunting. It was a pampered, secure existence. When he was a little boy his mother kept him in dresses and long curls; then she dressed him in Scottish regalia. Eventually, at the age of seven, he wore pants—short pants that were part of miniature sailor suits. Evidently, before age nine he had never taken a bath by himself. He had few friends as a boy; most of his time was spent around adults, often illustrious ones. Indeed, he was five when he met President Grover Cleveland. Cleveland wrapped his hand around Franklin's head and said, "My little man, I am making a strange wish for you. It is that you may never be president of the United States."

The Roosevelt family traveled extensively, sojourning annually in Europe; wintering in Washington, D.C., where the family rented the opulent townhouse of the Belgian minister on fashionable K Street; and summering at Campobello, a gorgeous sliver of an island off the rugged coast of Maine, where Franklin fell in love with the water and developed a lifelong passion for sailing. He had a twenty-one-foot boat there, *New Moon*, which his father gave him as a present. It was also there that Roosevelt began to fantasize about a naval career.

He learned to ride at an early age as well. At the age of two he was already cavorting about with a pet donkey and by the age of six with a Welsh pony. However much he was pampered, his parents sought to instill a sense of responsibility in the young Franklin. How? By giving him dogs to watch over: first a Spitz puppy, then a Saint Bernard, then a Newfoundland, and finally a gorgeous red Irish setter. At the same time, he became an avid collector of stuffed birds, which hung on his walls; of naval Americana, which as an ardent sailor he cherished; and, from the age of five, of stamps, another lifelong interest. Eventually, he would fill more than 150 albums and compile a collection totaling more than 1 million stamps.

When Franklin was nine, his father suffered a mild heart attack, and although James survived for a decade more, he became markedly feeble. For Franklin, who adored and idolized his father, this was nothing less than devastating. Five times over the next seven years the family sought out the warm mineral baths at Bad Nauheim in Germany, believed to have curative powers for ailing heart patients. James fervently embraced the restorative powers of the baths. So did Sara. And, predictably, so did the young Franklin, who would later seek the mineral waters at Warm Springs, Georgia. How did Roosevelt cope with his father's illness? As with everything else, surprisingly serenely. Here, though he was discreet about it, his sheet anchor was in part his Episcopal faith. He believed then, as he quietly would believe for the rest of his life, that if he put his trust in God, all would turn out well.

At the age of fourteen, he entered Groton, then the most prestigious prep school in the nation; tuition was exorbitant, affordable only by the very rich. The purpose of the school was more than to cultivate intellectual development; it was also to foster "manly Christian character," moral as well as physical, among America's most privileged boys. "Character, duty, country" was the daily creed; a monastic existence was the daily life. Roosevelt was bright and able to quickly absorb his studies—he would win the Latin prize. He was also a skilled debater. That was as far as it went, though, for he was neither an original thinker nor particularly introspective. But the school's founder, the Reverend Endicott Peabody, a charismatic minister, would become a profound influence on Roosevelt, more so than anyone else except for, as Franklin would one day put it, "my father and mother."

For Peabody, who embodied the ethic of muscular Christianity, the clash of sports was as central to the education of Groton boys as the classes themselves. Consequently, having grown up in the comfort and seclusion of Hyde Park, Roosevelt was a misfit; he had never before played a team sport and wasn't much of an athlete. It showed. Not surprisingly, he was put on a football squad reserved largely for misfits; it was the second-worst team. Baseball was little better; this time he played on the worst squad. However unremarkable he was, though, his passion never waned; by dint of enthusiasm, he even achieved a letter on the baseball team, not for his play, but because of his efforts as the equipment manager.

By the time he prepared to attend Harvard in the autumn of 1900, the ideals of Groton had become second nature to him: work hard and reap the benefits, plunge into competition, and embrace effort as the key to success.

In the autumn of 1900, Roosevelt enrolled at Harvard, America's most elite university, then under the leadership of its legendary president Charles W. Eliot. If Groton was where Roosevelt, the pampered only child, developed the social habits of mingling with his peers, Harvard was where he cultivated the ability to guide them. Still, he hardly shed the ways of the idle rich. His was the world of well-connected, sophisticated bons vivants; of mint juleps and polo matches; of riding with the hounds and in crosscountry steeple chases; and of tennis at Bar Harbor and sailing at Newport. As for Roosevelt himself? He lived off campus on Mount Auburn Street in a luxurious three-room corner suite (for the extravagant sum of $400 a year), owned a horse, and was a regular during the busy social season: almost weekly he attended the hunt balls, lavish black-tie dinners, and the endless debutante coming-out parties. When Porcellian, the most illustrious of Harvard's clubs, turned him down, he was crestfallen. However, he was chosen for Hasty Pudding, where he served as librarian, and for the fraternity Alpha Delta Phi. Moreover, he was elected to the editorial board of the *Harvard Crimson*, ultimately becoming its president, a great honor. His duties at the *Crimson* were extensive and often taxing—"the paper takes every moment of time" he wrote to his mother—but he acquitted himself admirably, all the while developing an understanding of the inner workings of the media, which would later serve him well when he entered the political arena. Academically, he coasted through, without challenging himself very much. Thanks to his education at Groton, he was able to skip the mandatory freshman curriculum. As to the electives, he eschewed theoretical courses like philosophy; instead, he gravitated toward history, government, and economics, a subject about which he would later remark, "Everything I was taught was wrong." And as at Groton, he won no academic honors, although his grades were solid.

During the late autumn of his freshman year, he received word that his father had suffered one more heart attack, then another. The family rushed to New York so that James might be closer to the specialists, but this did little for his worsening condition. With his loved ones collected at his bedside, he died at 2:20 a.m. on December 8, 1900. Though it was a great loss emotionally, the family would never want for anything material. Two years earlier, when her own father died, Sara had inherited an amount equivalent to roughly $37 million today. Upon James's passing, he left Sara and Franklin an estate that would be worth more than $17 million today.

Grief stricken, the family coped by traveling. Rather than going back to Campobello that summer, Franklin and Sara spent ten weeks abroad in Europe: first on an elegant cruise liner that took them through the majestic fjords of Norway and around the arctic circle, where they met Kaiser Wilhelm II. They then went on to Dresden, where Sara had gone to school as a girl, followed by time on the shores of Lake Geneva where they could breathe the crisp air. Finally, they went on to Paris, where they learned that President William McKinley had been assassinated. Their lives would never again be the same. They were not simply rich, but suddenly political royalty: the inimitable Theodore Roosevelt, their cousin, was now president.

That first winter without James was a difficult transition. Sara found life without him barren. She did her best to keep busy, supervising the estate's many workmen and overseeing its frequently intricate if not chaotic business affairs. But she soon prepared to focus her unwavering attention upon her son.

As the new year opened, Franklin spent three whirlwind days in Washington, D.C., in honor of his cousin Theodore's daughter Alice, at the White House; it was her coming-out party. The president also invited Franklin for a private talk over tea, twice. "One of the most interesting and enjoyable three days I have ever had," he wrote to his mother.

Shortly after Roosevelt returned to Harvard, his mother moved to Boston to join him. Rattling around in the house by herself, she found life at Hyde Park unbearable without her husband; she now wanted to be with Franklin. She moved into an apartment, made new friends, and joined the cloistered, elite world of Boston Brahmins. She also became a constant in Roosevelt's life, and far from resenting it, he enjoyed having her there. Not infrequently, he asked his mother to approve his dates.

Roosevelt loved the company of women. For a decade and a half he had scarcely any contact with the opposite sex and, in part due to the era of Victorian restraint, he had not much more once he arrived at Groton. Harvard was a different story. He fell in love with the lovely Frances Dana, though he was talked out of marriage by his mother because Frances was a Catholic, and the Roosevelts and Delanos were Protestants. Then there was Alice Sohier, the daughter of a distinguished North Shore family who lived in an elegant town house in Boston. He and Alice discussed marriage. An only child, Roosevelt exuberantly confessed he wanted six children. Alice balked at the prospect, confiding to an intimate, "I did not wish to be a cow." In the autumn of 1902, she backed out of the relationship and went instead to Europe. That was when he met Eleanor, a tall, "regal," "coltish looking" blue-eyed young woman, who was his fifth cousin once removed, and the orphaned daughter of his godfather, Elliott Roosevelt. Eleanor and Franklin's courtship was, in a sense, carefully choreographed.

Creatures of elegant New York society, they attended the premier horse show that autumn at Madison Square Garden, perched in the family box. Later, they lazed together on the manicured grass at Springwood, under the watchful eye of a chaperone. They took a dinner cruise aboard Roosevelt's motorized sailing yacht, the *Half-Moon.* And that New Year's Day they were in Washington as part of the inner circle as Theodore—who was her uncle as well as Franklin's cousin—stood in the East Room of the White House, warmly greeting long lines of supporters; soon, amid the polished silver and glittering candelabras, they dined with Theodore himself in the state dining room. But Franklin's mind was far away from politics. "E is an angel," a smitten Roosevelt wrote in his diary.

Eleanor's world was even more sheltered than Franklin's—and more tragedy-laced. When Eleanor was eight, her mother, Anna Rebecca Hall, who was often debilitated by migraines and bouts of dark depression, died of diphtheria. Two years later, her father, Elliott, died. A charming playboy who had dropped out of high school, he suffered from numerous inner demons, and his excesses knew no bounds: he was a dashing philanderer, and when he wasn't taking morphine or laudanum, he was drinking heavily, up to half a dozen bottles of hard liquor daily. One night he was even too drunk to tell a cabbie where he lived. Another time, he almost jumped from his parlor window. And on August 13, 1894, he lost consciousness, alone; he was dead the next evening.

From then on Eleanor lived with her maternal grandmother at their elegant brownstone on West Thirty-seventh Street or their estate on the Hudson—or she attended boarding school at Wimbledon Park in England. Hers was a solemn existence. Frequently surrounded by cooks, butlers, housemaids, laundresses, coachmen, and tutors, she had few friends and virtually no opportunity to meet other children, except for Theodore Roosevelt's daughter Alice. Unlike Franklin's mother, Eleanor's grandmother was a strict disciplinarian. Eleanor's life became an exercise in self-improvement: piano, dance class, lawn tennis, shooting, and riding. Like Franklin, she was also tutored in German and French, and she became fluent in French. Just as Roosevelt could chat easily in German, she could conduct extensive conversations in French. In time, she also excelled in Italian.

Still, she lacked self-confidence and considered herself an ugly duckling. But as the months passed, she shrewdly learned to compensate for her self-doubts. When she entered boarding school at the age of fifteen, in England at Allenwood—in many ways as prestigious as Groton—where classes were conducted entirely in French, she became the most popular girl in the school. She was earnest and eager and hardworking. She was also a quick study. The school's headmistress was an ardent feminist—this was rare for the times—and Eleanor learned to question the orthodoxy of the day and to freely express her thoughts, a scandalous liberty in the rigid, patriarchal age of Victorianism. Slender and sophisticated, already at a young age she was an ardent Progressive, taking an interest in political events. She would later comment that under the tutelage of the headmistress, who had a profound influence on her, she developed a "liberal mind and a strong personality." And unlike Franklin, whose success at sports was modest at best, she made the first team in field hockey.

In the cool autumn days of 1903, Roosevelt and Eleanor dated, always, of course, with a chaperone. He asked her to come to Cambridge for the big game—Harvard versus Yale. The next day, under a clear sky, the two ambled along the Nashua River. Roosevelt proposed; she accepted. When he told his mother at Thanksgiving, Sara was aghast, believing that he was simply too young. She entreated the young couple to keep the engagement secret for a year. However, she did not object to Eleanor, nor did she try to forbid the marriage. They accepted the arrangement. In the meantime Eleanor wrote letters to Franklin brimming with affection—she called him "boy darling," or "Franklin dearest." In turn her nickname was "Little Nell."

In September 1904, Franklin and his mother moved to 200 Madison Avenue, a massive brick town house near J. P. Morgan's stately mansion, and Franklin entered Columbia Law School. This was prelude. On October 11, a buoyant Roosevelt gave Eleanor an engagement ring from Tiffany's. She was just twenty, and their arrangement was now official. When their engagement was announced and they were receiving a flurry of congratulations, Theodore Roosevelt insisted the wedding take place in the White House "under his roof." They demurred. Instead the lavish wedding took place at Eleanor's great-aunt's twin town houses; there were top hats and elegant carriages, and Theodore himself was there to give the bride away. The couple had two honeymoons: the first was a modest week away; the second was a three-month grand tour that took them to London, Scotland, Paris, Milan, Verona, Venice, Saint Moritz, and the Black Forest. Roosevelt bought Eleanor a dozen dresses and a long sable coat, and, for himself, a silver fox coat and an old library: three thousand leather-bound books.

At Columbia Law School, as at Harvard, he was an undistinguished student, receiving B's, C's, and a D. Vaguely bored and wealthy, confident and even a bit cocky, he seldom let studies stand in the way of a good time. One Columbia professor remarked that Roosevelt had little aptitude for the law—actually, he had initially failed courses in contracts and civil procedure—and that he "made no effort" to overcome the problem with hard work. Nevertheless, he easily passed the New York bar examination in his third year, upon which he promptly dropped out of school; he never earned his degree. Meanwhile, at Christmastime in 1905, Sara told the newlyweds that she had hired a firm to construct a town house for them ("a Christmastime present from mama"), which would adjoin a second home: hers; the dining rooms and drawing rooms of the two homes opened into each other. Very much her own woman, Eleanor was deeply unhappy with the fact that Sara was making so many major decisions for her family. But Roosevelt was unsympathetic, acting as if there were no problem. As Eleanor herself explained, "I think he always thought that if you ignored a thing long enough it would settle itself." Three years later, Sara gave Roosevelt and Eleanor a second house, an elegant seaside cottage on the gorgeous shores of Campobello Island. The sprawling home had thirty-four rooms, manicured lawns, shimmering crystal and silver, and seven fireplaces, as well as four full baths—although no electricity.

All told, theirs was a lavish lifestyle. In addition to their three houses, they always had at least five servants, a number of automobiles and carriages, a large yacht, and many smaller boats; Roosevelt continued to love the water. As befitted their station, they belonged to exclusive clubs, dressed stylishly, and donated their money to various charitable causes. As for their five children? They were to be raised by governesses, nurses, and other caregivers. Eleanor, as serious as ever, was the stricter of the two parents. Her grandmother had always been quick to say "no" rather than "yes," and she was the same. By contrast, Franklin was warm, good-humored, and engaging. As his daughter Anna once said, "Father was fun."

He was more than fun. Early on, he confessed that he had little taste for the law. Nor was he content with summering at Campobello or sailing at Newport or spending his time at seasonal coming-out parties. With uncommon candor, he explained that he planned to run for office, and audaciously believed he would one day be president. First, he would become a state assemblyman—a low-paying part-time job in Albany—then assistant secretary of the navy, and finally governor of New York. Theodore had made it to the White House following exactly that path; why couldn't Franklin?

IT HAPPENED ALMOST AS he predicted.

Except at the start. The assemblyman who Roosevelt assumed would step aside to provide him with a seat declined his entreaties. Still, Roosevelt was determined. He first threatened to run as an independent, but was then persuaded to run for the state senate as a Democrat, in the Twenty-sixth District, which had elected only one Democrat to the office in fifty-four years. A committee of three nominated Roosevelt, and the local newspaper, the Republican *Poughkeepsie Eagle*, sniped that he had been "discovered" by the Democrats more for his deep pockets than for any other redeeming qualities. Roosevelt, in a style he would use again and again, motored around the district in an open touring car, which was painted bright red and owned by a piano tuner. Along with two other local candidates, he crisscrossed the district in this newfangled automobile, purring along at twenty-two miles per hour. He was attentive: as he bumped down the dusty, rutted roads, he made sure that the campaign car was pulled over and the engine shut off whenever a horse-drawn carriage or hay wagon appeared, lest it startle the animals or peeve a voter.

At the outset, he was not a great speaker. His words were too abstract, and he relied too much on flattery of himself and others. But he would speak anywhere—on a front porch, by the side of a road, on the top of a hay bale. Eleanor would describe his style as "slow," noting that "every now and then there would be a long pause, and I would be worried for fear he would never go on." With her discerning eye, she thought he looked "tall, high-strung," and even "nervous." However, he excelled at working a crowd—his energetic hands seemed permanently outstretched, ready to grip the next open palm. Still, the campaign was often poorly run. Once, while traveling in the eastern edge of the district, he arrived at a small town late in the afternoon, jumped from the car, headed straight to the hotel, and invited everyone in the bar to have a drink—on him. Only after the bartender began pouring did Roosevelt think to ask where he was: Sharon, Connecticut, not only the wrong district but the wrong state. Undaunted, Roosevelt grinned and paid up; and then proceeded to reuse the story and the joke for years. And he had no qualms about trading on his famous name, borrowing his cousin Theodore's pronunciation of "dee-lighted," and sometimes announcing to a crowd, "I'm not Teddy," his way of suggesting that he was the *other* Roosevelt. On Election Day, despite a last-minute rush by the Republicans, Franklin Roosevelt carried the district by more than 1,100 votes.

The Roosevelts rented a house in Albany, for a princely $4,800 a year. Eleanor, prone to recurring depressions, was at first reluctant about the house, about the job, and about politics in general, but she gritted her teeth and assumed that it was a wife's duty to be involved in her husband's interests—although when she had tried her hand at golf, Roosevelt had watched her swing and promptly dissuaded her.

He immersed himself in political life but did not always win over his fellow politicians. He particularly had trouble reaching the Irish-Catholic Democrats. Roosevelt's father had disdained Irishmen, even as workers in his household, and a leading New York politico, James Farley, claimed that Eleanor had once said to him, "Franklin finds it hard to relax with people who aren't his social equals." Eleanor strongly denied it, although in her own early letters she made less than temperate observations about Jews; once, of a party honoring the financier Bernard Baruch (who would later become a close ally), she wrote, "I'd rather be hung than seen there." And Roosevelt himself was at times clearly uneasy working with different classes outside his own tight circle. As he later acknowledged to his secretary of labor, Frances Perkins, "I was an awfully mean cuss when I first went into politics." Moreover, if he was a Progressive, he was a cautious one. It took him until 1912 to openly support women's suffrage, and he would not back a labor reform bill mandating a fifty-four-hour maximum workweek for women and children, even after the devastating fire at the Triangle Shirtwaist Company, in which more than a hundred female garment workers died.

Then came 1912. Two years after Roosevelt had won his state senate seat, he was running for reelection and Woodrow Wilson was running for president, against Theodore, who was a third-party candidate. Following politics rather than kinship, and, as ever, self-interest most of all, Roosevelt backed Wilson. He had been at the Democratic convention, working the room, ostensibly on behalf of Wilson, but equally on behalf of himself. One of the men he impressed was Josephus Daniels, a member of the Democratic National Committee and also the editor of the Raleigh, North Carolina, *News and Observer.* But that would be significant later. First, Roosevelt had to win reelection to the state senate, and suddenly that goal was in jeopardy. In September, Roosevelt fell seriously ill with typhoid fever in New York City. He was too sick to campaign, or even to get out of bed. Eventually he recovered, but his political career now seemed imperiled.

It was Eleanor who rescued him by contacting Louis Howe, a dogged Albany newspaperman and political impresario who was enthralled with Roosevelt. She asked whether Howe would consider taking over the campaign. Howe eagerly said yes. In truth, he didn't look like much, and seemed an odd partner for the patrician Roosevelt. He was squat, asthmatic, and stooped, with a pitted face and a cigarette wobbling between his lips; he was often unbathed as well. Yet he was a political genius who quickly became Roosevelt's virtual surrogate, taking out full-page newspaper ads and producing a direct-mail campaign of multigraphed letters bearing Roosevelt's signature. In effect he took over the last six weeks of the campaign. And in a dramatic departure, Howe remade Roosevelt into a full Progressive, supporting labor rights, supporting women's suffrage, and complaining about Republican political bosses. With Howe at the helm, Roosevelt won reelection by an even wider margin than he had achieved in 1910. When Roosevelt reached the White House, Howe became his secretary—the equivalent of today's chief of staff—and he did not leave Roosevelt's side until he died in April 1936.

The state senate was only a stepping-stone. Roosevelt had early on let it be known, to Wilson in particular, that he wanted a job in Washington. He turned down two offers—as an assistant secretary in the Treasury, and as a collector for the Port of New York—holding out for his desire: assistant secretary of the navy. His obstinacy paid off; Wilson gave him the navy job. He would be serving under Josephus Daniels, whom he had befriended during his state senate campaign. Roosevelt now held the same post that had launched his cousin Theodore on the way to the White House.

In the Navy Department, Roosevelt learned about the bureaucracy and the ways of Washington. He brought Louis Howe with him, and this enabled him to also keep tabs on New York. Roosevelt enjoyed the trappings and the ceremony, but as the number two man, he was on the periphery of power, and he knew it. Making the ships run on time was not the role to which Roosevelt aspired. He tried to make a bid himself for the U.S. Senate but failed. His candidacy was rebuffed by his own party and by the president himself—humiliatingly for Roosevelt, Wilson openly backed a rival candidate. Roosevelt was routed in the primary, and never forgave the man who had opposed him, James Gerard, who was the U.S. ambassador to Germany and a former justice of the New York state supreme court. Fortunately World War I intervened, and Roosevelt quickly devised plans for expanding the U.S. Navy (which were ignored) and also improved his ability to testify before Congress (which got him noticed). The efforts worked. By 1916, his stance as a "preparedness Democrat" made him an asset in Wilson's reelection campaign. Roosevelt was sent to stump in New England and the mid-Atlantic states, and it was here that he first began using his fire hose analogy, the idea of lending one's own hose to a neighbor whose house is on fire. Over time, he would tweak, amend, and refine this analogy, which became one of the most famous concepts of his political career. He would later use it during World War II to sell a wary American nation on his Lend-Lease policy for Great Britain.

For Roosevelt, when the United States finally entered World War I in April 1917 after the torpedoing of three steamships, the navy was the place to be. At that time it had 60,000 men and 197 ships in active service; at the end of the war it had almost 500,000 men and more than 2,000 ships, a staggering number. Roosevelt threw himself enthusiastically into the expansion and was so successful that he was forced to share some of his newly acquired supplies with the army, and "see young Roosevelt about it" quickly became a catchphrase in Washington. But Roosevelt, as ambitious as he was restless, was unsatisfied. He dreamed of seeing military action, again following in the footsteps of his cousin, but was thwarted at every turn by his superiors, who would not allow him to go overseas, let alone enlist in any branch of the armed forces. Instead, he put his persuasive skills to use, lobbying for the creation of a 240-mile underwater chain of explosives to foil German submarines. Roosevelt's position in the navy and his work to protect naval shipyards also endeared him to the leaders of Tammany Hall, which dominated New York Democratic politics.

In the capital, the Roosevelts were much in demand. Invitations arrived daily, and Eleanor quickly discovered that the social whirlwind required her to have a social secretary. In 1914, she hired Lucy Mercer to come in three mornings a week. Not long after that, having borne six children, Eleanor informed Franklin that there would be no more babies. To ensure this, Roosevelt was also informed that he was no longer welcome in his wife's bed.

Roosevelt was a tall, attractive man of thirty-four. When he had first run for the state senate, women had flocked to hear his speeches, even though they could not vote. Now he also had status, a touch of maturity, and roving interests. Lucy, Eleanor's part-time social secretary, was everything her employer was not, feminine and self-assured with a gentle voice and a "hint of fire in her eyes." She was also tall, slender, and blue-eyed, with long, light-brown hair. And although her family had long since exhausted its funds, she was nevertheless part of the same hallowed social set as the Roosevelts. Even as she worked in the Roosevelts' house, Lucy attended the same large dinners and parties as Franklin and Eleanor. Amid the guests, Roosevelt flirted and Lucy flirted back. From there, things quietly escalated. Roosevelt and Lucy went on cruises on the Potomac and long, private drives in Virginia—alone. Once, Alice Roosevelt Longworth, Theodore's oldest daughter, who had been Eleanor's maid of honor at her wedding, caught sight of them riding side by side in Roosevelt's roadster. Alice wrote to Franklin, mentioning that he had never noticed her: "Your hands were on the wheel, but your eyes were on that perfectly lovely lady."

Eleanor sensed trouble. Not long after a Potomac cruise hosted by Franklin and Eleanor, a suspicious Eleanor terminated Lucy's employment. She likely did it on the pretext of going away for the summer; she had no proof of any relationship, only her suspicions. Almost immediately, Lucy enlisted in the navy. Not unsurprisingly, her first assignment was secretarial duty at the Navy Department; she had left Roosevelt's house for his office. Possibly aware of the link between Roosevelt and Lucy, Secretary of the Navy Daniels removed her from her post and then from the navy only a few months later. Yet while distance may have banked their passion, it did not extinguish it. For nearly thirty years, Franklin and Lucy would continue to meet and write to each other. In his last conscious moments in April 1945, it would be Lucy, not Eleanor, who was with him. At the end, it was her voice that he heard and her face that he saw.

THE YEAR 1918 WAS when Franklin Roosevelt was at last determined to go to war. All four of his Republican Roosevelt cousins had signed up for combat. Just as the young Austrian painter Adolf Hitler was itching for action on the front, Roosevelt wanted at least to set foot in Europe, even if he were not in full uniform. Then a congressional delegation announced plans to inspect naval installations during the summer. Secretary Daniels dispatched Roosevelt to ferret out any potential problems.

While crossing the Atlantic on a destroyer, he heard bells sound for a U-boat attack, and he raced to the deck. The attack never materialized; the waters remained calm, and the destroyer was unmolested. Yet that outcome was not good enough for Roosevelt. His biographer Jean Edward Smith has observed: "As Roosevelt retold the story through the years, the German submarine came closer and closer until he had almost seen it himself."

He arrived in England a week after his cousin Quentin Roosevelt was killed in a dogfight over France. After his ship docked, Rolls-Royces whisked Roosevelt to London, where he met the king and the prime minister and came away with a strong dislike of the British Minister of munitions, Winston Churchill, "one of the few men in public life who was rude to me," he would later tell Joseph Kennedy. From there he went on to Paris, where he was deeply impressed with the presidential wines, "perfect of their kind and perfectly served." And at each location, letters awaited him, from Eleanor and also from Lucy Mercer. Then he headed for the front. He saw the scarred battlefields of Château-Thierry, Belleau Wood, and Verdun. At Verdun alone there had been some 900,000 casualties; partially and fully exploded shells had obliterated the forts and trenches, and the battlefield was an unrecognizable expanse of brown, churned-up earth. Roosevelt stared at it in silence.

He was still eager, however, to witness action. Once, a shell whistled and landed with a "dull boom" nearby. Roosevelt took off toward the sound, leaving behind a suitcase of important papers on the running board of his car. Yet for all his jaunty enthusiasm, the devastation wrought by combat made a lasting impression on Roosevelt. Later, he would mention the images he had seen in a walk through Belleau Wood: "rain-stained love letters," or men buried in shallow graves, with nothing more than a weathered rifle butt poking out of the ground to mark their resting place.

After France, he traveled to Italy, where he tried unsuccessfully to negotiate a command structure for the Mediterranean, then back to England. Determined as ever, on his return to Washington he planned to resign his post and head for the front. Again, another foe intervened:

Spanish influenza. Roosevelt was struck on board the USS *Leviathan*, collapsing in his cabin. His flu was compounded by double pneumonia. Clammy and sweating, Roosevelt lay in his bunk barely conscious, hovering near death. He lived. Many others were not so lucky. Death came often during the passage, and both officers and men who passed away on board were buried at sea. Then, when the ship docked, Roosevelt was transported by ambulance to his mother's New York town house. Four orderlies carried his prostrate body up the stairs. Eleanor had hurriedly arrived to attend to him and dutifully unpacked his bags. In the process, she discovered sheafs of love letters, neatly tied together, all from Lucy Mercer. These letters confirmed her worst fears, and as Eleanor would later put it, "the bottom dropped out of my own particular world."

According to various family accounts, Eleanor offered to give Franklin a divorce so that he might marry Lucy, but both Louis Howe and Sara Roosevelt were aghast at the idea and convinced him that it would derail his political career. Sara may well have threatened to disown him if he left Eleanor for Lucy. In the end, he stayed, as did Eleanor.

Roosevelt did not recover from either the pneumonia or the discovery of his liaison with Lucy in time to resign his post and enlist in the war. When peace came, he instead pressed his case to return to Europe to preside over the demobilization of the navy, and Daniels finally relented. Franklin and Eleanor were sent together. The trip was a watershed. When they were four days out of New York harbor, word arrived that Teddy Roosevelt was dead. And before the year's end, President Woodrow Wilson would be paralyzed by a massive stroke. His cherished dream of a League of Nations would collapse, and the 1920 campaign would begin. Roosevelt was there, giving the seconding speech for New York's Al Smith at the Democratic convention; moreover, he became the party's nominee for vice president, on the ticket with Governor James Cox of Ohio. Roosevelt again felt no shame in trading on his name: as he had done in running for the New York state senate, he adopted many of Theodore's characteristic expressions—"b-u-ll-y," "stren-u-ous." Yet the campaign soon foundered, and Warren Harding routed Cox and Roosevelt, with more than 60 percent of the popular vote and an impressive

404 votes in the Electoral College. Still, the loss at least proved to be a financial gain for Roosevelt. He became vice president of the Fidelity and Deposit Company of Maryland, for the hefty sum of $25,000 a year, largely for lending his name to the masthead. The Democrats, Roosevelt thought, would be wandering in the wilderness for the near future. With the future ahead of him, he preferred to decamp to his summer home on the island of Campobello, Maine.

IT BEGAN AS A vague malaise and a dull ache in his legs. Then came the exhaustion and shivering. He only picked at his dinner tray and was cold even under a heavy woolen blanket. In the morning, as he was walking to the bathroom, his left leg gave way beneath him. He shaved and made it back to bed. He could not know it then, but this was the last walk he would ever take unassisted.

By now, he had a fever, and the pain in his back and legs had increased. The family attempted massage, but to no avail. Within a week, his frantic doctors were desperate for even a glimpse of movement in one of Roosevelt's toes. They could not see any. In truth, he could not even use the toilet on his own; a catheter was implanted, which Eleanor got up to drain during the night. By the end of August, there was no improvement. By the end of September, significant muscle atrophy had set in.

He was eventually diagnosed with poliomyelitis, or infantile paralysis, although more recent medical speculation has suggested some form of Guillain-Barré syndrome. Whatever the cause, the outcome was the same. He was a paraplegic.

Nevertheless, on October 15, Franklin Roosevelt reached a milestone. He was able to sit up. He had been transported back to New York City and left the hospital in late October. An intensive exercise regimen was designed to enable him to use crutches. His now-useless legs were laboriously strapped into fourteen-pound steel braces, molded from his ankle to his hips. He could no longer balance on his own or extend one leg at a time. Instead, his crutches became his legs; he stabilized himself using his upper body, and half-dragged, half-swung his legs and his hips along from behind. At Hyde Park, the rope-and-pulley trunk elevator became his conveyance to the upper floors; dutifully, his mother had "inclined planes" installed and removed all the raised thresholds so nothing would impede a wheelchair. Sara Roosevelt hoped her son would retire to Hyde Park, but his political adviser Louis Howe had other ideas.

"I believe," Howe audaciously said, "someday Franklin will be president."

THE MAN WHO HAD fallen in a heap when he attempted to navigate on crutches across the slippery marble floor at his Wall Street offices, the man who could not lift even one arm and wave for fear of toppling, the man who had once towered over others but was now almost always the one who did the looking up—miraculously returned to politics in 1924 as a lead speaker for the Democratic presidential convention. What Roosevelt could no longer do with his arms, he did with his head, throwing it back, holding his shoulders high. Whatever parts of himself he could still move, he animated. And he now used his voice brilliantly. No longer halting, it had matured into a resonant tenor and was infused with a passion that he had previously lacked. It thrummed, it vibrated, it sang. And wherever he was, the audience felt it.

In November 1928, Franklin Roosevelt achieved what had once seemed to many to be impossible. He was elected the Democratic governor of New York. He did it by being carried up back stairs to deliver speeches and by riding in the back of a car, from which he could speak without standing up. Indeed, the simple act of standing up and sitting down required more effort for him than most men exert during an entire day. Day after day on the campaign trail, he disguised his disability and seemed to have gained a new equanimity. Frances Perkins, who joined Roosevelt on his run for governor and who would later become his secretary of labor, recalled him telling her once, "If you can't use your legs and they bring you milk when you wanted orange juice, you learn to say, 'that's all right' and drink it."

Roosevelt was now truly living what his cousin Teddy had preached: "the strenuous life." And he lived it not in a charge up San Juan Hill or on a big-game hunt in the western plains, but every waking hour of every day. He lived it from the moment he summoned his strength to hoist his useless legs from his bed into his self-designed wheelchair; he lived it when the sweat ran down his face as he said to himself, "I must get down the driveway" or "I must get to the podium" or "I must get across the room." He did it minute after minute and week after week, always refusing to give up or give in. As never before, he had become a man of conviction and determination. And when the country was on its knees because of the Great Depression, Governor Roosevelt seemed, however improbably, the man who might best be able to lift it back onto its feet.

ROOSEVELT'S POLITICAL OPERATIVES WERE already preparing their candidate for the presidential election only a few days after he was reelected as New York's governor. He formally announced his candidacy on January 23, 1932, and proceeded to win all the delegates in Alaska and Washington state in the first week. But he did not succeed in derailing his opposition. In his final speech before the Democratic convention, he promised "bold, persistent experimentation." "Take a method," he boomed, "and try it. If it fails admit it frankly and try another. But above all, try something." He arrived at the convention with a solid lead, but still about a hundred votes short of the nomination. After a night and a day of fierce lobbying and multiple votes, he finally won on the fourth ballot, claiming more than two thirds of the delegates after California and Texas switched to the Roosevelt column. He then made a dramatic flight to Chicago to accept the nomination, and his words to the assembled crowd thundered over the radio: "I pledge you, I pledge myself, to a NEW DEAL for the American people."

Whatever Roosevelt's promises, no one could overlook the desperate situation the country found itself in. The Great Depression was horrific. At least 25 percent of the American workforce was unemployed; in some industrial cities, unemployment was as high as 80 or 90 percent. International trade was devastated. In less than four years, the American economy had shrunk by $45 billion, or about 45 percent. Even more staggering than the numbers were the haunting images: the bread lines forming in every city; the evicted families, jobless and destitute and dirty, shuffling from one soup kitchen to the next; and the makeshift tents in the dead of winter buckling from rain and sleet, not to mention the filthy children who huddled by bonfires alongside the railroad tracks. And the great midwestern dust bowl was yet to come. Sometimes, the enormousness of the task and the despair must have seemed overwhelming.

But not to Roosevelt. In his race against Hoover, he gave twenty-seven major addresses, each covering a single topic, and he made his campaign about substance and about organization. Most of all, he believed he would win, and equally remarkably, everyone around him became a believer as well. The embattled incumbent president, Herbert Hoover, accused the Democrats of being the "party of the mob." Hoover also insisted that despite the Depression, no one was starving: "The hobos," he exclaimed, "are better fed than they have ever been." The voters went overwhelmingly against Hoover and for Roosevelt; it was a drubbing—the president carried only six northeastern states. Roosevelt's Democrats also gained a nearly three-to-one majority in the House and control of the Senate. On election night, Washington seemed to be his.

And there was this: we think of our presidents as robust, vigorous, capable of striding through any part of the country or indeed the globe. But Franklin Roosevelt could not stride. He could not even stand unbraced or unassisted. Never before or since has a disabled person run for the American presidency, let alone won. That he ran and won in a time of national turmoil is a testament not only to the skill of his campaign, but to something fearless and indomitable deep within himself.

~

"He has been all but crowned by the people," newspaperman William Allen White grandiloquently wrote. Actually, this was an overstatement. True, in the New Deal days he was the man whom millions loved, but he was also the man whom millions loved to hate. In his first hundred days in office, he undid the Temperance movement by repealing Prohibition and rebuffed both organized labor and veterans with his sweeping legislative proposals and executive orders. He remade the banking system and began to remake the government and economy. For Roosevelt, no dream seemed impossible. And to many, as inch-by-inch he restored confidence in the economy and tamed the worst of the Depression, it was nothing less than miraculous.

Yet the heady promise of those early days and months also could not be indefinitely sustained. By the mid-1930s, some of Roosevelt's presidential magic had begun to wear off. The jaunty, quick-witted president who seemed to relish sparring with his enemies now appeared at times baffled and weary, though he did rebound in 1936—an election year—with a string of legislative achievements reminiscent of the first hundred days of his term. By the end of his second term, however, as he confronted ever-rising difficulties with Congress, continued obstruction from a wary Supreme Court, a persistently sluggish economy, and the ominous sight of Adolf Hitler looming over Europe, he suddenly looked ordinary, much like any other two-term president. Yet once plunged into the throes of World War II, he emerged not only as a great statesman, but as one of history's originals.

Callous and cunning, he was careful never to get too far ahead of public opinion, even as he pushed, prodded, and manipulated his two very different wartime allies, Churchill and Stalin. Neatly attired and insouciant, he was the very picture of understated upper-class elegance and seemed strangely immune to mercurial passions—Francis Biddle once remarked that Roosevelt "had more serenity than any man I've ever met." And despite his useless legs, he was still a strikingly imposing figure, with his broad torso and wide shoulders. His charm was without peer. When he famously tossed his head back, or flashed a wide grin, his eyes flickered with emotion. When he chuckled with delight, so did those around him. His smile remained infectious, and his company was irresistible: Churchill felt it; so did Stalin; and so did General Dwight Eisenhower, Roosevelt's chief adviser Harry Hopkins, and Secretary of

State Cordell Hull. Roosevelt was a magnet to which thousands were drawn. How else to explain the nearly slavish devotion of those who supported his political endeavors, or the unwritten rule among the press corps never to report on his disability or photograph his wheelchair or his shriveled legs?

In spite of his disability, Roosevelt remained a man of constant action, loving to drive, loving his stamps, loving the interplay of politics. Largely motionless himself, he instead made motion orbit around him, perfecting the tilt of his head and using his cigarette holder like a conductor's baton. He was given to drumming his fingers when excited. He could infuse equal gusto into discussions of grave international issues such as the "survival of democracy," as he did into mundane politics such as the fate of a ward heeler in a Pennsylvania precinct. And when angered he could point a threatening finger or display a menacing scowl.

Like all great leaders, he was not above simple demagoguery or ruthless invective when it served his purpose: Roosevelt blithely referred to isolationists as "cheerful idiots"; when he appointed a Republican, he joked to the press corps that he couldn't find any dollar-a-year men among the Democrats; and when Ambassador William Bullitt fell out of his favor, Roosevelt encouraged him to leave Washington and run for mayor of Philadelphia—and then promptly instructed the Pennsylvania Democratic bosses to "cut his throat." He once derided Congress as "a madhouse," and denounced the Senate as "a bunch of incompetent obstructionists." The commander in chief even thought that his own vice president, Henry Wallace, who served with him for his entire third term, was a crackpot. And he liked to make fun of his secretary of state, cheerfully imitating Hull's lisp.

But intuitively, Roosevelt understood Adolf Hitler's bloodthirstiness as much as anyone—ironically, he and Hitler had come to power at the same time, in 1933—and knew that with each new battle and each month of the war, "we are fighting to save a great and precious form of government for ourselves and for the world."

∾

In 1933, after his first hundred days in office, Roosevelt had brilliantly managed to usher fifteen historic pieces of legislation through Congress. When it was necessary to hold firm, he did that; when it was necessary to compromise, he did that; when it was necessary to make a bargain, he did that as well. "It's more than a New Deal," his secretary of the interior, Harold Ickes, boasted: "It's a new world!" Even when a bleak recession and unemployment lingered and when he failed in his attempt to "pack" a restive Supreme Court, he never lost the adulation of vast segments of the public or the interest of the press.

Yet when it came to the darkening situation in Europe, Roosevelt flinched. Instead of showing his customary confidence, he played it coyly. Despite Hitler's onslaught, the ghastly memories of World War I remained as fresh as ever—the sights and sounds of exhausted armies shadowboxing from their trenches; the tedium of siege and the billowing clouds of dense, roiling smoke; and the stabbing bursts of gunfire that never seemed to fade away. America had buried over 117,000 soldiers in World War I, while Europe and Russia lost 10 million. Many Americans thought that was plenty, and two decades later they had little appetite for what they still thought of as Europe's wars. By the summer of 1939, with Europe bounded by France's Maginot Line against Germany in the west and the provisions of the Munich agreement in the east, Roosevelt had all but decided not to run for a third term.

But then came a stark phone call at 2:50 a.m. on August 31, 1939, informing him that ten armored German divisions had stormed across the Polish border, and that war had been declared. Roosevelt cleared his throat and rasped to his ambassador in Paris, William Bullitt, who was relaying the news from Warsaw, "Well, Bill, it has come at last. God help us all." It was then that Roosevelt began the process of reversing himself: he would ultimately decide to seek an unprecedented third term in office—breaking a tradition begun by George Washington himself. Over the next eight months, during the period known as the phony war, Roosevelt publicly promised to keep America out of Europe's conflict. "I've said this before and will say this again," he told the nation; "your boys will not fight in foreign wars." Anyone who suggested otherwise was perpetrating a "shameless and dishonest fake," the president said, adding, "The simple truth is that no person in any responsible place has ever suggested the remotest possibility of sending the boys of American mothers to fight on the battlefields of Europe." Still, he also did what he could to nudge Washington and indeed the nation at large closer to action and to the growing reality of future conflict. But whereas Churchill had lectured Neville Chamberlain about his policies of appeasement ("The government had to choose between shame and war," he bellowed. "They chose shame and will get war!") Roosevelt instead searched for a middle way. He informed members of the Senate Military Affairs Committee that if England and France fell, all of Europe "would drop into the basket of their own accord. . . . I cannot overemphasize the seriousness of the situation. This is not a pipe dream."

When Great Britain declared war on Germany, followed by France five hours later, Roosevelt took to the airwaves in a fireside chat, and said: "This nation will remain a neutral nation, but I cannot ask that every American remain neutral in thought as well. Even a neutral has a right to take account of facts." And though he told Congress in a personal address, "Our acts must be guided by one single hardheaded thought—keeping America out of war," he emphasized the urgency of repealing the Neutrality Act so that America could provide military support to the western Allies. (Congress responded by authorizing a so-called cash-and-carry plan, which allowed American manufacturers to sell arms to Britain and France so long as each country paid cash and sent its own ships to pick up the goods.)

Still, neutrality had a high price. The war news haunted Roosevelt. While poring over cables from abroad, or reading his morning *New York Times* and the *Herald Tribune*, he would mutter to himself over and over, "All bad, all bad." The first president to use the phone extensively—Harry Truman recalled how Roosevelt's voice boomed so loudly he had to hold the phone away from his ear—he often spoke to his emissaries in Europe or aides in the State Department. Day-in and day-out, the phone rang constantly, bringing him the latest news of Hitler's feints and moves. Then his days were filled with meetings: with the press, with the secretaries of state and the treasury, with the attorney general, with his personal secretary for afternoon dictation, and ever more frequently with senior members of the Senate. Invariably, Fridays were cabinet days, when the president met with the members who had the greatest political weight or the greatest measure of influence.

Predictably, he craved diversion where he could find it—in his nightly rubdown with masseur George Fox, in his collection of stamps and cherished naval prints, in his beloved tree plantings, in his frequent naps, in the movies he was "addicted to," and most of all in the cocktail hour that took place every afternoon at the White House, when he banished all talk of war and busied himself with mixes and shakers. But none of this was ever quite refuge enough.

"I'm almost literally walking on eggs," Roosevelt confessed early in 1940. The strain showed. The president's blood pressure shot up to 179/102. Then came a scare: one evening in February, during an intimate dinner with Ambassador Bullitt and the close presidential aide Missy LeHand, Roosevelt collapsed at the table—it was a small heart attack, which his longtime attending navy physician, Admiral Ross McIntire, quickly dismissed and hushed up.

As spring approached, the United States made one last-ditch effort to forestall all-out war. In March, Undersecretary of State Sumner Welles, a close adviser to the president, traveled to London, Paris, Berlin, and Rome to propose a plan of peace and security through disarmament. In hindsight, the proposal reeked of desperation. At the time, the Germans were scornful and the British were horrified. As the world watched, the United States seemed to be doing little more than awaiting Hitler's next move.

It would not have to wait long.

On May 10, 1940, Hitler launched his now infamous blitzkrieg—lightning war—against the Netherlands and Belgium, ravaging them by land and air. On day four of the German advance, Hitler ordered the old Dutch city of Rotterdam destroyed not for military reasons but for

Schrecklichkeit ("frightfulness")—the explicit use of terror to break a people's will to resist. After a day of ferocious bombing, some thirty thousand people lay dead beneath the rubble. Hours later, the Dutch surrendered unconditionally, and the Belgians followed within two weeks.

Then Hitler, unencumbered, turned his full force on France. Protected by Stuka dive-bombers, Nazi tanks and motorized infantry ripped through the Ardennes virtually unopposed, and Erwin Rommel's notorious panzers rapidly reached the Channel coast. In World War I, movement of the battle lines was often measured in yards rather than miles, and the French and British had managed to hold back German thrusts for four ghastly years, despite the carnage and millions of casualties. This time, the French, considered to have the best army in the world, were dumbstruck. They were overrun and had hardly fired a shot.

Churchill urgently cabled to Roosevelt: "The scene has darkened swiftly. The small countries are simply smashed up, one by one, like match wood. We expect to be attacked ourselves." Privately, Roosevelt told his aides that if Great Britain fell, the United States would "be living at the point of a gun." The question for Roosevelt, however, and for the world, was this: was he willing to publicly rally the nation to brave the German fury? His answer was silence.

Within weeks, German panzer units had trapped the British expeditionary force and the French First Army along the harsh English Channel on the French beach at Dunkirk. While the German officers waited for Hitler's final orders to annihilate the British, about 338,000 English and French troops escaped in an armada of small fishing boats and other craft, leaving behind nearly 2,500 guns and 76,000 tons of ammunition. Half of the British naval fleet, including its destroyers, had been sunk or damaged, and now England, fearing the worst, braced itself for an attack. Expecting the Germans to follow his troops across the Channel, Churchill proposed laying poison gas along England's southern beaches to try to thwart the Nazi forces at the shore.

Then on June 5, German forces prepared to turn south. At the Somme, the French line crumpled before the onslaught of German panzers. Four days later, the Germans crossed the Seine, facing only token resistance.

On June 14, the unthinkable happened: Paris itself fell. France was now finished, and its tattered government hastily retreated to Bordeaux. An armistice was signed on June 22, ceding a vast part of France to the Germans. The south of France remained in the hands of a puppet government in the resort town of Vichy. Meanwhile, the countryside was filled with refugees—and littered with corpses and the abandoned carts and luggage of the dead. Moreover, the Germans held 2 million French POWs.

In one audacious stroke, Hitler had outdone Kaiser Wilhelm and Napoleon: he had managed to sever the alliance of his enemies, drive Britain from the European continent, all but destroy the French army, and rewrite the Treaty of Versailles. Germany had either bullied its enemies or smashed them with its blitzkrieg. And its constellation of military forces was now feared from the Caspian Sea to the English Channel.

In vain, Great Britain sought to involve the United States. On the morning of May 15 the French premier, Paul Reynaud, telephoned the newly installed British prime minister, Winston Churchill, at 7:30 to convey, in English, a grim message: "We are defeated. We have lost the battle." Churchill had been imploring Roosevelt to help. The prime minister's immediate reply to Reynaud was: be steadfast; hang on until the United States joins the fray. Churchill then cabled to Roosevelt, saying, "The voice and force of the United States may count for nothing if they are withheld too long." Roosevelt did promptly ask Congress to agree to spend $1.2 billion more on defense in order to build more planes and to increase production facilities. He would also ask for another $1.9 billion a few weeks later. But for the moment, that was all. There would be no troopships of American forces, no public threats, and most critically, no declaration of war. In the days surrounding the fall of Paris, both a frantic Reynaud and Churchill made desperate, last-second pleas to Roosevelt to intervene. Where, they asked, was the might of the United States? In private, Roosevelt offered support, but in public the official American response remained a noncommittal, stony silence. It had become every country for itself.

AT THE OUTSET OF World War I, England's secretary of state for foreign affairs, Sir Edward Grey, had lamented, "The lamps are going out all over Europe; we shall not see them lit again in our lifetime." This, of course, was before America's entry into the first Great War. Now, it was as if history were tragically repeating itself, as one European nation after another was conquered by a rapacious Germany, and as America remained absent. In truth, militarily Roosevelt was hamstrung: far from being a powerhouse, his army was ranked eighteenth in the world, and he commanded not millions of battle-hardened troops like Hitler's, but a pathetic number of men—only about 185,000—many of whom trained with fake wooden rifles. Despite his plan for a large expansion of American airpower, his air forces were outdated and almost nonexistent. The navy was little better. And at one point, Roosevelt reviewed a contingent of national guardsmen training, their brightly colored regimental banners streaming in the wind. They drilled with broomsticks instead of machine guns, raced around in trucks instead of tanks, and were so out of shape that many collapsed from heat and exhaustion during the maneuvers.

Politically, the situation was equally desperate. On the heels of the Depression, Roosevelt had kept defense spending at minimal levels, even though a belligerent Third Reich was violating pact after pact and arming itself to the teeth. By 1940, the American nation remained in the grip of isolationism, and because that was an election year, Roosevelt was unwilling to muster his considerable persuasive powers to prompt an early American entry into the war. So as the summer of 1940 arrived, Britain stood alone, Roosevelt was running for an unprecedented third term on an antiwar plank, and the Nazis were unopposed wherever they went.

THE CONTRAST BETWEEN ROOSEVELT, appealing to the American people for a third term with pledges to keep the nation out of war, and a jubilant Adolf Hitler in Berlin could not have been more striking. Nor could the tenor of the two men have been more stridently at odds. For

Hitler, at the pinnacle of his power, anything and everything now seemed possible. When he toured the deserted streets of a defeated Paris—Nazi loudspeakers had warned all the residents to remain indoors—it was a visit to the tomb of Napoleon that most seemed to captivate the Führer. First he slapped his thighs giddily, followed by a prolonged pause, and then total silence. Standing before the remains of the emperor, the Führer was transfixed.

The German people felt much the same about Hitler. On July 6, he returned to Berlin and was welcomed as if he were a victorious Roman emperor. By the time his train pulled into the station at three o'clock, hundreds of thousands of well-wishers had lined the streets all the way to the Reich Chancellery. The roads themselves were strewn with flowers, and huge crowds of storm troopers shouted, "*Sieg heil! Sieg heil! SIEG HEIL!*" The sun shone brilliantly, and the people, cheering themselves hoarse and delirious with war fever, called again and again for Hitler to come out onto his balcony. Time after time he did. Hitler was now, one of his generals insisted, "the greatest warlord of all time." Little wonder that Hitler believed it was just a matter of time before Britain itself would fall or sue for peace. And little wonder too that he audaciously began to contemplate a final showdown with the Soviet Union in the fall, a titanic battle that would demolish Bolshevism. It would be, Hitler remarked, "child's play," another "lightning war." And, the Führer reasoned, if Russia was routed, "Britain's last hope would be shattered."

Until that moment arrived, Hitler remained content to smash Great Britain from the air.

Throughout August and September successive waves of German fighters took to the skies to bomb England into submission. The Luftwaffe had first sought to blast the Royal Air Force from the air, but the British fought back with everything they could: in a series of dramatic dogfights over the Channel coast and the cities of southern England, the RAF pilots went wing to wing against the Nazi fliers. With America on the sidelines, England's survival had now depended on these close-combat dogfights. When the Germans failed to annihilate the British air force, they then launched a terror-bombing campaign. Thus began the epic Battle of Britain.

Initially, the Germans had targeted ports, radar stations, airfields, and communication facilities. Then the Luftwaffe shifted to nighttime bombing and unleashed as many as a thousand planes a night. German bombs lit up London's East End and then London itself for fifty-seven consecutive nights. When they attacked the city of Coventry, most of its ancient churches were reduced to rubble, and so were seventy thousand homes. The RAF retaliated in kind, bombing Berlin. Hitler angrily announced, "If they attack our cities, we will simply rub out theirs." In response, Churchill said of Hitler, "This wicked man, this monstrous product of former wrongs and shame, has now resolved to break our famous island race by process of indiscriminate slaughter." His jaw jutting, the prime minister boldly promised, "We can take it." England did, but it wasn't easy.

The damage was unprecedented. Ten thousand lay dead, and more than fifty thousand were injured. In the German raid on the manufacturing city of Birmingham, more than 1,300 people were killed in a single evening. Buildings were reduced to charred skeletons; vast craters were left in the city streets. Children were fitted with gas masks. And night after night as the lights were extinguished across the city, some 177,000 Londoners took to makeshift bomb shelters in the stations of the city's famous Underground. Soon, the ground would shake and the sky would be ablaze, as firemen rushed to douse the walls of flame. Once day broke, weary citizens would stumble out from their subterranean world and gaze anew at another round of devastation.

Steadfast, impatient, fretful, Churchill himself would frequently make his way out from the cavernous yellow chamber where he met with aides and would hike up the stairs to a roof when he heard heavy bombing. There, clad in a thick siren suit and steel helmet, gas mask at the ready, he munched restlessly on a tired cigar and watched as his beloved London burned.

But come daylight, tens of thousands of tiny Union Jacks still flapped defiantly in the breeze from the windows of Londoners' houses—that is, those situated beyond the wreckage. "How much they can stand, I don't know," CBS newsman Edward R. Murrow reported in his sonorous voice. "The strain is very great." Yet the British gave as much as they got. Churchill was right; his people could take it. And they managed to inflict extensive losses on the Wehrmacht as well. By late fall, a stymied Hitler had decided that the key to winning the war lay not in the west, but in the east. He indefinitely shelved Operation Sea Lion, the Nazis' planned naval assault on Great Britain across the English Channel, and began to set his sights on invading the Soviet Union—a nation with which he had a nonaggression pact. The consequences would be fateful for the war, for the people of Europe, and eventually for the United States.

And though this was unknown at the time, also for the increasingly embattled Jews of Europe.

~

WHILE ROOSEVELT WAS STILL groping for a grand strategy, Hitler was finally settling on his own. Having achieved nearly total domination in the west, he now planned to attack eastward. He picked June 1941 to begin. He expected the battle to be over by the first frost.

Upon receiving word of the attack against the Soviet Union, Winston Churchill immediately sided with Stalin. And with impressive foresight, Roosevelt extended to the Soviet Union the ever-increasing quantity of American arms and supplies being sent to the Allied powers fighting against the Nazis. But for nearly six months, only two nations were at war with Germany. That would change after December 7, 1941, when Pearl Harbor was attacked and America finally entered the war. Suddenly, there were three: Great Britain, the Soviet Union, and now the United States.

~

ROOSEVELT AS COMMANDER IN chief was both a feast of a character and a massive riddle of a man. To be sure, not everyone loved the American president. "God damn Roosevelt!"—that was the least of what his critics said. Throughout the war, the genial president was castigated as a tyrant and a "paralytic cripple," as a fabricator of bogus promises and a dictator thirsting for global control, as a "Don Quixote of the present century living in his dreams" and as a feeble politician with a "warped" brain. Among wartime presidents, only Lincoln was as castigated.

While preaching freedom abroad, long after the direst days of the Depression, he also had to weather his own mounting problems at home. For example, in the summer of 1943 a simple fistfight in a remote corner of a Detroit park quickly escalated, prompting spasms of racial violence and race riots across the country. National morale was battered. "The whole world is watching our domestic problems," the *New York Times* direly reported.

In the meantime, the business of war was ceaseless. A never-ending parade of problems, appeals, complaints, and queries flowed into the Oval Office. Cartoonists lampooned the president's indecision and ridiculed him for allowing the nation to be so buffeted mercilessly. Yet against all this, against all the nagging policy disputes and temporary military failures, Roosevelt invariably retained his grace. Where an exhausted Abraham Lincoln had morosely wandered the halls of the White House muttering to himself, "I must have relief from this anxiety or it will kill me," and a disgusted George Washington resorted to invective against his political enemies, Roosevelt continued to display good humor and aplomb. It is little wonder that one of Roosevelt's political opponents wrote, "We, who hate your gaudy guts, salute you."

Roosevelt as chief executive remained a puzzle to friends and foes alike. This suited him just fine. He always grasped the symbolism of governance. Thus he spoke to blacks at Howard University, to foreigners at the Statue of Liberty, to the nation from his fireside. Often he acted not by following any grand design but by sheer instinct, hastily improvising makeshift arrangements. One of his greatest accomplishments, the Lend-Lease plan to keep Great Britain viable militarily after 1940, he devised on board a yacht while sailing the Caribbean. It was pure genius, a masterstroke. Under that benign name—Lend-Lease—Roosevelt created a mechanism to sidestep the entire government apparatus and open up the United States' military arsenal in the simple guise of a short-term loan between allies and international friends. Then he sold it, to the American people and to the Congress, genially and cheerily, but all the while never giving an inch of ground.

Not every policy, however, was as masterly. Time and again, he also temporized, unwilling to make a decision until a crisis arrived at his doorstep. Temperamentally, he might have been more at home in the quieter and quainter presidencies of Woodrow Wilson or Theodore Roosevelt, a time of simpler, more ad hoc government. But by the end of 1943, he would be responsible for creating, first, a structure for waging global war—overseeing the creation of the huge, imposing defense and war agencies that we know today—and laying the foundation for the very structure of modern presidential government.

Even here, however, he remained unpredictable. For example, he established the National Resources Planning Board, but then criticized it for dreaming up grandiose theories, particularly in economics. By the middle of the war, he had put together a first-rate, even stellar, cabinet, and surrounded himself with men like Hopkins, Hassett, Stimson, Marshall, Forrestal, Bowles, Byrnes, Nimitz, Eisenhower, and MacArthur. However, he frequently resisted delegating power to them, or even providing them with adequate coordination or administration. The result was a government often in conflict with itself. Stimson, the secretary of war, once groused that Roosevelt was "the poorest administrator I've ever worked under." Stimson concluded: "He wants to do it all himself." In truth, Roosevelt saw his job as head of state less as a matter of management and more as leading the American people. Thus he was also the sermonizer in chief, with his great, resonant eastern voice, articulating principles, fostering shared morals and momentum, and inspiring personal loyalty. In short, moving a nation.

And always, his remained the public face of humanity.

Nothing about him was textbook. He was a man of principle but also a man of expedience. He ably practiced the nuances of negotiation, but he was also a preacher, talking about the global brotherhood of man. And he was devious. With a mischievous air, he loved nothing more than keeping his own government off guard. He deliberately fostered disarray among his own people, believing that this led to more creative policy making: sometimes he would supply information to his aides; at other times he would deliberately withhold it, keeping them in the dark. He made copious use of his own personal desk drawer of intelligence, culled from bits of gossip and all the endless telegrams, correspondence, and memorandums that arrived daily in his office.

And as Hitler would one day learn, he also had an impeccable sense of timing: some days, he seemed strangely sluggish, dragging his feet on decisions, waiting interminably before acting. But he was just as likely, particularly when he was politically vulnerable, to move quickly, even before his staff and his cabinet were informed.

Given his style, it was almost predictable that as Roosevelt navigated the war, his government was in constant turmoil. No surprise, Walter Lippmann once described Roosevelt's leadership as "hesitant and confused," and a congressional critic gave a radio talk called "Roosevelt Versus Roosevelt," saying that the nation needed "fewer and better Roosevelts." Was this fair? Sometimes his presidential magic worked; sometimes not. Disorder, delays, and muddle were frequently the watchwords; problems were met principally by improvisation, not long-term strategy. Yet somehow it all came together. For example, in virtually the same breath he could be a consummate realist, speaking about winning the war as quickly as possible, but also speak fervently about the peace, when a successor to the ill-fated League of Nations would take over.

It was thus perhaps fitting that on April 13, 1943, Roosevelt dedicated the Thomas Jefferson Memorial on the two-hundredth anniversary of Jefferson's birth. While a stiff wind whipped across the tidal basin, the bareheaded president donned his black cape and rose on his braced legs to speak to the crowd. "Today, in the midst of a great war for freedom," he said, "we dedicate a shrine to freedom." Then he paid this simple tribute: "Jefferson was no dreamer." Indeed, these two presidents, one a son of Virginia, the other a New Yorker, had much in common. Jefferson was an aristocrat who spoke in the name of the common people, and so was Roosevelt. Jefferson was a schemer and a manipulator, and so was Roosevelt. Jefferson was a deft politician and a fierce partisan, and so was Roosevelt. Both gave birth to poetic words—founding documents, really—that brilliantly inspired the American people in their own time and generations later. And each could divide people as passionately as he united them. Each was also more than a touch hypocritical, even though both had a sublime quality. Finally, both men sought to peer over the political horizon.

As with the Depression, throughout the mind-numbing trials of the war, Roosevelt never shed his optimism. But unlike Hitler, neither did he have blinkers on. Secretary of the Treasury Morgenthau observed, "The amusing thing about the president is that he can state these facts coolly and calmly whether we win or lose the war, and to me it is most encouraging that he really seems to face these issues, and that he is not kidding himself one minute about the war." And as Isaiah Berlin said of Roosevelt, "He was absolutely fearless. In a despondent world which appeared divided between wicked and fatally efficient fanatics marching to destroy, and bewildered populations on the run . . . he believed in his own ability . . . to stem this terrible tide" of war. Berlin concluded that Roosevelt had the character and energy of the Axis dictators, but was "on our side."

Yet even his equanimity had its limits. Roosevelt sought respite from the war, often with a small group of intimates, on many weekends at Shangri-La, the presidential retreat in the Catoctin Mountains about sixty miles north of Washington. Invariably, his workload traveled with him. But once there, he could thumb through his beloved detective novels, nibble on cheeses and cocktail appetizers, and chat with friends, sometimes about matters of state but more often about trivial things. In contrast to Hyde Park, Shangri-La was rustic to the point of being ramshackle. For Roosevelt, this was grand. His eyes lit up with boyish glee, and he liked to inform his guests jokingly that one of the bathroom doors "did not close securely."

No one, however, neither his enemies nor his friends, should have been seduced by his geniality. He was as tough as steel—or just as aptly, as tough-minded as Abraham Lincoln, who weathered the heavens hung in black to win the Civil War. Actually, his adviser Rex Tugwell did compare Roosevelt's ordeal in the face of the Depression to Lincoln's struggle against disunion.

A good fight invigorated him—Roosevelt said mockingly that every senator was "a law unto himself"—and he dripped with contempt for his adversaries. Once, speaking before a cheering crowd at Madison Square Garden in October 1936, he said that his enemies were "unanimous in their hate for me!" Then he paused dramatically, and added, "and I *welcome* their hatred!" Another time he was subjected to sustained booing on Wall Street, and again in Cambridge when Harvard students gathered to see the university's most eminent alumnus as he glided by in his motorcade; in both instances Roosevelt continued on his way, waving and smiling warmly. Not unsurprisingly, he came to admire the populist Andrew Jackson, who like him had been increasingly regarded with venom by the rich.

Politically he described himself as "a little left of center," though it is worth remembering that he kept a folder labeled "Liberalism Versus Communism and Conservatism." Still, he was anything but dogmatic in his philosophy, willing to experiment with countless policies, or jousting with the secretary of state, or deriding economists speaking in "jargon, ab-so-lute jargon." But deep down, he was a liberal: when his critics insisted that the administration have a balanced budget, Roosevelt boomed, "Hell, a balanced budget isn't putting people to work. I will balance the budget as soon as I take care of the unemployed!" And there remained an indisputable fact: for a time in the 1930s, when American democracy seemed on the verge of dissolution, when the two political parties seemed drained of energy and the collapse of free institutions remained a very real concern, when millions of people had flocked to the new pied pipers of unrest, demagogues like Huey Long and Father Coughlin, and when society and humanity were in peril, Roosevelt rescued democracy at home. Now, as World War II raged and the Tehran summit began in earnest, the question loomed: could he do the same abroad?

During the war, this was the issue. It was always the issue.

~

IN TEHRAN ROOSEVELT WAS about to see exactly how far his personal magic could take him. At three o'clock on a warm Sunday afternoon beneath a cloudless blue sky, Stalin walked unaccompanied from his building and was met outside by a U.S. army officer who escorted him into a room where Roosevelt was waiting. Stalin—a short man with bristly gray hair, pitted cheeks, and a weather-beaten face, not to mention broken teeth stained from years of smoking—was dressed in a khaki tunic adorned with a star of the Order of Lenin on his breast. Roosevelt, seated in his wheelchair, was dressed in a handsome blue business suit. As Stalin extended his hand to take Roosevelt's, the president was struck by what a powerful figure he was. ("He was a very small man, but there was," one American noted, "something about him that made him look awfully big.") Roosevelt also noticed that Stalin looked "curiously" at his shriveled legs and ankles.

Throughout his career Roosevelt had believed in his ability to bond with political allies and adversaries alike, and he was determined to make a personal connection with the Soviet dictator. Well, he should have been; there was much at stake in this meeting. Coarse, cunning, and unscrupulous, Stalin was bound by neither morality nor sentiment: he was the architect of the gulag and the great purges; his regime had coldly executed hundreds of thousands of alleged "enemies of the people" on the flimsiest of evidence; and having started the war as Hitler's partner until the Nazis double-crossed him by invading the Soviet Union, he was also an unpredictable ally. Up to this point, Stalin had been insisting angrily that the Soviets were suffering a disproportionate loss of life, and the Americans therefore feared that even now the Soviet Union might make a separate peace with Germany. Almost incomprehensibly, the Soviets had lost 1 million men in their victory at Stalingrad alone, more than the United States would lose in the entire war. But bravery and sacrifice also took other forms. Thanks to Roosevelt, the United States was contributing crucial supplies and munitions to the Soviet war effort. In the latter part of 1942 alone, it had sent Stalin a staggering

11,000 jeeps, 50,000 tons of explosives, 60,000 trucks, 250,000 tons of aviation gas, and 450,000 tons of steel, as well as (soon) 5,000 fighter planes, and 2 million pairs of boots for the Russian soldiers fighting and bleeding in the gravelly, snowy wastes around Stalingrad. American tires were keeping Soviet trucks moving and American oil was keeping Soviet planes flying; American blankets were warming Soviet troops, and American food—millions of tons including wheat, flour, meat, and milk—was feeding them. Still, Stalin believed the Allies should bear a larger burden of the fighting: hence his intense determination that they make a direct assault on Nazi-occupied western Europe as soon as possible. Here, Roosevelt was sympathetic.

Nonetheless, Churchill had been lukewarm about this idea, preferring to invade Sicily or to focus on the Mediterranean, while out of necessity Roosevelt had deferred the idea until the United States had sufficient sea transport—cargo boats, tankers, destroyers, and escort vessels—for a major cross-Channel assault. But now, as 1943 drew to a close, with troops fighting on the mainland of Halu, the Allies were making significant inroads. The end of the war was within sight.

The next storm was about to break over Europe. And while meeting with Stalin, Roosevelt was looking ahead.

IN TRUTH, ROOSEVELT HAD wanted to see Stalin in person from the moment the Germans had lunged across the Polish border. He often said that at a meeting he learned more by watching a face than by listening to any of the actual words that were uttered. For years, even as president, he had disliked relying on long written missives. And his private secretary Grace Tully also noted that although he used the phone constantly—it was a lifeline—Roosevelt liked to watch facial expressions as well. Churchill too had recognized this early on and took many opportunities to sit down with Roosevelt in person in order to cement the Anglo-American relationship. But so far, Joseph Stalin had only sent his elusive deputy, V. M. Molotov, to the White House. That was not enough for Roosevelt. So it was that the first meeting of the Tehran conference would be an informal tête-à-tête between himself and Stalin, and it would take place in Roosevelt's rooms.

Roosevelt welcomed Stalin, repeating his long-stated wish that they meet in person. Surprisingly soft-spoken, even humble, Stalin countered with his own greeting and pleaded, once again, that his preoccupation with military matters had until now kept the two apart. Then the two men began to talk, and the topics ranged across the globe. True, Roosevelt wanted to talk about military issues, but above all he wanted to discuss longer-term diplomatic matters as well. Still, in deference to Stalin, the president asked about the eastern battlefront, where the Soviets were taking the brunt of the punishing German assault—it was "not too good," in Stalin's words. Stalin added that the Germans were bringing up fresh divisions and the Red Army was about to lose a crucial railway center. Roosevelt artfully asked, however: didn't the initiative still lie with the Red Army? Stalin nodded yes.

At Roosevelt's urging, they moved on to discuss broader matters: France, Indochina, China, and India. Again and again, the president was drawn to diplomacy; again and again, he wanted to talk about the future beyond the war, and specifically his concept of a postwar world managed by an international body led by the four great powers: the United States, the Soviet Union, Great Britain, and China. Then, almost as quickly as it had begun, the private meeting was finished; the two had spoken for about an hour.

It was enough time for them to feel each other out but, as far as Roosevelt was concerned, not enough to cement "any kind of personal connection" with Stalin.

~

THE FIRST MEETING OF all three leaders had been scheduled for four o'clock, in the large conference room at the Soviet embassy.

The leaders and their staffs gathered around a specially procured oak table. It was round, eliminating the issue of who would be seated at the head or the foot, but that did little to eliminate the subtle jockeying for global influence. Given this group's diversity, there was bound to be conflict. Also, there was no fixed agenda; the participants could discuss what they liked and avoid whatever they did not. Inside, the conference room itself was more suited to the chilly winds of Moscow than the sunny warmth of Tehran. Curtains billowed about the windows, tapestries hung from the walls, and the chairs were oversized. Each leader arrived with his aides, although Roosevelt was without George Marshall, who, confused about the scheduled time, was off sightseeing.

Churchill and Stalin had already agreed to defer to Roosevelt to open the session.

Roosevelt, who was sixty-two, began with a quip about welcoming his elders, and then noted emphatically, "We are sitting around this table for the first time as a family, with the one object of winning the war." Churchill spoke next; he was suffering from a cold, so his normally resonant voice was barely audible, yet he said eloquently that the three of them represented the "greatest concentration of power the world has ever seen," adding, "In our hands here is the possible certainty of shortening the war, the much greater certainty of victories, but the absolute certainty that we hold the happy future of mankind." Stalin was perfunctory, speaking about the "potential collaboration" of the three Allies, then thundering, "Now let us get down to business," by which he meant the American and British invasion of Europe, the opening of a true second front against Germany.

The Americans in turn wanted Stalin to signal willingness to commit his forces in the battle in the Pacific. Here, Stalin was sly, saying that he was too deeply engaged in Europe to join in the war against Japan, but that once Germany collapsed the Allies would march together in the Far East. Satisfied, Roosevelt then steered the conversation back to Europe and the projected invasion, emphasizing that the Allies should indeed stand by the decision, made in August 1943 at the Quebec Summit, to invade in May 1944, while also noting that the harsh realities of weather would impede a second front in France before late spring. "The Channel is such a disagreeable body of water," Roosevelt said; then, conscious of Stalin's concerns, he added, "No matter how unpleasant that body might be, however, we still want to get across it."

Churchill, who could well remember a dismal period less than three years earlier when Great Britain had been the only nation under assault from German bombs, testily interjected that when it came to the English Channel, "We were very glad it was a disagreeable body of water at one time."

Roosevelt plunged ahead with further discussion of the cross-Channel invasion, to be code-named Overlord. Given the projected timetable, what could America and Britain do in the interim to divert German resources and reduce the onus on the Red Army? An impassive Stalin, smoking profusely, had his ideas, averring that an invasion from the north could be preceded by an attack through the south of France. In a pointed reminder that the east still remained the central front of the war, he stated that in battling the Germans it had become clear to him that a big offensive launched from only one direction had a far lower likelihood of success. Attacking from two directions would compel the Germans to disperse their forces and would give the Allies a chance to link up and multiply their power by converging. Perhaps this thinking might be applied to the current plans?

Whereas Roosevelt seized upon this concept, Churchill balked. He did not want to pull out forces currently in Italy; as such, he had already suggested making alternative plans for the eastern Mediterranean, perhaps even enticing Turkey to join the war. But Stalin wanted no eastern Mediterranean routes; he believed Italy could be nothing more than a diversion, useless as a path into Germany because of the near impassability of the Alps. Ignoring Churchill, Roosevelt sided with Stalin. The British prime minister gracefully fell back, saying, "Although we are all great friends, it would be idle of us to delude ourselves that we all saw eye to eye on all matters." Meanwhile, Roosevelt implored the military staffs to begin work at once on a plan of attack on southern France to accompany the cross-Channel invasion.

Overlord and its tactics dominated the remainder of the afternoon, until the three leaders retired. They were to reconvene shortly afterward for dinner.

~

ROOSEVELT HOSTED THE DELEGATION next. In the past few hours, the president's Filipino cooks had built cooking ranges and had begun preparing a quintessential American dinner of grilled steak and baked potatoes. For their part, the Secret Service agents were relieved that it was American food being prepared in an American kitchen; at the Roosevelt-Churchill summit in Casablanca, all food and drinks were tested first by medical officers and then bundled together and placed under heavy guard to prevent poisoning or any other tampering.

As the three leaders gathered, the president began by mixing cocktails for what he affectionately called the "children's hour." His drinks—free-form, ever-changing combinations of alcohol and various accompaniments—were very much an acquired taste. This evening Roosevelt put a large quantity of vermouth, "both sweet and dry," into a pitcher of ice, then added a "smaller amount" of gin, stirring the concoction "rapidly." Stalin dutifully drank it—actually, he preferred wine to vodka—but said nothing until Roosevelt eagerly inquired how he liked it. "Well, all right, but it is cold on the stomach," the Marshal replied.

At dinner, the cocktails were replaced by wine and bourbon, which flowed freely for a long series of toasts.

But if on the surface the leaders were festive, there remained an icy undertow in their discussions. As the meal progressed, postwar Europe again became the focus. Coldly writing off Russia's ancient enemies, Stalin took control: he returned to a theme from his private talk with Roosevelt, this time publicly denouncing the French to the entire delegation gathered around the table. He declared the entire French ruling class to be "rotten to the core," adding that its members deserved "no consideration from the Allies" and should not be left "in possession of their empire." Churchill, firmly believing that France would have to be reconstructed as a strong nation, spoke up on behalf of the French. Roosevelt attempted to play peacemaker, but to no avail. Stalin then took up the more crucial issue of Germany, arguing for its "dismemberment and the harshest possible treatment" as the only means to prevent an eventual return of German militarism.

To emphasize his point, Stalin, himself the ruthless force behind countless purges—the slightest criticism of his regime was an offense against the state, and he himself once muttered, "Who's going to remember all those riffraff in ten to twenty years? No one!"—spoke about interrogated German prisoners of war. When these prisoners were asked why they had butchered innocent women and children, their reply was that they were doing only what they had been ordered to do. Then Stalin recounted an experience of his own inside Germany.

In 1907, he had been in Leipzig to attend a workers' meeting. But two hundred German delegates failed to appear, because the railroad clerk who had to punch their train tickets did not arrive at work and the German delegates would not board the train without properly punched tickets. The German mentality, Stalin declared, was too blindly obedient to authority. (In the interest of maintaining harmony, neither Roosevelt nor Churchill was daring enough to comment on the paradox of such a statement by an absolute despot who wielded power from the barrel of a gun.) Clearly Stalin was probing his allies, attempting to see exactly how far they could be prodded into punishing and remaking a postwar Germany. He even said he disagreed with Roosevelt's view that the Führer was mentally unbalanced, instead calling Hitler an intelligent man hindered by a primitive approach to politics.

This time, Roosevelt tried to steer the conversation back to less controversial topics, like the matter of access to the Baltic Sea. But suddenly, at about 10:30 p.m., just as he prepared to speak, no words came out of his mouth. There was a long pause.

To the horror of the participants, the president turned green, and "great drops of sweat" began to "bead off his face." Then he put "a shaky hand to his forehead."

A stunned silence descended on the gathering as everyone gazed at the American president, who was clearly in serious distress.

Saying little, Harry Hopkins leaped from his seat and had Roosevelt wheeled away from the table and back to his room. Roosevelt's physician, Admiral Ross McIntire, was dining outside. He raced to the president's room.

As it happened, only McIntire knew that a similar incident had happened once before, on an evening in February 1940, also during dinner. Was this a repetition of that ghastly dinner—except that this time, the presidential collapse was happening with the world's most powerful leaders present? At this pivotal time, the nation could not afford to have Roosevelt seriously ill.

In Roosevelt's room, McIntire hurriedly began his examination. Roosevelt explained that after the meal ended, he had felt faint. McIntire's diagnosis was surprisingly perfunctory: indigestion and excess stomach gas. He gave Roosevelt something to relieve the symptoms. If the president's discomfort was anything more than indigestion—and it almost surely was—McIntire apparently never pursued it. And by the next afternoon, Roosevelt was again meeting with Stalin to lay out his vision of a postwar world, before the two then joined Churchill for another round of conferences.

But even if the Americans could move on, untroubled, the night was surely a worrisome omen, as well as a grim reminder to Churchill and to Stalin that for Roosevelt, good health was fleeting.

WHILE ROOSEVELT SEEMED "FULLY recovered" from the attack of indigestion, and was, according to the Americans, "as alert as ever," the summit had once more snagged on the increasingly thorny issue of the cross-Channel invasion. Fearing that a direct assault could "wipe out civilization" and leave the Continent desolate, Churchill was still dragging his heels. For his part, Roosevelt, unable yet to commit vast forces for the planned assault on Europe, still wanted to focus on the postwar world and his concept of an international organization to resolve disputes. Stalin, however, mindful of his troops bleeding and dying on the unforgiving eastern front, kept returning to Overlord. Whether doodling on a pad with a red pencil (he liked to draw wolves' heads) or sitting impassively cradling a cigarette, he was relentless. He wanted an explicit date in May—as Roosevelt had promised—and he wanted a commander. To this end, a somber Stalin pointedly asked Roosevelt for the commander's name. The president acknowledged that he had not made a final choice, although everyone knew that the leading candidate, General George Marshall, was attending the conference.

Stalin saw this simply as stalling and fumed, "Then nothing will come out of these operations."

After some talk of Turkey and Bulgaria, the discussion again returned to Overlord. Now Stalin said accusingly to Churchill, "Do the British really believe in Overlord, or are you only saying so to reassure the Russians?" Churchill, chewing on a cigar, scowled and noted that "it will be our stern duty to hurl across the Channel against the Germans every sinew of our strength." As on the previous day, the session ended with Churchill's words.

Later, in private, the frustrated prime minister retorted, "Bloody!"

NOW IT WAS STALIN'S turn to be the host at dinner.

Through the long succession of toasts and amid tables groaning with a classic Russian meal—cold hors d'oeuvres to start, then hot borscht, fish, an assortment of meats, salads, compotes, and fruits, all accompanied by vodka and fine wines—the Soviet leader began goading Churchill. He alternately "teased" or "needled" the British prime minister, and even went as far as suggesting that Churchill still harbored warm feelings toward Germany and privately desired a "soft" peace. Despite the fact that it was Churchill who had mustered the facts against Hitler earlier and more cogently than anyone else, Stalin continued with his verbal barbs, almost always sanctioned and even aided by Roosevelt. The "acrid" exchanges accelerated, until Stalin riposted that the German general staff "must be liquidated." The whole force of Hitler's armies, he continued, "depended upon about fifty thousand officers and technicians." If these were "rounded up and shot at the end of the war," German military strength would be undone. Stalin made his remark with a "sardonic smile" and a "wave of the hand." But either Churchill's translator missed the Soviet leader's ostensible sarcasm or the prime minister himself decided that he had had enough. Furious, he icily replied, "The British Parliament and public will never tolerate mass executions. Even if in war passion they allowed them to begin, they would turn violently against those responsible after the first butchery had taken place."

Churchill added, "I would rather be taken out into the garden here and now and be shot myself than sully my own and my country's honor by such infamy." At this point, a previously silent Roosevelt sought to mediate by offering some humor of his own. He suggested a compromise: on the number fifty thousand, he could not support Marshal Stalin. Instead, only "49,000 should be shot."

Unremarked by any side was the glaring fact that when it came to human liquidations in this ghastly war, including an entire race of innocent civilians being inexorably butchered in the dark forests of Poland, fifty thousand seemed to be a very small number indeed.

ON THE THIRD DAY, all sides found a way to come together. Stalin made a less than subtle suggestion that failure to open a second front in Europe in 1944 could all but ensure that a war-weary Soviet Union would seek a separate peace with Hitler. However improbable it was at this stage of the conflict, his threat had the desired effect. This time, Churchill bowed to reality. By lunchtime, he and Roosevelt pronounced Overlord a go, with a possible side operation against the south of France. The Soviets, for their part, would organize an offensive to take place in May against German forces in the east.

That night, November 30, Churchill, although still ailing—by now he had a miserable bronchial cough and an intermittent fever—nonetheless was the host of the official dinner. It was his sixty-ninth birthday, and the trappings of the British Empire were on display. Crystal and silver glistened in the candlelight, Roosevelt and Churchill wore black tie, and the toasts were poignant. Usually, the person proposing a toast would circle the table to touch his glass to the toastee's. At one point, however, Roosevelt toasted the health of Churchill's daughter, Sarah. But it was Stalin who rose and walked around the table to clink glasses with her and bow. Sarah Churchill hesitated a moment, then left her seat to walk to Roosevelt's place, where she touched her glass to his, and he said with great charm, "I would have come to you, my dear, but I cannot."

As the evening wore on, for the first time Stalin rose to thank America publicly for the extensive shipments that were keeping the Red Army alive ("I want to tell you what the president has done to win the war"). He even acknowledged, memorably, that without Lend-Lease, "we would lose this war."

Then it was Churchill's turn. With Stalin sitting to his left and Roosevelt to his right, he recalled: "Together, we controlled practically all the naval and three-quarters of all the air forces in the world, and could direct armies of nearly twenty millions of men, engaged in the most terrible of wars that had yet occurred in human history." He paused, then added, "I could not help rejoicing at the long way we had come on the road to victory since the summer of 1940 when we had been alone."

It was Roosevelt, however, who would have the last word. At 2 a.m., he triumphantly raised his glass and said, "We have differing customs and philosophies and ways of life. But we have proved here at Tehran that the varying ideals of our nations can come together in a harmonious whole, moving unitedly for the common good of ourselves and of the world."

But whatever harmony was achieved at Tehran, it nonetheless remained elusive in a larger sense; for there was still much more war—and unfathomable moral tragedy—to come.

~

WHEN ROOSEVELT RETIRED TO his room on his last night in the Soviet compound, he fretted, worrying that he had not yet achieved his primary purpose: reaching a lasting, personal accord with Stalin. Despite his best efforts, he found the Soviet dictator "correct," "stiff," "solemn," with "nothing human to get hold of." In his own words, he felt discouraged. Then it occurred to him that for two evenings, he had watched Stalin needle and tease Churchill with obvious enjoyment. True, he had joined in, but with some restraint. For the most part, when Stalin had been blunt and Churchill had debated vociferously, he himself had patiently listened and mediated, joked and prodded. On the final day of the conference, seeking political gain, he chose an opposite course. He would mock the prime minister outright.

On his way to the conference room on that last morning, the president caught up with Churchill and said, "Winston, I hope you won't be sore at me for what I am going to do." The prime minister was somewhat taken aback; just days earlier he had enjoyed an intimate Thanksgiving dinner with Roosevelt in Cairo, where they had carved turkeys (two of them), drunk champagne while holiday music blared in the background, and eaten pumpkin pie. Amid the carnage of war, it was an evening of unforgettable friendship. Nevertheless, Churchill, a veteran of tough-nosed English politics, needed little help in imagining what was about to come next; as Roosevelt remembered it, the prime minister simply shifted his cigar and "grunted."

As soon as he entered the conference room, Roosevelt wheeled his way over to Stalin and the surrounding Soviet delegation. He appeared cagey, even intimate, as if drawing Stalin into his confidence; but Stalin was unmoved. Then, lifting his hand toward his mouth, as if covering a whisper, Roosevelt chuckled, "Winston is cranky this morning; he got up on the wrong side of the bed." As the Soviet interpreter repeated the words, "a vague smile passed over Stalin's eyes." Roosevelt immediately decided that he was on the right track. Once the group was seated at the table, he began to tease Churchill about his "Britishness," about "John Bull," about "his cigars, about his habits." The president watched Churchill turn bright red and scowl, and the more he did so, the more Stalin smiled. Finally, Roosevelt recalled, "Stalin broke out into a deep, hearty guffaw, and for the first time in three days I saw light." At last, the ice has been broken.

Having made his inroad, an ecstatic Roosevelt even took the liberty of calling Stalin "Uncle Joe" to his face, and the Soviet leader was not offended. What Churchill felt went unrecorded. However, it was the American ambassador Averell Harriman, an admirer of both Roosevelt and the Russians, who offered perhaps the most telling observation on the president's choices: "He always enjoyed other people's discomfort," Harriman would write.

THE SUMMIT WAS A success. Roosevelt left Tehran for Cairo, as did Churchill. Overlord had been agreed to; they had discussed the need for an international body to keep the peace; they had hashed out the fate of the Baltic states and the status of a postwar Germany; they had talked of reparations from Finland and of persuading the Turks to enter the war; and they had huddled over State Department maps of central Europe, hotly debating the contentious matter of the borders of Poland as well as its government-in-exile.

But there was still unfinished business, including one of Roosevelt's most important decisions of the war. On December 5, he rendered the much-awaited verdict that would set Operation Overlord and D-Day fully in motion: he formally selected the commander for the joint Allied invasion. His army chief of staff, General George Marshall, whom the president considered the most accomplished figure of the joint chiefs and who had accompanied Roosevelt to Tehran, was now anxiously waiting. Marshall knew that almost every sign suggested he would be the commander, and he wanted the job. Indeed, at one point during the Tehran conference, Stalin had personally congratulated Marshall on his upcoming command. Yet the more Roosevelt had thought about it, the more he worried about losing Marshall's discreet, wise counsel. He wanted him in Washington, not in the field, and decided this was a gamble not worth taking. So late on a Sunday morning, Roosevelt called Marshall into his room. After some small talk, the president finally asked the general what he wanted to do about Overlord. The taciturn Marshall, ever the good soldier, replied that it was the president's decision to make. "Then it will be Eisenhower," Roosevelt said. To ensure the finality of his decision, the president then instructed Marshall to start writing as he dictated a personal message to Stalin. The general put pen to paper and took down Roosevelt's words announcing the appointment of his military subordinate: "The immediate appointment of General Eisenhower to command of Overlord operation has been decided upon." Once Marshall wrote this, Roosevelt added an exclamation point and coolly affixed his signature. There would be no turning back. Marshall later gave Eisenhower the original signed note as a memento, adding by way of explanation, "It was written very hurriedly by me."

This was the start of a year of fateful decisions. But first, the president, tired but feeling confident, had to return the thousands of miles home.

ON HIS WAY BACK, Roosevelt had wanted to go to Naples to see the troops, but combat was still raging there, and the president was eventually dissuaded, electing to go to the islands of Malta and Sicily instead. At Malta, he would present a plaque to the inhabitants for resisting the Nazis; in Sicily, he would inspect the troops, decorate war heroes, and speak to his flamboyant but troubled general, George Patton, who had recently slapped a shell-shocked soldier in the face. Then Roosevelt went on to Morocco and the sea voyage back across the Atlantic.

On December 17, Roosevelt returned to the White House. He had been abroad for over a month. By Christmas Eve, he traveled north, to Hyde Park, and was preparing to deliver a fireside chat on Tehran. Surrounded by microphones and the glare of klieg lights, Roosevelt sought to prepare the American people for the final push against Germany; he spoke of a true "world war" and the "launching of a gigantic attack upon Germany," adding, "We shall all have to look forward to large casualty lists—dead, wounded, and missing. War entails just that. There is no easy road to victory and the end is not yet in sight."

Then came Christmas Day. For the Roosevelts it was spent listening to carolers and hearing the president read Dickens's classic *A Christmas Carol*. But in chilly upstate New York, the president was suffering through a bout of influenza, coughing and aching; his temperature would soon spike and he would feel "at loose ends." Still, it was the first time in eleven years that he had spent Christmas with his family in Hyde Park, and he was determined to enjoy every minute of it.

Yet on that same day, as wreaths and red ribbons dotted the elegant hotels and homes of official Washington, and as the fire crackled at Hyde Park and eggnog and other drinks and little cakes were served, a young lawyer in the Treasury Department was working overtime on a memorandum for its chief, Treasury Secretary Henry Morgenthau Jr. It had a long, but stunning title: "Report to the Secretary on the Acquiescence of This Government in the Murder of the Jews."

For all the talk of battle plans, empires, and postwar peace, the systematic murder of the Jews was one item that none of the Big Three had discussed in Tehran. The blistering report would be delivered to the secretary of the treasury at the start of the new year, and then in turn to the president himself.

2

"I Want to Sleep and Sleep Twelve Hours a Day"

As early as 1940 a jubilant Führer had told Hermann Göring, "The war is finished."

But as the Tehran summit ended and 1944 opened, the Nazis' successes were increasingly limited. Still, even if the Allies could see a clear path to victory, the war was anything but finished and its outcome was far from evident. On January 3, the British Royal Air Force launched another large air raid on Berlin. This time, however, the damage to the city was minimal, while the RAF lost twenty-seven planes and 168 crewmembers. British planes were being lost at a rate of 10 percent each month. And in Italy, the only active front in the west, the Allies were bogged down at the Germans' seemingly unbreakable Gustav Line. Yet more than ever, even as he acknowledged that "we have got a long, long road to go," Franklin Roosevelt was now looking ahead.

Driven by a conviction that even today history has trouble fathoming, Roosevelt had helped to forge an alliance out of desperation abroad;

had beaten back isolationism at home and kindled a democratic spirit when the days were darkest; and had emerged as the leader of free men everywhere. Hitler may have mocked him, but a sentimental Winston Churchill knew better, once calling Roosevelt "the greatest man I've ever known." So did legendary journalist Edward R. Murrow, who reported that, to the men fighting or preparing to fight in this war, "The name 'Roosevelt' was a symbol, the code word for a lot of guys named 'Joe' who are somewhere out in the blue with the armor heading east."

Yet there was to be nothing easy about this war, not in the beginning, nor in the middle, nor at the end. Actually, when Murrow spoke those words, the English-speaking Allied forces weren't headed east yet; they were slugging their way north, mired in the invasion of Italy. The advance there was brutally slow. Here was a soldier's hell: villages had to be taken house by house, while along the coastline the Germans holed up in impenetrable mountainous positions and targeted Allied soldiers one by one. Amid the billowing clouds of dense roiling smoke, the stabbing spurts of mortar fire, and the thunderous roar of bursting shells, one soldier quipped that this was "the winter of discontent." It was. For the drenched and shivering GIs, the mud, the muck, the sleet, and the valleys were enemies every bit as implacable as the Nazis. Vile storms turned clay roads into sheets of water; and with the troops wedged between the German lines, all the Allied advances bogged down. Jeeps were paralyzed by the swamps, and tanks were rendered virtually useless. Supplies had to be shuttled by mules, which sometimes picked their way over corpses much as they had done on the western front in World War I. And everywhere they turned, Allied soldiers were assaulted by the biting cold and howling winds.

Indeed, the plight of the men, crouched precariously on knife-edge cliffs, was heartrending. Trench foot was widespread in the damp, cold foxholes, and so was frostbite. Pounded by heavy storms, the soldiers were often thigh-deep in rainwater. When there was a lull in the shooting and the men could look up, they saw scavenger dogs feasting on the entrails of dead GIs. At night, they could hear the cries of the wounded pinned down by withering machine-gun fire and stranded out of reach

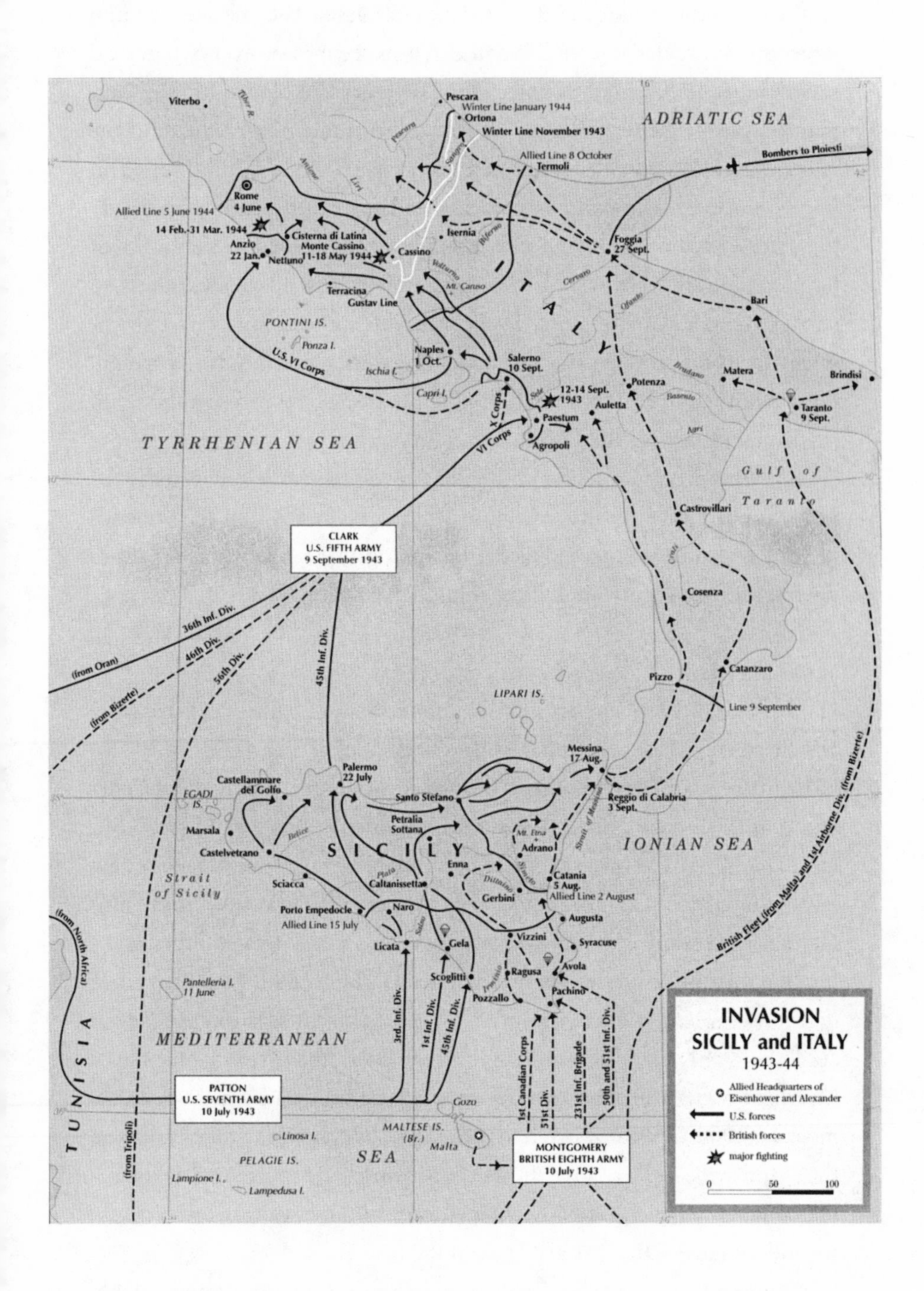
INVASION
SICILY and ITALY
1943-44
Allied Headquarters of Eisenhower and Alexander
U.S. forces
British forces
major fighting
0 50 100
ADRIATIC SEA
TYRRHENIAN SEA
IONIAN SEA
MEDITERRANEAN SEA
Gulf of Taranto
Strait of Sicily
ITALY
SICILY
TUNISIA
Viterbo
Pescara
Winter Line January 1944
Ortona
Winter Line November 1943
Allied Line 8 October
Termoli
Bombers to Ploiesti
Rome 4 June
Allied Line 5 June 1944
14 Feb.-31 Mar. 1944
Cisterna di Latina
Monte Cassino 11-18 May 1944
Anzio 22 Jan.
Nettuno
Cassino
Isernia
Foggia 27 Sept.
Terracina
Gustav Line
Mt. Caruso
PONTINI IS.
Ponza I.
U.S. VI Corps
Ischia I.
Capri I.
Naples 1 Oct.
Salerno 10 Sept.
12-14 Sept. 1943
Paestum
Agropoli
Auletta
Potenza
Bari
Matera
Brindisi
Taranto 9 Sept.
X Corps
VI Corps
Castrovillari
Cosenza
Catanzaro
Pizzo
Line 9 September
LIPARI IS.
CLARK
U.S. FIFTH ARMY
9 September 1943
36th Inf. Div.
46th Div.
56th Div.
45th Inf. Div.
(from Oran)
(from Bizerte)
Messina 17 Aug.
Reggio di Calabria 3 Sept.
Strait of Messina
Palermo 22 July
Castellammare del Golfo
EGADI IS.
Marsala
Castelvetrano
Santo Stefano
Petralia Sottana
Mt. Etna
Adrano
Enna
Caltanissetta
Catania 5 Aug.
Allied Line 2 August
Gerbini
Sciacca
Porto Empedocle
Allied Line 15 July
Naro
Augusta
Vizzini
Syracuse
Licata
Gela
Avola
Ragusa
Scoglitti
Pozzallo
Pachino
British Fleet (from Malta) and 1st Airborne Div. (from Bizerte)
(from North Africa)
Pantelleria I. 11 June
3rd. Inf. Div.
1st Inf. Div.
45th Inf. Div.
1st Canadian Corps
51st Div.
231st Inf. Brigade
50th and 51st Inf. Div.
PATTON
U.S. SEVENTH ARMY
10 July 1943
Gozo
MALTESE IS. (Br.)
Malta
MONTGOMERY
BRITISH EIGHTH ARMY
10 July 1943
Linosa I.
PELAGIE IS.
Lampione I.
Lampedusa I.
(from Tripoli)

of their comrades, cries that as the hours passed became weaker and fewer and more desperate. German defenses seem to be everywhere and nowhere, despite the continuous whine of American planes strafing German outposts and supply lines. Predictably, morale plummeted and the Allied casualties rose. Isolated in their cragged ravines, or trapped in barbed wire, or hemmed in by enemy mines, or buffeted by the steady *pop! pop! pop!* of enemy gunfire, the men were pushed to the limits of human endurance. Many of them succumbed to shell shock, others to sheer exhaustion or outright insanity. Some spontaneously wet themselves from the unrelenting strain. As the weeks and months wore on, GIs ruefully dubbed this stretch of what had been the ancestral home of the Roman Empire "the Purple Heart Valley."

But with the approach of spring, Roosevelt fervently believed the Allies would soon break the stalemate. Indeed, he hoped that the impending fall of Rome would signal the beginning of an operation far more profound: the long-awaited cross-Channel invasion, Overlord.

IT WAS TO BE the largest amphibious invasion in history, across the treacherous English Channel, and it was designed to be the decisive blow of the war. Far away from the Allied summitry, for the better part of a year the D-Day preparations had consumed military planners. Now, with Dwight Eisenhower at the helm, the operation would reach a new level of intensity. It had to. France was the only viable western route into Germany, and surprise was critical; Hitler knew the invasion was coming, but he didn't know where. Still, the Germans could field fifty-five divisions—eleven of them armored—whereas on the first day Roosevelt could land only eight divisions of his own. Thus, the sheer magnitude of Overlord was astonishing, and every operational detail was critical: almost 180,000 GIs transported in more than five thousand ships and one thousand wide-bellied aircraft, leaving from eleven ports and converging on just five beachheads. These men were all now waiting breathlessly for the signal—"OK, let's go!"

The key to the invasion was its location: Normandy, a formidable

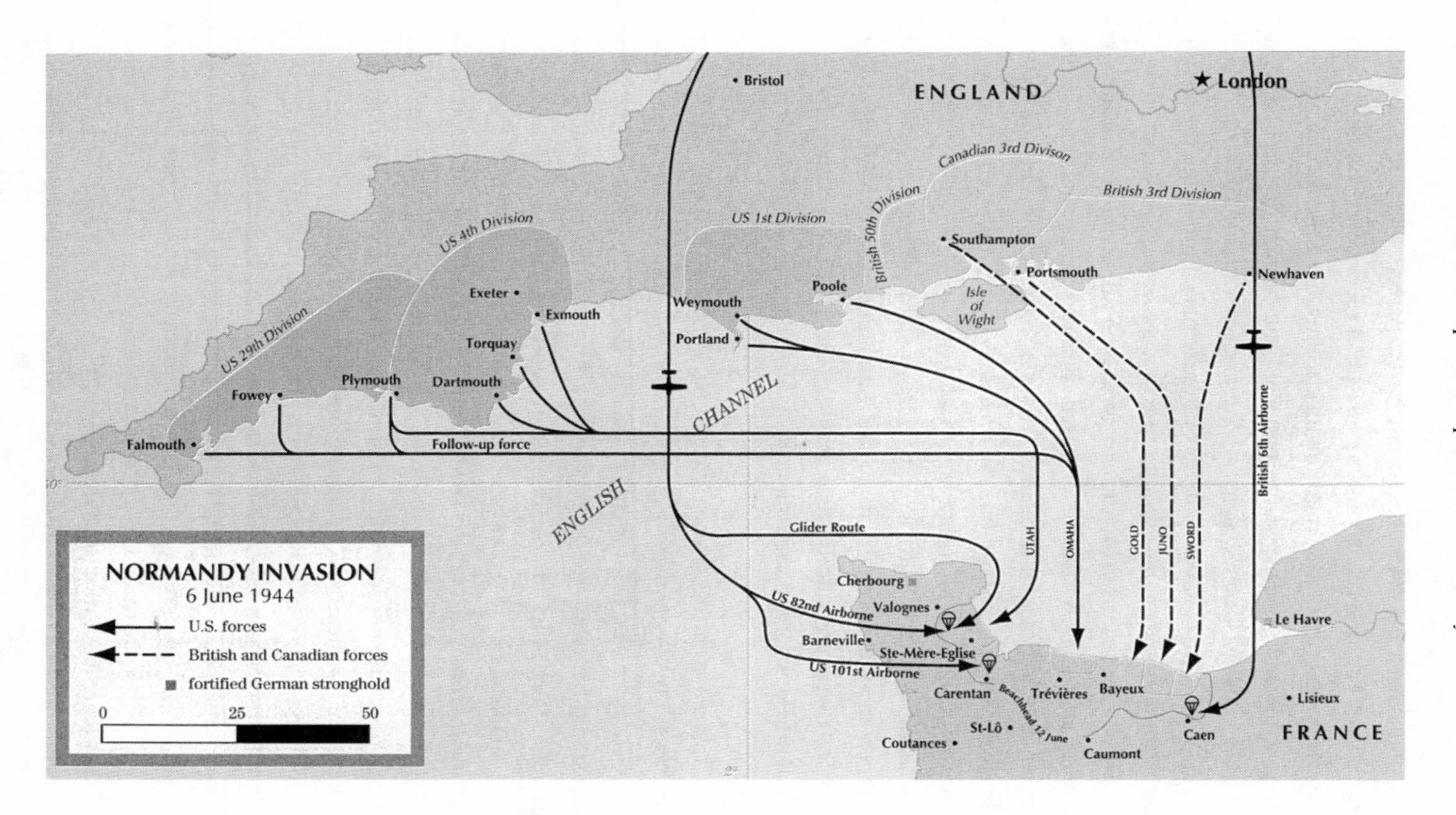
NORMANDY INVASION
6 June 1944
U.S. forces
British and Canadian forces
fortified German stronghold
0
25
50
ENGLAND
FRANCE
ENGLISH
CHANNEL
London
Bristol
Newhaven
Portsmouth
Southampton
Isle of Wight
Poole
Weymouth
Portland
Exmouth
Exeter
Torquay
Dartmouth
Plymouth
Fowey
Falmouth
British 3rd Division
Canadian 3rd Divison
British 50th Division
US 1st Division
US 4th Division
US 29th Division
British 6th Airborne
SWORD
JUNO
GOLD
OMAHA
UTAH
Follow-up force
Glider Route
US 82nd Airborne
US 101st Airborne
Le Havre
Lisieux
Caen
Bayeux
Caumont
Trévières
Beachhead 12 June
St-Lô
Carentan
Ste-Mère-Eglise
Valognes
Cherbourg
Barneville
Coutances

coastline with no ports, bracketed by two rivers and wide swaths of farmland. For months, thousands of Allied reconnaissance flights over coastal waters had sought to identify enemy bunkers and heavy artillery, while midget submarines patrolled the French beaches, attempting to examine German defenses. Meanwhile, to confound the Nazis, Roosevelt and the Allies spun an elaborate ruse. Employing the skills of America's movie moguls, counterintelligence created a virtual dummy army under the leadership of renowned General George S. Patton; comprised of strikingly realistic armored divisions fabricated from rubber, painted prefabricated airplanes, and perfectly scaled landing craft—buttressed by the continuous hum of radio traffic and even camp stoves that smoked—this phantom force was meant to dupe the Germans into believing that the Allies were preparing for an all-out assault on the French coast at Pas de Calais, rather than at Normandy. Most of Hitler's generals were convinced this was where the invasion would arrive.

And elsewhere in the United Kingdom, the true invasion force gathered.

It was a military caravan without parallel: tens of thousands of camouflaged tanks—landing ship tanks, swimming tanks, and flail tanks—as well as trucks, jeeps, artillery pieces, gliders, typewriters, medicine, Mustang fighters, and locomotives ("hundreds") were quietly positioned along miles of roadside in southern England, in expectation of the cataclysmic encounter to come. Meanwhile, hundreds of thousands of men, "tense as a coiled spring" and sealed off from the rest of the world, conducted poison gas drills, dug foxholes, were trained in demolition and wire cutting, and pored over detailed maps and photographs of enemy fortifications. By early June, their number would total nearly 3 million. They received copious distributions of invasion money, shiny wire cutters, gas masks, new toothbrushes, fresh cigarettes, seasickness pills, extra socks, and of course extra ammunition. To no one's surprise, two of their most treasured possessions became French guidebooks and condoms. At the same time, fifteen hospital ships were prepared to accommodate eight thousand doctors, and loaded on board were 100,000 pints of plasma; 600,000 doses of penicillin; and 100,000 pounds of sulfa. Some 124,000 hospital beds were also readied. In quieter moments, the GIs closed their eyes, crossed themselves, and bowed their heads in prayer; they knew what was coming.

But it was rarely quiet. Each night, convoys many miles long rumbled for hours on end. And with row upon row of office buildings and warehouses, sprawling guest facilities, and a myriad of dockworkers stacking supplies and provisions—100,000 packets of gum, 12,500 pounds of biscuits, 6,200 pounds of sweets, endless spare tires, huge reels of cable, and tens of thousands of wheels and wooden cases—it would have been easy to mistake the military nerve center of this ever-expanding armada for a vast commercial metropolis. Indeed, the logistics of Overlord were mind-numbing. It was as if the Allies were ferrying the entire population of Boston, Baltimore, and Staten Island—every man, woman, and child, and every car and every van—in total darkness over 112 miles of choppy waters in a mere twelve hours.

The command post for this onslaught was an innocuous-looking trailer not far from the Portsmouth dockyard, distinguished only by the presence of a red telephone that sat on a simple wooden desk—this relayed scrambled calls to Roosevelt and the War Department in Washington—and a green telephone that was a direct line to Churchill at 10 Downing Street.

By late spring, all would be in readiness. The only thing left would be for the man in the trailer, General Eisenhower, to give the final order for the assault. For Roosevelt, Eisenhower, and the Allies, there was no real contingency planning. As the general put it, "We cannot afford to fail."

Overlord was all or nothing.

~

AT THE SAME TIME, across the Channel, a pacing Erwin Rommel, one of Hitler's shrewdest and most daring generals, who had already sparred against the Allies in Egypt but had eventually come up short, was now firmly in command in France. Rommel felt that Germany's best chance was to stop the Allied forces dead in their tracks—on the beaches. And he was determined to do just that. For half a year, some

500,000 Germans had meticulously built massive pillboxes and deadly obstacles to await the Allies. Whenever possible, awaiting Rommel's orders were the elite of the Wehrmacht, the men who had raced into Czechoslovakia, who had brazenly stunned the Poles, who had overrun Norway and Belgium and outmaneuvered a dumbstruck France, and who, for good measure, had outflanked the Yugoslavs and the Greeks. Whatever private doubts Rommel may have harbored about the eventual success of an Allied invasion, he knew that he could make every yard costly. He also knew—or hoped—that even his second-class and third-class troops—a motley mix of children and old men as well as "volunteers" from Croatia, Poland, Estonia, Latvia, Lithuania, and the Crimea—could make up with *Fanatismus* ("fanaticism") what they lacked in actual training. Moreover, he knew that every Allied reinforcement, every grenade, every dose of morphine, every tourniquet, and every tin of food would have to brave the English Channel before it could reach Hitler's "Fortress Europe."

Finally, Rommel knew just how complicated amphibious operations were; anything could go awry and often did. True, the American general Winfield Scott had successfully landed at Veracruz in 1847, but his enemy, Mexico, was ill-prepared. Even Napoleon had dismally failed to cross the English Channel, and so had Hitler himself. Not since William the Conqueror in 1066 had a military landing succeeded—and unlike the Allies, William had been going the other way. Recent history also offered little reassurance. Frustrated by the weather and the water, the British were ignominiously defeated at Gallipoli in World War I, a memory that a quarter of a century later still haunted Churchill. And when a large Allied commando force had attacked Dieppe along the French coast in August 1942, the Nazis had cut them to pieces.

So for weeks on end, Rommel's men erected a formidable web of strongholds and defenses, connected by a vast system of tunnels. The pace was frenetic. They laid more than half a million advance barriers in the surf—"Belgian gates" and sharpened interlocking iron bars—designed to shred the hulls of the landing craft and thereby induce the

Allies to wait for low tide, when the grazing fire of German machine guns would be at its most murderous and efficient. They ingeniously flooded hundreds of miles of Normandy fields to create a natural killing zone, forcing enemy aircraft to crash-land. And they set booby traps of all kinds, including hundreds of thousands of land mines, designed to detonate when a wire was tripped or cut. There were also antitank ditches and countless rolls of barbed wire, creating what Rommel hoped would be a marathon of horrific obstacles that the Allied troops would have to breach before they could even reach the coastal fortifications of Hitler's famed Atlantic Wall. And of course everywhere there was concrete: concrete and steel reinforced walls, thirteen feet thick; concrete heavy gun nests for men keeping a vigilant watch; and concrete missile-launching sites. Meanwhile, in the distance deadly German panzer tanks waited to fire their guns and hurl the invaders back into the sea.

Was this the Nazis' counterpart of the Maginot Line? Or was it an impregnable twentieth-century version of the Union's defenses against Pickett's foolish charge at Gettysburg? Only time would tell. "The war will be won or lost on the beaches," Rommel solemnly told an aide. "The enemy is at his weakest just after landing [and] the first 24 hours of the invasion will be decisive."

It would be, he predicted, gazing into the distance, "the longest day."

UNTIL THAT DAY ARRIVED, there was nothing to do but wait. So Roosevelt waited, in the Oval Office, or the map room, or when motoring through the capital's streets. He knew the sights, sounds, and scars of a nation at war. These he could deal with. He knew winning the war could still "take an awfully long time." This he could also deal with. And he could deal with the shiploads of coffins that he knew would soon return home. But as the Allies prepared to launch their most important effort of the war, there was one fact he could not control: since his trip to Tehran, his own time was running out.

As Overlord was gearing up, he was all but a dying man.

~

He would never admit this to the outside world, and just as likely, never even to himself. Why? As America prepared for an operation that would decide the fate of Europe, was this an act of reckless indifference? Or of self-deluding conceit? Or was Roosevelt, the resolute and clear-sighted wartime leader, simply unwilling to accept any personal weakness, or unwilling to accept any defeat? Despite his handicap, he had always been a commanding physical presence leading the Allied coalition. Suddenly, though, in the early months of 1944, when his energy was most needed, the president looked and acted dangerously ill.

He was just sixty-two, yet he had been in the public spotlight for the better part of three decades, ever since Woodrow Wilson had appointed him assistant secretary of the navy. Now, ten years after he had assumed the presidency, Roosevelt was, in ways large and small, the picture of exhaustion. His cheeks were sunken and his hand quivered violently when he reached for his cigarettes. His face was the color of milky chalk, except for the skin under his eyes, which was so dark and discolored that in photographs it appeared perpetually bruised. In the morning hours he was too fatigued to work, while in the evening hours he felt too ill to sleep. When he sifted through position papers at his massive desk in the Oval Office, he far too frequently had a blank stare, his mouth drooped when he read the mail, and almost unthinkably, he fell asleep during dictation. As if this semi-stupor weren't troubling enough, remarkably, he once all but blacked out when signing his name, leaving nothing more on the paper than smudged ink and an incoherent scrawl. On another occasion, his Secret Service agents were stunned to find that he had fallen out of his chair and was sprawled helplessly on the floor. And always there were the headaches—headaches that plagued him daily—and the hacking cough that refused to go away.

After dining at the White House, one of Roosevelt's political allies confessed to being shocked at how "tired and worn" the president looked. Roosevelt's director of war information, Robert Sherwood, was even more forthright, describing the president as having "an almost ravaged" countenance. Sherwood, "shocked by his appearance," remarked on how much weight Roosevelt had lost and how "emaciated" his neck was. Winston Churchill confided to his own personal physician, Lord Moran, that the president looked like "a very tired man."

Predictably, there were rumors. However much Roosevelt and the White House staff carefully managed his public persona, it became known that he had to cancel a number of engagements, including press conferences, and this led to talk of grave illness. The White House said that Roosevelt had "caught the flu," which was true—it was a consequence of his globe-trotting and of his summitry with Churchill and Stalin at far-off Tehran the previous December. But the rest was fiction; the president was anything but fine. As his son Elliott would later write, "The influenza refused to let go. He felt perpetually tired." He added, "One trouble followed another—chronic indigestion compelled him to forgo combining business with eating; on occasion, he was drenched with sweat; a phlegmy cough racked his lungs."

Roosevelt had spent considerable time that winter in Hyde Park, but being there did little to improve his health. Already by January, the president was waking later and later in the morning. Roosevelt's trusted aide William Hassett noted in his diary on January 28, "The President again slept late." On January 25, Roosevelt did not come downstairs until almost 11:30 a.m. By the second half of March, back at Hyde Park, Roosevelt had begun to deteriorate rapidly. As the first gray of morning light spread in through the windows, the president would wake, tired and trembling. Unable to work, barely able to concentrate, he confined himself mostly to his bedroom, even eating all of his meals in bed on a tray. On March 24, Hassett noted, "The president not looking so well in his bedroom this morning, nor later when he held a press and radio conference—voice husky and out of pitch. This latest cold has taken a lot out of him." Every morning, in response to the inquiry as to how he felt, Roosevelt's characteristic reply was "Rotten" or "Like hell." By March 26, his temperature had spiked to 104 degrees. "Boss looks ill, color bad," Hassett again noted. As the president meekly picked at his food, his daughter Anna grew so alarmed that she confronted his physician, Admiral McIntire, who brushed off her concerns, citing the lingering effects of influenza and bronchitis. She knew better, however, and insisted that her father receive a full workup at Bethesda Naval Hospital. Reluctantly, McIntire arranged it—but he gave an order: not one word of the president's condition should be revealed to Roosevelt himself.

On March 28, 1944, as Roosevelt was eased into his limousine for the ride to the hospital, he muttered once more to Hassett, "I feel like hell!"

WITH A MOTORCYCLE ESCORT clearing the road, Roosevelt's motorcade rolled up Wisconsin Avenue to Bethesda Naval Hospital. There, he was lifted from his car and placed in a waiting wheelchair. He immediately put up a happy front, playfully waving and wisecracking as he was wheeled into the hospital and down the dimly lit corridor past the swelling crowd that had assembled to see the leader of the Allied armies. Whereas Roosevelt's personal doctor was an ear, nose, and throat specialist, specifically chosen because Roosevelt suffered from a chronic sinus condition—which he often notoriously groused about—here he was met by Dr. Howard Bruenn, a young, highly regarded cardiologist who was a lieutenant commander in the naval reserve. Austere and famously no-nonsense, Bruenn was disturbed at what he found. From the outset, he suspected that "something was terribly wrong." Flicking on the lights in the examination room, he found Roosevelt's face "very gray," "pallid," and saw that his lips and skin had a "bluish discoloration," which meant that the body and blood were not performing the most basic circulatory function, getting oxygen to the tissues. Roosevelt coughed constantly, and could not hold his breath for more than thirty-five seconds.

Listening to Roosevelt's heart and lungs with a stethoscope increased Bruenn's sense of alarm: as Roosevelt inhaled and exhaled, Bruenn heard rales, telltale rattling or bubbling sounds indicating that fluid was building up inside the president's lungs. Roosevelt was literally starting the slow process of drowning from within. This was not simple bronchitis or the lingering effects of pneumonia, as McIntire had led him to believe. In fact, from the outset, Bruenn recognized that Roosevelt was having trouble even breathing; simply moving him from one side to the other induced a disquieting "puffing." As the doctor later recounted, "It was worse than I feared."

The severity of Roosevelt's illness became even more apparent as the examination progressed. A quick scan of Roosevelt's records revealed that as early as February 1941, the time of the small heart attack, his blood pressure had been recorded as 188/105. What had happened after that was unknown; according to Roosevelt's medical history, McIntire had not taken the president's blood pressure since then. Today, in Bruenn's exam room, it was 186/108. But other changes were obvious. The X-rays and electrocardiogram revealed that his heart was seriously enlarged and his pulmonary vessels were engorged. And there had been a significant increase in the size of Roosevelt's cardiac shadow. If this weren't distressing enough, Bruenn's stethoscope also detected a systolic murmur, indicating that the president's mitral valve was failing to close properly.

Bruenn quickly made his diagnosis: Franklin Roosevelt, president of the United States, was suffering from congestive heart failure, hypertension, and hypertensive heart disease, compounded by acute bronchitis. Absent significant intervention, Roosevelt had no more than a year to live. Bruenn's words would prove to be prophetic.

Considering how deathly ill he felt, Roosevelt was remarkably incurious about his condition. Following McIntire's pointed orders, Bruenn never offered a word about his findings, and Roosevelt cheerfully went along with the charade, chatting about one topic or another—this was his standard way of avoiding distasteful subjects—but never inquiring about his health. Indeed, the charade continued that afternoon, when Roosevelt made sure to attend a scheduled press conference so as to dispel any public concerns. It was a brilliant performance. Waving off any worries about pneumonia, the seemingly bemused president flashed a smile, feigned a mock cough, and patted his chest to show how unaffected he was. As flashbulbs popped, the press fell for it, and even the *New York Times* reported, "The president's color and voice . . . were better."

Yet this was mere bravado, and he was anything but better. Met by Eleanor and their daughter Anna in his White House study afterward, he was visibly suffering and too tired even to talk. By 7:30 p.m., he had gone to bed.

In the meantime, determined to treat Roosevelt like any other patient, Dr. Bruenn dictated a memo outlining his recommendations. A few could be easily accomplished, such as restricting salt in his diet, undertaking a program of weight reduction, taking digitalis (though setting the dose was somewhat complicated and possible side effects included hallucinations and blurry eyesight), taking daily mild laxatives, and sleeping in a specially elevated bed to relieve his breathlessness at night. Roosevelt was also smoking as many as thirty cigarettes a day, and Bruenn's instructions were to significantly reduce this number and to limit his cocktails in the evening. But Bruenn's most significant recommendations were trickier, both because Roosevelt was president of the United States and because the Allied invasion of Europe was just two months away. He urged that Roosevelt have complete bed rest for several weeks, with nursing care, and that he avoid "tension."

McIntire, who had egregiously missed most of the president's ailments and was still resisting the idea that his patient had any kind of heart condition, all but exploded at the suggestion of bed rest. "The president can't take time off to go to bed," he snapped. "This is the President of the United States!" So he assembled a team of senior specialists to review Bruenn's diagnosis. McIntire's handpicked specialists sided with him, but Bruenn, believing the president's life was endangered, refused to back down. Finally, McIntire agreed to allow two outside specialists to examine Roosevelt. After seeing the president, they emphatically sided with Bruenn.

One of the consulting specialists, Dr. Lahey, indicated that he was also worried about the president's gastrointestinal tract. Lahey left no definitive record of what his concerns were, but on the basis of some materials he left behind, he may have found what he believed to be an inoperable and probably malignant tumor in Roosevelt's stomach. It was perhaps a secondary cancer, originating in a malignant mole over the president's left eye or a wen that had been removed from the back of his head. But the immediate danger for Roosevelt was his heart.

This medical team, then, was presented with an almost insuperable challenge. The president couldn't work—work could kill him—and he couldn't not work: the country needed him. What to do? They agreed on a scaled-down version of Dr. Bruenn's recommendations, including limiting callers to a minimum during his meals; this would be buttressed by a much more careful, daily program of monitoring his health. Bruenn now began to appear at the White House gates on alternate days to check on his patient. Within the first two weeks, the regimen seemed to be working—up to a point. X-rays showed a clearing of the lungs and a lessening of the bronchitis, probably helped by fewer cigarettes. Some of Roosevelt's color also returned, and his coughing stopped. There was even a decrease in the size of his heart. The president was also sleeping better and reported that he was feeling better. Still, he was far from well—but that did not stop McIntire from blatantly misleading the public and the press. On April 3, McIntire asserted that the president was fine, that the exam had revealed nothing of any real import, and that now the president needed only "some sunshine and more exercise."

The next day, however, Roosevelt's blood pressure rose to 226/118, and in contrast to his usual demeanor, Roosevelt was unusually listless, impatient, and expressionless; moreover, his concentration remained impaired. The normally stoic Roosevelt even confessed to Eleanor that he too was worried and suspected that the doctors didn't know what the problem was. When he suffered inexplicable pain in his rectal area, he himself feared that there was a malignant cancerous growth, though the discomfort eventually ceased. But he continued to take his pills without asking what they were for and continued to avoid any talk of his real diagnosis. Whether it was the strategy of denial that had worked so well for him with polio, or whether it was the denial that had cloaked his father's own ultimately fatal heart condition, it was the route that Roosevelt took. He preferred to remain completely in the dark.

By this stage, however, the president's medical team realized there was little choice. War or no war, president or not president, if Roosevelt were going to survive, something more needed to be done. The president was told he needed a significant period of rest. Away from the White House.

FOR ROOSEVELT, IT MUST have been a torturous moment. A significant rest, away from the White House? Against all the odds, he had overcome polio and been elected president, had confronted the Great Depression, and was now presiding over the coming D-Day invasion and keeping the Allied coalition together. But suddenly, the ravages of his own ill health were threatening to do him in. "I see no way out and I am furious," Roosevelt hotly told Churchill. Could the Allied effort survive his death? Roosevelt, like Churchill, knew well enough that wars could turn on such unexpected events: the death of a commanding general from friendly fire, an "error in strategy" or failed intelligence, or even a president's sudden loss of nerve. But Roosevelt also knew that the task of great commanders was to find ways to overcome obstacles, not to be thwarted by them. They needed to lead—even when impaired. And always, they had to move on. So it was for Roosevelt.

Though his doctors may have felt desperate, he felt challenged. Throughout his presidency, the mere act of standing up with his heavy metal leg braces locked in place—they weighed fourteen pounds—was an ordeal. Sweat pouring down his face, his jaw rigid, he often struggled to stand or to walk, swinging his hips forward in a halting, bowlegged gait. For years, he attempted to manage stairs on his own, muttering under his breath, "I must get down the stairs, I must." He never did. But if his body was broken, his spirit never was. As president, he often awed observers with his stamina. The nation, indeed the world, knew him not for his handicap, but for his vitality: his resonant tenor, his lilting cadences and singing phrases, his flowing cape, and his famous smile. And most of all, for the fact that he spoke and thought in the idiom of the times.

Thus he treated this obstacle like everything else he confronted in life: with unbridled confidence. He had faced down despair before, and was determined to do so again.

~

IN EARLY APRIL WINSTON Churchill's good friend, the financier and elder statesman of the Roosevelt administration, Bernard Baruch, offered Roosevelt his spacious mansion, Hobcaw Barony—a famous South Carolina plantation "between the waters"—as a secluded retreat for the president. Here, there were fish of all kinds and plentiful wildlife, from quail to fox, and alligators to turkey. Here, there were rustling streams, miles of beautiful fields and salt marshes, and dense forests filled with pine trees and century-old oaks festooned with Spanish moss. Here, away from the tug of war, the president could convalesce. Indeed, so peaceful was Hobcaw that Baruch didn't even allow telephone lines to be strung there. Roosevelt's bags were packed and his slow private train was prepared. "I want to sleep and sleep," Roosevelt said when he first arrived, on Easter Sunday, April 9, 1944, "twelve hours a day." It was supposed to be a two-week getaway.

Roosevelt stayed for a month.

~

AT THE VERY TIME that Roosevelt was wending his way down to South Carolina and the Allied forces were gearing up for D-Day, one particular sector of the Nazi empire was working at a frenetic pace: the gas chambers of Auschwitz. These represented the final, desperate push to eliminate the last remaining large population of Jews in Europe—every child and every mother, every father and every grandparent, anyone deemed unfit for heavy labor, or for medical experiments, or simply to live. This time, the intended victims were Hungarian Jews; their gassing would constitute the single largest mass murder in the history of the world. For Hitler, it was the realization of a long-held dream.

~

AUSCHWITZ. ON ANY MAP, there was nothing like it. It was, from its medieval beginnings, a border town, dividing peoples and cultures, Slavic and German. Its name, Oswiecim, ironically, was derived from the old Polish word for saint. The Slavic residents brought their culture; the German settlers who followed brought their legal system. Straddling two rivers, the Vistula and the Sola, Oswiecim evolved into a small trading center. Over the centuries, it would pass from Polish rulers to the Holy Roman Empire and then to the Bohemian kings of Prague, with Czech as the official language. It returned to Poland in 1457, having been sold for 50,000 silver marks. During the first partition of Poland in 1772, Oswiecim was claimed by Austria. Under the Hapsburgs, its name was changed to Auschwitz, and German became the official language. In fact, until the collapse of his empire in 1918, the Hapsburg ruler was, among his many other titles, the duke of Auschwitz.

While Oswiecim's residents were primarily Catholics, there were also Jews, with only a scattering of Germans. The city had no laws forbidding Jews to live or trade within its walls. Jews were not banished to ghettos, and over time the city developed a flourishing Jewish community. Jews owned banks and factories, worked as shopkeepers and tradesmen, and even owned a popular distillery. As time passed, Auschwitz became a center of Orthodox Jewish intellectual life and Zionist organizations, to the point that some Jews spoke of "Oswiecim Jerusalem." Actually, in its population, Jews equaled or even slightly outnumbered Catholics, and the city's political life reflected this balance: the post of deputy mayor invariably went to a Jew, but the mayor was always a Catholic.

The town's first workers' camp was built around the turn of the twentieth century to house the legions of migrant laborers. After World War I, it held refugees, primarily Poles fleeing from the newly formed Czechoslovakia. Then things began to change dramatically as the years before World War II saw the first genuine strains of anti-Semitism crop up among the residents. Jews were now forbidden to use a popular bathing spot along the Soła River, as well as the town park. Meanwhile, Polish residents quietly boycotted Jewish craftsmen, forcing some to close their shops. But no one could predict what would happen when, in 1939, Germany vanquished the Polish forces and annexed a vast area including Auschwitz, making it formally part of the German Reich.

It was then, at the beginning of 1940, that the town of Auschwitz, in the words of one German historian, "caught Himmler's eye."

Heinrich Himmler, the notorious SS *Reichsführer* (leader of the SS), was looking for places to build concentration camps for political opponents. The old workers' camp at Auschwitz was one of three suggested sites, but it was not the first choice. The buildings and barracks were dilapidated, the site was swampy and malarial, and the water supply was poor. But the site also had at least two redeeming features. It was already on a transportation route—it sat at a railway junction—and it could be segregated from the prying eyes of the outside world. So in late April 1940, Auschwitz became the Reich's seventh concentration camp. Everything flowed from this beginning.

By the end of 1940, Auschwitz had already grown so large that it colonized villages and absorbed forests, ponds, and farmland, until the camp's official "zone of interest" stretched over a sprawling fifteen square miles. And that was by no means enough. In the fall of 1941, construction began at a second camp area, in Birkenau, about one and a quarter miles away. Originally, Auschwitz had held mainly Polish political prisoners and Soviet prisoners of war. But in January 1942, Himmler announced the arrival of 150,000 Jews, one third of them women.

They came, always, by train.

~

IT HAPPENED LIKE THIS: As the packed trains pulled into Auschwitz, for several moments there was a gloomy silence, punctuated by tender whispers and sudden sobs and saddened glances. Gathering close, families huddled and started speaking in low voices. Mothers clutched sons, daughters held on to fathers, children gripped both parents' hands, kissing them repeatedly. Some prisoners were uncommonly composed, simply listening intently. Others were on the verge of panic, counting the moments in terror and anticipation. Still others felt as though this were an eerie dream; and a hush—"every human sound now silenced"—would descend on the cattle cars packed with human cargo.

The train lurched to a halt and the doors were flung open. Outside was a scene of chaos, confusion, and horror. For the Jews, after days of being trapped in their darkened cattle cars, squinting into the rush of bright floodlights lining the tracks was almost unbearable. So was the stench, like nothing they had ever smelled before. They couldn't know it at the time, but it was the odor of broiling human flesh and burning human hair. Outside they heard all kinds of noises, dogs barking loudly, and commands they couldn't understand. They were being ordered about in German; SS men with machine guns paced up and down the platform, and in staccato bursts, sentries yelled, *"Mach Schnell!"* When the Hungarians stumbled out of the cattle cars, disoriented and anxious, and timidly began asking questions, the Germans shouted back, *"'Raus, 'raus, 'raus!"* ("Out, out, out!")

In the distance, the prisoners could see tall chimneys dominating the skyline, and bright orange plumes of flame that seemed to shoot into the clouds.

Not knowing what else to do, the prisoners fiddled with their luggage, or whispered hesitantly to a family member, or quietly called out to a friend as though things were normal, when of course they were anything but. Meanwhile, a few camp prisoners with hollow eyes and gaunt bodies managed to slip through the lines of the newcomers, mumbling to old men that they must say they "are younger," and telling young boys to say that they "are older," and pleading with all to deny that they were weak, ill, famished, or fatigued. At the same time, a thick cordon of SS men, with eyes like ice, ominously strode back and forth. Soon they began to quickly interrogate the Jews, one by one, in pidgin Dutch, Slovak, Czech, or Hungarian. "How old?" "Healthy or ill?" While the prisoners shuffled into formation, a senior officer climbed onto the platform. The most notorious of these was the Nazi doctor Joseph Mengele. Thrusting out a finger, the senior medical officer would begin to point, left, right, left, right. Anyone who was fit, or robust, or who at least appeared robust, was put in one line. Everyone else—invariably grandparents, the elderly, girls, little children, and babies—was put in another line. One line meant the work camp. The other line meant the gas chambers. The prisoners were separated by sex.

After a packed trainload had arrived, Mengele asked one father, "Old man, what do you do?"

"Farmwork," he replied hesitantly. He was told to go right, until Mengele shouted for him to return. "Put out your hand!" Mengele slapped him violently across the face and shoved him into the other line—the line for slaughter. "*Schnell!*" ("Fast!"), he called out. "*Schnell!*" It was the last time the man's teenage son ever saw him.

The leashed dogs, German shepherds and Doberman pinschers, continued to bark.

Someone mustered the courage to ask about his luggage. Here the SS proved they were as cunning as they were remorseless. "Luggage afterward," came the brisk reply. Invariably mothers wanted to stay with their children. The SS said, "Good, good, stay with child." One husband wanted to accompany his wife—they had been put in different lines—and the SS calmly insisted, "Together again afterward."

After the selections were made, those slated to die were marched to one of five gas chambers, under a rain of baton blows at every step along the way. Yet they had no idea what lay in store for them; the Nazis had carefully concealed their true intentions at every stage. The prisoners were taken past a gate strung with barbed wire, through double rows of SS men lining a twisted path, and past ominous watchtowers housing German soldiers with machine guns. Each of the crematoriums was like its own Potemkin village, having a separate entrance and concealed partially by a handsome wicker fence, along with elegantly tended flower beds, which gave the entire structure almost a welcoming appearance, even an appearance of repose.

~

BUT THE INTRICATE LAYERS of false fronts seldom worked completely. Although their march to the chambers was shrouded in mystery, it was also laden with terror. Shivering and anxious, three hundred to four hundred terrified prisoners at a time were hustled to an underground staircase that led to a changing room. The snaking line seemingly stretched the length of several football fields. Still more prisoners usually huddled outside waiting for their turn.

They knew something was amiss—the whole area was ringed with armed SS men and snarling dogs—but for the most part, they remained composed. The reasons varied. They may have been exhausted by their long journey, or cowed by the surroundings, or simply paralyzed by fear. Or perhaps they were somehow seduced by the reassuring sight of a truck marked with a Red Cross parked alongside them. Few wanted to believe in the horror that awaited them. Few could have imagined that they would be reduced to ashes within several hours. In what world was such a ghastly fate possible?

Still, a mother might panic and a child might begin to cry uncontrollably, upon which they were promptly taken behind the building by SS guards. One camp inmate who managed to survive would recall lying in his barracks, his hands pressed to his ears, listening to people being shot outside and knowing that the falling snow was mingling with ashes from the crematorium.

The women, children, and old men were sent in first, and only afterward the healthier, stronger men. When they reached the undressing room they saw that it had the lulling appearance of an international information center. Innocuous-looking signs in French, German, Hungarian, and Greek were displayed, pointing the newcomers to the "Bathroom" and the "Disinfection Room." In the changing room itself there were orderly benches on which people could comfortably sit—by this stage a welcome respite—as well as clean, numbered coat hooks all along the wall. To complete the pretense, the Nazis told the prisoners to carefully remember the numbers so that they'd be able to find their personal effects more easily after they showered. As the prisoners looked around, they also saw signs with messages such as "Through Cleanliness to Freedom," "Lice Can Kill," and "Wash Yourself." To prevent any resistance, the Germans also promised the famished prisoners a meal just after "disinfection."

The deceit lasted until the very final moments. To Greek Jews preparing to undress in the anteroom outside the gas chambers, SS Obersturmführer Franz Hossler is recalled to have said, "On behalf of the camp administration I bid you welcome. This is not a holiday resort but a labor camp. Just as our soldiers risk their lives at the front to gain victory for the Third Reich, you will have to work here for the welfare of a new Europe. How you tackle this task is entirely up to you. The chance is there for every one of you. We shall look after your health, and we shall also offer you well-paid work. After the war we shall assess everyone according to his merits and treat him accordingly."

Still speaking in a calm tone, Hossler added, "Now, would you please all get undressed. Hang your clothes on the hooks we have provided and please remember your number. When you've had your bath there will be a bowl of soup and coffee or tea for all. Oh yes, before I forget, after your bath, please have ready your certificates, diplomas, school reports and any other documents so that we can employ everybody according to his or her training and ability." And finally, "Would diabetics who are not allowed sugar report to staff on duty after their baths?"

Despite the Nazis' best efforts, the children were inevitably terrified. The setting was too bizarre, too cold, too forbidding. Many mothers, by now almost delusional with hope, hurried to be first in line and get it all over with as quickly as possible, if only for the sake of their children. Still, even the sight of what looked like showerheads was not enough to dispel the doubts that crept in. Nor was the fact that sometimes the SS, actually wearing white coats, ladled out soap and handed out towels before they slammed the heavy doors to the gas chambers.

Typically at this stage, the prisoners began to whisper to each other.

The men were the last to be shoved into the chambers. As many as two thousand people were now tightly wedged like paving stones in a room built to accommodate only half that number. Two thousand was almost as many people as were cut down in Pickett's charge at Gettysburg, or about the same number as the Allied dead at the bitter battle of El Alamein in North Africa, or slightly more than half the number who died in the terrorist attacks of September 11, 2001.

All that remained was to wait.

The waiting, sometimes lasting two hours, was hell. It was punctuated by little moments of cruelty. The SS often amused themselves by flicking the lights on and off in the gas chamber, a perverse form of torture. When no water came out of the showerheads and the light was flicked off, the prisoners began to shriek hysterically; they now knew they were somehow going to die. But when the light was flicked on again, there was a sound, a huge collective sigh by people hopeful that the operation had been canceled and they had miraculously been given a reprieve.

They hadn't. The massive airtight door to the gas chamber was locked with an iron bolt that screwed tight. With ruthless efficiency, the SS opened a tin of Zyklon B and emptied it into a special cone. An SS doctor supervised the entire operation; he would watch through a peephole consisting of a double pane of glass and a thick metal grid strong enough to withstand the desperate blows of the suffocating prisoners. Now, the lights were turned off for the last time.

It was dark; no one could see.

The end began with a series of small actions.

After the bolting of the door, the gas quickly began to fill the room, not from the ceiling, as one would expect, but from the ground upward. Little children began to violently hug their parents—though too often, terrified boys and girls became separated from their parents and scrambled around, desperately calling for them. Their hearts racing, couples held hands. Then the screaming began. And so did a terrible struggle. Those standing nearest the gas fell dead almost immediately. But many of the others fought for life with every ounce of their strength. They huddled together, they screamed together, they gasped for air together. And tragically, they often struggled against one another bitterly in those final minutes. Instinctively, hundreds of people tried to push their way to the door, since they knew where it was. They hoped to force their way out; in the process, however, the weaker people, the aged, and the children were trampled, their crushed bodies piling up. Meanwhile, some victims sought to climb higher, because the higher they got the more air there was. Once again, the strongest were on the top, and in these last horrid death battles, as one survivor later observed, "the father had no way of knowing that his little son lay beneath him."

Children's skulls were crushed. Flailing in the dark, hundreds of people were battered beyond recognition. There was the stench of vomit and of blood—from noses and ears—and everywhere human excrement.

As the minutes passed and the steel door would not budge, the gas kept coming. Soon the bloodcurdling screams turned into a death rattle, and the death rattle turned into the faintest of gasps. Within minutes, everyone had collapsed, and the bodies began to shut down. Their hands moved weakly; their feet kicked pathetically; their eyes clouded over. After twenty minutes, the job was done.

Standing outside the heavy, reinforced door, the supervising doctors followed the killing. Most didn't watch. In the words of Hans Munch, one of the Nazi doctors at Auschwitz, "The door was thick. You could hear a noise. You could compare that noise to the sound of a beehive . . . a certain buzzing sound. And if you did this frequently, you didn't have to look. You would know only by listening."

When they were all dead, a ventilator sucked out the poison gas. In gas chambers five and six, where there were no ventilators, the doors were simply opened.

The bodies lay in great heaps, three feet or four feet high, or more.

After the dead were cleared away, the Nazis would repeat the process all over again within a matter of hours.

~

A LITTLE GIRL ON HER way to Auschwitz wrote, "Of what use is the sun in a world without day? Of what use is a God when his only duty is to punish?"

~

WHILE THESE KILLINGS WERE in progress, the surviving inmates, only months from their own deaths, simply waited. Noisy engines ran and horns roared to drown out the cries and other sounds of the dying, but the remaining prisoners knew better. As it happened, it was not the Germans or Poles, but a special squad of the *Sonderkommando*—invariably Jewish inmates pressed into service—who pulled the corpses out of the gas chamber. Their job was agonizing. It was also backbreaking. More often than not the bodies were so twisted together that they were difficult to disentangle. After ripping them apart, the workers of the *Sonderkommando* had to pry gold teeth systematically out of the gums of the dead; wrench wedding rings from their fingers; and, stepping over the mounds of bodies, separate those who had died clutching their loved ones. They even were ordered to tear open the anuses and vaginas of the cadavers to look for hidden jewelry. Mute, with dazed expressions, they meticulously cut off the flowing hair of the dead women, sorting it first into huge piles before stuffing it into large sacks. Sweating and numb with horror, the squads then carted the corpses in tubs, up to ten freshly murdered people at a time, to the ovens, where they were laid out on stretchers before being inserted. Because the ovens worked overtime, the crematoriums repeatedly overheated and failed, so specialists from Berlin were constantly being called in to repair the equipment. When the crematoriums were temporarily disabled, the corpses were instead burned in mass graves, or incineration trenches. Even for the Nazis, it was a laborious, complicated process.

With the SS guards supervising, the *Sonderkommando* had to repeatedly stoke great fires. With heavy steel hooks, they stirred the burning bodies. As the fire took hold of the corpses, there came the sweetish smell of burning flesh—"an inconvenient smell of smoke" was how one Nazi doctor once laconically described it—and the smoke slowly wafted into the camp and settled over the town of Auschwitz itself.

Chillingly, when the dead were reduced to ashes, these were never buried but were instead put to use. The fine, gray remains were used not only to fertilize the fields of the camp's farms, but also as filler for new roads and walking paths, and even for insulating the SS barracks against the frigid Polish cold. Any unburned bones, usually the pelvic bones, were smashed to dust. As for the piles of human hair? They were warmed on the rooftops of the crematorium.

No detail was too small for the German Reich, and at Auschwitz, the Germans seemingly overlooked nothing. The Nazis benefited immensely from the dead. The piles of leftover eyeglasses—whether the lenses were cracked or perfect and the frames bent or broken—were turned over to the state. The piles of human hair, whether coarse or fine, light or dark, were used to stuff mattresses, or spun into thread, or turned into rope. Hair was also made into felt for the Nazi machinery of war. Customers paid handsomely for these human products: the Bremen Wool Carding company offered 50 pfennig per kilo; the Alex Zink Felt Factory near Nuremberg was another purchaser. And fertilizer companies purchased bags of human bonemeal from the SS.

Then there was the luggage of the dead, which was laboriously collected and sorted. Here, again, no source of loot was overlooked. There were the stacks of food and the coats, shirts, socks, silks, minks, overcoats, black frock coats, blouses embroidered with gold, furs of all kinds, belts, and underwear; there were vials of medicine and hundreds of thousands of pills; and there were the cartloads of household goods and crates of chairs, tables, and rugs. Moreover, there were wads of cash in various currencies, lire, francs, English pounds, and black market dollars, not to mention the assorted clocks, glittering gems and other fine jewelry, and even little bottles of Chanel. There were, too, delicately perfumed soaps and eau de cologne. And that was hardly all. The volume of shoes alone was mind-numbing: farmers' shoes, merchants' shoes, soldiers' shoes, old shoes, new shoes, boots and rubbers, leggings and slippers, shoes worn right through the soles, shoes of gleaming new leather. They were black and gray and red, even white. There were high heels, low heels, shoes with open toes. There were evening slippers and Dutch wooden shoes, pumps and beach sandals and high laced women's shoes. There were the small buckle shoes of so many little children taken from their mothers. These personal effects were housed in thirty separate barracks surrounded by barbed wire; the storage grounds were called "Canada"—Canada because the inmates who came up with the name thought it to be a fabulously rich nation.

The effects of the dead became state property, and the German people its recipients. The treasures were immense: Every month more than a ton of jewels, melted nuggets of gold, and bundles of currency were loaded into heavy, lead-lined boxes, which were shipped to Berlin. German pilots and U-boat crews were awarded the wristwatches of the dead; so were Berliners whose homes had been reduced to rubble by the Allied air raids. Ethnic German settlers received countless household goods, French perfumes, toilet soaps, and textiles; tots in Berlin received the collected children's toys. The notorious Reichsbank received precious metals; the ambitious Reich Youth Leadership received money; the insatiable German manufacturer IG Farben received gold and silver. The troops on the eastern front received remodeled fur coats, while hundreds of thousands of men's shirts and women's blouses were sent to cities and towns inside Germany. As for such rare luxuries as diamonds and jewel-encrusted bracelets? The SS simply pocketed these themselves. Even the civilians of the town of Auschwitz wanted to profit from the repositories of goods; they asked camp administrators if the belongings of the dead might be for sale at a discount, or better still, be given away.

There had once been a time when the Germans rode the crest of a great age: they were champions of the arts and sciences, and lovers of literature. They supported the finest poetry, the grandest music, and the best of philosophy. But now, as D-Day approached, they specialized in one thing and one thing only: the science of murder.

3

Escape, Part 1

SOUTH CAROLINA WAS HARDLY Roosevelt's first trip south while he was in office. He returned time and again to heal in the waters at Warm Springs during his years in the White House, and after the 1940 election, Roosevelt had taken a ten-day cruise through the Caribbean for pleasure and relaxation. In fact, in the spring of 1944, he had originally hoped to go to the Caribbean again, to fish and sun himself at Guantánamo Bay in Cuba, though his fragile health and the exigencies of war made such a trip impossible.

Yet Roosevelt was not the only one taking a rest.

~

AS THE WAR GROUND on and the body count mounted and the D-Day invasion loomed, SS officers sought the quiet of a retreat to rejuvenate themselves. Taking a break from the savagery and killings, they were eager for a good time. And why shouldn't they have been? They were finally getting a respite from the god-awful business of war. To look into the frightened eyes of the near-dead or the soon to be dead, however hated these people were, was difficult for even the hardest of men. And the SS did so on a daily basis. To grasp the magnitude of their mission, a horrific reality that entailed the deaths of so many, week after week, day after day, even minute after minute, was no easier. Earlier in the war, a number of their colleagues cracked under the pressure. These officers were different, however. Tucked away in the heavily forested outer reaches of Upper Silesia in Poland, their operation was carried out under a veil of such secrecy that until recently, its location didn't appear on most maps, and even many of their colleagues were unaware of their work. For some, their days stretched from four in the morning to as late as midnight. They had to face the continued threat of nearby air raids, the maddening cacophony of barking dogs, the bright floodlights, the constant watch for insurrection, the ghastly smoke and smells, and always the demand to "do more." That was the business of their particular war.

By all accounts, though, these officers accepted their jobs with an alacrity that was almost hard to fathom. Also by all accounts, many of them approached those jobs with enthusiasm; for a number of them, this was the high point of their lives, a moment spiced, as it were, with the excitement of great events. And for a job well done, they were now being handsomely rewarded.

They were accompanied often by a bevy of young, attractive women—for the most part administrative specialists—and even babies and bright-faced children. Their bus rumbled eighteen miles or so past the outskirts of their camp, past the timbered slopes that ran alongside the Sola River, past small villages whose cottages were still untouched by war, through the mountains until they reached a small wooden bridge. Soon, they were at their destination: a peaceful Alpine-style recreation lodge tucked into the hills at the Solahütte retreat along the scenic river itself.

They were here for eight days of vacation.

~

THEY BOUNDED OUT OF the bus in freshly starched uniforms. Somewhere, a photographer took snapshots of their vacation, recording it for posterity. Over the next week or so—the time frame is inexact—the beaming officers and their female companions looked as if they were posing for travel posters, or as if they were summering in Maine or Martha's Vineyard, nestled among hills and fir trees; all that was missing were the swimsuits and the sound of gramophone music. The women, with their perfect white skin, frolicked, while the officers smoked and chatted. The feeling was comfortable—like a tranquil William Glackens painting—much as life had once been, decades earlier, before the war and the years of the crippling Depression. On the occasional warm afternoon, they would lie languidly in deck chairs on the lodge's wide wooden porch, blankets covering their legs; a few napped, some gossiped or sunned themselves or sipped a drink. Others cradled their children, or romped with their dogs like "Favorit," teaching them to sit or stay or lie down. Later, the men would go off by themselves, gathering on long benches around a metal table to drink wine and beer; some rolled up their sleeves before having yet another smoke.

Recapturing the simple pleasures of life, they were making the most of their time here, enjoying good company, good food, fresh air, and festive gatherings. And the rest of the world seemed quite far off. War? Impending invasion? All that was forgotten.

The air was clean and at last they could breathe deeply, eat well, and even find romance in a picturesque setting. And they sought rest not only now, but throughout the year. Come June, more vacationers would arrive. Then, the weather would be warm, the fields full of flowers. The young women, clad in identical white shirts and neat black skirts, would array themselves in a line, sitting on the railing of a pastoral wooden bridge, while merrily scooping up blueberries out of little bowls. One of their companions would entertain them with an accordion. When they were finished, they playfully held their bowls upside down in mock dismay.

The men accompanying them were handsome and well groomed, and the women looked demure and lovely; remarkably, despite the raging war they appeared so composed, so cultivated, so cultured. And in setting after setting, they posed for the camera. They posed during a sing-along—the officers and young women, about a hundred all told, crowding together on a hill, barely able to contain their giddiness. They posed when the accordion played, and when they danced to its tunes. They posed at outdoor time and shooting practice and in their summer clothes. They posed during moments of banter; or when a soft rain began to fall and they deliriously scooted for cover; or in the evening, when their dining table was covered with a crisply pressed white tablecloth, fine china, and elegant wineglasses, and filled with plentiful food. During the winter season, they posed during the ritual lighting of the Christmas tree. And later, they would even pose at a funeral in the snow, where coffins—too often a rarity on the battlefield—were draped with Nazi flags.

There was a time, however, when they did not pose: at the end of their vacation, when they returned to their bloody work. The juxtaposition was chilling, for these frolicking vacationers were otherwise the dreaded SS. Their place of work: Auschwitz. Indeed, even their holiday retreat, Solahütte, was a satellite facility of the camp, built during 1942 and overseen by Auschwitz SS Obersturmführer Franz Hossler, using Jewish forced labor. The vacationers drawn to the lodge and its environs included Joseph Mengele, who conducted ghastly medical experiments on the unsuspecting inmates; Carl Clauberg, who performed sterilization experiments with acid; and the former camp commandant, Rudolf Hoess. The women themselves were members of the SS *Helferinnen* ("helpers"). When all was said and done, their sole function at Oswiecim was to do one thing only: implement Hitler's Final Solution.

Or, more starkly: kill Jews.

~

SPRING ALWAYS SEEMED TO come late to Auschwitz. The omnipresent cold and the leafless landscape were a constant in so many brief lives. And the surviving Jews? As slave laborers, they had a life of unending terror and heartache. Those spared immediate execution and consigned instead to the labor camps often wore out in a matter of weeks, after which they too were dispatched to the gas chambers.

Those who remained could only gaze helplessly over the horizon of barbed wire. Every day, they were awakened in pitch blackness at 4 a.m., worked a backbreaking twelve hours with virtually no rest and only the meagerest food, and were then forced to endure endless roll calls at night. When the time for sleep finally came, sometimes after midnight, initially they had sacks filled with straw, and later crude, hard three-tier plank wooden bunk beds; usually six people and sometimes as many as eight were packed into a bed designed for three. In general, the SS crammed more than 700 people into barracks built for 180. There was no heat, no electricity, no paved floor—the floor was simply damp, boggy ground. And if the gas chambers did not kill the inmates soon enough, sickness did: spotted fever, dysentery, and typhus all flourished, but just as often a simple cold was enough to do the job. And many people's bodies simply seemed to decay from within. Open sores oozed on swollen legs. The ubiquitous lice were as big as fingernails and carried encephalitis within their nits and shells. They too were killers. Meanwhile, the barracks were overrun with vermin. Basic rampant filth and negligible sanitation also raised the butcher's bill.

Inside the camp, the prisoners' world seemed enveloped in darkness. During the winter, winds and snow lashed at their barracks, as they slept almost naked, with no blankets, in subzero temperatures, hovering between life and death. Their only pillow was a fist—that is, if they could even clench a hand. And sleep was hard to come by—there were continual outbursts of hacking coughs among the prisoners, and the deeper wheezing sounds made by the very ill. Often, a prisoner would wake in the morning and find the one next to him dead. Too weak to move even the pathetically light bodies of their comrades, sometimes too weak even to move themselves, the living just continued sleeping.

In the grim environment of Auschwitz, the Nazis' daily cruelties could turn even the gentlest prisoners into monsters. Emaciated prisoners were ready to kill each other for a mere crust of bread; sons were forced to select their fathers for the crematorium; mothers were forced to strangle their babies. Many of the prisoners were drawn from the intellectual class of Jews, comprising distinguished doctors, lawyers, accountants—respected professionals from every field. Yet even these formerly eminent figures had been reduced to animals by their treatment at the hands of the Germans, by the disgusting living conditions, the indiscriminate murder brought on by the slightest (or no) provocation, and the intentional, prolonged starvation.

The Nazis erased the identity of every prisoner, one more means by which they stripped the Jews of any remaining dignity. Once in the camp, the prisoners no longer had names; instead they were identified by numbers that were painfully tattooed in their forearms with a single needle. Remarkably, some seven hundred babies were born in the camp—they were registered as "new arrivals"—and they too received tattoos: on their buttocks or their thighs. Moreover, the prisoners had to wear whatever filthy rags they were given. The clothes might be much too large or much too small. It didn't matter. The same for shoes. Indeed, the clothes themselves were a health hazard; they were never washed but only steamed, and then only every six weeks, until they were falling apart. Even the underwear, when the prisoners had any, was invariably disgusting.

Daily roll call was a special hell. The few children in the camp who weren't immediately selected for the gas chambers had their own diabolical version of it. They were forced to stand for hours in water, until they had no choice but to urinate—or defecate—in it; this then became the water they were forced to drink. For everyone else, depending on the whim of the SS, roll call might last an hour, three hours, or all day—or night. Waiting for their numbers to be called, the prisoners were subjected to repeated harassment, isolation, and debilitating drills. Standing at attention for hours is difficult enough for a healthy person; for the weak and humiliated, it was almost impossible. There were some whose knees buckled, some who toppled over, some who simply couldn't stand straight. They were severely beaten by the SS, or, while standing half naked, doused with buckets of ice-cold water.

There was no letup from the cruelty.

No offense was too trivial to be punished. A poorly washed food bowl could lead to solitary confinement with only bits of bread and dirty water. A missing button was enough to send a prisoner to a tiny windowless cell, somewhat like a telephone booth, where he was forced to stand shoeless on cold stone. Dirty fingernails were punishable by a beating with a bamboo cane. Failure to take off one's cap when the SS walked by often merited fifty lashes with a whip, the dreaded "cat." And an inappropriate scowl or grimace was enough to result in a torture dating from the Middle Ages: dangling precariously from a post with the arms tied behind the back and raised high. Death was often the result. At one protracted roll call in 1940, eighty-four prisoners died from exposure and beatings.

Frequently the camp administration left the corpses of dead prisoners languishing in the courtyard as an example.

Yet, remarkably, there were prisoners who survived the first couple of weeks in the camp. They often clung to the notion that their living conditions might somehow improve, that the beatings might cease, that a modicum of normality would be restored. It was not to be. With cruel Orwellian logic, the SS formed a prisoner orchestra—it included many of the finest musicians from the capitals of Europe, and even the renowned director of the Warsaw Philharmonic—that played music while other prisoners trudged off to their work details in the chill early-morning darkness. Many of the work details were in effect graveyards themselves. The timber yard, the gravel pit, and the construction site all produced tremendous losses nearly every day.

The malnutrition was appalling. For breakfast, if one could call it that, prisoners were given an unsweetened coffee substitute or something that resembled herbal tea. For lunch, they had a thin, watery soup that might contain small bits of potato, parsnip, or millet. For dinner, the prisoners were allotted a couple of ounces of stale, moldy bread, and this was the last food they had until breakfast. All told, they were forced to live on only a few hundred calories a day. They died quickly, but the work continued uninterrupted, as fresh trainloads of Jews arrived daily.

And the SS was always exhorting the same thing, shouting at the prisoners, "To work! TO WORK!"

Life in the camp was in all ways brutal and sordid. Even using the toilet was perilous. Many prisoners could relieve themselves only in outdoor privies, regardless of the weather. Others, in barracks built later, had to share a single latrine with perhaps thirty or more inmates. Many of the prisoners had diarrhea, so there were long lines and endless waits, often for hours. The SS would shoot on sight anyone seen relieving himself anywhere other than in the latrine. Those unable to reach the crude holes in time were killed and their bodies were left lying in the feces and urine. The stench was suffocating. And so were the foul bodily odors that clung to the living prisoners.

So horrible was the situation that many prisoners tried to end their lives, hurling themselves against the electric barbed wire surrounding the perimeter of the camp.

And those who hung on, even those who had been hardiest and strongest, were quickly reduced to living skeletons, insane with hunger and scarcely capable of life. Their teeth decayed and fell out. Their hair and nails refused to grow. Their eyes became great sunken hollows in fleshless faces. When the day came that they could no longer walk, they tried to crawl; when they could no longer crawl, they tried to prop themselves up on their elbows; and when they could no longer do that, they sat up with frightened eyes, silent and shunned by the other prisoners, picking at discarded potato peels, until they just faded away.

No one at the camp thought of actually living; the inmates just thought of living a little longer.

As one of the Nazis put it, "This was the way of Auschwitz."

THERE WAS INDEED A "way of Auschwitz." Inside the tangled barbed wire walls stretched hundreds of one-story buildings, a state within a state, a fine-tuned apparatus created for one man, Adolf Hitler. From its seemingly innocuous beginning as a work camp in 1939, Auschwitz had become an institution with the muscle of an absolute despot and the heart of a monster. Technically its commandant, and the SS, answered to Berlin, but in truth they became independent overseers of death. True, their titular masters were Hitler and his notorious inner circle—committed Nazis such as Heinrich Himmler, Joseph Goebbels, Adolf Eichmann, and earlier Reinhard Heydrich—but in practice the administrators of Auschwitz largely answered to no one. It became the worst killing center the world had ever seen; its powers were nearly absolute. With undeterred abandon, they confiscated public property. They controlled their own funds and could effectively suspend any public official in their domain. They freely dispensed with anything resembling due process or international law as a mere nuisance. And operating in almost total secrecy, with the tap of a finger or the wink of an eye they decided the fate of almost 2 million innocent souls—nearly three times as many as the recorded dead in the American Civil War.

Even when the German Reich came under extraordinary pressure in 1944, even when Hitler's health deteriorated and disgruntled factions and cabals multiplied in the Nazi Reich, Auschwitz never faltered. Until the moment when the Nazis were overthrown, it was seemingly omnipotent.

In 1944, Auschwitz was far more than the single death camp called by this point Auschwitz II or Birkenau. It was an entire network of death, twisted experimentation, and slave labor: there was Auschwitz I, the parent camp; and also Auschwitz III, a sub-camp conglomerate that included Monowitz, a separate facility churning out synthetic rubber for the Nazi war effort. Eventually, an ambitious complex of some thirty subcamps affiliated with Auschwitz came into being. At these, the SS and the German private sector worked hand-in-hand with cold, ruthless efficiency. Attracted by the cheap slave labor—remarkably the SS charged the companies for each worker, but gave discount rates to state industries—an array of industries soon moved into the sprawling Auschwitz system: there were producers of consumer goods, manufacturers of chemicals, and fabricators of metals. There was the IG Farben synthetic oil and rubber factory operated at Auschwitz (IG Farben also held the patent on the Zyklon B used in the gas chambers). And there were the famous Krupp plant, the Siemens factory, the Silesian shoe company, the United Textile Mill Works, the Trzebinia oil refinery company, and the Reichsbahn. They were joined by the German Earth and Stone Works factory, the German Food Company, various coal mines, and the German Equipment Company. There was even a fish and poultry breeding plant, and an SS agricultural estate. But for the prisoners, these enterprises were almost interchangeable. They all involved the same hunger, hard work, and ruthless exploitation.

Chillingly, the lives of ordinary Germans in the camp or the nearby town remained largely untouched by the mass murder. With something oddly like the pioneering spirit of Americans moving west, German settlers arrived at Auschwitz and its environs from all parts of the old Reich: Hamburg, Cologne, Münster, Magdeburg, Munich, and even Vienna. These settlers had a buoyant belief in their own future, and a sense that it was their duty to bring enlightened German culture to the backward Slavic east. With joyous hearts, they came—or professed to come—in order to realize Hitler's expansive vision of constructing a new society, one resting not simply on money, status, or name, but on courage and the test of character.

And they had good times, too. While gaunt, terrified Jews shuffled into the gas chambers, or ate insects to relieve their hunger, or at the wave of an SS man's hand watched their loved ones prepare to die, the SS forces gathered nightly at the German House, a boisterous local pub directly opposite the Auschwitz station. On one side of the road, Mengele and his medical staff were overseeing the selection process; on the other side, the SS men drank thick beer, bedded willing young females in an adjoining hotel, and swapped jokes until midnight. Drunkenness was commonplace.

Indeed, the Nazi administration seemingly spared no expense to provide distractions and amusements for the "hardworking" SS. In the camp itself, they gathered for sing-alongs, music, and an assortment of entertainments (during the Christmas season, Jews in a chorus were compelled to sing "Silent Night"). The camp had its own concert wing, and enthusiastic bands from Germany regularly journeyed east to entertain the SS. Auschwitz also had its own theater, which featured carefree plays (what the Germans called "thief comedies") like *Disturbed Wedding Night* and *A Bride in Flight* and such belly-laughing amusements as *Attack of the Comics*. There was high culture as well, as when the Dresden State Theater presented *Goethe Then and Now*. And as if to dispel the lengthening shadows of the gas chambers, the Nazis brought in garden designers, landscape architects, and botanists to beautify the camp; these experts included a distinguished professor of landscape design from the agricultural college in Berlin.

In 1943, just a few weeks before a group of Hungarian Jews would be transported to Auschwitz, the Nazis held a raucous New Year's celebration at the Ratshof Pub in the town's market square. Dance bands had been brought from Berlin, and a renowned host from Austria. The celebratory feast consisted of an array of delicacies—goose liver and oxtail soup, "blue carp in aspic," roast hare and biscuit roulade, *Sekt* and pancakes and a jelly-roll cake. The revelry went on deep into the night, whereupon dessert was served (three different kinds), accompanied by a herring salad and rich coffee. And when the music stopped, the entertainment was hardly over. The camp had also provided a comedian.

WAS THERE EVER ANY sense of shame at Auschwitz? Or pangs of conscience among the Nazis? Or basic abhorrence? No. Nor were the Nazis hapless nobodies or simply cogs in a vast bureaucracy of death. At Auschwitz, the appetite for blood was never sated. With icy determination, the Nazi killers even complained about loopholes that prevented the deportation of some Jews to Auschwitz. By contrast, even during the long heyday of European and American slavery, some of the most eloquent thinkers of the time—like the young British prime minister William Pitt, often considered "the best brain that ever graced English politics," or the author Harriet Beecher Stowe, whose "little book" helped incite the American Civil War—raised their voices ever louder and more furiously in defense of common humanity. And against all those who sought to profit from slave labor, there were also some like the master potter Josiah Wedgwood, who embossed on a series of his famous plates the image of a chained Negro on bended knee pointedly asking, "Am I not a man and a brother?" There was almost none of this at Auschwitz or within the larger German administration or even among the German people themselves. Instead, the Germans took a line from one of Hans Christian Andersen's fabled tales, "everything looked as if it were outlined in flames, everything was enveloped in magic light," and grimly turned it on its head. Here the flames were consuming the slaughtered, and the magic light was the cruel glow as flesh met fire and was turned into ashes.

In Hitler's Manichaean worldview, the conflict between the forces of good and evil—namely, the Aryan race and the Jews—was destined to reach a climax. Whatever happened on the battlefield, there could be no relenting in the struggle to wipe out European Jewry. "Towards Jewry," Hitler once said, "there can be no talk of humanity." Thus, Adolf Eichmann would one day rue that the Nazis didn't "do more." Thus, Heinrich Himmler would boast that the SS remained "morally decent" in the mass murder of Jews, and would lament that this planned annihilation was "a glorious chapter" that would never be written.

But while the vast Allied armada was gathering in Britain for the D-Day invasion, and President Roosevelt was convalescing, one inmate at Auschwitz was determined that its story would be written, and read by the world. He was determined to warn Roosevelt and the Allies about the impending massacre of the Hungarian Jews and rally the forces of rescue and rebellion.

And he was determined to do something that had never been accomplished before: to escape from Auschwitz.

NO MAN APPEARED LESS suited to foil the Nazis or to carry the fate of Europe's remaining Jews on his shoulders than Rudolf Vrba. Indeed, at age nineteen, he was arguably less a man than a naive adolescent. What is not in question, however, is that by this young age he had lived more than a lifetime, and seen as much suffering as anyone on earth.

He was born in 1924 in Topolcany, Slovakia. In 1944 he changed his original name, Walter Rosenberg, to the more dashing and less Semitic-sounding Rudolf Vrba; to his friends he was known affectionately as Rudi. He came from modest beginnings. His father owned a sawmill; his mother was a dressmaker and homemaker, and quite proud of her cooking. She liked to tease him, and he liked to tease back. Physically, he was impressive: strikingly handsome with a mane of jet-black hair, he had a squarish build and seemed large despite his slender frame. Bushy eyebrows framed his lively dark eyes, and his face had a boxer's chin. He was at once sentimental yet calculating, hardheaded yet softhearted, and by the admission of others, "impetuous" and "impulsive." And since the age of seventeen, he had been either on the run or in a death camp.

His formal education was negligible, having been cut short. In Slovakia, owing to the Nuremberg laws restricting Jews, he was forced to leave his *Gymnasium* (high school), at age fifteen; his name was simply struck off the roll. Yet he never lost hope with regard to learning, or to anything else for that matter. Instead of giving up, he found work as a laborer and became something of an autodidact, teaching himself Russian and English. He also spoke German fluently, and eventually Polish and Hungarian as well. In the worst of times—and virtually all of his later adolescence had been the worst of times—he somehow always maintained his infectious grin and winning ways. They would serve him well when he needed them.

After the school doors were closed to Jews, there were other creeping restrictions. At first Slovakian Jews were unable to move and could live only in certain towns, and even there, in certain sections within those towns. Then travel was curtailed. Ghettos sprang up, and Jews were required to wear a yellow Star of David on their clothing. Then came the deportation laws; Slovakia's Jews were informed that they would be sent to work on reservations inside Poland. However, as the Nazi vise tightened around his country, Vrba was determined to make his way to freedom. In March 1942, while snow was still falling, he ripped the Star of David off his clothes, stuffed the equivalent of 10 pounds sterling into his pocket, hopped into a taxi driven by a family acquaintance, and headed not east, like so many others, but daringly west, for Britain, where he planned to join the Czech army-in-exile. Just before dawn, he crossed the border into Hungary and made his way to the house of a school friend. Within four hours, he was again sent on his way. He had tried to look the part of a gentile: he wore a business suit and carried the local Fascist newspaper under his arm. Using a second-class ticket, he had boarded an express train for Budapest. Yet the closer he got to freedom, the closer he drew to danger. After nearly being turned over to the police by a Zionist organization in Budapest (ironically, he received more help from a pragmatic Fascist, whose name he had been given by his schoolmate's family), Vrba tried to return to Slovakia as an Aryan. Instead, he was caught and savagely beaten by Hungarian border guards, who derided him as "a dirty, bloody Yid" and put him into a transit camp in Novaky. There he quickly learned the code of a concentration camp: bribes, greed, deceit.

Somehow, he escaped within a few weeks, wandering frantically through a thick forest, and making his way back to the town of his birth, where he stayed for several days until he was caught again. This time, he was handed over to the SS and sent to a dreaded death camp, Majdanek.

At Majdanek he saw row upon row of ugly barracks, ominous watchtowers, and electrified barbed wire. And he saw countless people from his hometown: librarians and schoolteachers, garage owners and shopkeepers, all in ragged striped uniforms, all with their heads shaved, all slated for slaughter. Then the shooting began. While loudspeakers blared dance music or martial songs, the SS marched men and women into separate lines at the edges of ditches, before mowing them down with machine guns. Dumbfounded, Vrba watched it all. He saw some who died with their eyes open, frozen in an expression of incomprehensible agony. He saw some who tried to crawl away after being shot. And he saw some who crumpled instantly, dying where they stood. Seventeen thousand died that day. Vrba's brother, Sam, was among them.

Just two weeks later, on the evening of June 30, 1942, Vrba was transferred southwest, to Auschwitz. At first, he naively thought Auschwitz would be a less dangerous place than Majdanek. He was quickly enlightened. Here, in his own words, he encountered "neatness and order and strength, the iron fist beneath the antiseptic rubber glove." His head was shaved, and he had a number tattooed on his arm—Rudolf Vrba was now prisoner 44070.

Whatever hope he had for survival was soon dispelled. Auschwitz was, he realized, a reeking slaughterhouse. But while some other prisoners reached the last extreme of loneliness, or spent their waning days in a robotic stupor, Vrba always kept his wits about him. While some shrieked and begged before their execution, Vrba always kept his emotions in check. While other survivors were heartbroken after their loved ones had been marched off, naked and shivering, to death, he somehow was able to summon up in his mind the remaining echoes of his former life. Driven, secretive, and iron-willed, from the outset he came up with a strategy for survival. Knowing that food meant strength—even if the tea tasted like sewer water and the lumpy bread contained sawdust—he resolved to eat as well as possible. He rapidly learned about the black market in the camp, a market that kept a lucky few alive—a person here and a person there—and brought countless others to unspeakable torture and death.

Vrba was fortunate. To start with, he was strong, so he was a desirable worker. Then, in August 1942, he was assigned to the special slave labor unit that handled the property of the gassed victims. He was now working in the camp's legendary storehouse, nicknamed "Canada" by inmates who imagined the actual Canada as an almost magical land of riches. Here, he sorted the possessions of the Jews transported to Auschwitz. He went through their bags after they had left the trains, and sometimes he entered the empty trains to clear away the bodies of the dead. Working in "Canada," Vrba had access to the SS food store, with its tall stacks of cans—marmalade, nuts, jam, vegetables, ham, beef, and fruit—assembled for the enjoyment of the SS and nearly all available to be pilfered. He learned that lemons were highly prized because they contained vitamin C. There was even, for the enterprising, steak.

When not plotting his survival, Vrba took careful notice of the apparatus of death. For the next eleven months, he had a rare vantage point of not only living in the camp, but of also being present for the arrival of most of the transports. He was stunned to see just how little the dazed and disoriented newcomers knew about Auschwitz as they feebly climbed off the trains. Sorting through their luggage, he learned that they had packed sweaters for the winter, shorts for the summer, sturdy shoes for the fall, cotton shirts for the spring—in short, clothing for a full year. They had brought gold and silver and diamonds to pay for goods or to make bribes. They also brought with them the basics of domesticity, items like cups, cutlery, and other utensils, an obvious indication that many believed they were simply being "resettled" somewhere in the east.

Not a day passed that Vrba didn't dream of escaping. He was always conscious that, although he had managed to survive so far, every day brought him "nearer to death in one form or another." Still, in the summer of 1943, he dramatically improved his position at Auschwitz when he was appointed a registrar at Birkenau's quarantine camp. There, he was provided with normal clothes, was afforded relative freedom to move about the camp without hindrance, and had access to better food. He made further contacts with a fledgling camp underground—which remained fledgling because its members were continually being killed off.

And patiently and diligently, he began to compile statistics of the mass murders being committed daily. His memory was phenomenal. He made a mental note of each transport that arrived, and carefully recorded the number of people. He committed to memory the sequence of tattooed identification numbers allocated to each group of victims on arrival. And by conferring with other registrars, he was able to calculate the amount of fuel burned, and hence the number of bodies being cremated. He also questioned the *Sonderkommando*, the group of strong, young male Jews picked by the Nazis to remove the bodies from the gas chambers and crematoriums (those chosen for the *Sonderkommando* who did not accept were gassed or shot). In this way he learned the details of how the gas chambers worked. Finally, though young, he became a courier for the resistance inside the camp.

If survival is a test of ability, he was the most able of all, maneuvering safely through crisis after crisis, escaping death and beatings and discovery; he seemed to have nine lives and bartered and sold them all. Once, he almost died; but he managed to be, for lack of a better term, "promoted" repeatedly, to the point where he became almost "a semi-permanent fixture" in the camp. Earning the trust of the Germans, to the extent that this was possible, he never went hungry; and while others cruelly starved to death, he was able to nibble on a piece of chocolate here and there, eat sardines from Portugal, or wash down a piece of yellow cheese with lemon-flavored water.

In another rarity, people even began to call him by his first name.

How did he deal with the suffering and death all around him? To have known that such things existed and to have withstood them must have been an inexpressible horror. And now, in the late summer of 1943, Vrba had remained alive in Auschwitz for over one year. He had, by his own admission, become "a little numb to suffering." This was an understatement. But then the world of Auschwitz turned. On September 7, four thousand Czechoslovak Jews from the Theresienstadt ghetto arrived. They came as families, men carrying luggage, children clutching dolls and teddy bears. The SS men joked with these newcomers. They played with the children. The prisoners were neither sent off to the gas chambers nor dispatched to the work camp. Nor were the families separated. And their heads were not shaved. They were allowed to keep their own clothes and to live in relative comfort in an adjoining camp built especially for them. Far from being beaten, they were pampered.

Gazing across the barbed wire, Vrba and the other starving survivors watched in amazement. While each day thousands of inmates wasted away, dragging their feet when it became too difficult to walk, and spitting up blood or black saliva, these Czechs seemed to lead an almost idyllic life. The children had a playground where the SS organized games for them. A little school had been set up in a wooden stable; it was run by a former Berlin sports instructor. The families were provided with soap and medicine and better food. And periodically guards, while tussling with them gently, would bring sweets and fruit for the frolicking children. The question, of course, was why.

The more Vrba dug, the more he learned. First came a little shock. Sleuthing around in the registrar's office, he realized that the Czech prisoners' tattoos bore no relationship to Auschwitz. Then came a bigger shock. He also saw that each prisoner was registered with a unique card that stated: "six months quarantine with special treatment." Special treatment was code for extermination.

Vrba soon figured it out. The Theresienstadt ghetto and its Jews were a distorted fantasy of the Third Reich. Theresienstadt was one place where the Nazis periodically allowed access for the observers of the foreign division of the German Red Cross, to dispel increasingly widespread rumors of mass executions. Indeed in late February 1944, Adolf Eichmann himself showed the Auschwitz family camp to the head of that Red Cross division as proof of Germany's humane treatment of these Jews. The Czechs were being used as pawns in the Nazis' fiction that the millions of Jews were not being exterminated in death camps, but merely being resettled in work camps in the east. Thus, these four thousand were kept separate—separate from the gassings and the systematic beatings, separate from the misery and monstrous cruelties. For six months, the four thousand thrived. They made friends, taught their children, had family suppers, fell in love, carried on life almost normally, and dreamed of freedom. But the end came as quickly as the beginning. On March 3, they were instructed to write postcards home faithfully reporting the comfort in which they were living—but the Nazis shrewdly stamped these cards with the address Neu Berun, a small town five miles northwest of the actual death camp, thereby preserving Auschwitz's secrecy. To complete the deception, the inmates were instructed to ask their relatives to send them parcels of food. And all the cards were to be postdated by three weeks.

Then suddenly, on March 7, six months to the day after their arrival, footsteps could be heard as SS guards surrounded the special camp.

Already, the *Sonderkommando* had been told to stoke the fires of the crematoriums.

In mid-afternoon, the trucks came. Immune to the cries of the children and flailing the prisoners mercilessly with clubs, a small army of

Kapos (trusties) forced them onto the transports and headed for the gas chambers. At the sight of the undressing room, the enormity of their fate became clear. They had smelled the smoke from the crematoriums for months. They knew what awaited them. Too late, they set upon the guards and fought back with their fists. But the end came as quickly as the beginning. The SS men were ready. Moving with quick, firm strides, they clubbed their recalcitrant victims with rifle butts, and when that didn't fully work, used flamethrowers. The naked prisoners, heads smashed and bleeding profusely from their wounds, were driven into the chamber. As the gas pellets clinked down through the roof, they began to sing first the Czechoslovak national anthem and then the Hebrew song *Hatikvah* until they gave themselves over to their execution.

Vrba was heartsick. Having hoped in vain for a rebellion among the prisoners, he realized now that his only course was to flee and to somehow warn the world. For months, Vrba had been secretly plotting his escape. He knew that every effort thus far had failed. However, he had no choice but to act.

AT THE START OF 1944, the Nazis began building an additional railway line at Auschwitz, one that led straight to the gas chambers. There would be no need for trucks, no need for selections; the train doors would simply open and men, women, and children would be shunted immediately to their deaths. Aghast, Vrba could see the new tracks from his office window, could watch these tracks "edging their way up the broad road." He saw prisoners slaving away on them day and night, even under arc lights to lengthen the working hours. He also noticed that other inmates were hammering and building; they were almost doubling the size of the camp. The expansion of Auschwitz could mean only one thing: the Nazis were preparing to receive a huge influx of Jews. The only place left with a large population of Jews was Hungary. This was corroborated by the SS, who said that the camp was expecting new transfers, and crudely joked about "Hungarian salami." Vrba knew what this meant. When Jews from the Netherlands were gassed, he had heard that the SS boasted about eating the cheese these victims had packed for the journey; when French Jews arrived, the SS feasted on sardines; when Greek Jews came into the camp, the SS had the halvah and olives they carried in their bundles.

Vrba and his friends estimated that 1 million Jews living inside Hungary were in jeopardy. Transporting and killing this many would be a record, even for Auschwitz. Still, it seemed not only plausible but possible. German newspapers, which some of the prisoner leaders found, were reporting that the German military had marched into Hungary "to restore order." A puppet leader had been installed, and the Nazis now controlled the Hungarians' fate. Slowly, Vrba absorbed these massive facts. Now he wanted to do more than simply expose the Nazis' crimes against humanity; he wanted to prevent further crimes. He ambitiously hoped to warn the Hungarians, to help raise "an army one million strong, an army that would fight rather than die." If the Hungarians knew what awaited them, Vrba believed, they could at least put up resistance before boarding the transports, and perhaps they could even be saved.

Painstakingly Vrba assessed every previous unsuccessful escape attempt, scrutinizing its flaws and seeking to correct them.

HE HAD FEW ILLUSIONS about the difficulty of cracking the Nazi defenses. But although he accepted that everyone else in the camp "might die," he always felt, almost as an article of faith, that he himself would somehow succeed. He knew the penalties of a failed escape: he had seen them at the end of his very first week in Auschwitz. Marching with his detachment toward the barracks one afternoon, Vrba saw two mobile gallows. Thousands of prisoners had been gathered, under the watchful eyes of Rudolf Hoess, the camp commandant. Then an *Oberscharführer* bellowed in a loud, carrying voice that two Polish prisoners had been caught trying to escape: "This is something which the camp administration will not tolerate." Surrounded by two columns of SS men, the two emaciated, dirt-smudged, barefoot prisoners were dragged out to the gallows; ostentatiously pinned to their tunics were notices that read, "Because we tried to escape." The prisoners' steps were accompanied by the increasingly loud crescendo from two dozen military drums, but the captives showed no signs of indignation or weakness or fear. Only on reaching the wooden stairs did they falter. One of them began to make a speech, but the din of the twenty-four drummers extinguished his words. Vainly, he continued to speak as the hangman slipped the ropes around both men's necks and pulled the levers. The trapdoors opened; there was first one dull thump, then another. To Vrba's horror, the prisoners fell only half a foot or so. They were not being hanged; they were being slowly strangled. The assembled men watched as the would-be escapees writhed frantically, then slowly, then not at all.

The drums stopped, and a black silence descended, broken only by the harsh order that Vrba and the rest of the prisoners stand at attention for another hour, staring at the corpses. The assembled Nazis withdrew. Underneath a setting sun, Vrba, swallowing every insult, looked at the dangling prisoners and cemented his own resolution to escape.

THE CHALLENGE FOR VRBA—AND it was a challenge—was that Auschwitz was divided into an outer camp where the inmates worked and an inner camp where they slept. In that sense, one had to escape not once, but twice. Like a medieval castle, the inner camp of Auschwitz-Birkenau was ringed by a moat: a water-filled trench six yards wide and five yards deep. In turn, this moat was surrounded by two separate high-voltage electrified barbed-wire fences fifteen feet tall. And beyond these physical barriers were human ones. Night and day SS men trained their machine guns on the prisoners from their watchtowers. Once dusk fell, arc lights brilliantly illuminated the barracks and the barbed-wire fences. If any prisoner managed to break through these barriers, sirens and whistles would blare as the outer towers sounded the alert. Within seconds, three thousand men and two hundred snarling dogs would be racing to seal off the entire area. And the open space that they had to patrol, between the inner and outer camps, was completely bare; it was explicitly designed to be a killing field. Any escapee crossing that dusty, empty plain would be easy prey, completely at the mercy of cross fire from the two sets of towers lining the perimeters.

One shred of hope for Vrba was that after a high alert, the troops and dogs would patrol the camp for only three days and nights. If the escapee wasn't caught by then, the Germans retrenched, assuming the inmates had broken out. At this point, the search would be turned over to the vast web of SS authorities beyond Auschwitz. "It was clear to me," Vrba later recounted, "that a man who could remain hidden beyond the inner perimeter for three days and three nights had a reasonable chance."

A reasonable chance perhaps, but no one had yet figured out a way to do this. So Vrba, as he lay on his hard plank at night before drifting off to sleep, began what he called his "first scientific study" on "the technique of escape."

Soon, Vrba found an ally. An inmate from Russia, big, burly Dimitri Volkov, took Vrba under his wing; Vrba had often given Volkov his bread and margarine rations and for months, with Vrba using his self-taught Russian, they had discussed great Russian writers. Then one day, their talk changed. Cocky, knowledgeable, a former army captain, and now a POW, Volkov gave Vrba a crash course in the essentials of a successful escape. Volkov explained that Vrba would need a knife to defend himself, and a razor blade in case he got caught—to slit his own throat. He would need a compass and a watch, so that he could time his journey and figure out where he was. And he should travel only at night; daytime was for sleeping. He would also need salt, because with salt and potatoes, he could "keep going for months." However, he should never carry money, because if he was starving he'd be tempted to buy food. Instead, Volkov said, he must stay away from people. Also, he insisted, Vrba should never get "drunk with freedom." In other words, as Volkov put it, "the fight only begins when you are away from the camp."

Perhaps his most practical advice—advice that would later save Vrba's life—was to carry Russian tobacco that was drenched in petrol and dried, and to spread it all over himself. The smell, Volkov promised, would foil the tracker dogs.

After Volkov finished giving his lessons, the two men never spoke again. Why? Was Volkov carted off to a gas chamber? Vrba never knew. But he had other teachers as well. In January 1944, five other inmates, including one of Vrba's Slovak friends, raced for freedom; they barely made it beyond Auschwitz. Within three hours, the SS had brutally killed them: they were shot with dumdum bullets that ripped their flesh to pieces. Their bodies, mutilated "beyond recognition," were dragged to the camp and placed in chairs by the SS. Signs sadistically draped to their bodies proclaimed, "We're back!"

It seemed as though Vrba's plans lay in ruins. But then he linked up with Charles Unglick, a former captain in the French army, who had fought bravely at Dunkirk. Unglick was one of those rare few at Auschwitz who seemed indestructible. Strong, wealthy, brazen, a "gangster" of a man, he managed to develop considerable influence in the camp, cowing the *Kapos* and bribing the SS. He bullied the *Sonderkommando* too. Unglick discovered that one of the SS guards was an orphan who had been raised by Yiddish-speaking Jews; soon, he devised an audacious scheme to pay off this guard with gold and diamonds taken from "Canada," hidden beneath a plank in his barracks. In return, the guard would smuggle both Unglick and Vrba out, and they would make their way through enemy lines to Paris. Why would the guard do it? Vrba was suspicious. Unglick insisted that the guard harbored secret sympathy for the Jews.

They set the date of their escape as January 25, 1944, at 7 p.m., three days hence. Standing at roll call that night, as the wind swept through and the inmates shivered, Vrba could barely contain his excitement while he awaited his rendezvous with Unglick and the SS guard. His last roll call, he thought. Freedom. And help for the Jews who still remained outside Auschwitz.

Seven o'clock came and went. Then it was 7:05. Then 7:10. Then 7:15. Vrba had a terrible premonition that everything had gone awry. As luck would have it, while he torturously paced the ground, he was called to visit a man who was one of his "block seniors," a noted Slovak intellectual. Vrba was so nervous he could barely think. Unsure what to do, he went to join the block senior, and they shared a bowl of goulash soup. As soon as Vrba returned outside to wait, another registrar ran to him, explaining that Unglick had been looking everywhere for him and badly wanted to see him.

Vrba raced back to the meeting point, but there was no Unglick, no lorry, no SS guard. Had they escaped? Back at Unglick's room, he ripped up the loose plank in the floor, and saw that the bag of gold and diamonds was gone. But he had no way of knowing what had happened. And he realized that his opportunity had slipped away.

Vrba returned dazed and disillusioned to his block. He made distracted conversation, mumbling incomprehensibly to the other prisoners, until perhaps half an hour passed; it was somewhere around eight o'clock. Then a dreaded shout broke the night: "Block Senior Fourteen!" "Block Senior Fourteen!"

Partly in darkness, partly in the glare of the camp lights, Vrba stumbled to the courtyard of Block 14. His heart stopped. There lay Unglick's body, with a single bullet hole in his chest, blood dripping all over his face and neck. Vrba hung his head. Not many lasting relationships were ever formed inside Auschwitz; few people lived long enough or had strength enough to cultivate them. But Vrba had given his friendship to Unglick. They had joked and dreamed together, and now he was devastated. As it turned out, the SS man had been playing Unglick all along; he simply pocketed the gold and diamonds, pumped a bullet through Unglick's heart, and announced to the camp administration that he had thwarted an escape.

Staring at Unglick's contorted body, Vrba was close to total despair. He had sought to cheat fate, but to no avail. Miraculously, he had survived the selection process. Miraculously, where countless thousands perished within weeks, he had survived Auschwitz's cruelties. Yet now, what had seemed to be his best and perhaps his only chance had slipped away. With Unglick's death, all of Vrba's hopes died.

Overcome with sadness and smoldering anger, Vrba sought to steady himself, at first to no avail. But his desolation was short-lived, for in the weeks to come another opportunity would present itself.

VRBA'S NETWORK AT AUSCHWITZ included other friends, and one in particular: Fred Wetzler, who was also a registrar and who came from the same town as Vrba in Slovakia. Vrba believed he could trust Wetzler "implicitly." Like Vrba, Wetzler was a rarity in Auschwitz. Twenty-five years old, he was immensely popular, even with the Germans. He had vast knowledge of the inner workings at Auschwitz, and seemed to know all the details of the camp. Vrba liked him and now was putting his life into Wetzler's hands.

Wetzler's plan for escape was unlike any other. Because the Nazis were expanding the camp to accommodate the influx of Hungarians, there was more chaos than normal. Wetzler learned from some fellow Slovaks about a large pile of wooden planks that had been stacked in the outer camp; this pile was, in effect, a specially prepared hideout amid the vast array of building material. Within the pile was a cavity, large enough to accommodate four people. The pile itself stood beyond the watchtowers and the electrified fences of the inner camp. So if one could securely remain unseen inside it for three days, then the search detail would be withdrawn. All that would remain was to race for safety. There was both madness and genius in this plan. Boldly, Vrba and Wetzler would be hiding in plain sight.

As it happened, four other Slovaks wanted to go first. To Vrba's delight, they succeeded. The SS search was frantic, and it intensified daily. Yet after three days the Slovaks had not been discovered. Vrba and Wetzler decided they would wait two weeks, and then make a run for it themselves. But seven days later, their hopes were dashed when the SS returned with the badly beaten escapees. Vrba watched in silence as one by one the men were brutally tortured in public with leather whips, before being marched off for further interrogation. It was, Vrba reasoned, just a matter of time before the SS would break them and learn about the precious hiding place.

But Vrba and Wetzler still wanted to make sure.

Vrba managed to maneuver himself into the punishment block, where one of the prisoners whispered to him that they had not revealed the existence of the cavity.

Could they be trusted? Were the SS playing an elaborate game, as they had done so many times before? Vrba and Wetzler decided they had to take a chance.

~

THE WHOLE VENTURE WAS fraught with peril, but the details were quickly put in place. Vrba had a brief opportunity to study a map of the upper Silesian region, committing to memory a rough route for their escape; they would follow the Sola River and then they would trudge along the train tracks, the same tracks that carried car after car loaded with Jews. From the storage rooms in "Canada," the two men had pilfered finely woven Dutch tweed jackets and overcoats, along with heavy boots and a white woolen sweater. They found the precious Russian tobacco, and carefully soaked it in petrol before drying it. Vrba had also managed to find a knife, which he squirreled away. They would bring bread and margarine as rations and a little vial of wine for liquid. Crucially, they also persuaded two other prisoners, both Poles, to slide the planks back over their heads once they slipped inside the woodpile. The logistic problems, they knew, were difficult. They also knew they would need stealth, luck, and impeccable timing. Fortitude too: for the first three days they risked discovery by the dogs.

The date they set was April 3, 1944, at two o'clock p.m., but they were foiled when a suspicious SS man stood outside the gate at Wetzler's compound, and Wetzler sensibly refused to go.

~

THE NEXT DAY, APRIL 4, flying twenty-six thousand feet above Auschwitz, a South African pilot in a reconnaissance plane turned on his camera. He had taken off from the Allies' air base at Foggia in southern Italy, and had flown due north. He was searching for bomb targets.

As he guided his plane over this section of Upper Silesia, the camera clicked, taking twenty exposures of the Monowitz slave labor camp, where the IG Farben manufacturing plant was located. Just under three miles away from Monowitz were the death chambers at Auschwitz. On this same day, Auschwitz would receive a trainload of Jews from the northern Italian city of Trieste, still under German control. On board were 132 deportees. Of these, 103 were immediately sent to be gassed.

The photography took no more than a couple of minutes. The undeveloped film was then sent to the British Royal Air Force station west of London, where intelligence personnel developed it and studied the grainy pictures. They were looking for specific industrial installations that might be bombed. But as they examined the roll, three of the images showed rows of huts. These were the first known photographs of Auschwitz.

Over four more days, Vrba and Wetzler tried and failed. Each time, they were foiled when something unexpected went wrong: an accomplice was held up or there was a delay. Did the SS suspect something? Vrba and Wetzler had no way of knowing.

Finally, they resolved to make their break on April 7. That morning they went about their routine as if everything were normal. But once more in the early afternoon Vrba made his way toward the woodpile. All around, there was hammering and building, sweating and swearing, and chaos. Tense with fear, Vrba was suddenly surrounded by two SS men he had never seen before. They began commenting on his clothes, calling him a "tailor's dummy." True, as a registrar Vrba was an exception at Auschwitz, allowed to dress almost as he liked. Nevertheless, these Nazis objected to his coat, and haughtily began to rifle through his coat pockets, discovering a fistful of cigarettes. Vrba froze. Had his plan been foiled even before it began? Struggling to keep his composure, he began to sweat profusely. He knew if they opened up his coat, they would see his suit underneath. A deeper search would reveal the watch that he had stolen for the journey; at that moment, it was underneath his shirt, perilously pressing against his skin. If the watch alone was found, he would surely be executed for attempting to escape. And there were also the matches and knife that he had hidden.

A few ripped buttons, and all would be lost.

However once they had gone through the pockets, the Germans left his coat buttoned. Instead, they began laughing at him, taunting him, and striking his shoulder with a thick bamboo stick. Vrba visibly winced, his mind clouded with pain. With a sneer, the Germans stepped back to examine him further. They told Vrba that it was time he saw the inside of Block 11, where prisoners were taken to be disciplined. He stood still, not moving a muscle, terrified. Then, suddenly, one of the men struck him full across the face and shouted at him, "Get out of my sight!" Too stunned to think, barely able to speak, Vrba awaited their next move. Then, just as quickly, the Nazis decided they didn't want to make the trip to Block 11. Instead, they would report Vrba to the political department and he would be picked up after roll call.

Vrba was now a wanted man, with only hours remaining before he would be pulled out of line.

Vrba raced back to his section gate, then doubled back toward the woodpile. Trying to saunter over, Vrba saw them all, waiting. The Poles were standing on top working; Wetzler was below. They gaped when they saw Vrba, but otherwise there was silence; no one exchanged a single word or a sound. They were now moving very quickly, having only seconds to complete their deception. The Poles slid the wood planks to one side and gave a tiny nod. Vrba and Wetzler stood still for a moment, then they quickly picked their way to the top of the pile, dropped their legs into the opening, and slid into the cavity. They heard the planks being wrestled back into place over their heads, and then the sound of feet as the Poles scrambled off the pile.

Inside, it was pitch-black. The air was stuffy. The two men were forced to sit birdlike, in an uncomfortable, cramped position. For about fifteen minutes, Vrba and Wetzler didn't move a muscle and didn't say a word.

All they could hear was the scratchy sound of their own breath.

~

FIFTEEN MINUTES PASSED. THERE was no commotion outside; nothing had changed. Then, Vrba got to work. To foil the dogs, he filled the narrow spaces between the planks with the powdery Russian tobacco. It required nearly an hour of painstaking work. When it was finished, Vrba and Wetzler sat alone with their thoughts. It was only 3:30 in the afternoon. The moment of truth would come at 5:30 p.m. when the roll call began and the prisoners lined up. Vrba was at once scared yet excited. Nervously he kept fingering his watch—by now his eyes had adjusted to the dark—looking at the time, holding it up to his ear to make sure it hadn't stopped. Finally, he forced himself to put the watch away. He did not need it in the woodpile, nor did Wetzler. Both men could tell the time simply from the noises filtering in from outside. The routine was always the same. And sure enough, crouched in the gloom, they heard the tramp of boots of the prisoners returning for roll call.

By 5:25, Vrba was convinced the SS already knew they were gone, and were debating how to respond. By 5:30, Vrba's heart was racing. For some reason, no one had sounded the alarm. By 5:45, it was still eerily quiet. Vrba expected that at any moment they would hear the planks being pulled away and would look up into the barrels of machine guns. By six o'clock, there was still no siren.

"They're toying with us," Vrba whispered. "They must know where we are."

Wetzler was afraid to say a word. He nodded his head in agreement.

Then suddenly there came a high-pitched wail. The siren had sounded.

~

WITHIN MINUTES, AS THE half-light that precedes dusk fell over the camp, Vrba and Wetzler could hear the pounding of SS boots while their pursuers took up positions across the ground. The kennels were emptied and the two hundred specially trained dogs began combing the grounds of Auschwitz-Birkenau, barking frantically. It was an impressive display of force on the part of the Germans; they were crawling all over the surrounding countryside and were everywhere among the hundreds of low, single-story barracks. Thousands of men were now knocking down doors, lifting floor planks, and racing from building to building. Vrba knew what this meant: Every barracks would be promptly searched. Every building and structure, from the latrines to "Canada," would be examined, for three days. Every prisoner would be checked and rechecked, for hours on end; many would be brutally tortured. Vrba and Wetzler were gripped alternately by exhilaration and terror. Exhilaration at the prospect of success; terror at the prospect of getting caught.

The terror only grew. At first, the Germans were far away—Auschwitz was a huge, sprawling complex—but they soon drew closer. Suddenly, the two men heard an SS officer shout, "Look behind those planks!" Vrba and Wetzler froze as they heard the Germans scrambling up their woodpile. A shower of grit and fine dust rained down on them. The two men clamped their hands over their noses, fearful that they would sneeze. The dragnet was closing in, much as they had expected. Now in addition to the hoarse wheezing of the guards, they could hear the panting and frenzied sniffing of the dogs and the scraping of their claws as they slipped from plank to plank, just overhead. Himmler himself had once boasted that the dogs of Auschwitz had been trained "to tear a man apart."

Even through the darkness, Vrba could see that Wetzler's eyes were gleaming and his teeth were clenched. Their luck, it seemed, had run out. Vrba clutched his knife more tightly. He had vowed not to be taken alive.

~

THE MEN HEARD NOTHING; the dogs smelled nothing. Somehow, the Russian tobacco had worked, and no one had thought to move aside the boards. The dogs scampered away, trailing the many scents to another sector of the camp. They were followed by the guards, until the search was little more than a distant sound. For Vrba and Wetzler, this was a triumph. But they knew it was only the beginning.

Throughout the night, the men and the dogs searched, again and again sweeping around the woodpile. And to muffle their own sounds, Wetzler recalled, he and Vrba tied strips of flannel across their mouths and pulled them tight whenever either man felt a tickle in his throat.

And then they heard another, more familiar agonizing sound: the clang and clatter of trucks carrying new victims to the gas chambers. Vrba mentally counted. First there were ten, then twenty, then thirty, then forty, then fifty, then sixty. Even in the midst of an intense search, the business of death continued apace at Auschwitz. Vrba and Wetzler could picture the line for the "showers"; they could imagine the wrenching cries and whimpers of the Jews. Then they heard nothing until the "monotonous sound" of the dead bodies being loaded one after the other into the ovens. As it happened, they were hiding right near Crematorium IV.

Hour after hour, they listened as the *Sonderkommando* opened the iron doors of the crematorium and slid the bodies, already shrunken and contorted, into the flames to be turned into ash. Hour after hour, they smelled burning flesh and hair. This had been a transport of Belgian Jews; 319 souls, including 54 children, had been immediately gassed.

The second day was worse. The searchers were more desperate and Vrba and Wetzler more terrified. They'd had nothing to eat or drink for over twenty-four hours. They were filthy, unshaven, and exhausted. They would nod off to sleep for a few moments, only to be snapped back to reality by more sounds of the chase. They were now hearing different noises: the Nazis restlessly exchanging passwords, the sentries pounding around the outer ring, the officers barking commands to search here and search there.

As THE TWO MEN approached their third day in the woodpile, the intensity of the search slowed. All around them, the SS were conducting sweeps and the chase continued—until two o'clock in the afternoon. As they strained their ears to listen, Vrba and Wetzler heard two German prisoners exchanging rumors about where the escapees were. These men were convinced that, rather than being miles away, they were still in the camp, biding their time. One of the men evidently looked over toward the woodpile.

"You think they could be there?" he asked his companion.

The other man, probably shaking his head, said the dogs would surely have smelled them.

No, the first man insisted. "What if they found a way of killing the scent?"

"It's a long shot," came the reply.

The two men climbed onto the pile and began yanking away the planks of wood. Vrba and Wetzler, had a sickening sense of déjà vu—this was like the first day. Once more, Vrba drew his knife. Holding his breath, he flattened himself against the wall of the cavity, as if he could somehow disappear. The Germans were now within inches of finding their quarry. Yet just before the next plank could be moved, there was a tremendous noise from the other side of the camp. The Germans raced off toward the commotion, presumably believing the escapees had been caught. Vrba and Wetzler were still safe.

For Vrba and Wetzler hiding in their woodpile, a few hours away from possible freedom, April 9 was a day of silence. But it was far from quiet at Auschwitz. As it happened, on that day the trucks once again rumbled up the road, carrying victims to be gassed and then burned; but this time they were transporting a special group of Jews: those who had been housed in the Majdanek concentration camp, the first camp that Vrba had been sent to, where he had spent two weeks before his deportation to Auschwitz. Now, with the vengeful Soviet army pushing westward, the SS had furiously evacuated the camp and was preparing to abandon it. In a triumph of Nazi perfidy, the Germans doggedly sealed up wooden cattle cars filled with the evacuees, even as they torched all their own records, and dismantled Majdanek. In a vain attempt to cover up their crimes, they also exhumed and burned the remains of eighteen thousand bodies that had been buried in the forest—the Germans had machine-gunned these victims in the woods on a single day—November 3, 1943—which lived on in Nazi lore as "the Harvest Festival." They had not been able to dispose of the tens of thousands of shoes of other victims. These shoes rose in piles, like mounds of grain. Many were baby shoes, so tiny that two could easily be cradled in a grown man's palm.

For eight days, the train from Majdanek had crept westward along the worn rails, whistles blaring. For the prisoners, the journey was agony. Denied water and medical help, the evacuees, thin and hairless and clad in little more than rags, were under no illusions. This time, some fought back. At a station en route, twenty of them managed to cut their way out of the train and sought to escape. The SS methodically shot them all. Meanwhile, ninety-nine of the evacuees never reached Auschwitz at all; amid the sickening stench of sweat and waste, they simply died along the way. As for the survivors? They were weak, exhausted, some all but unable to move, worse than wild animals. On arrival, they were either gassed at once or tattooed and detailed for slave labor until they could be killed later.

BUT IT WAS NOT just the sounds of death that filled the air. Early in the evening, Vrba and Wetzler heard a distant humming in the sky. The hum turned into a rumble, the sound of heavy aircraft, coming closer. Soon came a series of whistles. The woodpile shook as the ground was peppered with explosions. Vrba and Wetzler held their breath. Had the camp finally been discovered? Were the Allies at last going to bomb the watchtowers and the electrified wires? "Was this," they wondered, "the end of Auschwitz?" For a fleeting moment Vrba entertained the delirious idea that they were being liberated. The explosions were answered by staccato bursts of antiaircraft fire, guns from the camp furiously firing into the sky. The woodpile shook, more grit rained down, and brilliant flashes bathed the cavity in a harsh, blinding light. But Auschwitz itself was not under attack; actually, it was industrial targets several miles away that were being pelted by the Allied bombs. The camp was untouched, and after the noise of the planes faded away, Vrba and Wetzler once again heard the clink of the grills and smelled the crematoriums setting flesh aflame.

They passed the day of April 10 in silence. At a little before 6:30 p.m., three days since the first siren had sounded, they heard shouts passing from watchtower to watchtower, around the camp: "*Postenkette abziehen!*"—"Cordon down!" It was the order calling off the internal search at Auschwitz. The guards would go back to their posts and barracks; the dogs would go back to their kennels. The search was over. Now, it would be up to the SS network outside the walls of Auschwitz to catch the escapees.

~

ON APRIL 9, MAJOR Hartenstein of the Waffen SS had already dispatched a telegram to Berlin with news of the escape. All Gestapo units in the east, all criminal police units, and all frontier posts were to be on the lookout for two Jews. With the same brutal efficiency that they applied in managing the camp, the Nazis sent the report over the wires, spreading their tentacles. In the event of capture, a "full report" was to be delivered to Auschwitz.

~

INSIDE THE WOODPILE, VRBA and Wetzler were hesitant to move, fearful that the end of the search could be a trick to drive them from their hiding place. In the chill evening air, they shivered—and waited.

By nine o'clock, the two men heard no sounds out of the ordinary, nothing to suggest that anyone thought they were still inside Auschwitz. After their days of crouching in dirt and darkness, they stood up stiffly and began to push against the remaining planks of their "roof." They pushed and the planks did not move. "Grunting, straining, sweating" together, they brought every ounce of their strength to bear on one section of wood. They managed to raise it an inch and grip their fingers around the boards. Finally, they heaved the wood to the side and were startled to see a string of brilliant stars dangling in a "black, winter moonless sky."

Had the two German prisoners not tried to search the woodpile and moved some of the boards, Vrba and Wetzler might have been completely trapped, unable to get out.

Carefully, the two men replaced the planks and then sat down on the woodpile to gaze back. For a fleeting moment Vrba saw Auschwitz from the outside—just as the hundreds of thousands of victims who arrived at its gates saw it. As he looked up from the flat ground, there were the bright lights ringing the camp that cast a shimmering glow punctuating the darkness. There were the dreaded silhouettes of the watchtowers, ominously rising into the sky. And behind the wire and the walls, behind that cordon of light, was mass slaughter on a scale never before witnessed in history.

Vrba and Wetzler climbed off the woodpile, lay down on their bellies, and began crawling toward a small forest of birch trees. Once there, they dropped their heads and ran. They never looked back.

4

Escape, Part 2

ON MARCH 24, FRANKLIN Roosevelt gave a statement to the press. His voice was husky and out of pitch because of the fluid filling his lungs and the slow constriction of his congestive heart failure. But if his voice was weak, his words were strong. Despite being ill, Roosevelt spoke firmly of the "wholesale, systematic murder of the Jews of Europe," describing it as one of the "blackest" crimes of all history, a crime which "goes unabated every hour." He promised, "None who participate in these acts of savagery shall go unpunished." He added that knowingly taking part in "the deportation of Jews to their death in Poland" would make a person "equally guilty with the executioner." And Roosevelt spoke specifically about the Jews of Hungary and those Jews from other nations who had found a haven inside Hungary's borders as being "threatened with annihilation," on "the very eve of triumph over the barbarism which their persecution symbolizes."

The next day, 599 Jews from the Netherlands reached Auschwitz; 239, including the elderly and all the children, were gassed on arrival.

In the meantime, two weeks later, while Vrba and Wetzler were hiding in their woodpile, Roosevelt was preparing to depart for Hobcaw Barony, the Wall Street financier Bernard Baruch's secluded 16,000-acre estate, in a desperate attempt to regain his health. Hours after Vrba and Wetzler fled Auschwitz, Franklin Roosevelt was waking up at Hobcaw Barony, in a wide, white-columned house built to resemble George Washington's Mount Vernon estate. While the weather was a touch cool, the sun shone frequently, and Roosevelt had no doubt already joked with Baruch that it was time to round up the fish and drive them toward shore so he could get out on a boat with a hook, bait, and a fishing pole.

The barony was old, but its name was even older: Hobcaw was a Native American word meaning "between the waters." The Spanish had first tried to settle the area in the 1500s, but they abandoned the land after three quarters of their colonists died during the first winter. Later, the British built a fort on the site during the Revolutionary War, and British gravestones still stood at the woods' edge.

Until the start of the twentieth century, Hobcaw had been part of the great Carolina Low Country rice empire. By the 1940s, abandoned rice fields were home to ducks, turkeys, and even the occasional eagle, exactly as Baruch desired. In 1905, he had bought the land for a winter hunting retreat. A South Carolinian by birth, Baruch kept and cultivated his accent even after his family moved to New York when he was ten. From his humble start as an office boy, he rose to the pinnacles of power, becoming a financial adviser and confidant to six presidents. In Washington, he frequently held court with top officials on a bench in Lafayette Park, overlooking the White House. And now the president had come to his door, hoping to rejuvenate himself.

Hobcaw was quiet and away from the prying eyes of Washington, yet the White House was leaving little to chance. Given the precariousness of his health, for his entire stay the president would be accompanied by doctors Bruenn and McIntire. He had also brought his little terrier dog, Fala.

Preceding his arrival, there was a flurry of activity at the plantation to make the necessary accommodations. For a month the presidential railcar had sat in readiness, while marines tirelessly combed the woods and the Coast Guard patrolled the nearby inland rivers. Meanwhile, the Secret Service detail was busy hammering. The agents constructed wooden ramps to enable them to move the president around on each side of the house. They put up a sizable fence on the large fishing pier. They even jerryrigged a slide from Roosevelt's second-floor bedroom to the outside in case of emergency, namely fire; actually, the slides traveled with the president everywhere he went and were ready to be used at the White House if the stairways ever caught fire. Roosevelt was terrified of fire.

At Hobcaw, Roosevelt kept to a simple routine, but his aristocratic heritage was on full display. In a bedroom painted a subdued green, he looked out his window across a shaded lawn sloping down to the bay. He slept late, usually until 9:30 a.m. but sometimes later, and went to bed early, at 9:30 p.m. Every morning he flicked on the reading lamp by his mahogany bed and took his time reading the newspapers. When he felt up to it, he fiddled with his correspondence. Daily, a special plane from Washington brought documents that required his presidential signature, and Roosevelt got into the habit of addressing those at dusk, before his customary one or two martinis and his seven o'clock dinner.

But mostly, he rested.

In the afternoons, the president napped after lunch and then later frequently took little outings: he cruised up the Waccamaw River in Baruch's yacht or fished from the pier or at the freshwater pond at Arcadia. He took jaunts to see the plentiful wildlife, like snipes, opossums, snakes, or, just as often, deer and wild boars. He traveled to see the exquisite Belle Isle Gardens, where there were magnificent trees and an old fort. On some days, there was no destination other than simply to drive. He was crazy about driving. And once, in a rare moment of solemnity, he paused at the tip of the plantation, where he saw the weathered markers of British soldiers who had fallen during the Revolutionary War. Another afternoon was spent on the coastal beach of the neighboring Vanderbilt plantation, where Roosevelt watched as other men stood at the water's edge and practiced surf-casting, sending their fishing lines out into the waves, while nearby his little dog Fala dug holes in the sand. Roosevelt also spent several hours fishing around Winyah Bay in a Coast Guard patrol boat.

And he sunned himself on the tremendous bayside terrace of Baruch's mansion. From there, he could watch the moss-covered oaks swaying in the breeze, gaze out on the azaleas in bloom, or follow with his eyes as Fala bounded across the lawn and played with a black cat. Roosevelt now stayed permanently in his wheelchair. His leg braces had been all but discarded; they came out only for public appearances. And during this month, he was all but out of public view.

When he wasn't sleeping or sightseeing or fishing, there was plenty of time for socializing. These were some of his happiest moments. At the noontime and evening meals, he was surrounded by those whose hearts burst with affection for him. He enthusiastically ate with his little group, including his daughter and his cousin, not to mention his two doctors and assorted officials who came down from Washington, D.C. Eleanor also made the journey to briefly check up on him. One afternoon, Roosevelt entertained the Australian prime minister and his wife. Each day feeling a little stronger and a little better, he would rumble incessantly about whatever topic entered his mind, keeping his company spellbound with stories about politics and policy and the old days, especially the virtues of catching bass and bream; he and his old friend Baruch also freely reminisced. Dr. Bruenn called Roosevelt "a master raconteur," and this was not far off the mark. At lunch and dinner alike, in Bruenn's words, Roosevelt "animated the conversation."

Even in his condition, he was a feast of a character, dwarfing those around him. And he was playful, teasing the small pool of reporters who idled around with the ostensible purpose of covering him. Once, he ordered them a round of bourbon.

The trip, however, was not without problems. Every day one of

Roosevelt's bitterest foes, William Ball, the editor of a Charleston newspaper, the *News and Courier*, wrote pieces lambasting him. The president typically shrugged these off; but Baruch, with his southerner's penchant for manners, traveled sixty miles to Charleston to tell Ball that the harsh editorials should stop as long as the president was visiting.

~

WHATEVER RESPITE HOBCAW OFFERED, difficult problems remained to be solved. There were questions of what the peace would look like; questions of surrender; questions of battle on the Normandy shores; questions of the Japanese threat, at home and abroad; and questions of the mounting loss of life under the Nazis, in combat and among innocent civilians alike. Could the United States and the Allies act? Would they act? These were all issues awaiting the president's leadership. And many wondered, would Hobcaw Barony give Roosevelt the same opportunity for rest and inspired thinking that the USS *Tuscaloosa* had provided in the Caribbean at the start of 1941, when he developed his audacious policy of Lend-Lease to save the British war effort? For the president and those who depended on him, there was nothing left to do but wait.

~

HOWEVER, AT AUSCHWITZ THERE were two men who refused to wait, who were running as hard as they could among the towering birch trees until they stumbled into open ground. Hurling themselves to the grass, Vrba and Wetzler now began to crawl. They knew they were working against the clock; they could not afford to be visible when daytime arrived. They also knew there were land mines in the area, but there was nothing they could do about that. Eventually the two men reached what they first thought was a stream; in fact it was a moat of—what? Ashes of the dead? Vrba cautiously put out his hand. He touched sand, smooth white sand. He knew that sand, any sand, was deadly. "Once we trod on it," Vrba thought, "our footsteps would be arrows for the patrols to follow as soon as it was light." But there was no choice, the sand stretched in a wide ring. So Vrba and Wetzler raced forward, plunging toward an area of land thickly covered with low scrubby bracken. In the dark, the men could not run, nor could they crawl. They could make out the shape of signposts, but neither of them felt brave enough to strike a match and read what any of the signs said. Dawn was fast approaching, starting to break in the eastern sky. They were dirty, had barely slept in three days, and were weak from hunger. But they pressed on, gasping for breath at every step. In the distance, they saw the contours of a forest. Thick trees offered cover and seclusion. If they could get that far, perhaps they could keep a jump ahead of the Germans.

Then Vrba saw another signpost. Were they near a town? He carefully scanned the German words: "Attention! This is Auschwitz Concentration Camp. Anyone found in these moors will be shot without warning!"

Somehow, they were still inside the camp. It had never occurred to Vrba just how huge the complex of Auschwitz was. By now, a bright pink light threaded the sky. Vrba and Wetzler were completely exposed. They knew they needed to get to the forest.

Then they heard the faint sound of German, and cursing and shouting. Just over a quarter of a mile away, they saw a work detail of emaciated women shuffling along, being beaten by armed SS men. Even here the scent of death clung to Auschwitz. Wetzler and Vrba flattened themselves on the ground, panting in fear. But the sounds did not come closer. The prisoners and the SS overlords moved on; the fugitives remained unseen. Yet for now, they knew they could not stand up again. For the next two hours, they remained flat on the ground, crawling and slithering through a field of young corn, through hollows, dips, and ditches. Meanwhile, the darkness had become the first sliver of dawn, and the first of dawn became daylight. The sun was overhead when they finally reached the forest and made their way into the thick firs. At least they now had the cover of the trees. They pushed on as quickly as they could until, right in front of them, they heard dozens of voices. Vrba and Wetzler dived into some bushes, and, peering out, saw a large party of Hitler Youth, knapsacks slung over their shoulders, out for a hike and a picnic.

Near the two men's hiding place, the young Germans sat down underneath the trees and began to munch on their sandwiches, laughing, playing, and swapping jokes. Vrba and Wetzler slowly crawled into a bush, and lay still. "We were trapped," Vrba recalled, "not by the SS this time, but by their children!"

Then a hard rain began to fall.

The rain became a downpour, and the Hitler Youth grabbed their knapsacks and raced off. The ground was soaked, and so were Vrba and Wetzler. Undeterred, they marched through the mud and the muck for several hours, eluding yet a second SS patrol with another band of female prisoners, until they finally found a thick patch of bushes. By now, although the cocktail of adrenaline and fear had been keeping them going, they were so tired they could barely think.

Burying themselves inside the brush, the two men drifted off to sleep for the first time in four days.

AS THEY SLEPT, THOUSANDS of SS troops were combing the countryside or were on heightened alert looking for the two Jewish escapees, just as they had looked for all the other fugitives they had caught. No Jews had ever successfully escaped from Auschwitz.

The telegraph wires of the SS continued to chatter with nearly unprecedented urgency. The Waffen SS major, Hartenstein, cabled reports of the breakout to an agitated Gestapo command post in Germany. Copies of the telegram raced across the Nazi realm, landing on the desks of the SS administrators at Sachsenhausen, of every Gestapo chief, of each of the SD (*Sicherbeitsdienst*, or Security Service) units, and of each criminal police unit. Of course, it also went to all the headquarters along the borders. The upper reaches of the Third Reich and even Himmler himself had been informed of the escape. And the telegram underscored the priority of the search: Vrba and Wetzler were explicitly named and identified as Jews. The telegram closed: "Request from you further search and in case of capture full report to concentration camp Auschwitz."

~

VRBA AND WETZLER HAD no idea of the full extent of the search for them, but if previous escape attempts had taught them anything, it was that prisoners on the run were a top priority. They also knew that eventual capture and torture, followed by public execution, were only one possibility. Vrba remembered that the Soviet POW, Dimitri Volkov, had warned him to stay away from people, and for good reason: German soldiers and citizens alike were told to shoot Jews, or for that matter "unidentifiable loiterers," on sight. In turn, the Polish citizens were told that if they helped prisoners escaping from Auschwitz, or aided partisans fighting the Nazis, they would be executed.

Vrba calculated that they had about eighty miles of Polish countryside to cross before reaching the relative security of the Slovak border. As much as possible, they would follow the current of the Sola River, which flowed in an almost straight line from south to north. But still, every inch from here on in was laden with difficulty. For one thing, as they were acutely aware, by this stage they both stood out conspicuously. They were unwashed, they stank, and they were extremely pale. Their faces bore evident traces of suffering. Despite their Dutch overcoats, they looked ragged and unkempt. They had no papers. And they had no food or water except what they could forage.

But they had no options except to stumble forward until they were in friendlier territory.

At first, they knew only what they could see before them, which was nothing but inky blackness stretching from the horizon behind them to the one beyond. Then, a few hours later, they looked up and, to their horror, saw the dark, familiar outlines of watchtowers, huts, and labor materials. Watchtowers? Huts? After two nights and a day on the run, they had yet to leave the confines of Auschwitz; they had merely gotten as far as one of the satellite camps. And they knew that as soon as dawn broke, the towers would be manned and they would be visible on the flat, open ground. Hearts pounding, they backed away from the watchtowers. Finally, as the sky lightened to gray, Vrba and Wetzler spotted a wooded area. Slipping into it, they found a cluster of bushes. Quickly, they began breaking off branches of trees to cover themselves. Concealed by these branches and the bushes, they heaved a sigh, and once more rested, believing they had found a safe spot.

Actually, they hadn't. When the smoky light rose off the ground and the sun climbed overhead in the morning, the two men awoke with a shudder. They were not in a patch of woods; they were in the middle of a park. And not just any park, but an elite one, reserved for only the SS and their families. Along the paths near the bushes, SS officers in their green uniforms fondled their girlfriends or strolled beside their wives; SS dogs wagged their tails and romped over the grass, racing up to sniff the bushes; and SS children, all dressed up, their blond hair seemingly perfectly in place, frolicked and giggled, running in all directions. Lying motionless in the bushes, Vrba and Wetzler watched it all, wondering if their luck had run out and this would be their end.

Suddenly, two children, who had been playing nearby, ran right up to the bushes. Vrba and Wetzler found themselves staring directly into their wide, round eyes.

"Papa," one child cried out. "There are men in the bushes. Funny men."

Vrba and Wetzler had already glimpsed the father, wearing the uniform of an *Oberscharführer*, a pistol in a holster slung low across his hip. The two men pulled out their knives. The father raced over to the bushes and stared, looking at them from head to toe. Then he turned around and shooed his children away. The last Vrba saw, the *Oberscharführer* was speaking in hushed tones to his stricken-looking wife. They had lucked out; the German had assumed they were Nazi homosexuals, having a tryst. For now, the search had faltered. Having survived this scare, Vrba and Wetzler were acutely aware that the Nazi net had to be drawing ever tighter around them. They stayed put until dark, then they headed in what they believed was the direction of the Bezkyd mountains.

~

THE BEZKYD (BESKIDS) MOUNTAINS—TO this day the origin of their name remains a mystery—traced the frontier of Slovakia to the east and Poland to the north, and stretched from Czechoslovakia in upper Moravia all the way to the Ukraine. At their high point along the Polish-Slovak border they were about 3,500 feet above sea level, with a landscape consisting of long, rolling hills covered with forests and pastures. Giant fir trees rose into the sky, and cool, snow-fed mountain creeks cut across the valleys. Meanwhile the hillsides were dotted with little villages.

Throughout the day and into the evening, Vrba and Wetzler marched on.

In the distance, they saw lights flickering. They thought it must have been the town of Bielsko; if so, they were going in the right direction. Their plan was to sidestep the town, and hence its people, and continue south toward the border. But as the lights of the town were extinguished one by one, until it was pitch-black, Vrba and Wetzler lost their way. One of their greatest fears was that somehow they would get turned around—and end up moving back toward the Germans. With their next steps, they might as well have been. Rather than avoiding the town, they wandered too far west, and soon found that they were picking their way down its main streets. The sun was slowly rising, and it was just a matter of time before they were discovered by a patrol of armed militias. Bielsko was exactly the wrong town to be in. Jews there were not allowed to declare that they spoke Yiddish, and during the war the town had extinguished most of them. Moreover, though it was in Poland, about 85 percent of its inhabitants were German-speaking.

Scanning for patrols, they crept out of the town. But they could not get back to the safety of fields and forests. Their only option was to head to the small neighboring village of Pisarovice. Yet now they were no longer walking in the motionless hours before the first light of dawn. By the time they reached it, day was breaking. If they were seen, that would amount to a death sentence; indeed, wandering through a small village was exactly how the four Slovaks who had broken out of Auschwitz before them had been captured. Vrba and Wetzler knew their only option, chancy as it was, would be to seek help. If they knocked on the door of an anti-Semite, someone who hated the Jews as much as the Nazis did, they were finished. If it was the home of a German, they were equally done for. Even the home of a sympathetic Pole was a risk.

Having no other choice, they saw a neat but weathered house tucked away on a street where chickens freely ambled about. They slunk into the backyard and, hoping against hope, anxiously rapped on the door.

The door opened a crack, and an elderly woman with a young girl at her side called out to see who was there. She was a solid-looking peasant and clearly a partisan. Vrba and Wetzler greeted her with the traditional Polish words, using their best Polish accents: "Praise be to the name of Christ." "May His name be praised forever, amen," she replied, and invited them in.

"I'm afraid my Russian is not very good," she said hesitantly, "but you speak Polish well. Now you must be hungry." She invited them into her kitchen, where they had a small meal of boiled potatoes washed down with substitute coffee. She was a talkative woman, wasting little time in detailing the situation for them. The open country, she explained, was constantly patrolled by the Germans; therefore, traveling in the daytime involved incalculable risks. Thus, she stressed that they would need to spend the evening here. The safe haven of the mountains was a number of hours away. As if signaling that Vrba and Wetzler could trust her, she added that one of her sons was dead and the other was in a concentration camp. Whether it was Auschwitz or another camp, she didn't say.

Then suddenly the door opened. Vrba and Wetzler leaped to their feet, prepared to fight or to run. But the caller was only an elderly man, smoking an ancient pipe, who said good morning and asked them if they could help chop a pile of wood. Grateful to still be alive, they happily got to work. It was like a dream. Never before had they been so thankful for a place to work, a place to eat, and a place to go to bed. That night, the old Polish woman provided them a meal of "potato soup and potatoes" before leading them to a barn, where on a mound of hay they blissfully drifted off to sleep.

At three o'clock in the morning Vrba felt a hand on his shoulder, shaking him.

It was the old woman, speaking quickly, telling them that it was time to leave. She gave them coffee and pressed 4 Polish marks into Vrba's hand. He demurred, remembering his friend Volkov's advice not to take any money. She insisted that he take it, "just for luck."

Now on the eighth day of their journey, they marched off in the darkness, toward the snow-flecked mountains.

They walked at night, when it was colder, by threads of starlight or the round glow of the moon, searching for natural ruts in the fields or the dirt. They slept during the day, hiding as much from the wild animals that roamed the woods as from people. The hours of exhaustion and tedium dragged on, but they never stopped. Almost miraculously, two days later they were at the halfway point en route to Slovakia. Their goal was always the same: to wander for hours without seeing a soul.

Standing in the mountains, they could see a town in the valley below them. After the stench of Auschwitz, they could now take deep breaths; the air was crisp and clean. Nearby was the Sola River. As for the village, they remembered from what the captured Slovaks in Auschwitz had told them, that there was a heavy, well-armed German presence. They gazed down at the town, knowing that they could make plans to go around it. Suddenly, there was a sharp noise, like a violent clap of hands, or a firecracker. A bullet whistled directly over their heads. On a neighboring hill, they saw the glint of guns. A German patrol, with dogs barking, was coming after them—fast. Their only hope was to somehow make it to the top of the hill and then to the valley below.

They stiffened for a moment, then ran, their feet slipping on the wet rocks and the heavy spring snow. Around them, bullets ricocheted off the rocks; the patrol was in hot pursuit and closing in fast. Wetzler found shelter behind a large boulder, but Vrba tripped and landed with his face pressing into the snow. He was too terrified to move. He heard a shout, "We've got him!" followed by the sounds of boots and dogs coming down the hillside. But they didn't have him. Vrba leaped up, threw off his heavy damp overcoat, and raced for the boulder. From below, the Germans began firing again; the dogs howled. Together, Vrba and Wetzler took off, plunging into a swift, icy stream at the bottom of the valley. It was a shock to their systems—the water was freezing, and twice, Vrba slipped and was sucked under the current. Yet they were propelled through the water and the rocks by the thought that the river would wash away their scent and confound the dogs. Soaked and scared, Vrba and Wetzler then pulled themselves ashore and began to run, through thick snow that sometimes reached as high as their waists. Deep under the tree cover, when they could no longer hear the baying of the dogs, they slid, exhausted, into a ditch and buried themselves under shrubs.

For what seemed like an eternity, their hearts pounding, they listened and waited.

Every twig that cracked, every rustle of wind, every clump of snow that plummeted to the ground from a sagging tree limb sent waves of fear through them. But within hours, the barking died down and there were no more sounds of footsteps. The Germans had been thwarted. For the first time, Vrba and Wetzler could taste freedom. Now, they had to make it to the Polish border and somehow slip across into Slovakia.

The nights remained cold, and they shivered while they slept. There was almost no food to scavenge, nothing to fill their stomachs but snow and icy stream water. They had barely enough to survive. And they had to be on guard constantly, keeping to darkened, out-of-the-way back roads and twisting, curving paths. By this stage, they feared everyone. They could easily imagine being shot or axed in some nameless overgrown field. Complicating matters, Vrba's feet were grossly swollen—he had to sleep in his boots—and he had trouble even walking.

Their best-laid plans were increasingly coming unglued. And then, while trudging through a field, they came face-to-face with an old hunched Polish woman, tending her goats. Vrba and Wetzler stared at her in silence and she stared back. All the while, Vrba was making quick calculations in his head. He didn't have a good feeling about this woman, yet they were running out of time. He was hobbling badly. They needed food desperately, and they needed guidance to the border. And every day that they delayed announcing the news about Auschwitz, more Jews would be slaughtered. What to do? If she made trouble, they would strangle her—or use their knives. So they gambled. "We are heading for the Slovak border," Vrba told her. "Can you show us the way? We've escaped from a concentration camp." Then came the startling words; his voice trailed off as he added, "From Auschwitz."

For the first time, he had said it: he had spoken of the place to someone on the outside.

Carefully studying these two filthy, sweaty stragglers, the old woman registered neither fear nor surprise. Inexplicably, she seemed as distrustful of them as they were of her. They didn't know it at the time, but the Gestapo frequently disguised themselves as escapees or Jews, seeking to ferret out Polish partisans or Polish "traitors." Thus, suspicion fed suspicion. Fear fed fear.

"You'll have to wait here," she declared in a controlled voice. She said she would send them food "right away" and a man to help them in the evening. Vrba and Wetzler scanned their surroundings and realized that they were on a hill between a bridge and a darkened forest. They did some quick calculations: The forest was much closer than the bridge. If a German patrol came, it would have to cross the bridge, and that would give both men enough time to spot the patrol and escape into the forest, most likely before the Germans spotted them. Meanwhile, they would wait.

After two hours a boy of about twelve crossed the bridge and skipped up the hill, carrying a wrapped package of cooked potatoes and some meat. The two men wolfed it all down, eating with their hands. A satisfied smile crossed the boy's face. "My grandmother," he told them, "will be back when it's dark." As quickly as he had come, the boy skipped away. But Vrba and Wetzler were still dubious, wondering if all of this was an elaborate ruse. They heatedly debated whether to continue waiting—or leave. Believing that they could disappear into the woods quickly if necessary, they once again decided to wait.

The sun dipped under the horizon, and night fell. The cold returned. They counted the hours until finally the old woman arrived with a male companion, dressed in well-worn peasant clothes. He was brandishing a pistol. Vrba's nerves were on edge, his feet throbbing; he now feared the worst.

No one spoke until the woman gave them more food, which they again furiously ate, grabbing it with their fingers and shoving hunks into their mouths, barely taking time to chew one mouthful before swallowing and gulping another. Watching the spectacle, the Polish man let out a loud chuckle. As he put the gun away, he laughed and said only escapees from a concentration camp "could eat like that." Then he explained his own fear that Vrba and Wetzler might have been Gestapo agents acting as "decoys." He invited them to come to his house and stay there, and then promised that he would get them safely across the border.

They trudged off down the hill into the valley, past carefully tended little cottages, and into the man's home. By now, Vrba's feet were in agony. He could not even pull off his boots. Taking his razor blade, the one he kept for suicide should the need ever arise, he carefully cut through his boots to relieve his swollen feet. The man gave him slippers to wear, and then something even more precious: an actual bed to sleep in. The next day they were in good spirits, resting and waiting in his house. After supper he informed them that it was time to go.

They left the house, closed the door, and in a quiet single line, headed south toward the Slovak border.

∾

THEY WALKED IN SILENCE until suddenly the man stopped. He told them that a German patrol passed this point every ten minutes. They would have to hide in the bushes until the next one appeared and then make a dash. Within minutes, the three men heard voices and footsteps. It was the German unit, passing so close that the men could have reached out and touched them. Yet the patrol looked neither left nor right and quickly vanished. The three men continued; they still had a long way to go. After two days of walking, they came to a quiet clearing. Their guide paused, pointing a finger. "See the forest over there? That's Slovakia." It was only fifty yards away, but it might as well have been on the other edge of the universe. He informed them that yet another German patrol would soon appear, and that as soon as it passed, they should make their move. "I'm glad I could help," he added, and then, looking at Vrba's feet, he said, "I hope those slippers hold out." With those words, their guide turned and vanished into the night.

For two unspeakable years Vrba and Wetzler had held on to their hopes and nurtured them. They had learned to sleep virtually with one eye open, and to live day-by-day with closed hearts. They had wondered if they would or would not survive. And they had wondered if the outside world would ever come to their rescue. Now it was they who were coming to the outside world. After watching the Germans march past them, they dashed as fast as they could, careening over the border to freedom. It was April 21, 1944.

They had three weeks to warn the Hungarians, Roosevelt, and the rest of the world about the deadly truths of Auschwitz. Thus would begin an extraordinary, and at times devastating, cataract of events.

VRBA AND WETZLER KNEW that they could no longer keep to forests. They had to make contact with local Jews. That meant they would have to walk to a town, without papers, and ask for help. They were strangers and obvious escapees, and Slovakia was a German-controlled, collaborator nation. Their opportunity came within hours. They emerged from the trees into a field, and in front of them a poor farmer straightened up and stared. Vrba and Wetzler decided to trust him. "We need help," Vrba told him. "We must get to Cadca." The farmer grinned, "You'd better come to my place first because you're not going to get far in those clothes." He allowed them to stay in his cottage, he gave them some farm clothes from his meager supply, and he told them that the best way to reach the town was by train. In three days, he would be taking the train to the local market with his pigs. "You help me along with them and nobody will ask any questions." So for three days, until the pigs were transported and sold, Vrba and Wetzler waited. The farmer was as good as his word. He took them to the office of a local Jewish doctor named Pollack, ostensibly to get treatment for Vrba's feet. Because there was a desperate need for medical care, the Nazis had not deported Pollack to Auschwitz. Instead he was practicing at the headquarters of the Slovak army, Germany's ally. Actually, Vrba knew Dr. Pollack; they had almost been on the same transport out. Now Vrba was the one to tell the doctor that all his "resettled relatives," who had presumably left for the north or the east, were in fact dead. Shaken, Pollack bandaged Vrba's feet.

The next morning, Vrba and Wetzler were on their way to Zilina, to meet with Jewish leaders. Vrba was still shoeless and wearing the bandages.

At the Zilina headquarters of the Jewish Council, Vrba and Wetzler were received in luxury and comfort unlike anything they had ever experienced. The council consisted of men of countenance and erudition, with contacts in all the right places—and it showed. Meeting with the spokesmen for Slovakia's Jews, Vrba and Wetzler ate in an intimate dining room where the table sparkled with shiny plates and cutlery, and they were served "the finest meal" they had ever eaten. After dessert, they smoked cigars, sipped sherry, and passionately talked nonstop, recounting all the sordid details of Auschwitz. In a fever of excitement they explained everything. Nevertheless, at one point the ebullient Vrba paused, looked up at his hosts, and suddenly realized that they seemed strangely moody and cautious.

Indeed, they didn't seem to believe a word he was saying.

It became clear to him that they were laboring under the delusion, or at least clinging to the vain hope, that Slovakia's Jews—indeed all the Jews of Europe—were merely slaving away in work camps or concentration camps and would be able to return home after the war. But as it happened, the Jewish Council kept methodical records; every name of every Jew taken by the Nazis in Slovakia was recorded by hand in large ledgers. The council members began by asking Vrba on what date he had left. "June 14, 1942." The nodding began. Then the next question, "Where did you leave from?" "Novaky." More pages in the ledger were flipped. "Can you name any of the people on the transport with you?" Vrba gave them thirty names of people in his own wagon. Every name was in the ledger.

For hours, the incredulous men of the Jewish Council grilled Vrba and Wetzler in separate rooms, calmly checking and rechecking every detail. Vrba's memory was phenomenal. Despite the initial setback, he flung himself into the facts. It was soon clear that these were not perverse products of his imagination; everything he said stood up to scrutiny.

As Vrba and Wetzler painstakingly took their hosts through the hell that was Auschwitz, the council finally understood that a further crisis was coming. Pale and trembling, the members went from disbelief to horror, from horror to sadness, from sadness to urgency. By the evening's end, Vrba and Wetzler's report amounted to sixty single-spaced pages; it also included remarkably detailed sketches of how Auschwitz and Birkenau were organized, and drawings showing the long rows of barracks, and where the crematoriums were. It was ready for dissemination to the world. While SS trains continued to roll northward, clicking monotonously over the rails, the Jewish Council promised Vrba and Wetzler that the report would be in the hands of the Hungarians the very next day. Thereafter, it would, they believed, be only a matter of time before the report was given to the British and the Americans as well.

That night, Vrba and Wetzler slept blissfully on soft beds, bubbling with excitement and comforted by the thought that the Hungarian Jews would be quickly alerted. It was April 25, 1944. On April 28, Oskar Krasnansky, a chemical engineer and a leading Slovak Zionist in Bratislava who had traveled to Zilina to question Vrba and Wetzler, gave their report to Rudolf Kastner, head of the Hungarian Jewish rescue committee. When Vrba asked about the report and if it had reached the Hungarians, he was soothingly told, "Yes, it is in their hands."

Thus would commence one of the war's great dramas.

MEANWHILE, ROOSEVELT'S TWO WEEKS at Hobcaw were quickly extended to three, and during the third week, the president indulged in a secret delight. His old love, with whom he had once had a passionate affair, Lucy Mercer Rutherford, drove over from her winter home at Aiken; Bernard Baruch had to give her his gasoline ration coupons for the trip. The clandestine visit, with its romantic overtones, was arranged by Roosevelt's daughter Anna; whether it was platonic or otherwise is a fact lost to history. What has not been lost was that Roosevelt adored Lucy and she adored him. Lucy's name never appeared on the visitors' log at Hobcaw, but she may have stayed up to a week. Roosevelt's son Elliott would later write, "Lucy drove over from her nearby home in Aiken to extend the care and love she had not lost for this lonely, ailing, cheerful man. Her visits were taken as a matter of course by the Hobcaw group, but Mother was not told a word . . . her trusted counselor, Bernie Baruch, was an accomplice in keeping the secret."

Still, Roosevelt's stay at Hobcaw was not without its problems. On April 28, Roosevelt was informed that his good friend and cabinet member, Secretary of the Navy Frank Knox, had died of a heart attack; he was seventy. Clearly rattled by the news, Roosevelt then had his own scare.

After lunch he began to sweat profusely. His entire body then began to convulse, and he felt acute pain in his abdomen. He was also nauseated. His neck hurt terribly and his blood pressure perilously rose to 240/130, a new high. With his combative spirit, Roosevelt resisted panic; so did his doctors. Dr. Bruenn diagnosed this as yet another malady, gallstones, and sent him to bed for two days. Bruenn and McIntire also decided that Roosevelt couldn't go to Knox's funeral in Washington, D.C., but would instead have to spend an extra week convalescing. Later that day, to dampen the gnawing pain, Roosevelt was given a hypodermic injection of codeine so that he could briefly give a statement to the press about Knox's death. Yet the pain stubbornly persisted for three more days.

Despite the public pronouncements by his doctors, it was clear that Roosevelt's body was breaking down. His blood pressure was still high, and he was taking daily doses of digitalis. And he was still barely able to work.

~

ON THE NIGHT OF April 27–28, while an ailing Roosevelt was writhing in pain in South Carolina, Allied assault forces were conducting their most important military exercise of the war, along a peaceful stretch of land on the southwest coast of England, known as Slapton Sands. Code-named Operation Tiger, it was the central part of a weeklong, full-scale dress rehearsal of Operation Overlord. It was held in the strictest secrecy, and measures were taken to ensure that it would be as authentic as possible, right down to the use of live ammunition and live naval fire. Even the ramparts that had been erected were patterned after the Allies' best descriptions of Rommel's Atlantic Wall in Normandy. Moreover, the Devonshire shore, and the chalky cliffs in the background, bore a striking resemblance to Utah Beach itself.

The night's joint exercises involved large forces, some thirty thousand men all told, who were slated to go to France as a team. There were assault forces O for Omaha, G for Gold, U for Utah, J for Juno, and S for Sword. There were infantry divisions, combat engineer divisions, and the Seventieth Tank Battalion. Separately, there were Ranger battalions; naval beach battalions; the Eighty-second Airborne; and chemical battalions to decontaminate anything hit by poison gas. And there were medics and even grave registration crews to take care of the dead; on the actual D-Day, the soldiers would be instructed not to stop to help the wounded—that agonizing task was to be left to the medics and registration crews.

During the exercise, the troops were assembled in marshaling areas, briefed on their mission, and then loaded aboard landing crafts. So were the tanks, ammunition, and other supplies. Eisenhower's commanders were cutting no corners, or, on this evening, so it seemed. All together, 337 ships were involved. The voyage was calculated to be exactly the same length and take approximately the same time as the crossing of the English Channel to Normandy. As the men, a number of them already sleep deprived and drenched in sweat, were being ferried toward the shore for the landings, they readied themselves for the intense preparatory bombing of the coastal areas that was to come. The earlier practice for the amphibious landing operations had already involved live fire above the beaches, so that the soldiers would be prepared for whatever Rommel might have waiting for them. The beaches were supposed to have been declared clear before the men landed, but as a result of signal errors, some of the craft reached shore before the shelling had stopped. These troops rushed the beaches only to be blown up by ammunition from their own guns.

Now, it was two hours after midnight, and a bright moon lit up the sky.

Cradling their guns or lighting cigarettes, the men were struck by how placid the water was. The air was brisk, and the visibility was fair; morale among the men was high. Some hours earlier, during the last flickers of daylight, assault forces of the U.S. Fourth Infantry Division had successfully disembarked and gone ashore on Slapton Sands. Now with HMS *Azalea* in the rear, the convoy of ships prepared to make the night assault. It was an imposing sight as eight Allied landing ships moved steadily toward Slapton Sands. On board were many elements of the invasion: engineers; chemical experts; quartermaster troops; waterproof tanks; and jeeps.

Earlier in the day, Eisenhower himself had watched some of the exercises. At last, everything seemed in readiness.

But little did the troops or their commanders realize that across the very same water, German listening posts on Rommel's Atlantic Wall were steadily picking up the increased chatter of American radio traffic about the training assault. Though this was only an exercise, this was one of Eisenhower's worst nightmares; the Germans had been alerted to the Allies' activity.

Suddenly, everything went wrong. Nine supercharged German torpedo boats emerged like ghosts out of the darkness into Lyme Bay; moving stealthily and painted black for nighttime camouflage, they glided, unimpeded while observing radio silence. For the Americans, this was a disaster in the making. It began with human error. When, just after midnight, one of the accompanying British picket ships spotted the German torpedo boats—which by then had breached the Allies' westward defenses, another egregious oversight—the report quickly reached a British corvette, but not the American vessels. Because of a typographical error in the orders, the U.S. ships were using a different frequency from the British naval headquarters ashore. These mistakes would be costly.

Within the hour, there was mayhem.

For a few moments, some of the Americans assumed these hundred-foot German attack ships might be part of the exercise. Actually, in their codebooks was a special signal, "W boats attacking," to be used if they spotted a convoy of German vessels. Suspecting nothing, however, they took no defensive actions, and the surprise was complete.

The Germans' E-boats began firing torpedoes. The next thing the Americans felt was a furious jolt. Then there was a deafening sound.

Geysers of water spewed into the air as the German torpedoes punched wide holes in the unprepared American ships. As the soldiers watched in horror, the LST 531 was hit and quickly burst into flames. The torpedoes tore through the starboard side, exploding first in the tank deck and then in the engine room. At this stage there was little the Americans could do. Within seconds, more torpedoes hit their mark. It seemed as though the fires might be containable, but then they quickly began to spread at almost exponential speed; the flames were being fed by the gasoline in the vehicles aboard. Savage explosion followed explosion. And men were running, stumbling, or crawling. The heat and smoke were so intense that gasping firefighters were forced to abandon their efforts. Soon, the crackling of flames mingled with the wild screams of the soldiers—while pleading for help, they were roasting alive. The sounds and sights were appalling. Severed limbs and headless bodies were strewn about. And with the gamey scent of charred flesh filling the air, blood was mingled with the salty water.

The sky throbbed with flashes of bright yellow and white light—the Germans were sending up magnesium flares. The Americans sought to return fire, but to no avail. When that didn't work, the decision was made for the ships to go their separate ways. This dispersal didn't work either. Elsewhere, German torpedoes tore into a second ship, LST 289, though here at least the damage was not fatal. Everywhere on LST 289 were blackened holes, twisted steel, and flaming oil; the ship lost its stern, but after recoiling, it somehow survived and hobbled into port. From another ship, American troops watched dumbstruck as a surface torpedo screamed toward LST 58, then barely missed it. A third ship, that had been struck earlier, LST 507, was not so lucky. As the men scrambled to unleash its guns, there were two thunderous explosions and great columns of fire rose from the vessel's belly. Soon, water shot through a hole in the ship's hull and over the sides, and the electric power was cut. As the alarm began to sound for the men to abandon ship, suddenly the ship buckled, then began to roll. In desperation, men ran about on the decks. Within only six minutes, the vessel sank. In the course of the battle, five other ships would be damaged as well.

There are many ways to lose one's life in war, and this was among the cruelest. Trapped below the decks and engulfed by flooding water, hundreds of frantic soldiers and sailors went down with their ships. In the chaos, others appeared to be better off; they managed to leap into the sea. But many of them soon drowned anyway, because they had not been taught how to put on their life preservers; they had wrapped these around their waists rather than under their armpits. Many other men drowned because their overcoats were waterlogged. They struggled a bit, then in almost slow-motion, disappeared underwater. Still others were shocked by the freezing water. While shrieking for help, they slipped into the sea, succumbing to hypothermia.

Some men were crying hysterically—they couldn't swim and were terrified of water.

Few of them made it.

And for those who did, clinging to life rafts, they were shaking and sobbing quietly to themselves, thanking God that they had somehow survived. They may have gotten out in the nick of time, but they suffered the agony of remembering what they had seen, and of not knowing what had happened to their comrades. There was also fear about what the next few hours would bring, and whether they would be found.

If the exercise went disastrously awry, so did the rescue. As the night wore on, more men, puking their guts out on the rafts, simply gave up, sometimes only minutes before the rescue ships made their way into Lyme Bay. It took as much as an hour for an Allied flotilla to dash westward, to reach Slapton Sands. When these seamen arrived, they were stunned at the carnage. At first the entire scene seemed suspended in an eerie, unnerving stillness. Hundreds of bloated, burned corpses floated and bobbed in the water. Most were fully clad, with steel helmets firmly fastened. Indeed, many had such badly charred hands and blackened faces that from a distance the rescue workers thought they were "colored troops." And there were hundreds of pieces of unrecognizable flesh that had simply bled into the water.

It was also frightfully hot as the atmosphere was still thick with the odor of smoke and heated air. Ammunition was exploding. Meanwhile, the sea was covered with oil, and fires continued to burn furiously, hissing and sparking and crackling. The bodies, the wreckage, the twisted steel, and the other remains—life preservers, guns, ammunition cartridges, sinking tanks, burned jeeps, and grotesquely mangled trucks—were all lit by the infernal glow.

Many of the numb, exhausted survivors were swallowing a toxic combination of blood, fuel, and salt water. Hanging on to their life rafts, they fought off the urge to sleep and continued to drift for hours in the mist and the "unbearably cold" water, waiting to be rescued. Some never were.

Throughout the evening and early morning, rescue teams—some

with tears in their eyes—sought to save as many of the living, and to recover as many of the dead, as they could, but often in vain. One navy man recalled, "It was the saddest thing I ever saw," and a British rescuer deemed it "a ghastly sight." For days, bodies would continue to wash ashore. The dead totaled 749—551 soldiers and 198 sailors—and 300 others were wounded; this was the most costly training exercise in the entire war. In fact, more men were lost in this mock assault than in the actual battle of Utah Beach. For that matter, more Americans died at Slapton Sands than on all of D-Day's beaches besides Omaha.

Attended by his naval aide Harry Butcher, an infuriated Eisenhower, pacing in his office, was promptly informed of these terrible losses. Butcher remarked to Eisenhower that he was concerned about "the absence of toughness and alertness" of the young American officers in the exercises. In this, Butcher was not alone: many witnesses considered Slapton Sands a bad omen. And for Eisenhower and the Allied high command, there was another profound concern. Ten officers aboard the sunken ships were among the very few who knew exactly where the D-Day landings would take place—and all of these ten were now missing.

It quickly became a race between who would find these officers first: Eisenhower or Rommel. If they fell into the Germans' hands, it would be a disaster of the worst order. The Americans and the British, "in a panic," immediately began a thorough search of the bay to find them.

Eisenhower knew that the fate of the invasion was potentially at stake.

~

AWAKENING THE NEXT MORNING, a recuperating Roosevelt knew about none of this. No one had called him. His codeine shot had worn off, but not his pain. Still intensely uncomfortable, he remained under the doctors' orders to stay in bed. For once he complied, bringing to mind a wry cable he had sent to Churchill the previous December, when the prime minister was laid low with pneumonia. "The Bible says you must do just what [your doctor] orders," the president had written from

Washington, "but at this moment I cannot put my finger on the verse and chapter." It was perhaps significant that over the fireplace in his room was an etching depicting his alma mater, Harvard, winning a crew race against Oxford in 1876. Now, of course, Roosevelt was in an altogether different kind of contest: holding out until Overlord could begin a second front. But as his commanders moved Allied armies and naval convoys around like pieces on a chessboard, Roosevelt, nestled in the Baruch mansion, could scarcely move himself.

Nevertheless, his determination never flagged. As the days passed, the president's health improved. His face noticeably brightened—one reporter observed that the "tired seams were smoothed from his face"—and his spirits and demeanor had also improved considerably. He cut his drinking back to one and a half "cocktails per evening," and tanned himself "brown as a berry." The *New York Times* editorialized "We can all be glad he has had a chance to enjoy a month of rest and relaxation from the almost overwhelming burdens which his office forces him to carry. He earned every hour of it." William Hassett, Roosevelt's aide, agreed, noting that his boss was "radiant and happy," insisting he had had a complete rest. But Hassett added one disquieting note: "He is thin, and although his color is good I fear that he has not entirely shaken the effects of the flu, followed by bronchitis, which have bedeviled him for many weeks now."

After Roosevelt's train reached Washington on Sunday morning, May 7, he jauntily wrote to Harry Hopkins, that he had "slept 12 hours out of the 24, sat in the sun, never lost my temper, and decided to let the world go hang."

He added playfully, "The interesting thing is the world didn't hang. I have a terrific pile in my basket, but most of the stuff has answered itself."

5

"This Is the Year 1944"

THAT WAS NOT QUITE true. One supreme irony of the war was that a man who couldn't walk, and whose health was failing, was now symbolically carrying the free world on his back.

In the spring of 1944, amid the rising crisis for the Jews and the escalating military situation on the ground, Franklin Roosevelt had been president of the United States for an unprecedented eleven years—three years longer than George Washington, six years longer than Abraham Lincoln. For all those who knew him, or for those under the Nazi thumb in distant parts of the globe who knew of him, he remained the most extraordinary and enigmatic political leader perhaps on the earth. Like his wartime partner, Winston Churchill, he was an overwhelming personality and a superbly convincing figure. With just a subtle, well-timed hint, he could rouse deep passions and even outsize affection. In the run-up to his third term in 1940, Roosevelt sent a message telling the Democratic delegates that he would not be a candidate unless he was drafted. And the loudspeaker at the convention had shouted back, "We want Roosevelt . . . THE WORLD WANTS ROOSEVELT!"

His conversations were an intoxicating blend of earthy wisdom and carefully rendered humor. His wartime summits were marked by a subtle blend of diplomacy and a thespian's gift of charm—he invariably knew when to give in, or when to hold firm. And his fireside chats galvanizing a nation to arms were the stuff of legend. So was his cunning, which was well hidden, and his steadfast defense of democracy, which was not.

Despite his deteriorating health, his prodigious determination and singular focus on winning the war were almost without equal. Perhaps they had to be. In the western theater alone, many millions fervently depended on his leadership: the British, the free French, the Belgians, the Dutch, the Danes, and the Norwegians; the embattled peoples of Luxembourg, Poland, and Czechoslovakia; the Greeks and the Turks; and increasingly, the Italians and Hungarians as well. There was also Joseph Stalin, the Soviet leadership, not to mention the peoples of the Soviet Union; and, of course, the dwindling numbers of European and Soviet Jews.

Roosevelt was sixty-two, and more than ever, the burdens of leadership sat heavy on him. Weary from the incessant fatigue and fighting, he was now trying to lose weight to relieve his painful gallbladder. His face was haggard and gaunt, and his shirt collar gaped around his neck. His blood pressure continued to rise and his skin had taken on a grayish hue. With victory in sight, there was now a race between his own body, the enemy within; and the Axis powers, the enemies without. Did he ever brood, feeling that opportunities were slipping away? He never said so—never to his aides, never to his intimates, never to the nation or the world at large. Never while scribbling notes in the corners of memorandums or while mixing drinks during his beloved cocktail hour. Never while cherishing his dream of a peaceful postwar order. And however much he was ailing, however much he may have had trouble juggling all the competing demands on him, Roosevelt knew one thing: under the strain of the Allied assault, Berlin, the center of the Nazi Empire, was trembling, and Hitler's Third Reich itself was increasingly at the point of collapse.

Now, Roosevelt felt, he had to keep pushing. Moreover, he believed there was a spillover effect. As the War Department stated, "We must constantly bear in mind the most effective relief which can be given victims of enemy persecution is to ensure the speedy defeat of the Axis."

~

WAS THAT TRUE? IRONICALLY, this narrow focus on the battlefront was just what the Nazis were counting on as they prepared their death machine at Auschwitz to slaughter an unprecedented number of victims under the cloak of secrecy. Now, in May 1944, a crisis would come to a head: between the battlefield, with Operation Overlord looming, and the gas chambers in Auschwitz.

~

IN SLOVAKIA, VRBA AND Wetzler's report had been typed. One copy was given to a courier bound for Istanbul. Another copy went to the Slovak Orthodox Jewish rabbi, who promised to try to smuggle it into Switzerland, because from there it could reach the west. A third copy was passed to the Vatican's chargé d'affaires in Bratislava. But arguably, except for Roosevelt himself, the most important recipients would be the Hungarian Jews. One of the men who had questioned Vrba, Oskar Krasnansky, translated the report into Hungarian and gave it to the head of the Hungarian Jewish Rescue Committee, Rudolf Kastner. So by early May 1944, the committee head and his advisers had the report. But there the report stayed, hidden. Remarkably, these men made no move to release it, to share it, or to publicize it in any way in Budapest or beyond. Why?

As Vrba and Wetzler were reaching freedom, Adolf Eichmann and the Germans were at the Nazi headquarters in Budapest concocting a colossal Ponzi scheme to confound the Jews and Allies alike, all the while weaving further threads of entrapment, mass death, and disposal. They began by bartering with the leaders of the Hungarian Jews in what would become known as "blood for goods." The Germans proposed that Hungary's Jewish population would be spared death if the Nazis received hard goods, such as trucks: ten thousand trucks (likely to be used against the Soviets), along with tea, soap, coffee, and sugar. Desperate for any possibility of escape, desperate to live, the Hungarian Jewish leaders grasped at this German straw. They dispatched Joel Brand, a member of Hungary's Relief and Rescue Committee, to negotiate on their behalf; on May 19, he arrived in a small plane at Istanbul bearing a stunning offer. As a goodwill gesture, he said, the Germans were even willing to release a few thousand Jews as soon as the Allies agreed to the plan. But absent an agreement, the Jews would be killed. The British, deeply suspicious, detained Brand and began a detailed interrogation of him in Cairo.

For their part, the Soviets balked, believing it was a ruse by Germany to establish a separate peace with the western Allies. The Americans and British were also deeply skeptical; the American OSS called the offer an "incredible Nazi black maneuver." Still, no one could be certain whether the Nazis were seriously contemplating "saving" any of Hungary's Jews or this was simply an elaborate attempt to divide both the Jews and the Allies.

By then, however, it hardly mattered. The first trains from Budapest had already long since left for Auschwitz, and were now arriving there at a relentless pace.

The mass uprising that Vrba and Wetzler had believed would take place in Hungary was not to be. In fact, by sending Vrba and Wetzler's report to the Jewish leaders in Hungary, who at that moment were focused on the chance of making a separate deal with the Nazis, the Slovakian Jews were unwittingly playing into Hitler's hands. And so, hundreds of thousands of Jews unknowingly boarded railcars that chugged slowly toward death.

~

As ELIE WIESEL NOTES, Roosevelt knew in broad brushstrokes about this impending tragedy—though it would be months before the full Vrba-Wetzler report reached the White House—and so did Churchill. The Vatican also knew about it, and so did Switzerland. And so did the *New York Times*—even without the Vrba-Wetzler report. Only the intended victims remained in the dark. "Panic in Hungary would have been better than panic which came to the victims in front of the burning pits in Birkenau," Vrba later wrote. "Eichmann knew it," he added, "that is why he smoked cigars with the Kastners, 'negotiated,' exempted the 'real great rabbis,' and meanwhile without panic among the deportees planned to 'resettle' hundreds of thousands in an orderly fashion."

Thus, even as the D-Day forces massed across the English Channel, Hitler's plans for the destruction of every Hungarian Jew within his reach were set in motion—though these Jews were previously believed to be untouchable. If May was the month of waiting for Overlord in the west, in the east, it was the end of all waiting for the last remnant of European Jewry: the Hungarian Jews.

SINCE THE OUTSET OF the war, the pro-Nazi Hungarian government had largely allowed the huge and still intact Jewish community—some 750,000 people—to exist unmolested. For an enraged Hitler, this was intolerable, doubly so because he feared Hungary might negotiate a separate peace with the Allies. So through a combination of browbeating and blackmail—he even took the extraordinary step of threatening the family of the Hungarian head of state—Hitler forcibly established a puppet regime in Hungary, ready to do his bidding. With the German takeover complete, on March 19, 1944, German storm troopers massed in the streets of Budapest, accompanied by the feared masterminds of genocide, the SS. That night, their footsteps could be heard echoing across the country. With that, the fate of the Jews seemed sealed.

Within days, under a scrupulously conceived cloak of deception, the country was divided into six zones. By April 15, Hungary's entire Jewish population had been moved into ghettos. In the following days, Jews were relentlessly hustled into detention centers or herded into cattle cars. As for the seemingly fortunate ones who managed to hide safely, many were quickly hunted down.

With breathtaking speed, a way of life was hurtling to a close. Anguished men prayed while terrified mothers hastily wrapped food for their journey and tenderly bathed their children. Preparing for the worst, they stitched valuables into small cloth sacks or strung them under garments. Having little idea what awaited them, they packed their luggage, being careful to bring along the baby's best outfits as well as diapers, toys, teddy bears, blankets, and all the other sundry things that only a parent invariably remembers. Now came the sleepless nights—and not knowing what lay next. A resettlement camp somewhere in a distant region? Separation from their loved ones?

Then came the terror.

In the provinces, in Baja or Ruthenia or Kecskemet, there was chaos and confusion. In city after city, Nazi storm troopers swarmed through the streets, launching bruising roundups: families were dragged from their homes, leaving behind unfinished bowls of soup, a slab of dough waiting to be kneaded, and books and bags and other belongings strewn in the corridors or streets, awaiting looters or the ready fingers of the Hungarian police. And ahead of them—though few wanted to admit it to themselves and few, if any, could fully comprehend what lay in store—was the last stop, the place where Jews from all across Europe were gathered for slaughter. Many were wearing their finest clothes, as if they were off to the theater or to a wedding.

"*Alle Juden, 'raus—'raus*!" the SS shouted. "Keep order. Do not push. Anyone who attempts to resist will be shot!"

Soon, the railway stations were choked with thousands and thousands of grim-faced, muttering people. The elderly, the sick, women cradling infants, the rich and the destitute alike—none were exempt. Although two trainloads had left in late April, the first large-scale deportation began on May 14: a train packed with about four thousand Jewish men, women, and children in forty sealed boxcars—this was like trying to stuff a busload of people into a walk-in closet. Without regard for age or infirmity, and certainly without pity, eighty were crammed into each car until there was no light and little air. Then the doors were nailed shut. Day after day, these cattle cars made their way northwest. Such roundups were repeated not only across Hungary, but in Italy, Belgium, the Netherlands, France, and Poland itself.

Once the cattle car doors were slammed shut, the SS shouted the order to go; then there was a high-pitched squeal, and the train started to move. When the locomotive was only a blur of smoke on the horizon, those inside tried to wrestle with their uncontrolled emotions: a combination of fear and despair, resignation and resolution, collective panic and individual grief. Was this, they queried each other in hushed tones, a journey to a Nazi work camp? Or to an SS gun to the head? Few had any answers; fewer had the courage to speculate.

They didn't know about earlier transports, such as a train that had arrived with six thousand corpses, whose eyes were still strangely open and whose mouths hung slack, as if gasping; these people had suffocated. Nor did they know about the train carrying four thousand frightened children under the age of twelve, cruelly separated from their parents and each desperately craving not so much food or water as a simple, human hug; all of them were executed. Nor did they know about the cries of other thousands as they were deliberately and slowly asphyxiated in specially designed railway cars.

Each train made its way fitfully, lurching forward between prolonged, unnerving halts. The people were piled together so tightly that they crushed one another. They were unable to bend or budge; they had no food and virtually no water, nor any toilets. As the days passed, there was a suffocating stench of feces and urine, and everywhere, it seemed, there was sweat and filth. The trip took two to three days, sometimes as many as five; for the elderly and ill, it was often shortened: hundreds died standing up, or wedged into a corner of the boxcar by their neighbors.

Through the slits, these deportees could see thin shafts of light, then the tall weathered cliffs of the Tatra Mountains, and then the names of the last Hungarian cities that slowly disappeared behind them. When they passed the border at Kaschau (Kosice) around noon on the second day, silence descended over the cattle cars. Typically here the deportees rose to their feet and, shuddering, clutched each other. Few said a word. They knew they were passing the point of no return.

Pushed to the limits of human endurance, at every stop they begged hysterically for water, but rarely was any forthcoming, and anyone who tried to approach the train to help was forcibly warded off by the SS. And it was not just thirst that was unendurable; it was also the elements. To the deportees in their weakened state, when it rained the cool air was brutal; on warmer days, body heat and the stagnant air were overwhelming. The deportees cried out for a handful of snow, a bit of bread, a spoonful of soup, a sip of coffee—anything to quench their thirst or fill their bellies. Nursing their babies, young mothers groaned throughout the night and cried out for food and water. And then there was the silence when the feeble crying of another infant ceased.

In Zilina, people with tears in their eyes lined the tracks, watching the trains roll by. Decades later they could still remember the confusion of arms plaintively reaching out through the slats as the train moved away.

Inside the cattle cars, sleep became all but impossible, despite the hunger and thirst and exhaustion. As the sun dipped down and night fell, civilized Hungarians—doctors, accountants, shopkeepers, homemakers, grandparents—became an unruly, agitated mass, sprawled across the musty floor. They felt miserable, ashamed, and frightened. Disputes, usually over nothing more than a slight brush from someone nearby, broke out. Curses became commonplace as the night wore on. So did screams. Unable to sleep, someone would impulsively try to climb to his feet, only to topple over from fatigue; deprived of all sustenance, the deportees now struggled to make their limbs obey even simple motor commands. Sadly, not only did their judgment become impaired; so did their compassion. Treated like animals, some became like animals. Little wonder: by now, their senses were numbed and their starving bodies were literally feeding on themselves.

A whistle blew and the train began to chug doggedly along the single-track railway through the tree-lined banks of the Lubotin, the winding river that accompanied it. Peering through the slits, those inside could now see towns with Slovak names, then Polish names, and with each mile, everything became more remote and unfamiliar. The weather turned colder and more unforgiving. The shuddering halts became more frequent, until the train was crawling. And suddenly, with a jerk, in the evening, the locomotive slowed at a quiet vista.

Thickly forested, slashed by deep ravines and filled with mist, their destination almost resembled a scene in a Grimm Brothers fairy tale. As far as anyone could see, there were birch trees, then great gusts of white smoke and hazy, distant objects. But as the smoke slowly lifted, the night was lit up by rows of red and white lights lining the tracks. For the passengers, arrival brought an odd serenity; their doubts would finally be resolved. One small girl thought to herself, "Nothing can be worse than these cattle cars," while another asked her father, "Will there be playgrounds there, Daddy, like there are at home?"

But any such serenity was short-lived. People, now huddling, began to pray, or weep, or whimper. Some were silent. The next stage came abruptly. First there was a thud, then a trampling of feet, then a barking of commands in an unknown language. Then came the squeak of the train wheels stopping, and the opening of the cattle car doors with a thundering clap.

Outside was an ominous sign over the entrance to their destination: *Arbeit Macht Frei* ("Work Makes You Free"). In the distance, blazing flames shot thirty feet into the sky, and towering clouds of smoke hovered above them. The stench was ungodly.

This, they were soon to learn, was Auschwitz.

And though none could have known it at the time, most of them had less than an hour to live.

∾

VRBA AND WETZLER AT least had some effect. During the third week of May, as the deportations continued, leaders of the Slovak Jewish underground wrote a long letter pleading with the outside world to "bombard the death halls in Auschwitz" along with the main deportation routes. Yet in the west, including the White House, their pleas ultimately fell on deaf ears.

For Roosevelt, first things came first. That meant crushing the Germans on the beaches of Normandy.

MEANWHILE, ABOUT NINE HUNDRED miles west of Auschwitz, in little English towns called Falmouth and Dartmouth, Portsmouth and Newhaven, the men of the largest Allied invasion in history gathered into companies—and marched. For hours on end, tearful crowds lined the streets to watch them. Whistling and roaring, women waved handkerchiefs, men flashed the V-for-victory sign, and children climbed lampposts or trees and called out to the GIs at the top of their lungs. Quartermasters handed out cartons of cigarettes as the ships' loudspeakers ordered men to board. Here came the tanks and the big artillery pieces, which rolled over narrow country roads that only a few decades before had carried little more than horseback riders, donkey carts, and the occasional carriage. Here came scores upon scores of jeeps, trucks, half-tracks, bicycles, and even locomotives. And then here came the troops. The crowds may have been boïsterous, but for the most part, the men were strangely quiet; many of them were scared. Many expected to die.

Over the course of two years these gum-chewing soldiers had dug foxholes together, had swapped stories about their wives or girlfriends, had played poker or drunk beer together. They knew one another's tastes and fears and whether anyone snored at night or groaned under his breath at his commanding officer. They knew who cheated at craps, and who could hold his liquor. They knew they could rely on their companions, and they knew that in the waters of Normandy, they would give their lives for each other. As one officer gibed to another, "I'll see you in France."

~

To the south, Rome had yet to be taken, but flying from the recently captured air base at Foggia in Italy, the Allied heavy bombers now ruled the skies over central Europe, pounding enemy targets far beyond German airspace: in Hungary, Slovakia, Romania, southern Poland, and even Upper Silesia at the outskirts of Auschwitz. And from their bases in southern England, another fleet of six thousand bombers and fighter planes, seemingly enough to block out the sun, gunned their engines and readied to provide life-sustaining air cover for the invading force.

Roosevelt's commander for Overlord, General Dwight D. Eisenhower, had set D-Day for June 5—a month later than originally planned.

Throughout these ghastly war-torn years Roosevelt had always managed to put up a confident front; the American people, in fact all the Allied nations, were accustomed to newsreels showing his hearty laugh, his mile-wide smile, and the gleam in his eyes. But if publicly he always projected an air of confident leadership, privately he agonized. After the bombing of Pearl Harbor, behind closed doors at the White House, a drawn and pale Roosevelt had buried his head in his hands, muttering that he would go down in history as "a disgraced president." He was so despondent that his body convulsed, and he could barely eke out the words to speak to his aides. Later, when the invasion of Italy began, his hand shook violently as he lifted the phone to receive word that the operation had commenced. Now, during the final preparations for D-Day, Roosevelt was determined to keep his composure and inform the American people about the impending carnage. A jittery Eleanor Roosevelt was seemingly less confident, writing poignantly, "Soon the invasion will be upon us. I dread it."

Roosevelt, however, did not dread it. At one point, he had planned to fly to England for the start of the invasion, but his health made this impossible—Churchill would thus write to him on June 4, "How I wish you were here." Instead, Roosevelt went to Charlottesville, Virginia, where he would plan one of the most important speeches of his career: his comments to the nation on the invasion's beginning.

~

OUTWARDLY CALM, ROOSEVELT KNEW that even the best plans could go awry, and in this case they did. Across the ocean on Saturday, June 3, an anxious Eisenhower was lighting up yet another cigarette—a notorious chain-smoker, on the best of days he often smoked as many as sixty Camels. Meeting at Southwick House with his meteorologists, he learned that this day was not among the best. Eisenhower already looked worn, and well he should have. Earlier that day reports from the Associated Press had erroneously declared: "Flash. Eisenhower's headquarters announces Allied landing in France." And now the weather report was not good. In the Channel, the waves were increasingly tumultuous and clouds had begun to form. Then came the wind. It started to drizzle, and soon the drizzle thickened into a downpour. The chief meteorologist told Eisenhower that June 5 would be little better. The day was expected to be frightfully gray, with great gusts of "force 5 winds" and such poor visibility that the Allies' air superiority, crucial to the success of the operation, would be severely compromised. Moreover, the weather was worsening so quickly that predicting more than twenty-four hours ahead was useless.

Gone now were Eisenhower's unblinking gaze and infectious grin. Instead, a fretful Eisenhower, his eyes looking downward, announced that they would revisit the decision later on Sunday morning, hoping that the weather would clear. By late that night, however, the storm had intensified; winds were howling, and a torrential rain was rattling the shutters of Southwick House and even shaking his personal trailer. The invasion was postponed for at least twenty-four hours.

The weather, the waiting, and the deep anxiety took their toll. And it was no better across the Atlantic. It is tempting to think of Roosevelt tranquilly smoking cigarettes and putting the final touches on his D-Day speech. Nothing could be further from the truth. Over the weekend, Roosevelt's secretary sensed that every "movement of his face and hands" revealed the president's nervousness. For his part, Roosevelt leafed through the pages of his Book of Common Prayer in search of a

D-Day invocation. But the moth could not resist the flame. Upon receiving news of the delay, an anxious yet unwavering Roosevelt returned to the capital on Monday morning, awaiting the latest developments. They came in fragments. As he contemplated the "what next" of the invasion, more ships continued to sail out of their harbors, thousands of landing schedules were finalized, and in the fog of the distant English Channel, a tremendous fleet of vessels were already rocking in the choppy waters.

"You know I'm a juggler," FDR once insisted about his ability to handle multiple crises. "I never let my right hand know what my left hand does." But with the date for the D-Day invasion still undecided, and the Germans lying in wait along their vast coastal fortifications, this proved more difficult than even he imagined.

ON THE EVENING OF Sunday, June 4, while Adolf Hitler was cocooned in his mountain retreat in the Bavarian Alps, Eisenhower slipped quietly into his headquarters at the old country mansion, Southwick House, for the meeting that would decide the outcome of the war. Meanwhile, a chill, ill-tempered rain fell in thick sheets and continued to rattle the rooftops.

Conferring in a mahogany-paneled room with his principal aides, Eisenhower was briefed again on the bad weather. By now, the gaudy optimism that had characterized the initial planning for D-Day had long since evaporated. According to his chief meteorologist, within hours, just before dawn on June 5, there would be a break in the storm. Winds would die down, and for roughly thirty-six hours there would be more or less "clear weather." How clear? That was uncertain. And any long-range prediction was daunting; by Wednesday, storm clouds would develop again. That would force a delay until June 19—two full weeks.

This left only a narrow window for the invasion. How long, Eisenhower wondered glumly, could this operation be left dangling? "What do you think?" he asked his chief of staff, Walter Bedell Smith. "It's a hell of a gamble," Smith answered, "but it's the best possible gamble."

Eisenhower fixed his gaze on the British commander, General Bernard Montgomery, asking, "Do you see any reason for not going tomorrow?" Montgomery shot back one word: "Go!"

But there was no unanimity. Eisenhower's deputy, Arthur Tedder, dispensing with tact and ignoring the chain of command, had protested that an invasion on June 6 was "chancy." He recommended postponement—again. Listening, Eisenhower cocked an eyebrow and then polled everyone in the room. Those present, shaken and fatigued by the gravity of the decision confronting them, split down the middle: seven for, seven against. Eisenhower again waved a hand and wandered around the conference table, which was surrounded by huge maps. His agony was visible. The decision was now his and his alone.

"I am a born optimist and I can't change that," he once said. But on this day, optimism was almost impossible. If the weather reports were wrong, his troops could be hurled back into the ocean from the start; moreover, stormy skies would delay or preclude the desperately needed air cover and hinder the naval bombardment that could offer some measure of protection. For his men who made it ashore, tired and bottled up on the beaches, this would mean disaster, a repeat of the bloody 1942 Dieppe raid, and on a far larger scale. But if the Allies waited, the risk magnified that the Germans would learn the secret of where Overlord was going to take place. This too would be fatal. As it was, the Allies had already had a bad scare at Slapton Sands. In either scenario, with the Germans dug in, gains and losses would be measured in terms of yards on the beaches of Normandy, rather than in terms of hundreds of miles on the road to Berlin. And if the Germans were waiting, fully prepared, his men could be cut to pieces.

The room felt silent, except for the sound of Eisenhower's footsteps. Meanwhile, the mansion itself was shaking from the howling winds and withering rain. By almost every criterion, it seemed inconceivable that the Allies could initiate the assault in such conditions.

"I don't like it, but there it is," Eisenhower said almost inaudibly. There was a hush in the room. It was 9:45 p.m. He continued, "I am quite positive that the order must be given." It was given, but in effect, only conditionally. Eisenhower decided to reconvene his men once more, around 4 a.m. When he gave his order, however, five thousand ships left port and began furiously streaming toward France. If they were to be recalled, the general could not wait until dawn.

Back in his trailer, Eisenhower slept poorly. He climbed out of bed at 3:30 a.m. and shaved hurriedly before driving through the muck and mud once again to Southwick House. By now, the rain was widespread; these late-spring thunderstorms stretched over a swath of hundreds of miles, extending as far as the Austrian Alps—where Hitler had been asleep for just half an hour. Nevertheless, the meteorologist reiterated his new predictions; the weather would clear shortly and the skies would stay clear for a day or two. Pacing once more in the mess, Eisenhower knew that a definitive decision had to be made.

He paused, finally stopping in his tracks, sat on a sofa for a full five minutes, then pronounced softly: "OK. We'll go." At these three words, cheers echoed through Southwick House. And with this simplest of antiphons, he initiated the most imposing amphibious assault in the annals of war. The invasion would be launched at dawn on June 6.

In the meantime, as the eve of the D-Day invasion neared, an increasingly confident, even cheery Roosevelt returned to Washington from Charlottesville.

Whenever Eisenhower, the supreme Allied commander, traveled, he carried lucky charms in a zippered purse that included a silver dollar, a French franc, and an English crown piece, each of which he would finger nervously. But Roosevelt needed no such things, for his lucky charm was now Eisenhower. Whatever doubts the president may have harbored about his commanding general earlier in the war—once prompting Eisenhower himself to mutter, "Tell Roosevelt I am the best damned lieutenant colonel in the U.S. Army"—Eisenhower had grown on him. The president knew that Eisenhower, despite his temper, was fearless, pugnacious, and selfless. He knew that, like himself, Eisenhower was incurably optimistic. He also knew that Eisenhower was a realist, a master of the "sensible compromise," able to navigate around the petty whims that threatened to divide general from general, commander from commander, ally from ally.

And all this had paid off. The Allies had prevailed in North Africa in 1942; had heroically slogged their way through Italy in the winter of 1943; and, in the final hours before the assault at Normandy, had seized Rome. True, Roosevelt knew that this victory had come at a price. For four months there had been a sullen test of wills: the Allies had pushed and prodded, but without success. The desperate fourteen Nazi divisions gave no ground, tenaciously pinning down 150,000 Allied troops at Anzio, until the Allies finally routed them on May 23. Rome was captured soon thereafter. Once the ancient symbol of Western civilization, it was now the symbol of the unstoppable Allied advances. After months of sleepless nights, of hovering between anxiety and exhilaration, Roosevelt finally sensed opportunity. He was ecstatic.

Speaking on the air from the sparsely furnished Diplomatic Reception Room in the White House, Roosevelt gave one of the most important fireside chats of his presidency. Exulting in this triumph, he saluted the capture of Rome. "The first of the Axis capitals is now in our hands," he buoyantly told the American people. "One up and two to go!" But the ultimate prize remained Berlin. About the cross-Channel invasion itself, Roosevelt said nothing. After his speech, he stayed up late and relaxed by watching a movie before being lifted into bed shortly after eleven o'clock. He of course knew what would come next. Meanwhile, waves of Allied paratroopers had already begun jumping from their transport planes. And tens of thousands of soldiers were already crossing the choppy waters of the English Channel under a moonlit sky. South of the Isle of Wight, thousands of warships and transports were heading in never-ending streams toward the French coast.

It was Eisenhower who once scribbled in a note to himself, "We've got to go to Europe and fight." As Roosevelt drifted off to a fitful sleep, this was finally what was about to happen.

~

THE PLANES WENT FIRST. In the dark of night, nearly nine hundred wide-bellied C47s were arrayed across the sky, wave upon wave in V formations, three hundred miles long, crossing the Channel at an altitude of five hundred feet, low enough to elude Nazi radar. Inside, the men of the 101st and Eighty-second airborne divisions smudged black streaks on their faces and hugged their parachutes. It was an awe-inspiring sight to be flying in a tight formation, nine planes wide, without lights, without radio activity; and the atmosphere felt almost tranquil. But that feeling was short-lived.

When the planes emerged from a bank of clouds at the coastline, machine-gun fire and tracers were arcing everywhere around them. Then came the explosions—deadly German 88-millimeter shells—that lit up the sky. The planes began to bounce from the enemy fire before they took evasive action, rolling and spinning, ascending and descending. Out of necessity, they quickly broke formation. For the first few moments, it was bedlam. In their planes, dumbfounded men slipped to the floor. Some men began to throw up. Everywhere there were shouts. While passengers and cargo tumbled in all directions, bullets tore through the planes' wings and fuselages. Above and below, to the right and to the left, aircraft exploded or were cut in half; or cockpit windows shattered and pilots were killed by shrapnel, sending their planes helplessly spiraling to the ground. Virtually every plane was hit, but almost miraculously, a majority kept flying. As they approached the drop zone, the pilots flicked on the green lights.

Over the whine of gunfire and the screeching of the planes themselves, the jumpmasters began to give the signal for the men: go.

One by one, the paratroopers leaped out of the planes, pulled their rip cords, and began floating down in the darkness.

As they dropped like confetti from the sky, below them figures were running in all directions, shouting, gesturing, and aiming rifles. They were Germans.

ELSEWHERE, GERMAN ANTIAIRCRAFT BATTERIES received sporadic reports of separate, scattered paratrooper landings with no discernible pattern, from northwest of Caen to both sides of the Vire River, from the east coast of the Cotentin Peninsula to Montebourg, all the way into neighboring Belgium. Was this the long-awaited invasion? A Resistance operation? A diversion? The Germans were baffled, especially when they found that these drops were dummy parachutists, some of which, on landing, began playing recordings of firefights. For the Wehrmacht, the drop turned into a maddening exercise: eventually believing that up to 100,000 paratroopers might have landed, they spent hours combing the woods and beating the bushes in search of an enemy "that was not there." But in fact the Allies were there.

Starting at one o'clock in the morning, under pale moonlight, small teams of Allied paratroopers began silently maneuvering through the outskirts of villages or in dense woods: wherever they could, they severed communication lines. Moving quickly, they then began to damage telephone poles with gammon bombs, as well as shred underground communication wires. Bit by bit, the Allied paratroopers were disrupting and confusing the Germans and hemming in Nazi patrols stretched across numerous northern French towns. When they had an opportunity, these paratroopers seized bridges or cleared fields in anticipation of the Allied reinforcements that would soon be following. To the extent that the nearby German units realized that enemy paratroopers were indeed landing, they believed this too was a ploy.

The full magnitude registered only when a German private looked up and saw that the sky was "filled with planes."

By 3 a.m., the paratroopers were no longer alone. And now the Germans had to worry about far more than planes.

Like great birds, blackened gliders appeared overhead, winging their way on fierce crosswinds to reinforce the Americans. They carried bulldozers—to be used to create landing strips—jeeps, antitank guns, motorcycles, folding bicycles, more ammunition, and, just as important, troops. But then, in an instant, everything seemed to go wrong.

On the ground, the Germans' fire was withering. From a distance, the paratroopers began to hear earsplitting sounds: tortured scrapes, followed by deafening crashes and the crunch of tearing wood; some of the gliders were breaking into pieces. Then came the anguished cries of dying men. Gliders were built for abuse, but not this kind. After flying in circles, gliders now were bouncing off treetops or smashing into tree canopies. Other gliders plunged into rocky walls or nearby barns; the debris was scattered across acres of fields. Still others skidded into roads or each other. Some sank in marshes or in areas that Rommel had flooded. Then there were those that ended up in hedgerows.

Casualties were high, for both the gliders and the paratroopers. One of the most heartbreaking sights was of paratroopers, their chutes unfurled, dangling helplessly from trees, looking like "rag dolls shot full of holes." And too often, things were little better on the ground. Whether they landed in apple orchards or weed-choked yards, men were scattered in small, isolated pockets. Communication between units was almost nonexistent. The crumpled field radios were dead. When the men blew whistles or bugles, these were drowned out by the staccato sounds of antiaircraft fire. And they had little in the way of physical protection. Their extra ammunition was soaked; they lacked bazookas or their machine guns jammed and their demolition equipment failed. They had no mortars, mine detectors, or antitank guns for larger-scale defense.

But there were isolated signs of hope. As one American paratrooper engaged in a firefight, there was a sudden, inexplicable lull in the action. The sound of enemy fire stopped and was followed by a loud crack echoing through the night—a lone gunshot. First one, then two, then eventually a dozen enemy troops emerged with their hands held high, grinning, laughing, and slapping each other's backs. They were Poles who had been forcibly conscripted by the Nazis. Instead of engaging the Americans, they had executed their unit's German sergeant and promptly surrendered. They would not be the last such fighters to do so.

By now, scattered across Normandy, about eighteen thousand Allied paratroopers and glider troops were gearing up for a fight. Before daylight they quickly destroyed bridges over the Dives River and, after a bitter battle, took the German gun battery at Merville. At Sainte-Mère-Église, the Eighty-second Airborne fought tenaciously, holding the village despite suffering heavy casualties. Confronted with stubborn German resistance, one soldier pugnaciously announced in his finest French: "*Nous restons ici!*"—"We are staying here!" Heroic victories had also been gained at Chef-du-Pont and Pegasus Bridge. And the units began securing their principal goals; they destroyed German cannons inland and held crossroads and bridges, controlling the precious exit routes from the beaches.

Meanwhile, Hitler was still asleep and the Wehrmacht remained disoriented. In a telling coda, one German officer concluded, "We are not confronted by a major action."

IT WOULD BE HARD to imagine a worse delusion. Since midnight, the Allies' seaborne armada had been crossing the choppy waters. First came the landing craft and cruisers, then the destroyers and great columns of minesweepers, then the bombardment ships and battleships. Then there were transports, Coast Guard rescue vessels, PT boats, and blockships, so many that they seemed to form a runway from the Isle of Wight to the Normandy shore. Many of the ships displayed a large O, for Omaha Beach, brightly painted on the hull; others had U, for Utah Beach. As they approached shore, a whistle began to sound and officers started to shout, "Report to your disembarkation areas!"—upon which the troops climbed down the waterlogged nets, scrambling to their Higgins boats.

What their airborne brethren had initiated, they were about to continue.

It was still dark, and the early morning hours remained cool. As the boats rocked madly in the water, the men huddling against each other started to vomit and the frigid spray stung their eyes and drenched their weapons. But it was their expectations that most consumed them: in their boats, these men were keyed up and ready to go. Around 5:20 a.m. dawn began to break. Soon thereafter, as the sun rose, they heard a roar, and the first waves of bombers flew overhead.

H-hour was to be 6:30 a.m.—an hour after the first fingers of daylight.

~

AT THE ATLANTIC WALL, the unsuspecting German defenders raised their binoculars. Suddenly, emerging out of the morning mist, just on the horizon, were the Allies' landing craft, hundreds of them, jostling in the water. They were coming and coming fast. All along the bluffs, German soldiers aimed their mortars and raced to their communications radios. "Target Dora, all guns!" they shouted. "Target Dora, all guns!"

To their disbelief, this armada grew gigantic as it closed in. "We could not see the sea anymore," one French witness recorded, "only ships all over." By now, that was practically understatement. Out in the channel hundreds of guns in the battleships and destroyers were awaiting the order to fire. The air bombardment was scheduled first, unleashing a series of explosions that seemed to roll along the shore. Though terrified, the men in the Higgins boats began to cheer. Minutes later, they were clutching their ears: the line of battleships had opened fire. The first salvo alone was a series of thunderous explosions, as if the heavens and the sea had unleashed some primordial wrath. "This was the loudest thing I have ever heard," one correspondent wrote in marvel. "Most of us felt this was the moment of our life."

It was. The first salvo was followed by a chorus of guns from across the Allied fleet, enveloping the entire shoreline in flashes of explosions and a thick canopy of smoke. Dust and debris rose in billowing clouds. Windows shattered in nearby houses, and Germans scattered all along the bluffs, looking for safety. Then they fired back.

At 6 a.m., tanks started to swim ashore, negotiating the strong headwinds and swirling tidal currents. Rockets whistled above, while the big guns of the battleships continued to belch out fire. The Allies' shells set off land mines along the shore in rapid succession and ignited crackling brushfires among patches of dry beach grass. The heat and noise were unparalleled. "Their roar," one soldier recorded, "was like the final crescendo of a great symphony." For many of the men about to spill out of the Higgins boats, it seemed like insanity, a prelude to certain death; no one could survive such an enfilade of fire. In front of them, the beaches shook from the fury of the bombardment.

Eisenhower was fond of the aphorism that plans are everything before the battle, and useless once it has begun.

Now the battle had begun.

The opening assault wave hit the Normandy beaches at 6:30 a.m. The U.S. First, Fourth, and Twenty-ninth divisions slogged their way toward Utah and Omaha beaches, while the British and Canadian troops disembarked an hour later onto Sword, Juno, and Gold beaches. It would be hard to imagine more thorough planning than what the Allied troops had been put through in advance of D-Day; it would be equally hard to imagine so many things going wrong. From the outset, basic elements of the plans quickly fell apart. No planners had anticipated that such large numbers of troops would become seasick even before the battle began; before the first shot was even fired, the men in the opening group were exhausted, cramped, and disoriented from bobbing up and down in the choppy seas for some four hours. Virtually no one had expected that some men would die senselessly when they barreled from their landing craft too soon and struggled through water that was chest-deep—even though it was low tide—and were weighed down by the sixty-eight pounds of waterlogged gear they were carrying. Others inadvertently plunged into water over their heads. Many were simply sucked into underwater shell craters and drowned before coming close to the shore—they never stood a chance. On landing, still others were barely able to move, too exhausted from using their helmets to bail out the water that kept rising and threatening to sink their landing craft after the boats' pumps had failed.

Far too many tanks were outfitted with flotation devices that worked magnificently in trial runs but failed miserably in the dense, unruly waves breaking on the Normandy coastline. And along Omaha Beach, the Allies' naval bombardment was fleeting and frequently misplaced; rarely did it adequately lay cover fire across the beach. Curiously, the Allies' air bombing was little better; it was far off the mark and failed to dislodge the German beach defenses along the bluffs. As a consequence, the incessant enemy fire that hit the American troops was ghastly; some companies had a 90 percent casualty rate within a few minutes of landing.

And it was not only the firing at the shoreline that proved to be so deadly. True terror came again when the men of the Sixteenth Infantry reached Omaha's grass-covered slopes. The assault was more like a slow-motion re-enactment of General George Pickett's disastrous charge across no-man's-land at Gettysburg than a well-ordered action of World War II. Along this ten-kilometer stretch, many of the officers were cut down or wounded even before they stepped onto the beach. From the minute that the Higgins boats dropped their ramps, the Germans ferociously unleashed mortar fire, artillery fire, and machine gun fire. They also used mines wound tight with wires, so that a German soldier sitting in a bunker could detonate the mine for maximum impact when a landing craft reached the shore. Worse still, with one exception, every unit ended up in the wrong place. The men were buffeted by winds of eighteen knots and waves that were kicking up as high as six feet; in fact, in the aftermath of the storm, there were whitecaps rising as far as twelve miles out from the coast.

Meanwhile, heads and arms of the dead were bobbing up and down in the water. It looked like a slaughter.

Photo reconnaissance had also grossly fallen short. The Americans were, as a practical matter, blind, unable to decipher whether the German fire was coming from the little, weathered cottages dotted along the shore, or from the maze of concrete emplacements burrowed into the top of the bluff.

Also, the assault troops were like overloaded pack mules—one private who weighed 125 pounds was carrying over a hundred pounds of gear ashore, including a drum of flamethrower fluid and a cylinder of nitrogen. As a result, the men found it impossible to fire their weapons, or sometimes even to stand up straight; they were soaking, confused, and unable to wade through the wet sand and the web of mined obstacles before them. Among the first ashore was Company A; of its two hundred men, some 60 percent—the now famous Bedford boys—all came from the same little Virginia town. Within fifteen minutes they were reduced to a couple dozen; the rest were strewn across the battle-scarred landscape, or their bodies were washing helplessly onto the shore. With frightening speed, another company lost 96 percent of its men in the attempt to haul grenades, dynamite charges, machine guns, mortars, mortar rounds, flamethrowers, and other equipment ashore. As the minutes ticked by, the beach was littered with burning landing craft and corpses, corpses with no hands, corpses with no feet.

The original plan had been for the troops to occupy the bluff by 7:30 a.m. Instead, everywhere on the beach, there were shreds of flesh and thousands of abandoned gas masks, grenades, bazookas, radios, rifles, machine guns, and ammunition boxes. And at the bottom of the Channel were hundreds of tanks, jeeps, and self-propelled artillery that had simply sunk.

There was no letup from the melee. Soon, the beach was jammed with the dead and the dying. In the water itself, the Allied landing craft were exploding or bursting into fire. Dead men were floating facedown, while the living were slogging through the sea with their faces raised, gasping for air. Some of the men in the sea pretended to be dead, hoping the Germans would stop firing and the tide would simply take them in. Said one sergeant, simply, "God, it was awful." Onshore, the Germans in the pillboxes concentrated their gunfire on the beach, while the Americans huddled behind whatever obstacles they could find, often in ankle-deep water, or crawled aimlessly through the muddy, bloodstained beaches on their elbows and knees. Frantically, they dug in the sand to open up makeshift foxholes or trenches where they might wait out the mortar fire. Many men wet themselves. Others broke down sobbing. From their nests on the bluffs, German snipers coolly picked off Americans who, after a hush, bravely took turns racing out to the water's edge, hopscotching around clumps of the dead to drag wounded men to safety. It was a sickening sight. Leaderless and directionless, GIs sought to evade machine-gun fire only to be exposed to mortar fire; they sought to evade mortar fire only to be exposed to light cannon fire. "I became," one private recalled, "a visitor to hell."

The wounded had their own special hell. Some had been hit in the chest, or they were bleeding from hip to shoulder, or their upper jaw might be shattered and a cheekbone left exposed, blood pouring from the wound. In rare cases, their buddies gave them morphine shots and stayed with them until they exhaled a final breath. Some men were burning inside their gear because the fuel tanks had been lit on fire; they dashed, often in vain, into the water. Too frequently, men died forlorn, utterly and totally alone, a final, attenuated prayer on their lips. One dying soldier simply cried, "Mother, Mom," before his eyes froze, his lifeless gaze locked onto the clouds above.

To receive first aid from the medics the wounded had to be taken out not to the rear, as had almost always been the case in battle since the advent of warfare, but forward, toward enemy fire. That added to the psychological toll. With chaos swirling around them, some men snapped or lapsed into shock. The din alone was terrifying: a naval barrage behind them, artillery and mortar fire before them, aircraft overhead, and the noise of engines and calls and cries of the wounded all around them. For some, it was simply too much.

Standing on the bridge of the cruiser *Augusta*, watching his men, General Omar Bradley was convinced that Omaha Beach was "an irreversible catastrophe," and he prayed that the men could simply "hang on." He knew the beach was already too congested, that hundreds of landing craft were circling aimlessly offshore, that sending in reinforcements could actually compound the problem. Yet retreat was not a feasible strategy; to leave a gap of thirty-seven miles between Utah and Gold beaches would have imperiled the entire invasion.

Remarkably, the Allies kept coming. At 7:30 a.m. the main command group waded onto the shore, only to have their numbers almost immediately cut down. Exposed to enemy fire, pinned down, and realizing that the previous assault plans were worthless, the remaining commanders began improvising. The men couldn't stay where they were; that was madness. Yet they had no way to flank the Germans or push forward—or move backward for that matter. There was no discernible route to climb through the heavily mined swamp or to scale the bluffs to pry the Germans out of their trenches. And there were thick rolls of barbed wire in front of them. On its face this was a crisis of unconscionable proportions.

But in fits and starts, small groups began making their way up the bluffs, and slowly pockets of leadership—colonels and generals, but also lieutenants as well—began to form, waving their hands and shouting and screaming for their men to keep moving. One colonel blustered, "We might as well get killed inland as here on the beach." At the same time engineers meticulously began to lay tape to show where the Allies had cleared minefields, while other men swam across antitank ditches filled with water. Each moment they were waiting for the Germans to counterattack. A counterattack would have, with minimal effort, "run us right back into the Channel," as one battalion commander said. But it never came.

Instead, came the most exhilarating sight of all: three Americans pinned down behind the foundation of what was once a house looked up at what had to have seemed like a marvel—Americans doggedly making their way along the crest of the German-held bluffs.

They had made it to strategic high ground.

THE AMERICANS WERE RELENTLESS. As larger landing craft began to arrive, tanks, half-tracks, jeeps, trucks, and self-propelled artillery streamed ashore. Not long after H-hour, Operation Overlord was moving into full swing. The Allies were pounding Hitler's men again and again and, despite high casualties, were inching forward. And elsewhere, at Gold, Juno, and Sword beaches, the Allies were progressing nearly unimpeded.

Eisenhower himself was up before 7 a.m., having already been informed that things seemed to be going "by plan." For a few minutes he lay quietly in his bed, smoked a cigarette, and with a broad grin flipped through a dime-store western novel. He chatted with his close aide Harry Butcher. Then he began his customary pacing.

It was around this time that General George H. Marshall, the influential army chief of staff, picked up a phone to awaken President Roosevelt.

THE WHITE HOUSE OPERATOR took the call first, at 3 a.m. Washington time. Asking General Marshall to hold a moment, she promptly rang Eleanor, and requested that the first lady rouse the president. Aside from the soft rustling of the Secret Service agents in the hallways, and the never-ending hubbub in the classified map room where top-secret dispatches came in at all hours, the White House was quiet, a quiet that Eleanor found nerve-racking. She herself had been too anxious to sleep. Now she eased open the door to the president's bedroom and explained that Marshall was on the phone and the invasion was under way. The president promptly sat up in bed, pulled on a sweater, and put the phone to his ear. Marshall briefed him on the progress of the invasion thus far; actually, Eisenhower had already buoyantly told Marshall that "the light of battle was in [the troops'] eyes." Roosevelt flashed a smile, and from that point on, he began working the telephone lines.

MEANWHILE, WORD ABOUT THE invasion was filtering out across the nation and the world. Transocean, the official mouthpiece of the Nazis, was actually the first to announce that Overlord had begun, stating that British parachute troops were landing on the French coast. With the help of its translators, the Associated Press immediately followed suit, putting the news out on the wire. The BBC quickly joined in. Not to be outdone, the *New York Times* put a special "late city edition" on the streets by 1:30 a.m.—it was aptly called a "postscript." There was no actual story yet, only a headline in full caps: "HITLER'S SEA WALL IS BREACHED, INVADERS FIGHTING WAY INLAND; NEW ALLIED LANDINGS ARE MADE."

Within half an hour, people were beginning to stir, already forming long lines at newsstands or, coffee in hand, sitting in pajamas by their radios, turning up the volume and nervously awaiting the latest battle news. At 2 a.m. eastern time, news came. The radio stations, as jittery as the American people, interrupted their regular programs to declare: "German radio says the invasion has begun." This report, however, was both confused and fragmentary, actually warning that the Germans' announcement might be a trick to flush out the French Resistance. Within hours, that notion was dispelled. Americans could listen to the actual recording of Eisenhower reading the orders he had given to the troops on the eve of the invasion. It had first been broadcast over loudspeakers on the transports in southern England; now the American people could listen to the same stirring words the Allied troops had heard before their ships left the English coast.

Addressed to the "Soldiers, Sailors and Airmen of the Allied Expeditionary Force!" the message was: "You are about to embark upon the Great Crusade, toward which we've striven these many months. The eyes of the world are upon you. . . . You will bring about the destruction of the German war machine, the elimination of Nazi tyranny over the oppressed peoples of Europe, and security for ourselves in a free world.

"Your task will not be an easy one. Your enemy is well trained, well equipped and battle hardened. He will fight savagely.

"But this is the year 1944! Much has happened since the Nazi triumphs of 1940–41. . . . Our home fronts have given us an overwhelming superiority in weapons and munitions of war, and placed at our disposal great reserves of trained fighting men. The tide has turned! I have full confidence in your courage, devotion to duty and skill in battle. We will accept nothing less than full victory!

"Good luck!"

The American people hung on every word. For their part, the GIs, earlier, had folded up the order and slipped it into their pockets. Many of those who survived stuck it on their walls when they returned home.

∾

THE *NEW YORKER* MAGAZINE proclaimed this "a colossal moment in history," and it was. For the whole country the suspense was "agonizing." Workers audibly gasped when they heard the news broadcast over loudspeakers. As the night turned into dawn, the anticipation heightened. It was quickly becoming a day not only of prayer but of quiet hope and restrained rejoicing. Let news of the invasion race across the nation from ocean to ocean, the American people exulted. Let it be proclaimed in the newspapers, and sung in thousands of newscasts across the country, that Roosevelt's Allied armies were moving forward on the verge of a great triumph.

The news became unstoppable. So was the delirium. The kings of Norway and England addressed their nations. In Belgium and the Netherlands, the respective premiers did the same. So did Charles de Gaulle, who addressed the French. Then, after an hour of making calls, President Roosevelt lifted the phone one more time and gave the White House operator a simple message: begin waking up all of his aides and tell them they were expected to be at their desks immediately. Soon thereafter, the president's old hands, men like Steve Early and Pa Watson, got to work in the West Wing, to keep control over the documents and messages that were flooding in. In the clatter of the map room, the officers who manned it around the clock in three shifts sought to keep up with the rapidly changing battle. And throughout the White House's tiny offices and partitioned cubbyholes, Roosevelt's staff struggled with the tide of concerns coursing in.

In these stirring, emotion-packed hours, Roosevelt could feel that the Allies were on the way to a great triumph, even if some of the first reports were less than heartening. It brought to mind a comparable moment at the White House seventy-nine years before, in early April 1865, when Abraham Lincoln was presented with several captured Confederate flags after the victory of Five Forks. "Here is something material," he had rejoiced, "something I can see, feel and understand. This means victory, this *is* victory."

Now, as afternoon began on the beaches and a new round of troops continued to come ashore, more than ever Roosevelt too had begun to believe. At 9:50 a.m., he wheeled himself into the Oval Office and briefed the speaker of the House, the cantankerous, wily Sam Rayburn. At 11:30 a.m. his military leaders—General Marshall, Hap Arnold, and Admiral King—filed in, to stand near his massive desk and feel the weight of history. They were far away from the battle, and the details they had were still scanty. Things were going badly at Omaha Beach, though on the other fronts the troops were steadily thrusting forward. Yet by the time Roosevelt was picnicking outside with his daughter shortly after midday, under the cooling shade of his favorite magnolia tree, it was clear that the tide was decisively turning in favor of the Allies.

Later that afternoon, the president held his regular press conference for nearly two hundred correspondents who eagerly bustled in. Initially, there was a hush. They could make allowances for the fact that he had been up most of the night—he had slept only four hours—but even so, they saw that he looked deathly tired. His face was heavily lined and gaunt; his cheeks were sunken. Sitting in his large green swivel chair, however, Roosevelt maintained his fine form, and he had dressed the part: he wore a snow-white shirt, with the initials FDR embroidered on his left sleeve, and sported a dark blue dotted bow tie. And he had a yellow-amber cigarette holder cocked in his mouth, indicating to more than one of the journalists in the room that he was "pleased with the world." Pads and pencils in hand, the reporters recorded Roosevelt's every word, while the president's dog, Fala, playfully bounded on the furniture. Roosevelt was in good spirits, grinning broadly and joking that the assembled reporters themselves were "all smiles."

Nonetheless, he struck a cautionary note. "You just don't land on a beach and walk through—if you land successfully without breaking your leg—walk through to Berlin," he said, adding, "and the quicker this country understands it, the better." He concluded, "This is no time for overconfidence."

But beneath his words, there was confidence. As to specifics, Roosevelt was vague, indicating only that the invasion was "up to schedule." And how was he holding up? Roosevelt hesitated, his eyes sparkling, and flashed another broad smile. "Fine—I'm a little sleepy."

After meeting with one of his top Pentagon officials, John J. McCloy, Roosevelt was wheeled past the office of White House physician Ross McIntire—which contained a dentist chair, a rubdown table, and closets filled with various medications—and taken past the spacious indoor pool he had recently built, on his way to a 7:30 p.m. dinner with Eleanor.

Later in the evening, just before 10 p.m., Roosevelt once again took to the airwaves, this time to lead the nation in prayer. His words were brief (only ten minutes) but lyrical, and among the most captivating of his presidency. Like a priest watching over his flock—an estimated 100 million Americans were fastened to their radios—he solemnly prayed first for "our sons, pride of our Nation." This day, he pointed out, the Allies had set out on a mighty endeavor, "a struggle to preserve our Republic . . . our civilization and to set free a suffering humanity." He continued, his voice at its mellifluous best: "Lead them straight and true; give strength to their arms, stoutness to their hearts, steadfastness in their faith. They will need Thy blessings. The road will be long and hard. For the enemy is strong. He may hurl back our forces, success may not come with rushing speed," to which he added commandingly, "We shall return again and again."

As for the Allied troops, "They fight not for the lust of conquest," he added emphatically. "They fight to end conquest. They fight to liberate."

And sensing the mood of a still anxious country, he saved his most trenchant words for last, a soaring invocation for all the people at home, for the parents yearning for their sons to return untouched from battle, for the wives yearning for their husbands to make it through safely, for the boys and girls waiting for their fathers to walk through the front door, all of whom intuitively understood what was at stake. "Some will never return," Roosevelt intoned gently. "Give us faith in Thee; faith in our sons; faith in each other; faith in our united crusade."

The nation agreed.

~

SINCE DAWN, THE NATION had been marking the day. In cities across the land, bells rang. For the first time since the funeral of Chief

Justice John Marshall in 1835, Philadelphia's mayor rapped the Liberty Bell with a wooden mallet, and the sound was broadcast from coast to coast over the web of radio airwaves. Meanwhile, on Broadway the show did not go on; the theaters stayed dark for D-Day. There were no baseball games. The New York Stock Exchange halted for two minutes of silent prayer before trading began. Macy's was closed, but in a burst of patriotism, the store rigged up a radio outside to give updates about the invasion throughout the day. In Columbus, Ohio, citizens paused for five minutes to join the national prayer: every truck, every bus, every car, every worker, and every pedestrian froze in place. And across the rest of the nation, in small towns and large, air raid sirens screeched, factory whistles hooted, and telephone switchboards were overwhelmed with friends and families calling each other.

The *New York Times* editorialized, "We have come to the hour for which we were born." Mayor Fiorello La Guardia of New York City announced, "It is the most exciting moment in our lives." Worshippers carried their Bibles to churches, or rushed to synagogues across the nation. In office buildings and on assembly lines, men and women spontaneously halted work, put their hands over their hearts, and prayed before returning to their tasks. At the same time, masses of people flooded to the hospitals to donate blood. Across the globe, there were wild celebrations. In England, people spontaneously stood and sang "God Save the King"; in Moscow, the Party elite and common people alike danced in the streets; and in Rome, newly liberated Italians waved American, French, and British flags.

As early as December 16, 1943, the *New York Times* had commented that Germany was "suffering severely," and that 1944 could well be the year when it would "collapse."

If all went as planned, for Roosevelt, D-Day would be the greatest day of his presidency.

6

"Could We Be Granted Victory This Year, 1944?"

ROOSEVELT MAY HAVE BEEN far away from the battle, but in his mind's eye he was able to visualize the carnage now taking place on the beaches of Normandy. A former assistant secretary of the navy, as president he routinely liked to drop by the White House map room with Admiral Leahy. This low-ceilinged basement room had previously been a coatroom for women and then a billiard room, with score beads draped along a makeshift wire strung between the walls and cue sticks racked alongside. But after Pearl Harbor, it was transformed. Now it held detailed charts of the Atlantic and Pacific military theaters that were updated two or three times daily to reflect the ever-shifting locations of the enemy and Allied forces. Here, Roosevelt could examine the rapidly changing military tides marked by little multicolored flags, curved arrows in thick grease pencil, and differently shaped pins. The special pins marking the location of the Big Three particularly delighted him: Churchill's pin was in the shape of a cigar,

Stalin's was a briar pipe, and his own was a cigarette holder. As D-Day progressed, Roosevelt watched with satisfaction when the grease pencil markings moved steadily off the beaches and out into the French countryside. At this moment, everything was in the hands of Eisenhower and his men.

Seven months earlier, en route to the summits in Cairo and Tehran, Roosevelt had taken a detour and spent the day with Eisenhower viewing the ruins of the ancient city of Carthage. There, he was able to gaze at the hideous remnants of the bloody North African campaign that the Allies had waged against Rommel and Kesselring: burned-out shells and tanks littering the plain, blown-up ammunition dumps, blackened tank traps, and uncleared minefields left over from the battle for Tunisia. As he rode with Eisenhower in the backseat of a dusty Cadillac, the general recounted at great length the pitched, often bewildering winter campaign the Allies had fought at Tebourba, Medjez-el-Bab, and the Kasserine Pass, as well as the spring struggles when they finally choked off the Axis forces at Tunis.

Reaching back into history, Roosevelt mused aloud about whether the U.S. and German tanks might have been fighting on the same ground involved in the legendary battle of Zama, where the great Roman general Scipio Africanus had defeated Hannibal and the Carthaginians on the vast, open plain. Would the Allies defeat the Germans on D-Day as the world's earliest republic had routed the Carthaginians? Roosevelt surely hoped so.

Munching on a sandwich, Roosevelt had then joked, "Ike, if one year ago, you'd offered to bet on this day the president of the United States would be having his lunch in the Tunisian roadside, what odds would you have demanded?"

Now, Roosevelt could well have been asking, what were the odds that a president who three months earlier had appeared to be dying would be presiding over the destruction of Hitler's vaunted Wehrmacht?

~

Destruction was the word. The long wait, the huge buildup of forces, and the intricate planning by Roosevelt, Churchill, and their military command—all were now paying dividends. Along many miles of the Normandy coast, villages were all smoke and flames. The Allied armies had jabbed, bruised, and pushed forward against the Nazi defenders. Within hours, thousands of Allied planes crisscrossed the sky above, while below the beaches were swarming with men, tanks, and amphibious supply carriers, as well as fresh supplies that were arriving as quickly as the sea and tide would allow. On Utah Beach, the troops had met with little resistance, and what resistance they did meet was second-rate: the Germans quickly folded. At the British and Canadian sites—Sword, Gold, and Juno beaches—the fighting also went better than expected. Even at Omaha, despite the dead and wounded strewn along the beach, despite the gridlock of intermingled vehicles and bodies, despite the agonizing hours of bloodshed, by the day's end some thirty-four thousand American troops were able to gain a foothold on French soil.

The Germans were not only outmatched but outsmarted. Remarkably, Rommel wasn't even at the front. On June 5, he had chosen to be at his home near Ulm, spending a day of repose strolling with his wife, Lucie. She was trying on the new sandals that he had bought for her birthday. As a result, on D-Day itself, the vaunted German commander was nowhere to be found. He was not alerted about the attack until 10:15 a.m. He then spent the next several hours madly racing over four hundred miles of road to his ornate command post at La Roche Guyon, cursing himself and shouting at his driver, "*Tempo! Tempo! Tempo!*"—"Faster, faster, faster!" With the Luftwaffe a mere shell of itself, Rommel was reluctant to fly. Incredibly, he didn't arrive at his headquarters until after 6 p.m. By then, the beaches, bluffs, and artillery nests had been all but cleared. Meanwhile Hitler, pale and delusional, was cloistered at Berchtesgaden, reminiscing about the old days and watching newsreels during the evening. Actually, when the news of the invasion arrived, he was asleep and his staff was afraid to wake him. When he finally arose from his bed at 10 a.m., he vainly believed he could crush the invasion, but he delayed the dispatch of two panzer tank divisions, which were stationed 120 miles away from the beaches, until it was too late. "We waited for orders, and we waited," the commander of the Twenty-first Panzer Division later lamented. "We couldn't understand why we weren't getting any orders at all."

So the tanks stayed in place, vulnerable to the Allied bombing runs. And when their orders finally arrived, they could only crawl along under a shroud of tall oaks in the roadside woods until darkness came to avoid the relentless bombardment from overhead; some panzers were pulverized anyway. In the meantime, the German forces across Normandy were powerless against the Allied air attacks that pummeled the railroads, highways, marshaling yards, and bridges, and which bottled up the German reinforcements in the interior. Incredibly, Hitler's other top general, Field Marshal von Rundstedt, continued to believe throughout the morning that the landings were a diversion.

The contrast between the Americans and the Germans couldn't have been greater. At noon, an invigorated Eisenhower was crouched over maps in his command tent. He turned on his heel, shuffled over to his door, pushed it open, and looked up into the sky, magnificently declaring, "The sun is shining."

And thousands of Allied planes were ruling that sunny sky—they flew ten thousand sorties on D-Day. What they saw as they returned home was unforgettable: the French countryside was littered everywhere with white parachutes and pieces of crushed gliders, while along the coast hundreds of landing craft were disembarking tens of thousands of men. It looked as though small cities had been erected on the Normandy shore. As one GI said, it was "the greatest show ever staged."

By nightfall the Allied forces were rushing forward in such numbers that they seemed to be springing up like King Aetes's mythical warriors rising from the soil Jason the Argonaut had scattered with dragon's teeth. After capturing Gold Beach, the British had thrust about six and a half miles inland and linked up with the Canadians on their left. At Juno Beach, Canadian tanks sprinted inland, as far as ten miles, so quickly that they had to halt and wait for the infantry to catch up. Their forward elements penetrated deeper into France than any other division, advancing to within three miles of the outskirts of the city of Caen. At Sword Beach, after all the smoke and haze had cleared, and the fighting had died down, 29,000 British troops waded ashore, with only 630 casualties. At Utah Beach 23,000 men came ashore with only 210 killed or wounded. Nearly 18,000 paratroopers had landed during the night, though their losses had been great. When the sun finally set over Normandy, some 175,000 men—Americans, British and Canadians—were established on French soil; to be sure, in some places they had only a narrow foothold, and some of their positions were isolated, but nonetheless their presence stretched across fifty-five miles. And behind them, a million more men would be coming within a few short weeks—actually, by July 4.

One American pilot remarked, watching the beaches and sea filled with a seemingly endless stream of American men and matériel coming ashore in France, "Hitler must have been mad to declare war on the United States."

The supposedly impregnable Atlantic Wall, a product of Hitler's fanatical vision and thousands of frantic man-hours, had taken four years for the Germans to build, and months for Rommel to reinforce. With the exception of Omaha Beach, which took a day, the Allies cracked it in under an hour.

Now, the Allies were methodically on the move. And the Germans were left to retreat, regroup, and watch.

ON JUNE 6, AS the Allies made their way in from the beaches, two more escapees from Auschwitz—Czeslaw Mordowicz and Arnost Rosin—arrived at the Slovakian border; actually, they thought the war was over. Like Vrba and Wetzler, they were met by Slovak Jewish leaders and interviewed by Oskar Krasnansky. They had fled the camp on May 27; by that time, the Hungarians were arriving en masse. The two men told of a spur railroad track being completed by crews "working night and day." This new track allowed transports to be brought straight to the crematoriums, without the bother of the selection process. And with the crematoriums overwhelmed, "great pits" were dug, "where corpses were burned day and night." As Rudolf Vrba would note, "Wetzler and I saw preparations for the slaughter. Mordowicz and Rosin saw the slaughter itself."

Inside Auschwitz, while the Allies were overrunning Normandy, on July 6 Nazi records noted that 496 Jews arrived and 297 of them were gassed.

~

AT THE SAME TIME, in Amsterdam, Netherlands, a Jewish businessman, Otto Frank, hiding with his wife and daughters and friends in the annex of a house on Prinsengracht, hung a map of Normandy on the wall. He followed whatever news reports he could get and used colored pins to mark how far the Allies had advanced into France and toward the Low Countries.

But even as the German war machine was slowly retreating from the beaches of Normandy, over 850 miles away, the trains continued to chug north and east, past the glory that was once Vienna, past ancient Kraków, pulling into the Auschwitz station. The disabled, the sick, the children, the elderly—all were being gassed at the astounding rate of two thousand every thirty minutes—adding up in a few hours to more people than were lost in the first day's assault at Normandy.

By the day of the invasion ninety-two trains in the last month alone had carried almost 300,000 Hungarian Jews to death. This was as though all the inhabitants of Boston were forced onto the Metroliner and taken to Washington, D.C., to be brutally murdered—or as if the bloodshed at Normandy were repeated more than 10,000 times.

And inside the dank, drab, stuffy rooms of the "secret annex" in Amsterdam, hidden behind a hinged bookcase that disguised a door, a young Jewish girl destined for immortality, fourteen-year-old Anne Frank, waited with her family, often looking at the map on the wall. With her chestnut eyes and unceasing curiosity, Anne was all audacity and eloquence. Despite the innumerable difficulties of a life in hiding, she worked on her studies, fell in love, and did chores. Despite the madness swirling all around her, she pondered great philosophical and political questions about war and peace ("the whole globe is waging war . . . the end is not yet in sight") and ruminated about the fate of others, "real slum kids with running noses." And despite her own terror, she never lost her compassion, worrying about her father's "sad eyes" and about the wretched victims sent to "filthy slaughterhouses."

She and her family had survived the howling Nazi mobs, and the unnerving stillness in the streets after the many roundups of Jews. They had survived the endless waiting—waiting anxiously for the dreaded SS to knock on the door; waiting wistfully for deliverance by the Allies; waiting, waiting, always waiting. Anne had survived, in her own words, wandering "from one room to another, downstairs and up again, feeling like a songbird whose wings have been brutally clipped and who is beating itself in utter darkness against the bars of his cage." And they had all survived their many quarrels, during which "the whole house thunders!"

Now, after their years of hiding from the Nazi terror, of being caged like hamsters in four small rooms, of always keeping silent when the SS walked by and even fearing to cough loudly when they had flu, D-Day was the most delirious day of Anne's life. Often, to keep her sanity, she would climb a steep ladder to the attic, sit at the skylight and look at her beloved chestnut tree or listen to the birds, wistfully pondering the lives of the people living freely in the house opposite hers.

Free people—an almost unfathomable concept. The house across the street, owned by gentiles, might as well have been an ocean away. But perhaps no longer. Taking pen to paper, she wrote in her diary on June 6, "This is *the* day. The invasion has begun!" She eloquently continued: "Would the long-awaited liberation that has been talked of so much, but which still seems *too* wonderful, *too* much like a fairytale, ever come true? Could we be granted victory this year, 1944? We don't know yet, but hope is revived within us; it gives us fresh courage, and makes us strong again."

"Oh," she wrote, "the best part of the invasion is that I have the feeling that friends are approaching. We've been oppressed by those terrible

Germans for so long, they've had their knives so at our throats, but the thought of friends and delivery fills us with confidence!"

But were friends coming to free them? Anne Frank didn't know—nor did the Jews of Hungary, nor, for that matter, did Roosevelt or Churchill—that on D-Day both British and American intelligence agents were poring over air reconnaissance photos: photos that showed in chilling detail the buildings at the main camp of Auschwitz. Three photographs in particular revealed the death chambers in Birkenau. Indeed by the end of June, the reconnaissance images were so detailed that the intelligence agents could make out the ramps and people walking to the crematoriums, and with the use of a magnifying glass, even the prisoners' tattooed numbers. Examining these aerial photographs could have been the critical first step toward bombing Auschwitz. Yet the analysts skipped over the apparatus of death—as it happens, their superiors had given them no reason to examine that part of the camp closely. They instead focused on their actual mission: the nearby synthetic rubber and oil plants, part of the so-called oil war. Those targets were crucial to the air campaign intended to strangle Germany's war machine.

And in the dark recesses of a distant Polish forest, the trains continued to roll into Auschwitz with melancholy regularity.

As June wore on, the war was far from over, even though there were increasing signs that the Nazi Reich was crumbling. On the eastern front, Stalin made good on his promise to Roosevelt at Tehran. A new summer Soviet offensive inflicted a series of calamitous defeats on the Germans: the Soviets rapidly pushed westward, cutting off the Third Panzer Army in Vitebsk and encircling the Ninth Army two days later near Bobruysk. Meanwhile, in the air, the Allied sorties continued. During the first four months of 1944, their planes had dropped 175,000 tons of bombs against Germany, while on June 6 alone, the Allied

Mediterranean Air Force flew more than 2,300 sorties; they pounded rail yards and oil refineries in the Balkans and in Romania, again and again. Inside the Reich, chaos was intensifying. Munich, Bremen, Düsseldorf, and Duisberg were among the cities that suffered serious damage or even destruction; Germany's glittering cultural centers were slowly being turned into wastelands.

And in light of all this, far from becoming a latter-day Caesar, Adolf Hitler himself was now sickly and prematurely aged. He was hunched like an old man; his left arm trembled uncontrollably, and there was shaking in his left leg. His once piercing eyes were red, his once black hair had turned gray, then white, and the skin on his face sagged. Tormented by persistent gastrointestinal distress, and unable to sleep, he was taking as many as twenty-eight different pills a day. His physical decline was matched by his mental deterioration: fits, incessant tantrums, unchecked egomania, and out-of-control paranoia. It was a fact that not once in 1944 did he show his face to deliver a speech—he intuitively understood that he no longer had the favor of the nation. And only twice did he address the country on the radio. Not, however, after D-Day.

Ranting and raving, he remained in seclusion at his retreats with his Nazi inner circle, zealots like Martin Bormann, Joseph Goebbels, Albert Speer, and Hermann Göring. To the ordinary German, however, he had all but vanished. Once idolized by millions, he was, by his own admission, friendless except for his German shepherd, Blondi, and his mistress, Eva Braun. There was the fact that he was losing touch with reality, hoping for victory against all the evidence, and hoping for his latest weapon—thirteen-ton V-2 rockets that could reach the speed of sound just thirty seconds after liftoff and which carried a one-ton warhead—to descend from the upper reaches of the atmosphere to rain destruction on the enemy.

There were the ever-lengthening rosters of the war dead that he dismissed or outright ignored. And of course, there was always the fuel for the Nazi regime, the one thing that kept him going above all else: his hatred for the Jews. At this stage, with the Nazi empire deteriorating, only one thing seemed to work—its machine for killing these defenseless civilians. And that machine remained shrouded in as much secrecy as the Führer himself.

~

DESPITE OF ALL OF Hitler's fury against the Jews, which intensified as the war ground on and the Nazis' military fortunes ebbed, the Führer was always careful to couch what he said in vague statements. To be sure, when he was still addressing entranced, cheering crowds in Berlin, or when he spoke to intimates in the evening hours at his Wolf's Lair tucked away in the Prussian forest, he always whipped up his audience to greater extremes of enmity against the Jews. His message was menacing, his countenance terrifying. Little by little he personally laid the groundwork for the most terrible industrialized genocide the world had ever seen. This was undeniable.

But shrewdly, he wanted it to be deniable.

So, a question: why did he bother to conceal his own deep involvement in the mass murder of Jews? Driven as much by intuition as calculation, however mad, he sensed that the German nation was unprepared to learn of such evil amid their most civilized of surroundings. True, they heard his tirades regarding the "life-and-death struggle between the Aryan race and the Jewish bacillus," and his dark hints about the "Final Solution," but usually he was indirect, speaking in ambiguous, sweeping generalities rather than making precise statements. In such a manner, he reasoned, the Nazis could preserve all the outward traits of a cultured people—including, so they thought, a conscience.

Even when surrounded by his henchmen at his cherished late-night tea, Hitler never actually talked about the physical extermination of the Jews. He would speak of Jews as "the scourge of mankind," but never about the death mills at Dachau and Chelmno. He would say that if only there were no more Jews in Europe, "the unity of the European states would no longer be disturbed," but he never spoke about Auschwitz. He would declare that "the Jews are everywhere" and that all the Jews "from Berlin and Vienna should disappear," but never mention the millions who had actually been murdered. Thus, his terrible secret was, on the surface, maintained.

There was another, equally diabolical, reason for his secrecy. The less the horrific facts of Hitler's program of annihilation emerged, the less likely the world community was to be aroused. Some might say this and some might say that, but for Hitler, it all amounted to empty talk. In his view, Roosevelt and Churchill from time to time mouthed humane pieties about the ill-treatment of the Jews, yet lacking firm details, these condemnations had no teeth. The same was true of any declarations of concern made by the frequently cowed Catholic Church or by the International Red Cross. And there was a third reason for the secrecy, too. The less the Jews themselves knew, the more pliant and more docile they would be as they were taken east in the slow-moving cattle cars toward their imminent slaughter.

~

BUT BY MAY AND certainly by June 1944, the hard questions could no longer be dodged. Particularly after D-Day, and as the Vrba-Wetzler report was about to become known, the question of the Jews would, for many, become as vexing as the war itself.

Yet this development had been a long time coming.

A long time coming, in no small measure, because of the lengthy, complicated process by which the Final Solution emerged in Nazi policy. A long time coming, also because of the too often tepid response with which each fresh report of atrocities and massacres was received in the White House and the marble corridors of decision making in Washington.

So, how to understand the enormity of the Holocaust, and the enormity of the slow response by the White House? And how to understand those who were woefully blind or purposefully blind, or who simply turned their backs on the sheer evil of the crime? It begins with understanding the history of the unfolding war, the history of the Jews in prewar Europe, and the history of Roosevelt's presidency.

And it ends with the long, tortuous road that stretched to the spring of 1944.

Part Two

The Road to 1944

Hitler in the map room with his generals.

7

Beginnings

TO LATER GENERATIONS, THE full dimensions of the Final Solution are clear. But in the swirl of the early days of World War II, the information available to the Allies was haphazard, frequently baffling, and prone to being misunderstood. The popular concept is that the Final Solution began solely with the death camps. This is untrue. To be sure, its sordid beginning lay in Hitler's early pronouncements. But the Final Solution was at first less a policy than a process, influenced by the vicissitudes of the battlefield and the whims and vagaries of the Nazis' henchmen in the newly conquered territories. Only in time would it take on the fully industrialized character that we know of today. And only late in the war, after Roosevelt died, would there be the images captured permanently by the camera's unblinking lens: The pictures of bodies, some bloated, some barely there at all, some so skeletal that all that remained were white, shrunken torsos in which every rib could be counted and the last remnants of skin were pathetically stretched over feeble bones. The pictures in which starvation had reduced bodies nearly to the point of nothingness. The pictures of hollow eyes frozen in horror, eyes that pleaded, if not for help, then at least for mercy.

But by the time these pictures were taken, it was too late. And once again, the question would loom: how did it happen?

The seeds of genocide had been planted for some time. On January 30, 1939, the sixth anniversary of his takeover of power, a sweating, ebullient Hitler appeared before the Reichstag to deliver one of his most significant speeches, a speech he would return to time and again. Every seat was taken. "I have very often in my lifetime been a prophet," he boasted, "and was mostly derided." There was wild cheering. He continued: "[In] my struggle for power it was in the first instance the Jewish people who received only with laughter my prophecies that I would . . . take over the leadership" and then also "bring the Jewish problem to its solution." There was more cheering. His voice rising, his hands thrusting into the air, he declared, "I want today to be a prophet again." And what was his terrible prophecy? If "Jewry inside and outside Europe should succeed in plunging the nations once more into a world war, the result will not be the bolshevization of the earth and thereby the victory of Jewry, but the annihilation of the Jewish race in Europe!"

Here was his cherished word—*Vernichtung* (annihilation)—one that he would use again and again. Actually, just nine days before, meeting privately with the Czechoslovak foreign minister, Hitler had boldly insisted that "the Jews here will be annihilated." Who could not believe him? For here, experience told the tale. Promptly on becoming chancellor in 1933—the same year Franklin Roosevelt took office—Hitler systematically started to rob German Jews of their basic rights, rights that were formally stripped away by the infamous Nuremberg laws of 1935. In every way imaginable, Jews were being hounded out of public life. By order of the state, Jewish retail establishments were closed. Jews were barred from schools, concerts, and theaters, and even prohibited from driving automobiles. Jewish lawyers and doctors were forbidden to practice. Jewish peddlers were outlawed. Jewish banks were subjected to moblike shakedowns. And the stench of anti-Semitism was pervasive. So were torment and distress. Nazi storm troopers, or sometimes simply brown shirted hooligans, vandalized private Jewish homes and smashed Jewish businesses. The main synagogue in Munich, a gorgeous old building, was torched, while vandals desecrated Jewish cemeteries. And this was just the beginning. Male Jews with Aryan-sounding names were required to add "Israel" to their name; females had to add the name "Sara." Jews were required to have "J" embossed on their passports. Far from condemning such actions, Hitler rarely wasted an opportunity to egg on the anti-Semites: Jews were, he insisted, "lice," "vermin," "parasites." A Jew was, in a familiar Nazi saying, a "bacillus." Jews were "vampires," corrupting everything that was noble and good and bleeding "all nations to death."

If there was any doubt about the growing savagery of the Nazi regime, it was dispelled on November 9–10, 1938, the infamous "night of broken glass." *Kristallnacht* was a descent into barbarism believed unthinkable in the heart of a supposedly civilized state. Under Hitler's reign, the tinder had been there, awaiting a match. It came by happenstance when a seventeen-year-old Polish Jew, driven mad by the forced deportation of his family, not to mention the summary expulsion from Germany of eighteen thousand Polish Jews, calmly shot a low-level German diplomat in Paris. The next morning, the Nazi press in Germany whipped party fanatics into a frenzy, calling for retaliatory violence against all Jews. Local party leaders soon followed suit. On November 8, the Nazi SS chief Heinrich Himmler acidly declared, "We will drive [the Jews] out more and more with an unprecedented ruthlessness." With that, the furies were unleashed.

Goebbels commented in his diary, "If only the anger of the people could now be let loose!" When he conferred with Hitler at a reception that evening, the Führer evidently agreed, muttering that the Nazi storm troopers—the SA—should "have a fling." While Hitler quietly retreated to his Munich apartment, Goebbels, having been given the green light, joined the fray; at 10 p.m. he made a speech calling for riots against the

Jews. At 1:20 a.m. all police chiefs were instructed by the SS, by telex, to arrest as many male Jews as possible and not to hinder the destruction of synagogues.

Within hours angry demonstrators massed in the roadways, and the sky was lit up by the flames of burning synagogues. All across the country, Nazi mobs, drunk with power, rampaged, smashing windows of shops belonging to Jews. Party activists scrawled anti-Semitic slogans on the walls of stores and private homes. Some SS men donned civilian clothes and joined the rioting. At the same time, assault squads, the dreaded *Stosstrupp Hitler*, began marching up and down the streets of Munich, chanting and punching their fists in the air, and hunting down and murdering Jews; all told, about a hundred were killed. In Berlin, fifteen magnificent synagogues were torched; by the end of the evening, hundreds across the country were destroyed. Fire brigades were pointedly instructed to stand aside and let the synagogues smolder. Back in his hotel room, Goebbels rejoiced as he listened to the crackling fires and the shattering glass echoing in the night—they were from shop windows being smashed and heavy chandeliers crashing down. "Bravo," he thought to himself. "*Bravo!*"

More than eight thousand Jewish-owned shops were pillaged. No one managed to count exactly how many apartments were broken into and left a shambles. Looting was rampant; but often merchandise was simply hurled into the streets for the sheer delight of it. Gilt-framed mirrors were wrecked, oil paintings were cut up, heirlooms and antiques were mutilated. Clothing—girls' dresses, boys' school clothes—was scattered about. Individual Nazis made off with their victims' cash and savings, and seized radios, books, pianos, medical supplies, toys, and anything else of value.

Nor did the mobs stop there.

Nothing seemed to satiate them. Anguished women were roughed up, slapped, and molested. So were the elderly. Even children, hiding in cellars and attics and whimpering uncontrollably, were not exempt. They too were manhandled, or simply hung upside down and punched, while SS hooligans clapped and laughed. Meanwhile, in Berlin and all across Germany, crowds watched as fires burned and millions of pieces of broken glass were strewn everywhere, littering the streets and sidewalks.

Thirty thousand Jews were arbitrarily rounded up and arrested; the next step for them was a concentration camp. In the meantime, their businesses were simply expropriated by the state. Thus German Jews began a frightful existence: living from day to day, wondering what horrors the next day would bring. "How can this barbarity be happening in the 20th century?" one Jewish woman asked herself. In Washington, President Roosevelt agreed, saying, "I myself could scarcely believe that such things could occur in the 20th century."

For the Nazis, this was another step on their road to genocide. One German official—the governor of Berlin, Hans Frank—trenchantly put it, "I ask nothing of the Jews except that they disappear."

THEREAFTER, THE FULL FORCE of the racist Nazi laws intensified. A Department of Racial Purity was created, which initiated a detailed census of the Jewish population. And the daily humiliations were endless. Jews were no longer able to enter parks—signs announced, "Dogs and Jews Not Allowed"—go to restaurants, or even use public toilets. For that matter, city benches were forbidden as well. Jewish musicians were not allowed to perform works by non-Jewish composers. With no warning or pension, Jewish civil servants were dismissed. The same for Jewish teachers and travel agents. Jews were even forbidden to create art. Jews could no longer marry Aryans, have sexual intercourse with Aryans, or work with Aryans. And virulently anti-Semitic children's books were widely disseminated; Ernst Heimer's *The Poison Mushroom*, for example, depicted Jews as disgusting, repugnant swindlers with "criminal eyes," "infested" beards, "filthy" ears, and noses bent "like the number six." The message was straightforward: Jews were poison for the German people, the cause of all misery and distress. Unsurprisingly in this atmosphere, there were some twenty suicides a day among Jews.

Before the Final Solution, Hitler had first busied himself devising an economic solution. On the day after Kristallnacht, he dined with Joseph Goebbels at a popular Munich restaurant, the Osteria Bavaria, where he sketched out a program of oppressive economic measures against the Jews. It was not enough that the Jews had been terrorized or that some had been murdered. Now, he decreed with a straight face, they would be responsible for repairing the damage to their homes and their stores without any assistance from German insurance firms. Actually, the insurance companies would make payments—Hitler saw to that—but these would be to the state, not to the Jews. This ruling was onerous in the extreme, for the damage done on Kristallnacht was estimated to be several hundred million marks. Quickly thereafter, ubiquitous signs proclaimed, "BEWARE—DO NOT SHOP IN JEWISH STORES."

But removing the Jews from the economy was not enough. Soon, the Nazis began considering ghettos, and whether all Jews should wear special badges.

AFTER KRISTALLNACHT, GERMAN JEWS were desperate. Much as they had loved their native land, Germany, tens of thousands began to flee. The problem, however, was where to go. During the tense days of July 6–14, 1938—Hitler had already annexed Austria—President Roosevelt convened the Évian Conference. Thirty-two countries sent representatives to Évian, Lake Geneva. The delegates stayed at Hotel Royal, a luxurious French resort, and discussed whether they could increase immigration quotas for Jews. But despite daily reports of Nazi outrages against the Jews, despite the brutalities perpetrated on innocents by Nazi thugs, the participating nations remained unmoved at the bargaining table. At the conference there were rare disclaimers and expressions of sympathy, but with Europe blundering toward war, the delegates did little more than gaze into foggy crystal balls. They made no decisions of any consequence; instead, it seemed they spent most of their time gambling at casinos, getting massages, taking mineral baths, riding, and playing golf. Their indifference was striking. According to his supporters,

Roosevelt had the best intentions—the lead U.S. delegate was not a professional diplomat but his good friend and confidant Myron C. Taylor—yet the outcome of the conference was a disaster. Rather than helping the Jews, the civilized nations had ratified their reluctance to open their arms. They offered only veiled remarks and vague promises.

Despite being hampered by isolationist sentiment, America struggled to do more. Roosevelt at least recommended that his consular service remove unnecessary red tape from visa applications by those wishing to come from Germany. And by some measures, he did successfully raise the refugee issue as an international humanitarian concern; indeed, *Newsweek* went as far as to claim that the administration had signaled "active opposition to international gangsters."

But the help stopped there. The U.S. quota for German immigrants remained unchanged at just under twenty-five thousand annually. Even in 1938, despite its claims, the administration admitted ten thousand fewer immigrants than the legal limit. To the Jews, a closed border was frequently, in effect, a death sentence. And the message from the United States seemed to be this: although it was a nation mainly of European immigrants, America wanted little part of the increasingly desperate refugees. Roosevelt himself, when questioned if he had considered where Jewish refugees from Nazi Germany might go, and whether he would contemplate a relaxation of immigration restrictions, flatly said: "That is not in contemplation; we have the quota system." One participant at the conference, the future Israeli prime minister Golda Meir, wrote about her mixture of "rage, frustration, and horror." For his part, Chaim Weizmann pointedly warned Britain's Anthony Eden that "the fire from the synagogues may easily spread from there to Westminster Abbey and the other great English cathedrals," adding that failure to rebuke the Nazis would mean "the beginning of anarchy and the destruction of the basis of civilization." He was of course right.

Still, such pleas fell on deaf ears, and the Nazis rejoiced. "Nobody wants them," boasted the German newspaper *Völkischer Beobachter*, while a triumphant Hitler gloated, saying, "It is a shameful spectacle to see how the whole democratic world is oozing sympathy for the poor tormented Jewish people, but remains hardhearted and obdurate when it comes to helping them."

Somehow, eighty thousand Jews in Germany, in the direst of circumstances—the government refused to allow them to take their money or possessions with them—managed to elude the talons of the Nazis and pick their way across the borders. Penniless and scared, they reached England, the United States, Latin America, and notwithstanding numerous British impediments, Palestine. Some even went as far as Japanese-occupied Shanghai, which welcomed them with the least red tape.

But those who escaped or were granted refuge were very few compared with the tens of thousands flooding into foreign consulates throughout Germany to apply for visas, desperate to flee. For his part, quietly behind closed doors, Roosevelt did what he could to let more in—within limits. Between 1933 and 1940, almost 105,000 refugees from Nazism made it to safety in the United States. No other country took any such number, though tiny Palestine did admit 55,000. And after Kristallnacht, Roosevelt allowed all German and Austrian citizens who were in the United States on visitor permits to remain when the permits expired. Still, this didn't even come close to reaching America's capacity to help, or circumventing the low monthly quotas for immigration.

Indeed, on May 13, 1939, six months after Kristallnacht, the luxury liner *St. Louis* vividly dramatized the situation. At precisely 8:13 p.m. the ship had set sail from Germany for Cuba flying a Nazi flag, with Hitler's portrait hanging prominently in the social hall, and 937 hopeful Jewish refugees on board—among the last to escape from Germany's ever-tightening restrictions on immigration. On reaching Havana two weeks later, however, the passengers, except for twenty-eight, were told they could not disembark; as it happened, in Berlin, Nazi propagandist Joseph Goebbels had maliciously spread the word that the Jews were criminals and a threat to Cuba, whipping up a storm of protests against them. In any case, Cuban anti-Semites needed little goading. The Jews' landing permits were denied. For seven days in the blistering heat the ship remained in the Havana harbor, while intermediaries sought to negotiate admission for the passengers. Meanwhile, friends and relatives anxiously gathered on the beaches, straining to see the refugees lining the rails of the *St. Louis*. Some even hired dinghies and motorboats to go out and meet the ship. Baskets of bananas, books, and other articles were also delivered to the liner. They were futile gestures. The Cuban government was unmoved by the negotiators. Within the week, the ship was turned away. In protest, one survivor of Buchenwald slashed his wrists and fell into the ocean.

On June 2, the *St. Louis* sailed north, making for the Florida coast. At this point the captain, Gustav Schroeder—a gentile and an idealist—held out hope that the United States would admit the passengers, four hundred of whom were women and children, and many of whom actually had quota numbers for eventual entry into America. For weeks while the world watched, the *St. Louis* cruised just offshore, close enough to Miami that the refugees could see the "shimmering towers" of the city's skyline, as the *New York Times* reported. The sky was a rich blue, and the azure water sparkled; yet the days were filled with confusion and trepidation. Knowing that a forced return to Germany meant certain death, the terrified passengers sent an urgent telegram to Roosevelt asking for help. Roosevelt never replied. Nor did the White House even comment on the matter. The Jews sent a second telegram to Roosevelt, who a few days earlier had been at Hyde Park. Still no answer. Instead, the president spent the week busily occupied with other meetings, other events. On board, the refugees tried to keep their spirits up, but they were like survivors of a shipwreck, isolated from the one great nation in a position to help them.

As the days went by, the news became grimmer. The State Department took the lead, insisting that it would not "interfere" in Cuban affairs, and that the passengers would not be allowed to come ashore. Reportedly, to underscore the message, the Coast Guard even fired a warning shot just off the bow of the *St. Louis*. Miserable and depressed, its captain knew he had little choice but to return to Germany. As the ship turned toward the open Atlantic, the hundreds of refugees watched forlornly while Miami receded in the distance. According to some historians, at this point a Coast Guard vessel shadowed the *St. Louis* to prevent any passengers from jumping overboard and swimming ashore—or for that matter, committing suicide. On the ship, the passengers' dread was palpable. Once more they pleaded with world leaders to give them asylum. In the end, it was not a humane America but an imperiled Belgium, the Netherlands, France, and England that each agreed to take a limited number of the passengers. But within a year, the first three of these countries were overrun by the Nazi Wehrmacht. And eventually at least 254 passengers, if not a majority of the *St. Louis*'s roster, perished in Nazi concentration camps.

For the Nazis, and Hitler, the *St. Louis* affair was a rousing propaganda triumph, proving once again that the Allied countries didn't want Jews any more than Germany did. For the United States, and Roosevelt himself, it was a humiliating episode, all the more so because as long as the United States and other countries were willing to let the Jews in, for the time being, the Nazis were still willing to let them leave. Moreover, Roosevelt was, many believed, anything but unsympathetic to the plight of the Jewish refugees. In his own administration Jews constituted a significant proportion of senior aides, which prompted anti-Semites to deride Roosevelt as "a Jew," and to refer to his New Deal as the "Jew Deal." "In the dim distant past [my ancestors] may have been Jews or Catholics or Protestants," Roosevelt once quipped, "what I am interested in is whether they were good citizens and believers in God. I hope they were both."

But Roosevelt was unwilling to confront xenophobic public opinion, a vaguely anti-Semitic State Department, and an isolationist national mood.

~

BY CONTRAST, AS MORE of Europe fell under Nazi dominion, there was rising concern among the American public to rescue the greatest number of European children as possible, particularly English children. No less than the Jewish refugees, these children faced severe immigration restrictions as a legacy of the quotas Congress had established in the 1920s. Yet in this case, buoyed by public support, the administration exercised considerable creativity to help the British children. The idea was to let them enter the United States not as immigrants but as temporary visitors, since visitors' visas were exempt from numerical limitations. On radio, an impassioned Eleanor Roosevelt argued this way: "The children are not immigrants. The parents of these children will recall them when the war is over. . . . Red tape must not be used to trip up little children on their way to safety." However, the State Department balked at even this proposal. In the summer of 1940, advocates of the refugees pressed their case for weeks, but to little avail. Then, Eleanor interceded directly with the president, who in turn personally raised the matter with Cordell Hull, the secretary of state.

The next day, with the stroke of a pen, a new ruling was issued. The British refugee children would be admitted as visitors, subject to the (largely rhetorical) provision that "they shall return home upon the termination of hostilities." Actually, however, it was unclear how to even get the British children to the United States. They were still in England, and the British government was unable to spare warships to escort any unarmed merchant ships carrying them. For their part, the Americans were reluctant to send U.S. ships through waters infested by Nazi submarines. In the end, Congress broke the logjam, amending the Neutrality Act to allow U.S. ships to evacuate the joyous British children.

Why the British children, and not the German Jewish children? This was precisely the question an indignant congressman, William Schulte of Indiana, asked. Seeing this as a matter of conscience, with evangelical fervor he drafted a bill calling for a visitor's visa for any European child under sixteen. But the anti-immigration forces clung ever more tightly to their arguments; as a result, he faced stiff opposition and the bill was bottled up in committee. The reasons behind the opposition varied. For the most part, public opinion sharply distinguished between the British children, who were mainly Christian, and the German children, who were mainly Jewish. Here, of course, was a classic formula for inaction. It was a sad fact that the whiff of anti-Semitism remained in the American landscape, and at this stage, only bold political leadership could maneuver around it. The Roper polls consistently found that the American people looked askance at Hitler's treatment of the Jews in Germany, but the majority of Americans also looked askance at helping the Jews or increasing their immigration quotas. And in a further sign of the times, in New York City, hooliganism against synagogues was not uncommon.

Even after German troops stormed across the Polish frontier in September 1939, anti-immigration forces continued to muster arguments against increasing entry quotas or relaxing entry rules. They persisted in the spring of 1940 when the Germans invaded the Low Countries, and stories abounded that beforehand, the Nazis had successfully placed spies in the targeted nations. Such rumors were worrisome, and a weary, war-conscious President Roosevelt took them to heart, especially when, as if in the blink of an eye, the conquered European capitals were surrounded by barbed-wire fences and 2 million Germans occupied these countries.

On May 16, the day after the Netherlands unthinkably surrendered, Roosevelt appeared before a joint session of Congress. "These are ominous days," he intoned. "We have seen the treacherous use of the fifth column." In other words, he was talking about ostensibly peaceful visitors who were actually part of enemy units. Cable after cable and intelligence report after intelligence report seemed to confirm his preoccupation with subversion. He was told that in Norway, thousands of Nazi agents were disguised as diplomatic attachés, newsmen, university professors, and even refugees. He was told that so-called German tourists provided help to German troops in Norway. About the Netherlands, he was told that unknown numbers of agents had infiltrated the country and had played a significant role in facilitating Germany's stunning parachute landings.

This had a profound effect on Roosevelt's attitude toward refugees. In a fireside chat ten days after he spoke to Congress, Roosevelt gave one of his most muscular speeches of the war, firmly insisting that national security was more than simply a question of military weapons.

"We know of new methods of attack," he declared, pausing for emphasis. "... The Trojan horse, the fifth column that betrays a nation unprepared for treachery." He paused again. "... Spies, saboteurs and traitors are all actors in the new strategy." Another pause, and then he said, his voice booming: "With all that we *must* and *will* deal vigorously."

He did. Roosevelt authorized the illegal use of wiretaps for monitoring subversive activities, and he enjoined the State Department to tighten the restrictions on refugees. In theory this made sense; no president could ignore the sobering possibility of spies in the nation's midst. In reality, however, the policy was often bewildering. Every generation has illusions that baffle its successors, and this was the case here. It is hard to accept that Hitler's principal victims, the beleaguered Jews trying to cling to life, were German spies, any more than the British children were. Yet tragically, as the Nazis' grip tightened in German-occupied territories, the official anti-immigration policy in the United States gathered in volume and strength.

That it did so was largely the responsibility of one man: Breckinridge Long, President Roosevelt's head of the visa section in the State Department.

IN AN ADMINISTRATION FILLED with oversize personalities and raw talent, Breckinridge Long was a bit of an anomaly, despite his imperial presence. His speech was clipped, his mouth was turned down in what seemed to have been a permanent frown, and he was suspicious and distrustful of everyone. He was tall and powerfully built, and had narrow eyes, a striking shock of white hair, and an acerbic tongue. His pedigree seemed impeccable. Just as the president proudly traced his roots to Teddy Roosevelt and Hyde Park, Long, a midwesterner, could boast that his lineage stretched to two distinguished southern families:

the Longs of North Carolina and the Breckinridges of Kentucky. Among his relatives was the distinguished John C. Breckinridge, who had been a U.S. senator, the youngest vice president in American history, and later the Confederacy's secretary of war. Long was born in Saint Louis, Missouri, in 1881; his mother was Margaret Miller Breckinridge and his father William Strudwick Long. Young Breckinridge attended the finest schools, receiving his BA and MA from Princeton. In between, he studied law at Washington University.

He soon opened a law office in Saint Louis, built a thriving international practice, and amassed a considerable sum of money. He married well, too, and had a daughter. He acquired the tastes of a country gentleman and loved the outdoors, particularly foxhunting and sailing; he also bred horses. He was a collector as well, of English antiques, fine art, and models, such as little ships. In his practice he spoke meticulously, each word neatly sounded out, and colleagues and rivals sensed that his words carried authority. An ardent Democrat, he soon engaged in politics, supporting Woodrow Wilson in 1916, and assiduously promoting the League of Nations. By this stage, he was rapidly advancing through the political hierarchy.

In 1917, when Long was thirty-six, Wilson rewarded him by appointing him assistant secretary of state, overseeing Asian affairs. Just as important, he befriended another rising star, the brash, charismatic assistant secretary of the navy, Franklin Roosevelt. Roosevelt would return to New York to run for governor, and in 1920 the dour but ambitious Long left the State Department to run for the senate in Missouri. Long was decisively trounced in an election that was an overwhelming Republican triumph. Undaunted, he ran again two years later, but once more lost. The postmortems indicated that as a politician, Long had a built-in tension that he could never easily reconcile. Socially he could be warm and cordial, even charming; his friends good-naturedly called him "Breck." Professionally, he was incorruptible, able, and austere. However, he had an abiding dislike of the give-and-take of politics, a fatal weakness in any politician.

For the next eleven years he practiced law, but like a dog returning to his bone, in 1932 he couldn't resist the tug of politics once more. He threw his weight behind Roosevelt and gave handsomely to Roosevelt's presidential campaign, for which he was rewarded with the ambassadorship to Italy, a plum assignment. Forging friendships with all the right people, he had clearly learned how to navigate in the tumultuous 1930s.

But Long's tenure, then and later, was marked by controversy. When Benito Mussolini marched into Ethiopia in 1935, Long, mesmerized by Mussolini, advised against retaliatory restrictions of oil shipments to Italy. Critics whispered that Long was shamelessly pro-Mussolini. This may have been an overstatement, but the words stung. After three years, he resigned his ambassadorship, although he remained ensconced in Roosevelt's administration. In 1938, Long became a delegate of a State Department mission to Brazil, Argentina, and Uruguay. Suddenly, his rise was meteoric. A year later, he landed in the State Department, and a year after that he became one of the most influential assistant secretaries of state, responsible for, among other things, overseeing immigration and the all-critical Visa Division. Under his tutelage, much of the State Department soon mirrored not only his strengths but his weaknesses as well.

Long's unwavering belief was that all refugees were potential spies and constituted a menace to U.S. national security. To be sure, the Germans had assiduously sought to infiltrate spies into potential refugee populations, and in this regard Roosevelt himself shared Long's fear. But Long's diary entries paint a much more revealing picture, in which he seems less a scion of the establishment and more a relic from the Know-Nothing South of the 1840s. In slur after slur, he made it clear that he thought ill of virtually anyone who didn't have his social values or come from his social class; didn't think much of liberals; disliked Catholics, New Yorkers, and eastern Europeans; and despised Jews most of all. To run afoul of his anti-immigration hysteria often came with a cost. He even interpreted the desire to allow British refugee children into the United States as "an enormous psychosis" on the part of the American people.

For all his zealotry and nativist sentiments, it was Long who bordered on being paranoid, seeing himself as under assault from "extreme radicals," "Jewish professional agitators," and "refugee enthusiasts." Here, perhaps he was right. But despite the fact that many of his subordinates were equally indifferent to the plight of the refugees in Europe, he believed that many of his colleagues were waging a campaign against him. Deep within him lurked a dark vein of stubbornness. This flaw, and it was a flaw, meant that once he made up his mind and adopted a position, he treated virtually any attempt to argue him out of it as an assault on his integrity.

Yet even when refugee policy—in particular, whether to admit Jews or not—had become a costly war of attrition in government circles, Long proved himself to be an effective bureaucratic infighter. In the summer of 1940, he had successfully upended Roosevelt's 1938 policy softening the most restrictive immigration policies, which were a legacy of the worst months of the Great Depression. This reversal was just a start. Within a year, convinced Germany was loading the United States with Gestapo agents, he mounted a double-pronged assault against opening the door to immigrants, tightening visa controls and cutting the number of refugee admissions by 50 percent. He said, "I believe that nobody, anywhere has a right to enter the United States." The next year, the number was reduced once more, to one fourth of the original quotas. As it happened, Long was as inventive as he was dogged. His department unabashedly devised an insidious regulation known as the "relatives rule," which subjected all would-be immigrants to an almost impossibly strict review by the State Department's so-called Interdepartmental Committee. Purportedly a means of expediting decisions, the committee in fact operated in the strictest secrecy and became a means for inaction.

In most cases visas were not granted, but the department seldom refused applications outright—that would only have produced noisy protests. Rather, it set up a line of obstacles that stretched from Washington to Lisbon to Shanghai and that simply wore out the persistence of the fleeing refugees. One outraged American publication wrote, "Owing to the department's inertia and its obstructionist tactics only a handful [of refugees] have been saved. The record of delays, misleading reports, promises, more delays, refusals of consuls to act on instructions presumably sent from Washington—all this is bitter knowledge among persons engaged in the business of trying to salvage political émigrés."

Soon, the flow of refugees was reduced to a mere trickle—this at a time when Jews were being murdered first in the hundreds, then in the thousands, then in the hundreds of thousands, and then in the millions.

Applicants from Germany, the Soviet Union, and the Italian territories—those who most needed to find a safe haven—were required to surmount impossibly complex regulations. Most never did, no matter how needy or desperate they were. As time went on, Long's campaign was increasingly relentless—and devious, too, as when he testified to the House, "The historic attitude of the United States as a haven for the oppressed has not changed. The Department of State has kept the door open." Then came his most influential and notorious policy, in the form of a secret intradepartmental memo, which he circulated in June 1940, first addressed to James Dunn and Adolf Berle Jr. "We can," Long brazenly wrote, "delay and effectively stop for a temporary period of indefinite length the number of immigrants into the United States. We could do this by simply advising our consuls to put every obstacle in the way and to require additional evidence and to resort to various administrative devices which would postpone and postpone and postpone the granting of the visas." The refugees despaired, and for good reason. Only 10 percent of the quota for immigrants from Germany and Italy was filled, and 200,000 people were shut out. Critics pointed out that by his actions, Long was indirectly assisting the Nazis, but faced with these barbs Long simply shrugged his shoulders and pressed forward.

How wide was the support for Long's policies in the government itself? True, Long was thin-skinned, humorless, and narrow-minded, but he was never personally interested in encomiums. As it happened, his stridency won him some supporters, but it alienated others. One Treasury Department official, Randolph Paul, would later describe Long and his colleagues as an American "underground movement . . . to let the Jews be killed," while Josiah DuBois Jr. would bristle at the mere mention of Long, outright calling him anti-Semitic. The president's own Advisory Committee on refugees was so "wrought up about" Long that its chairman insisted on meeting with Roosevelt to vent his grievances. And Eleanor herself sent a heated memo to the president, saying, "I am thinking about these poor people who may die at any time and who are asking only to come here on transit visas and I do hope you can get this cleared up quickly." A rattled Roosevelt sent a note to his undersecretary of state, Sumner Welles: "Please tell me about this," he inquired. "There does seem to be a mixup."

There wasn't, but that didn't matter. It might seem that Long's actions would threaten to swamp the State Department in a tide of indignation, but Long enjoyed the support of the most important constituency of all: Roosevelt himself. To mollify the critics, and on Welles's recommendation, the president met with Long on October 3, 1940, at noontime; it was a lengthy meeting for the president, a half hour. Long, never a man of great patience, seemingly lost what little he had. He was unrepentant. But he was suave enough not to appear deaf to the cries of victims in Europe. He smoothly shifted the focus of the discussion and persuaded the president that countless refugees were in fact nefarious German agents seeking to infiltrate the shores of America. In any case, he also painted a fanciful picture of a sympathetic, yet careful procedure in the State Department, one that operated efficiently to rescue the deserving while weeding out the dangerous. However unimaginative Long was, his gift for manipulating the political process can hardly be exaggerated. By the end of his presentation, he had received the president's unqualified approval. Perhaps at this stage the president believed the refugee issue was manageable. It wasn't, because Hitler wasn't. But with his fears stoked, the president was unwilling to compromise the war effort.

That day Long proudly noted in his diary—his bureaucratic syntax notwithstanding—that Roosevelt was "wholeheartedly in support of the policy which would resolve in favor of the United States any doubts about admissibility of any individual."

~

A WEEK LATER ROOSEVELT MET with James G. McDonald, the chairman of the President's Advisory Committee on Political Refugees. If Long was no pushover, neither was McDonald. A man of great principle, he had been the high commissioner for refugees for the League of Nations in the 1930s, and he had no great love for double-talking bureaucrats or foot-dragging heads of state. In 1935 he had resigned his post in the League because of the organization's reluctance to help Jews in Nazi Germany. He was equally impatient with Long, whom he regarded as an anti-Semite. Yet McDonald had great admiration for Roosevelt and saw the president as an untiring advocate for refugees. Roosevelt had no illusions about what McDonald wanted. He knew that McDonald's committee, though it lacked political clout in the government, had painstakingly sifted through lists of endangered refugees, examined affidavits and records submitted by friends of endangered antifascists, and submitted selected names to the State Department for action.

But on this day, McDonald got nowhere. He thought he would have the president's undivided attention. He didn't. Instead, Roosevelt sought to defuse the situation by playing the role of an amiable raconteur. He simply recounted one story after another, each having nothing to do with why he and McDonald were meeting. Unable to get a word in, McDonald finally dispensed with tact and started to openly criticize Long, only to have the president frostily snap at him. Don't, Roosevelt bristled, "pull any sob stuff."

If Roosevelt was a cautious humanitarian, Long was a consummate realist, coldhearted where Roosevelt was warm-blooded, callous where Roosevelt was spirited. Yet theirs was a relationship every bit as significant as Dwight D. Eisenhower and George Marshall's, Sumner Welles and Cordell Hull's, or Harry Hopkins and Roosevelt's. Buoyed by his support from the president, Long happily sparred with James McDonald; jousted with Henry Morgenthau, secretary of the treasury; and collided with Joseph Buttinger, the refugees' advocate. Nor did he shrink from crossing words with Eleanor Roosevelt herself. His clash with Eleanor began on a warm August day in 1940 when a small Portuguese liner, the

SS *Quanza*, pulled into New York harbor. It had 317 passengers, and it was far from its usual South African run. It was instead evacuating eighty-three war refugees from occupied France.

Here was the *St. Louis* redux, on a smaller scale—another opportunity for America to save lives. The passengers were a broad array, including "Negro seamen," American ambulance drivers, members of the eminent Rothschild family, the editor of *Paris Soir*, a Japanese journalist, a seventeen-year-old Czech figure skater, a Parisian opera star, and a French movie star as well as the refugees.

Predictably, every passenger holding an American visa was allowed to disembark. As for the refugees? Grouped together and scared, they begged to be allowed in, but were flatly told by officials: "Impossible." What was needed? All the proper papers, which, given the bureaucratic labyrinth that had been established by the State Department, were virtually impossible to obtain. Having little choice, the *Quanza*'s captain decided to sail on to Mexico rather than return to Europe, which was, as one refugee said, "a German concentration camp." But when they arrived at Veracruz, the Mexican authorities were no more willing to accept the refugees than the Americans had been.

By now, the passengers were in "complete despair." Shrewdly, the *Quanza*'s captain sailed back to the United States, docking at Norfolk, Virginia, where ostensibly the ship would be loaded with coal to prepare for the voyage home. This gave refugee organizations precious time to plead for help. They did, appealing directly to Eleanor Roosevelt. She in turn personally confronted the president, and asked him to do something. Something, but what? Roosevelt quickly dispatched an envoy, Patrick Malin, to assess the situation. Working in the name of the President's Advisory Committee on Political Refugees, Malin hurried to Norfolk. He collected the documents of everyone aboard, and in the end certified that anyone without documents was a political refugee, entitled to stay in America. The passengers were jubilant. "Mrs. Roosevelt saved my life," one refugee proclaimed. Others nodded their heads in agreement.

This was a rare political victory over Breckinridge Long, but a short-lived one. "It was a violation of the Law," he insisted in his diary. "I would not give my consent. . . . I would have no responsibility for it." Afterward, Long redoubled his efforts, piling up one obstacle after another to keep refugees from getting visas. It was, Joseph Buttinger told Eleanor Roosevelt, a "ghastly situation." Eleanor agreed, and once again sent a personal note to the president to do more. "FDR," she scrawled, "can't something be done?" This time Roosevelt ignored her. Yet as reports of Long's obstructionism piled up, as lines of desperate Jews lengthened at consulates in western Europe, as the news reports of Nazi oppression mounted, Eleanor thought that surely the issue couldn't have been simpler. She all but exploded, telling the president: "Franklin, you *know* he's a fascist!"

The president was curt in responding. "I told you, Eleanor," he said crossly, cutting her off. "You *must* not say that."

"But he is!" she shot back.

How serious was the matter? Eleanor later told her son that her inability to admit more refugees was the "deepest regret" of her life.

THROUGHOUT THE STATE DEPARTMENT, at the highest levels, officials were either uninterested or uninformed or unconcerned. As a consequence, Long's attitude affected far more than just visa policy: it helped define the government's entire response to the European Jewish crisis. So long as he had his way, the United States would remain a timorous bystander.

For Roosevelt, the pressure from without—to do something, to help the Jews, to streamline procedures—was overpowered by the pressure from within: a government apparatus tugging at him to address national security first, and humanitarian matters only as a distant second. Baffled observers wondered why Roosevelt's conscience, his very essence, did not compel him to shoulder his way into action. Where at least was the anger? Where was the Churchillian eloquence that, for example, railed against the "villainy of the Nazi outrage"? Publicly, the refugees' advocates put on a brave face. But behind closed doors they were discouraged.

There were a few notable public dissenters. *The Nation* editorialized, "The record is one which must sicken any person of ordinarily humane instincts." It continued: "It is as if we were to examine laboriously the *curricula vitae* of flood victims clinging to a piece of floating wreckage and finally to decide that, no matter what their virtues, all but a few had better be allowed to drown." But such voices were few and far between.

In the face of all this, it is little wonder that as late as January 1943, 78 percent of respondents in one poll thought it would be a "bad idea" to let in more immigrants *after* the war; or that in August 1940, 15 percent of respondents had considered Jews "a menace to America." Increasingly desperate Jews, squeezed between the Nazis' deceptiveness and the U.S. government's apathy, had to find another route for help.

BUT BY THE END of 1940, in addition to the refugees' plight there was desperation of another form. England, the only leading nation now at war with Hitler, was rapidly depleting its munitions and other matériel. Running out of options, Churchill pleaded for immediate help. But Roosevelt, as with the refugees, was inclined to caution. In May 1940, as Hitler's forces marched westward across Europe, the president refused Churchill's urgent request for destroyers. There was nothing America could give that would be of greater help to England. Roosevelt, however, was unwilling to take this step.

Nevertheless, the president did stand up to his own military chiefs so that America could supply England with airplanes; 22,000 thirty-caliber machine guns; 25,000 automatic rifles; nine hundred 75-millimeter howitzers; 58,000 antiaircraft weapons; 500,000 Enfield rifles (left over from World War I); and 130 million rounds of ammunition. But for the time being, that was as far as Roosevelt was willing to go. Thus, as German planes and troops beat France into submission, there were growing whispered questions about him. These questions went to the heart of his response to the Nazi threat. Why, interventionists wondered, was this eloquent liberal, this enemy of totalitarianism, standing passively by, first during the horror of the Munich agreement and now during the agonizing fall of France? Why was this graduate of Groton and son of Harvard, who fought relentlessly for the impoverished at home, now coldly ignoring the plight of Hitler's victims cramming American consulates abroad? Why, it was asked in London, was there a hiatus in action at the White House—and where was the bold improvisation for which Roosevelt was so famous? Finally, why was America all but following a policy of "America first"?

Moreover, did Roosevelt not see that his pursuit of political popularity at home had exacted a heavy toll—that he was sending a signal to Hitler that America was sitting this one out?

In truth, Roosevelt's was a double game. At the same time as he was trying to rearm England, he was continuing to insist to the American public that the United States would not fight. But in pandering to the Americans who wanted to stay out of the war, the president was unable to turn the country around on the question of involvement. That, however, was about to change.

Caught at a crossroads, with Paris about to fall, the French government fleeing, and Mussolini's Italy declaring war and attacking at the Côte d'Azur, the president argued that, in effect, America would at least enter the war by proxy. Speaking at a commencement in Charlottesville, Virginia, he declared in stirring words that it was a "delusion" for the United States to contemplate existing as "a lone Island in a world dominated by the philosophy of force." He repeatedly emphasized America's responsibility to arm and supply those nations now firmly committed to standing against Germany, although he mentioned no names. "We will," Roosevelt said, "extend to the opponents of force the material resources of this nation; and at the same time, we will harness and speed up the use of those resources in order that we ourselves may have equipment and training equal to the task." After pausing for emphasis, he concluded, "Full speed ahead!"

In Britain, a resolute Churchill huddled by the radio, taking in every one of the president's words. On hearing "Full speed ahead!" the prime minister all but jumped for joy. If America wasn't going to join the fight, then at least it would help Britain stay in the fight. "We all listened to you last night," a grateful Churchill wrote to Roosevelt, "and were fortified by the grand scope of your declaration. Your statement that the material aid of the United States will be given to the allies in their struggle is a strong encouragement in a dark but not unhopeful hour." Now, there was no turning back. America was headed toward a war footing, even if the president protested otherwise. The Roosevelt administration moved cautiously at first, then more decisively, calling for compulsory military training, the draft, the creation of a million-man army, and the use of the U.S. Navy to deliver supplies to Britain. To be sure, there were detractors. One isolationist, Senator Burton Wheeler, whose choice of words would later prove unfortunate, railed against America's getting involved in the "Holocaust of Europe's wars," while William Borah, the Senate's longest-serving member, delivered a scathing attack against Roosevelt, insisting that America would now be "taking sides," and that this would be "the first step to active intervention." And the aviator Charles Lindbergh, the nation's most prominent isolationist, continued to be a spokesman for antiwar fervor.

Roosevelt sat back and waited, believing that the rapidly changing international situation would eventually mute the isolationists. By now, Austria, Czechoslovakia, and Poland had all but disappeared as states. France had fallen; the Low Countries were occupied. Norway, Denmark, and Finland lived under the swastika. And it was just a matter of time before Greece would be threatened and the Balkans overrun. Everywhere, it seemed, there were fields of danger. At home, public opinion still remained mixed, but antiwar sentiment was softening. In July 1940, a Gallup poll found that 61 percent of Americans felt the most important task was to stay out of the war, but 73 percent supported giving all possible assistance to England short of entering the conflict.

What would it take to get the nation into the war? Lacking Roosevelt's firm voice to steer it, the country stayed divided, and a great debate raged. There were those who wanted no part of the war whatsoever. There were those who were haters—hating the Jews, despising the British, or sympathizing with the Fascists. There were left-wing isolationists, who saw war as an unmitigated evil; and right-wing isolationists, who saw this war as a plaything of the dictatorial Roosevelt. There were mothers who simply couldn't bear the thought of their boys dying on far-off battlefields. And then there were those who wanted to fight the Nazis immediately.

There were still others, an increasing number, who supported Roosevelt's campaign pledges: help Britain, provide material aid, but stay out of the war.

The isolationist groups were the most vocal, particularly the America First Committee. It had a hefty membership of sixty thousand and was growing like "a house afire." Yet bit by bit, indignation over the Nazis' conquests deepened, and the ranks of isolationists in Congress thinned.

And after the evening of November 5, 1940, when Franklin Roosevelt was reelected president, America moved one step closer to war. As he had done in 1932 and 1936, a glowing Roosevelt, his necktie loosened and coat off, perched himself in the dining room of his boyhood home in Hyde Park and tabulated the voting returns. Elsewhere in the residence, family and friends nibbled on toast and forkfuls of scrambled eggs, while in the smoking room Teletype machines whirred, spitting out the figures. At midnight, while Luftwaffe bombers were attacking London, there was a loud whoop from the crowd waiting at Hyde Park, a band blared out songs of triumph, and ebullient Democrats paraded by torchlight across the lawn. Meanwhile, Roosevelt grandly puffed on a cigarette, waving his arms and grinning broadly. "We are facing difficult days in this country," he told the well-wishers. "But I think you will find me in the future just the same Franklin Roosevelt you've known a great many years." Through a combination of his own ambition and vanity and the urgency of the world war, Roosevelt had achieved something that had eluded all other presidents, including his cousin Theodore—a third term as president. On Election Day, the largest number of Americans ever went to the polls—50 million. Actually, Roosevelt won reelection by the smallest margin since Woodrow Wilson in 1916, but he still had enough of a mandate to come to the aid of a beleaguered Europe, if he so chose.

The question was: would he take it?

~

BACK IN WASHINGTON ROOSEVELT, as his train crawled into the capital, briefly basked in the adulation of his supporters. With his customary panache, the president doffed his old familiar campaign fedora to greet the roaring crowd. On the route from Union Station to the White House, children climbed on trees and boxes to get a better view as the presidential limousine rolled by. And hundreds of thousands of cheering spectators crowded Pennsylvania Avenue, waving little flags and chanting over and over again, "We want Roosevelt! We want Roosevelt!" until the president's car disappeared into the grounds of the executive mansion. Yet despite his reelection, the president seemed strangely inattentive, even a bit irritable. The strain of his third presidential campaign had taken a toll on him, and increasingly, the situation in Europe was doing the same. "The more I sleep," the president muttered one day, "the more I want to sleep."

However, sleep was a luxury he didn't have.

During the Battle of Britain, while the Germans were ruthlessly bombing their cities, the British were also losing merchant ships in frightful numbers. In just ten days in mid-July 1940, the Germans sank or damaged eleven British destroyers. Before November 3, the British would lose over 400,000 tons of shipping as a result of sinkings. Churchill was despondent. Three times in June he had urgently requested destroyers from the Americans, calling the situation a "matter of life and death." King George VI himself contacted Roosevelt to beg for aid "before it is too late." Yet Roosevelt fretted about political reaction from Congress. On July 21, 1940, Churchill again sent Roosevelt an impassioned request for fifty or sixty U.S. destroyers, to be provided "at once."

"Mr. President," he wrote, "with great respect I must tell you that in the long history of the world this is a thing to do *now.*"

Roosevelt wanted to help, and so did some prominent Americans who called themselves the Century Group. They waged a national campaign to provide political running room for Roosevelt to take action.

But Congress remained firmly resistant—Senator Claude Pepper, Roosevelt's ally, stonily informed the president that a bill allowing destroyers to be transferred to Britain "had no chance of passing." Eventually Attorney General Robert Jackson came up with the idea that Congress could be bypassed altogether. The president, Jackson argued, could provide the destroyers—in truth, they were old destroyers badly in need of refurbishing, and only half a dozen of them would be brought into action by the end of 1940—on his own authority by "trading them" for access to British bases in the Caribbean for ninety-nine years. Roosevelt agreed, and sent a wire about the breakthrough to Churchill, who also immediately agreed. Only then did the president inform Congress. Almost innocuously, he announced the deal from the sitting room of his private car on the presidential train, forty-five minutes from a dilapidated ordnance plant he had been inspecting in West Virginia. With a mischievous smile, his eyes rolling, he made the stunning announcement to a few reporters, declaring this to be "the most important action in the reinforcement of our national defense since the Louisiana purchase."

Immediately, there was an uproar. The *St. Louis Post Dispatch* denounced Roosevelt as "America's first dictator." Not to be outdone, the Republicans' presidential nominee of 1940, Wendell Willkie, called Roosevelt the most "arbitrary of any president in the history of the U.S." On the floor of the House, Representative Frances Bolton wondered aloud if Roosevelt could do this without consulting Congress adding, "God alone knows what he will do" when America's boys were drafted.

Nevertheless, the arrangement for the bases was at best a stopgap. Although Hitler had shelved his planned invasion of Britain—Operation Sea Lion—for the time being, the Nazis' onslaught was continuing. By December, cables from Whitehall to the White House poured in through special coding machines, detailing the withering German attacks. Landmarks, factories, houses, corner pubs, and the House of Commons were damaged or obliterated. And there was an equally devastating problem: Britain was now running out of money. Germany could boost its war effort by plundering the industrial powers it had conquered—France,

Belgium, the Netherlands, and Czechoslovakia—and could draw slave labor from Poland. But if Britain suffered economic strangulation, it could be defeated within the year.

Roosevelt's cabinet met hurriedly on December 3 and struggled with the question of how to help a beleaguered Britain. The cabinet members glumly concluded that within thirty days a financially strapped England would deplete its gold and dollar reserves, and be unable to pay for much-needed supplies. American army chiefs agreed that the United States' defense production facilities could be boosted, but financing remained a question, as did transferring military assets to Britain. Henry Stimson, the secretary of war, argued that the time for temporizing was over, and that the whole matter should be presented to Congress. His colleagues agreed. What they couldn't agree on was how Roosevelt would react. Would he be willing to take this to Capitol Hill? Or would that only give ammunition to the isolationist barons in the legislature?

In England, Churchill labored for weeks on another impassioned letter to the president, one that the prime minister described as among the "most important" of his life. He began with a dazzling overview of the strategic equation. On its own, he argued, Britain would be unable to match the German armies massed across Europe. Nevertheless, he observed that "the decision for 1941 lies upon the seas." However, confirming what Roosevelt's cabinet already knew, he said that the moment fast "approaches when we shall no longer be able to pay cash for shipping and supplies." Churchill hastened to add that England could withstand "the shattering of our dwellings" and "the slaughter of our civilian population by indiscriminate air attacks." But what it could not withstand was a "less sudden and less spectacular but equally deadly danger"—the inability to feed its people and import the munitions that it needed. He added a hopeful note: "You may be assured that we shall prove ourselves ready to suffer and sacrifice to the utmost for the Cause." And he put the matter to the president squarely: "If, as I believe, you are convinced, Mr. President, that the defeat of the Nazi and fascist tyranny is a matter of high consequence to the people of the United States . . .

you will regard this letter not as an appeal for aid, but as a statement of the minimum action necessary to achieve our common purpose."

The letter was sent across the Atlantic as Roosevelt was in the Caribbean on a ten-day cruise aboard the USS *Tuscaloosa.* He knew that further evasion in public and further manipulation in private would no longer suffice, and he was well aware that the enemy was watching him closely, taking his measure. He was also keenly aware that he had a momentous decision to make. Once and for all, he needed to show the world—Axis powers and friends alike—what he stood for. Churchill's letter would crystallize his course of action.

On board the *Tuscaloosa*, the president worked only a couple of hours a day. Otherwise, he spent time with colonial officials, played poker, fished, sunned himself while reading detective stories, napped after lunch, and relaxed by watching movies; he saw Betty Grable in *Tin Pan Alley* and Gary Cooper in *Northwest Mounted Police.* To be sure, each day background papers and briefing documents were brought to him by navy seaplanes, but to those who watched him, it appeared that he simply set them aside. By all accounts the weary president was, in Harry Hopkins's words, "refueling" himself.

But on receiving Churchill's letter, Roosevelt had grave misgivings. He ceased being social: for two straight days, he shut himself off and sat alone in his deck chair, brooding "silently," reading and rereading the letter, wondering how the United States could help Britain. He could send arms, planes, and guns to Britain as a gift, but that would never be accepted by the American people. He could lend money to Britain, but that idea wouldn't be accepted either. He could ask for repeal of the Neutrality Act, but for him, that was still politically a nonstarter. At no point did he ask for his cabinet's advice. Nor did he request any studies by his staff. Nor did he pick up the telephone and sound out his influential allies in the Senate—or for that matter, consult with his good friend, his eyes and ears, the tough-talking, wily Harry Hopkins. It seemed the only advice that he took on the *Tuscaloosa* came from Ernest Hemingway, who sent word to him about how to catch big fish using a pork rind. (When the president tried Hemingway's method, he failed.)

Finally, one evening Roosevelt had an epiphany regarding the question of Britain's troubled finances. For some time he had been mulling over how to lease cargo ships to Britain for the balance of the war. If the United States could do this for ships, why not for planes or guns or other weaponry? If Hitler was truly to be stopped, he reasoned, the United States should simply lend Britain whatever it required, and at some undefined point in the distant future, after the war had ceased, the English would return whatever they had borrowed, or repay not in dollars but in kind. Inspired by the "fire hose" analogy that he first used in 1916, Roosevelt believed he had found his solution—famously dubbed Lend-Lease. It was unclear whether the program was even legal, but as Hopkins noted, "there wasn't a doubt in his mind that he'd find a way to do it." It proved to be one of the boldest strokes in Roosevelt's long, storied career, and the ensuing couple of weeks would constitute one of the most critical periods in his presidency. Henry Morgenthau, his secretary of the treasury, went so far as to call it Roosevelt's "greatest effort of all his years in office." Actually, the approach was pure fiction—it was unrealistic to suppose that after the war the British would return a fleet of weathered, rusty vessels or tens of thousands of battered tanks and dirt-smudged guns. In truth, the plan constituted an outright gift. But politically, the Lend-Lease was a brilliant concept, and militarily, even more so.

And it was vintage Roosevelt, another example of how he could boldly circumvent his entire bureaucracy, and Congress for that matter, when he set his mind to it.

~

WHEN HE RETURNED TO the White House on December 16, the president convened numerous meetings with his restless aides. Here was Roosevelt at his best—focused, thinking big, deft. After ironing out the details, he called reporters into his office for a press conference, claiming that there wasn't any "particular news." But of course there was. He dismissed any talk about sending arms, guns, and planes to Britain as a gift. No, he insisted, there was a far better way. Strictly from the

American point of view, he said, the United States should ramp up its production facilities and only then "either lease or sell the materials, subject to mortgage" to the British.

In a deceptively playful tone he continued, "Now what I am trying to do is to eliminate the dollar sign. That is something brand-new in the thoughts of practically everybody in this room—get rid of the silly, foolish old dollar sign." Reporters began shaking their heads. What on earth was the president talking about? Roosevelt told them. "Well, let me give you an illustration: suppose my neighbor's home catches on fire, and I have a length of garden hose four or five hundred feet away. If he can take my garden hose and connect it up with his hydrant, I may help him to put out his fire. Now what do I do? I don't say before that operation, 'Neighbor, my garden hose cost me $15; you have to pay me $15 for it.' . . . I don't want $15—I want my garden hose back after the fire is over. All right. If it goes through the fire all right, intact, without any damage to it, he gives it back to me and thanks me very much for the use of it."

In other words, he intimated, America's arsenal and war matériel were no good if they were simply lying in storage; they would be of far greater use on the battlefield in the hands of the fighting British. After the war America would then be repaid "leaving out the dollar mark and substituting for it a gentleman's obligation in kind." The president smiled. "I think you all get it."

Not entirely. But as Roosevelt laid out his plan, it was quite clear that the reporters were the orchestra and he was their conductor. The reporters peppered him with questions. Did this mean America was inching toward getting into the war? Roosevelt shook his head. No. Did this mean, as Congress would later ask, that the U.S. Navy would have to help in convoying munitions? No again. How about a congressional nod—would he need to seek it? Yes, he would. So adroit was Roosevelt that the press failed to ask him the single most important question: what did "in-kind" repayment actually mean, and wasn't this really an outright gift?

Reaction abroad was striking. Churchill called Lend-Lease "the most unsordid act in history," and a Nazi spokesman ridiculed Roosevelt's policy of "pinpricks, . . . insults, and moral aggression."

Now, for Roosevelt, it was time to sell the Lend-Lease program to the nation, in one of the most significant fireside chats of his presidency. On Sunday, December 29, at 6:40 p.m. he visited the White House physician's office, as he did before many major speeches, for treatment to clear his sinuses and keep his vocal cords moist. He may even have had a quarter-solution cocaine wash, which was legal at the time, flushed through his nose. Then Arthur Prettyman wheeled the president into the oval Diplomatic Reception Room, where technicians had finished setting up the tangle of wires and microphones for Roosevelt's address to the nation. He was maneuvered behind a simple wooden desk bearing only microphones emblazoned NBC, CBS, and MBS. Clustered nearby was a small, transfixed group: his most important cabinet members, Secretary of State Cordell Hull, Secretary of War Henry Stimson, and Secretary of the Treasury Henry Morgenthau; his closest family members, Eleanor Roosevelt and his mother, Sara; and a key ally from the Senate, the shrewd, hard-bargaining majority leader, Alben Barkley.

The assembled listeners could see that Roosevelt's tan was gone and there were circles of fatigue under his eyes, but he was relaxed and his voice as musical and robust as always. At nine o'clock, when he started to speak, people poured out of diners and movie theaters to hear him. They crowded around radios in their living rooms and turned up the volume. The rare few who owned television sets turned them on. For the speech, some 70 percent of Americans hung on every word.

"This is not a fireside chat on the war," Roosevelt told the nation. Rather, "it is a talk on national security; because the nub of the whole purpose of your president is to keep you now, and your children later, and your grandchildren much later, out of a last-ditch war for the preservation of American independence." He paused for emphasis. "Never before since Jamestown and Plymouth Rock has our American civilization been in such danger as now. . . . The Nazi masters of Germany have made it clear that they intend not only to dominate all life and thought in their own country, but also to enslave the whole of Europe, and then to use the resources of Europe to dominate the rest of the world."

The president was unsparing in his assessment of Nazi aggression and of those, at home and abroad, who sought to justify it. "The experience of the past two years has proven beyond doubt that no nation can appease the Nazis. No man can tame a tiger into a kitten by stroking it. There can be no appeasement with ruthlessness." He derided those who insisted that the United States should throw its influence "into the scale of a dictated peace," "a negotiated peace," with a "gang of outlaws." This would only, he said, "lead Americans to pay tribute to save your own skins." America must not, he now preached, "acquiesce" in Europe's defeat, "submit tamely" to an Axis victory, or "wait our turn" to be the target of an attack later on. This would only embolden Germany and the Axis powers in their unremitting drive to subjugate the world, the outcome of which would be "all of us and all the Americas . . . living at the point of a gun."

Yet he remained sly. For those who believed this was a prelude to America's directly entering the war, he resoundingly dismissed such ideas as "deliberate untruths." Yes, he acknowledged, there was a profound "risk in any course we may take," but Americans had no choice but to abandon the notion of "business as usual." To drive this point home, he added, "We well know that we cannot escape danger, or the fear of danger, by crawling into bed and pulling the covers over our heads.

"Our national policy is not directed toward war," he continued. "Its sole purpose is to keep war away from our country." And then came one of the most memorable phrases of his presidency, or any presidency: "We must be the great Arsenal of Democracy! For us this is an emergency as serious as war itself." With great flair—this was a speech that had gone through seven drafts—Roosevelt continued. Americans must show "the same resolution, the same sense of urgency, the same spirit of patriotism and sacrifice as we would show were we at war." And for those who thought he displayed a callous indifference to Europe's suffering, he continued: "The history of recent years proves that the shootings and the chains and the concentration camps are not simply the transient tools but the very altars of modern dictatorships. They may talk of a 'new order' in the world, but what they have in mind is only a revival of the oldest and the worst tyranny." He ended with an equally eloquent injunction for the United States to undertake "the mightiest production effort" in its history. "I call for it in the name of this nation which we love and honor, in which we are privileged and proud to serve."

That same evening, the Nazis were firebombing London with the greatest fury since the outset of the war. The historic Old Bailey was struck and burned. So was Dr. Samuel Johnson's house off Fleet Street. Much of the old City was left a smoking ruin. Off Gresham and Basinghall streets, the restored timber roof of the ancient Guildhall, one of the administrative centers of London, was ablaze; the building dated back to 1411 and had survived the great fire of 1666 but now was little more than a charred shell. Although it was two o'clock in the morning and Nazi planes were perilously circling overhead, tens of thousands of Londoners turned on their radios and listened to Roosevelt. By the time he finished his fireside chat and was winding down by watching movies before going to bed, the White House was awash with telegrams—those supporting the speech outnumbered critical messages by a hundred to one.

With this speech, and at his subsequent inauguration, Roosevelt seemed to be on the pinnacle of his political prestige and reputation. His rating in the polls had soared, and in 1939 and 1940, Congress had passed virtually every national security measure that he had requested. He had thwarted his critics in the Democratic Party and outmaneuvered his adversaries in the Republican Party. He had boldly reshuffled his cabinet and changed vice presidents. He had won a third term as president. He had deepened his relationship with Winston Churchill. And as he prepared to shepherd the Lend-Lease bill through Congress, his ability to wield influence on the national scene was every bit as great as it had been during the euphoria that surrounded him in 1933. Having done much to legitimize the national tendency toward no military action and no foreign wars, he now, in 1941, sought to entangle the nation's military affairs with Britain's, and above all to defeat the isolationists.

Yet strangely, even then, not only did the nation still seem divided, but so did Roosevelt himself. On New Year's Eve 1940, Churchill wrote: "Remember, Mr. President, we do not know what you have in mind, or exactly what United States is going to do, and we are fighting for our lives."

READING THESE WORDS, ROOSEVELT knew he somehow had to reassure Churchill. On January 19, he handed a private communiqué to Wendell Willkie, whom he had defeated in the election and was now asking to serve as an emissary to England. The message was to be passed privately to Churchill. Scrawled on the paper was a verse from Henry Wadsworth Longfellow's "The Building of the Ship," which Roosevelt had jotted down from memory. In Britain, there was still snow on the ground when Churchill opened it and began to read.

Dear Churchill,

Wendell Willkie will give you this. He is truly helping to keep politics out over here.

I think this verse applies to your people as it does to us.

Sail on, O Ship of State!
Sail on, Thou Union, strong and great!
Humanity with all its fears,
With all the hopes of future years,
Is hanging breathless on thy fate!

As ever yours,
Franklin D. Roosevelt

As the New Year began, Roosevelt still had to secure the passage of Lend-Lease, now in the form of a congressional bill, HR 1776. It was once said about the British Parliament that it could do anything except change a man into a woman; the same could have been said about the powers granted by HR 1776. The bill gave the president sweeping authority to exchange or lease or lend any article to any government. At the same time, the administration presented this not as a measure that would inevitably drag the United States into hostilities, but as a necessary measure if the nation wanted to stay out of Europe's nightmare. Roosevelt's critics didn't believe him. "Never before has the United States," the fiery Senator Burton Wheeler blustered over the radio, "given to one man the power to strip this nation of its defenses." The influential *Chicago Tribune* agreed: "This is a bill for the destruction of the American Republic. It is a brief for an unlimited dictatorship with power over the possessions and lives of the American people." However, it was Charles Lindbergh who provided the most prominent voice for the isolationists. Handsome, trim, charismatic, a popular hero who had bravely flown the Atlantic and held people the world over in his spell, he called on the United States to seek a negotiated peace, not pass a bill that would prolong the bloodshed on both sides of the Atlantic: "We are strong enough in this nation and in this hemisphere to maintain our own way of life regardless of . . . the other side."

As 1941 opened, the America First campaign was persistent; yet so was the interventionist Committee to Defend America. Both sides distributed bright little buttons, colored posters, and of course pamphlets. Both sides marched on Washington carrying their broadsides. Both sides testified before Congress and took to the radiowaves.

In the end, the isolationists were no match for the president. After he applied all his influence, the Lend-Lease bill passed both houses by stunning majorities. As early as March, congressional opposition buckled. The public was with the president.

But when Churchill called Lend-Lease "Hitler's death warrant," Hitler snickered.

And then he prepared for his next move.

~

DESPITE HAVING WEATHERED THE Battle of Britain, many in England continued to fear a cataclysmic Nazi assault across the Channel. And on the European Continent, the people of the Balkans also lived in terror of being seized in the Nazi fist coming their way. Indeed, if one looked at the map, it seemed just a matter of time before Hitler would grab Gibraltar or isolated Malta and then race across northern Africa and the Near East. Spain was under increasing pressure, and so was Greece. The Nazis continued to sink British and American vessels in the Atlantic at a terrifying pace—ships were being lost to German U-boats three times faster than American shipyards could replace them. Portugal and Turkey were threatening to join the Axis. Even Vichy France was being drawn more tightly into the Nazi orbit. It was as though Hitler were gleefully pushing rooks and bishops around a chessboard, while the Allies clung desperately to a handful of pawns. Step by step, Hitler had outflanked and suffocated his isolated adversaries. Step by step, he continued to spread the swastika from one nation to the next.

On April 6, 1941, Hitler struck again, ordering a lightning assault on Yugoslavia and Greece. Despairing and confused, the two nations were nonetheless defiant. As the sun climbed into the sky over the Yugoslav capital, Belgrade, Hitler told his army that the "hour is come," and long columns of tanks and motorized troops rolled through the streets. The Luftwaffe strafed the defenseless capital while German ground forces took Skopje, and then they set their sights on the undefended Monastir Gap, the gateway to Greece. From his pillbox, one defiant Greek general boasted, "We will hold them with our teeth," but teeth, or guns, or courage for that matter, were hardly adequate. Fourteen German divisions quickly massed against the defenders. The western world, including the United States, could not help admiring the courage of the Greeks, which recalled that of the ancient Greek city-states. But the Greeks were outmatched and outgunned as waves of German forces kept coming. In distress, the Greek cabinet fled to Cairo. For their part, British army units mounted a stiff defense, but to little avail. Soon they and the Greek units alike were retreating south along one-lane mountain roads choked with smoking vehicles and mud. On April 17, 1941, Yugoslavia surrendered. In under a week, so did Greece. In a telling omen, the Germans discovered a scrawl in chalk on one building, "After Thermopylae, the three hundred were killed." Actually, the casualties here were, of course, much worse; 17,000 people lay dead and the Germans took 300,000 Yugoslav prisoners and 270,000 Greeks. Meanwhile, Yugoslavia, where partisans were strung up on lampposts, was carved into pieces; portions were handed over to Germany's allies, Hungary, Italy, and Bulgaria, while client regimes were formed in Serbia and Croatia.

There seemed to be no end to Hitler's cruel appetite. Next came a German blitzkrieg from the air against Crete: 16,000 paratroopers and camouflaged mountain soldiers and 1,200 planes swooped down on the island's dumbstruck defense forces. It was a stunning measure, the first full air assault in modern military history. The Greek forces on the island and their British allies tenaciously fought back. They hit the Germans with whatever they could—hundreds of Germans were killed in the air and on land—but they too were ultimately outnumbered and overwhelmed. By the end of the month, Crete belonged to the Nazis. Having now conquered the eastern Mediterranean, Hitler was expected to set his sights on the oil-rich Middle East. And as Churchill informed Roosevelt, the loss of Egypt and the Middle East would entail incalculable risks.

In this situation, Roosevelt countered the Nazis as best he could. For the moment, America's military was still weak, its reach still limited. On May 3, Churchill, fretful after having witnessed defeat after defeat, directly asked Roosevelt to intervene—Churchill wanted the United States to join the war as a "belligerent power." Roosevelt only counseled patience and deflected the request. Instead, he once again sought to reassure the prime minister that the United States was trying to do everything "that we possibly can" to help Great Britain. On May 10, the same evening that the president was composing this reply, five hundred German bombers inflicted their worst damage to date, destroying huge tracts of London including the symbol of British democracy itself: the House of Commons; even the venerated statue of Richard the

Lionhearted was reduced to ruins. While the wreckage was still smoking, Churchill, his head sunk in despair, waded into the rubble and wept.

Meanwhile, the president pushed and prodded, employing both exhortation and threats. But in Berlin, Hitler and the Nazis were unmoved. To the Führer, Roosevelt was a demented cripple, lacking the guts to lead the American people into war and the stomach to endure mass casualties. Whatever threats and speeches the president may have been making, they rang hollow. When Roosevelt issued a "proclamation of unlimited national emergency" at the end of May 1941, Hitler dismissed it as bluster. Hitler could read a map as well as anyone, and the map showed how the world's most powerful democracy, which was calling on smaller nations to resist being swallowed up by the mighty German armies, was itself protected by the buffer of the Atlantic Ocean. Hitler as well as his translators could listen, and they all knew about American isolationism. And they knew that the American president had not asked for repeal of the Neutrality Act, that he had not requested heightened war authority, and that he continued to insist that the war be won "by keeping the existence of the main defense of the democracies going—and, that is England." Finally, Hitler knew that America had simply watched as the Germans infiltrated Bulgaria and crashed across Yugoslavia and Greece.

In truth, Roosevelt was intending to prepare public opinion inch by inch for eventual hostilities. He was preparing to quietly meet with Churchill on two battleships off the coast of Newfoundland and was endorsing secret joint conversations between the American and British military staff.

But absent decisive action, the Führer remained emboldened and unintimidated.

MEMBERS OF ROOSEVELT'S ADMINISTRATION also doubted the president. Roosevelt's strategy, they thought, was one of neither war nor peace. And some continued to wonder if Britain could survive the unremitting German onslaught. "It has been as if living in a nightmare,"

Averell Harriman wrote to Harry Hopkins, "with some calamity hanging constantly over one's head." Behind the president's back, his most senior lieutenants schemed to push Roosevelt into doing more. Henry Stimson, the secretary of war, sat down with the president and insisted that he show more moral leadership, take more firm action, put more resolve behind his words. To Stimson, the president seemed "tangled up." And Henry Morgenthau trenchantly observed, "The president is loath to get into this war. He would rather follow public opinion than lead it." Roosevelt himself confessed to his cabinet that he was "not willing to fire the first shot." And, having repeatedly said America would stay out of the war, he also admitted, "I am waiting to be pushed into the situation."

Until an actual push came, Roosevelt would remain noncommittal. But for the time being, Hitler was unwilling to take the bait; Nazi ships even refrained from overly provocative acts against the Americans in the Atlantic.

And for Roosevelt, remaining noncommittal meant remaining noncommittal to everyone—the English, the Mediterranean nations, soon the Soviet Union, and of course, the embattled Jews of Europe.

8

Mills of the Gods

IN THE SPRING OF 1941, while Roosevelt was searching for a strategic path, Adolf Hitler found one. Hitler, a product of boiling rage, of recklessness and raw vision, refused to let the Nazi armies stand still before the German conquest was total. Hunched over his desk in the Chancellery, he had nearly absolute power. Between bedtime and breakfast, he could, by arching an eyebrow or waving a hand, alter the fate of millions of people, unseat ancient monarchies or overthrow heads of state, or leave a countryside scorched and cities in flames. On a whim, he could allow a country to live—or call for a whole race to be killed. He had instincts of a tyrant. He was also convinced that he and he alone had the instincts of a statesman, and the tactical sense of an unconquerable general. He cowed everyone around him—his increasingly narrow inner circle, Göring, Goebbels, and Himmler, who were his sycophants; his ally, Mussolini, who was indulged but little more than an afterthought: and the figureheads

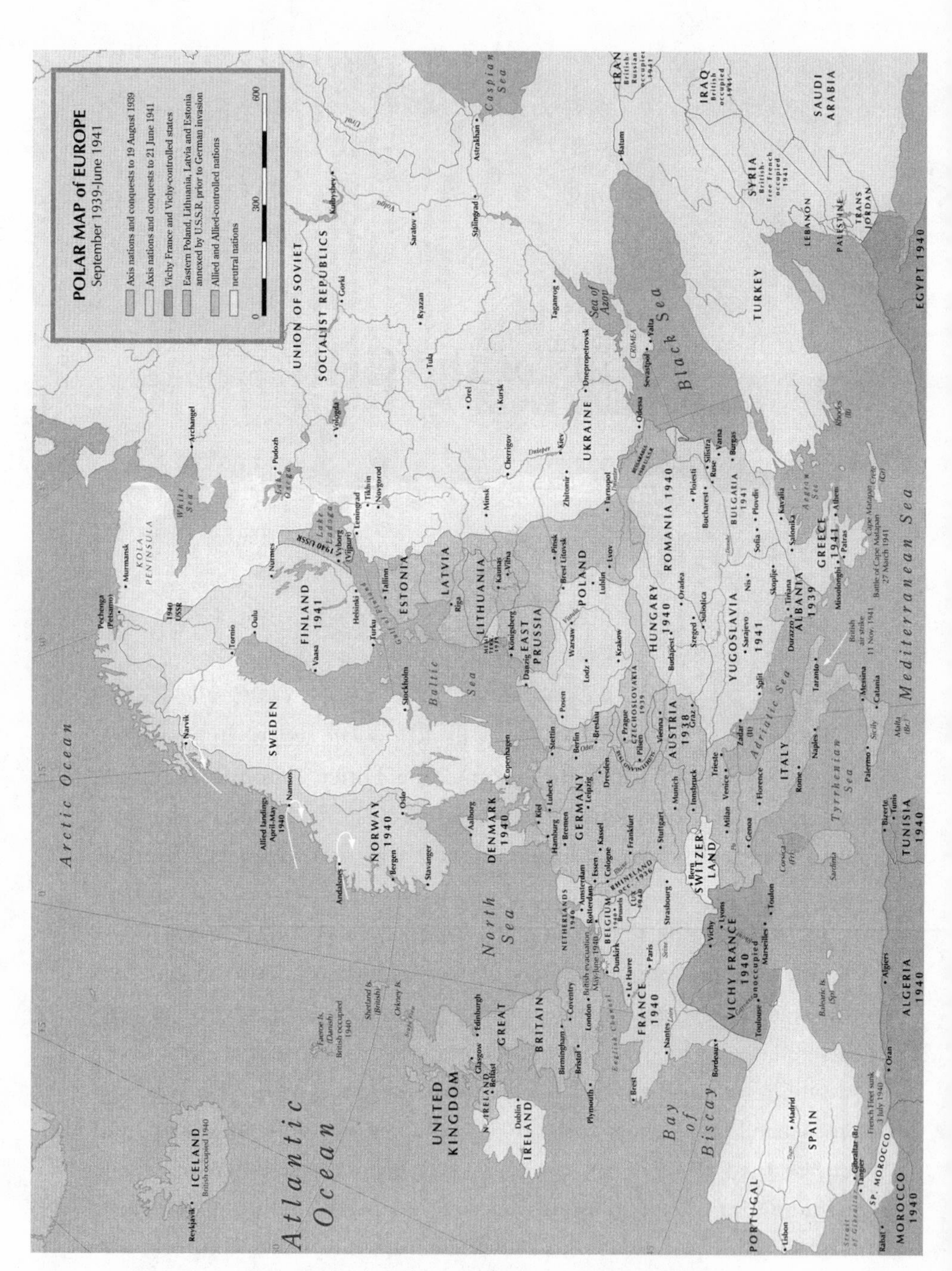

Territory controlled by the Axis powers, 1941.

of the conquered satellite nations, who were treated like naughty children.

His generals, all professional men, should have been different. They weren't. Time after time, as he harangued his military leaders about politics, history, and strategy, they stood silent, in awe of the Führer. Hadn't he resuscitated Germany's fortunes? Hadn't he taken the nation out of the depths of despair and vaulted it to the zenith of power? Hadn't he shown how to blend propaganda with diplomacy, and then exert pressure from the air and power on the ground? It was perhaps no surprise, then, that at the end of March 1941, when Hitler gathered his generals to hear another of his tirades, "they sat there before him," as one observer recalled, "in stubborn silence, a silence broken only twice"—when those assembled raised their hands in salute as the Führer swept in through a rear door, and afterward when he departed. The generals did not voice any objections. Remarkably, they did not utter a single word.

They should have. For before May began, Hitler finalized one of his most stunning decisions of the conflict: to open up a two-front war. On June 22, Nazi forces would launch an all-out assault against the Soviet Union. Intoxicated by his previous success, Hitler was sure nothing could stop them. "We have only to kick in the door," he screeched to his staff, "and the whole rotten structure will come crashing down." A mesmerized Goebbels agreed: "Bolshevism will collapse," he thought, "like a house of cards."

The decision had been under review for months. On its face, it was sheer madness. For one thing it meant double-crossing his ally; as recently as November 12, the flag of the Soviet Union—the red-and-yellow hammer and sickle—had fluttered alongside the swastika in the Reich's capital when the Nazis received a Soviet delegation to discuss carving up large portions of the globe. Moreover, Hitler himself had once stated, in *Mein Kampf*, that one should never fight a two-front war. And his own generals insisted that the first lesson of military history was: "Don't invade Russia." And for good reason. Russia was a colossus with a thousand-mile frontier and a storied history of swallowing up would-be conquerors: the Ottoman Empire got nowhere against Catherine the Great, and Napoleon did little better against Czar Alexander.

But where other invaders found Russia a merciless graveyard, the Führer saw possibilities. For Hitler, the opening of a second front was designed to be more than simply a turning point of the war. It was to be a final blow that would subjugate the despised Soviet Union, force Britain to sue for peace, and forestall America's entry into the conflict. On paper, it seemed like a workable plan. Hitler's army was the best in Europe; Stalin's, after his repeated purges of his top generals, was seemingly the worst. In truth, both American and British generals believed the Red Army could fall in as little as six weeks once Hitler's onslaught began. Also, Hitler's plan included seizing the oil fields of the Caucasus, thereby giving Germany crucial resources to fight. And control of the Soviet Union would open up access not just to oil, but also to its other vast resources: wheat and agriculture from Ukraine, gas from Romania, even fruits from the Crimea. It would also provide slave labor for Germany. And it would give Hitler *Lebensraum*—living space—for the German people in the east. But could it be done?

Many had doubted that Hitler could rout opposition parties in Germany, but hadn't he done that? Few thought he could corral dissidents and Jews alike, but hadn't he done that? And who could fail to be impressed by his nearly complete control of Europe from the English Channel to the Balkans? In fact, the more he had considered it, the more reasons he had to invade the Soviet Union now. Britain refused to be beaten, and remained a defiant force. For all his timidity, Roosevelt appeared to be paving the way for an eventual military confrontation and would be in a position, as Hitler himself acknowledged, "to intervene from 1942 onwards." And though the Soviet Union remained a member of the Tripartite Pact, Hitler despised Bolsheviks and believed the Soviet Union was being ruled by "the international Jew." He also was convinced that the Soviet Union was ripe for the picking, and he imagined that its suffering, superstitious people pined for the old days of the czars and were waiting for an opportunity to cast away the iron hand of the Bolsheviks.

Still, Hitler's decision was not made overnight. As far back as December 1940, Hitler had summoned his field commanders to tell them what he had already confided to his high command: be ready to outline an unparalleled land assault against the Soviets. "The German Armed Forces must be prepared, even before the ending of the war against England, to crush Soviet Russia in a rapid campaign," his military directive Number 21 insisted. The invasion's code name was Barbarossa, in honor of the medieval Holy Roman emperor Frederick I, who had won titanic victories in Europe and was considered one of Germany's greatest kings. With a combination of moral certitude and contempt, Hitler sat his generals down and lectured them about the inevitable death struggle, a "holy war" between National Socialism and the dreaded Bolshevism. And by striking east, he emphasized over and over, Germany could win the war in the west. Britain would sue for peace, and America would stay on the sidelines. Thus he outlined one of the most audacious military efforts ever carried out, a war of annihilation that would entail 3.2 million men plunging across a front 1,800 miles long; an as yet incalculable number of planes, armored vehicles, and tanks; and a battlefield that would extend from the Baltic Sea in the north to the Black Sea in the south, and over miles of open plains in between.

Time was running out. By early spring, Undersecretary of State Sumner Welles began passing on reports to the Kremlin that Hitler planned to strike the Soviet Union. Meanwhile, the Allies' intelligence continued to pick up the chatter of reports of German divisions hurriedly shifting to the east. But in the fog of war, no one could discern Hitler's true motives. After all, there were still rumors of a spring assault against Britain, even as Hitler met with a Japanese delegation and dropped broad hints that conflict with the Soviet Union was unavoidable. Only slowly did Stalin begin to prepare for the worst. "Depending on the international situation," he told officers in the Kremlin, "the Red Army will either wait for a German attack or may have to take the initiative." But the attack came far sooner than he had expected.

During the third week of June 1941, the Nazi ambassador in Moscow received a blunt cable from Berlin. German guns had opened fire on all Soviet borders at 3:30 a.m., and now, at 6 a.m., two and a half hours after the initial salvos and barrages had begun, the sky was lit a fiery red. The ambassador climbed into his car and was driven to the Soviet Foreign Ministry, where he read the cable aloud to a pale, quivering Molotov. At first the foreign minister showed little emotion, his exhausted eyes, framed by dark circles, remained unblinking.

But then he quietly exploded. After ripping up the communiqué, and spitting on it, the tense Molotov responded: "This is war." At the same time, while President Roosevelt was asleep in the White House, a shocked and indignant Stalin fell into a state of near collapse.

IT WAS THE DECISION of Hitler's life, and in many ways the decision of the war. In planning the invasion, the Führer came to believe that Napoleon had been stymied largely because he focused on Moscow. The Nazi generals disagreed; they thought that capturing Moscow would sever the head of the Soviet snake, leaving the country unable to fight west of the Ural Mountains. But as always, Hitler had the last word. So the Germans' assault took place in the north, south, and middle, and from the start, it seemed that Hitler had destiny on his side. On the first day, German forces destroyed whole armies and more planes than they had managed to neutralize during the entire Battle of Britain.

In Germany, Goebbels exulted in his diary, "Now the guns will be thundering. May God bless our weapons." Meanwhile, Hitler's proclamation reverberated over the radio: "The hour has now therefore arrived to counter this conspiracy of the Jewish, Anglo-Saxon warmongers." In the days that followed, the Wehrmacht continued to strike the Soviets with unheralded ruthlessness and force. Like a "swarm of crawling locusts"—Winston Churchill's term—they hit the Soviets with everything they had; all told, the Germans deployed over 3 million men, 3,600 tanks, 600,000 motorized vehicles, 7,000 artillery pieces, 625,000 horses, and 2,500 aircraft. And the surprise was complete. Six hundred tanks—three panzer divisions—along with motorcyclists, armored cars, and infantry, steamrollered a defenseless Soviet rifle division in the north.

In the center, the Germans deployed even more men, and 1,500 tanks. Confused and cut off, in the days that followed, the dumbstruck Soviet troops radioed in vain: "We are being fired upon. What should we do?" They received no reply. It was the same in the south: another German army made short work of the hapless defenders there. Columns of tanks stretched for miles along hardened roads, past burning Russian villages, while German commanders barked orders and artillery echoed in the distance. At the same time, the Luftwaffe dominated the skies. After the initial onslaught that destroyed a thousand Soviet planes, which were reduced to little more than twisted, smoking metal on the ground, eight hundred more planes were destroyed in the air.

The enormity of Russian disaster was staggering. While whole villages were put to the torch, German armored columns sped along parallel paths, then crisscrossed, ensnaring entire Soviet divisions, sometimes even entire armies. The city of Brest-Litovsk, central to the Soviet frontline, quickly fell. By the week's end, the Germans had taken both Lithuania and Latvia. In the north, where Leningrad was the strategic prize, the Nazis had pushed close to Ostrov. In the center, most of White Russia had fallen. And Minsk was surrounded and fell within five days. Within a matter of months, some 3 million Soviet soldiers would become captives of the Germans. Most would never return home. And by mid-July, as the Germans pressed on to Smolensk, they were only two hundred miles from Moscow; by mid-October, they would be within forty miles of it. By every criterion, this was war on a grand scale; the Nazis seemed to be unstoppable. They raced along the Baltic toward Leningrad, while General von Rundstedt swept into the Ukraine. From Riga on the Baltic Sea to Bialystock in the center, from Odessa to Sebastopol along the Black Sea in the South, the German march continued.

The Führer had grandiloquently predicted that this would be France all over again, a lightning campaign accomplished within eight weeks, before the first snows set in. Now, his prophecy seemed to be coming true. German infantry moved so quickly across Soviet territory that runners had to bring telephone wires to forward positions—the Nazis were outstripping the primitive Soviet communication system. Hitler now stood astride as master of Europe as had no one else in history. Not Bismarck, not Napoleon, not even Julius Caesar had seized so much territory and conquered so many people. A continent now lay in the Führer's grip.

And the Nazis were after more than land or territory. As part of his conquest, Hitler had authorized Heinrich Himmler to terrorize civilians and slaughter all Soviet political officers. Pillaging entire villages, the Nazis became unspeakably cruel. That, however, was just the beginning. During the early days of this Nazi conquest, Hitler and the Reich made one other fateful decision: once and for all, to deal with the problem of the Jews.

~

HITLER'S PURPOSE IN INVADING the Soviet Union was not only to seize territory and riches, but also to create a new imperium in the east, under which his murderous prophecy about the "Jewish question" would finally be fulfilled. As the Wehrmacht pushed forward along a two-hundred-mile swath, genocide was now in the air. For the Jews, the dying soon began.

Interestingly, the Final Solution had at one time been conceived as a territorial solution. Hitler originally planned to resettle the European Jews from beyond the Urals in the freezing, windswept wastes of Siberia. There they would, as Hitler's biographer Ian Kershaw memorably noted, be worked to death as slaves and starved to death as subhumans. The same was true for the 5 million to 6 million Jews of the Soviet Union. With uncharacteristic candor, Hitler boasted to his personal lawyer and Governor General of occupied Poland, Hans Frank, that the Jews would be "removed," just as the Führer had prophesied in 1939.

If that was the theory, however, the reality was far different. In the conquered territories of the Soviet Union, Nazi *Einsatzgruppen*—mobile killing squads—were told to exterminate all "extremist elements," which largely meant Communist functionaries such as commissars, and, of course, "Jews in the service of the party." Yet the intended barbarity was ambiguous. What exactly did "service of the party" mean? Different elements of the German army had different interpretations.

The number of those killed was at first small but then quickly escalated. The *Einsatzgruppen* wasted little time in getting to work; two days after Operation Barbarossa began, men from the security police lined up 201 Jews in a Lithuanian village and shot them dead. Within three weeks, the killing squads could boast nearly 3,500 victims; by August, more than 12,000 male Jews had been murdered. Joseph Goebbels, reading the detailed reports of the executions, was ecstatic. "Vengeance," he wrote in his diary, "was being wreaked on the Jews and the big towns of the Baltic."

The vengeance was just beginning. The Nazis' atrocities were soon being copied by anti-Semitic locals. One of the first pogroms that set the tone took place in the Lithuanian town of Kovno (Kaunas). Jews were herded together and pushed into the town center, while crowds of murmuring enthusiastic onlookers gathered. Then the violence started. One by one, Jews were savagely clubbed to death; meanwhile, the Lithuanians egged the killers on, clapping and cheering. There was no pretense of a trial, or of any reason for the executions, except the fact that the victims were Jews. Approving German officers stood by on the sidelines grinning and joking, a number snapping photographs for posterity—or to send home to their families. The savagery was a public spectacle; women even hoisted children onto their shoulders or held them up to witness the mayhem. Robespierre, the bloody mastermind of the Terror during the French Revolution, likely would have approved; the SS certainly did. For forty-five minutes, the butchery continued, with a relish that was almost hard to fathom, until there were no more Jews left alive. Then one of the villagers leaped onto a mound of the dead and began to dance, while serenading the crowd with the Lithuanian national anthem on an accordion. When it was all over, an entire segment of the town had been annihilated.

From then on, the Nazis, vain, cruel, and megalomaniacal, strutted about in their uniforms and took particular delight in such actions by the local populations, goading them on. The Nazis repeated that this genocide was just and necessary in the life-and-death struggle against the Jews. Goebbels scornfully insisted that the Jews were "vile," they were "lice," and the only way to cope with them was with brutality. "If you spare them," he reasoned, "you later will be their victim." The professional military officers, whose voices were of considerable influence and who should have exercised better judgment, agreed. For example, the commander in chief of the Sixth Army exhorted his men to be bearers "of a pitiless racial ideology" and "avengers" upon the Jewish "subhumans." In Berlin, Hitler was more philosophical about the carnage: "If there were no more Jews in Europe," he said, "the unity of the European states would be no longer disturbed."

So it began. At the outset, true, the victims were mainly men. But as time passed, the massacres included defenseless women and innocent children, and the killings often amounted to little more than forcing naked Jews to kneel at the edge of a pit before spraying them with submachine-gun fire.

On September 29 and 30, 1941, the Jews of Kiev were instructed by the Nazis to gather at the Jewish cemetery, with all their possessions, money, documents, "valuables," and "warm clothing." From there, they would—or so they believed—be loaded onto trains and resettled. But then events took a sudden, unexpected turn. The Germans had prepared for only five thousand or six thousand to report; more than thirty thousand came. The panic-stricken victims were formed into a long, snaking line and told to give up their luggage, their coats, their shoes, their valuables, and then their other garments—even their underwear. Each article of clothing had to be meticulously put in the appropriate pile. Shoes here. Coats here. Pants here. Hats here. Socks here. Belts here. Valuables here. And on it went. Once they had undressed, they were instructed to stand on a mound of freshly plowed earth, above the high, narrow mouth of a deep ravine whose name would live in infamy: Babi Yar.

The Germans lined up old men and old women, pointing at their slack bellies and breasts with rifle butts; they lined up mothers carrying small children; and they lined up schoolchildren.

Then they lined up machine gunners.

The killing squads did their bloody work, and this became a blind, wanton slaughter. Machine-gun salvo was followed by machine-gun salvo, hour after hour, for two days. And throughout those two days, not far from an ordinary stretch of road and a small, innocuous town, the naked corpses of the victims tumbled into a pit. As the pit filled with the dead, their bodies were heaped on one another in deepening layers, their blood staining the earth. Many were killed outright by the machine-gun fire, although many others were only wounded and became like confused animals trapped in a maze, scurrying this way and that. In one of Babi Yar's more despicable cruelties, children were simply grabbed by their legs and thrown alive into the pit.

It was too much for one watchman, who witnessed in horror this scene of "human grief and despair." That evening, as the sun began to set, people with plows and spades were put to work and the Germans copiously buried the victims under thick "layers of earth." But because such great numbers of the victims were still alive, the earth continued to move long afterward: the wounded, writhing and trembling, were still frantically shifting their arms and their legs. And eerie sounds emanated from the ground. Moans could be heard, as could the muffled voices of victims calling out to one another in pain. Sobbing could be heard, and choking. And so could one little girl crying: "Mammy, why do they pour the sand into my eyes?"

Arrogant and willful, German soldiers and the SS continued to make their rounds, holding torches aloft and "firing bullets" from their revolvers into anyone who still appeared to be alive. Other Germans strode over the bodies, stepping on limbs and bellies, looking for valuables. For hours individual pistol shots rang out into the air as a group of loitering soldiers traded jokes and snickered into the night.

In all, more than thirty-three thousand Jews were murdered. Remarkably, one young girl was somehow alive. Keeping very still, she heard the whimpering and wheezing of the few who remained, until one by one they stopped breathing. She heard the SS, barking orders. She heard Germans examining the dead. And she felt pain like nothing she had ever felt when an SS man kicked her breast with his heavy boot and stepped on her right hand until the bones "cracked." Lying with her mouth up, she began to gag—it was the dirt; she was gradually being buried alive. But, panting and panicked, she managed to dig herself out with a last desperate effort, "scramble over the ledge," and then make her way to freedom. Many years later, she alone would bear witness to the terrible crimes of Babi Yar.

In a cruel twist of fate, the slaughter at Babi Yar was made possible in part by Hitler's personal decision to send his vaunted panzer divisions to capture Kiev, in the south, rather than continue on toward Moscow. Hitler's panzer commander had flown to Berlin and pleaded with the Führer to move north, but Hitler wanted Kiev. His forces had taken 650,000 additional Soviet prisoners by September 27, two days before the killings began at Babi Yar. The Soviets' collapse at Kiev was, at the time, the greatest defeat ever visited on an army.

But there was more to come.

EACH EXECUTION IN A German-occupied city or a town would beget more executions, and the same crimes would be repeated again and again. In Poland, Nazi-dominated Warsaw was filled with death and disease and despair. People continued to ask how Hitler could have become so strong, how he could have taken over Poland and Czechoslovakia and France and attacked the Soviet Union. They asked about the United States, and why it had not joined in the war. However, most people had no answers, only a more profound sense of exhaustion. The constant hunger made their stomachs churn and their heads ache; but here, not even starvation was enough for the Nazis. One day, German policemen, seeking to send a message, dragged thirty trembling Jewish children to clay pits filled with water and held them under until they drowned. Meanwhile, a newspaper reported that Jews were moving through the ghettos "like ghosts." All across the east, thousands of Jews sought refuge in small, cramped closets or crawl spaces, or even in dank sewers or damp, cold abandoned buildings; but roving bands of

Nazis or collaborationists went from building to building looking for them. Their last refuge was crumbling: "We feel like beasts surrounded by hunters," lamented one fifteen-year-old. Life had become a kind of blind man's bluff.

The hunters became ever more deadly. Wherever the Germans held sway, they hired assassins, sanctioned torture, and relished the sight of blood. That October in the Ukrainian port city of Odessa, nineteen thousand Jews were pushed into a town square surrounded by a wooden fence. This time there were no shootings. Instead, the executioners methodically doused their victims with gasoline, then roasted them alive in a huge fire. The victims were left to howl in agony and die an agonizing death, until nothing remained of them except singed flesh and bits of dry, white bone.

Over only four months, an astonishing half a million Jews would be massacred.

~

AS WINTER SETTLED IN, the situation was little better for those still alive. In Warsaw, seventy children, the cold air stabbing at their lungs, shivered and froze to death in the streets. Indeed, frozen human corpses were now a "frequent sight." Half-insane with grief, mothers would cuddle their dead children, seeking to warm the "inanimate" little bodies. Perhaps even more heartbreaking was the sight of a child huddling against his mother, stroking her face and tugging at her sleeves, thinking she was asleep when in fact she had quietly perished.

In England, the fiery Winston Churchill gave a public voice to the Jews. "None has suffered more cruelly than the Jew," he wrote in a famous tract in the *Jewish Chronicle*. "He has borne and continues to bear the burden that might have seemed to be beyond endurance. He has not allowed it to break his spirit: he has never lost the will to resist. . . . Assuredly in the day of victory the Jew's suffering and his part in the struggle will not be forgotten. . . . It will be shown that, though the mills of the Gods grind slowly, yet they grind exceedingly small."

~

For all the carnage, though, the Germans still were not planning the Final Solution. Rather, they continued to contemplate a form of territorial solution, removing the Jews somewhere deep in the east. "Emigration" and "evacuation" were the watchwords. "Where the Jews are sent to," Hitler maintained, "whether to Siberia or Madagascar, is immaterial." But when Hitler's rhetoric became more fiery, the rest of the world stayed largely mute, writing his words off as bluster or bluff, or simply wary of the consequences of an actual confrontation. Once more, Hitler had been underrated by his neighbors and his foes.

Not only Hitler himself but also his high command was increasingly focused on the problem of the Jews. Murderous words increasingly poured from their lips and from their pens. Each instruction, each technical problem in dealing with the Jews was examined. Each bureaucratic obstacle to making Europe *Judenfrei* was analyzed. In Poland, Nazi authorities flirted with the idea of one large camp into which the Jews would be herded to labor in coal mines. But every solution raised a new problem or conundrum: in this case, what about those who couldn't work? (Of course, there was always the option of deporting the Jews eastward.) But to what district were the Jews to be relocated? (By late fall, the lightning war that Hitler had anticipated in the Soviet Union was proving to be a delusion.) What about transportation? (Trains were already in short supply.) What about the possibility of eliminating the Jews by starving them to death? (But even this required territory for them to be rounded up in.) That the war against the Soviet Union was stalled—the Nazis tried to capture Moscow, but their broad assault would fail—led the Germans to examine other options for handling the Jews.

Meanwhile, though there was not yet a coordinated, comprehensive decision about genocide, Adolf Eichmann, a dauntless figure, began preparing an overall plan for the "complete solution of the Jewish question," and Hermann Göring continued to clamor for a "final solution." At the same time, Himmler and Reinhard Heydrich initiated the creation of an extermination camp in Riga, Latvia, a network of prison and labor camps that could accommodate up to 10 million, though they then abandoned it because of local partisan warfare. Nevertheless, revenge and reprisal were never far from Hitler's thoughts.

In September, Hitler agreed to start deporting German, Austrian, and Czech Jews to the east. The solution to the Jewish question, he said, must be "energetic" but must not cause "unnecessary difficulties." At the same time, in Kraków, Poland, Hans Frank insisted, "As far as Jews are concerned, I want to tell you quite frankly that they must be done away with one way or another." And Himmler maintained that the Jews must be exterminated "down to the very last one."

It was around this time, in the fall of 1941, that the Nazis began to contemplate the use of poison gas.

The bridge to industrialized mass murder was about to be built.

THE MASS SHOOTINGS AND other forms of slaughter increasingly took a toll on the killers themselves. Even the much touted SS discipline was unable to prevent the stress created by the butchery; drunkenness and disorderly behavior increased among the Germans; and there were rumbles of protest from the army itself. One Nazi official, a Dr. Becker, went as far as to complain about the "immense psychological injuries" and "damages" to the men's health. Wilhelm Kube, the commissioner general of White Russia, agreed, singling out the policy, which he called beastly, of burying alive seriously wounded people, who then "worked their way out of the graves." Moreover, the German authorities came to believe that there had to be a cleaner and less public way of killing than mass shooting. There was. In East Prussia in 1940, the Nazis had used gas vans for "euthanasia," that is, to murder people who were physically and mentally handicapped. At institutions in Germany, Austria, and Poland that housed the deformed, the disfigured, or the chronically ill, the Nazis piped in carbon monoxide from trailers or put the victims directly into carbon monoxide chambers. In other cases, elderly people were asphyxiated by exhaust fumes administered through specially designed tubes. The Germans experimented with other methods as well, including stationary killing installations.

Then, in 1941, fifteen mobile gas vans were delivered to the *Einsatzgruppen* for use against the Jews in the occupied countries of the east. No technical detail was too small to escape the Nazis' attention. The Germans fretted about the weather—the vans could be used only in "absolutely dry weather." They fretted because the gas caused constant headaches—it was debilitating their executioners. And they fretted about appearances—they camouflaged the vans as house trailers, outfitting them with neatly painted window shutters. Some even fretted about the nature of their victims' deaths; Dr. Becker noted in one memorandum that, with proper use of the gas, "death comes faster" and the recipients fall asleep "peacefully."

In an experiment with another toxic substance, on the night of September 2, 1941, several hundred Soviet prisoners of war at Auschwitz were marched into the cellars of Block 11 in pitch darkness, packed in, and gassed with Zyklon B. Auschwitz was then being used primarily as a concentration camp for the Nazis' political opponents, mostly Poles.

Word soon raced out to the leadership of the Third Reich: this trial was deemed a success.

~

ON JANUARY 2, 1942, less than a month after the United States had officially entered the war, the Germans prepared for a conference on the shore of the beautiful Wannsee, a lake on the western rim of Berlin. The purpose was a "joint conversation" about the remaining work connected with the "final solution." It would be, in the words of one Nazi official, a "great discussion." But before it was to take place, the Germans carried out yet another experiment in gassing. Under a darkened sky on the evening of December 7, 1941—as Japanese aircraft were laying waste to the United States fleet at Pearl Harbor—seven hundred Jews were being ferried in trucks along a rutted road near the Polish village of Chelmno. They were told the usual story: that their destination was a railway station some five miles away, from where they would be sent to agricultural or factory work in the "east." They never arrived. Instead, fearful and confused, they were detained overnight in a small, shabby villa on the outskirts of the village.

The next morning, eighty of the prisoners were dragged into a special van, which sped off toward a clearing in the thick Chelmno woods. By the journey's end, they were struggling in vain for air. While the van was parked with the engine running, carbon monoxide was piped into the rear, killing them. Inside, after the doors were opened, there was a sickening stench of waste and sweat. This bloody work continued for four days, a thousand dying each day, four thousands all told. The bodies were pitched into a mass grave in a clearing in the woods. As President Franklin Roosevelt was announcing to the world that December 7 was "a date which will live in infamy," the Germans were inaugurating, under the greatest secrecy, the first days of the "final solution."

The number of Jews slaughtered in the Chelmno woods was nearly twice the number of Americans killed by the Japanese in the attack on Pearl Harbor. From that day, the Nazi gas vans began working overtime, without pause, without interruption; more than fifty communities in Chelmno would be wiped out. One local resident drily observed, "*Ein Tag—ein Tausend*": "One day—one thousand."

In Kraków, Hans Frank, having recently returned from Berlin, enthusiastically informed his cabinet of the imminent decisions about the Jews. "Do you think they will be settled in the Ostland, and villages?" he asked rhetorically. "We were told in Berlin: why all this bother? We can do nothing with them either in the Ostland or in the Reichskommissariat." So what was to be done?

Berlin had answered with bravado: "Liquidate them yourselves."

AND BY NOW, NO Jews were exempt. Previously, exceptions had been made for German Jews who had Aryan partners, German Jews who were decorated war heroes, and people who were only part Jewish (*Mischlinge*). When a train bearing a thousand such German Jews had come into Riga, no less than Heinrich Himmler placed an urgent call, seeking to prevent their extermination. It was too late; they were all killed.

After the Wannsee conference, however, there would no longer be any such confusion.

ON JANUARY 20, 1942, a fleet of limousines sped into a lakeside suburb of west Berlin, past clean, sturdy houses, where the walks were swept and smoke rose from the chimneys, onto a quiet residential street, just across from the popular Wannsee beach, and entered into the tree-lined driveway of a spacious, elegant stone villa. Goebbels himself lived only a few hundred yards away. Built in 1914, the villa was now owned by the SS and used as a conference center. One by one, representatives of all the key Reich ministries emerged from the cars to discuss the Final Solution. Here were officials from the ministries of the Interior and Justice, from the eastern territories and the Foreign Office, from the office of the Four-Year Plan and from the general government, and of course from the Gestapo. Here too, were representatives of the Reich Chancellery of the Nazi Party and the Race and Resettlement Office, as well as of the Nazi Party Chancellery. There was the secretary for the conference proceedings, whose task was to produce a written record of all that took place. And here came the cold-blooded killers: the dour bureaucrat Adolf Eichmann, along with Dr. Rudolf Lange, the SS *Sturmbannführer*, who was invited because he had successfully executed so many German Jews in Latvia.

When the participants assembled at midday, theirs was a daunting task. The German offensive against the Soviet Union, begun under a cloud of euphoria, had stalled short of Moscow. Temperatures there had plummeted to twenty below zero, blackening the German attackers' skin with frostbite; even the crankcases of their vehicles froze. While the Germans were forced to seek shelter, the Soviet army began a punishing counteroffensive. Hitler had proclaimed that the Soviet territories west of the Urals would become a German garden of Eden, but the reality was that this would be a long war, and it was unlikely that the Soviet Union would ever be completely conquered. Moreover, the Japanese attack on Pearl Harbor had prompted the Führer to declare war on the United States, meaning the Germans were now confronted with a true two-front war. None of this, however, distracted the conference from its cherished goal: establishing the Final Solution for the European Jewish question.

Even to the Nazis, the idea of deporting all the Jews of Europe to the eastern territories and then killing them seemed like lunacy. German resources, in men and matériel, were already severely stretched. Moreover, some German officials were horrified at the prospect of killing valuable workers and irreplaceable craftsmen who could help with the war effort. Also, a mass deportation of the Jews—which would involve gathering, registering, documenting, and transporting millions of people—was a formidable logistical task. The technical obstacles alone were mind-boggling—at Chelmno, for example, the experimental gas chambers often malfunctioned: deaths that were supposed to take no more than fifteen minutes sometimes took hours; routinely, some victims were still alive when the doors were opened. As to coordination, the railways, the bureaucrats, the Gestapo, and the military would all have to work in unison, toward a single, almost fathomless objective. From scratch, the Germans would have to create something never before accomplished: an entire industrial apparatus of destruction.

Death camps would have to be built in distant places. Intricate timelines would have to be drawn up. Impounding policies would have to be developed. For the endless stream of deportations, interim transit ghettos would have to be erected. And the Germans would have to depend on the tacit "unrecorded cooperation" of many thousands of disparate people—from unquestioning administrators and diligent secretaries to watchful bureaucrats and SS officials—all of whom would have to carry out their jobs unhesitatingly and in town after town and city after city, send Jews on their way to "resettlement." Local populations would either have to collude outright with the ongoing mass murder or somehow be cajoled into cooperation, or at least into connivance—turning a blind eye. Nor could the involvement of all the necessary Germans be guaranteed.

At the conference, amidst the ornate marble pillars and gorgeous mahogany paneling, not to mention the oversized fireplaces and light-filled French doors, Heydrich made it clear to the participants that the Final Solution would be far more encompassing than previously imagined. Emigration and evacuation were no longer sufficient. Nor were shootings. He calmly explained that the Final Solution would now extend to all of the 11 million Jews scattered throughout Europe and beyond. With an expressionless face, he then presented a meticulous list of the numbers of all the Jews involved, including the 330,000 Jews in Britain; including the 4,000 Jews of Ireland; including the Jews of the neutral countries—55,500 in Turkey, 18,000 in Switzerland, 10,000 in Spain, and 8,000 in Sweden—and including the remaining 34,000 in Lithuania, where 200,000 had already been murdered by the *Einsatzgruppen.*

No number was too large to be considered, or too small. No country was exempt. The greatest number of Jews listed was 2,994,684, in the Ukraine. The second-largest number was 2,284,000, in Germany. Third was Germany's ally, Hungary, which had 742,800. Fourth was unoccupied France, which had 700,000, a figure that included France's North African colonies: Morocco, Algeria, and Tunisia. The smallest number was 200, in Italian-occupied Albania. There was even an entry for the estimated number of Jews in the United States. The list also included Estonia, for which the laconic notation was "Without Jews."

As they sat around the polished table, Heydrich, one of the cruelest and most brutal mass murderers in the Reich (he referred to Jews as "terminal subhumans"), outlined the mechanism for the Final Solution. Europe, he said, would be "combed from west to east." Evacuated Jews would be brought "bit by bit" to what he called "transit ghettos" before being transported farther east. Jews would be separated by sex, by their ability to be slave laborers, by their locality. And in countries such as Hungary, which thus far was protecting its Jews, it would be necessary to "impose an adviser" on Jewish questions.

The participants made another key decision. Heydrich's right-hand man, Adolf Eichmann, would be put in charge of coordinating all aspects of the Final Solution. His representatives—in effect, his emissaries of death—would fan out to capitals all across Europe, while he would dispatch instructions from Berlin. In turn, he would be apprised of each deportation being planned and carried out. On such details did the fate of millions hang. Almost overnight, tens of thousands of miles of rail lines would come under his aegis, and so would a vast bureaucracy of murder. There would be an elaborate system of confidentiality to obscure the true nature of the Final Solution. Within months, the railway telegraphs would be chattering, and Eichmann would have men positioned in France, Belgium, the Netherlands, Luxembourg, Norway, Romania, Greece, Bulgaria, Hungary, and Slovakia.

As the meeting drew to a close, shafts of bright light came through the windows, and Eichmann, Heydrich, and another colleague warmed themselves in chairs by a nearby stove. Uncharacteristically, Heydrich began puffing on a cigarette. They sipped brandy, and as Eichmann would later recount, they sat together like comrades, winding down "after long hours of effort." With such power and pedigree, and soon racial purity, they believed the Nazis' Third Reich was invincible. The destruction of the Jews, they felt, would one day arouse awe, testify to the greatness of their heritage, and cover them with glory.

Ten days later, nine years after his rise to power, Adolf Hitler spoke before a huge, cheering audience at the Sports Palace in Berlin. His words, broadcast by radio in Berlin and all across the Third Reich, were also received in Washington and London. His message was as chilling as ever. "The hour will come when the most evil universal enemy of all time will be finished . . . for one thousand years."

AS THE WANNSEE CONFERENCE came to an end, and as eastern Europe was mostly sealed off from the rest of the world, the SS were scouring remote villages west of the Bug River on the former border between Germany and Poland. In three of these sites, men were soon hammering and swearing, sawing and building, turning old labor camps into new death camps. With such work, and much plotting and intrigue, everything seemed to unfold in precise, formalized detail. The Germans consulted architects and builders, the Gestapo, leaders of industry, and experts in pest control. While sipping sherry and eating caviar, they marveled at architects' miniature models. And while the slave workers struggled in the muck and cold and darkness to erect the camps, the SS strode around like Roman Caesars, urging the prisoners to work harder and faster. If workers died of exhaustion, or of typhus or other maladies, it was no matter; the work continued.

Where there had once been only enveloping woodlands, or existing work camps, the sites would constitute one of the most ambitious construction projects ever conceived. But this was no ancient Versailles, with its finely clipped hedges and bubbling fountains. Nor was it like the great imperial forums of Rome, where crowds once thronged to festivals, or, for that matter, the dazzling temple complex at Karnak, Egypt. Nor, for that matter, was it like the sumptuous Russian Winter Palace, or Sa'adabad, the Ottoman Sultan's summer estate outside Constantinople. Devoted exclusively to death rather than life, in history it was unique to Adolf Hitler and the Third Reich.

Each of the first four sites, though remote, was a spur on a railway line, which linked it to many towns where half-starved Jews were now confined. The first, Belzec, was tied to Lvov and Kraków, and encompassed the whole of Polish Galicia. It had six gas chambers designed to look like a bathhouse; this was prettified with geraniums, and as a "thoughtful little witticism," a Star of David was painted on the roof. Belzec was capable of killing fifteen thousand people a day. By rail, all of Warsaw could be brought to Treblinka, which had no fewer than thirty gas chambers capable of dealing with twenty-five thousand people a day. Sobibór was deep in the woods but was accessible by rail for large Jewish populations dispersed across Chelm. The fourth, in existence since December 1941, was Chelmno itself.

By comparison, a fifth site was not tucked away in a remote village at the edge of eastern Poland, where houses were clean and small and flowers bloomed in almost every yard. Rather, it was a sizable town with a significant railway line, with ties to each major country in Europe—to France as well as Belgium in the west, to Yugoslavia as well as Italy in the south, to the Reich itself, as well as to the annexed railway network in Poland. Prior to the spring of 1942 it had been a work camp, but then construction began for a new camp located in a forest of towering birch trees (Birken), which the Germans called Birkenau. Auschwitz-Birkenau, as it then came to be called, would soon provide slave labor for the Nazi war effort spread across eastern Upper Silesia—in synthetic coal factories, rubber factories, military and industrial enterprises, and coal mines.

In June 1942, the Germans put in place their program for the deportation of Jews from western Europe to the camps. That July, the first transports were under way, and Jews from the Polish and German ghettos began arriving at the camps by the trainload. That summer, new gas chambers were built and the system of industrialized mass murder was put into operation. By now, what had once been fitful and episodic, haphazard and frequently improvised, had become methodical and consistent. The Final Solution had commenced with stunning speed.

By the year's end, the SS was able to report initial successes in the Final Solution. At the close of 1941, only about 500,000 Jews living in the conquered Soviet territories had been executed. But by the end of 1942, some 4 million Jews were dead.

IT WAS LIKE AN earthquake splintering a continent—a turning point after which human history would never be the same. And yet it went largely unrecorded. In the United States, there were factories to gear up and soldiers to train. And the Allied world had focused its attention and its war machine on the Pacific in the east and on North Africa in the west. In North Africa, the British were already squaring off against Rommel.

And waiting for the Americans.

~

THE LARGER TRUTH WAS that in 1942 the United States had already been at war with Germany for months, but had yet to fire a single shot. That, however, was about to change. While British forces were slugging it out with Rommel in North Africa, beginning in the spring officials both in Washington and in London had spent innumerable sleepless nights debating the logistics of opening up a second front against Hitler. "We've got to go to Europe and fight," Dwight Eisenhower bellowed, "and we've got to quit wasting resources all over the world." Eisenhower, Secretary of War Henry Stimson, and Army Chief of Staff George Marshall were adamant in their belief that only one vast, direct assault would be sufficient to roll up and cripple Nazi forces in Europe. They wanted to spend the next six months building up an assault force in Britain, and then in the spring of 1943 launch a cross-Channel invasion. Their thinking was straightforward: Marshall and Eisenhower dreamed of one decisive battle, a land attack with the largest force they could muster "as soon as possible," and with America's greatest tank commanders smashing Germany's famed panzers on the open ground of northern Europe.

Churchill thought otherwise. He did not feel that the Allies were ready to fight the Wehrmacht in France. Moreover, he remained haunted by the Somme, a ghastly battle of World War I in which the British saw sixty thousand of their finest young men wiped out in a single day. Thus he favored a peripheral attack, perhaps in the Mediterranean, in North Africa, or in southern Italy. It would test the waters and, in his words, it was better "to go round the end rather than through the center."

Undaunted, Eisenhower and Marshall drew up preliminary plans for the great cross-Channel assault. It had two code names: Operation Bolero for the buildup of Allied forces, and Operation Roundup for the actual invasion of France, scheduled for 1943. With considerable fanfare, it was presented to the president at the close of March 1942. As a fallback should the Soviet army collapse—a fear that plagued Roosevelt—they had also designed a limited emergency operation for later in 1942, intended to divert German resources. Would Roosevelt sign off on these plans? A skeptical Stimson thought not; he was worried that the president lacked "the hardness of heart" to undertake such a large-scale operation at this point. However, Roosevelt surprised them, not only approving the plan but immediately sending George Marshall and his own personal aide Harry Hopkins to London to meet with Churchill and discuss it.

Speaking with the Americans at 10 Downing Street, Churchill and his staff were reluctant. Still, they also knew how important the proposed plan was to the president; actually, Roosevelt had already wired to the prime minister: "What Harry and George Marshall will tell you all about has my heart and mind in it." To Marshall's surprise, by the end of the weekend Churchill was unusually cooperative. With a nod, a wink, and a smile, Churchill insisted that he was "open to" the Americans' alternatives. Moreover, he seemed to have approved Bolero. "All well," Hopkins cabled to Roosevelt. In truth, the weekend had been a masterly exercise in stage management by a prime minister who had rallied his people on the brink of catastrophe. Now, with the American delegation, he was seeking to buy time.

Jubilant over Churchill's seeming change of heart, Roosevelt cabled to Joseph Stalin and invited the Soviet foreign minister to Washington to discuss plans for a second front. Vyacheslav Molotov arrived at the White House on the afternoon of May 29. It was a Friday. With two interpreters present, Roosevelt went out of his way to make Molotov happy; he had confessed in a memo to the Joint Chiefs, "At the present time, our principal objective is to help Russia. It must be constantly reiterated that Russian armies are killing more Germans and destroying more Axis material than all the 25 united nations put together." Roosevelt was charming; Molotov, peering owlishly through his round glasses, was persistent and pugnacious. Roosevelt wanted to make Molotov happy; Molotov wanted to make Stalin happy. In the end, Roosevelt complied. Without stipulating when and where a second front would be opened, he directly told the Soviet foreign minister to inform Stalin that "we expect the formation of a second front this year."

Machination now followed machination. From London, Churchill, his eyes wide, watched all this with mounting interest—and concern. In truth, he had sensed what was coming and on hearing about the outcome of Roosevelt's meeting with Molotov, he was aghast. Now he moved quickly. On June 10, Churchill promptly informed Molotov, who was then visiting London, that he opposed a cross-Channel invasion anytime during 1942. The next day, the British cabinet voted to postpone an invasion of Europe until 1943 or later. And Churchill decided to fly to Washington immediately to discuss military strategy with the president himself. The prime minister arrived in Washington on June 18 and flew to Hyde Park to see the president the next morning. He did not know that Roosevelt was already feeling political pressure, trapped between a desire to satisfy Marshall and Eisenhower and a hope of somehow reassuring his closest ally, Churchill. In a sudden turnabout, the president blurted to Marshall that the time had come to "reopen" the question of invading northwest Africa.

As Roosevelt and Churchill settled down to business at Hyde Park, the prime minister began to pepper the president with questions about the strategy for the proposed invasion. Were there enough craft to transport the men? Where would they land? How many men would be needed? What was the actual plan? Wagging a finger at Roosevelt, his eyes twinkling, Churchill raised question after question. Nor did Roosevelt have the answers. At that point, Churchill began to wonder aloud whether there might be other options for relieving the pressure on the Soviet Union. He mused, "Ought we not to be preparing within the general structure of Bolero some other operation by which we may gain positions of advantage, and also directly and indirectly to take some of the weight off Russia?" It was then that Churchill suggested what was already on Roosevelt's mind: a military operation in French northwest Africa.

The two men returned to Washington by train on June 20 and met again the following morning in the president's study. In the middle of the meeting, an aide quietly slipped into the room and slid a piece of paper into the president's hand. A shaken Roosevelt read the message and silently gave it to the prime minister. Staring at it, Churchill looked careworn. Tobruk, the seemingly impregnable British garrison in Libya, had fallen to General Erwin Rommel's Afrika Corps. The information was sketchy, and only over the next eighteen hours would the full magnitude of the defeat become clear. For a valiant thirty-three weeks the British at Tobruk had managed to hold off the German siege; now thirty thousand British officers and men were being rounded up as prisoners of war and Rommel was poised to push on to the strategic prize of Egypt. With this victory, Rommel also took possession of vast dumps of ammunition, food, and, most important, gasoline. With Hitler's blessing, Rommel boasted "I am going to Suez!"

Churchill was despondent. "Defeat is one thing," he later wrote; "disgrace is another." In later years he went so far as to acknowledge that the fall of Tobruk was "one of the heaviest blows" he experienced during the war.

The president sensed this. After a long silence, Roosevelt finally said, "What can we do to help?"

Churchill composed himself and said to Roosevelt, "Give us as many Sherman tanks as you can spare, and ship them to the Middle East as quickly as possible." The president immediately agreed, and within days the United States was shipping three hundred tanks and one hundred self-propelled guns to the British Eighth Army in Alexandria.

The disaster of Tobruk had an immediate effect on Churchill, fixing his opposition to a cross-Channel invasion in 1942. Roosevelt, also stricken by the news, intuitively understood this, and now in earnest turned the discussion to the idea that he had hinted at in previous days to Marshall: a smaller-scale invasion of French North Africa. It would at once, he reasoned, bolster the British in the Middle East and force the Germans to shift troops from the eastern front where they were fighting the Russians.

A jubilant Churchill embraced the idea, booming to the president, "HERE is the true second front in 1942! HERE is the safest and most fruitful stroke that can be delivered!"

All that remained was to inform Marshall and Eisenhower, and begin putting the operation into place. It would be code-named Torch.

~

THIS WAS CLASSIC ROOSEVELT, making ad hoc decisions based not on extensive studies but on intuition and a gut feeling. His top advisers, who would have to carry the plan out, were vehemently opposed. They could point out, with good reason, that months earlier when Roosevelt had written out a list of alternatives for military action, this plan wasn't even included. After he learned of the final decision, Eisenhower wrote in his diary that July 28, when the order was signed, would go down as "the blackest day in history." Secretary of War Stimson was convinced that Torch would be a disaster, another bloody Gallipoli. Marshall concurred. They had other considerations as well. Roosevelt had promised Molotov that the second front would be opened in 1942. But Torch was no second front. Moreover, the invading forces wouldn't even be fighting Germans. Their enemy would essentially be French colonial troops defending France's North African empire—troops the Americans were hoping to lure over to the Allied side.

Politically, Torch was problematic. It intensified Stalin's paranoia regarding his capitalist partners, and his feeling that they were shaky. Militarily, it was every bit as vexing. Eisenhower and Marshall worried about the risks. The target was, as Eisenhower put it, the rim of a continent where "no major military campaign" had been conducted for centuries. It was a forbidding thousand-mile stretch of sand, rock, and mountain that extended from Casablanca on the Atlantic to the narrow spit of land at the Mediterranean pointing toward Sicily and southern Italy, with the Tunisian coast somewhere between. There, the Vichy French ruled like Ottoman sultans in Casablanca, Oran, Algiers, and Tunis. The Italians and Germans ruled like Julius Caesar in Tripoli and Cyrenaica. And Rommel's armies, at El Alamein, some 160 miles northwest of Cairo, reigned like Roman legions in the provinces.

There was also a question of preparation. Rather than a systematic buildup over many months, "we had only weeks," Eisenhower complained. For him, this was an uncharacteristic understatement, but time was short. Then there was the question of where to land. For Africa, unlike Europe, they had only meager information about the terrain; in truth, it was riddled with unknowns. And none of the options were very attractive; the beaches of Algeria were protected from the elements but otherwise were a risky landing site: there was a strong possibility that the Nazis would thrust through Spain to cut off the Allied invaders via Spanish Morocco. To land on the ledge of Africa from the Atlantic entailed possibly encountering ferocious weather, particularly the towering eighteen-foot whitecaps that crashed ashore on the beaches of Casablanca. And to land from anywhere in the North Atlantic, hundreds of boats and thousands of troops would have to thread their way through blackened waters infested by predatory U-boats. And however determined the Americans were to create a second front, it would divert U.S. naval power away from the Pacific. To Eisenhower's way of thinking, striking at the periphery of German power, rather than at its core, would prolong the war—a fatal mistake. Finally, critics of Torch worried once again that a desperate Stalin would make a separate peace with Hitler. This time for good.

Roosevelt was willing to let his generals fret. On August 6, the definite decision had been made, and it included appointing Eisenhower as commander in chief of the Allied expeditionary force. Roosevelt's "secret baby"—Henry Stimson's words—would move forward. Whether it prolonged the war or not—most historians think not—and whether it was preferable to a full cross-Channel invasion or not, Torch had the undeniable benefit of finally bringing U.S. ground troops into the fight against the Axis powers in 1942. Churchill and Roosevelt understood this, even if Eisenhower and Marshall did not. Only later did Marshall concede, "We failed to see that the leader of democracy has to keep the people entertained."

Actually, entertainment was an inelegant euphemism. More accurately, Roosevelt had conceived of the operation as a way of uplifting the American people. Thus, he wrote to Churchill on August 30, "I feel very strongly that the initial attacks must be made by an exclusively American ground force." Those assaults would be supported by British air and transport units, and there was concern about how the Americans would be distinguished from the British; as Churchill quipped to Roosevelt, "in the night, all cats are gray." Roosevelt was reassuring. "We're getting very close together," he told Churchill. Churchill shot back that if convenient, British troops could "wear your uniform. They will be proud to do so."

Roosevelt said, "Hurrah!"

Churchill agreed the next day: "OK, full blast."

When would the attack take place? At the outset, Roosevelt had planned for late October; clasping his hands as if in prayer, he had pleaded with Marshall, "Please make it before Election Day." But Eisenhower and his colleagues were still working out details to the very end—for weeks, the Americans and the British wrangled over the specifics of the operation—so the assault was postponed until five days after the election: November 8. It was to be Roosevelt's first major military operation of the war—ordered against the counsel of his military advisers.

For the president, it needed to be a triumph.

9

Giant Cemeteries

HE WAS A MAN who had probably never imagined that anyone's life might depend on him. He had neither epic ambitions nor epic flaws; indeed, on almost every level he was a puzzle. Proud of his lineage—Eduard Schulte was German through and through—meticulous, iron-willed, driven, and secretive, he was possessed by an inner vision that he dared not share with anyone. He was a titan of industry, but he had a hidden side that would astonish his colleagues and the elegant social set—the men in white tie and tails and the women in furs—with whom he mingled. No doubt he himself was surprised when, in a time of Nazi barbarism, his unlikely hands would potentially come to hold the fate of hundreds of thousands of innocent Jews and the future of the Final Solution.

Physically he was impressive—six feet tall with broad shoulders. His skin was pale; his nose was like a beak; his eyes were dark, sad, and brooding. And he had a confident gait even though he walked with a pronounced limp, the souvenir of an accident that had almost killed him—he had accidentally slipped under a railway car—necessitating the amputation of his left foot, and then eventually of his entire leg.

Little in his background suggested that he would play a central role in the drama of the Final Solution. The Schultes had lived in Germany since the seventeenth century, and his grandparents grew up among the spired churches and lush green parks of Westphalia. Schulte's own childhood home in Düsseldorf was luxurious and decidedly aristocratic. The family dined out at exclusive clubs and entertained extravagantly. Like others in their social set—their friends were eminent lawyers, bankers, physicians, and artists—they enjoyed the first flush of prewar prosperity. Their surroundings were always stylish and the children, including Eduard, were taught the finest of social graces; later in Eduard's life, his motto became "*Anstand und Würde*" ("decency and dignity"). The Schultes' passion was hunting—they owned a weekend getaway outside the city, and Schulte would eventually buy land for a hunting lodge the size of a small resort. And they collected gold watches.

The Schulte household was run by a staff of servants, including a cook; a butler; a gardener for the sprawling grounds, which needed daily cultivating; a tutor for the children; and a hefty woman who bathed the children and took them on strolls for exercise. At Christmastime, the family feasted on oysters and champagne, and the children rode their toy rocking horse or enthusiastically played with a large collection of sturdy, green-enameled clockwork trains. When not nibbling on raisin cakes in one of the many local coffeehouses, they also vacationed, often, but only in Germany—usually in the Black Forest.

Schulte's family was Protestant, and politically conservative, so after World War I his parents voted for the right-wing National People's Party from 1919 on. Yet in religion and politics the Schultes were neither doctrinaire nor overly ideological; they eschewed excessive religious observance—Schulte himself, even after he had children, did not go to church—and read the *Frankfurter Zeitung*, one of Germany's most prominent liberal dailies. And one of Eduard's closest childhood friends was a Jew, a fact that would shape his views for many years to come;

together, the two would hop onto bicycles, explore Düsseldorf, and swap their dreams and stories. Schulte was never an anti-Semite.

From his earliest years, Eduard was an achiever. He read *Robinson Crusoe*, thrilled to James Fenimore Cooper's *The Deerslayer*, and lingered for hours over the large glossy pictures in Theodore Roosevelt's African safari stories. As he grew older, he was poised for success, standing out as a model student at the elite Düsseldorf municipal *Gymnasium*: there, he studied Latin and then turned his attention to Greek. He absorbed enough that he was able to read Homer in the original, and could recite passages from the *Odyssey* by heart. Typical of most Germans of his day, his English was spotty at best. He also showed an inclination toward leadership: rarely boastful, he was able to ingratiate himself with those above him, and to dominate—or inspire—those below him.

As a boy he fantasized often about what he wanted to do in life, imagining himself deftly negotiating his way out of crises. And he thought about money; ambitious and single-minded, he wanted to be rich. Soon he conquered the musty particulars of the German banking system and showed an impressive talent for the stock market. In the spring of 1913, after earning a degree in stock exchange law, Schulte moved to Berlin, where he became a junior employee of one of Germany's largest banks. Three years later, he joined the office of supply in the Prussian war ministry; though still young, he was responsible for the production and sale of soap in Germany, a mundane-sounding but significant position. His rise was swift. He married in 1917; had two sons, Wolfgang and Ruprecht; and by the age of thirty had become a general manager at Sunlicht Soap, where he flourished. More than ever, he could rejoice in his good fortune.

Then failure struck. The economy slowed, inflation was high, and Eduard was laid off. No job prospects captured his interest. The Bavarian civil service offered him a position; he turned it down. The pay was only a small fraction of his salary at Sunlicht, and he had no desire to spend the rest of his working days huddled over stacks of government papers. For a while, little stirred his imagination. He wandered along the streets of Berlin, until one day he bumped into a family friend. On the friend's advice, Schulte applied to be the general manager of one of Germany's oldest corporations, the industrial giant Giesche, which was the leading producer of nonferrous metals, particularly zinc. Old, conservative, and distinguished—the official history of the corporation filled three hefty volumes, and its tentacles were seemingly everywhere—Giesche also produced chemicals and dyes; maintained river barges; and owned basalt quarries. With little overstatement, the *New York Times* called Giesche one of the "oldest industrial undertakings in the world" and one of the "most valuable" in Europe. Schulte's application was a long shot—he was not quite thirty-five years old—but he wangled a series of interviews, and soon thereafter, he was hired as the head of the corporation.

At the outset, after World War I, Giesche was deep in debt and unable to finance the modernization of new mines. Through careful management, Schulte was able to secure much-needed loans, and shrewdly, he forged a partnership with the legendary American financier Averell Harriman and Harriman's Anaconda Copper Mining Company. Giesche had headquarters in Breslau (Wroclaw), where Schulte moved with his family; and also in Poland, in the town of Kattowitz (Katowice).

Breslau was a bustling city—the largest and most significant in eastern Germany—and it had been one of Germany's most impressive cultural centers. Now, in the mid-1920s, it teemed with daily newspapers, baroque buildings, open-air concerts in the summer, and ice skating in the winter. There was also a thriving university. Yet for all of its activity, Breslau was not another Munich or Hamburg, nor was it as cosmopolitan as Berlin, London, or Paris. The air was dirty, the streets were narrow, and large factories belched plumes of black smoke into the sky. The surrounding region, once prosperous, was now impoverished compared with a flourishing western Germany. Moreover, as the worldwide economy stalled, many of its residents had a sense of dread.

For Eduard, however, life couldn't have been better. His family moved into a spacious ten-room apartment bought by the corporation in a wealthy suburb, in a building that was architecturally the equal to thousands in Paris, London, and Berlin. The home was ideally located: within a few minutes in each direction there was a school for the children, a tennis club where the family played, and a park where they strolled. In the summers, they took excursions to the Giant Mountains. And when Schulte took business trips to Berlin, London, Switzerland, or New York City, a posh hotel suite always awaited him—in New York he stayed at the Waldorf Astoria; in Berlin, at the exclusive Coburg. He made money and invested it wisely. In the great crash of 1929 he lost it, and in 1932 the zinc market collapsed. However, by 1935, Giesche, now intertwined with the Nazi government, was again filling its coffers, and Schulte was once more a rich man.

He felt right at home with the widespread ethic of German purity, yet he ridiculed the hand kissing and smoking jackets so prevalent among Germany's gentry. Still, he was both fussy and vain and cared deeply about his appearance. He wore his hair carefully cropped—he did this to hide the fact that he was going bald—and his teeth were crooked, to his great annoyance. He dressed well, bringing back the finest materials from London for tailored suits. Nor did he have the look of someone with a serious disability, despite his amputation. At home he exercised regularly with a punching bag to keep fit. He also relished solitude, and hunting on his country estate.

His marriage to his wife, Clara, was enduring. The two functioned as a team. In many ways they were opposites, however: he was a practical businessman, with little love for theory; she was an intellectual who loved the life of the mind and had studied at the Sorbonne and in London. Where he was reserved, aloof, a masterpiece of understatement, she was warm and sensitive—she was also prone to depression. Where he avoided the limelight, she frequently made herself the center of attention—at gatherings around the fireplace in her home, she was an engaging raconteur, and she formed a salon in Breslau to discuss current events. But they were alike in at least one regard: he worked hard, often sixteen hours a day, and she kept an equally busy schedule, writing two historical novels.

A German first, Schulte was intensely patriotic. He was no great admirer of democracy, and he thought that Germany's defeat in World War I was a debacle. Beyond that, laconic and aloof, he studiously kept his political views to himself; scratch the surface, however, and there were indications that after Hitler's rise to power in 1933, Schulte no longer fitted in with Germany. Ironically, he had been skeptical about the overrepresentation of aristocrats in the previous government. Then, as Germany's economic crisis worsened, as the number of hungry people increased—at one point, over 15 million Germans were on welfare, and in Berlin there was the spectacle of the world's longest bread line stretching down the Kurfürstendamm—the problem for Schulte was no longer the right or the left. It was the inexorable growth of the Nazi Party, which had all but eviscerated both sides.

For Schulte, the alarms were everywhere. Dissension and intrigue now honeycombed the nation. There were the Nazi hooligans parading through the streets; there were the signs that Hitler seemed to be talking first out of one side of his mouth and then out of the other; and there was the casual brute force routinely used against real and imagined political enemies. The trouble with Germany, it was argued, was not simply Jews but deceit, traitors, and foreign conspiracies. One afternoon, a Polish worker was beaten to death by storm troopers in front of the Schulte family's eyes. It was blind, wanton slaughter. Then came the Night of the Long Knives: in June 1934, Hitler's henchmen arrested and murdered scores of his presumed political adversaries. Over several days, the Nazi SS and Gestapo—the notorious secret police—systematically eliminated opponents of the regime; a number of the vice chancellor's closest colleagues were murdered, some eighty-five all told; unthinkably, the vice chancellor himself was placed under house arrest on trumped-up charges while two of his associates were shot. The body of one opponent, a state commissioner, was discovered in a wooded area outside Munich, hacked to pieces, evidently by pickaxes. And the cabinet and the courts had blessed these extrajudicial killings, reversing centuries of German law. Meanwhile, thousands more were rounded up for the sole vice of their political opinions.

Yet for most Germans, this seemed to be the dawn of a wondrous new era of regeneration and prosperity, of Germany's long-awaited resurgence and growth. The provocative extremes of poverty and wealth were lessened; and nationally, there was an outpouring of patriotic fervor, as well as an all-out mobilization of resources. Most Germans were ecstatic. They saw the new government as unencumbered by outworn sentiments, outdated strategies, and the ineffectual ways of the old aristocratic regime. It was, they thought, an era destined to last a millennium. Where the old state had been impoverished and ripping open at the seams, the Nazis now began to forge the Germans into a single nation. Foreigners might have mercilessly lampooned Hitler, but like no other politician he knew how to appeal to the Germans' simmering resentments. And the people cheered.

But not Schulte. Increasingly exhausted and dispirited, he concluded that the Nazis were little more than "gangsters," monsters who would "ruin Germany." But with his disgust came caution—rabid Nazi sympathizers were everywhere. Most of his colleagues at Giesche were enthusiastic about the Nazis; so were the gardener and the charwoman at home; he feared that even his children would eventually be—they were forced to join the Hitler Youth. Still, he knew that if he wasn't careful with his opinions, the Nazi state would tighten its net around him, and the more he struggled to be free, or to speak out, the more he would become entangled in its mesh. By this stage, not even his closest friends knew what strong emotions ran just beneath the surface.

Because of such misgivings, his options seemed limited. Some around him argued that it was Hitler who would be co-opted by a benign government, and not vice versa. Others said Hitler was the German counterpart of Franklin Roosevelt, the man who at long last could feel the pulse of the people, genuinely able to inspire the masses, and defend their interests. True, at times the Nazis seemed to be prophets of death as much as of life, and progenitors of medieval terror as much as of progress, but wasn't all this for the betterment of the state? Schulte thought otherwise, but he held his tongue.

As time passed, the Nazi Party's iron hand only tightened its grip. There was no tide of indignation at home that could threaten to swamp the party, no backlash from the center. Hitler plunged ahead. He eliminated unemployment, built superhighways, presided over the Olympic Games, and began to rearm Germany. He cultivated the image of a peacemaker, and in the nation he had a receptive audience. Yet he also harangued the German people rather than consulted them; at times he compelled them rather than persuaded them; and he told them tales rather than the truth. However, the people, seemingly intoxicated by his conquests, blithely followed his lead. These were heady days for the Nazis, a time of apparently high purpose and creativity. Hitler's diplomacy reunited the Germans, and his armies revolutionized warfare—inventing the famed blitzkrieg and bringing the nations of Europe into the Nazi orbit. Over time, Hitler's victories would spread the German boot from the Rhineland to Austria, from Czechoslovakia to Poland, and even to Paris.

For the most part, Schulte remained uneasy about anything that smacked of activism against the regime; it was too dangerous. To be sure, there were times where he might rasp impatiently against the Nazis to his wife, Clara, but to the outside world he had to pretend otherwise. He adapted like a chameleon to the changing world. Still, these were bitter years for him.

Actually, he had seen Hitler clearly from the beginning. One day in 1933, as the election campaign in Germany approached its climax and swastikas decorated telegraph poles, he was invited to Hermann Göring's private residence for an extraordinary meeting between the regime itself and representatives of Germany's banking elite and industrial titans. The Nazis needed money.

Krupp Steelworks was there; so were the director of United Steel and the head of IG Farben. That Göring hosted this meeting at his famous Präsidentenpalast spoke volumes. Göring had been a flying ace in World War I and was now Hitler's charismatic public face in the Reichstag, Germany's lower parliament. Most of the invitees, seated in carefully arranged chairs, beamed in anticipation of what they were about to hear. The Führer kept everyone waiting for fifteen minutes, and then dramatically entered. He shook Schulte's hand and everyone else's, and then launched into a stinging diatribe about the urgent need for rearmament, about the evils of liberalism, and about the pitfalls of Bolshevism and social democracy. He would, he said, restore the Wehrmacht to its former glory. He snapped that Germany needed a "new spirit" and a new "political system," then paused to let the implications sink in. He attacked his partners in the governing coalition—the right-wing German nationalists—who, he insisted, would have to stand aside for the National Socialists; then he darkly hinted that an "armed takeover" of the government might be necessary. As quickly as he had entered, he left the meeting. At that point Göring made a stunning announcement to the men who sat before him: the next elections, in March 1933, would be the "last" for the decade, if not for the century.

An enthusiastic industrialist, Gustav Krupp von Bohlen und Halbach, having already expressed "the unanimous feeling of the industrialists in support of the Chancellor," rose to pledge 1 million marks to the regime, while the others promised 2 million more. As for Schulte? He was mute the entire time, doing his best to digest Hitler's monologue. As he got into his limousine after the meeting, he couldn't help thinking that Hitler was a "raving lunatic" who was putting Germany, even the world, on the path to ruination. And when, as Göring had promised, the Nazi Party held the last parliamentary vote for a decade, Schulte saw his fears coming true.

Alienated more than ever, in 1938 Schulte took long absences from Giesche, spending months abroad. On one warm July afternoon, Schulte found himself in London, strolling on Heath Street with Julius Schloss, an old friend and business colleague who had taken the unusual step of emigrating to England. Crowds were milling about in the streets, and the two ambled into Jack Straw's Castle, a local pub. Schloss had no great love for Hitler, and, quite suddenly, Schulte decided to unburden himself. War was imminent, Schulte said. The annexation of Austria was just the beginning, Czechoslovakia would be next, and then Poland and beyond. Schloss thought otherwise, suggesting that Germany's generals and bankers would do whatever they could to prevent war. Schulte shook his head; no, Hitler had cowed the opposition, and the German people were pliantly falling in line behind him.

Might not Germany moderate itself? Schloss wondered.

No, Schulte said. Hitler had cleverly hidden his "ultimate aims."

The two were silent, and then Schulte continued. If he were Jewish, he exclaimed, he would board the next train out of Germany, as quickly as possible. But, he sighed, he was German. His family, and everything else he held dear, was there. And he couldn't see himself living in New York or Paris or London.

Then, after temporizing, he insisted that he would stay in Germany until "the bitter end."

But after Kristallnacht, after the takeover of Austria—the infamous *Anschluss*—after the rape of Czechoslovakia and the overrunning of Poland, Denmark, Norway, the Netherlands, Belgium, and France, the bitter end seemed bitter indeed. In Berlin, Schulte slowly absorbed these brutal events. By 1940, to him all this was not glory, but Germany bleeding from every pore. And the image of a continent being squeezed in Hitler's fist was now a ghastly one. Surrounded by fanatical Nazis, he felt marooned, depressed, alienated from his own nation. The brownshirted mobs grew more belligerent by the day, and it seemed that the Führer's mystique grew more powerful by the hour. Meanwhile, over the years, Schulte had watched with increasing dread the Nazis' rearmament, the slayings of their critics, the burning of books, the establishment of concentration camps, the screaming taunts of the Nazis' supporters, and of course the war.

And then came a fateful party attended by Heinrich Himmler.

~

SCHULTE HIMSELF WAS POSITIONED in the middle of the war effort. The Polish branch of Giesche in Upper Silesia was deemed by Germany to be a "vital military plant," and so Schulte was immediately elevated in the Nazi ranks. Also, Schulte's number two man at Giesche, Otto Fitzner, was a fanatical Nazi. Handsome, hard-charging, and hardworking,

Fitzner, a trained engineer, was a veteran of World War I and on the fast track in the new German order. Through careful maneuvering, he had a rapid ascent in the Nazi hierarchy: first as a senior commander in the SA, then in the SS, then in an honorary appointment to Heinrich Himmler's staff, and then as head of the metal industry branch within the Ministry of Economics. After that, he received an all-important appointment as head of the civilian administration overseeing Upper Silesia. Fitzner even once met Adolf Eichmann and was one of the first Germans to learn about the deportations of Jews. Few thought to question his access to some of the most sensitive information in the Third Reich. Yet—though this was unknown to the Nazi high command—Fitzner had at least one weak spot: he was prone to bragging. He also assumed that Schulte was an equally fervent Nazi. Unwittingly, Fitzner became a pipeline of information to Schulte throughout the war.

Schulte had other sources as well; the governor for Lower Silesia, who later was made head of the SS, was a friend of his, as was a senior executive at Daimler-Benz, which sold Mercedes automobiles. And through Giesche he came to know a number of German generals. In the bustle of wartime Berlin, he maintained contact with several highly placed acquaintances, and in the city's clubs he backslapped and drank with diplomats and generals. Despite the insistence on secrecy in the Nazi regime, talk was still a common currency in the hubbub of war. For Schulte, separating fact from fiction was the main challenge.

Schulte's determination to gather information soon became an obsession, and his obsession soon became a desire for action, and he concocted a dramatic role for himself: to undermine the Nazi regime.

At great risk, Schulte slowly dribbled out the Nazis' secrets to the west. On his frequent business trips to Switzerland, he passed on his assessments about conditions and plans in Germany, along with bits of gossip, to a member of the Polish secret service, who in turn passed the information on, via secret radio transmitter or diplomatic mail pouch, to the British. From there, it was relayed to the Americans in Washington.

How important was this information? Schulte was only one of hundreds, if not thousands, of informants. But the time would soon come when he emerged as one of the most important—if America and the Allies would only listen.

In Germany, Schulte now regularly turned his radio on and listened to the crackle of the BBC, even though if the Gestapo found out, this was a crime punishable by execution. Under the strain, he became moody and high strung, yet he remained determined. In Switzerland, he passed on information about the fateful Hitler-Molotov-Ribbentrop meeting. He relayed information about the mammoth German preparations for Operation Barbarossa. He provided assessments about the dependence of German industry on raw materials, and made off-the-cuff observations about Hitler's relationships with his generals.

But his most stunning information would come, quite by accident, from a dinner party in a remote region of Poland. At stake were the lives of millions and, as he stumbled on this information, his own life.

ON THE MORNING OF July 17, 1942, Schulte was in his office riffling through a newspaper, mulling over the reports from the front lines. The beloved German general Erwin Rommel was squaring off against British general Bernard Montgomery at El Alamein; German forward units had pushed their way as far east as the Donets River in the Soviet Union; and Franklin Roosevelt had severed relations with Germany's ally Finland. Schulte was just about to summon his secretary when his deputy, Otto Fitzer, eased his way into the office, bearing startling news. Heinrich Himmler, chief of the SS and, second only to Hitler, the most feared man in the Third Reich, had "important business" in the area. Schulte stiffened. Himmler was known as a talented organizer; was he coming to inspect the Giesche works? Fitzner reassured him: no. Instead, Himmler was visiting "Auschwitz." To Schulte, this was puzzling: there was nothing of any significance in Auschwitz.

The more Schulte thought about it, the less sense it made. True, eastern Upper Silesia teemed with activity. Coal mines, synthetic fuel and rubber factories, and several hundred other military and industrial plants had relocated to the area from Germany, attracted by tax breaks and the ability to increase profits by using slave labor. Giesche itself was a beneficiary. But Auschwitz? Once part of the Holy Roman Empire, Auschwitz was an unremarkable town, now known principally for social misery, wretched economic conditions, and a distillery that dated back to 1804. There was a concentration camp, situated on swampy, malarial ground, but as far as he was aware, this camp consisted primarily of an old Austrian garrison dating back to World War I and now used to house Soviet POWs.

One significant thing it did have was a railway junction: located between the coal mining area around Kattowitz, and the industrial area of Bielsko, it had rail lines leading directly to Kraków and Vienna. And it had one other benefit: it was easy to close off against the outside world. But either Schulte knew none of this, or he didn't piece his knowledge together.

NOR COULD SCHULTE YET know that Himmler, this former chicken farmer who came to control the entire Nazi concentration camp system, would, outside of Hitler and Stalin, be responsible for more European deaths than any other man in history. Self-absorbed, scheming, and provincial, he was anything but the image of Hitler's ideal Aryan. Pudgy and sickly looking, he had an owl-like face, a recessed chin, bad eyesight, and poor posture. A notorious hypochondriac, he also suffered frequently from stomach cramps, not to mention blinding headaches, for which he took a hodgepodge of alternative medicines.

He was born in 1900, and his beginnings suggested a far different path in life. His father taught Latin and Greek at the renowned Wilhelm Grammar School in Munich; and Himmler himself was an eager, hardworking student, though he would also retreat to his room and fantasize about great feats of chivalry and crusading knights. Then came World War I. He enthusiastically joined a Bavarian regiment in 1918, wanting to be a part of a war in which each hill, each ridge, each crest frequently had to be stormed with bayonets, and where the battleground was soaked with German blood. But to his lasting chagrin, he never saw action; his division was demobilized first. Equally disappointing, the discredited monarchy, trembling and ineffective, began to disintegrate.

The postwar era was chaotic, and as inflation and unemployment soared, his father's finances severely suffered. Himmler was unable to study at Munich University. Instead, he had to settle for earning an agricultural degree that led to a second-rate job as an assistant in an artificial fertilizer factory. He left the job within a year. But then, as Adolf Hitler found his calling, so too did he: as a professional Nazi.

Jumping at the chance to again wear a uniform—even if only on weekends—he joined the German combat league, the fanatical paramilitary organization that supported Hitler's abortive Munich putsch in 1923. In the process he had a falling-out with his father, who considered the Nazis "lower-class rowdies." Nevertheless, when a year later the Nazi Party, now banned, was forced to go underground, Himmler quickly signed up, becoming a courier.

Meanwhile, he spent his free time patching together a philosophical worldview from a smattering of disparate, often paranoiac sources. He sifted through astrological writings in search of guidance; he absorbed numerous anti-Semitic works; he zealously delved into a study of witchcraft and witchcraft trials. And he fell in love with a radiant, blue-eyed, silky-haired blond nurse, Margarete Boden, who was eight years his senior and whose guiding tenet was "A Jew is always a Jew!" In any other European country, he might have been just another enlightened eccentric, the sort whose ideas fall from penny machines at county fairs—or from lunatic racists. In 1928, he started a small chicken farm on the outskirts of Munich with fifty laying hens, but the project failed from the start. The hens produced barely any eggs, money was tight, and his marriage suffered. He had to struggle to get by on his meager party salary of 200 marks a month. Now deputy director of Nazi propaganda, he despised democracy and was an ardent anti-Semite and an extreme nationalist.

In 1929, Hitler promoted Himmler to deputy leader of the SS—the so-called protective squads—whose responsibility was to protect the Nazi hierarchy. By this stage in Hitler's Germany, treachery was everywhere. Himmler would, notoriously, engineer the murder of two Nazi mentors during the Night of the Long Knives: Gregor Strasser and Ernst Röhm, of whom he was once a devoted follower. Seizing his chance, he built the SS into a racially exclusive empire, some 200,000 strong, serving his every whim. Himmler deftly maneuvered his way, through all the dismissals and intrigues, into Hitler's inner circle. By now, his very glance had come to symbolize the terrifying chill of a knock at the door or, one day, the haunting menace of the gas chamber. He once even boasted that if Hitler asked him to shoot his own mother, he would do it and "be proud of his confidence." Little wonder that Himmler's SS men wore a death's-head badge on their caps.

Pretentious and imperious, he was also particular. For the Nuremberg rally in 1929, he urged each local SS leader to bring an adequate number of clothes brushes. Cunning and moralistic, he also dabbled in such racial theories as the "hereditary health" of future SS wives, and, using a magnifying glass, he personally scrutinized photographs of every applicant for the SS to identify any dubious racial characteristics. He saw himself not as a monster or a demon, or even as a soulless technocrat, but instead as a heroic patriot and a "decent" person. He was also a fanatical nature worshipper. Though he neglected his wife, daughter, and adopted son—he also fathered two illegitimate children—he always put on the appearance of a warm and devoted father; they affectionately called him "Heinie." And he insisted that executing Jews was a matter of "total cleansing" for the Fatherland and a duty that could not be avoided. In keeping with this warped credo, he maintained that the SS murdered "decently" as well. Despite his ideological hatred, he nevertheless drew a distinction between killing Jews for "political motives," which he maintained was valid, and manslaughter or criminal murder for "selfish, sadistic, or sexual" motives, which was not. But whether he was growling to subordinates, or exploding with wrath, the cornerstones of his life were cunning, zeal, burning ambition—and death.

While Schulte was left to puzzle over why Himmler was at Auschwitz at all, Himmler was busying himself with the industrialized mechanism of genocide.

~

FOR HIMMLER, IN THE early weeks of July 1942, the work seemed endless. There were the secret directives about resettlement that he sent from Berlin to the head of the SS and to the lieutenant general who was the leader of the German police forces. There were the meetings with the head of the concentration camp inspectorate and an SS major general, who was a hospital chief, to discuss medical experiments on Jews at Auschwitz, experiments that Himmler warned were "most secret." There were the appointments he made and still had to make, such as earlier selecting Rudolf Hoess as the commandant of Auschwitz. And there was his visit to the camp itself.

He had been there once before, on March 1, 1941. At the time, his interest was surprising, given that he had not previously shown the slightest concern about the camp and had called off a visit scheduled for October 1940. Still, he had given orders to expand the camp to accommodate up to thirty thousand inmates, as well as to build the much larger camp that would become Birkenau. For his second visit, on July 17, 1942, a warm sunny day, he swept into Auschwitz in an open black Mercedes, driven by a chauffeur and surrounded by a large entourage. Treated like a visiting head of state, he paused for a moment and smiled, surprised and pleased when the camp orchestra played a famous aria from the Czech opera *The Bartered Bride*. An inmate was shocked to observe that Himmler moved with the grace and charm that one would expect to see at an English garden party.

That day, with an air of indifference, his expression vaguely bored and slightly amused, Himmler watched the complete process of gassing, from start to finish. With the pride that an architect shows for his work, he lingered while inspecting the existing gas chamber and the construction site for an expanded set of larger, newer gas chambers and crematoriums—a vast improvement over the old system of burying bodies in huge pits from which, after thaws and rains, the decomposing corpses would often emerge like zombies sprung to life. Then, his rimless glasses glinting in the sunshine, he strode onto the Auschwitz rail platform, where he heard a high-pitched whistle, followed by the arrival of two trains bearing Dutch Jews. He watched as the SS doctors decided the Jews' fates: the able-bodied women and men were beaten as they trudged off to the barracks; the remainder were slated for death. He watched as naked women's heads and bodies were methodically shaved and their hair carefully jammed into sacks to be sold as filling for luxury mattresses bound for Germany. He watched as 449 people were crammed into Bunker 2, and the door sealed. And he looked through the observation window as they began to shout, scratch, and vomit, defecate, and urinate on themselves before they died. Himmler watched it all, without saying a word and without giving any sign of remorse. In twenty minutes it was over.

After that he continued with the rest of his itinerary: he visited the building of a dam, the agricultural laboratories, the farm plantations, the herb gardens, and the experimental plant. He spent time in the hospital block, where he was briefed on the medical experiments that he had, just days before, ordered to be carried out, including the castration of men by X-ray and the sterilization of women by injection. He had a lengthy discussion with camp doctors about the high mortality rates and the continued spread of disease among the prisoners, caused by inadequate sanitation, an insufficient diet, and insufferable crowding; Himmler showed neither interest nor sympathy. He saw the living quarters and kitchens, and even climbed the gate tower to look at the drainage systems. And he toured the IG Farben synthetic rubber and oil plant, Buna.

That evening, a satisfied Himmler prepared for supper at Auschwitz before making his way to the Giesche Villa.

~

AT DINNER IN THE mess, Himmler sat down with Fritz Bracht, the Nazi Party's chief of Upper Silesia, as well as the camp's high command.

The tables were set with ample quantities of food, and Himmler, in his "best sparkling form," chatted gaily with the German officers about their careers and their families, as if they all had just come from a sports match rather than the gas chamber. After dessert was served and the final drinks were downed, the party climbed into Mercedes-Benzes and disappeared into a forest of pine and birch trees near Kattowitz, en route to an elegant villa that now served as Bracht's residence. Owned by Schulte's firm, Giesche, the villa seemed like a perfumed garden. It had tall, sun-filled windows and an azure swimming pool, as well as a golf course—amenities seldom available in wartime. Inside were drawing rooms, lounges, and dining rooms with dark mahogany paneling and polished floors. The doors were thrown open and the guests entered: the men wore their uniforms and the few women present wore jewels and haute couture. Himmler (who rarely drank) helped himself to a glass of red wine, lit a cigar, and held court. By all accounts, far from being cold or haughty, he was at his most charming, leading a sweeping discourse about everything from pedagogy for children to new styles of houses to his inspections of battle lines.

There, perhaps for the first time, Himmler openly talked with the guests—it is believed out of earshot of the women—about the plans for a much larger construction at Auschwitz. He and his guests also openly talked about Hitler's plans to systematically murder all the Jews of Europe and beyond—every last man, woman, and child.

The next day, back at the camp, Himmler picked his way through the section devoted to sorting the belongings of condemned Jews; later he looked on with a mixture of satisfaction and cold efficiency as a camp prostitute guilty of theft was whipped on her bare backside. Delighted with everything he saw, he promoted Hoess to lieutenant colonel, and informed him that he must now expeditiously begin building the enhanced crematorium complexes; more Jews, he warned, would be coming in vast numbers. Indeed there would be no letup—Jews would arrive at Auschwitz from France, Scandinavia, Belgium, the Balkans, and eventually Hungary.

Before leaving he made sure to exchange a few amiable words

with Hoess's wife and her little children. Back in Berlin the next day, on July 19, he wrote urgently to Friedrich Wilhelm Kruger in Kraków, commanding that the "resettlement of the entire Jewish population" be completed by December 1, 1942. At this stage, 400,000 people were still jammed into the ghetto of Warsaw, an area only two and a half miles long by a mile wide, which had previously housed only 160,000 people; after Himmler's order, 6,000 a day, every day, were assembled for "deportation" to the east.

~

A WEEK AND A HALF later, word about Himmler's dinner party and the plan to exterminate all of European Jewry filtered through to Schulte. He was stunned. Eliminate them? All of them? The numbers were incomprehensible. Until that time, when Hitler talked about the Jews, Schulte had taken the Führer's words to mean, for example, that the Jews would be resettled in a place like Madagascar. In any case, although the German nation might be deaf to the cries of Hitler's victims, Schulte was not.

It was then that he resolved to board the next train to Zurich and somehow pass the fateful news on to the Allies—and, he hoped, all the way to Franklin Roosevelt—as soon as possible.

For Schulte, it was a race against time.

~

UP TO NOW, IT was almost as if Schulte were in a theater, watching a frightening movie. No longer. On July 29, 1942, he quietly boarded the train at Breslau and eased himself into his first-class compartment; there he stayed, lost in his thoughts, as the train made its way south. Here—unlike in wartime Germany and Poland, where a thousand British planes had devastated Cologne and Allied air attacks had relentlessly struck Danzig—the landscape remained relatively unscathed. The train raced past picturesque whitewashed villages and a forest of tall pines. In Böblingen and Herrenberg, there were groves of trees, orchards, sheep, and pastures. In Ehningen there were churches with delicately shaped onion towers. By Bondorf and Neckarhausen, the train moved parallel to a nearly empty highway, then along the Neckar River.

At Singen the train stopped and the conductor announced that everyone had to get off for border control.

Was this trouble?

One by one, the passengers climbed out of the train and were waved into a nondescript room in the station, where two police officers scrutinized their passports. The check took about twenty minutes; then the passengers reboarded the train. Overhead, the sky suddenly darkened and the day turned cloudy just as Schulte saw the Rhine and the Swiss border beyond. Even on a cloudy day, Switzerland, with its natural seclusion and the beauty of its valleys, had an aura of health and freedom completely incongruous with the rest of the war. Its rugged mountain peaks rose into the sky. The air itself was a swirl of colors and delicate odors.

Soon, Schulte saw a little wooden house with a Swiss flag flapping in the wind. He was almost there.

~

SCHULTE COULDN'T SHAKE OFF the thought that for what he was about to do, the Gestapo could hunt him down, abduct him, or kill him. Yet when the train came to a stop inside Zurich's main railway station, the Hauptbahnhof, and a porter escorted him to his limousine, Schulte knew that he could not turn back. The car sped past Zurich's elegant stores and the headquarters of its largest banks. Then it turned to the right and slowed on reaching his hotel. The manager greeted him warmly, and Schulte was escorted to his usual suite, which had splendid views of the shimmering lake. Tapestries adorned the walls, and the public spaces had Tudor paneling; in Schulte's rooms a flower arrangement and a bottle of red wine awaited him.

Schulte picked up the phone. It was mid-afternoon.

~

EVEN IN NEUTRAL SWITZERLAND, there was little doubt that this was a continent at war. Though it was the height of the season, and the middle of the day, the streets were deserted—save for men striding about in uniform. Everything was rationed. Some of the smaller shops had been closed. A number of the larger businesses were struggling to survive—hotel owners, for instance, were facing the fact that only one tenth of their rooms were occupied during peak season. Gasoline was scarce. Meat was also in short supply. And of course, as in other nations across Europe, there was a blackout at night. But in what was perhaps a portent, there were indications of American culture around the city: not far from Schulte's hotel a Mickey Rooney comedy was playing.

Schulte had wrestled with the question of to whom to pass on his information. It had to be someone discreet—otherwise Schulte would be risking his life—but at the same time someone with the necessary connections and influence. It also had to be someone who would share Schulte's sense of urgency. He mulled over names: Poles, Swiss, Americans. In the end, he felt it had to be someone with ties to a major Jewish institution in America, who could then send the information to the White House.

He set up a meeting with a well-placed Jewish contact in the world of high finance.

That night, Schulte had a late dinner with a Jewish woman named Doris, with whom he was having a passionate affair. While they were picking at their food, Doris noticed that he looked anguished. Schulte laconically told her that "there were problems."

The next morning Schulte rendezvoused with his contact, and wasted little time in detailing Hitler's plan to exterminate the Jews of Europe. Not just thousands. Not just hundreds of thousands. But every man, woman, and child within the grasp of the Third Reich. He urged his contact in the strongest terms that this information had to be relayed immediately both to the leading Jewish organizations in America and to the U.S. government itself. He stressed that if immediate action wasn't taken, the Jewish people would be wiped out. A great crematorium had been built, and the Nazis were planning to take 3 million to 4 million Jews to the east, where they would be gassed with prussic acid. He stressed that this information came from unimpeachable sources in the upper reaches of the Nazi regime, but that otherwise the plan was enshrouded in the greatest of secrecy.

Schulte's contact sat stunned. As fantastic as the scheme sounded, he knew the Jews of eastern Europe were being rounded up and murdered in pogroms. Yet this was death on a scale almost unimaginable. This was not the Russians massacring Polish officers, or Lithuanian mobs herding Jews toward freshly dug pits for mass shootings, or roving Nazi squads assassinating anyone in their path. This was death on a level never before devised. Had anyone other than Schulte told him this information—the war was rife with rumors—he might have been skeptical. Schulte, however, was an impeccable source.

One problem—and it was a considerable problem—was that the contact was not close enough to the appropriate diplomats or to the Swiss Jewish leaders. He instead suggested another colleague, a Jewish journalist who was respected in all the right circles in Switzerland. Schulte agreed.

Wasting no time, the contact called the journalist immediately. Told he was out of town, he quickly tracked him down, leaving a message that it was a matter of "life and death."

When he finally reached the journalist, Benno Sagalowitz, Sagalowitz agreed to take a train to Zurich the very next day. But for the time being, Schulte was unwilling to meet with Sagalowitz himself. It was too dangerous. And in any case, he had an important conference in Berlin, which he could ill afford to miss, if only to keep up appearances. He authorized his contact to use his name—but only with Sagalowitz.

While Schulte was on a train heading home, his contact met with Benno. He explained to Benno that Schulte, a well-placed German industrialist, had a dire message to convey. With that, he pulled out a folded piece of paper from his pocket, and began to read its shattering contents. "I've received information from absolutely trustworthy sources," he said, his voice breaking with emotion, "that Hitler's headquarters is considering a plan to kill all remaining European Jews."

After relaying the whole sordid story, he underscored what Schulte had stressed: "action" must be taken at once. And by "action," he didn't mean diplomacy or the standard protest by the State Department or a warning from the Allies; he meant something more dramatic, such as rounding up German citizens in the United States.

Benno paused, digesting what he had just heard. "May I quote him," he said, "when I pass it on?"

The contact shook his head. "Under no circumstances."

For Benno, there were many unresolved questions. Was this just propaganda, much like the apocryphal stories of atrocities in World War I: babies being bayoneted or eaten alive by Germans, and nuns being violated? Benno reflected on what he had been told and thought not. Just a week earlier, he had clipped an article from a leading Swiss newspaper about a message that Winston Churchill himself had delivered to American Jews in Madison Square Garden. Churchill had urgently warned that more than 1 million Jews had been killed, and that Hitler would not be satisfied "until the cities of Europe" where Jews lived had been turned into "giant cemeteries." Wasn't Schulte confirming this? Hadn't Hitler been underestimated time and again? Moreover, the Führer was at the zenith of his power—most of western and eastern Europe lay in his grasp, and his forces seemed as unstoppable in North Africa as in northern Norway. In the Soviet Union, Nazi forces had reached the outskirts of Moscow. The Continent was close to despair, and even the remaining neutral nations were pervaded by a deadly tonic of fear and rumors.

Benno believed only one man could make the difference between life and death for millions of Jews. Like Schulte, he resolved that President Roosevelt should be reached as quickly as possible.

BUT HOW TO DO this, when it seemed that just about everyone in the free world was vying for the American president's attention? It turned out that the responsibility would fall on the shoulders of a young émigré lawyer working in a musty office at the former Hotel Bellevue in Geneva. Sagalowitz's contact was just thirty years old, and his name was Gerhart Riegner.

Small, scrawny, with a wry smile and slicked-back hair, he had been born in Berlin to a comfortable middle-class Jewish family with deep roots in German culture. He practiced law like his father and had studied at the Sorbonne, passing the bar in Paris. Then setback followed setback: Hitler came to power and, as in Germany, France lost its tolerance for Jews. French authorities passed an edict that forbade foreigners to practice law until a decade after they were naturalized. At his wit's end—he had even considered moving to Palestine—Riegner sought the advice of an eminent legal philosopher, who suggested he go to Geneva and take up international law. Riegner followed this advice and moved to Geneva. There, in 1936, he found a position with the League of Nations. He had the grand sounding portfolio of "monitoring" the rights of minorities guaranteed by the treaties ratified at the close of World War I. But as Hitler's power was on the rise, the League's was on the wane, until the organization all but withered away. Nevertheless, Riegner's determined efforts caught the eye of one founder of the World Jewish Congress, who asked him to take over the day-to-day work of that organization at Geneva.

It was a daunting prospect. Suddenly, Riegner, polite, conscientious, reserved, and a refugee himself, was in a position to report on the escalating persecution of Jews, as well as to run one of the most significant "listening posts" in Nazi-dominated Europe, particularly as fragmentary information about massacres began to trickle in. Actually, the World Jewish Congress was more fiction than fact. Founded in 1936 to protect the rights of Jews in Europe, and to "mobilize the democratic world against Nazi atrocities," it had virtually no budget, no authority, and no diplomatic reach. It had a meager office in New York, and an equally meager one in London. It had few emissaries abroad and had to confront an unsympathetic public and an overwhelmed western alliance. Its calls for protests and economic boycotts of the Nazi regime went nowhere, and its denunciations of mounting anti-Semitism were all but unheeded. More often than not, its only authority stemmed from its chief architect—its general secretary—and whatever persuasive powers he could muster.

Initially, the World Jewish Congress had its headquarters in Paris, but after France was overrun by the Germans, it was forced to move to Geneva, where it already had a liaison office. In 1940 most of Europe had already fallen under Nazi occupation, and even in neutral Switzerland, Riegner never felt quite safe. Thus, he always carried a rucksack filled with basics, "ready to flee into the mountains" in case the Germans pursued him. It included a fake Bolivian passport, complete with ID, and an emergency visa for the United States. Moreover, he knew that Switzerland was a reluctant host nation and that as far as his own security was concerned, the clock was always ticking. Indeed, within a week of his meeting with Sagalowitz, the Swiss police began turning back Jewish refugees who had managed to cross the border. Riegner was also attuned to the other worrisome signs around him. His first brush with anti-Semitism had occurred when he was just five and a fellow pupil derided him as a "dirty little Jew." He could vividly recall the Nazi hooligans who gathered outside his parents' home in Germany in 1933, chanting over and over, "Jews out! Jews out!" while he huddled, terrified, in his bathroom. There were also the indelible images of the brownshirts smashing the windows of Jewish homes and stores, hauling out Jews, chasing them down, and beating and taunting and finally killing them.

Riegner and Sagalowtiz had talked for five hours over lunch, dissecting every detail provided by Schulte. Riegner wanted to satisfy himself about Schulte's reliability; Sagalowitz reassured him. After lunch they strolled along one of Lake Geneva's beautiful beaches and paused to watch boats gliding in the water. It was a cloudless day, and the sights and smells were intoxicating. At first, hearing Schulte's warnings secondhand, Riegner was incredulous. His initial reaction was that there had to be some mistake; it made no sense. To be sure, he knew about the initial hazy reports of pogroms, and then the more extensive and specific reports of Nazi persecutions. He knew about the arrests and deportations, the harsh use of ghettos and capricious imprisonments, the forced labor and the summary slayings, and insidious accounts of "mobile gas vans." And he knew that three times Hitler had given speeches proclaiming openly that he would exterminate the Jews of Europe.

Indeed, he recalled that in early 1942 one of his colleagues had written a letter with a terrifying conclusion: "The number of our dead after the war will have to be counted not in thousands or hundreds of thousands but in several millions." Then in June 1942, Riegner himself became aware that more regions across Europe were being emptied of Jews: in France, Belgium, Austria, the Netherlands, Germany itself, and now Poland. That raised the question: where were the Jews going to be settled? No one, it seemed, knew.

What was unique about Schulte's report was that it came not from Jewish victims or Jewish authorities, but from a German industrialist with access to Hitler's inner circle. And gas chambers? This was the first Riegner had heard about them. And for the first time, here was evidence that the Nazis had a coordinated extermination plan extending across all of Europe and beyond.

The streets were half deserted. Now, for Riegner, the time for hesitating was over. He and Sagalowitz were terribly shaken. Both men were well aware that they might be accused of the worst kind of panic-mongering. But if this news was true, every day and indeed every hour now mattered. Like Schulte, Riegner believed this news had to get to President Roosevelt, and get to him fast.

But first, he had to find a sympathetic ear. It was then that Riegner began to make his plan. He and Sagalowitz decided to meet again in Zurich, on Monday, August 3.

Thus would begin the efforts to formulate what history would remember as the "Riegner Telegram."

~

OF COURSE, NEITHER RIEGNER nor Schulte knew that Hitler's scheme had already begun, and that, in secret, the murderous Nazi machine was now operating at a grueling pace. Treblinka, Sobibór, and Belzec were already killing Jews en masse; and the Nazis had begun their assault on the Warsaw ghetto, where the Jews would heroically fight and fail. By now, 1.5 million Jews had already been killed.

FOR HIS PART, AN agitated Schulte was now back in Breslau, leading a double life, playing his roles flawlessly. In one life, he continued to display his normal swagger, and kept up his work routine as always. There was the thorny question of delivering zinc for the production of ammunition, as the War Ministry was now demanding; there was his own schedule of appointments and conferences; and always there was the question of having enough supplies of raw materials. In his other life, he was working night and day, or as best he could, to obtain further information about the Nazis' plans to murder each and every Jew in Europe—and he was fervently hoping that his contacts in Switzerland would heed his message.

There was another message that he hoped they would heed as well. From his familiarity with the inner workings of the Third Reich, he knew that simple statements or diplomatic démarches would have little effect on Hitler and his regime. The Nazis held Roosevelt in contempt and respected only force. Thus only dramatic action or a crushing blow could sway the Nazis, such as a widely publicized arrest of hundreds of thousands of Germans living in America—not unlike the internment that FDR had imposed on the Japanese Americans after Pearl Harbor—or an Allied bombing attack.

As the enormity of the risk he had taken sank in, Schulte couldn't help wondering if one day the SS might knock on his door, coming for him.

FOR RIEGNER, THE STRAIN was almost unbearable. Nevertheless, as European Jewry was being taken apart piece by mangled piece, he was determined not to be defeated by the magnitude of his task. After careful thought—by his own account it took two days for him to make "sense of the whole thing"—he decided to approach both the American and the British consuls in Geneva and ask them to pass on the information to their respective governments, as well as to send a coded message to Stephen Wise, who was one of the United States' most prominent Jews and a close personal ally of President Roosevelt. On the morning of August 8, he made his way to the British consulate, where he passed on Schulte's information. By 4:48 p.m. on August 10, a coded cable was being relayed to the Foreign Office in London; it reached there at 6:25 that same evening.

Later in the day, Riegner arrived at the American consulate, where he met with the vice consul, Howard Elting Jr.

By now, the normally composed Riegner was in a state of "great agitation" as he blurted out the Nazis' extraordinary plans. "There has been," he said, "and is being considered in Hitler's headquarters a plan to exterminate all Jews from Germany and German controlled areas in Europe after they've been concentrated in the East—presumably Poland." He continued, "The number involved is said to be between 3½ and 4 million and the object is to permanently settle the Jewish question in Europe." The dapper Elting—he had black, wavy hair and wore three-piece suits—was at first taken aback; the report seemed "fantastic." Riegner nodded in agreement: he had at first felt this way as well. Yet he stressed that it coincided with the recent mass deportations, and with everything else they knew about Germany's actions toward the Jews.

At that he handed Elting a summary of the message and urged that it be telegraphed as soon as possible to Washington and other Allied governments, as well as to Stephen Wise. Whatever doubts Elting may have had were overcome by Riegner's earnestness. Wasting little time, Elting immediately passed on Riegner's information to the American legation in Bern, adding that in his "personal opinion," he thought Riegner was "a serious and balanced individual." Moreover, he recommended that the report be "passed on" to the State Department.

Told to draw up a formal report for the secretary of state, Elting highlighted his belief "in the utter seriousness of my informant."

Adolf Hitler in 1936 triumphantly reviewing his honor guard in Berlin.

Kristallnacht, on November 9–10, 1938, a chilling first sign that the Nazi regime would make attacking Jews a priority. Horrified residents watched a synagogue, one of many torched, go up in flames.

With the seizure of territory in the Soviet Union in 1941, the Nazis began executing Jews en masse. Members of the SS look on as a Ukrainian Jew is executed in cold blood.

4

It was at the Wannsee Villa in 1942 that the Nazis, in the greatest of secrecy, planned a systematic, industrialized means of mass murder: the Final Solution. After the plans were drawn up, the Germans retired to the library to sip sherry.

5

The train tracks leading to the main entrance of Auschwitz.

6

Heinrich Himmler, third from the left, with Rudolf Hoess next to him facing the camera, inspects the Monowitz-Buna complex by Auschwitz on July 17, 1942.

Gerhart Riegner, after a clandestine meeting with Eduard Schulte, a highly placed German industrialist, wrote a fateful cable in August 1942 to alarm Roosevelt and the United States government about the impending slaughter of European Jews.

7

From June 1940 onward, Breckinredge Long and the State Department put up roadblock after roadblock to keep Jews from being able to come to the United States, which amounted to a death sentence for them. At one point Treasury Secretary Henry Morgenthau dramatically confronted Long, telling him, "Frankly, Breck, the impression is that you are anti-Semitic."

8

A close ally of Roosevelt's and one of the most prominent Jews in America, Rabbi Stephen Wise was "demented with grief" over the fate of the Jewry. He was a moving spirit behind efforts to prod the White House to do more. Here, pictured on the right, he is at a rally of 47,000 people to raise public awareness about the persecution of European Jews.

9

10

Jan Karski, a member of the Polish underground, infiltrated one of the death camps and witnessed firsthand the Nazi atrocities against the Jews. In July 1943 he met with Roosevelt—a meeting that had great impact on the president's thinking. Nonetheless, the Polish ambassador said that the president did not commit to any concrete action.

11

Henry Morgenthau, only the second Jew in history to hold a cabinet post, was reluctant for years to raise Jewish issues with Roosevelt. But faced with the alarming facts about the Final Solution and the administration's reluctance to get involved, he decided to risk his cherished friendship with the president. He hotly protested to FDR in January 1944 about the government's "acquiescence in the murder of the Jews."

12

The War Refugee Board was hastily created in January 1944 by Franklin Roosevelt. Secretary of State Cordell Hull, Morgenthau, and Secretary of War Henry Stimson gather here along with Executive Director John Pehle. The board would save at least 200,000 lives, prompting Morgenthau to lament "the terrible 18 months" of delay before the board was created.

13

The gassing of the Hungarian Jews in the spring of 1944 was the worst single mass killing in the war, carried out with frightening speed. Here they undergo selection on the ramp to Auschwitz-Birkenau. Humanitarians, eventually joined by the War Refugee Board, frantically called on the White House to bomb the death camp.

14

Raoul Wallenberg, a Swedish emissary sent to Hungary in June 1944 by the War Refugee Board, employed every method at his disposal to save Jews there. He even confronted one SS officer and threatened that he would "swing from the gallows" if he carried out the execution of a group of Jews. Wallenberg was an example of a humanitarian exerting creative methods on behalf of European Jews—the kind of creativity that had been missing from American policy.

Franklin D. Roosevelt, Joseph Stalin, and Winston Churchill at the Tehran conference in Tehran, Iran, November 29, 1943. It was here that the Big Three agreed on a strategy for 1944—mainly that a second front in France would be opened up in the spring.

16

Franklin Roosevelt with General Dwight Eisenhower and General George Patton in Sicily after the Tehran conference. In one of the most important decisions of the war, Roosevelt told Eisenhower simply, "Well, Ike, you are going to command Overlord."

17

The Allied military high command met to plan Operation Overlord in England in 1944. The meeting was intense and fraught with questions. When the weather kicked up on June 4, one of the generals remarked, "It's a hell of a gamble." Eisenhower later gave the order: "Okay, we'll go."

Rallying the men, Eisenhower met with paratroopers of the 101st Airborne on June 5, 1944. He was blunt and to the point. “Go get ’em,” he bellowed.

19

At 7:30 a.m. at Omaha Beach on June 6, 1944, American soldiers waded through the water from their Allied landing craft. Casualties were atrocious, German fire was unremitting, but the men kept pushing forward.

Gliders brought a continuous stream of supplies to the Allied troops at Utah Beach.

Allied troops continued to advance at Omaha Beach, and within a week more than 300,000 reinforcements had arrived in France. Nevertheless, Germany managed to hold out eleven more months.

22

By the spring of 1944, the Allied mastery of the skies was nearly complete. A number of German cities lay in ruins, including Ludwigshafen, pictured here. It was then that the debate over bombing Auschwitz intensified.

23

Assistant Secretary of War John McCloy (on left) resisted all of the cries to bomb Auschwitz as well as military efforts to rescue an endangered Jewry, prompting Morgenthau to attack him as an "oppressor of the Jews."

24

Nothing could quite prepare the Americans for the ghastly sights they found when they liberated Ohrdruf and other Nazi concentration camps. Dwight Eisenhower and his generals view the charred bodies of prisoners at Ohrdruf on April 4, 1945. General Patton was so sickened that he vomited. Below, bodies of prisoners at Ohrdruf are stacked like cordwood.

25

26

Winston Churchill, Franklin Roosevelt, and Joseph Stalin at the Yalta conference, Livadia Palace, February 9, 1945, to discuss the postwar architecture of the world. Roosevelt acknowledged he felt "more bloodthirsty" than ever toward the Germans, but his focus was on the establishment of the United Nations. Visibly deteriorating, Roosevelt had only two months left to live.

Ten days after Schulte had arrived in Zurich, it seemed to all involved that it would be just a short time before Roosevelt, Churchill, and the world would learn about Hitler's plans for the Jews.

They were sorely mistaken.

ARGUABLY, IN PERHAPS NO other aspect of the war would the White House be able to receive such authoritative information from deep inside the Third Reich. Yet in his August 11 cover letter accompanying the Riegner report, the American minister in Switzerland, Leland Harrison, sought to bring this drama to a premature close by attaching a watered-down message characterizing the report merely as "war rumors inspired by fear and what is commonly understood to be the actually miserable condition of these refugees who faced decimation as a result of physical maltreatment, persecution, and scarcely endurable privations, malnutrition, and disease."

Riegner's telegram wound up not in the Oval Office but on the desk of the State Department's division of European affairs, where it was generally dismissed by the administration officials. One official, the prickly Paul Culbertson, didn't even think the Bern legation should have "put this thing in a telegram." His colleague, the bland, colorless Elbridge Durbrow, took an even harder line, commenting that the Swiss legation should refuse even transmitting such messages "to third parties," and noting, with tragic certitude, that "American interests" were not involved. As to the veracity of the German industrialist's disclosure? It was "fantastic," yet another war rumor. Was there any curiosity about who the German industrialist was? Remarkably, there was not. Was there any interest in how intimate he was with Hitler's inner circle? Equally remarkably, there was not. As for Riegner, who was a known quantity? He was simply treated as erratic, impetuous, a nuisance. The State Department's routine would go on virtually unchanged by the Riegner report. It was as though the men in Washington had covered their eyes and ears and were simply waiting for the whole mess to disappear.

For the State Department now, the only decision left was whether to relay the Riegner report on to Roosevelt's ally Rabbi Stephen Wise, as Riegner had requested. The answer was no.

"Never did I feel so strongly the sense of abandonment, powerlessness and loneliness," recalled Riegner, "as when I sent messages of disaster in horror to the free world and no one believed me." No doubt Schulte would have been in equal despair.

10

Riegner

IN THE DAYS THAT followed, there was some second-guessing within the State Department about the Riegner Telegram, but only about process, not content. One department official, Paul Culbertson, didn't like the idea of sending it on to Rabbi Stephen Wise, but he cautioned that "if the Rabbi hears later that we had the message and didn't let him in on it he might put up a kick." His solution was to pass it on but damn it with a form of faint praise, adding that the "Legation has no information to confirm the story." Others, like Elbridge Durbrow, took the opposite view. He continued to declare the allegations in the telegram "fantastic." Even if the killings were about to take place, he worried about the "impossibility of our being of any assistance." His advice? To bury the report and move on. Which is exactly what they did.

Moreover, Durbrow wrote a memo in which he declared that in the future the Swiss legation should refuse to pass on any more such message "to third parties," unless it clearly involved "American interests."

This memo would be prophetic: within the next six months, the State Department would go to great lengths to strangle any further flow of information from Switzerland about mass exterminations.

Four days later, the State Department bluntly informed Leland Harrison, the U.S. minister in Switzerland, that Riegner's message would not be passed on to Wise, because of its "unsubstantiated nature." A week later Riegner was told the same thing; nevertheless, he was counseled that if he could supply "corroboratory information," his message would receive further consideration.

Riegner's last, best hope of getting word to Roosevelt was still Wise. Yet Wise remained in the dark.

WHO WAS STEPHEN WISE and why was he so important? On paper and in person, no man seemed more suited to publicize the Riegner Telegram than Wise. He was by turns brilliant, headstrong, imperious, and inflammatory. He was also perhaps the most well-known leader of the Jewish community in America in the 1930s and the 1940s. To his admirers, he was a seasoned diplomat and a much heralded truth teller, an unwavering defender of the downtrodden. To his detractors, he was dogmatic, on the wrong side of history—or a nuisance. But neither his friends nor his foes could ignore his connections, which were considerable; his following, which was extensive; or his commitment, which was unshakable.

Born in Budapest in 1874, he was the grandson of the chief rabbi of Hungary, and this lineage conferred a touch of royalty on him. His parents spoke German, and when he was a young child they immigrated to New York. He became a remarkable union of two diverse threads of Judaism that were uneasily interwoven; he embraced the New World—he graduated from Columbia University—even as he maintained his ties to the Old World: he was ordained in Vienna as a Reform rabbi. He headed a synagogue in Portland, Oregon, and later founded the renowned Free Synagogue of New York, a temple that quickly became as fashionable as it was famous—Wise was given the latitude to preach in any direction he wanted, and in a break from the past, dues were completely optional. An ardent political liberal, he was committed to social justice. He pushed for child labor laws, was an outspoken defender of workers' rights, demanded benefits for striking employees, and tirelessly promoted free speech and civil rights. He formed an unshakable alliance with Christian reform leaders, and struggled on behalf of such social issues as honest city government and free labor unions. He pushed for Negro rights as well. Growing bolder with each cause, among his many accomplishments, he helped to found the National Association for the Advancement of Colored People—the NAACP. And like Lord Byron, he one day woke to find himself famous.

In private, Wise could be humorous, affectionate to his friends, and loving to his family. In public, he was charismatic, energetic, candid, and legendary as an orator, not only in the Jewish community but beyond. Whether he was defending the Jews or pleading for the poor, he was always eloquent, his voice filled with robust timbre. To the long-suffering masses, his was a rousing message: no longer need you feel inferior; no longer need you feel scorned or alone. Physically, he fitted his part. Tall and powerful, he had the build of a steelworker, the sturdiness of a Roman wrestler, and the presence of a statesman. With his magnificent thatch of hair, and with his muscular arms outstretched, he was a mesmerizing speaker. And because of his ability to mingle easily in the worlds of both religion and politics, his political power quickly grew.

As a young man on business in Europe in 1898, Wise had met the towering founder of modern Zionism, Theodor Herzl, and soon thereafter he broke with most Reform rabbis and became an early Zionist, committed to the establishment of a Jewish state. Wise also became a deputy to the future Supreme Court justice Louis Brandeis, and together the two men helped prod president Woodrow Wilson to support the Balfour Declaration of 1917, which enshrined England's support for a Jewish national homeland in the ancient land of Palestine. In the ensuing years, Wise's fingerprints seemed to be everywhere in American Jewish life: he was at one time or another president of the World Jewish Congress, Riegner's organization, which Wise had helped found in 1920; the

American Jewish Congress; the Jewish Institute of Religion, a prominent theological college; and the Zionist Organization of America—as well as editor of *Opinion* magazine, not to mention a driving force of the journal *Congress Weekly.*

When the Great Depression came, Wise spoke out early and often for unemployment insurance and ample measures of relief. By then, he had already solidified a relationship with Franklin Roosevelt, whom he supported for governor of New York in 1928, notwithstanding the fact that the Republican candidate was Jewish. "I never voted as a Jew," Wise later said, "but always as an American." As an early and vocal supporter of President Franklin Roosevelt's New Deal, Wise cultivated ties to such formidable Democrats as Roosevelt's advisers Henry Morgenthau Jr., Felix Frankfurter, Frances Perkins, and Harold Ickes. But though Wise became a street-savvy participant in the upper echelons of American politics, his personal relationship with Roosevelt was complex and ambivalent. Where Roosevelt was in his gut pragmatic, Wise was a radical; where Roosevelt freely tapped into politicians of all stripes if they could be of help to him, Wise was inclined to divide the world into those who were right and those who were wrong; where Roosevelt was an amalgam of candor and obfuscation, Wise was put off by those who were indirect. In a sense, Roosevelt was all ego, Wise all superego.

When Roosevelt took an uncertain stand regarding the Tammany Hall political machine in New York City during his bid for the presidency in 1932, a disappointed Wise refused to back him. A year later, however, the president won Wise over with his charm and his New Deal. From then on, Wise was under Roosevelt's spell; and from then on, he never faltered in his support for the president. He called Roosevelt "boss," but actually Roosevelt was his hero. "He re-won my unstinted admiration," Wise later gushed, "and I spoke of him everywhere I went with boundless enthusiasm." He never looked back. In 1936, Wise wholeheartedly supported Roosevelt for a second term; in 1937 he was unfazed by Roosevelt's Supreme Court packing debacle and by the mounting congressional opposition to the president; and in 1940 he supported Roosevelt's third term. For better or for worse, Wise's trust in Roosevelt was absolute.

After Hitler came to power in 1933, Wise, by turns meticulous and melodramatic, became an implacable opponent of Nazi Germany. While *Time* magazine seemed entertained by Hitler's grandiosity, dismissing him as a "bristle lipped, slightly potbellied," comical figure who often "stroked his tuft of brown mustache," and who looked like Charlie Chaplin, Wise knew better. From the outset, he knew that the demons had been let loose. When the brownshirts—the storm troopers—wearing their high-crowned caps and red swastikas were assaulting and bludgeoning Jews, men as well as women, young as well as old, who failed to thrust out an arm in the stiff *Heil* salute as Nazis paraded in the streets singing "*Deutschland erwache!*" ("Germany awake!"), Wise knew that these were not the antics of a lunatic fringe but the beginning of a terrible chapter in European history.

Zealously speaking out against Hitler, Wise also sought to engineer a movement to boycott German goods; urged Roosevelt to more strongly oppose the Nazi regime; and was the driving force behind many anti-Nazi demonstrations by Americans, including mass protests in New York City, one of which, at Madison Square Garden, drew over fifty thousand people. His ability to assess people was at times impaired—he remained in awe of the president, chronically unable to be objective about him, let alone critical. In the 1930s he was convinced that Roosevelt was as emotionally committed as he was to helping the persecuted Jews—true, Roosevelt did nothing to dissuade him of this, even appointing him to the Advisory Commission on Political Refugees chaired by James G. McDonald. In the 1940s, Wise believed Roosevelt would stop at nothing to somehow save the millions of victims in the Holocaust. On the basis of varying degrees of evidence, he believed in Roosevelt's fervent support for the Zionist movement.

Was Wise's euphoria about Roosevelt built on shifting sands? Yes and no. Early in the war the president had lifted Americans' hearts with his fireside chats; couldn't he now do the same to help the Jews? Yet in pressing for his personal cause, Wise had setbacks. When he had sought to change congressional opposition to the 1924 immigration act, he failed, receiving minimal assistance from Roosevelt. When he sought to alter British policy in Palestine, he again fell short—once more, he lacked the backing of the administration. Then in 1941 and 1942, Wise was devastated by the fragmentary reports trickling out of Europe about the Nazis' atrocities against Jews. May 1942 was particularly bitter, especially when he heard the staggering account, smuggled out, which asserted that 700,000 Polish Jews had already been massacred by the Germans. Learning about this, Wise was more grief-stricken than ever.

As a member of the president's advisory committee, Wise pushed and prodded the State Department to provide emergency visitors' visas for Jews threatened by the Nazis, to the point of jousting ferociously with the department and irritating the administration. The frustration began to wear on him. So did age.

At sixty-eight years old in 1942 he was "far from being well," as he confessed to a colleague. He had an inoperable double hernia, which necessitated frequent X-ray treatments; an enlarged spleen; and a bone marrow disease, which often left him pale and weak. Though his condition made it difficult for him to fly, Wise nonetheless pushed his body to the limit, traveling widely, usually by train.

As the months passed, a hard question lingered. Among a growing number of Jews there was a gnawing suspicion that Wise was too prone to vacillation, too establishment for the radicals, and too radical for the establishment. There was also a persistent view that his trust in Roosevelt was misplaced, that Wise was wedded to a president who, when it came to the Jews, offered lip service rather than action. Even Wise's attempt to unify the American Jewish community would fall short; for one thing, conservative Jews would oppose his vocal liberalism, his support for the New Deal, and his Zionism.

Yet whatever his failings, his concern was real and so was his passion. And the fact remains that Wise was one of the pivotal civic and civil rights figures in the nation, and one of the most important Jewish leaders in the world. If anyone had been put on this earth to save the

Jews, it seemed to be Wise. If anyone could persuade Roosevelt to take action, or to mediate between the warring factions at the State Department, it would be Wise. And if anyone could march into the Oval Office and wave the Riegner Telegram before Roosevelt's eyes, it would be Wise.

But in August 1942, thanks to the State Department, Wise was still a bystander.

IN WASHINGTON, AS LURID accounts of Nazi atrocities continued to arrive, the professional diplomats seemed to keep doing what they did best: immaculate in their striped trousers, wing collars, and pince-nez, they shuffled papers, composed cables, and assembled in conferences. And they took their time.

Although Riegner's message may have stalled in Washington, it continued to attract attention in London. At first, the Foreign Office hesitated, taking no action for a week. But Riegner had, sensibly, also requested that his report be passed on to Samuel Sydney Silverman, a highly respected British barrister who was a member of Parliament and also the chairman of the English section of the World Jewish Congress. Covering his bases, Riegner had added one extra line in the cable he sent to the British: "PLEASE INFORM AND CONSULT NEW YORK," by which he meant Wise.

On August 28, Silverman did just that; he cabled Riegner's information to the United States, addressing it directly to Wise. It was one thing to block a message from a relatively unknown Swiss Jew like Riegner, quite another to bottle up a report coming from a British MP. This time, while administration officials were adjourning from work for brandy, cigars, and conversation, Silverman's message sped its way through both the State Department and the War Department. It landed on Wise's desk on a Friday, while he was preparing for the Sabbath. Wise, of course, had no way of knowing that the State Department already had the Riegner Telegram, nor that it had been decided not to transmit the contents to him.

For several days, Wise urgently conferred with a number of colleagues, all of whom were "reduced to consternation" by the graphic accounts. Then he made his decision. On September 2, Wise passed Silverman's cable on to Sumner Welles, the undersecretary of state. Wise also added a personal touch, saying he deemed Riegner a scholar of "entire reliability," "not an alarmist," and "a conservative and equable person." He asked the undersecretary to request that the American minister in Switzerland quietly confer with Riegner about the possibility of additional corroborating information.

And he suggested that the Riegner Telegram be brought directly to President Roosevelt's attention.

WHY DID WISE NOT bring the matter up with the secretary of state, whose wife was in fact half-Jewish? Wise calculated that he would get a better hearing from Welles than from Cordell Hull. For several years the State Department had been riven by antagonism and jealousy stemming from the recurrent bureaucratic clashes between these two titans. And time after time, Welles, rather than the secretary himself, had proved to be the one who ultimately had Roosevelt's ear. This was not surprising. Fifty years old, Welles was tall, dignified, and blond. And he had all the right connections. He was a graduate of Groton and Harvard; he summered in Bar Harbor; and he was related to Senator Charles Sumner of Massachusetts, the great foe of slavery and unwavering advocate of freedom. More important, for many years Sumner Welles had been a close friend of the president—the *New York Times* would write that FDR was "personally fond" of Welles—as well as of the first lady, who as much as anyone else in the administration had an abiding concern for the plight of the Jews. An instinctive humanitarian, Sumner Welles also increasingly became a champion of the Jews.

Hull's résumé was also impeccable: born in a log cabin, he was now seventy-one, a former congressman, senator, and chairman of the Democratic National Committee, as well as the longest-serving secretary of state; he also worked on the foundation of what would become the United

Nations, earning a Nobel Peace Prize. Yet, not unlike FDR, he was in failing health. Too often he seemed tired, out of step, little more than a figurehead at the State Department. For one six-week period, his poor health forced him to turn over the running of the department to his subordinates. And the fact that his wife was half Jewish, far from being helpful, was actually a hindrance, because he went out of his way to prove that he was not swayed by special interests; indeed, he was one of the authorities that turned away the *St. Louis*, with its German Jewish refugees, in June 1939.

So as Wise considered how best to thread his way through the maze of government intrigue and reach Roosevelt, Welles seemed to be the right guide indeed.

THERE IS A TIME to be eloquent, and a time when eloquence is wasted. For the most part, State Department officials, from Breckinridge Long to the Division of European Affairs, thought Wise was crying wolf—or that the issues he was raising were a meddlesome sideshow. They were exceedingly skilled at smoothly uttering pious platitudes while doing nothing; already, the Division of European Affairs had suppressed another telegram coming to Wise from London, one which called for urgent steps as a response to Riegner's report.

By contrast, the British were serious about the threat, and had been for some time; indeed as early as 1933, the British ambassador in Berlin spoke fervently about his "great uneasiness and apprehension" regarding a country where "fanatics and eccentrics have got the upper hand."

That same year, in the United States, Senator Millard Tydings of Maryland had introduced a resolution calling on Roosevelt to "communicate an unequivocal statement of the profound feelings of surprise and pain experienced by the people of the United States upon learning of the discriminations and oppressions imposed by the Third Reich upon its Jewish citizens." The State Department blocked the measure, claiming heatedly that the president would be put in an embarrassing position, and asking how Roosevelt could explain how there were still lynchings in America (even, it was pointedly noted, in Maryland)? Secretary of

State Hull made sure that the resolution died in committee. Just three months after taking office, Roosevelt himself acknowledged that the Jews in Germany were being treated "shamefully," but added, "We can do nothing," except to help those who are American citizens. Unable to find a more comprehensive answer, he joked to James Paul Warburg, a member of a leading American Jewish family, "You know, Jimmy, it would serve that fellow Hitler right if I sent a Jew to Berlin as my ambassador. How would you like the job?"

By now, however, these issues of 1933 seemed relatively small. More information continued to arrive about the destruction of the Jews—from Switzerland, from the Polish government in exile, from London, from sources in distant Palestine. Almost by the day, the picture as a whole was becoming unmistakable, even if some of the details were wrong or outdated. Still, officials at the State Department remained unmoved. Ray Atherton, the chief of the European division, planted seeds of doubt in Welles's mind, insisting there was no reliable evidence about how many Jews were being "deported east." As to "extermination"? Here again, he questioned the evidence. Actually, the State Department officials were convinced that the Jews, silent and afraid, were being used as slave laborers in the Nazi war effort, not unlike the Soviet prisoners of war as well as the captive Poles.

Unwilling to breast the tide, Welles picked up the phone on September 3 and called Wise. He requested that Wise keep the Riegner Telegram under wraps until it could be "confirmed."

Fatefully, Wise relented.

He did so having no idea how long the government would drag its heels. In the meantime, the Nazis' roundups went on, the cattle cars continued to roll eastward, and hundreds and then thousands of Jews were being murdered each day.

~

EVEN AS HE ADHERED to his promise to Welles to keep Riegner's report out of the news, Wise continued to undertake furious behind-the-scenes measures to help the imperiled Jews. The strain began to show. He confessed to a good friend, the distinguished clergyman John Haynes Holmes, "I am almost demented over my people's grief." He wasn't sure what leverage he could use, whom he could talk to, or what steps to take. One day in New York City, he exchanged views with a colleague who had just received word by cable from Switzerland that the Warsaw ghetto had been "evacuated" and that 100,000 Jews had been "bestially murdered." The cable had said that the corpses of the victims were being used for "artificial fertilizers." The missive ended with an urgent plea: "Only energetical steps from America may stop these persecutions. Do whatever you can to cause an American reaction."

The phrase "only energetical steps from America" must have rung like a Klaxon. Wise's colleague confided that he was "physically broken down from this harrowing cable." So was Wise. Touched by a sense of earthly doom, he saw this cable as a confirmation of Riegner's report. A copy of the cable was passed on directly to Franklin Roosevelt as well as Eleanor Roosevelt. But there was no response. Wise had also asked the distinguished Supreme Court justice Felix Frankfurter to speak with Roosevelt personally; Frankfurter would not.

The dimensions of the threat were so large that Wise next took the lead in organizing a temporary committee of influential Jewish leaders to prod the administration into greater action. They did whatever they could. Wise also asked Myron C. Taylor, Roosevelt's emissary to the Vatican, who had been the president's representative at the Évian Conference, to make an appeal to the pope. Taylor did, but the Vatican curtly informed him that the pope would not "descend to particulars" and in any case had already warned that "God would bless or condemn rulers" depending on the manner in which they handled their subjects. Meanwhile, in New York City, Wise met with the President's Advisory Committee on Political Refugees, which had been in existence since 1938; but the group had little influence, then or now. However, he did manage to secure a meeting for his own ad hoc group with Sumner Welles and other officials on September 10.

With a heavy heart, an increasingly pessimistic Wise boarded the train for Washington, D.C.

~

WISE HAD A FULL schedule. On September 10, 1942, he sat down with Sumner Welles, Vice President Henry Wallace, Dean Acheson (who would later become the legendary secretary of state), Assistant Solicitor General Oscar Cox, and others, laying before them the "awful cables"—the Riegner Telegram, for one. Apparently unable to grasp the information, the vice president said that he had heard the Jews were being shuttled to the Russian front, where they were used as laborers, principally to build the Nazis' defenses. For his part, Cox wondered if this was the last straw, if the time was rapidly approaching when at least a United Nations War Crimes Commission would be established—a minor step to be sure, but something. And at least Welles promised to dig deeper. Though it took him four weeks, in early October he personally instructed the U.S. chief of mission in Switzerland, Leland Harrison, to meet with Riegner and get to the bottom of matters. He had also forwarded, as a "TRIPLE PRIORITY MESSAGE," recently received intelligence about the Jews of Warsaw being killed in special camps.

Now, suddenly, there was movement. This time Harrison passed on information to Welles that Jews were in fact being rounded up and sent to "an unknown fate in the east." For the first time, the concentration camp Belzec was identified by name. And a gravedigger's account of gassings appeared in a Jewish newspaper, published in late September. Prodded by Myron Taylor, the Vatican suddenly acknowledged that it had received unverified reports of "severe measures against non-Aryans"—though it remained hesitant to take any further steps. The Roman Catholic Church, stiffly doctrinal, filled with ambitious prelates, was unwilling to place itself at the mercy of Hitler's armies. At this point, however, the varied information had begun to trickle into the White House, and for the administration some of the hard questions could not be dodged or easily explained away, even if the complete details of the Final Solution were not yet fully understood. To be sure, war stalked Europe everywhere; so did misery and hunger and deprivation. The Continent had been transformed into a reeking slaughterhouse—and America was warily eyeing its pending North Africa campaign. Yet this reign of Nazi terror against the Jews seemed to be something entirely different, something altogether new, something crying out for action.

The action came in the form of a statement. On October 7, 1942, the White House, echoing Roosevelt's warning in August that war criminals would face "fearful retribution," released a statement that the president was aware of a continuation of Nazi war crimes. Straddling the middle ground—his armed forces were soon to be committed to North Africa—President Roosevelt promised what he could, but little more. He declared that war criminals would be subjected to "just and sure punishment" at the war's end. The United Nations would establish a commission for the investigation of war crimes. Finally, Roosevelt warned the Nazis and those assisting them "to deter those committing the atrocities" and let them "know that they're being watched by the civilized world." What the president did not do was ask for a thousand sanctuaries across Europe, or call on Italy, Hungary, Romania, Bulgaria, and Vichy France to refuse to cooperate in the deportations.

THE KILLING AND DYING continued. Wise and his colleagues found little consolation in the White House measures. Weary of his struggle, and exhausted by the demands of alerting the public, Wise pressed on, speaking at a mass rally against the Nazis' perfidy. He also lobbied the Department of the Interior to make the Virgin Islands available for refugees fleeing Hitler's terror—a small gesture but still something. However, Roosevelt demurred, turning down the request. Meanwhile, in Switzerland Riegner and a colleague compiled a nearly thirty-page account with the most detailed information yet, including corroborating documents, and information from Schulte. They personally brought it to Leland Harrison and watched as Harrison began to read the first page. The report pulled no punches. "This policy of total destruction," it announced, "has repeatedly been proclaimed by Hitler and is now being carried out." "Poker-faced," Harrison took his time, methodically scribbling notes in the margins as he read. When he was finished, he looked up and asked for the name of the German industrialist close to Hitler's inner circle who provided much of the information. Riegner and his colleague hesitated, and their initial silence betrayed their dilemma. To reveal Schulte's name was to potentially expose him to getting caught or killed. It also meant violating the promise Sagalowitz originally made to him. But not to reveal it was potentially even worse—that would deprive the report of its unimpeachable veracity.

In the end, they relented. They handed Harrison a sealed envelope containing a single slip of paper on which was written: "Managing Director Dr. Schulte, mining industry. In close or closest contact with dominant figures in the war economy."

They added that a high official at the International Red Cross, one of Europe's leading intellectuals, had independently confirmed the information provided by Schulte. From then on, a torrent of further corroboration continued coming from various sources. A Swedish businessman traveling through Warsaw learned that half the Jews there had been killed. For its part, a small publication, the *National Jewish Monthly*, had begun to put together the disparate pieces of the genocidal puzzle. Where were all the Jews, it wondered, particularly if they were being used as laborers? In the Polish ghettos? No—because reports indicated that 300,000 Jews had vanished "without a trace." In Nazi-controlled White Russia? No—because Soviet guerrillas reported that all the Jews there had been cleaned out. In Germany? No—because German dispatches boasted that the German Third Reich was "Jew-free." The monthly concluded that "the Nazis may be resorting to wholesale slaughter, preferring to kill all the Jews rather than use their labor."

Shortly thereafter, another publication, the *Jewish Frontier*, also hotly questioned whether Jews were really being used as labor. "A policy is now being put into effect, whose avowed object is extermination of a whole people," this publication insisted. "It is a policy of systematic murder of innocent civilians, which in its dimensions, its ferocity and its organization is unique in the history of mankind." In England, the archbishop of Canterbury agreed, declared that he was unconvinced by the "forced labor" explanation, and that a planned program of annihilation was almost certainly under way. William Temple, who would soon become the archbishop's successor, declared that it was hard "to resist" this appalling conclusion.

And as it happened, in Geneva, Paul Squire, the American consul, had received jolting photostats of letters from Warsaw written both in German and in partial code, providing evidence that the Germans were exterminating the Jews in frightening numbers. Incredibly, these photostats, forwarded via diplomatic airmail pouch, took more than three weeks to reach the State Department and then took nearly as much time to be brought to Sumner Welles's attention.

True, the information pouring in was at times confusing and contradictory; Auschwitz largely remained a carefully guarded secret, and the other killing centers were not yet fully understood. Yet by November 1942, the essentials of the Final Solution were emerging with alarming clarity.

IN GERMANY, THERE WAS increasing clarity as well. Despite his insomnia Adolf Hitler continued his normal routine. When he was not leaning over maps of the dismal eastern campaign or berating his commanders, there was late-morning small talk with his aides and rambling monologues about the state of the war and the "sacrifices" and "heroic struggles" of the German people; then there was afternoon tea and more small talk; in the evening there would invariably be films, often two of them, procured by his propaganda minister, Goebbels. As ever, Hitler was moody; as ever, he was puritanical: a vegetarian who eschewed nicotine, he also looked askance at foul language. "*Um Himmels willen!*" ("For heaven's sake!") was as profane a phrase as he ever uttered. And as ever, he thought of himself as cultured: he would listen to records, usually Beethoven's symphonies or selections from his beloved Wagner—leaning back in a chair as if in a daze, his eyes closed.

These days, guilty of the murder of millions, he was increasingly wrapped in illusion, isolated from the German citizenry at home and from the German soldiers at the front, seldom appearing in public. But he could not escape military realities, much as he tried to. His war effort was crumbling, and the war was turning decisively in the Allies' favor.

The British had stepped up their nightly bombing raids: Munich was hit ferociously, and so were Düsseldorf, Bremen, and Duisburg. Afterward, crowds would swarm through the streets, numbed, shocked, and grumbling. And across Germany, increasingly long lines of women stood for hours waiting for daily rations, frustrated and hungry. On the eastern front, the battle for the immense prize of Russia was now being fought at Stalingrad. Hitler had been led to believe that this action would be over within ten days. Instead, the huge German army was caught in a prolonged, intense campaign in the snowy wastes of the Volga bend. In the city itself, with Soviet flags off in the distance, fighting took place house by house and smoking ruin by smoking ruin, in the cellars, in the muck of the sewers, in bombed-out plants, and in still-blazing department stores. The stench of corpses was palpable. In this savage battle, the Germans and Russians often circled each other at point-blank range, or engaged in hand-to-hand combat, until one unit or another was annihilated. As this dance of death continued, medical supplies ran out and food ran perilously short.

This agony was increasingly felt even in Berlin: the cheering crowds had fallen silent and the once exuberant citizens now shuffled hesitantly down the boulevards and read lists of the dead posted at newsstands and in shop windows. For Hitler, the North Africa campaign was proving to be little better; despite Rommel's upbeat reports, his men were short of weapons, equipment, and luck. Rommel, undertaking a mass retreat, had been forced to break off his offense at El Alamein in the direction of the Suez Canal only three days after it had begun, though this did not prevent Hitler from grandiloquently awarding the Desert Fox a field marshal's baton.

Against this background, on September 30, 1942, Hitler, casting himself as a returning prophet, appeared at the Berlin Sports Palace to prop up the Germans' sagging morale and delivered a halting, rambling address to begin the Winter Relief Campaign. He frequently paused—this was his trademark—while the huge, packed audience roared, "*Sieg heil! Sieg HEIL!*" After deriding Roosevelt as "this demented man in the White House," he offered this prospect: "My comrades, you have no idea what is concealed under the simple words of the communiqué of the Highest Leadership of the Armed Forces." Then, with unrestrained candor he referred to his pronouncement before the Reichstag on September 1, 1939, when he had declared, "If Jewry is starting an international world war to eliminate the Aryan Nations of Europe, then it won't be the Aryan nation which will be wiped out but Jewry." He paused again for applause—the audience had been handpicked by the Gestapo—and then, with a flourish, added: "In Germany too the Jews once laughed at my prophecies. I don't know whether they are still laughing, or whether they will have already lost the inclination to laugh, but I can assure you that everywhere they will stop laughing. With these prophecies I shall prove to be right."

This hate-filled tirade was broadcast to millions of Germans, and also received by the BBC and transcribed on the American wire services. Hitler was speaking not only to the German people, but ultimately to the world.

BY THIS STAGE, THE bureaucrats' inertia and callous indifference could not overcome the preponderance of information about the massacre of the Jews. Nonetheless, with their characteristic skepticism, a number of key officials in the fractious State Department continued to question reports about the Final Solution. Sumner Welles, however, no longer needed to be convinced. He now had two options before him: take the matter up directly with the White House, or take it up with Stephen Wise. He chose Wise. On November 24, he urgently telegraphed Wise and requested that he come immediately to meet at the State Department. Later that day, Wise sat down in Welles's office, and the undersecretary handed him several reports accompanied by his own grim conclusion. This was not, he made clear, a matter of long, slow-moving lines of refugees or laborers trudging eastward. "I regret to tell you, Dr. Wise," Welles said, his voice laden with emotion, "there is no exaggeration. These documents confirm and justify your deepest fears."

Welles insisted that he could not release this information to the news media himself—"for reasons you will understand," he said, only partially convincingly—but suggested there was nothing preventing Wise from doing so. He added, "It might even help if you did."

Wise agreed. No longer bound to secrecy, he promptly called a press conference early that evening. The *New York Times* showed up, and so did the *Washington Post* and seventeen other newspapers. He walked the reporters through the details. The Nazis were transporting Jews from cities all across Europe to Poland for annihilation. Of the half million Jews in Warsaw, only 100,000 remained. And the Nazi "extermination campaign" had already wiped out 2 million Jews.

That night, a dejected Wise took the train back to New York, where he continued to publicize the details to whomever would listen. The next afternoon, he held another press conference to, as he put it, "win the support of a Christian world so that its leaders may intervene in protest" against the treatment of Jews in Hitler's Europe.

And suddenly, he had allies in the unlikeliest of places. In London, the Polish government in exile released a graphic statement about Jews being shunted into cattle cars and being deported to "special camps" at Sobibór, Treblinka, and Belzec. Under the guise of "resettlement in the east," the statement continued, the mass murder of Jews was occurring. And in the far-off holy city of Jerusalem, the Jewish press released its own harrowing account of gas chambers in concrete buildings and, perhaps for the first time anywhere, a report about Jews being taken "to great crematoriums at Oswiecim, near Cracow."

Oswiecim, of course, was the Polish name for Auschwitz.

The following day, seventeen newspapers carried Wise's information, though all but five relegated it to inside pages. Nevertheless, it was the most publicity that the catastrophe had generated to date. The gifted correspondent James McDonald's special cable to the *New York Times* stood out. It was headed "Himmler Program Kills Polish

Jews—Officials of Poland Publish Data—Dr. Wise Gets Check Here by State Department." McDonald wrote, "The most ruthless methods are being applied" to liquidate the Jews. "All persons, children, infants and cripples among the Jewish population of Poland are being shot, killed by various other methods or forced to undergo hardships that would inevitably cause death" as a means of carrying out Himmler's program of extermination. In his dispatch, McDonald also provided frightening details. "The people are packed so tightly" in the freight cars, he said, that they die of suffocation; or they die from lack of water and food. "Wherever the trains arrive half the people are dead." And the remainder were then mass-murdered at the camps. "Neither children or babies are spared. Orphans from asylums and day nurseries are evacuated as well." McDonald added that the few survivors were "only the young and relatively strong," who then became slave laborers for the Germans, and even they didn't last long. The newspaper also carried a UPI dispatch about Wise receiving confirmation of this from the State Department.

And although there were those who would later insist that they didn't have any actual knowledge about Auschwitz, the *New York Times* also carried the wire story from Palestine about the killings at "Oswiecim."

On December 2, a Day of Mourning and Prayer was solemnly observed throughout the United States and in twenty-nine other nations. There were memorial services and religious services, local radio programs, and special printed materials. There were searing speeches and lunchtime services and impromptu meetings. There were silent groups who stood in contemplation in the cold. In New York City, which had the largest Jewish population in the nation, Mayor Fiorello La Guardia took the lead in sponsoring the day's activities. They were impressive: many shop windows were adorned with memorial notices, and that morning half a million workers in factories and stores rose to their feet and halted production for two minutes; radio stations also ceased broadcasting and went silent for two minutes. Starting at noon, Americans listened to a sixty-minute radio program. Later in the day, NBC broadcast a moving fifteen-minute memorial service on its stations across the country.

The White House and an irritated State Department, which had hoped to sweep the whole matter under the rug, were soon flooded with telegrams and letters crying out for the administration to do something. Reading one of the newspaper accounts, Eleanor Roosevelt remarked that she was stricken "with horror" and indicated that as never before had she appreciated the totality of the carnage. And in the war cabinet in Britain, there was a growing intention to condemn the Germans.

In Germany, the Nazi leadership itself couldn't help noticing all this activity. "The question of the Jewish persecution in Europe is being given top priority by the English and the Americans," Goebbels remarked in his diary. "At bottom, however, I believe both the English and the Americans are happy that we are exterminating the Jewish riff-raff."

WISE WAS ENCOURAGED BY the heightened attention to the genocide. He now felt free to compose a letter to Roosevelt himself, asking for a face-to-face meeting with the president for his temporary committee. "Dear Boss," he wrote, "I do not wish to add an atom to the awful burden which you are bearing with magic and, as I believe, heaven inspired strength at this time." But it was now clear that the "most overwhelming disaster in Jewish history" was taking place in Europe. And "it would be gravely misunderstood if, despite your overwhelming preoccupation, you did not make it possible to receive our delegation." He closed the letter with a mixture of sorrow and desperation: "As your old friend, I beg you will somehow arrange to do this."

Roosevelt did. He arranged to meet Wise and four colleagues on December 8. It was one of the rare face-to-face discussions the president had with any Jewish leaders about the Holocaust.

AT NOONTIME, THE DOOR to the Oval Office was flung open, and Roosevelt received Wise and his colleagues. The president, in a half jocular manner, detailed his plans for a postwar Germany—he was already looking ahead, clearly confident that victory was within the Allies' grasp. Wise then pulled out a two-page letter and solemnly read from it: "Unless action is taken immediately, the Jews of Hitler's Europe are doomed." What was to be done? The message asked Roosevelt to deliver a stern warning to the Nazis that they would be held in strict "accountability for their crimes." It also outlined a request for a commission to be formed to sift through the evidence of the Nazis' atrocities and "report it to the world."

"Do all in your power," Wise pleaded, his voice tinged with melancholy, "to bring this to the attention of the world and all in your power to make an effort to stop it." He then handed the president a twenty-page memorandum entitled "Blueprint for Extermination," which gave a horrifying summation of the Nazis' activities, including a country-by-country analysis provided by Riegner. Roosevelt's reply left little doubt that he had been fully briefed on the Final Solution, or at least on what the U.S. government and Wise knew about it.

"The government of the United States is very well acquainted with most of the facts you are now bringing to our attention," the president said. "Unfortunately we have received confirmation from many sources. Representatives of the United States government in Switzerland and other neutral countries have given us proof that confirms the horrors discussed by you."

Unhesitatingly, and buttressing the White House statement of October, Roosevelt said the government would indeed issue a warning about war crimes. He did not, however, want to make it appear that the German nation as a whole was complicit in the mass killings. He pointed out that Hitler was "an insane man," and that Hitler's inner circle was "an example of a national psychopathic case."

Were there any other recommendations? he wondered. Wise and his colleagues had none. Beyond their request for a warning and a commission, they had settled on no other specific requests. They should have known better; the president's time did not come lightly, and this was their one opportunity. Then the president began bantering about a host of topics unrelated to the genocide; by all accounts, he did 80 percent of the talking, merely filling the meeting time without making further commitments. This, of course, was part of his magic and political genius. His demeanor, which one might have expected to be somewhere between anger and despair, was neither; he was his usual unruffled self. In any case, Wise and his colleagues scarcely noticed. At 12:30 p.m. an aide slipped into the Oval Office, indicating that the meeting had come to an end. "Gentlemen," Roosevelt boomed as they were walking out, "you can prepare the statement. I am sure that you will put the words into it that expressed my thoughts."

Shaking hands with each of the participants, Roosevelt closed with his own heartfelt remark, "We shall do all in our power to be of service to your people in this tragic moment."

BUT THERE WAS ONE thing in his power that Roosevelt did not offer to do. Unwilling to detract from the war effort or to risk political capital, he neither offered to make a speech personally denouncing the Final Solution nor offered to make it the topic of a fireside chat, as he did with such wartime issues as rationing and rubber. Nor did he offer to undertake anything to counteract the State Department's obstructionism—though he had recently instructed Robert Murphy to send him direct reports from Africa before Operation Torch, pointedly saying, "Don't bother going through State Department channels. . . . That place is a sieve." Instead, the initiative again fell to Wise, speaking as a sort of proxy for Roosevelt, and then to the British.

Once more, Wise convened a press conference and announced to the scribbling reporters that the Jewish leaders had just met with the president, who was "profoundly shocked" to learn that 2 million Jews had been murdered as "a result of Nazi rule and crimes." Moreover, Wise continued, the American people would hold the perpetrators of these crimes "to strict accountability in a day of reckoning, which will surely come."

At last, there seemed to be momentum: as Roosevelt had indicated, nine days later, on December 17, the United Nations, consisting of the three main allies—the United States, Britain, and the Soviet Union—and the governments of eight occupied countries, issued a dramatic joint declaration about the agony of the Jews and condemning genocide. Describing the Germans' actions as "bestial," the declaration used the "strongest possible terms." It received extensive publicity and its impact was significant.

In London, the tough-minded British foreign secretary, Anthony Eden, himself heavy with despair, read the declaration to the House of Commons. "I regret to have to inform the House," he said, "that reliable reports have recently reached his Majesty's government regarding the barbarous and inhuman treatment" of the Jews. Line by line, he calmly read the declaration's graphic words: "None of those taken away are ever heard of again. The infirm are left to die of exposure and starvation or deliberately massacred in mass executions." So shocked were the members of Parliament that they all then stood, heads bowed, in a moment of silence. Speaking over the BBC, Count Raczynski, a member of the Polish government in exile, denounced the German nation for "accepting the destruction of an entire race" that had contributed so much to the glory of German civilization.

Yet in Washington there remained doubters, inside and outside the government. This stern declaration had arisen less from Wise's meeting with Roosevelt than from the actions of the British war cabinet. In fact, when the proposal for the statement was forwarded from the British to the State Department, one official dryly wrote that he had "grave doubts" about the "desirability or advisability" of issuing such a statement; in any event, he described the reports, which came largely from the Riegner cable, as "unconfirmed."

Horror at the atrocities was not shared by everyone in the public either. In the press, perhaps because Roosevelt's personal voice was lacking, there continued to be skeptics. There were also those who vociferously opposed assisting the Jews: for example, the editors of a highly influential Protestant publication, the *Christian Century*, conceded that "beyond doubt, horrible things are happening to the Jews in Poland," but considered it uncertain whether "any good purpose is served by the publication of such charges." When, three weeks later, the United Nations condemned the annihilation of the Jews, the *Christian Century* continued to close its eyes, conceding only, "The right response to the Polish horror is a few straight words to say that it has been entered in the books," and maintaining that the best way to help the Jews was through "redoubled action" on the war fronts.

Newsweek saw it differently. When that November Roosevelt sought new war powers legislation that would enable him to defer laws impeding "the free movement of persons, property and information into and out of the United States," Congress was uncooperative. The president and Vice President Henry Wallace met with the influential Sam Rayburn, the speaker of the House, and Rayburn insisted that the war powers bill would never make it through the Ways and Means Committee. Roosevelt quietly dropped the matter, without much of a fight. The intent of the bill was simply to ease the way for industrial and military advisers to enter and leave the United States, but were it to be passed, it would raise the specter of America's opening the floodgates for Jewish refugees.

"The ugly truth," *Newsweek* concluded, "is that anti-Semitism was a definite factor in the bitter opposition to the president's request."

But anti-Semitism was only a partial explanation. For instance, the *New York Times* wrote an editorial expressing a view that Roosevelt increasingly held himself: "The most tragic aspect of the situation is the world's helplessness to stop the horror while the war is going on." In other words, short of a complete victory over the Nazis, there seemed to be little the Allies could do except "denounce" the perpetrators and promise "retribution."

Was this one of those historical moments in which events acquire a momentum all their own and begin to exert an irresistible pressure? It was not. Eduard Schulte had risked his life to get his message to Roosevelt and to urge the Allies to lay waste to the Nazi death camps; he did eventually get the message to Roosevelt. But then instead of real action there was only a belated denunciation of the Nazis and surprisingly little sustained debate about what steps to take next. In retrospect, the lack of follow-through on the mounting evidence of the Final Solution was the moral equivalent of Neville Chamberlain's astonishing statement over the BBC on the eve of what became known as the rape of Czechoslovakia: "How horrible, fantastic, incredible it is that we should be digging trenches and trying on gas masks here because of a quarrel in a faraway country between people of whom we know nothing."

STILL, IF ROOSEVELT'S EYES were averted, it was also true that in the fall of 1942, he had his hands full. The public was unhappy with his conduct of the war both at home and abroad. And the president had to struggle to boost the morale of the American people and sustain and strengthen their spirit as the nation prepared to mark the first anniversary of its entry into the war.

On the domestic front, rationing was becoming a way of life. Sugar became scarce; so were meats and coffee. The supply of butter was cut back, and cigarettes were rare. A black market for household goods flourished. And nationwide gas rationing—in most cases the ration was only five gallons a week—was put into place to save rubber, which was needed for the war effort. Though wages were fixed, food prices kept rising, and inflation was eating away at the economy. Farmers complained bitterly. So did owners of small businesses, who were being squeezed by the weight of heavy regulation. As store shelves remained empty, housewives, too, failed to understand why so many items like canned foods, hairpins, cameras, and even alarm clocks were restricted or rationed. The administration called on Americans to be patriotic. Nevertheless, the public was in a foul mood, and Roosevelt paid the price in the congressional elections. His party lost forty-four seats in the House, nine seats in the Senate, and a number of governorships.

In mid-September, Roosevelt himself made extensive visits to munitions factories, navy yards, and army bases, hoping to raise morale.

Yet the Germans were increasingly bogged down in the death struggle at Stalingrad, and it was becoming clear to Roosevelt that the war was reaching a turning point. In mid-October he jauntily wrote to King George of Great Britain, "On the whole the situation of all of us is better in the autumn of 1942 than it was last spring. . . . While 1943 will not see a complete victory for us, things are on the upgrade while things for the Axis have reached the peak of their effectiveness."

But in the European theater, against the Nazis, the Americans had yet to fire a shot. Still slugging it out against the Japanese in the Pacific, American forces needed to prove themselves against the Axis powers.

They would do that in North Africa.

IT WAS A PARTICULARLY inhospitable place to fight.

The sun beat down relentlessly on the rock-studded terrain while vast mounds of desert glinted in the daylight, and the heat caused men to hallucinate. Away from the coast there were few roads. Meanwhile, what narrow passages did exist were strewn with mines. And when Erwin Rommel was placed in command of the German Afrika Korps in Libya, the British never saw it coming.

Like the dashing General Nathan Bedford Forrest in the Civil War, Rommel was an extraordinary strategist and a master of the lightning strike, always able to exploit even the smallest opening. Like Napoleon, he was worshipped by his men—they would follow him to the gates of hell if need be. And like Genghis Khan, he continually courted death, leading from the front and always on the move. Mercurial, slender, courageous, and chivalrous, he was perhaps Germany's most capable general. His fame filled the world; even Churchill grudgingly admired him. Prone to debilitating headaches, a nervous temperament, elevated blood pressure, and pain in his joints—it was rheumatism—he was nevertheless outstanding among the German high command: a rare courageous voice, he pressed the Führer to bring the war to a close early on, albeit to little effect.

Still he fought and fought hard. For fourteen months, before any Americans had fired a shot, he and the British seesawed over hundreds of miles of desert. Initially, he outmaneuvered, outfoxed, and overwhelmed the British, chasing them all the way back to Egypt; they left behind only the isolated British fortress at the Libyan port of Tobruk. Throughout the summer and autumn of 1941, Churchill did everything he could to reinforce that improvised fortress, which was hanging on for dear life against Rommel's flank. This was Britain's line in the sand.

Meantime, often under a bright moon, there were endless thrusts and withdrawals, but no knockout blow for either side. For the Allied soldiers there was also no rest. They had to figure out how to make their way through hundreds of miles of searing wilderness; and for them, as for the British navy, the compass and the stars became their navigators. Nighttime always entailed a gamble: huge columns of tanks would pause, not knowing whether the opposing force was fifty miles away or just around the bend. Dust, too, was an implacable foe; it was everywhere—on the men's goggles, in their boots, in their underwear, and caked in their hair. The men looked out over miles of landscape where the only sights were ugly patches of arid earth, the tracks left by vehicles, and debris—mangled tank treads and blown-out tires from previous skirmishes. Because of the heat and wind, night and day the men were covered with layers of stench and dirt and a film of perspiration. Then there were the insects, buzzing and swarming over their rations as soon as the tins of food were opened.

It was under these conditions that Rommel had taken Tobruk in June while Churchill was meeting with Roosevelt, and then had begun advancing toward Cairo. It was up to the British to halt the Germans and then to begin the process of pushing them back. And to wait for the Americans.

On October 23, while the British launched a heavy counterattack against Rommel at the Second Battle of El Alamein, and a bloodthirsty Soviet army at Stalingrad was pushing the Nazis back, the Americans at last joined the fray and set out for North Africa. A fleet of 670 vessels—cargo ships, warships, and troop transports—bearing an assault force of over 100,000 men prepared to make its way across the Atlantic. Over 100 ships alone would be coming from the United States. Meanwhile, tension grew in Washington and London; one key to success was ironclad secrecy. To be sure, the American troops were still untested; they would learn by being bloodied by the enemy.

Eisenhower himself was so anxious and fatigued that he had shoulder

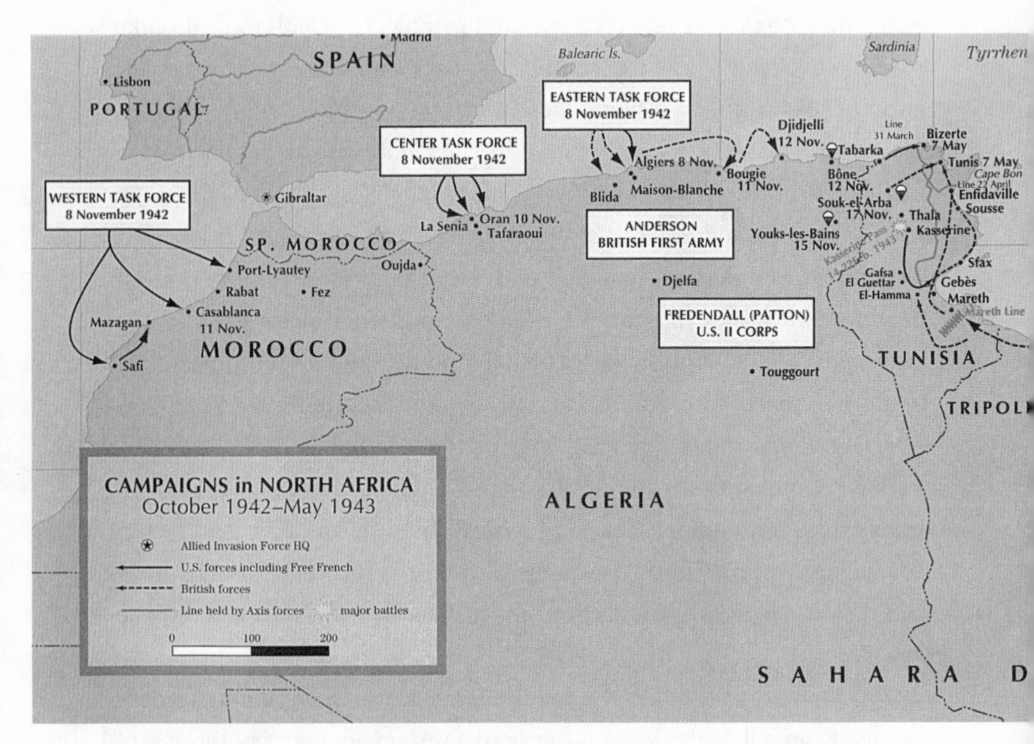

The movements of the Allied and Axis troops during the North Africa campaign

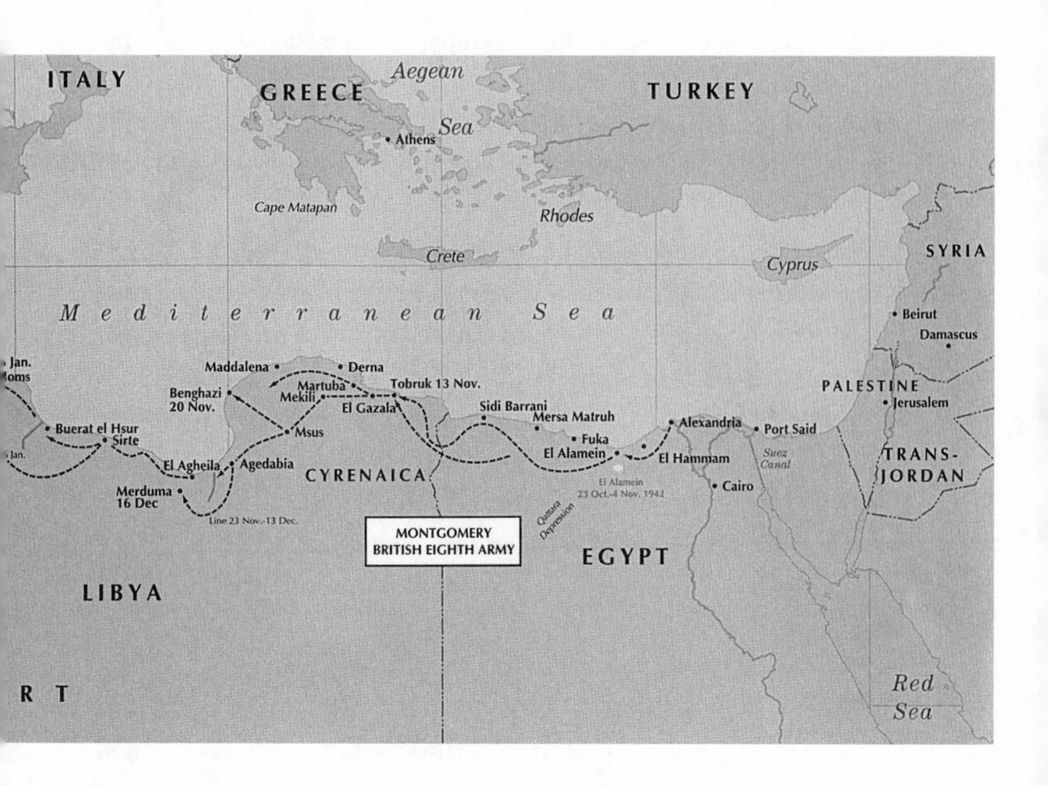
ITALY
GREECE
Aegean Sea
TURKEY
Athens
Cape Matapan
Rhodes
Crete
Cyprus
SYRIA
Mediterranean Sea
Beirut
Damascus
Maddalena
Derna
Martuba
Tobruk 13 Nov.
Benghazi 20 Nov.
Mekili
El Gazala
Sidi Barrani
Mersa Matruh
PALESTINE
Jerusalem
Buerat el Hsur
Sirte
Msus
Fuka
Alexandria
Port Said
El Alamein
El Hammam
Suez Canal
TRANS-JORDAN
El Agheila
Agedabia
CYRENAICA
El Alamein 23 Oct.-4 Nov. 1942
Cairo
Merduma 16 Dec
Line 23 Nov.-13 Dec.
Qattara Depression
MONTGOMERY BRITISH EIGHTH ARMY
EGYPT
LIBYA
Red Sea

spasms from hours of leaning over maps and reports; moreover, his breath smelled: he had begun chain-smoking three packs of cigarettes a day; and on some days he walked with a stoop.

The plan called for landing the army under the cover of darkness, and he was well aware that never before had a night landing on a hostile coast been undertaken so far from a home base. On the eve of the campaign, he lay on a cot in a command post deep in the tunnels under the Rock of Gibraltar. He wrote hesitantly: "We are standing . . . on the brink and must take the jump." For his part, General George Patton was more confident. He bellowed to his men: "I'm under no illusion that the God-damn Navy will get us within 100 miles of the beach. . . . It doesn't matter. Put us in Africa. We'll walk!"

Meanwhile, four thousand miles away, in the rustic hills of the Catoctin Mountains, Roosevelt was trying in vain to relax at the presidential retreat, Shangri-La—today's Camp David. The president fiddled with his stamp collection, shuffled cards for solitaire, read light novels, and parked himself comfortably on his screened porch. Yet gone were his usual wisecracks and jokes; gone was his typical ebullience. Had he been able to walk, he surely would have been pacing back and forth. He couldn't shake his nervousness about the invasion.

Saturday night at Shangri-La was zero hour: sunrise on the North African coast.

EISENHOWER KNEW THAT OUT of the entire year, less than two weeks would be suitable for a landing at Casablanca on the Atlantic coast and Oran in western Algeria, where two legs of the three-legged assault would take place, comprising 35,000 Americans and 39,000 British respectively. The third leg, including a force of 10,000 Americans and 23,000 British, would occur at Algiers in the mid-Mediterranean.

With a bit of swagger, the American troops thought they had been thoroughly drilled for modern battle; they were not. In truth, though crafty and courageous, they were green. Moreover, not only was their training inadequate but the coordination between the services was still haphazard. They didn't yet know the benefit of digging, or the art of camouflage. Nor had they learned to hate the enemy (Eisenhower's words). True, the army had provided the finest equipment it could for the young GIs. They had new multiple gun mounts and amphibious tractors, improved Sherman tanks, and the very best submachine guns. They were even bringing with them the latest advance in rocket launchers: the bazooka. And they were equipped with all the comforts that the quartermasters could think of: sun goggles, stepladders, magnifying glasses, mosquito bars, rubber boats, bed socks, bicycles, extra wool blankets for the cool North African evenings, dust goggles and dust respirators for the inevitable sandstorms, inflatable dinghies for additional transport, and even black basketball shoes. And of course American flags to plant on the beaches.

Before the troops were set to arrive, Eisenhower's deputy Major General Mark W. Clark and Robert Murphy of the State Department thought they had negotiated an arrangement with the French colonial forces to minimize resistance to the invasion. The hope was that the French would have little appetite for fighting the Americans and would also be eager to strike a blow against the Nazis. In any case, Roosevelt had instructed his advisers to let the French know that the Americans would be coming not as conquerors, but as liberators. Yet the situation in North Africa, a volatile mix of the Vichy government's supporters and sympathizers, anticolonialists and free French, was chaotic and confusing. Roosevelt couldn't shake the thought that if the Vichy French forces in North Africa opposed the landings with either conviction or tenacity, the mission could falter, or many thousands of men would be cut down in the fighting.

The convoy of six hundred ships was traveling under radio silence. Just before disembarkation, an uplifting note from Roosevelt was delivered to all the ships for the troops to hear. "Upon the outcome depends the freedom of your lives: the freedom of the lives of those you love." The president radioed a similar message for the Frenchmen of North Africa. Before the first fingers of daylight, they were surprised to hear an extended message from Roosevelt, recited in French, crackling over BBC airwaves out of London, "My friends," he said, "who suffer day and night, under the crushing yoke of the Nazis, I speak to you as one who was with your Army and Navy in France in 1918. I've held all my life the deepest friendship for the French people." He eloquently continued: "I know your farms, your villages, and your cities. I know your soldiers, professors, and workmen. I . . . reiterate my faith in liberty, equality and fraternity." He closed with a rousing call to the French to assist the invasion: "We do not want to cause you any harm." And finally: "*Vive la France éternelle!*"

Before sunrise, at 3 a.m., between the call to prayer in Rabat to the south and Algiers to the west, a fleet totaling over eight hundred warships and transports started to gather along the coast of Africa.

~

MEANWHILE, FOR ROOSEVELT, NEITHER his stamps nor his novels relieved his tension. Nor did the company of Harry Hopkins and a few good friends. Throughout the day and into the evening, he was unable to mask the strain on his face. Repeatedly, he locked his eyes on the telephone, awaiting news that the invasion had begun. Just before 9 p.m. on Saturday, November 7, the phone finally rang. Roosevelt's secretary, Grace Tully, reached for it. It was the War Department.

Roosevelt prepared to pick up the phone, almost as if in slow motion. His hand was shaking.

~

HE LISTENED IN COMPLETE silence for a few minutes, then roared, "Thank God. Thank God. That sounds grand. Congratulations. Casualties are comparatively light—much below your predictions." And then he said again: "Thank God." With a grin, he wheeled his chair around to face his guests. "We have landed in North Africa," he told them. "Casualties are below expectations. We are striking back!"

As it happened, fortune was on the Allies' side. Remarkably, the Atlantic was placid. Equally remarkably, they had no problem with German U-boats. Some of the landings went like clockwork, with men rapidly moving inland, confronting only minor opposition. And at Casablanca, American battleships and cruisers laid waste to the unsuspecting French flotilla in the harbor. Still, there were snags. Weighed down by almost two hundred pounds of ammunition and equipment, the troops struggled through the surf until finally many of them discarded their barracks bags; as morning broke the next day, the ground was littered with these waterlogged sacks and other equipment.

There were other problems. In some cases soldiers landed miles from their planned destinations. And to the horror of the Americans, the French sided with the Axis, struggling back. Sporadic firefights broke out, particularly at Oran and along the Atlantic beachheads, where the French mobilized for a counterattack. Some vessels got lost. Some landings were delayed or mishandled. And to Roosevelt's dismay, the proud, irate French broke off diplomatic relations with the United States, while an outraged Hitler used the invasion as a pretext to seize the southern zones of France that had been under the control of the Vichy regime. On the night of November 11, armored German units made it official, racing across the armistice line in France; clashes were minimal and they encountered little opposition. Now the Nazis controlled all of France.

But there were bound to be mishaps, and for the most part the Americans prevailed: the operation was a stirring success. By midday on November 8, Algiers was surrounded and then overrun—Oran too. What the inexperienced American GIs lacked in training, they made up for in numbers, overwhelming the opposition. Casablanca quickly fell. So did the critical port of Rabat. And the Allies were pushing into the rocky hills of Tunisia.

Roosevelt had been right all along. Morale did matter. In America, the mood was euphoric. Capturing the country's mood, *Newsweek* wrote: "*This is it!* Those were the words that raced through the mind of the nation at nine o'clock on the night of Saturday, November 7. . . . From one end of the country to the other there spread a feeling that now the United States was going to show the world—as it had always done before." At sporting events, the games stopped while the landings were announced and the crowds roared. At home, people pulled out maps and traced the path of the coastal invasions. In coffee shops and at YMCAs, children did cartwheels while parents scratched their heads, wondering how to pronounce the names of exotic North African places they had never heard of before. And everyone, it seemed, smiled at the headlines in the newspapers.

Now came the second phase of the operation. On November 12, Eisenhower, hoping to forestall any further resistance as well as to establish political order, offered the former Vichy commander in chief, Admiral Jean-François Darlan, the position of high commissioner for all French North Africa; in turn, Darlan would have to persuade the French soldiers to cease fighting and lay down their arms. If all went according to plan, the French would also take part in helping to liberate Tunisia. Darlan accepted. The hostilities ended. And for the American commanders in North Africa, this seemed to be a pragmatic arrangement—a way of preventing unnecessary bloodshed. As Eisenhower had written to Marshall, he was loath to think about "every bullet we have to expend against the French" rather than against the Germans.

Yet to their consternation, virtually overnight this decision proved to be an unmitigated blunder; Roosevelt and the British confronted a storm of protest. Across the political spectrum critics asked: Didn't Darlan represent everything the western powers despised? He was a Fascist to the core, and a collaborationist to boot—when the Nazis invaded France, he had quickly joined their side. When the Jews were being rounded up in France, he never issued a word of protest. And now Eisenhower and Roosevelt were putting their stamp of approval on what had become known as the treacherous "Darlan deal." Wasn't this too high a price to pay? The whole affair was clumsily handled.

To many, it appeared as though the West was prepared to deal not only with Fascists, but with the Führer himself. The fact that Marshal Henri-Philippe Pétain, the head of the Vichy government in France, curtly refused to accept the Allied landing and the liberation compounded matters. "We are attacked," he said. "We shall defend ourselves; this is the order I'm giving." At a minimum, critics felt, Darlan was treacherous, and this was an unconscionable bargain—promising freedom to the people of France and then putting their enslaver in control of them.

Nor were these just the clamorings of liberal columnists and left-wing activist groups. Roosevelt's own secretary of the treasury, Henry Morgenthau, denounced Darlan as "a man who had sold thousands of people into slavery." Roosevelt's former opponent in the presidential election, now his ally in the war effort, Wendell Willkie, agreed. "Shall we be quiet when we see our government's long appeasement of Vichy finds its logical conclusion in our collaboration with Darlan, Hitler's tool?" he asked. From London, Charles de Gaulle, leader of the free French, added his voice, saying in a terse one-sentence note that the "United States can pay traitors but not with the honor of France."

At the outset Roosevelt was nonchalant about the outcry; then he was flummoxed; and soon it was clear that the criticism stung. Eisenhower sought to contain the damage; he cabled to the president that if they backtracked on the deal, the French armed forces would resist "passively" and even "actively." However, this did little to quell the tumult. Roosevelt found himself backed into a corner; the whole affair was proving to be a morass. He eventually issued a statement asserting that he would accept Eisenhower's arrangement only for "the time being," adding that no "permanent arrangement" should be made with Darlan. "We are," the president went on, "opposed to Frenchmen who support Hitler and the Axis." He repeated himself again and again: the arrangement was only "a temporary expedient," and was justified solely "by the stress of battle."

Meeting with the president at the White House, Morgenthau lamented that the North Africa deal was "something that afflicts my soul." Roosevelt retorted with a Bulgarian proverb: "My children, you are permitted in time of great danger to walk with the devil until you've crossed the bridge."

But the moral issue lingered. How long was it acceptable to hold hands with the devil? For a sprint? For a marathon? And what if the devil took you on a detour?

This was not to be the last time these questions would be asked.

Now the contretemps appeared to have no end. Roosevelt was alternately chagrined, irritable, and resentful of the outcry against him. He looked haggard and tired. To those around him, he seemed haunted by his critics. In the morning he would open the newspapers and, barely containing his disgust, lash out at hostile editors, sneering as he read aloud every word of every unfavorable article and every unfavorable column. But on some days, he simply acted as though the North African campaign hadn't happened, refusing to talk about it at all. At still other times, he sought refuge in his usual pleasures: taking relaxing drives through the countryside; writing playful notes to his aides; bantering during his beloved cocktail hour. Eventually, he escaped Washington altogether, taking the train to Hyde Park to clear his head.

As it happened, Roosevelt would be rescued, politically, by a young French royalist from an Algerian family who assassinated Darlan on Christmas Eve, shooting him twice. Feeling revived, Roosevelt reported to his former boss at the Navy Department, Josephus Daniels, "I'm happy today in the fact that for three months I've been taking it on the chin in regard to the Second Front and that that is now over."

It was. Roosevelt's broad smile returned. As 1942 came to a close, the war seemed to be at a critical juncture—a mere two years after his invention of Lend-Lease to aid a desperate Britain, and just a year after the nightmare of Pearl Harbor. In incalculable numbers, the Germans were fighting and dying on the eastern front in the Soviet Union. At El Alamein, the British Eighth Army had gained the offensive and Rommel was in full retreat. With the success of the North Africa campaign, it was just a matter of time before the Germans were defeated south of the Mediterranean and North Africa was cleared of Axis forces. Despite setbacks—the American soldiers were later routed badly by Rommel's panzers in the foothills of the Kasserine Pass—the overall campaign had brought numerous benefits. It boosted the confidence of the war-weary British. It helped forge a genuine military alliance between the British and the Americans that would be indispensable when they opened up the European front. And it broke in the American army: for in North Africa, the officers and men of the U.S. Army, who had been in need of seasoning, were learning fast—there they gained experience. Also, it enabled Eisenhower to quickly weed out incompetent commanders. Finally, it paved the way for the forthcoming invasion of Sicily and the Italian campaign.

A euphoric Roosevelt, leaning back in his seat, inhaling deeply on a cigarette, relished every bit of his successes. He regaled reporters with stories about the planning for Operation Torch. He explained wryly that a second front didn't happen overnight, nor could it be simply bought "in a department store, ready-made." More than ever, a sense of victory began to fill Washington. It was just a matter of time before Allied troops would enter France, and Roosevelt was viewed as a master of the great gameboard of international policy. At home, the economy was also improving: thanks to the war effort, millions of Americans had risen above the poverty line, and unemployment had all but come to an end. And in Britain, as the year came to a close, church bells pealed to celebrate the successes in North Africa.

"Now, this is not the end," Churchill said to the British people. "It is not even the beginning of the end. But it is, perhaps, the end of the beginning!"

∾

ON DECEMBER 13, 1942, the rich baritone voice of Edward R. Murrow came over the air on a CBS radio broadcast. Even with the static crackling as the transmission lines carried his words over an ocean, listeners could sense the drama when he began: "This . . . is London." Millions of Americans were glued to their radios as Murrow uttered these words—"What is happening is this: millions of human beings, most of them Jews, are being gathered up with ruthless efficiency and murdered. . . . The phrase 'concentration camp' is obsolete, as out of date as 'economic sanctions' or 'nonrecognition.' It is now possible to speak only of extermination camps."

The terrible secret, for anyone who wanted to listen, was a secret no more.

~

ON DECEMBER 31, 1942, unlike the year before, Roosevelt's New Year's Eve at the White House was a festive occasion. There were cocktails and friends and family. There was dinner and a private screening of the movie *Casablanca*, starring Humphrey Bogart. There was good cheer. Just before the clock struck midnight, and as 1943 was about to begin, the president and his guests assembled in his second-floor study. Champagne was served. Roosevelt lifted his glass and offered his usual toast: "To the United States of America!"

Then, at Roosevelt's suggestion, drinks were raised once more. This time the president delivered a new encomium for the postwar world: "The United Nations!"

11

1943

BERLIN AT THE START of 1943 was quiet. On several fronts, from Africa to the Soviet Union, German forces were under attack, their gains were being reversed, and their casualty lists, already long, lengthening. But in the capital, for the moment no air raid sirens split the air; there were no whistles as the Allied bombs descended from the night sky, and no shuddering, thunderous explosions below. The antiaircraft guns lay silent. Flak did not go up and then rain down again. The streets were clear of debris; the bunkers were unused. It was the calm before the storm. And the German high command knew it. The Nazis would soon dispatch Joseph Goebbels, chief propaganda minister, to the Berlin Sportpalast, a huge arena in one of the city's southern suburbs. Standing in for the increasingly reclusive Hitler, Goebbels would speak before a handpicked crowd, surrounded by a raft of garlands and Nazi banners, while an ingenious loudspeaker system piped in recordings of ovations and cheers—the Nazi propagandists' equivalent of a comedy laugh track. Above the dais hung a banner that read: "Total War—Shortest War." This was what Goebbels had come to sell.

Gesturing, sometimes shaking his fist, sometimes placing his hands on and off his hips, Goebbels employed every oratorical trick. When volume was needed, his voice boomed. When he sensed a slight loss of attentiveness, he lowered his tone, forcing the audience to listen closely for every word. His message was uncommonly frank: bars and nightclubs would be shut down, luxury stores, beauty salons, and high-end restaurants would be closed. "We can become gourmets once again, when the war is over," he said. "Thrift" and "austerity" were the new watchwords. Then came the frenzied climax. Calling on his listeners to assent to total war, Goebbels rhetorically asked them to affirm their belief in the final victory of the German people. "Do you want a war more total and radical than anything we can even imagine today?"

"Yes!" came the reply, with wild applause.

"Are you determined to follow the Führer through thick and thin to victory and are you willing to accept the heaviest personal burdens?"

At that, the audience rose and shouted, "Führer, command; we follow!"

"You have given me your answers," Goebbels replied. "You have told our enemies what they needed to hear."

Across the Atlantic, in Washington, D.C., there were also signs of total war. Gone was the timidity of an isolationist America, sitting the war out as the European Allies were swallowed by the Nazi war machine. Gone, too, was the near frenzy defense of the early 1940s, when America was gearing up its "arsenal of democracy."

When the Nazi army had crossed into Poland, Washington, D.C., was a city with fifteen thousand outdoor privies and miles of slums with tarpaper shacks. But there were also the stately homes lining the soft hills of Kalorama and the ornate marble facades of government office buildings. On nice days, visitors could still stroll through the grounds of the White House. The gates were only a recent addition, and for years, the White House lawns had been a favorite spot for picnickers. When the Japanese bombed Pearl Harbor, Secretary of the Treasury Henry Morgenthau initially planned to protect the White House by having the

Secret Service pile sandbags at all the entrances and place machine guns at every door. Every staff member was also issued a gas mask; the president dutifully hung his from his wheelchair.

In consultation with the British, after the Japanese attack, the White House architect oversaw the construction of a bomb shelter with a tunnel to the East Wing and the Treasury Department. It was designed to withstand a five-hundred-pound bomb, and it had diesel engines to generate electricity and supply filtered air. Antiaircraft guns were also hauled up to the roofs of government buildings. But there was a hitch. The army was so short of antiaircraft weaponry that military planners decided to install mainly replicas made of painted wood. As for the few real guns on the rooftops? Only after the war was it discovered that the ammunition stacked up beside them was the wrong size. Unlike Berlin, Washington was not a city ready to shoot a damaging flak into the sky or to direct a counterassault from a bunker at the zoo. In any case, there was no need for all this: an ocean away from the conflict, Washington was safe and had always been safe. Yet by 1943, it was nonetheless a city transformed.

As during the Civil War, life in the capital continued largely uninterrupted. True, there were shortages and ration cards, and boys were shipped off to war. But schools remained open and so did offices; football and rugby games were played; picnics were held; movies arrived regularly in theaters; and the only visible rubble was from the monstrous construction projects engulfing the city and its environs.

The greatest transformation took place across the Potomac, just beyond Arlington National Cemetery, where the Pentagon had been built by an engineer who had overseen the construction of New York City's La Guardia Airport. To erect the five-sided behemoth as many as thirteen thousand men worked around the clock. Three hundred architects alone had space in a large abandoned aircraft hangar—they had to prepare the designs fast enough to keep up with the builders, who frequently came by and snatched unfinished plans straight from the drafting tables. By early 1943, the Pentagon was complete. It was at the time the largest building in the world, designed to hold forty thousand people and all their accompanying files, phones, typewriters, and every other instrument of bureaucratic war. And on the first day, it was still too small. The military continued to utilize other office space across the river in Washington.

The city itself was growing fast. The sidewalks were crowded with marines and sailors, and the United States was spending $300,000 a day on the war. Temporary office buildings lined the National Mall, which soon resembled a trailer park. And more than fifty thousand people arrived in the city each year, most looking for jobs. It was also crowded. Traffic was abysmal, housing even more so. Government workers actually slept in shifts in the rooms that they shared. And many lived in real trailer parks lining roads like U.S. Route One. It was a city running on grit and improvisation; it was disorderly and chaotic, and yet it was emerging as the most powerful capital on earth and the place that would take the lead in winning the war. But not quite yet.

Having already struck at the "underbelly" of the Axis in North Africa, the Allies were still not ready to make an all-out attack through northern France, nor would the coming months bring immediate victory. It was increasingly clear, though, that a reversal of the Nazis' fortunes was coming, and that it would be at once sweeping and, in time, irreversible—or at least this seemed clear to many, including the president.

So it was no surprise when President Roosevelt, making his way to the podium for his annual report to Congress on January 7, 1943, seemed more upbeat than ever. "Last year," he said, to a cascade of applause, "we stopped" the Japanese. "This year, we intend to advance." On the European front, he was equally confident: "The Axis powers knew that they must win the war in 1942—or eventually lose everything. I do not need to tell you that our enemies did not win the war in 1942."

"I cannot prophecy," he then intoned. "I cannot tell you when or where the United Nations are going to strike next in Europe. But we are going to strike—and strike hard." The applause mounted, and Roosevelt continued. This time it was his turn to taunt Hitler. "I cannot tell you whether we are going to hit them in Norway, or through the Low Countries, or in France, or through Sardinia or Sicily, or through the Balkans, or through Poland—or at several points simultaneously.

"But," he continued, "we and the British and the Russians will hit them from the air heavily and relentlessly. . . . Yes, the Nazis and the fascists have asked for it" (he paused for emphasis) "and" (another mesmerizing presidential pause) "they—are—going—to—get—it."

And more than anything else, Roosevelt felt sure enough of himself to talk about the eventual peace that would follow. "I have been told that this is no time to speak of a better America after the war. I'm told it is a grave error on my part.

"I dissent.

"Let us all have confidence, let us redouble our efforts. A tremendous, costly, long enduring task in peace as well as in war is still ahead of us. But, as we face the continuing task, we may know that the state of this nation is good."

~

A WEEK LATER, ROOSEVELT WAS at the Dar-es-Saada villa in liberated Casablanca. The villa was complete with an air-raid shelter, hastily made out of a swimming pool, and security was tight. In the two-story living room, the tall French windows could be covered by sliding steel curtains designed to protect against bullets or shrapnel. An armored division under the command of General George Patton guarded the compound, which was surrounded by barbed wire. And beyond the barbed wire lay an outer ring of antiaircraft batteries.

Elliott Roosevelt, who had been summoned in advance of his father, recalled being informed that the town of Casablanca itself, only recently taken from the Germans, was still "riddled" with French Fascist spies. The Secret Service, trying to plan for every contingency, had detailed an endurance swimmer to fly in the president's clipper plane. The idea was that if the plane was shot down at sea, this agent would stay afloat with Roosevelt for as long as possible.

The original hope had been for a tripartite conference, but Joseph

Stalin had demurred because his forces were in the process of a massive counterattack at Stalingrad, which cut the German army in two and trapped some 300,000 Germans. So instead, it was to be Roosevelt and Churchill once again, and Roosevelt had wanted to go someplace warm. The decor of the villa was lavish—the downstairs bedroom reserved for President Roosevelt was, Elliott recalled, "all frills and froufrou, with an adjoining black marble bathtub." On entering it, the president, gazing around, "whistled." "All we need is the madam of the house," he joked.

What Roosevelt actually got was Churchill, in the adjacent villa, and the usual retinue of military aides, from General Marshall on down. Much of the talk was speculation. The Germans had yet to be completely defeated in North Africa, although that moment was rapidly approaching as the British general Montgomery pushed west across Libya.

Obstacles, however, remained. German U-Boats still patrolled the Atlantic, and the Soviet Union might still collapse (though such a collapse was far less of a threat than it had been at the start of the German invasion, it was still not beyond the realm of possibility). Ensuring that Lend-Lease matériel reached the Soviets was a priority. Given these realities, Roosevelt's promise to the Soviets of a second European front was clearly impossible in 1943. The only time for an attack was summer, and on the military calendar, the relevant dates were fast approaching. As of now, there was no logistical base to support an invasion, and the beleaguered German Luftwaffe was still a presence in the skies. For his part, Dwight Eisenhower, having just undertaken the North African landings, reluctantly stressed that an assault force for the continent could not be readied until the following year, 1944; there were still too many inefficiencies in the Allies' shipping.

As the military talks progressed, it became clear that any immediate invasion of France was a long shot, if not a pipe dream. What to do? They discussed the other possible point of attack in the Mediterranean. Here, the British pushed for an invasion of Sicily. They argued that it would open up the shipping lanes and prod Italy out of the war, and that, with forces already positioned in North Africa, such an attack could be accomplished quickly. Marshall, a strong proponent of a second front in France, still held out for some buildup toward a cross-Channel invasion. However Roosevelt agreed with Churchill: the next objective would be Sicily. And the invasion would happen that year.

Once more, the British, led by Churchill, had won Roosevelt over. As Eisenhower would recall, Churchill "used humor and pathos with equal facility, and drew on everything from the Greek classics to Donald Duck for quotation, cliché and forceful slang to support his position." Still, Roosevelt, as always, was aware of his delicate position between Churchill and Stalin, and was always calculating what was needed at any moment and what might give him the upper hand. By choosing Sicily and forgoing a second front in Europe, "We have been forced into a strategic compromise which will most certainly offend the Russians," he mused, adding, "so that later we will be able to force a compromise which will most certainly offend the British."

Roosevelt then wanted to see the troops, the men fighting and dying for democracy, but his generals vetoed a visit to the front lines. Instead he traveled eighty-five miles by jeep to see the troops at Rabat, noting on his return, "Once in a jeep is enough to last quite a time." The president also hosted the ninety-year-old grand vizier of Morocco and the nine-year-old sultan. The grand vizier arrived bearing gifts; a gold dagger for Roosevelt and two gold bracelets and a towering tiara for the first lady. Roosevelt winked at his son the moment he spotted the tiara. "We could both picture her presiding at the White House with that doodad on her head," Elliott noted wryly. In return, as his gift, Roosevelt presented the grand vizier with a framed photo of himself.

Over dinner, in French, Roosevelt began formulating his idea of a Moroccan New Deal. He proposed to the grand vizier that there should be plans for developing local natural resources—phosphates, cobalt, manganese ore, and oil—and then using a significant portion of the resulting revenue to raise local standards of living. Roosevelt even suggested that Moroccans could come to study at American universities, and that American firms might be hired to start the development projects.

The climax of the summit was to be the tricky question of French politics. There was a controversial joint photography session with the two rivals for the leadership of the French government in exile; Charles de Gaulle, the symbol of the Resistance; and General Henri-Honoré Giraud, the North African compromise leader. But it was at the conclusion of this ceremony that the real sparks flew. Roosevelt and Churchill met with reporters on the lawn at Casablanca. The president, after referring to the venerated Civil War general U.S. Grant, whose initials were often said to mean "unconditional surrender," uttered one controversial sentence: "The elimination of German, Japanese, and Italian war power means the unconditional surrender by Germany, Italy, and Japan."

Once these words were spoken, there was no turning back. Unconditional surrender became the guiding precept for the remainder of the war.

Debate has raged ever since whether this was a statement made spontaneously by Roosevelt in the heat of the moment, or whether it was a result of discussion and deliberation, an evolving strategy designed in large measure to reassure Stalin and to boost the Allies' morale. Actually, Churchill was aghast. There was a distinct possibility that this demand for "unconditional surrender" would prolong the war by hardening the Axis opposition and snuffing out those who might push for a quicker, more flexible negotiated peace.

But this was almost an academic question. For Adolf Hitler in Berlin, "surrender" was not an option. He continued to believe only in unconditional victory.

~

ALTHOUGH THE GERMAN FRONTS were crumbling, never had his belief been stronger. The enraged Führer, intoxicated more by illusion than by fact, was now driving his generals to despair. In his mind, the war was still at the Nazis' high-water mark of October 1942, when he had commanded more of Europe than any leader since Napoleon. In the east, his veteran troops had reigned over vast swaths of Soviet territory, advancing to within forty miles of Moscow. In the west, he reigned over the crown jewel of Europe, northern France, including Paris. In the southeast, he had secured the tallest peak of the Caucasus, Mount Elbrus. To the south, the Mediterranean remained within his iron vise. In the north, Sweden was marginalized while Norway was still governed by the jackboot. Except for some swarms of unruly guerrillas, the Balkans were also part of the Third Reich. And in North Africa, all he had to do was give the word, and Rommel would push on to Alexandria and the Suez Canal.

But all that was in the past. The reality, as 1943 unfolded, was far more sobering. In the Soviet Union, the Germans' situation was rapidly deteriorating. Hitler had failed to provide adequate winter gear for his troops, and as the bitter Moscow winter set in, the Germans' weapons froze, as did the men themselves. Snow alternated with rain, and ice with mud; and the exhausted Germans lapsed into despair. Within months, the Nazis' casualties would total well over 1 million. All the previous successes—the *Anschluss*; the blitzkrieg in Poland and France—could not stave off tragedy in the freezing streets of Russia. One German general ruefully commented that in Moscow "the myth of the invincibility of the German army was broken."

In Stalingrad, the situation was equally dire. The Red Army successfully outmaneuvered the Germans forty miles to the west by the Don bend. With his troops on the verge of utter collapse, Hitler exhorted his commanders to stand and perish; in desperation, he cabled to Field Marshal Friedrich Paulus, "Surrender is out of the question. The troops will defend themselves to the last!" (Earlier, he had heatedly pounded his fists and shouted to his staff, "I won't leave the Volga!") Nevertheless, after furious attempts to reprovision the embattled Nazi troops, surrender is exactly what Paulus did. Twenty-two German and two Romanian divisions—the flower of the German army—were left to shiver and perish in the alleyways of Stalingrad. Of the 300,000 men of the Sixth Army, there were only 91,000 tattered survivors to surrender; and only 5,000 would ever return to Germany.

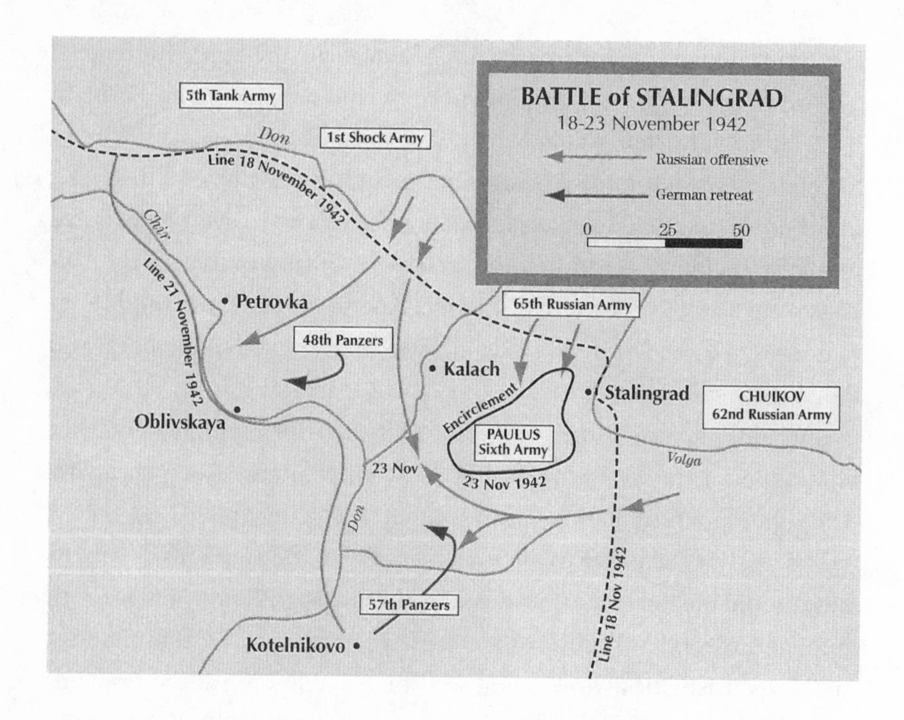

For the Nazis, the situation was also bleak in the Mediterranean. Here was the endgame for Rommel, the famed Desert Fox. Hitler demanded that he hold North Africa rather than relinquish it. That order too was ill-fated. Montgomery furiously counterattacked, and after suffering heavy casualties, Rommel ignored Hitler's message to "hurl every gun and every man into the fray. . . . Victory or death," and undertook a mass retreat. As Montgomery's armor slashed at the German columns, Rommel's escape route became a death trail: every gully, every flattened knoll, every escarpment was littered with burned-out vehicles and exploded tanks. Collecting himself, Rommel, with almost reckless gallantry, did what he could, striking at II Corps in a series of brilliant thrusts at the Kasserine Pass—a sobering defeat for the still inexperienced Americans—and later hurling his men four times at Montgomery. Reinforced by 110,000 troops and hundreds of tons of supplies, he jabbed, probed, and dug in wherever he could, but his last-ditch stand was to little avail.

Soon, nothing could stem the magnificent advance of the Allied columns. Having started two thousand miles apart, American troops and the British Eighth Army, moving like a great human scythe, were finally united, cutting off Rommel's escape path.

Tunis itself would fall, and an exhausted Rommel, in waning health and depressed, would be hastily summoned back to Germany to spare him the mortification of his drubbing; he relinquished control of his forces and never returned to his once sacred sand of North Africa. The remaining Nazi forces quickly began to crumble, and almost 250,000 prisoners were seized, over 100,000 of them German. To both Roosevelt and Churchill, Tunis was as important a victory as Stalingrad. Stalin himself seemed to agree, wiring to Roosevelt: "I congratulate you and the gallant U.S. and British troops on the brilliant victory which has resulted in the liberation" of Tunis.

Grudgingly, Hitler also acknowledged the importance of the Allies' victory. With understatement, he told some of his officers that the Germans' efforts in Tunisia had postponed the Allies' invasion of Europe by six months. Moreover, having once declared that holding Tunis was crucial for the outcome of the conflict, he insisted that if he had not made a stand in North Africa, the Allies would already have gained a foothold in Italy and raced into the main chain of the Alps at the historic Brenner Pass.

"That," he said, "would inevitably have led rapidly to the loss of the war."

By this stage, Hitler's foul moods and towering rages were notorious. At Wolf's Lair, walled off from the German people and even from his generals, surrounded largely by yes-men and lackeys, he now listened only to the advice of party sycophants, his personal physician, and his astrologist, all of whom were under his spell. Despite his exhaustion and ill health, however, his resolve never wavered. He remained ruthless, even as every element of his strategy was collapsing around him. Goebbels remarked, "We have not only a leadership crisis, but strictly speaking a 'Leader Crisis'! We are sitting here in Berlin . . . [and] I can't even report to him about the most urgent measures."

On February 20, 1943, one of Hitler's aides was struck by how the

Führer's appearance had changed. "In the intervening fourteen months," the aide observed, "he had aged greatly." He watched in horror as Hitler's left hand shook wildly; he also noted that Hitler's speech was hesitant, and his manner "less assured." Actually, Hitler's decline was far worse than the aide realized. He was increasingly haunted by stomach ailments. His eyes were cloudy and he moved like an old man. More and more often, his left leg spasmed and he dragged his feet and stooped as he walked; he was by all accounts developing Parkinson's disease. And he was beset by bouts of depression and sleepless nights. Desperate to prevent further degeneration, he was taking twenty-eight pills a day; they didn't work.

Nevertheless, with merciless determination, Hitler still thundered back and forth, pacing melodramatically and screaming about his cowardly commanders—about their stupidity and ineptitude and lack of patriotism, about their reluctance to push their men to the breaking point or their lack of imagination on the battlefield. And everywhere he looked, he saw betrayal, incompetence, and most of all weakness. Coarse and unreasonable, he berated his aides and advisers. Fanatical and stubborn, he considered no tactical matter too small for his attention, however foolish his interference might be, which only compounded the strategic difficulties.

Listening to the dismal reports from the front, his days were frantic. Evenings were calmer, though even then he fidgeted with his spectacles or twirled his red pencils. Then typically, he would linger at the fireplace lecturing his tired and often bewildered officers. As he launched into yet another dull, rambling monologue, his face was invariably weather-beaten, yet his eyes were strangely alive and his expression was curiously upbeat. The script rarely varied. There were the objects of his hatred: bureaucrats; Germany's royal family; intellectuals; industrialists; stockbrokers; the beautiful city of Saint Petersburg (he refused to call it Leningrad), which was to be sealed off, bombarded, and starved out; lawyers; the Luftwaffe; and his own inner circle, which had let him down: Göring and Speer, to name but two. There were also the objects of his great affection: peasant girls; the average soldier; the countryside;

the soil of Germany; his cherished Volkswagens ("the people's cars"); the simple worker; bright-eyed infants; his dog Blondi; Mussolini. And there were his rivals: Roosevelt, that "torturous, pettifogging Jew"; Churchill, that "unprincipled swine" and "old whore"; Stalin, that "half beast, half giant" who he nevertheless thought was a model of leadership. Of course, there were incessant generalizations about whole peoples—the English, whom he secretly admired even as he despised them (his inspiration for exploitation and domination remained the British Empire); the Russians, who were less than human; the Americans, whom he held in disdain. And there were the ones he invariably came back to—the cause of all the world's woes: Jews.

WHAT IN THE END explains the depths of depravity in Hitler and his Nazi regime? Was it in fact the purest unbounded expression of megalomaniacal power and breathtaking inhumanity the world has ever seen? Or was Hitler merely a right-wing rabble-rouser who somehow became the personification of a nation that ran amok? What is certain is that everything about him seems to defy analysis. Among history's long roll call of dictators and despots, Hitler stands alone, dwarfing Caesar and Genghis Khan, Idi Amin and Pol Pot; he literally created the paradigm for totalitarian dictatorship in the twentieth and twenty-first centuries. But in the end history is left with the same haunting, unanswerable questions. Why did Hitler commit these unimaginable crimes? How, in one of the most civilized nations in Europe, did he ascend to power and remain in power while executing such policies of carnage and killing?

And how did this one time disheveled nobody plunge the world into cataclysmic war?

Almost everything about him defies easy categorization. One of his favorite movies was *King Kong*. He was a loner all his life, with virtually no friends and no confidants—Goebbels was the closest thing he had to a friend. His relationship with his mistress, Eva Braun, seems to have been at most tepid; he kept her with him as a companion, and married her only at the end—just before providing her with poison and then shooting himself. Actually he showered far more emotion on his dog Blondi. He worked hard, and often, to teach himself the manners that enabled him to enter refined Germanic circles, but no matter how hard he tried, he remained crass and self-absorbed. He was also chaste and puritanical, and he neither drank nor smoked; in a number of ways he was reminiscent of the French revolutionary despot Robespierre.

He was also a notorious neurotic who was obsessed with germs. Once, when he was informed that a former whore had touched him, he was horrified and rushed to take a bath—he was terrified of venereal disease. The German nation and foreign emissaries alike regarded his icy, enigmatic stare as mesmerizing. Well, it should have been: he spent hours before a tall mirror, refining it. The same was true of his elaborate gestures. He was a spellbinding speaker; his orations were like the music of his cherished Wagner: he would start tentatively, then gradually speed up and produce cascades of powerful rhetoric.

The keystone of his life is his beginnings. He was born at Braunau am Inn, Austria, on April 20, 1889, on a chilly and overcast Easter Sunday—the son of a respected fifty-two-year-old Austrian customs official, Alois Hitler, and his third wife, Klara Poelzl, a young peasant girl. Both came from the backwoods of Lower Austria, and the family had a comfortable middle-class life. Nevertheless, as a child Adolf was resentful and lazy. He was also moody and prone to outbursts. Pictures of him as a baby depict Hitler looking almost bewildered. What stood out then, as they would later, were his remarkable eyes, eerily staring out into space.

His father was humorless and dictatorial; he was also a bad-tempered drunk, who frequently beat the young Adolf. The boy alternately feared and despised him; by contrast, he passionately adored his indulgent, hardworking mother, and would carry her picture with him all his life, even during his last days in the bunker. She may well have been the only person he ever loved. "I had honored my father," he wrote in *Mein Kampf*, "but loved my mother."

The family moved several times, then they settled in the small provincial city of Linz; for the rest of his life, Hitler always considered

Linz his hometown. His family sent him to a *Realschule* for secondary schooling—unlike the more traditional *Gymnasium*, it was based on "modern" subjects. But here he was maladjusted, his record was mediocre, he had no close friends—nor did he seek any—and others considered him high-handed and hot-tempered. Only the rousing stories of great Germanic feats kindled any interest in him; he was instinctively a nationalist from the very start. His father adamantly insisted that Adolf become a civil servant, while the rebellious Adolf wanted to be an artist—to which his father responded, "*No*, never as long as I live!" Fate intervened, however. On January 3, 1903, his father sat down, poured himself a glass of wine, suddenly collapsed, and just as quickly died.

At the age of sixteen, Hitler dropped out of school to pursue his dream of becoming a painter. His doting mother agreed. But Hitler drifted. He idled away his days, nurturing fantasies about a future as an eminent artist. In the evenings he went to the theater or opera and stayed up long past midnight. In the mornings he slept late. He would then spend his time sketching and dreaming—that is, when he wasn't trying his hand at poetry.

Increasingly, he developed an affected manner and began to wear a dark overcoat and fedora and wield a magnificent black cane. Relatives implored him to find a job; he scoffed at the idea. Instead his fantasy world intensified, and so did his artistic ambitions. Suddenly he began to dream about moving to Vienna and attending the Viennese Academy of Fine Arts. These were, by his own account, his "happiest days," almost like "a beautiful dream."

The dream soon ended, when his mother developed fatal breast cancer. He looked after her as much as he could before packing his bags and boarding a train for Vienna in September 1907 to sit for the entrance exam at the Academy of Fine Arts, where he was one of more than 100 candidates. He made the first cut, only to fail the next stage of tests. When he asked the director of the academy why he flunked, the Rector calmly explained that Hitler's talents lay not in painting but in architecture.

By this stage, his mother had died at the young age of forty-seven, and Hitler was prostrated with grief. He was also broke; his mother's sickness almost completely depleted the family savings. In his own words, "poverty and hard reality" now stared him in the face. He had enough savings to get by for a year, but little more.

Once again, he packed his bags and left the cozy provincialism of Linz, this time permanently, moving to Vienna.

From 1908 to 1913 Hitler, looking disheveled and run-down, kicked around in anti-Semitic, cosmopolitan Vienna, pursuing the mundane life of a small-time artist. Barely eking out a living, he had long since given up his visions of becoming a great painter; now he nourished the futile hope that he could somehow become a consequential architect. But failure begat failure: he was a dropout, had no real qualifications and no real hope of gaining any, and he had no real friendships. And he had contempt for a society that regarded him as an unstable crank. In truth, at twenty-five years old, he was little more than a vagabond. By his own admission, he was "the nobody of Vienna." At one point he had been so down and out that he was wearing lice-infested clothes and living with tramps and drunkards in a seedy hostel dormitory. To earn money he shoveled snow, carried bags for passengers at the railroad station, and did other odd jobs; he even entertained the idea of peddling a sensational "hair restorer." Whenever possible, he hawked his sketches and paintings. And whenever he could, he sought solace in reading the racist trash that was so prominent on Vienna's newsstands; he greatly admired the radical anti-Semitic nationalism associated with the pan-German leader Georg Ritter von Schönerer.

Later Hitler moved to the Men's Home, a modest step up from the hostel. Fellow drifters nicknamed him "Ohm Paul Kruger," after the Boer leader renowned for his resistance against the British.

His main passion remained music: Beethoven, Bruckner, Mozart, and Brahms. Vienna had some of the finest opera houses in all of Europe, yet when Verdi and Puccini played to packed houses at the Court Opera, Hitler was unimpressed—they were Italian. Beset by grandiose visions and dilettante dreams, Hitler's only love was for Germanic music, above all for his cherished Wagner, whose works were for him almost a mystical experience. In Wagner, Hitler insisted over and over, he heard the "rhythms of a bygone world"—a world of epic battles and blazing redemption, of philosopher kings, Teutonic heroes, knights, and a heroic Germanic past. And slowly, his own worldview was evolving.

Hitler was not yet a vegetarian, but he was, increasingly, a prude. Vienna hummed with culture, commerce, writers, thinkers, and academicians. Moreover, it had sexual codes intended to maintain the pristine character of the Germanic people. But it also had a seamier, more illicit side: decadence, sin, prostitution. To Hitler, Vienna had lost its clean, righteous high purpose and had become a new Babylon. Here, amid the red-light district, he hated the openly erotic art of Gustav Klimt, and the spectacle of tranvestite young men, "powdered and rouged," sauntering into shadowy bars. And he hated the prostitutes seeking customers in the city's scruffy tenement blocks, or the entertainers making love to men and women sprawled naked on bar counters showered under spotlights, as well as the brawny whores brandishing whips and the women offering *Mutter und Tochter* ("mother and daughter") sex.

Hitler himself was a deviant, yet in a different way. Terrified of disease and dirt, he was also seemingly frightened of women. He never dated and had no girlfriends; actually, once, at the opera house, a girl showed sexual interest in him. He scurried away. And homosexuality disgusted him. So did masturbation. Prostitution too, though it nevertheless strangely fascinated him. More than once, he was seen lingering on the Spittelberggasse, staring at the voyeurs fondling one another; still, he ranted about moral decadence and the evils of selling sex.

He was, meanwhile, developing politically. Already a strident German nationalist, he hated the Social Democrats and was horrified by the multilingual parliament; he also despised the multinational Hapsburg state, and he developed a distaste for the mixing of foreign peoples which, he lamented, corroded "this old site of German culture." Although he was barely scraping out enough money to live on—he brazenly insisted he could no longer paint for hire unless the spirit moved him—he compensated for the frustrations of his indolent life by sitting in cheap cafés and haranguing anyone who would listen about his grand visions of a greater Germany. Increasingly, while the accounts of this remain vague, he was seduced by the crackpot racial theories of Karl Lueger, the demagogic, anti-Semitic mayor of Vienna ("the greatest German mayor of all times"). He now believed all of society's ills could be traced to "the Reds"; then, fleetingly, he lit on "the Jesuits"; then finally he arrived at "the Jew." By his own account, this was his "greatest transformation of all." Whether it was chaos or corruption in cultural life or politics, it all came down to the "seducer of our people"—the Jew, systematically undermining the centuries-old purity of the perfect Aryan race.

Was Hitler alone in thinking this? Not in Vienna, which remained one of the most prejudiced, anti-Jewish cities in Europe. Toxic anti-Semitism was seemingly everywhere: at Easter, Jews were repeatedly accused of ceremonial child slaughter; and in the press, Jews were routinely described as being responsible for prostitution and perversion.

One day he packed his bags for a brief stay in Munich, which he exalted as a truly "German city." And then came World War I.

For the first time he had a sense of belonging to something meaningful, and something to be committed to. "I fell down on my knees," he later wrote, "and thanked heaven from an overflowing heart for granting me the good fortune of being permitted to live at this time." He fought for four years on the western front as a dispatch runner, winning the Iron Cross several times—one of these decorations was first-class, very rarely awarded to an enlisted man; ironically, it was a Jewish officer who nominated him. His comrades referred to him as "the artist." Suddenly, Hitler found his voice and his worldview. He was at once courageous and pitiless. Where others were overwhelmed by the human suffering, he saw opportunities for making an improved, racially cleansed Germany. When others bantered about sex with French girls, he retorted moodily, "Have you no sense of German honor?" When others routinely drank and swapped stories, he would sulk alone in an earthen dugout.

But then, on the night of October 13 and 14, Hitler was temporarily blinded by a mustard gas attack. His war had ended. And soon thereafter, it was over for a militarily defeated Germany.

From the outset, Hitler was tormented by Germany's capitulation and became obsessed with the so-called criminals who had surrendered. Here, November 8, 1918, stands as a formative day in his life. Still blinded by mustard gas, he was lying in a military hospital in Pasewalk when a Protestant chaplain cleared his throat and announced the armistice to the men in the ward. Hitler was devastated, calling this a "monstrous event." He was convinced that the German army had been "stabbed in the back." In truth, the notion of backstabbing was nothing more than propaganda—the German armed forces had fallen apart in the preceding four months. Meanwhile, across Germany, there was now industrial unrest, burgeoning press censorship, and severe food shortages. Protest and rebellion mounted. As the fighting was ending on the front, a chaotic Marxist-inspired insurrection consumed Germany: naval insurgencies broke out at Kiel; revolts burst out across the country; and a day later, Berlin itself was in chaos. Munich was also in turmoil. It was a nascent civil war.

In Munich, Hitler was mortified to see a provisional Soviet-style executive council attempting to govern. They were accompanied by widespread riots fomenting rebellion. At the same time, outspoken Jewish revolutionary leaders like Rosa Luxemburg preached the overthrow of the regime, with the aid of a Red army totaling tens of thousands of men, largely disenchanted laborers. Moreover, the executive council was led by Eugene Levine, another Jew, giving rise to the hysterical notion that Jews were running a secret international organization directed at fomenting world revolution. Thus sprouted the seeds of Hitler's genocidal anti-Semitism and rabid anti-Bolshevism.

Yet the revolution was quickly stillborn, stymied within weeks by the regular army as well as veterans called back to service. For good measure, counterrevolutionaries murdered Luxemburg, and cities like Munich became armed camps crisscrossed with barricades and barbed wire. Hitler, now devising his own form of anti-Semitism, began to refer to Jews as a disease of society, much like parasites.

While already a committed anti-Semite, his paranoia regarding the Jews metastasized even further. In June—at the army's behest—he attended Munich University, where he took anti-Bolshevik "instruction courses." Before long, he developed a reputation as an expert and was himself lecturing troops, speaking against Bolshevism and the Jews with such fury that his superiors suggested he not be so vehement. But he had "stumbled across his greatest talent," and for the first time was speaking publicly about the "Jewish question." In September 1919, Hitler informed a participant in his lectures that anti-Semitism was based on "facts," and the indisputable conclusion was that there should be a "removal of the Jews altogether."

Having impressed his superiors, in the summer of 1919 Hitler was assigned to so-called educational duties, which, in the hypercharged atmosphere of postrevolutionary Munich, consisted principally of spying on political parties from the extreme right to the far left. One day, fatefully, Hitler was sent to investigate a small group of nationalistic idealists, about five hundred strong—they were known as the German Workers Party. Hitler lost his restraint on listening to one speech, and took the rostrum himself. The chairman of the German Workers Party in Munich was so impressed with Hitler's speaking that he commented, "Goodness he's got a gob. We could use him."

Use him they did. On September 16, 1919, Hitler—this Bavarian hothead; this failed, frustrated artist; this ill-educated rabble-rouser; this corporal who was passed over for promotion to be sergeant—entered the then insignificant racist German Workers Party—he was given membership number 555—which soon changed its name to the National Socialist German Workers Party (NSDAP). By the summer of 1921, having ably kindled the fires of resentment and hatred, he made himself chairman of a movement that had a paltry three thousand members. Within months, he was recognized as its Führer, or leader.

Among his first acts was to give the new party its greeting, the ritualistic chant "*Heil!*" ("Hail!") or "*Sieg heil!*" ("Hail victory!"); and its new symbol, the swastika, which became emblematic of the mythical master Aryan race. The group's credo was outlined in a twenty-five-point program, which railed alternately against the Versailles Treaty and the Jews. But its real power stemmed from Hitler himself. Humorless and histrionic, he mesmerized audiences with his eloquent, clear-toned voice and his gift for self-dramatization. Hitler augmented his power by the use of strong-arm squads that roughed up opponents and maintained order at his meetings. These squads would later become Hitler's notorious black-shirted personal bodyguards, the SS (*Schutzstaffel*); and the storm troopers, the SA (*Sturmabteilung*), organized by Ernst Röhm—Nazi street fighters who eventually would murder their political opponents, often in broad daylight.

In 1923, Hitler nursed dreams of greater glory. Convinced that the Weimar Republic was on the verge of collapse, he plotted the overthrow of the Bavarian government. Storming into a seemingly inconsequential beer hall in Munich, he brandished a Browning pistol, then fired it at the ceiling while shouting that he was heading a new provisional government to carry out a revolution against the "Berlin Jew government." Then Hitler and two thousand armed followers marched through Munich, hoping for popular support; instead, they were met by a hail of police fire. Fourteen of Hitler's followers were killed, and the attempted "beer hall putsch" came crashing to an end. Wounded, Hitler himself fled and hid from the police; in the melee he had somehow dislocated his left shoulder. Tracked down and arrested, he was sentenced to five years' imprisonment in the Landsberg fortress. He remained as defiant as ever. As if he were an outsized Danton being led to the guillotine, he shouted to his accusers: "Pronounce us guilty a thousand times over: the goddess of the internal court of history will smile and tear to pieces . . . the court's verdict."

He was right. In prison he was pampered by every comfort the warden could provide, including a large, luxuriously furnished room with breathtaking views of the landscape outside, as well as a sturdy desk and writing materials, which he put to prodigious use. After melodramatically announcing in July that he was withdrawing from politics, he used this time to dictate the subsequent bible of the Nazi Party to his loyal follower Rudolf Hess: *Mein Kampf*. *Mein Kampf* was a crude and crazy patchwork of racial myths, anti-Semitism, and half-baked social Darwinism ("The racial question gives the key not only to world history but to all human culture"). However, it struck a chord and sold over

10 million copies while being translated into sixteen languages, and was even issued in braille for the blind. It would also make this once nearly starving artist an exceedingly wealthy man.

Within a shout nine months, Hitler was released. When he appeared at the prison gate his acolytes cheered him as a triumphant hero; his jailers gathered to bid him an emotional farewell; and as he left, he even stopped briefly for photos to be taken. At this same time, Hitler—he had been banned from speaking in public, and his party had been outlawed—shrewdly resolved that his path to power would not come from muscle alone; instead, he paid lip service to the nation's laws. But this was flim-flam. He was determined to rebuild the Nazi Party, construct a populist mass movement, and, in a blueprint that dictators would follow in years to come, wield parliamentary strength with extraparliamentary intimidation and terror. In effect, his goal was to legally subvert the Weimer Republic by making use of the German constitution itself.

It happened in stages. In 1925, the ban on the Nazi Party was lifted. Hitler quickly outmaneuvered the "socialist" north German wing of the party under Gregor Strasser, and established himself as the party's leader. His claim rested less on any clear program of National Socialism than on his own charismatic personality—that is, on the cult of the Führer. Within a year, his appeal stretched beyond Bavaria, and he had followers from the left as well as the right. Yet in the 1928 elections, the Nazi Party was still an eccentric minority; it won a mere twelve seats—2.6 percent of the vote. Then came the Great Depression, which made Hitler a national figure and helped sweep him into power.

In hindsight, World War I and the Depression made Hitler's rise possible. More convincingly than anyone else in Germany, he offered the defeated nation an enticing future. Thus, a new door of history had been pried opened. To be sure, in 1932 famine and slaughter stalked every great capital. But for a Germany in turmoil, there was a significant difference: reeling from global events, the German middle class was devastated by the Depression. Germans saw a lifetime's worth of savings wiped out within hours; the national currency was ruined; inflation spun out of control. Soon, people of all classes flocked to the Führer's vision of national liberation through strength and unity. He received the support of the press tycoon Alfred Hugenberg and, in surprisingly great numbers, of the younger generation. And he offered himself as Germany's savior. Social dissolution, mass unemployment, hysteria, and burning hatred now became Hitler's best friends.

In 1932, the Nazis received a surprising 18.3 percent of the total votes—6.5 million votes—and 107 seats in the Reichstag, making them the nation's second-largest party. Hitler's movement, unlike the other parties, could plausibly claim to have garnered support from all sections of society; this was all the more remarkable given that just a few years earlier his supporters had been only a few lunatics. Actually, even in January 1932 National Socialism was still disreputable. Among well-born Germans the Nazi Party was considered uncouth: they clearly saw that Nazi street fighters had butchered the party's detractors. Still, in the autumn of 1932, while Americans were voting Franklin Roosevelt into the White House, German aristocrats were reevaluating Hitler. Then, in a much-publicized address, Hitler spoke before a group of high-level industrialists at a prominent club and told them they had nothing to fear from radicals in his party. Now, in increasing numbers, they began to contribute liberally to his campaign.

Hitler officially acquired German citizenship. Then he became a candidate for the presidency, receiving over 13 million votes, four times more than the Communist candidate. In the meantime, the Nazis emerged as the largest political party in Germany, obtaining 230 seats in the Reichstag. Though the former field marshal Paul von Hindenburg became president, Hitler, having positioned himself as an agent of change, was a force that could no longer be ignored.

Yet he did not come to power in 1933 simply by a triumph of will. To be sure, he had won over more than 13 million full throated supporters in the country. But he was aided by a willing cabal of nationalists, militarists, and industrialists who had helped propel him to prominence. Equally surprising was the support he received from leading intellectuals, performers, writers, and artists. There were those, like the former chancellor, the urbane and well-connected Franz von Papen, who were genuinely disgusted by Hitler; however, they mistakenly believed that the responsibility of governing would somehow tame his radicalism. They were wrong. They also thought that it would restore the "tranquility required for a business revival." After failing to persuade Hitler to join a coalition government, and then securing his promise of "moderation," a desperate von Papen persuaded the reluctant von Hindenburg to nominate Hitler ("that Bohemian corporal") as his Reich chancellor. On January 30, 1933, Hitler was sworn in. Quite by coincidence, a cameraman captured Hitler's countenance for history: it expressed pure bliss.

Germany's democratic experiment had been abandoned without raising a fist. Goebbels enthused "Hitler is Reich Chancellor. Just like a fairytale." That night delirious Nazi hordes marched through the Brandenburg Gate in celebration. Meanwhile, there were those who muttered that disaster was just around the bend. Fearing for their safety, if not their lives, some of Hitler's political opponents made hurried plans to leave the country. Still, even among his harshest critics, few believed that the Nazis would rule for very long. And in the United States, some observers, like the distinguished columnist Walter Lippmann, seemed spellbound by the new Reich chancellor; Lippmann called one of his speeches a "genuinely statesmanlike address," and added: "We have heard once more through the fog and the din, the authentic voice of a genuinely civilized people."

Upon coming to power, Hitler moved quickly to outwit and outmaneuver his enemies. Within a matter of months, he put Germany under martial law. Conservatives were muscled out of the government, the free trade unions were ousted or outright abolished, Social Democrats were barred from political life, and of course Jews were targeted for a series of ever more punitive steps. Then came the regime's tactics of systematic intimidation. Demanding loyalty, the chancellor purged the ranks of some of Germany's most distinguished professors. He bullied his political opponents and silenced all but the most outspoken. Those who stubbornly refused to stay quiet were promptly arrested. Shockingly, four thousand people, including Reichstag deputies, were put behind bars. The most vociferous of his opponents met another fate: Dachau, the first of the concentration camps.

On March 5, 1933, Europe's ruling class watched with dismay as Germany held its last free election, which was perhaps the most violent in European history. Swastika banners hung from buildings, and Nazi posters were everywhere. Meanwhile, military music blared from public-address systems, and trucks full of brown-shirted Teutonic youths drove through the streets. When the storm troopers weren't breaking down doors or clubbing their opponents, they were marching with torches around the clock. In retrospect, the democratic opposition never stood a chance. Hitler gained an unimpeachable majority for the first time, with more than 17 million votes. Then, through a combination of propaganda and terror, he moved quickly to solidify his position as the undisputed dictator of the Third Reich. Having cowed his opponents, he now seduced the Weimar Republic's leading opinion makers. With the sure touch of a master politician, he mollified the old order by paying tribute to President von Hindenburg at the Potsdam garrison church, where Frederick II of Prussia, the revered Frederick the Great, lay buried. For those Germans who cherished Weimar's "golden years," the symbolism was profound.

Two days later, the members of the Reichstag entered the Kroll Opera House in Berlin, raised their hands, and voted to give Hitler the absolute authority he craved. The Enabling Act, in effect a far-reaching constitutional amendment, was passed overwhelmingly, 444 to 84. Germany was a dictatorship. Hitler now had the power not only to make laws but to control the nation's finances and conduct its diplomacy.

By early spring, the fanatical hero worship had reached a level scarcely ever seen in Germany, or anywhere else. Poems were written in Hitler's honor; trees called "Hitler oaks" were planted. Schools were named after Hitler, as were town squares. All across the nation his forty-fourth birthday—he was young; his deputies were even younger—was celebrated with song and dance and boundless adulation. And on May 10, Germany shocked the civilized world when university faculties collaborated in the lighting of huge bonfires: they were burning books—psychology, philosophy, history—considered unacceptable by the regime.

When von Hindenburg died at the age of eighty-six in August 1934, Hitler united the positions of Führer and Reich chancellor—illegally. He now had all the powers of the state in his hands. All German officers were required to swear an oath of loyalty to him, an oath that bound them not to the government or even to the nation, but to the caprices of a single individual whose stability, even then, was suspect. Hitler was the unquestioned ruler of Europe's most influential country. In the process, he allowed his leading acolytes, the cold henchmen Himmler, Göring, and Goebbels, to preside over their own fiefdoms of arbitrary power. Yet many Germans believed his rule would not last more than a year.

But within three years after Hitler assumed power, his regime was secure: he destroyed the left and co-opted the conservatives. He won even more adulation after abandoning the Versailles Treaty, building up the national army to five times its permitted size, and pressing Great Britain to allow Germany to increase its naval program. And after remilitarizing the Rhineland, he seemed to be a deity reborn. Dazzling success followed dazzling success—the Rome-Berlin Pact of 1936, the *Anschluss* with Austria, the liberation of the Sudeten Germans in 1938, and the dismantling of the Czechoslovak state in 1939. Presented with these bloodless victories and Germany's glorious territorial expansion, the German people closed their eyes to the concentration camps, the alarming Nuremberg racial laws, and the persecution of political dissidents. And they ignored all the other evidence that Germany had become a barbaric gangster state.

There were many ironies: among those who had to flee Germany for their lives was Ernst ("Putzi") Hanfstaengl, who had not only given generously to Hitler's electoral efforts but also provided Hitler with asylum after the failed Nazi putsch of 1923. And during the Night of the Long Knives, Hitler would orchestrate the murder of some of his closest allies, including his onetime right-hand man, Ernst Röhm.

How did his dictatorship compare with others? The question is too little asked. In the 1930s, Hitler's regime was very different from Stalin's: the Soviet Union was a bureaucratic dictatorship from the top down, made possible by a ubiquitous secret police—the KGB—and widespread terror at all levels of society. By contrast, Hitler's National Socialism, although it too had a secret police—the SS—nonetheless drew its strength from an overwhelming popular sentiment, becoming in effect a populist dictatorship. While the democracies were still saddled by the Depression, the German economy flourished, fueled in good measure by the country's military rearmament. The pace was frenetic: Germany's income had doubled, production had risen 102 percent, and the *Volk* were riding on a crest of affluence and euphoria. Even the Germans' birthrate soared, indicating their belief in this expanding prosperity. Along with his successes at home and triumphs abroad, Hitler had the advantage of being a transcendent politician, the object of a cult of adoration. And Hitler never let the German people forget that theirs had been a nation humiliated and scorned in 1918; so he expressed their resentments, their frustrations, and their aspirations. Curiously, in a global stage where Hitler's contemporaries were such towering figures as Churchill and Roosevelt, not to mention other colorful leaders such as Haile Selassie, Benito Mussolini, and Philippe Pétain, Hitler was among the most popular heads of state in the world, at least until 1940.

Not unlike Roosevelt, or for that matter Churchill, Hitler was a born thespian, always acting, always onstage. He was also a master of duplicity, once saying, in response to a proposal of President Roosevelt's, that no one wanted peace more than he did, and that the National Socialists had no ambition to *germanisieren* ("Germanize") other nations. He worked diligently to cultivate a sense of mystery and awe about himself: There was inevitably his delayed entry into a packed hall and his artfully chosen phrases and elaborate gestures. At the outset of a speech he liked to pause, letting the tension rise; then he would pause again in a frenzied moment of hesitation, followed by bursts of impassioned rants that sent his followers into a thrall. And there was his contrived love of the people: Hitler kissing the hands of ladies; Hitler, the friendly uncle, giving chocolates to children; Hitler the simple man of the people shaking the calloused hands of peasants and laborers.

His philosophy of National Socialism was sui generis. For Hitler, the Germans were a "people"—or *Volk*. And his *Volk*, while they came from many places inside and outside Germany, all had the same impeccable pedigree: German "racial stock." As Führer, he was the guardian of the *Volk*'s true home. Thus his dictum—*Ein Volk, ein Reich, ein Führer*.

Increasingly, as he rose to power, Germany bore Hitler's stamp. He had many accomplices along the way who were happy to go along with his every obscure and ephemeral delusions, and eventually with his genocide. Even the professional generals shamelessly pandered to his tactical blunders, no matter how desperate the situation was. The vast majority of Germans—and herein lies a tale in itself—blindly submitted to his will as well.

The writing was on the wall from the start. It was Hitler who determined the arc of the war from those early, heady days of triumph as he came to believe entirely in his own myth and omnipotence. And what did that omnipotence mean? When the time came, he was willing to kill anyone in the way of his power: the British, the French, the Poles, the Dutch, the Hungarians, the Belgians, the Czechoslovaks, the Greeks, the Soviets, the rich but also the poor, the strong but also the weak, husbands as well as wives, grandparents as well as grandchildren, his closest allies, and at the end his own "cowardly" people. And always, always: the Jews.

At the end of 1943—when the war was almost certainly lost and the German army was falling into disarray, when the morale of the soldiers, already low, plummeted, and some of his most illustrious generals were now hesitant to follow his orders, when the Allies had reached Naples and Roosevelt and Churchill were steadily gearing up for the invasion of France, when the Soviets were ready to push westward and Germany was being punished by nightly bombing raids, when the German people were destitute—Hitler buried himself in an unreal world at Wolf's Lair and then in the *Führerbunker*. There he planned and directed attacks by nonexistent armies and was almost entirely consumed by illusion, paranoia, and misanthropy.

One goal seemed to motivate him above all else: the gas chambers of Auschwitz.

~

BACK IN WASHINGTON, D.C., and London, there was increased pressure to assist the beleaguered Jews of Europe. But President Roosevelt was preoccupied with military strategy—the next step for the U.S. forces now in North Africa was to push hard into Italy—and the State Department was more obstructionist than ever. On February 10, 1943, the department would become involved in one of the worst scandals in its history. A shocking cable—telegram 354—bearing the secretary of state's name was sent to the Bern legation in Switzerland. It instructed the legation to cease transmitting future reports from private individuals unless there were "extraordinary circumstances." This was diplomatic doublespeak; the real intent was to impede the flow of information from Europe to the United States about the ongoing Holocaust. In effect, the State Department was now using the machinery of government to prevent, rather than facilitate, the rescue of the Jews.

Thus far, Congress had been largely silent. Perhaps the members felt they couldn't legislate virtue; nor could they command armies, bombing raids, and generals the way Roosevelt did. Yet now they took a stand.

In late February 1943, Alben W. Barkley, the Senate majority leader, proposed a resolution. A lawyer, a Methodist, and a liberal Democrat, Barkley was one of the nation's most respected political voices; he was also a close ally of Roosevelt's and had been the chairman of the Democratic convention that renominated the president for a historic third time in 1940. He would later become Harry Truman's vice president. Able to immerse himself in the small legislative details, he was by temperament and conviction anything but a freewheeling legislator. But when roused, he was a risk taker, and as time went on he would become a Zionist and a passionate defender of the Jewish people. On March 9, the Senate voted on his resolution expressing the American people's indignation about the "atrocities" and "mass murder of Jewish men, women and children," and condemning "these brutal and indefensible outrages." The measure passed overwhelmingly.

Meanwhile, across the Atlantic there was also a drumbeat of outrage. The much respected Archbishop of Canterbury, William Temple, himself only a year away from his own death, addressed the House of Lords on March 23. He made his way to the rostrum, and then in a clear, resonant voice, issued an urgent plea for immediate rescue steps to be undertaken. He bemoaned all the months that had been lost—the endless delays in taking action; the diplomats' heedlessness and procrastination; the blinders that politicians wore—and warned, "The Jews are being slaughtered at the rate of tens of thousands a day. . . . We at this moment have upon us a tremendous responsibility. We stand at the bar of history, of humanity and of God."

In a scathing editorial, an influential American weekly, the *Nation*, agreed: "In this country, you and I and the president and the Congress and the State Department are accessories to the crime and share Hitler's guilt." It added, "What has come over the minds of ordinary men and women that makes it seem normal and indeed inevitable that this country should stolidly stand by and do nothing in the face of one of the world's greatest tragedies?"

Then, as night fell on March 9, a record-setting audience of forty thousand came to Madison Square Garden in New York to watch a performance called "We Will Never Die," a memorial to the Jews butchered by the Nazis. Outside, thousands of others stood, stamping their feet in the chill evening air, hoping for a repeat performance. The event was no ordinary pageant; Edward G. Robinson was the narrator; the actors included Frank Sinatra, Burgess Meredith, and Ralph Bellamy, along with Paul Muni lending his voice. And it was produced by the legendary impresario Billy Rose, a close ally of the White House; and the author was Ben Hecht, an Academy award–winning screenwriter, playwright, and novelist, who had worked on Alfred Hitchcock's *Notorious* and the 1932 classic *Scarface*.

As the production began, the hall went dark, and then dazzling rays of light fell on the stage. In the background were two massive tablets forty feet high, etched with the Ten Commandments. In the foreground were the actors, dozens of them, standing erect and silent. They then began speaking. They spoke of Jewish contributions to mankind: Moses, Maimonides, and Einstein. They spoke of the Jews putting their lives on the line for the Allied armed forces. Then came a depiction of a postwar peace conference—much like what Roosevelt envisioned—in which the Jewish dead reappeared to narrate their stories of mass murder at the clutches of the Germans. In an ethereal tone, out came the haunting plea: "Remember us." Amid audible weeping in the audience, out came the haunting voice: "The corpse of a people lies in the steps of civilization. Behold it. Here it is!" Out came the call for conscience: "And no voice is heard to cry halt to the slaughter, no government speaks to bid the murder of human millions end."

The performance, also broadcast widely on radio, became a sensation. There was extensive coverage in newspapers and newsreels. The pageant toured nationwide to considerable acclaim; there were presentations in Philadelphia, Chicago, and Boston, and at Los Angeles' legendary Hollywood Bowl. When it came to Washington, D.C., it was seen by Eleanor Roosevelt, six Supreme Court justices, several cabinet members, more than three hundred senators and congressmen, military officials, and even foreign diplomats. All together, over 100,000 Americans saw the pageant.

It was almost impossible for the American mind to grasp the full horrors of Hitler's butchery. Yet Eleanor Roosevelt was so moved by the drama that she devoted one of her "My Day" columns to it. " 'We Will Never Die,' " she wrote, was "one of the most impressive and moving pageants I have ever seen. No one who heard each group come forward and give the story of what had happened to it at the hands of a ruthless German military, will ever forget those haunting words: 'Remember Us.' "

No one? Despite all the attention this play and the other measures received, one thing was missing. There was no proposal for actual steps to rescue Europe's trapped victims.

In fact, when the pageant's producer, Billy Rose, had asked for a brief statement of support from President Roosevelt that could be incorporated into "We Will Never Die," the White House demurred.

~

THEN, ON FEBRUARY 13, the *New York Times* carried a major story about the first significant opportunity to rescue Jews.

Headlined "Romania Proposes Transfer of Jews," a dispatch from London announced the Romanian government's willingness to free seventy thousand Jews, moving them from Transnistria to a place of the Allies' choosing, preferably Palestine. The Romanians themselves were willing to provide ships to give the Jews safe passage. Why were they doing this? And why now? The simplest reason was hard cash. The war-strapped Romanians were asking for approximately $130 per refugee, along with transportation and related expenses. But a more crucial reason was that the Romanians could interpret the shifting fortunes of the war as well as anyone; they were calculating that the war was turning the Allies' way, and that sooner or later the Axis powers would buckle—notwithstanding the German propaganda minister Joseph Goebbels's pronouncement, the very same day, that "the German people stand erect as on the first moment of the war." Thus, Romania was hoping to curry favor with the Allies by releasing the Jews, and thereby lessen the retribution to be exacted on it for collaborating with the Nazis. Its offer was a sign that Axis countries outside Germany were increasingly worried about the price to be paid for inflicting incalculable suffering on the innocent, especially on the Jews. To indicate the government's sincerity, the *Times* reported, the bishop of Bucharest and the papal nuncio would supervise the transfer; moreover, to ensure safe passage, the ships would bear the insignia of the Vatican.

For humanitarians everywhere, all this seemed almost too good to be true.

~

One renegade activist outside the government was unwilling to wait for the Allies' governments to initiate action. Peter H. Bergson, a Palestinian-born Jew, had been applauded and revered by his admirers, but he was distrusted, disliked, and even hated by his critics. Bergson—his name was originally Hillel Kook, and his late uncle had been the chief rabbi of Palestine—had first come to America hoping to campaign for a Jewish army, but then shifted his focus to rescuing the Jews from annihilation. Suspicious of the administration, intense yet charming, he was a charismatic orator and a dynamic leader of his movement. He was also a virtuoso in overcoming adverse odds. Rather than work through the State Department or the White House, he sought to build nationwide support for the embattled Jewish people through high-profile measures, including large display advertisements, mass demonstrations, and processions. Three days after the article about the Romanians appeared in the *New York Times*, his group took out an almost full-page ad in the *Times* with an arresting headline:

FOR SALE TO HUMANITY

70,000 Jews

GUARANTEED HUMAN BEINGS AT $50 APIECE

The ad was blunt. It was also embarrassing to the administration. Romania, it announced, "is tired of killing Jews. It has killed 100,000 of them in two years," but it was now willing to "give Jews away practically for nothing."

It called on readers to write to their members of Congress and inform friends, demanding action "Now, While There Is Still Time." Tucked away in the ad was the principal demand: that the "United Nations immediately appoint an intergovernmental committee" to devise ways to bring the extermination to a halt. Within days, Bergson's committee took out another ad, in the *New York Herald Tribune*, which also called for establishing an intergovernmental rescue commission. This set off a new wave of publicity. In turn, a galvanized Stephen Wise and the

American Jewish Congress partnered for a "Stop Hitler Now" demonstration. Seventy-five thousand flocked to this rally, once more jamming Madison Square Garden and also demonstrating outside, carrying signs or holding hands. Mayor Fiorello La Guardia addressed the meeting, and messages were read from the former presidential candidate Wendell Willkie, New York's governor Thomas Dewey, and the archbishop of Canterbury. This time, Wise and his group presented a detailed eleven-point program to be forwarded to Roosevelt. One *New York Times* columnist, Anne O'Hare McCormick, wrote that "the shame of the world filled the Garden Monday night." Taking a cue from Bergson, Wise sought to stir the conscience of Americans by immediately dispatching letters to the sounding boards of public opinion: Roosevelt, Secretary of State Cordell Hull, every member of the Senate as well as the House, and prominent newspaper editors. These dispatches included the eleven proposals for a rescue.

The president, however, gave a bland stock reply, writing that "this government has moved and continues to move, so far as the burden of the war permits, to help the victims of the Nazi doctrines . . . of oppression." As to the Romanian Jews? The secretary of the treasury, Henry Morgenthau, urgently brought the *New York Times* article to the White House for presentation to Roosevelt. It was the same story all over again. Professing ignorance, Roosevelt told Morgenthau to bring the matter to the State Department's attention. At the department, Undersecretary of State Sumner Welles said he would examine the facts. Predictably, the inquiry was cursory. Two weeks later the State Department insisted that the *Times'* story was "without foundation," that it had originated primarily not with the Romanian government but with the "German propaganda machine," and that it was intended to sow confusion and doubt among the Allies. At the Nuremberg trials after the war, this was found to be untrue.

Nonetheless, the administration was now feeling the political pressure. Two days later, the State Department leaked classified information indicating that the United States and Britain were engaged in discussions to convene a diplomatic conference for a "preliminary exploration" of the refugee problem. It was to take place in Bermuda in late April.

In the meantime word came from Geneva about a new round of massacres. Bulgarian Jews were now being deported en masse.

ON MARCH 27, WHILE an armada of British planes inflicted the heaviest raid on the German capital to date—a thousand tons of bombs fell on Berlin in all, reducing segments of the city to collapsing blackened ruins—President Roosevelt met in Washington with his special assistant Harry Hopkins; Secretary of State Cordell Hull; the British foreign secretary, Anthony Eden; Lord Halifax, the British ambassador; and Sumner Welles. Political genius lies in seeing over the horizon, anticipating a future invisible to others. Thus, an animated Roosevelt talked principally about the postwar peace that would follow the defeat of the Axis powers, and about the United Nations to be formally established—the body that would, in the president's words, help "police the world" for many years to come. But political genius also entails wrestling with unpleasant truths. At one point Hull interceded, mentioning that seventy thousand Jews in Bulgaria were now facing imminent extermination unless the Allies could manage to smuggle them out.

Here, however, was Romania redux. Anthony Eden counseled caution about offering to take all the Jews out of Bulgaria. "If we do that," he argued, "then the Jews of the world will be wanting us to make similar offers in Poland and Germany." Of course, wasn't that exactly what the United Nations should have wanted? As it turned out, no. Eden added, "Hitler might well take us up on any such offer and there simply are not enough ships and means of transportation in the world to handle them." A half century later, such callousness seems incomprehensible. Here was humanitarianism turned on its head: The fear seemed to be, not that the Jews would be marched to their deaths, but that they would be sent to the Allied nations; and no one, not even Roosevelt, objected to this line of thinking. Actually, the president simply recommended that the whole matter be turned over to the State Department.

What lay behind Roosevelt's silence, his seeming refusal to see, hear, or speak evil of the death camps? In fact, Eden's logic, and Roosevelt's reticence, reflected the prevailing wisdom at the State Department in the spring of 1943. As though the death camps were a passing phase, the department's R. Borden Reams wrote, "There is always the danger that the German government might agree to turn over to the United States . . . a large number of Jewish refugees," overwhelming America's ability to absorb them. In that case, he argued (ludicrously), the problem of "their continued persecution would have been largely transferred from the German government to the United Nations." The implication seems to have been that the gas chambers or work camps were preferable to placing any burden on the United Nations. Reams's attitude called to mind the startling observation by the British parliamentarian Sir Thomas Moore, early in the war, that he had been unable to find any trace of abuses by the Nazi regime. ("If I may judge from my personal knowledge of Herr Hitler," he declared, "peace and justice are the key words of his policy.")

To be sure, there remained almost insuperable practical problems, but these were a matter more of military capability and imagination than of anything else. Saving the Jews from the Nazi saturnalia of blood was the challenge: whatever the Allies decided to do, it was quite clear that Hitler had no intention of releasing a single Jew, let alone tens of thousands. At this point, the Allies had no means of rescuing the Jews who had not yet been deported. As it turned out, however, they weren't even trying.

In truth, if a deal had somehow been negotiated, the Jews could simply have walked across the mountains and the Balkans en route to Turkey. Moreover, just ten days after the meeting in Washington, the British announced their intention to move more than twenty thousand Polish refugees—non-Jews—to a safe haven in East Africa. And later in the year, similar help would be extended to thirty-six thousand non-Jewish Yugoslavs.

Why, the frantic Jewish leaders asked, couldn't the same be done for Hitler's Jewish victims?

~

IN THE EARLY SPRING of 1943, Stephen Wise contacted the White House requesting a meeting with Roosevelt. Ominously, the White House turned down the request.

For now, any hope of rescue for the Jews lay in the coming Anglo-American Bermuda conference on refugees. Meanwhile, four huge new crematoriums were put into operation at Auschwitz, and the slaughter of the Jews continued.

~

TRAINED TO HANDLE FOREIGN affairs with grace and subtlety, the diplomats convening in Bermuda were in the right place. For twelve days, they stayed at Horizons, a luxurious plantation built in 1760. It was perched on a rise amid twenty-five acres of exotic gardens, a profusion of swaying palm trees, spreading, manicured lawns, and hibiscus, with breathtaking views of shimmering turquoise water. Here, in sunlit reception rooms and sumptuous suites cooled by ceiling fans, the delegates would do their work. Bermuda had particular advantages. Originally, it was suggested that the conference be held either in Canada or in Washington, but both venues were vetoed as being too vulnerable to the hue and cry of pressure groups. By contrast, wartime regulations curtailed all access to Bermuda, which meant that the delegates were far from the prying eyes of the press—and from what the State Department considered noisy, showy humanitarian groups.

Roosevelt had hoped that Associate Justice Owen J. Roberts would be the chairman of the American delegation, but Roberts demurred because of his schedule. Roosevelt had replied: "I fully understand but I'm truly sorry that you cannot go to Bermuda—especially at the time of the Easter lilies!" Instead, he appointed Princeton University's president, Dr. Harold W. Dodds, to serve as chairman. Dodds would be buttressed by the influential chair of the Foreign Affairs Committee, Congressman

Sol Bloom; and the straight-talking future majority leader, Senator Scott Lucas of Illinois. Wise and other prominent Jews had hoped Jewish groups could be heard at the conference; instead, the administration only allowed George Warren, executive secretary of the President's Advisory Committee on Political Refugees, to serve as a technical adviser. In hindsight, the critics were right—the conference was doomed from the start.

On its face, it seemed as though London and Washington were competing for public recognition of their concern for the Jews, and that the conference started out strong. The participants agreed that there should be steps to encourage neutral European states to take in refugees; to secure transportation for moving refugees to sites in Europe and Africa; and to call on the Intergovernmental Committee on Refugees to carry out the conclusions arrived at in the conference. Yet from the outset, any specific emphasis on Jews was "strictly prohibited" because of fears that the Allies would object to any "marked preference" for any "particular race or faith." Moreover, the delegates were warned that the Roosevelt administration had no power "to relax or rescind" immigration laws (ignoring the fact that the administration had yet to even fill its legal quotas).

Once the conference began, it was clear that the administration was moving, as the historian James MacGregor Burns so aptly put it, "with wooden legs." Congressman Bloom suggested that the Germans be approached to see if they would free an agreed-on number of refugees "each month." But this only raised indignant shouts and went nowhere. A stickler for propriety, the State Department insisted it would oppose any negotiations with Germany. But what about approaching the satellite Axis countries such as Romania and Bulgaria, which might be willing to make separate deals? This wasn't even discussed. How about providing food to the half-starved victims of the Germans? Delegates quickly scrawled a line through this proposal; it was rejected outright. As to the possibility that Germany might release a sizable number of refugees of its own accord, again, the delegates stuck their hands in their pockets and pushed their glasses to the ends of their noses: this proposal was rejected for fear that Hitler might "send a large number of picked agents" into Allied territory, or because the Allies lacked the ships to accommodate a sizable exodus of Jews.

The reality, of course, was more complicated: a good number of ships that carried military supplies and men eastward across the Atlantic were actually empty on their return to the United States, but no one pointed this out with any conviction. What, then, were the conferees willing to agree to? Today, it is almost startling to read the recommendations, as freighted as they are with impediments. First, there was Spain. The British argued early and extensively that the estimated six thousand to eight thousand Jewish refugees there—these were the lucky ones who had escaped the mass roundups in neighboring France during the previous summer and managed to cross the Pyrenees mountains to safety—should be transported to a reception camp in North Africa. For the most part, they were currently in prisons and camps, where the conditions were wretched. In a rare moment of insight, it was pointed out that some three thousand of them were healthy enough and able enough to perform military work for the Allies. Yet the Americans were still hesitant, arguing that their ships were already overburdened. Again and again, the conferees came back to the view that the refugees might somehow compromise military operations; the Americans even insisted that North Africa could become a field of future military operations. But as they muddled along, the British felt strongly that if the conference could not find a way to accept at least this proposal, then an enraged public opinion throughout the world "would come to the conclusion that the allies are not making any serious endeavor to deal with the refugee problem."

Confronted with this taunt, Dodds, the chair of the American delegation, dispatched a hasty note to Breckinridge Long, asking him to give the proposal a second look. Speaking frankly, he added that the concept of a "refuge in Africa" under American administration "appears to be the only new contribution we can make that would impress public opinion."

War needs now jostled uneasily with humanitarian objectives, strategic considerations with a desire for public approval. Regarding the British proposal, public approval won out. Long passed the proposal on to the War Department, which rejected it, fearing that a significant mass of European Jews would raise the ire of the local Jordanian population. General Eisenhower, however, had no such objections and eagerly approved the plan. The conference followed Eisenhower's lead—"subject to military considerations." But when the proposal made its way back to Washington, Roosevelt expressed hesitation, describing the policy as "extremely unwise." Only after extensive discussions with the British did Roosevelt give his go-ahead: in July. In the end, only 630 Jews found a haven in North Africa.

For the most part, among these highly educated and well-connected delegates, plan after plan was raised and rejected. Plan after plan was quibbled over and endlessly dissected. Plan after plan was put off, pending future study. The conferees would not pledge funds, would not commit ships for the transportation of refugees, would not promise any changes in immigration laws; it was a collective failure of imagination.

But as the conference itself hurtled toward adjournment, the delegates were keenly aware they needed to have a list of "concrete recommendations." Those that they did have were few and modest. The first stated their objection to approaching Hitler about letting out potential refugees. The second asserted the two governments' desire to secure neutral shipping for "transport" of refugees. The third was that the British weigh the possibility of allowing refugees into Cyrenaica in eastern Libya. The fourth was a proposal to take Jews from Spain to depots in North Africa. The fifth recommended a declaration by the Allies about the postwar status of refugees. The sixth was a plan for reorganizing the largely inconsequential Intergovernmental Committee.

There were no serious dissenting voices. George Warren, the technical expert, later remarked that he had been "shocked by the strong resistance" to rescue action. In retrospect, it was as if the delegates were dealing with the nonviolent anti-Semitism of 1933 rather than the death mills of 1943; a time not of Treblinka and Dachau but when signs were displayed in Germany's motion picture theaters and restaurants reading

"*Juden unerwünscht*" ("Jews not welcome"); a time not of deportations and the Warsaw ghetto but when placards hung outside butcher shops saying "*Für Juden kein Zutritt*" ("Jews not admitted"); a time not of Auschwitz, but when Jews could not enter dairies to buy milk for their infants or pharmacies to fill their prescriptions. Perhaps for this reason, though the conference had arisen out of a desire to assuage public opinion, the delegates surprisingly agreed to keep the recommendations secret. They would release a one-page bulletin to the press, but the bulletin would announce only that they had carefully analyzed a range of possibilities and were making confidential suggestions to their governments.

Before going back to Princeton, the Americans' chairman, Dodds, publicly announced that the best way to help the refugees was to "win the war."

BAFFLED HUMANITARIANS EVERYWHERE WERE shaken and angry. The *Jewish Outlook* despaired that the conference had "destroyed every hope." In the House of Representatives, Congressman Samuel Dickstein angrily insisted that "Not even the pessimists among us expected such sterility," while in the Senate, an independent-minded Republican, William Langer, said that "two million Jews in Europe have been killed off already and another five million Jews are awaiting the same fate unless they are saved immediately." The renowned Christian theologian Reinhold Niebuhr warned President Roosevelt about the "deep pessimism" that followed the conference. And Rabbi Israel Goldstein, normally known for his moderation, blasted: "The job of the Bermuda conference apparently was not to rescue victims of Nazi terror, but to rescue our State Department."

The fact was that the president had been troubled about the plight of the Jews ever since Hitler took power in 1933. When pushed and prodded, he had verbally attacked the Nazis numerous times for their crimes and warned that the guilty would be sorely punished. It was clear, however, that at least thus far the deterrent effects of his warnings had been small.

And now, it was the president's circumspection, rather than any unwavering moral indignation, that set the tone of administration policy over the next crucial months. Little wonder that the State Department took weeks, even months, to deal with issues, or simply to answer correspondence. And every month, every week, tens of thousands more innocent lives were lost in Hitler's machinery of death. Why then, was Roosevelt not shocked into creative action? How was it that he seemed incapable of confronting the crux of the problem—the millions of Jewish men, women, and children held hostage by the Nazi regime and slated for the gas chambers?

Lacking answers, it fell to the Jews themselves to act. They did so, heroically, in Warsaw.

~

BY JULY 1942, THE Nazi death machine was in full operation in the Polish city of Warsaw. Already, Jews from the city and surrounding communities had been herded into the Warsaw ghetto, a space of ten blocked-off streets backing up to the Jewish cemetery on one corner and the rail yard on the other. When the war began, 350,000 Jews, roughly one third of the city's total population, lived and thrived in the Polish capital. Warsaw's Jewish population constituted the largest Jewish community in Poland, and in Europe. After New York City's, it was the second-largest single Jewish community in the world.

Within one week of the fall of Warsaw in late September 1939, the Germans established a *Judenrat*, a Jewish Council. Within two months, all Jews had to wear white armbands with a blue Star of David. Their schools were closed, their property was confiscated, and Jewish men were rounded up for forced labor. The ghetto was established in October 1940. Some 400,000 Jews from the city and surrounding towns had one month to move into an area of 1.3 square miles. On block after block, buildings overflowed; a single room was now home to seven people. The conditions were brutal. The ghetto was surrounded by a ten-foot wall, topped with barbed wire. There was to be no passage between the ghetto and the rest of the city: *Judenfrei* Warsaw. Inside the wall, there was never enough food; children starved to death, their emaciated bodies curled in doorways and on stoops. In less than two years, 83,000 Jews died of hunger and disease. Still, the Jews maintained their dignity, secretly praying and studying.

Then the first mass deportations began on July 22, 1942, as train after train pulled out of the station, bound for the killing center at Treblinka. By September, 265,000 Jews had been forcibly removed from the ghetto and sent to this death camp. And despite the Nazis' efforts to isolate the Jews of Warsaw, those who remained now knew where they were going. On September 11, an underground newspaper published an account by an escapee from Treblinka. It concluded, "Today every Jew should know the fate of those resettled. . . . Don't let yourself be caught! Hide, don't let yourself be taken away! . . . We are all soldiers on a terrible front!" Death was waiting—the only alternative was to fight. Confronted with these harsh truths, two Jewish underground organizations began to act. They formed armed resistance groups, numbering about 750 men. Their weapons were simple pistols and explosives, smuggled in from contacts in the Polish Home Army.

But the Nazis were moving equally fast. It was Heinrich Himmler who gave the order to liquidate the ghetto in the fall of 1942. Able-bodied residents were to be sent to forced labor camps near Lublin. The rest were to be destroyed. On January 18, 1943, after a hiatus, deportations resumed. However, this time the resistance was ready. Jewish fighters armed with pistols maneuvered their way into a transport group. They waited until the signal came; then they opened fire on the German escorts. The Germans quickly fired back, but in the confusion, the remaining Jews fled. Three days later, the Germans halted deportations. Now the preparations inside the ghetto began in earnest. Jews started building underground bunkers and shelters, ready to hide and fight if the Germans tried to make good on their promise to fully liquidate the ghetto.

Months passed, and the Germans set a date for the liquidation: April 19, the eve of Passover—a symbol that could not be mistaken. They planned for their final operation to take only three days. Yet when

Nazi SS units and police stormed the ghetto, they found the streets silent and the buildings deserted. Nearly all the Jews still alive had retreated to hiding places or underground bunkers. Then the Jewish fighters struck; in the words of one, "We suppressed our emotions and reached for our guns." They trained their pistols and their most lethal weapons, an assortment of homemade bombs, on the stunned Germans, who, unprepared, hastily pulled back outside the ghetto walls. Six Germans and six Ukrainian auxiliaries had been killed. When the Nazi forces returned, this time their task was total destruction: to raze every building and to demolish the ghetto block by block. To do so, they used flamethrowers. As flames overtook the walls and smoke billowed from the windows, Jews hiding inside were forced to jump to their deaths. The Germans, seeing them, began firing, riddling their victims with bullets as they stood on balconies to jump or as they plummeted helplessly through the air. If any made it to the ground alive, the German forces opened fire there. Yet despite the appalling carnage, small groups of Jews managed to elude the Germans and to fight them for nearly one month. In the unyielding words of one combatant, "We fight like animals for naked life."

They did. It wasn't enough. By May 16, the ghetto had been liquidated, and the German commander ordered the Great Synagogue on Tlomacki Street to be destroyed. Over fifty-six thousand Jews had been captured; most were sent to the Majdanek camp outside the city of Lublin. The Germans recorded that seven thousand Jews were killed in the uprising—among them the escapee from Treblinka who had brought news of the death camp and its gas chambers. Another seven thousand from inside the ghetto were sent to Treblinka. Nearly all were gassed immediately on their arrival.

Miraculously, a few Jews inside Warsaw did survive. Some hid in the ruins of the ghetto, attacking German patrols when the opportunity arose. Some slipped out, escaping to the Aryan side. Others, rather than be captured, took cyanide pills. And even after the ghetto was demolished in September 1943, "a few individuals continued to live in dugouts, totally cut off from nature, light, and human company." News of the uprising spread. In the months that followed, the ghettos in Bialystok and Minsk rose up against the Nazis, as did prisoners at the killing centers in Treblinka and Sobibór. The attempts were futile and ended most often in more death, yet by the fall of 1943 Treblinka and Sobibór were being dismantled.

But perhaps the most poignant coda to the battle was this: two days after the uprising at Warsaw began, a radio message was wired from a secret Polish transmitter. Only four sentences were sent before the signal was cut. They ended with two words: "Save us."

The message was received in Stockholm and then relayed around the world. But in London and Washington, no notice was taken. And in Bermuda, where the conference was under way, silence was the only reply.

MEANWHILE, AFTER A LONG struggle, the Allied armies continued to make stunning progress. The president's single-minded pursuit of military victory was starting to pay off. The campaign in North Africa had come to a close on May 13, and the Allied victory was complete. As nearly a quarter million Germans and Italians were taken prisoner, the question now loomed: what next? That was on Roosevelt's and Churchill's minds as they once again met in Washington to hash out the details of the next phase of the war. This was the Trident conference. By this stage in 1943, sensing that the end was near, the British and the Americans were convening so frequently, in so many places, that it was as if they were actors in a touring theater production. In January, Roosevelt had met with Churchill, Giraud, and de Gaulle in Casablanca; in March, he had met with Eden in Washington; in May, he met with Churchill and the combined chiefs of staff; and Churchill, Marshall, and Eisenhower would also meet in Algiers at the end of May. Summer would bring no respite: Roosevelt and Churchill and their staffs would convene again in Quebec in late August, and once more at the White House in September. Then, these meetings would spread out across the global stage: Roosevelt and Churchill would of course fly to Cairo in late

November; Roosevelt, Churchill, and Stalin would memorably gather in Tehran at the end of November; and finally, Roosevelt and Churchill would meet up once more in Cairo in early December.

Yet no matter how tiring his far-flung travels were, Roosevelt was inwardly triumphant and now looking ahead, pondering the broader questions of the historical record. He wrote to a good friend, Librarian of Congress Archibald MacLeish, the renowned poet, insisting that someone needed to capture the story of the global struggle, to recreate "the public pulse as it throbs from day to day . . . The processes of propaganda—the parts played by the newspaper emperors, etc." He continued: "It is not dry history or the cataloging of books and papers and reports. It is trying to capture a great dream before it dies." In this regard Roosevelt's secretary of war, Henry Stimson, played to Roosevelt's great dream as well, recalling the harrowing trials that the American people underwent during the Civil War in the ghastly spring of 1864, when the United States pressed on despite the terrible losses in the Wilderness campaign. "We are facing," Stimson told Roosevelt, "a difficult year at home with timid and hostile hearts ready to seize and exploit any wavering on the part of our war leadership." For the moment, however, Roosevelt was not wavering, and as the Trident conference in Washington began, history took a backseat to military policy and the invasion of Italy.

For two weeks, he and Churchill wrangled with strategy—particularly the timing of the cross-Channel invasion. Here was Casablanca all over again. Old arguments were rehashed. Old biases were summoned up. Roosevelt and his staff were itching to assemble a large force in England and to hit the Germans directly with an assault through France itself; Churchill and his military advisers wanted to push on in the Mediterranean, prod Italy to quit the war, and then slug their way into Germany through what they referred to as Europe's "soft underbelly." The debates were intense and often acrimonious; at one point, a despairing Churchill threw up his hands and moaned that Roosevelt was "not in favor of landing in Italy. It is *most* discouraging." But both sides had merit. For the Americans, the most fundamental criticism remained this: Italy was a path to nowhere. In this sense, to the American high command, the Italian campaign was a costly sideshow recalling the World War I song, "We're here because we're here because we're here." In their view, an operation in Italy amounted to wishful thinking, the vain hope that Germany could be defeated by attrition. Even in the best-case scenario, once having taken Italy, the Allied armies still had to drive across the Alps to get to Germany. Nor, the Americans argued, was this a good use of resources: because of its jagged landscape, harsh weather, and treacherous mountain passes, Italy was ill suited to offensive maneuvers. Moreover, it would tie up many more Allied troops than it would Kesselring's German divisions.

Yet the invasion of Italy was almost guaranteed by the massive commitment of armed forces in the North Africa campaign. The invasion of France could not really be waged until the spring of 1944—even Roosevelt knew this—so, once North Africa was stripped of Axis forces, it seemed counterproductive to haul the Allies' mammoth war machine back to Britain. And Italy was a ripe target there for the taking. If the Allies did not move on into Sicily and Italy, it would be like the situation they had faced in 1942 all over again, just on a different continent: they would sit out the remainder of 1943 and much of 1944 doing little except firebombing "soft" targets—the Nazis' cities and civilians—and "hard" targets such as rubber and oil facilities.

There were other benefits as well. By conquering Italy, they would conquer airfields that would allow Allied airpower to blast targets spread across the Balkans and Poland, including the sprawling network of factories so crucial to the Germans' war machine. Finally, there was the all-important question of morale, which Roosevelt understood better than anyone else; here, Italy was a natural extension of North Africa. The Italian campaign in 1943 would demonstrate that the United States and Britain were finally on the offense on the Continent itself, and that liberation was merely a matter of time.

While they were deadlocked early on, Roosevelt sought to break the ice by taking Churchill to the wooded presidential retreat in the Catoctin Mountains, Shangri-La. There, Roosevelt spent a few hours with his stamp collection, and early the next day he invited Churchill for a relaxing fishing excursion nearby. These activities buoyed both Roosevelt's and Churchill's spirits, but nonetheless, they remained at an impasse on strategy. In the days that followed, Churchill paced up and down in his room, worked nights and slept during the day, and fretted constantly, until he was ready to go home. But suddenly, at the brink of the conference's close, Roosevelt and Churchill each compromised. For his part, Churchill grudgingly agreed that the main effort would be the invasion of France—Overlord—and that it could not be postponed indefinitely. A target date—May 1, 1944—was established. Thus the military buildup in Britain for the great assault would be significantly accelerated. For his part, Roosevelt consented to move against Italy, but with the condition that they would use forces already dedicated to the Mediterranean—in that way, Italy would not detract from the cross-Channel attack. Once Sicily had fallen, seven divisions would be quickly shifted from the Mediterranean to France.

After Churchill departed on May 27, Roosevelt left for Hyde Park, where for three straight days he slept for ten hours a day.

As it happened, he would have at least two serious illnesses during the year. The first he wryly called "Gambia fever or some kindred bug," which he told Churchill he had contracted in "that hellhole of yours called Bathurst"; with the second, he reported to Churchill that it was "a nuisenza to have the influenza." After he recovered, he boasted to Churchill that he had felt like a "fighting cock" ever since.

But this was wishful thinking. There was more sickness to come.

~

MILITARILY, THINGS WERE NOW set in motion. Finally, the Italian campaign commenced. For days, Allied forces had been pouring out of Benghazi, Tripoli, Alexandria, Haifa, and Beirut. After that, the Allied bombing of Sicily opened up to soften enemy defenses. Meanwhile, the wind was gusting fiercely before the sun rose.

The invasion of Sicily began on July 10.

On the first day, 175,000 troops hit the beaches after braving forty-five-mile-per-hour winds. Within two days, nearly 500,000 men—along with tanks and landing craft—had come ashore, where they faced only 60,000 dumbfounded Germans. After its victories in North Africa, the British general Bernard Montgomery's veteran Eighth Army was now the tip of the spear, driving through the east coast. There, it rapidly seized one of the prizes of antiquity, ancient Syracuse, before plowing into the vast and important Plain of Catania (*la Chiana de Catania*).

The Germans, under Field Marshal Kesselring's command, put up a stiff resistance. Meanwhile, General George Patton's indefatigable Seventh Army landed in the south, where it was to cover Montgomery's left flank. Instead, Patton, independent-minded as ever, ignored orders and relentlessly proceeded to drive northwest, all the way to Palermo. Nothing could stop him, not rock ridges, not muddy valleys, and certainly not the Italian defenders, most of whom either surrendered or offered only a feeble fight. Thronging to their balconies, the Sicilians themselves greeted the invaders ecstatically, hanging white flags from their windows and handing out baskets of fresh fruit and bundles of freshly cut flowers.

The German troops, the cream of the Nazis' army, were a different story. Slowly pulling back, they laid waste to bridges, desperately counterattacked, and positioned themselves to fight on every hilltop and crag. At the easternmost point of the island was the strategic objective: Messina. While Montgomery's men slugged it out on the coast against fierce resistance, U.S. forces pushed forward. For their part, the American and British engineers were unstoppable. Working marvels, they heroically brought heavy equipment over narrow, primitive roads and laid down trestles over deep cavities.

Then, on July 17, the Allies began psychological warfare, air-dropping leaflets like confetti onto the streets of Rome and other once-Fascist cities; these messages were signed by Roosevelt and Churchill and were designed to increase the pressure on Italy to part ways with Hitler. The leaflets proclaimed: "Mussolini carried you into this war as a satellite of a brutal destroyer of peoples and liberties. Mussolini plunged you into a war which he thought Hitler had already won. In spite of Italy's great vulnerability . . . your fascist leaders sent your sons . . . to distant battlefields to aid Germany in her attempt to conquer England, Russia, and the world. . . . The time has come for you to decide whether Italians shall die for Mussolini and Hitler—or live for Italy, and for civilization."

As it turned out, the Italians were not ready to die for Mussolini or for Hitler. Under the blistering assault of the Allies, the morale of many Italians had already disintegrated. In towns across the country strikes and riots broke out, and Mussolini's lock on power quickly began to ebb and crumble. Just two days later, on July 19, while Montgomery and Patton were pounding through Sicily, the Italian dictator met with Hitler at a resplendent country villa. The indignant Führer insisted that Sicily must become "another Stalingrad." But the Fascist Grand Council would no longer have any of it. Before the sun began to climb on Sunday, July 25, the council held a hastily arranged meeting with Mussolini, at which there was a dramatic vote of no confidence. Within hours, Italy's king, Victor Emmanuel III, summoned Mussolini to his palace, and angrily said, "At this moment you are the most hated man in Italy. The soldiers don't want to fight anymore." Emerging from the meeting, Mussolini was reeling; then he was promptly detained by his former allies, the *carabinieri*—Italy's ancient national police—stuffed into an ambulance, and spirited off to confinement in a distant mountain resort in central Italy.

Long demoralized, the people of Italy were jubilant.

NOR WERE THEY THE only ones. After hearing the news of Mussolini's arrest over the radio, Roosevelt, in high spirits, positioned himself before an array of microphones in the Diplomatic Reception Room to give his first fireside chat since February. He began speaking at precisely 9:25 p.m. "The first crack in the axis has come," he boomed. "The criminal, corrupt fascist regime in Italy is going to pieces. The pirate philosophy of the fascists and the Nazis cannot stand adversity." With military precision, he then outlined the "almost unbelievable" production by the democracies in comparison with that of 1942: 19 million tons of merchant shipping during the year; naval ships, 75 percent higher;

munitions output, 83 percent higher; planes, an expected 86,000, nearly double the output for the previous year. He could not help boasting, yet he wisely tempered his words with realism. "The plans we have made for the knocking out of Mussolini and his gang have largely succeeded. But we still have to defeat Hitler and Tojo on their own home grounds. No one of us pretends that this will be an easy matter."

As to Italy? "Our terms," he said, "are still the same. We will have no truck with fascism in any way."

And then came his final uplifting flourish, a retort to Goebbels's fanciful speech in Berlin about the necessity for total war: "We must pour into this war the entire strength and intelligence and willpower of the United States."

Meanwhile, in the days that followed, Roosevelt was preparing to quickly drive a wedge between Italy and Germany. His pragmatic side once again on display, Roosevelt signaled that he was ready to make a deal with the mercurial new premier of Italy, Field Marshal Pietro Badoglio, a figure in the mold of Darlan, who had already opened secret discussions with the Allies in Spain and Portugal. Putting aside his earlier pronouncement at Casablanca about the demand for unconditional surrender, Roosevelt hinted at favorable treatment for the people of Italy. He told the press on July 30: "I don't care who we deal with in Italy so long as it isn't a definite member of the fascist government, so long as we get them to lay down their arms, and so long as we don't have anarchy." Underscoring his desire to conclude a separate peace and bloody the Germans—and keeping in mind the sentiments of the active Italian American voters at home—he added, "Now his name may be a king, or present Prime Minister, or a mayor of a town or a village."

He soon found out. Before dawn on September 3, 1943, British forces streamed onto the Italian mainland, and Roosevelt's gambit paid off—for the time being. In an olive grove near Syracuse, the new Italian government changed its allegiance and "declared war" on the Nazis—then fled Rome in a panic. The Nazis promptly retaliated. Hitler, irate at the Italian double-cross, sent sixteen battle-hardened divisions screaming down the spine of Italy; they quickly poured over the Brenner Pass and just as quickly encircled Rome. And in a daring raid on the mountain resort in Abruzzi, ninety German glider paratroopers, led by the Waffen SS, kidnapped Mussolini and restored him to office. Meanwhile, Rome was occupied and the Italian army disarmed. At the same time, the Nazis seized all of Italy's gold reserves, and Kesselring proclaimed Italy under German control. The Germans also began immediate persecution of any surviving Jews.

Six days later, the Allies struck back. On September 9, the shimmering sands of Salerno witnessed a stunning sight: American and British forces were landing en masse—actually, the Americans had disembarked at night—to begin their race for Naples. On the perimeter of the beachhead, the German coastal defense was fierce: thick smoke was everywhere, and the Americans faced thundering tank fire and heavy artillery. Meanwhile, the Germans cockily taunted the Allied troops, in English, over loudspeakers.

Counterattacking, Kesselring put up dogged resistance—he almost even split the American Fifth Army in two—while Rommel was dispatched to organize northern Italian defenses. It was not enough. Though Berlin radio boasted about the prospect of another Dunkirk, on October 1 Allied forces gained control of Naples, and the Germans were forced to conduct a hurried, painful retreat. From there, the Americans and British began making their way, over narrow roads and through rough terrain and weathered hilltop towns, toward Rome and Tuscany.

And with each slow, bloody yard as they worked their way north—Italy had suffered one of its most frightful winters in more than twenty years—the Allies were closer to being able to open up the second front with the invasion of France.

There was another considerable benefit. The Allies captured an invaluable complex of airfields at Foggia; this in turn provided them not simply with mastery of the skies, but also with fighter cover for the ground troops. It did one more thing. It enabled them finally to employ heavy bombers over the Balkans, over Austria, and even as far off as Poland.

Including the area around Auschwitz, some 620 miles away.

12

"The Acquiescence of This Government in the Murder of the Jews"

AMID WARTIME SUMMITRY AND wartime strategy, sobering reports from the military fronts and nagging reports about Allied squabbles, and continuing troubles at home, Roosevelt invariably kept his composure. To be sure, as the war ground on there were times when his legendary patience was tried. "I get so many conflicting recommendations," he once confessed, "my head is splitting." Nor was he above grumbling about his own problems. And not a day went by without harrowing reports of bloody battles that left a trail of corpses everywhere. Nor was there a day when he couldn't read about his own men, wounded or dead or taken prisoner. At sixty-two years of age, and after the unremitting complications of three years of war, he sometimes had bouts of lethargy or suffered from shortness of breath or an irregular heartbeat—or contracted debilitating influenza. But for the most part, to the American people he seemed indomitable. His energy, or rather his determination, did not wane. There was, as always, his broad smile and the infectious tilt of his head. There was his hearty laugh and his storytelling, as if he didn't have a care in the world. And at his ritualistic cocktail hour, there was always his good cheer. True, he had to curtail some of his favorite relaxations. Where he once fiddled with his stamp collection for hours before bedtime, now he was forced to study reports about tank production or preparations for Normandy. Where he once could count on a late-afternoon dip in the White House pool, now, surrounded by aides and a mass of documents, he confronted a mountain of work that never seemed to quit—the memos; top-secret papers; personnel complaints; and letters from the public—some four thousand a day and never-ending. In his own way he was a tireless worker, but more than that, he was an incurable charmer. At times he seemed to revel in his own personal glory—a prima donna, he did not relish yielding the spotlight for long—but his political leadership was undeniable, and his ardor for the American people was unquestioned.

How did he keep going? For one thing, the pendulum of war was swinging decisively in his favor. News from the fronts was increasingly positive. The Allies' blistering bombing of Germany commenced with a vengeance: by day American aircraft began pounding German cities, while the British did the same at night. For another, Roosevelt always found a way to relax. He had his beloved cocktail hour, where any talk of politics or war was strictly forbidden; his movies, which he could never get enough of; and his card games, which he loved to win. When he could, he restricted his schedule in the White House. When he felt it necessary—and he often did—he retreated for weekends at Hyde Park, where he slept late, postponed any work until afternoon, and took leisurely drives through the countryside that left him feeling glorious.

But then came a mass rally in New York City on behalf of the European Jews; a meeting with Stephen Wise; and an almost hour-long discussion on July 22 in the Oval Office with a member of the Polish underground, Jan Karski. Sometimes, illusions die hard, and that was the case with the world turning a blind eye to the plight of the Jews.

But now this was one illusion that was dying.

~

NEAR THE END OF July, humanitarians, disgusted by the inaction of the Bermuda conference, sought to take matters into their own hands. For three straight days, some fifteen hundred people gathered at the Hotel Commodore in Manhattan to discuss a program of action to help the Jews who still survived in Nazi-occupied Europe. Earlier, Wise had been the guiding force, but this conference was organized by Peter Bergson. One by one, an impressive roster of speakers, Jews and non-Jews alike, representing diverse backgrounds and political views, took their places on the rostrum. There was the mayor of New York City, Fiorello La Guardia, railing impassionately. There were distinguished writers such as Max Lerner and Dorothy Parker, eloquent and incisive. Even the former president, Herbert Hoover, participated by telephone.

As was often the case, the president had waited for a crisis before acting. Impelled by public pressure, Roosevelt sent a message to be read at the end of the conference. But its promises were, in Doris Kearns Goodwin's words, "vague" and "noncommittal." He cited the administration's "repeated endeavors" to save the European Jews; but the delegates to the conference knew better. He further promised that the government's endeavors would not "cease until Nazi power is forever crushed," yet the conferees asked themselves what those endeavors were, and whether the Jews would still be alive by the time Nazi power was overcome.

Eleanor Roosevelt, who had been sympathetic in the past, also sent a message to this emergency conference, but this time she too was off the mark. She insisted that she was glad to help "in any way," yet was uncertain what specific actions could be carried out. Then she offered the sort of stock phrases that the State Department so often used. The American people, she averred, were "shocked and horrified" by the Axis powers' actions toward the Jewish people, and would be willing to do all they could "to alleviate the suffering of the Jewish people in Europe and help them reestablish themselves in other parts of the world if it is possible to evacuate them."

But there were measures that could have been taken right away, ones that would not have hindered the military efforts of the Allies. Over three long, scorching days, each of the advocates of rescue laid these out in meticulous detail. Mayor La Guardia pointed out that the time was long overdue for the United States to open up its gates to greater numbers of immigrants. "Our own government," he said, "cannot urge other nations to take the initiative before it takes action on its own." More fundamentally, the speakers underscored the need for a specific governmental agency that would have the sole purpose of saving Jews. It would fight the bureaucratic battles, provide the political muscle, and take the necessary risks. Former president Hoover weighed in further, pointing out that additional measures were also needed: for starters, protection by the Allies for Jews who managed to smuggle themselves into neutral countries; more refugee sanctuaries in neutral territories; and seeking to compel Axis satellites not to deport Jews. Further, the conferees suggested threading the needle of Middle Eastern politics and putting pressure on British-controlled Palestine to take more Jews.

On its conclusion, the conference turned itself into a new organization, called the Emergency Committee.

The committee's leader, Peter Bergson, met privately with Eleanor Roosevelt in August. His heartfelt appeal on behalf of the Jewish people made an indelible impression. The next morning (August 8, 1943) she wrote in her column "My Day": "The percentage killed among them far exceeds the losses among any of the United Nations. I do not know what we can do to save the Jews in Europe and to find them homes, but I know that we will be the sufferers if we let great wrongs occur without exerting ourselves to correct them." She fell short of calling for decisive actions, but, more importantly, she relayed a letter from Bergson that outlined the need for a special governmental rescue agency.

Yet a distracted Roosevelt was unmoved. He scrawled a note to Eleanor: "I do not think this needs any answer at this time. FDR."

~

TIME WAS NOT A commodity the Jews could afford.

Never was this more evident than on July 28, 1943, when Roosevelt met Jan Karski, a thirty-two-year-old leader in the Polish underground who risked his life to uncover the horrific events unfolding in Poland.

Karski was trim, handsome, fearless, with piercing eyes. And he had a photographic memory. Earlier in the war he had been captured by the Gestapo and tortured nearly to death—he slashed his own wrists so he wouldn't give away secrets—but had somehow been rescued by a Polish commando team. Now, working with Jewish leaders, Karski, who spoke German, had been given the daunting mission of witnessing conditions in the Jewish ghettos and at the actual extermination camps themselves. Disguised first as a Jew, wearing tattered clothes and the blue Star of David, he was smuggled into the Warsaw ghetto, where, as he noted, "there was hardly a square yard of empty space as we picked our way across the mud and rubble" and where "Hitler youth hunted Jews for sport, cheering and laughing." Then, dressed as an Estonian militiaman, he was infiltrated into what he believed to be the Belzec concentration camp, which was about a hundred miles east of Warsaw. Actually, he may have been in a transit point at Izbica. He knew from earlier reports that every Jew who reached the camp was doomed to death, without exception. But how?

He set out to discover this firsthand.

After seeing the atrocities with his own eyes, he made a harrowing trek across Europe by train, from Warsaw to Berlin to Vichy to Paris to Spain and then back to London, carrying his reports in microfilm tucked into the shaft of a simple house key, which contained hundreds of documents.

His observations were searing. Karski was struck by how even a mile away from the camp he could hear terrifying "shouts," "shots," and "screams." And in the camp he saw chaos, squalor, and "the hideousness of it all." He saw elderly Jews, shivering and sitting silently on the ground, motionless, without a stitch of clothing on them. He saw small children clad in a few rags, crouched and utterly alone, staring up with "large frightened eyes." He saw how on any given night two thousand to three thousand dehumanized, starving Jews were forced to sleep outside in cold, raw, rainy weather. He watched as, for three ghastly hours straight, the Germans, alternately swinging and firing their rifles, stuffed 130 wailing Jews into freight cars that were designed to carry forty soldiers each at a maximum—forty-six cars in all. He watched as they were asphyxiated with quicklime, dying "in agony" as the thick, white powder ate away their flesh.

In a sense, what the German Eduard Schulte had hoped to begin, earlier in the war, the Polish Jan Karski now hoped to finish—if only the Americans would act.

Karski well understood that for many Americans, it would at first be difficult to comprehend the sheer scope and savagery of Hitler's efforts to wipe out Jewry. In fact, when he met with the Supreme Court justice Felix Frankfurter, a stunned Frankfurter, himself a Jew, found the account difficult to believe. Karski would later write, "I know that many people will not believe me, but I saw it, and it is not exaggerated. I have no other proofs, no photographs. All I can say is that I saw it, and it is the truth." Clearly this was no mere collateral damage or an unfortunate by-product of the ravages of war as the State Department often suggested. And when Roosevelt asked if the published reports of Jewish casualty figures were true, Karski replied, "I am convinced that there is no exaggeration in the accounts of the plight of the Jews. Our underground authorities are absolutely sure that the Germans are out to exterminate the entire Jewish population of Europe."

He informed Roosevelt that 1.8 million Polish Jews had been slaughtered, and that Polish Jewry would cease to exist within months unless there was some kind of intervention by the Allies. What could be done? Karski suggested the same policy that Schulte had proposed earlier on: retaliating against German civilians "wherever they could be found."

Roosevelt asked detailed questions about Polish partisan activities, as well as about the morale of the German soldiers. Karski then methodically ticked off a list of concentration camps, naming each of them, including Auschwitz itself.

Roosevelt was, by all accounts, stunned by Karski's firsthand reports. Indeed, the two spoke for an hour—thirty minutes over schedule. Cordell Hull later acknowledged that Roosevelt had been "completely absorbed." Roosevelt told Karski to tell the Polish underground, "You have a *friend* in the White House." Karski was impressed by Roosevelt's fervor. But then, as Karski walked out of the White House, the Polish ambassador mentioned to him that the president had uttered nothing but platitudes.

~

WERE THEY NOTHING BUT platitudes? There was little doubt that the president was consumed by the task of winning the war and crushing Hitler. He was reluctant to let anything divert time, attention, or resources from that goal. But there was also little doubt that whenever other humanitarian needs arose—as when refugees in Yugoslavia and in Greece were pleading for help—the U.S. government was able to muster transportation and find solutions.

It was also the case that the successful invasion of Italy opened up a slew of opportunities for Roosevelt—and, as it happened, for the Jews, although these same opportunities involved political and military problems. With the Allied soldiers fighting their way through Italy, Roosevelt was anxious to secure the actual assistance—or at least the tacit support—of the peoples of the Mediterranean. Here lay a chance for a concerted effort by antifascists, and here lay the predicament. These were nations riddled with ancient enmities and insuperable suspicions—toward the great powers, and toward each other.

The greatest prize was Palestine, at once a coveted haven, at the same time a quagmire. For the Jews ensnared by the Nazis, the escape lines largely were not westward to Britain and America, but southeastward across the Mediterranean. Thus, of all the opportunities for Roosevelt concerning the Jews, the most hopeful sanctuaries for them seemed to be in Palestine—in the ancient cities of Jerusalem, Haifa, and Acre. The fear, of course, was that any such plan would antagonize Muslims in countries where battles were still raging, thus somehow thwarting the president's single-minded focus on victory.

So, time and again, Roosevelt, seeking to avoid a politician's purgatory, straddled the fence. His position was uncomfortable, precarious, awkward, and probably inevitable. He sometimes paid lip service to the dream of Palestine as a Jewish homeland. But not unlike Lincoln, who until as late as 1862 considered the notion of resettling American blacks in Haiti or Africa, Roosevelt also flirted with the idea of Jews being resettled in more distant places, like Cameroon, and later Paraguay, and still later Angola in Portuguese West Africa. For Lincoln nearly a century earlier, such a policy was doomed, just as it was doomed for Roosevelt.

As 1942 came to a close, Roosevelt again thought about Palestine. "What I think I will do is this," he told Morgenthau. "First, I would call Palestine a religious country. Then I would leave Jerusalem the way it is and have it run by the Orthodox Greek Catholic Church, the Protestants, and the Jews—have a joint committee run it. . . . I actually would put a barbed wire around Palestine."

Bristling with energy, he continued, "I would provide land for the Arabs in some other part of the Middle East. . . . Each time we move out an Arab we would bring in another Jewish family. . . . But I don't want to bring in more than they can economically support."

However, in 1943 this proved to be mere talk. When Roosevelt received Zionist delegations, such as when he met with the Zionist leader Chaim Weizman in June 1943, there were violent reactions in Saudi Arabia, Syria, and Egypt. In 1943 Roosevelt also sought to prod Jewish and Arab leaders to meet with one another, but this attempt foundered on the shoals of Arab intractability—Ibn Saud refused to cooperate—and the War Department's own hesitations. In late 1943 Roosevelt tinkered with a new concept—a trusteeship for Palestine that would transform it into a certified holy land administered by the three dominant religions, Judaism, Christianity, and Islam—but this idea proved to be unworkable.

Roosevelt was once quoted as saying that he had never approved of Britain's 1939 white paper restricting Jewish immigration. But whenever he himself was confronted with the choice between stability in the Middle East and rescuing Jews, he invariably opted for peace—or stability. Such was the terrible calculus of global struggle. And so, in a situation characterized by continuing feuds and endless delays, the dismal impasse remained.

Meanwhile, the Nazi death machine continued unabated. There was no getting around the haunting question raised by the editors of the *New Republic*. On August 30, they wrote this: "The failure of the democratic powers to make any sustained and determined effort to stay the tide of slaughter constitutes one of the major tragedies in the history of civilization."

They added: "And the moral weakness which has palsied the hands of our statesmen is nowhere more vividly disclosed than in the now conventional formula . . . that only victory will save the Jews of Europe."

And then this: "Will any of these Jews survive to celebrate victory?"

IN SWITZERLAND, A TIRELESS Gerhart Riegner, for one, hoped so. For some time in the spring he had been working on a "wide rescue action" for Jews from Romania and France. There were now two significant, if slim, opportunities. In Romania itself, the hope was that children there could be transferred to safety in Palestine "if funds were made available." Moreover, food, medicine, and other relief could be dispensed to the Jews in Transnistria, a part of Ukraine under Romanian control; this was a variation of the earlier proposal under which Romanian officials would let seventy thousand Jews in Transnistria depart for the sum of $170,000. At the same time a second opportunity was presenting itself in France, where the cattle cars continued to roll and large-scale deportations were still underway at a staggering pace. Here, Riegner contemplated a daring rescue of fugitive Jewish children who were concealed in safe houses and other hiding places; plans were being readied to help them flee to safety in Spain. In both cases monies for the measure would be provided by American Jewish organizations rather than the government. At no time would the money move into or out of Axis territory. All the U.S. government had to do was guarantee repayment by transferring funds from America to accounts in Switzerland, which Romanian officials would collect after the war.

Back in the United States, Stephen Wise then spent eleven weeks fervently negotiating with the State Department to approve Riegner's plan.

But the plan went nowhere. First the State Department insisted that the proposal was too vague. Then it fretted that money might be used to pay ransom, which the government opposed. Finally, the State Department acknowledged that its real reluctance about a wide-scale rescue plan was not that such a plan would fail, but that it would succeed; there was a quota of only thirty thousand under the terms of the Palestinian white paper, and the department maintained that it did not know of "any other areas to which the remaining Jews could be evacuated."

Not until June did the State Department finally discuss the plan with the Treasury Department, which was the agency responsible for issuing the licenses required for transferring funds overseas. Hearing the State Department's objections out, the Treasury Department was nonplussed. It moved quickly and, on July 16, indicated that it would on its end issue the license.

Nevertheless, with the State Department dragging its heels, the impasse continued.

~

CONCERNED, WISE WAS ABLE to arrange for a private meeting with Roosevelt at the White House on July 22. Laying out his vision of the plan, he sought to assuage any of the president's fears that somehow the plan could hinder the prosecution of the war; he pointed out that the funds would not be tapped into until the war was over. Deeply moved by Wise's plea, Roosevelt quickly signed off on the plan, telling Wise, "Stephen, why don't you go ahead and do it?" When Wise fretted aloud that Morgenthau might object, the president promptly rung him up: "Henry," he enthused, "this is a very fair proposal which Stephen makes about ransoming Jews." In truth, at this stage Morgenthau needed little convincing.

Three weeks later Roosevelt sent Wise a follow-up letter asserting that the plan was ready to be enacted, and that only some details remained to be ironed out between the State Department and the U.S. mission in Bern.

Yet the past was repeated once again. For six and a half weeks, the State Department surreptitiously delayed the license. Indeed, it would hold up the license for a full eight months after the initial request for funds, by which time Riegner's rescue plans would be tragically outdated: by then Adolf Eichmann had pressured the Romanians into canceling the arrangement.

TWO DAYS AFTER WISE met with Roosevelt, the Allied bombing campaign laid waste to Hamburg, leaving it a flaming, smoking ruin. An astounding forty-two thousand German civilians were killed in the Hamburg bombings, a figure dwarfing the number of British civilians who had died during the murderous blitz. Weeks earlier, Düsseldorf and Cologne had fared little better. The same was true of the Ruhr, Berlin, and the Ploiesti oil fields in Romania, which Roosevelt enthused was "a smashing victory." In a message to Congress, Roosevelt, with almost boyish glee, once again took an opportunity to mock Hitler, just as the Führer once mocked him: "Hitler . . . started boasting that he had converted Europe into an impregnable fortress. But he neglected to provide that fortress with a roof. The British and American air forces have been bombing the roofless fortress with ever increasing effectiveness." Meanwhile, as German casualties mounted on the home front, Joseph Goebbels was forced to acknowledge that the Allies' offensive was "a catastrophe of hitherto inconceivable proportions."

The Allied targets were numerous—and multiplying: oil refineries, rubber facilities, transportation facilities and vehicles, ball bearing factories, shipyards, ammunition dumps, dams, and airplanes. And of course there was collateral damage to civilians. Roosevelt never had any qualms about the inadvertent bombing of German civilians, though he hastened to say that the United States was not bombing civilian targets "for the sheer sadistic pleasure of killing." His hope was to degrade the German military and destroy the morale of the German people.

Yet while the president balked at the thought of explicitly bombing

German targets as a reprisal for the murder of the Jews, the Nazis openly insisted they were liquidating the ghettos as reprisals for the Allied bombing campaign.

ON AUGUST 17, 1943, Roosevelt met for the fourth time with Churchill, first at Hyde Park, where they sipped scotch and munched on hot dogs, then more formally at Quebec City.

The Quebec conference principally dealt with the coming Normandy invasion. The president and the prime minister discussed the gritty logistics of crossing the Channel. They talked about landing craft, fuel pipelines, movable harbors, and the tons of matériel that would be deployed. They talked about who would command Overlord, agreeing that it would be an American. And then, cautiously looking ahead, Roosevelt raised the matter of Hitler's surrender. He wondered if the military chiefs had made backup plans in case Germany collapsed unexpectedly. The British assured the president that plans were in place if needed.

One other topic loomed large at Quebec: the atomic bomb. In October 1939, the renowned scientist Albert Einstein had written an urgent letter to Roosevelt telling him about the pioneering work by Enrico Fermi and Leo Szilard with uranium and urging preliminary research on an atomic weapon. Among other things, he emphasized the extraordinary destructive potential of nuclear fission and a nuclear chain reaction, and said it was "conceivable—though less certain—that extremely powerful bombs of a new type may thus be constructed": bombs so stupendous that they could demolish "whole ports" and their surroundings. He also pointed out that the Nazis might already have begun work on an atomic weapon themselves.

An atomic weapon in the Nazi arsenal? Few notions were more alarming. Because of the dread that the Nazis would get there first, the possible advance of weapons technology—despite all the problems it involved—had thus become one of the imperatives of the war. Roosevelt took action, establishing an advisory committee on uranium to explore a once unimaginable weapons program. But while a new generation of conventional weaponry was being developed and began rolling off American assembly lines—radar-guided rockets, amphibious tanks, bazookas, proximity fused shells, napalm, SCR594 ground radar—the scientists working on the atomic bomb appeared baffled in the early stages: the theoretical problems were complicated enough, the operational ones even more so.

In that first year, the advisory committee's work was halting and seemingly futile. The distinguished scientist Niels Bohr forlornly compared its work to that of the "alchemists of former days, groping in the dark in their vain efforts to make gold." He did not overstate. By contrast, the British were more optimistic; they believed that a working bomb could be constructed from U-235. With ample resources devoted to it, they estimated that the first weapon could be available by the end of 1943.

Churchill gave the go-ahead in Britain, but Roosevelt hesitated to expedite the research in the United States. Pearl Harbor changed everything. The president scribbled a laconic note on White House stationery to an aide: "Okay—returned—I think you'd best keep this in your own safe.—FDR."

The research in the United States now took on new urgency. The British soon arrived in Washington with a gleaming black metal box full of scientific secrets, while the Americans quickly reshuffled agencies and personnel. Eventually, the president established the National Defense Research Committee, whose members were eminent scientists, and finally comprehensive research on atomic fission began. Under the auspices of the army, the Manhattan Project was born, code-named after a secret headquarters in a nondescript building at 270 Broadway in Manhattan. Meanwhile, the Army Corps of Engineers began building huge, futuristic research facilities that amounted to the stuff of science fiction: atomic cities laboring in the greatest secrecy. When Henry Stimson, the secretary of war, went to Capitol Hill for funding, Senator Sam Rayburn waved him away and said: "I don't want to know why." The funds for the project were buried deep within the War Department budget.

Nobody knew which method would successfully produce the U-235 isotope and plutonium. Diffusion? Electromagnetism? Heavy water? Different pilot programs worked on different components of the problem. At the Metallurgical Laboratory of the University of Chicago, Fermi racked his brain, delving into plutonium research. At the Standard Oil Company, equally tenacious physicists worked on the centrifuge method. At Columbia University Harold Urey blazed a different path, conducting gaseous diffusion research. Foremost in the minds of the scientists and officials alike was the frantic requirement for speed. They couldn't let Hitler get there first.

The president of Harvard, James B. Conant, came to an appalling conclusion: that the Germans might be a year ahead of the Allies. "Three months' delay," he direly mused, "might be fatal."

From the outset, the Americans and the British agreed to cooperate, quickly combining their programs. Concerned about the ongoing German air attacks over Britain, Churchill balked at the risk of constructing the enormous facilities needed to develop the atomic weapon in Britain. So Roosevelt promptly agreed to shoulder the burden, approving tens of millions of dollars for the research at home. Henceforth, all the research and development was conducted in the United States; the government would spend nearly $2 billion on the Manhattan Project and employ 120,000 people. Actually, as work on the atomic bomb progressed, and the lights flickered into the late hours in the Los Alamos laboratories in New Mexico, Germany decided to shelve its own program, favoring instead its vaunted V-1 and V-2 rocket bombs. In January 1942, as the Germans at Wannsee formalized their decision to go ahead with the Final Solution, Albert Speer, the Third Reich's armaments minister, decided that the cost of constructing an atom bomb was too high and the project itself too fraught with peril. In any case, Hitler, arrogant as always, scoffed at nuclear science as "Jewish physics" and evinced little interest in an atomic weapon.

It was in Quebec that Churchill and Roosevelt reaffirmed their commitment to share the results of the Manhattan Project: they would both keep the results under wraps, and each would refrain from using the awesome weapon without the consent of the other. At the same time as the two leaders reached this understanding, thousands of Robert Oppenheimer's scientists and technicians were working in the many sectors of the vast project.

By December 30, 1944, Roosevelt would receive a report saying that the first bomb would be ready "about August 1, 1945," and would be the equivalent of ten thousand tons of TNT.

Here, as in so many other aspects of the war, the Allies were outstripping the Axis powers.

THREE AND A HALF months had come and gone since the Treasury Department had undertaken to help rescue the Romanian Jews—the Riegner plan—and what Morgenthau called "the relatively simple matter" of getting the American minister in Switzerland to issue a license. Incensed at what he considered the State Department's treachery, Morgenthau wrote directly to Cordell Hull. Meanwhile, intrigues were seemingly everywhere. John Pehle, Morgenthau's foreign funds control chief, lamented about the State Department: "The way they kick this stuff around . . . All of a sudden, right in the middle of something, they will refer it to the Intergovernmental Committee and nothing will happen." Then Britain's Foreign Office stepped in—the State Department had insisted on consulting it—expressing its concern about "disposing" of anything like "70,000 refugees," the number envisioned by the Riegner plan.

Confronted not simply with the State Department's objections but with the Foreign Office's message, Morgenthau memorably said that they were "a satanic combination of British chill and diplomatic double-talk, cold and correct and adding up to a sentence of death." And of the State Department's position, Morgenthau's aide Ansel Luxford noted, "That is a stock reply when you hit the Jewish problem. . . . You can find one million reasons why you can't get them out of Europe, but if somebody put their mind to getting them out, you can spend the next 10 years on what you're going to do with them."

A distressed Morgenthau himself agreed, baldly asserting, "When you get through with it, the attitude to date is no different from Hitler's attitude." This was echoed by Morgenthau's advisers. Randolph Paul said, "I don't know how we can blame the Germans for killing them when we are doing this. The law calls it *para delicto*, of equal guilt." Herbert Gaston added, "We don't shoot them. We let other people shoot them, and let them starve."

For some time, the tough-minded Oscar Cox of the Lend-Lease administration—he was "haunted by the suffering of refugees"—had been pressing Morgenthau to push for a separate rescue agency, what the speakers had called for at the Emergency Conference rally at Madison Square Garden earlier in the spring. Such a "War Refugee Rescue Committee" would, Cox maintained, "attack the whole problem afresh." Cox was in a position to know: he had drafted the Lend-Lease Act and the legal opinions concerning Japanese-American internment, and had prosecuted the captured German saboteurs who sneaked into the United States earlier in the war. While mulling it over, Morgenthau nonetheless still clung to the idea that somehow the State Department could pick up the slack. But it would not.

He scheduled a Monday morning meeting with the secretary of state and Breckinridge Long. Hoping to clear the air, Hull protested that the problem stemmed more from bureaucratic inertia than malfeasance. "The trouble is," he explained, "the fellows down the line," adding, "I don't get a chance to know everything that is going on." This, of course, was as true of Morgenthau as of Hull, yet the Treasury Department was able to act within a day, as opposed to within months. Hull also launched into a contorted monologue, blaming just about everyone else for thwarting well-meaning American initiatives for refugees—he mentioned the British, the Nazis, the Latin American countries, and of course bureaucrats within the department.

Hearing Hull's explanation, Breckinridge Long pulled Morgenthau aside and asked if they could speak privately in another room; there he quickly sought to cover his tracks, distancing himself from the very policies that he had promoted for years. He too blamed "people lower down in the State Department," even going so far as to blame one official

(Bernard Meltzer) who Morgenthau knew was among the few voices in the State Department actually pushing to rescue the Jews in Romania.

Hearing Long openly prevaricate so brazenly, Morgenthau did not restrain himself. "Well, Breck," he said, looking his colleague in the eye, "as long as you raise the question, we might be a little frank. The impression is all around that you, particularly, are anti-Semitic!" Taken aback, Long protested, "I know that is so. I hope that you will use your good offices to correct that impression, because I am not."

"I am very, very glad to know it," Morgenthau replied. But he wasn't about to back down. He added that the State Department was no different from the British Foreign Office—about as withering a charge as he could level.

If Morgenthau's prodding constituted pressure from within—after five months' delay, an embarrassed Long finally approved the license for the relief and rescue programs—there were now mighty forces increasing pressure from without.

~

ON NOVEMBER 9, 1943, twelve influential senators—they were led by Guy Gillette of Iowa and six of them were members of the influential Senate Foreign Relations Committee—picked up the idea begun by Peter Bergson and favored by Cox; they introduced a resolution calling on the president to create a "government rescue agency" to save the surviving Jewish people of Europe from extinction at the hands of the Nazis. Their resolution also increasingly found support in the House, where the straight-talking California Democrat, Will Rogers Jr., was the principal sponsor. If the Gillette-Rogers resolution reached the floor of either the House or the Senate, it would raise an embarrassing debate on the administration's mismanagement of the Jewish plight. As the measure gained support, Oscar Cox warned the State Department that Congress would eventually seize the initiative and do what the administration "should have done a long time ago."

Soon, five days of hearings on the resolution were held in the House Foreign Affairs Committee, chaired by Sol Bloom—a close ally of

Roosevelt's who had been a delegate at the ill-fated Bermuda conference. While Bloom denied that he was opposed to the legislation, his attitude from the outset was tepid at best. He repeatedly pointed out the expense of rescuing up to 100,000 people. "You have to figure at least $2000 a person," he said, "so that would be $200 million." This led Congressman Andrew Schiffler to angrily retort, "I do not think money is of primary importance."

Actually, Bloom straddled the fence. To the proponents of the resolution, it seemed clear that the chairman was seeking to kill it, or at least choke it off. But confronted with the mounting public pressure, Bloom sent a telegram to the editor of the *New York Post*: "I personally agree that the resolution should pass."

The most explosive moment of the five-day hearings came on November 26, when Breckinridge Long testified at a closed session. Why closed? Long insisted on secrecy because the Nazis might thwart a possible refugee aid operation if they knew what he discussed.

His testimony, lasting a grueling three and a half hours, was a masterpiece of showmanship. Citing little-known facts from the State Department's impenetrable visa system, he convinced the committee members that the administration was doing everything possible in its power to thwart the Nazis and save the Jews. He sought to use reason: "There has been," he said, "an agency of the American government actually attending to these affairs for a little more than four years." He sought to use emotion: "I have thought many times of the very definite and pertinent fact that there is no man or woman in this room that I know of whose ancestors were not refugees. Mine were, every one of them." And he sought to use intimidation: "I think your committee will desire to consider . . . whether any action on your part would be interpreted as a repudiation of the cause of the Jews."

A number of the members of the committee were seduced by Long's seeming sincerity and honeyed words. One after another, these members fell over themselves to thank Long for his dedication and tireless efforts. Moreover, the committee hearings foundered on the politically charged question of whether the resolution should call for immediately opening

Palestine to Jewish refugees. At one point Representative Karl Mundt worried aloud that the legislation had become a "hot poker." In effect, Long's testimony managed to strangle the rescue resolution in the committee and prevent it from reaching the House floor. But worried about antagonizing American Jews, Bloom, the committee chairman, decided to ignore the concern for secrecy and instead released the entire transcript of Long's remarks. His plan, or at least his hope, was to quell the discontent from Jewish groups and individuals.

It instead backfired. A furor immediately broke out.

During his testimony, Long had not been above flagrantly misleading the committee. For one thing, he claimed there was no ocean transportation available for refugees, when in fact Portuguese and Spanish passenger ships were coming to America three-quarters empty. For another, he claimed that the United States had taken in about 580,000 refugees since Hitler had come to power, which prompted a front-page article in the *New York Times* headlined, "580,000 Refugees Admitted to United States in Decade." The truth was a very different story. This figure, as David S. Wyman notes, encompassed all visas, whether in fact used or not, whether permanent or temporary, whether provided to Jews or not; and it referred only to visas that were authorized, not to the number of refugees who actually entered the United States. The more accurate number was less than half that, and many of those refugees were not Jews. Indeed, in the previous year only 2,705 Jews fleeing Nazi persecution had been admitted to the country, the equivalent of one hour's worth of the gas chamber's at Auschwitz.

Now, the *New York Post* called Long's testimony "false and distorted," and members of Congress erupted at his chicanery. A baffled and angry Emanuel Celler could barely contain himself; he spoke for many when he said that Long "drips with sympathy for the persecuted Jews, but the tears he sheds are crocodile." He called for Long's resignation, and concluded, "The State Department has turned its back on the time-honored principle of granting havens to refugees."

So, far from being derailed, the Gillette-Rogers resolution continued to pick up steam in December. Watching these events closely, the Senate

Foreign Relations Committee was ready to skip hearings altogether and act on the resolution before the full Senate after the holiday recess—on January 24, 1944. "The problem is essentially a humanitarian one," the committee reported, unanimously. "It is not a Jewish problem alone. It is a Christian problem and a problem for enlightened civilization."

The report continued: "We have talked; we have sympathized; we have expressed our horror; the time to act is long past due." Senator Gillette confidently predicted that the resolution would sail through the Senate "without a dissenting vote."

Meanwhile, administration officials, especially in the Treasury Department, were carefully monitoring the situation as well. Morgenthau said, "This is a boiling pot on the Hill. He can't hold it; it is going to pop, and you have either got to move very fast, or the Congress of the United States will do it for you." He and others worried that the president, FDR the humanitarian, FDR the redeemer, FDR the war leader, could be deeply wounded by an open airing of these questions and take on a new sobriquet: FDR, complicit in the Holocaust.

All that would change on Christmas Day.

~

RETURNING FROM HIS SUMMIT in Tehran, where he had met with Stalin for the first time, a triumphant but weary Roosevelt boarded a train in Washington and journeyed north to Hyde Park for the holidays. On the surface, Christmas Day was a magical affair. For the first time in more than a decade, Roosevelt was spending Christmas with his family in their beloved home. The upstate New York air was chilly but clean. The house was adorned with red ribbons and wreaths and a dazzling tree. The family thrilled to the sounds of local carolers, even as Roosevelt delighted his guests with a reading of Dickens's *A Christmas Carol*, each word delivered with his trademark upper-class Eastern accent.

Yet he was also suffering from influenza—again. First came the coughing. Then the chills. Then the aching.

By the time he went to bed that night, most of official Washington was sipping eggnog or eating goose or climbing into pajamas. There was, however, a notable exception. Little did Roosevelt know that at the same time one young lawyer in the Treasury Department, Josiah DuBois Jr., was working overtime on a memorandum for the secretary, Henry Morgenthau. It was one of the most significant memorandums in America's history.

He wrote, "One of the greatest crimes in history, the slaughter of the Jewish people in Europe, is continuing unabated." He spoke of "the tragic history of this government's handling of this matter" and the fact that officials in the State Department "have not only failed to use the governmental machinery at their disposal to rescue Jews from Hitler, but have even gone so far as to use this governmental machinery to prevent the rescue of those Jews." He warned that "time is most precious" yet said the State Department had been "kicking the matter around for over a year without producing results; giving all sorts of excuses for delays upon delays." He laid out in shocking detail the chronology of the government's indifference, complicity, or obstructionism (or outright anti-Semitism), and prominently mentioned the Riegner memo arising out of Eduard Schulte's efforts. He mocked Breckinridge Long's "pious remarks" and noted that Long twisted the facts. He recounted the sordid story of the State Department cable that ordered the suppression of information coming from Switzerland about the Holocaust. He quoted, at length, members of Congress who were critical of the administration.

He concluded: "If men of the temperament and philosophy of Long continue in control of immigration administration, we may as well take off that plaque from the Statue of Liberty and black out the lamp beside the golden door."

After finishing the eighteen-page memo, he underlined its explosive title: "Report to the Secretary on the Acquiescence of This Government in the Murder of the Jews."

~

THE MATTER NOW FELL to Morgenthau. How likely was he to assume the mantle of the conscience of the administration? As it happened, fate and the fickleness of history would make this the supreme moment of his illustrious life.

Henry Morgenthau Jr. was a product of generations of German Jews, devout Jews who were learned Hebrew teachers and businessmen, ritual slaughterers and impassioned rabbis. Weathering financial straits in Germany in 1866, his family looked across the Atlantic to seek greater opportunities and emigrated to the post–Civil War United States. One grandfather, an unsuccessful inventor (his inventions included a label machine), forever teetered on the verge of bankruptcy. By contrast, Morgenthau's ambitious, visionary father, Henry Sr., had a distinguished career. Wealthy and tough-minded, vain and manipulative, he yearned to become secretary of the treasury. He almost did. He was a self-made real estate mogul, and an early supporter of Woodrow Wilson during Wilson's first presidential campaign. During World War I, he received the plum assignment of ambassador to Turkey, where he tirelessly struggled to induce the United States to intervene when the Turks carried out their murderous campaign against the Armenians of forced marches and wholesale killing, beginning in April 1915. Moving easily in and out of establishment circles, he was a friend of Steven Wise's as well.

Henry Sr. had lofty goals for his quiet, recalcitrant son. Born in May 1891 to riches and privilege, Henry Jr. seemed destined for success. But as a youngster, he had a run of bad luck. Sent to school at Exeter, he was despondent. It turned out he suffered from a cognitive impairment—or in today's terms, a learning disability—that made writing a challenge and talking a chore; he lasted only two years in school. His father provided him with a tutor, but that didn't work either. He entered Cornell with an eye to receiving an architecture degree. Once again bad luck struck; he dropped out. At his wit's end, his father found a construction site where he set Henry up as a timekeeper, hoping this would at least give him an entrée into real estate. That backfired as well when Morgenthau contracted typhoid fever.

By temperament, he was shy, introverted, and prone to self-doubt. Socially, he was awkward. And he could be withdrawn, even brooding. Moreover, his health was also often impaired. He suffered from debilitating migraines and nausea, and slept fitfully. When he was diagnosed with typhoid fever, his father acted boldly and shipped Henry to a ranch in Texas to convalesce. There he realized that his great passion was farming, one of the few matters his father had no interest in, but the young Morgenthau pursued it ardently. He returned to Cornell to study architecture and agriculture, graduated this time, and in 1913 bought a dilapidated thousand-acre apple and dairy farm in Dutchess County, New York. By his own account, it was a "desperate move" to carve out his own unique identity, away from his overbearing father. It did more than that; suddenly he made a series of wise decisions.

In 1916 he married Elinor Fatman, the well-connected and wily granddaughter of one of Lehman Brothers' founders. A former drama student at Vassar, she was shrewd, perceptive, and, like Henry Sr., ruthlessly ambitious. They purchased another thousand acres in Dutchess County, creating Fishkill Farms, where, to his father's chagrin, Henry lived as a gentleman farmer; they reared three children as well as an abundance of apples, rye, corn, cabbage, and beef cattle.

Morgenthau soon became close with his famous neighbor, the amiable Franklin Roosevelt, who was then eyeing Albany as he plotted to become governor of New York. Once, when the Morgenthaus were invited for tea at Hyde Park, Roosevelt's mother, Sara, observed in her diary, "Young Morgenthau was easy and yet modest and serious and intelligent." She added, "The wife is very Jewish." Roosevelt and Morgenthau's friendship quickly blossomed, as did their wives'. Where Roosevelt was talkative, Morgenthau was painfully reticent; where Roosevelt was brash and self-assured, Morgenthau bristled easily at social slights; where Roosevelt was good-humored, Morgenthau was dyspeptic, even dour. Playfully, Roosevelt called his good friend "Henry the Morgue." He once suggested that Morgenthau run for sheriff of Dutchess County. But Morgenthau had hitched his wagon to Roosevelt's star, and as time went on, Roosevelt increasingly prized Morgenthau for his unwavering discretion, his solid intelligence, and his absolute loyalty.

Their friendship deepened and intensified in 1921 after Roosevelt's political career suddenly seemed to be in ruins following his paralysis.

Over time, Morgenthau became a virtual member of Roosevelt's family and had an especially close relationship with his sons.

Morgenthau also contrived to become Roosevelt's ideal of a farmer. On a whim, he purchased the little-known journal *American Agriculturist*, and began touting the success of Fishkill Farms; this was pure bunk—actually, the farm was hemorrhaging money. It didn't matter to Roosevelt. Now, when Roosevelt looked at Morgenthau he saw not only friendship but a shared affection for Dutchess County, for its soil and trees.

And Morgenthau remained tireless in his support for Roosevelt. The two were perhaps the unlikeliest of allies: Roosevelt, the invalid graduate of Groton who never really left home, who measured men and events by the old-fashioned standards of noblesse oblige and aristocratic responsibility. Morgenthau, the insecure, wealthy New York Jew seeking to climb his way into the WASP establishment. Balding, he was well tailored, cared about the cut of his suits, and cultivated a patrician demeanor.

For all their noble instincts, Roosevelt and his wife were hardly immune to the prejudices of their time; once, after attending a function for the Wall Street financier Bernard Baruch, Eleanor complained, "The Jew party was appalling." For his part, Morgenthau was discreet about his Jewishness. Not surprisingly, he tended to avoid the synagogue and stayed away from the Jewish country clubs in Westchester County. He was also hesitant about Zionism. Keenly aware of the prejudices of the day, Morgenthau always insisted that he wanted to be thought of not as a Jew, but as "one hundred percent American."

Still, his courage and sincerity were without question. So was his hard work. When Roosevelt ran for governor in 1928, Morgenthau packed his bags and became Roosevelt's de facto chauffeur and manager, driving the candidate 7,500 miles around the state in a beat-up old Buick. Meticulously planning Roosevelt's campaign stops, he even hired entertainment for key events. Once elected, Roosevelt repaid Morgenthau by making him chairman of his farm advisory committee, and after that, conservation commissioner. One of Morgenthau's most cherished possessions was a black-and-white photograph of the two of them smiling jauntily in an open car. Roosevelt had signed it: "From one of two of a kind."

Then Roosevelt was elected president in 1932. Morgenthau lobbied to be made secretary of agriculture, his lifelong dream, but midwestern party bosses scoffed at the idea because Morgenthau was Jewish, and a New York Jew at that. America wasn't ready for it, so neither was Roosevelt. As a consolation, he appointed Morgenthau governor of the Farm Credit Administration. But then, a year later, Morgenthau got an even greater chance at glory, when William Woodin, Roosevelt's first secretary of the treasury, became fatally ill. Once again, Morgenthau lobbied hard, going to the president himself. In his own words, he "put it on the line." This time Roosevelt complied, first appointing Morgenthau undersecretary of the treasury, then making him only the second Jewish cabinet member in history.

There were doubters. Critics scathingly chalked these appointments up to cronyism and even nepotism. *Fortune* mocked the new secretary of the treasury as the pampered son of a Jewish philanthropist and said he had few accomplishments except for spending "most of his life farming." Gladys Straus, a prominent New York Republican donor, jibed that Roosevelt had somehow found "the only Jew in the world who doesn't know a thing about money," while even Morgenthau's father insisted, "He's not up to it." The conservative budget chief Lewis Douglas grumbled about his "stupidity and Hebraic arrogance."

To his detractors, Morgenthau was prickly, stiff, ill suited for the job. Roosevelt thought otherwise. Finicky and ill-humored, Morgenthau was sometimes a nuisance, but as the president's longtime adviser Louis Howe once noted, where others were concerned only with their own agendas, Morgenthau was always committed to Roosevelt's best interests. And in an administration with such towering establishment figures as Henry Stimson, Cordell Hull, Sumner Welles, Dean Acheson, and his rival Harry Hopkins, as well as such intimates as Missy LeHand and Grace Tully, Morgenthau was unique. Keen, tough-talking, principled, he was almost always instantly responsive to the president's changing moods, and even when he wasn't, as the only cabinet member with a deep-seated friendship with the president—on his calendar, he had a regular lunch with Roosevelt every Monday—he maintained almost unparalleled access to the president. As World War II began, Roosevelt joked to Morgenthau, "You and I will run this war together." More than once, Roosevelt and Morgenthau playfully exchanged jocular little notes at cabinet meetings. A jealous Cordell Hull complained that Morgenthau was trying to be the second secretary of state; and Morgenthau felt free to sarcastically mock the views of Secretary of War Henry Stimson behind his back.

In bureaucratic battles, Morgenthau was blunt, rarely sugarcoating his words. When the economy began to sour in 1938, it was he who warned Roosevelt about "a depression within a depression." When Hitler broke promise after promise in the 1930s, and made one territorial demand after another, it was Morgenthau who felt the United States had no choice but to intervene in Europe: "If we don't stop Hitler now, he is going right on to the Black Sea," he insisted to Roosevelt: "Then what?" And while officials like Hull and John McCloy believed there was a significant difference between the evil Nazi regime and the everyday German people, Morgenthau saw Germans as "a war loving race" and the entire nation as guilty of war crimes.

Still, as close as Morgenthau was to the president, he remained politically something of an orphan. His constituency was essentially one person: Roosevelt. A frown from the president sent Morgenthau into a funk; a grin, or a playful presidential word, made his day. And he knew that the president, so prone to evasion in private, so protean in his beliefs, had volatile moods and reveled in playing one adviser against another. Indeed, every day Morgenthau woke up worried that the president was trying to "get rid of him," and he wrestled with the gnawing fear that it could be his last day in the administration. Once, he complained that the president was "bullying" and "browbeating" him.

His fears and insecurity were heightened, and he became more reluctant to press the president on the plight of Jewish refugees, when he heard from Leo Crowley (the head of the Foreign Economic Administration) that Roosevelt had said, "This is a Protestant country, and the Catholics and Jews are here under sufferance." Sufferance? Those words only made him more insecure, and it didn't help later when he proposed to the president a long-term plan calling for a weak postwar Germany stripped of all heavy industry so that it could never again menace the world; Stimson recorded in his diary that Morgenthau was "a very dangerous advisor" who was "biased by his Semitic grievances." For his part, McCloy said that Morgenthau should have no business dictating the terms of the peace, for the simple reason that "he is a Jew." (Actually, Roosevelt himself once remarked that for all he cared, the Germans could eat from "soup kitchens.")

Early on in the war, Morgenthau discreetly sought to help Jewish refugees. But as the administration learned more about the hideous death march of the Holocaust—about the cattle cars, the piles of corpses, the murder of children and the elderly, the orphans living in terror and dying in terror, and the almost incomprehensible scope of the Final Solution—Morgenthau had an awakening. Incensed about the State Department's reluctance to come to the aid of the refugees, he bluntly told Hull, whose wife was half Jewish: if you "were a member of the cabinet in Germany today, you would be, most likely, in a prison camp, and your wife would be God knows where." (As it happened, one defiant woman, whose husband was Jewish, was beheaded in Germany in 1943.)

So when Morgenthau received the memorandum from his aide Josiah DuBois, he immediately appreciated its gravity.

Would he take it to Roosevelt? He once told an aide that his friendship with the president was what he valued "above everything else." And he had also once lamented that "Roosevelt was not the greatest—let's put it this way—on this Jewish problem." Having spent his entire political life tethered to the president, and having stubbornly resisted being thought of as a token Jew in the cabinet, he now had to decide if he would risk all by bringing the matter straight to Roosevelt.

But that was exactly what he would do.

~

For morgenthau this situation had all the earmarks of a full-blown election-year scandal and more importantly a moral blight of historic proportions on the president's record. Absent a change in policy, Morgenthau believed that Roosevelt would share the responsibility for the extermination of an entire people. Moreover, DuBois had said that if Morgenthau didn't take any action on the report, "I'm going to resign and release" it to the press. The effect of that, combined with the pending debate in the Senate, would be devastating for the president.

Morgenthau pondered his next steps. He now knew he had to speak directly with Roosevelt. To pave the way, he discreetly met with Cordell Hull for a second time to feel him out; predictably, the meeting went nowhere. So he called Sam Rosenman, Roosevelt's speechwriter and trusted aide. A sharp exchange followed. Rosenman had his doubts. He also worried about negative press coverage, insisting that everything be off the record. Morgenthau winced, then exploded: "Don't worry about the publicity! What I want is his intelligence and courage—courage first and intelligence second."

Morgenthau convened an unusual meeting of the Treasury staff at his home, away from the watchful eyes of the press and the intrigues of the bureaucracy. The idea was to develop a strategy to persuade Roosevelt to approve a separate American rescue agency. He also invited Oscar Cox, who had long been a vigorous proponent of such an organization; Ben Cohen, a key member of Roosevelt's brain trust; and Rosenman. Morgenthau's assistant, Harry Dexter White, said that Roosevelt would never pay attention to the problem unless he was forced "to make a decision." Morgenthau felt that if the facts were properly laid before the president, he could be cajoled into doing the right thing.

Now Morgenthau moved to put everything into place. For starters, he decided to drop DuBois's politically charged title and replace it with a more neutral heading: "A Personal Report to the President." Everything else in the memorandum stayed the same. He also signed off on Cox's proposal to preempt legislation on the Hill by setting up the refugee board through an executive order.

Meanwhile, at another Treasury Department meeting, White took stock of where things stood, and provided an overview of the political labyrinth of refugee policy. To this point, Britain had dominated a number of decisions by the Allies on the Jewish question in Europe. Only Roosevelt, he maintained, could provide the leadership to overcome not just American resistance but British resistance to helping the surviving remnants of European Jewry. In turn, only Morgenthau had the stature to persuade the president to take decisive action on the proposed rescue agency. Having already reached this decision on his own, Morgenthau agreed.

Things were now moving very quickly. With a tinge of anxiety—he couldn't shake his fear of alienating the president—Morgenthau hastily arranged a rare Sunday meeting at the White House. For Roosevelt, it was to be an otherwise light day: tea with the crown prince of Norway, a visit to the doctor, and dinner alone.

AT 12:40 P.M. ON January 16, 1944, Morgenthau, his general counsel Randolph Paul, and John Pehle were escorted into the upstairs oval room of the White House family quarters, where Roosevelt greeted them. They carried a copy of the report, as well as a copy of the proposed executive order setting up the agency. Almost certainly, Rosenman had already briefed Roosevelt on the purpose of the weekend meeting. For his part, Roosevelt, though dapperly dressed, was still ailing from the aftereffects of the flu.

The president asked Morgenthau to give an overview of the report, then responded. As in the past, Roosevelt defended Long, asserting that he did not intentionally seek to block rescue measures; nonetheless, he acknowledged that Long had "somewhat soured" on refugees, seeing them as a security risk. Morgenthau quickly countered that according to the attorney general, in the entirety of the war, only three Jews admitted to the United States were in any way "undesirable."

Then he told the president what he had been saying to anyone else who would listen for weeks now. If Roosevelt did not act, Congress would step in and take matters into its own hands.

The president briefly examined the executive order and proposed one change: the new agency would be headed by Morgenthau, Secretary of State Cordell Hull, and Leo Crowley. But then, because only the army had the ability to provide assistance to refugees and dispense relief, Roosevelt suggested that Secretary of War Henry Stimson serve on the agency, rather than Crowley. For the president, Stimson would provide the added benefit of injecting caution into the efforts of the War Refugee Board (WRB), as the agency would be named. Morgenthau agreed.

Otherwise, Roosevelt speedily signed off on the new agency. As a measure of the president's heightened interest, he proposed that Sam Rosenman, a former judge and now the president's eyes and ears on significant issues, be kept in the loop; he and Morgenthau also talked about the possibility of rescuing Jews by getting them into Spain, Switzerland, and Turkey. In hindsight, the challenge of persuading Roosevelt seems to have been far easier than Morgenthau expected: Roosevelt needed little convincing. Increasingly isolated on this issue, confronting a mounting political scandal, preparing to run for a fourth presidential term, and concerned about the Senate's moving against him, the president understood that he could no longer put the rescue organization aside. Moreover, by this stage of the war, Roosevelt knew that there were opportunities to save Jews.

Yet hard questions persist. Why had it taken fourteen months from the time Stephen Wise met with the president to discuss the shocking facts of the ghastly Nazis' extermination campaign? (Morgenthau himself called this period "those terrible eighteen months" and later exploded to his staff, "The tragic thing is that—damn it!—this thing could have been done last February.") Why was so little imagination or effort devoted to rescuing the Jews, and so much imagination and effort put into covering up their terrible fate? Why was this president, who so masterfully was able to lift Americans' hopes and mobilize popular energy to attack the Great Depression and lead the United States in another world war, coming so late to this matter? Why didn't this president, who so ably understood that his departments, Treasury and State and War, were "large and far-flung and ingrained" in their practices; who once mockingly laughed about intransigence at the Pentagon, scoffing "Oh, don't worry about all those *people* over there"; and who once said that trying to change anything in the navy was like punching a featherbed ("You punch it with your right and you punch it with your left until you are finally exhausted, and then you find the damn bed just as it was before you started punching"); and who by a contest of wills and skillful timing knew how to outwit and outsmart the foot-dragging bureaucracy and recalcitrant officials, why did he not do more earlier? Why, it was asked by critics; why, why?

But now the president acted. On January 22—two days before the Senate was scheduled to debate the Gillette-Rogers resolution—Roosevelt issued Executive Order 9417 formally establishing the War Refugee Board (WRB).

The order stated: "It is the policy of this government to take all measures within its power to rescue victims of enemy oppression in imminent danger of death" as well as to provide "relief and assistance consistent with the successful prosecution of the war."

Part Three

The Fateful Decision

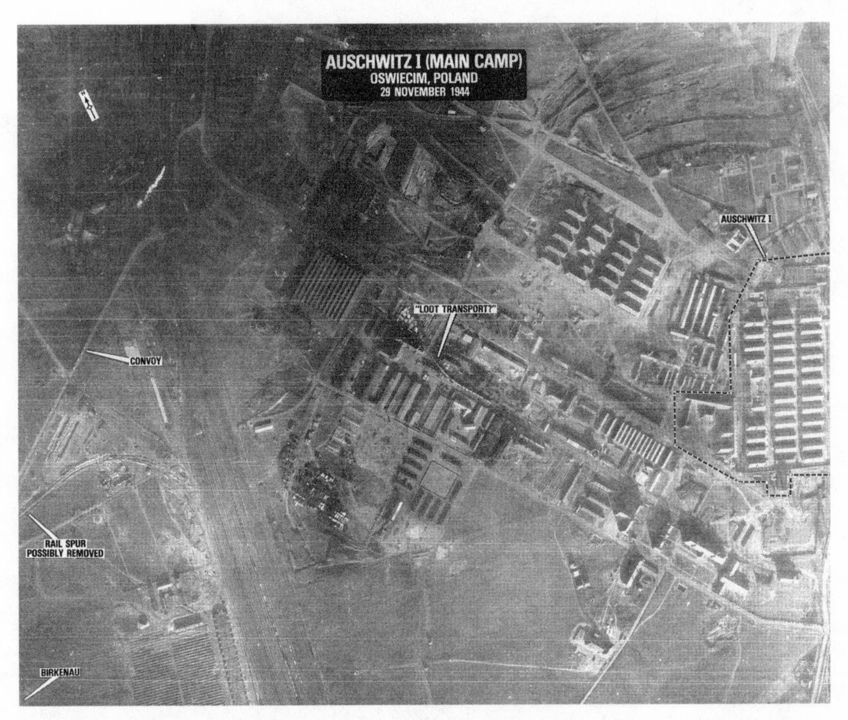

A U.S. Army Air Force reconnaissance photo of Auschwitz from November 1944.

13

Trapped Between Knowing and Not Knowing

FEBRUARY 1944. EUROPEAN JEWRY had been nearly annihilated.

How to appreciate the magnitude of it all? But for an accident of birth or the grace of a passport, untold others could have perished. The rolls of the death camps could easily have included: Edward G. Robinson; Billy Wilder (among the best filmmakers of Hollywood's golden age, he fled Germany when Hitler came to power); Mae West; Ingrid Bergman; Gertrude Stein; the artists Mark Rothko and Marc Chagall; Leonard Bernstein; the great songwriter Irving Berlin; the founding CEO of Neiman Marcus, Stanley Marcus; the chairman of Sears, Lessing Rosenwald; Jack Benny; Arthur Miller; Martin Buber; Jonas Salk; Hank Greenberg of the Detroit Tigers; Sid Luckman of the Chicago Bears; and the tennis player Helen Jacobs. They could have included, as well, no less than one of the greatest minds who ever lived, Albert Einstein; J. Robert Oppenheimer and Edward Teller, fathers of the atomic and hydrogen bombs; Milton Friedman, the Nobel Prize–winning economist; Eugene Meyer, owner of the *Washington Post*, and his granddaughter Katharine Graham, its publisher; the Sulzberger-Ochs family, owners of the *New York Times*; and the publisher Alfred Knopf. The list, a panoply of greatness, could go on: Ayn Rand, the writer; Hannah Arendt, the philosopher; J. D. Salinger, the novelist; Louis B. Mayer and Samuel Goldwyn, the movie moguls; Henry Morgenthau Jr.; Felix Frankfurter, the Supreme Court justice; and General Maurice Rose. Some people might never have been born: Bob Dylan, Nora Ephron, Barbra Streisand, Michael Douglas, Michael Bloomberg. A tapestry of science, arts, sports, humanities and politics. Anchors of the second half of the twentieth century into the twenty-first. And it is impossible to know how many more like them perished.

Five million Jews were now dead, 2 million of them at Chelmno, Belzec, Treblinka, and Sobibór. And Auschwitz was working overtime.

AS 1944 OPENED, THE Allies seemed unstoppable. Indeed, by the end of January, after a nine-hundred-day siege, the Red Army had slashed through the Leningrad blockade. In February, it trapped and destroyed ten German divisions in a pocket near Cherkassy and took Estonia, and the next month it reached the Bug River in Poland and the Dniester. Within weeks, it would seize Sebastopol, pause, then recapture Odessa as well as the Crimea. In Italy, the Allies landed at Anzio and were lunging for Monte Cassino. Meanwhile the Americans and British carried out unremitting bombing raids over France and the Netherlands, not to mention raids on Hamburg and Nuremberg and directly over Berlin—the first major daylight bombing of the Nazi capital itself. In late February alone, during a seven-day bombing campaign called "Big Week," the Eighth Air Force damaged or destroyed 70 percent of Germany's aircraft production facilities and 290 German fighters, degrading Germany's industrial backbone in the process. And with the onset of spring, the Strategic Air Forces flew twenty-one thousand sorties in April against bridges, railroads, and other German supply lines. As Sir

Arthur Harris, chief of the British Bomber Command, observed, "The Nazis entered this war under the delusion that they were going to bomb everyone else, and nobody is going to bomb them. . . . They sowed the wind, and now they are going to reap the whirlwind!"

And all this, of course, opened opportunities for the WRB.

FUNDED LARGELY BY PRIVATE donations, the War Refugee Board (WRB) was founded frightfully late, and in millions of instances too late. Nonetheless, after the appointment of a new interim director, Morgenthau's hard-nosed counsel John Pehle, the board got down to business. Provided with both institutional backing, $250,000, and, finally, genuine moral authority—it nominally consisted of the secretaries of the treasury, state, and war, but for all practical purposes it was run by Morgenthau's department—it quickly injected into the administration's efforts a spirit that had for so long been woefully lacking.

The WRB rapidly developed multipronged plans for the rescue and relief of Hitler's victims, wherever they could be found. Speed was one watchword; action was another. Morgenthau himself remarked that the board was made up of "crusaders." While there remained influential opponents of the WRB—one State Department official snidely commented, "That Jew Morgenthau and his Jewish assistants like DuBois are trying to take over this place" (actually DuBois was Protestant)—converts to its way of thinking were now found even in the least likely places.

As early as February 11, 1944, staff officers gathered around a large oak table in the secretary of war's conference room to discuss the new WRB and how to explain it to commanders in the field. "We are over there," one officer protested, "to win the war and not take care of refugees." John McCloy's executive assistant, Colonel Harrison Gerhardt, snapped back: "The president doesn't think so. He thinks relief is a part of winning the war." So the WRB scoured Europe for opportunities. The board was nothing if not ambitious. That spring, Pehle proposed that the Spanish government open its borders to the pockets of Jews fleeing Nazi-occupied France; notably, here the WRB had the support of the War Department. Meanwhile, the WRB financed a series of covert operations to protect the thousands of Jewish children remaining in France; the agents provided counterfeit birth certificates, work permits, and baptismal certificates—anything and everything that would do the job. And soon, an escape route was organized, over the Pyrenees from France into Spain.

For refugees seeking to make their way to Palestine, the WRB representative pressured Turkish officials to allow two hundred Jews every ten days to use Istanbul as a way station; this measure rescued some seven thousand in all. In the Balkans, under Pehle's aggressive leadership, the WRB opened a land route for the Jews in Bulgaria and a sea route for those in Romania. The Romanian government, desperate to quit the war, was finally prodded into evacuating forty-eight thousand Jews (out of the original seventy thousand) from Transnistria to the Romanian interior, saving their lives by taking them out of the way of the German troops frantically retreating from the front lines. In Switzerland the WRB bribed border guards to let refugees slip into the country; all told some twenty-seven thousand Jewish refugees made it. In a small but symbolic step, the Irish government was induced to take in five hundred Jewish refugee children; approaches were also made to Portugal and Sweden to accept fleeing Jews.

Not every battle was won. Later, Pehle came up with a sweeping proposal for the president to announce that the United States would now temporarily accept "all oppressed peoples escaping from Hitler." Would the president accept it? Pehle dictated a memo for Roosevelt, arguing that no rescue program could succeed unless refugees had some prospect of a haven. In reality, he assured the president that very few refugees would come to the United States. But he pleaded with Roosevelt to understand that to induce other countries to fling open their doors to aid the Jews, Washington had to set an example. The solution, Pehle recommended, was for the president to do what he had done so many times before: take unilateral action and sidestep a reluctant Congress, in this case by issuing an executive order allowing refugees into the country on a temporary basis. Morgenthau strongly endorsed this proposal.

But the secretary of war, Henry Stimson, vehemently dissented, and Roosevelt agreed. "I fear that Congress will feel that it is the opening wedge to a violation of our immigration laws," Stimson said. The president vetoed Pehle's draft, and instead approved only a far more modest compromise. Two days after Normandy, he offered temporary haven to 982 refugees, principally Jews from southern Italy, a number of whom had survived the horrors of Dachau and Buchenwald. In August 1944, they would be housed in a shabby, run-down shelter at Fort Ontario in the town of Oswego, New York, where they would remain through the frightfully cold winter like prison inmates, behind a barbed-wire fence and guarded by the army. Ironically, Roosevelt was proud of this measure, saying to Morgenthau, "I know the Fort very well. It . . . is a very excellent place." Actually, it was not. Oswego proved to be a meager step at best, and to most observers, including the refugees themselves, it was a dismal failure. But in the face of continuing nativist sentiment in the public and during an election year, it was as far as the president would go.

But an even greater challenge for the WRB, if not for Roosevelt himself, had come in March.

Hungary.

In early March, Hitler, suffering from a cold, his left leg trembling and the vision in his right eye blurred, called for Joseph Goebbels to come to the Berghof. Now badly losing the war, the Führer was nonetheless adamant about putting an end to the ongoing "treachery" in Hungary. For some time the Hungarians, watching the Nazis' fortunes wane, had put out feelers both to the western Allies as well as to the Russians. Admiral Miklos Horthy, the seventy-five-year-old Hungarian head of state, had also allowed the almost 1 million Hungarian Jews to exist largely unmolested, and thousands of Jews from Poland, Slovakia, and Romania had already sought refuge in Hungary.

Two weeks later after the meeting with Goebbels, while Hitler was bullying Horthy to sign a joint declaration consenting to the military occupation of Hungary, the German armies were readying for their last invasion of the war.

The next day—March 19, 1944—Adolf Eichmann's men entered the capital accompanied by throngs of German troops. Hungary was now firmly a Nazi client state. With the takeover complete, the stage was set for the largest single mass murder in human history—the destruction of the country's 750,000 Jews.

The Nazis wasted no time. In a matter of days, two thousand Jews were siezed. Within a month, the first deportation train carrying over three thousand Jews, sandwiched together in horrific surroundings inside forty cattle wagons, departed. Their destination was Auschwitz, the centerpiece of the Final Solution.

An astounding number of lives were at stake.

MORGENTHAU AND THE WRB exhorted the president to make a strong statement about Hungary; the staff of the WRB drafted it. But could the president deliver it? Roosevelt was now seriously ill, his lungs filled with fluid and his heart faltering, yet he was also still smarting from Morgenthau's report on the government's acquiescence in the fate of European Jewry. Thus, on March 24, just a few days before his fateful visit to Dr. Bruenn at Bethesda Naval Medical Center, the president went to great lengths to articulate the government's goal. That was to provide assistance not simply to the Jews facing Nazi brutality in Europe, but as Roosevelt's aide William Hassett explained, the aim had been "enlarged also to include an appeal on behalf of all who suffer under Nazi and Jap torture." Roosevelt spoke in a raspy voice, but his statement was nevertheless his most compelling to date.

"In one of the blackest crimes of all history," the president said, his usual sonorous tones sounding out of pitch, "the wholesale systematic murder of the Jews of Europe goes on unabated every hour." He continued: "As a result of the events of the last few days hundreds of thousands of Jews, who while living under persecution have at least found a haven from death in Hungary and the Balkans, are now threatened with annihilation as Hitler's forces descend more heavily upon these lands." Knowing that the D-Day invasion was not far off, he added, "That these innocent people, who have already survived a decade of Hitler's fury, should perish on the very eve of triumph over the barbarism which their persecution symbolized, would be a major tragedy."

There would be, Roosevelt promised, swift punishment of the Nazis. "It is therefore fitting that we should again proclaim our determination that none who participate in these acts of savagery shall go unpunished." Nor was he simply warning the Nazis; he was warning the satellite countries as well. "All who knowingly take part in the deportation of Jews to their death in Poland . . . are equally guilty with the executioner. All who share the guilt shall share the punishment." He reached out to the German people to separate themselves from Hitler's "insane criminal desires." He exhorted those under Nazi rule to hide Hitler's victims and to "record the evidence, to convict the guilty." And he maintained that the United Nations would "find havens of refuge for them," until the tyrant Hitler was driven "from their homelands."

The statement was electrifying. Suddenly the Final Solution was receiving the treatment it had long merited. There was a front-page headline in the *New York Times*: "Roosevelt Warns Germans on Jews; Says All Guilty Must Pay for Atrocities and Asks People to Assist Refugees." In the days that followed, Roosevelt's statement was translated into numerous languages throughout the Continent. It was broadcast many times by the BBC, as well as by numerous underground channels. Neutral radio stations quickly followed their lead. It was widely read behind enemy lines, and was even printed by many publications in the Nazis' satellite nations. Perhaps most important, the WRB saw to it that Budapest was blanketed with the statement: many thousands of leaflets were dropped by air over Hungary.

The board also arranged for air drops warning that war crimes would be prosecuted. At the same time, the WRB enlisted the eminent Archbishop Francis Joseph Spellman—Spellman was a confidant of

Roosevelt's as well as his liaison to Pope Pius XII—to record a radio broadcast instructing Hungarian Catholics that persecution of the Jews was an explicit violation of church doctrine.

And three days later, hoping to give Hungary further pause, Roosevelt again warned that "Hungary's fate will not be like that of any other civilized nation—unless the deportations are stopped." To add bite to Roosevelt's words, the WRB prodded General Eisenhower to make his own statement, to be disseminated in June, after the Normandy invasion. Roosevelt quickly approved the WRB's warning to the Nazis not to harm innocents ("whether they were Jewish or otherwise"). Eisenhower slightly watered down his statement, but still, his injunction was as direct as the president's.

"Germans! You have in your midst a great many men in concentration camps and forced labor battalions.

"Germans! Do not obey any orders, regardless of their source, urging you to molest, harm or persecute them, no matter what their religion or nationality may be.

"The Allies, whose armies already established a firm foothold in Germany, expect, on their advance, to find these people alive and unharmed. Heavy punishment awaits those who . . . bear any responsibility for the mistreatment of these people.

"May this serve as a warning to whoever at present has the power to issue orders."

MEANWHILE, IN TERROR AND anticipation, the Jews of Hungary waited. They waited, listening to the pitched whistles as the cattle cars rolled out. They waited for the Allied armies to save them. Hearing whispers of distant liberations, they waited for the Soviets to free them. Had they known, they would have also waited for those who were trying to rouse the world into action: the German industrialist Eduard Schulte; the Swiss humanist Gerhard Riegner; the activist Rabbi Stephen Wise; the Palestinian agitator Peter Bergson; the Polish agent Jan Karski; the escapees from Auschwitz, Vrba and Wetzler; the cabinet secretary Henry

Morgenthau and his assistant John Pehle; the WRB; the archbishop of Canterbury; and the Polish underground. They waited for the bombers to fly overhead and the GIs to advance on the ground; and for the Axis satellites to seethe with discontent and for the Nazi regime to collapse. They waited for the camps to be bombed into submission. And most of all, they waited for the remarkable president of the United States, Franklin Delano Roosevelt, to come to their aid.

In the late spring of 1944, hundreds of thousands of Jews, the last remnants of a cornerstone of European civilization, hoped that the waiting would soon be over.

They did not have much time.

THUS WOULD BEGIN ONE of the most momentous decisions of Roosevelt's presidency, and of the war. While American, British, and Canadian GIs were rushing onto the beaches of Normandy and punching through the German defenses, the fateful question arose: should the Allies bomb the rail lines to Auschwitz, or even Auschwitz itself?

ON MAY 10, 1944, several weeks after the United Press reported that 300,000 Hungarian Jews had been forced into assembly camps, the *New York Times* published one of its most stunning reports, a wire from Istanbul headlined "Jews in Hungary Fear Annihilation." Joseph Levy wrote, "Although it may sound unbelievable, it is a fact that Hungary, where Jewish citizens were comparatively well treated until March 19, is now preparing for the annihilation of Hungarian Jews by the most fiendish methods. Laughing at President Roosevelt's warnings, Premier Doeme Sztojay's puppet Nazi government is completing plans and is about to start the extermination of about 1 million human beings who believed they were safe because they have faith in Hungarian fairness."

The article went on to quote a neutral diplomat who was lamenting "the most abominable crimes" being perpetrated. Despite his affection for Hungary, he all but called for "Allied bombings of Budapest" to put an end to the barbarism.

A few days later, the *Times* published another report, this time that the first group of Jews had been removed from the Hungarian countryside to "murder camps in Poland."

Roosevelt's reaction? Although the president had just returned from a month's rest in South Carolina, he was still exhausted and ailing. His voice had lost its fire; his aides could sometimes hardly hear him. The following morning the *New York Times*, under the headline "Roosevelt Is Reported Avoiding 'Killing Pace,' " said that the president's physician, Ross McIntire, believed Roosevelt would need to continue "to take it a little easier than usual."

For now, that meant it would fall to others in the administration to wrestle with the issue of Auschwitz.

ON JUNE 2, 1944, four days before D-Day, Secretary of the Interior Harold Ickes wrote to Franklin Roosevelt about what he deemed "an urgent necessity." The question was the internment of some 120,000 Japanese Americans, who nearly two and half years before had been forcibly removed from the West Coast to ten "relocation camps"—Roosevelt himself actually referred to these facilities as "concentration camps." They were in remote places, and they were primitive at best: there were outhouses rather than basic sewer facilities, and as many as twenty-five people lived in a space designed for four. At the desert camps, summer temperatures reached 115 degrees; in the winter, the temperature plummeted to 35 degrees below zero. And every camp was surrounded by rows of barbed wire and patrolled by armed guards.

Ickes now enumerated his arguments: that there was no justification for the continued internment; that the ban on Japanese Americans living on the West Coast was clearly unconstitutional, as the Supreme Court was likely to decide later in the year; that it was hindering efforts to have American POWs better treated by the Japanese; and that the entire process was psychologically damaging to the Japanese Americans. Ickes even wrote, "The continued retention of these innocent people in the relocation centers would be a blot upon the history of this country."

And it was not just Ickes who was alarmed. Eleanor Roosevelt had long been pressing her husband to close the camps and begin a program of educating Americans about the tenets of democracy. Now, she joined with Ickes in asking Roosevelt to rescind Executive Order 9066, signed in February 1942, which established the camps and the internment system. The president took his time in responding. On June 12, he made his decision. The camps would remain open for now, and "the whole problem for the sake of internal quiet should be handled gradually." In other words, for the moment, the order would stand.

No one was more relieved by the decision than Assistant Secretary of War John McCloy, known as "the department's point man for domestic security." After his own trip to the White House on June 12 to discuss a proposal to return a "substantial number" of Japanese Americans to California, he reported back to the West Coast military commander, "I just came from the President a little while ago. He put thumbs down on this scheme. He was surrounded at the moment by his political advisors and they were harping hard that this would stir up the boys in California and California, I guess, is an important state." After all, 1944 was an election year, and like the Jewish question, this could prove to be a damaging embarrassment.

The roots of the United States' internment of Japanese Americans could be discerned well before the strike on Pearl Harbor, and indeed in the very man to whom Roosevelt gave the job: John Jay McCloy. In some ways, McCloy's life was similar to Roosevelt's. Both lost their fathers at a young age to heart disease; both had strong-willed mothers. But where Roosevelt avoided practicing the law, McCloy immersed himself in it, rising through the ranks of one of New York's top firms. And there were other key differences. When heart disease largely incapacitated Roosevelt's father, young Franklin had no material worries or wants; his financial well-being was secure. By contrast, when John McCloy Sr. suffered a fatal heart attack, there was no income; there was not even any life insurance to fall back upon, because McCloy's employer, PennMutual Insurance, would not write a policy for its own supervisor of applications and death claims.

When McCloy was twelve, his mother sent him to a boarding school, Peddie, in Hightstown, New Jersey, which educated the sons of men in the "middle ground" in the industrial and economic world. At Peddie, McCloy discovered an affinity for tennis, earned high marks, and gained admission to Amherst College in Massachusetts, in the western Berkshires. Afterward, he applied to Harvard and was accepted for the fall of 1916.

During World War I, McCloy was in the Reserve Officers' Training Corps (ROTC) and was shipped off to Plattsburgh. He specialized in field artillery and was first sent to Fort Ethan Allen in Vermont. There he caught the eye of Brigadier General Guy Preston. But despite General Preston's urging, McCloy declined a career in the military and returned to Harvard Law School. After failing to gain a top slot in a Philadelphia firm, he made his way to Wall Street, eventually settling at the firm of Cravath, Henderson, and de Gersdorff.

There, he worked on corporate reorganizations and securities issues, for which he traveled across Europe. The following year, he married the sister-in-law of an influential New York congressman. Cravath sent McCloy to open an office in Paris, where he received a legal assignment at the international court at The Hague. The defendant, Bethlehem Steel, a Cravath client, claimed that a 1916 explosion in New York harbor, which had destroyed millions of dollars' worth of Bethlehem munitions, had actually been the work of German secret agents. To McCloy, the case read like a spy thriller, and he was hooked.

McCloy spent the better part of the 1930s pursuing the alleged German saboteurs across Europe, at some times even tailing them with his wife. The case was finally resolved in favor of McCloy's client by the Supreme Court in 1941. Yet the effects of the episode lingered long after. It made McCloy exceedingly conscious of any alleged subversive activities, and it also made him very sensitive to the concept of a "fifth column," the term used for domestic disloyalty—here, his views were much like Breckinridge Long's. When he joined the War Department, he was quickly promoted to an assistant secretary of war.

As German troops marched across Europe, McCloy was, in the words of his biographer Kai Bird, "obsessed" with sabotage: "Throughout early 1941, he was forever passing on to army intelligence rumors about various suspected saboteurs and their possible connection to a rash of strikes on American defense factories." By November 1941, when he was reading army reports that claimed the Japanese had "a well-developed espionage network along the Pacific Coast," McCloy, in Bird's phrase, "did not doubt it."

The sneak attack at Pearl Harbor stoked McCloy's deepest fears. The day after the bombing, McCloy called Stimson at home to deliver the report that "an enemy fleet was thought to be approaching San Francisco." It was quickly found to be a false alarm. But the belief spread that Japanese agents had infiltrated Hawaii and the West Coast. Nearly 1,400 Japanese aliens were detained in the first five days after the assault, and newspapers such as the *Los Angeles Times* breathlessly reported the likelihood of Japanese raids along the West Coast. By January, a congressman from Los Angeles was demanding that all Japanese be "placed in inland concentration camps." Compared with German Americans and Italian Americans, Japanese Americans on the West Coast were a small minority, only about 120,000, and two thirds had been born in the United States. But that made them a more manageable target, and their concentration on the West Coast served to heighten their visibility.

The uneasiness approached hysteria after the release of the Roberts Commission Report on January 24, 1942. Charged with investigating the Pearl Harbor attack, the commission concluded that the Japanese strike force had been aided by espionage agents based in Hawaii. The commission offered no substantiating documentation, but the allegation was enough. The army's general in the region, John DeWitt, began speaking of the Japanese as "an enemy race."

But there were dissenters—influential ones. In Washington, no less than the FBI's J. Edgar Hoover sharply objected; in his view, the claims made by army intelligence showed signs of "hysteria and lack of judgment."

On February 1, 1942, the two sides—for and against removal of the Japanese—met in Washington, D.C. The attorney general and Hoover argued strenuously against internment. The military argued for it. And sitting quietly in the room, as the civilian representative for the War Department, was John J. McCloy.

Finally, as the back-and-forth continued, McCloy interrupted the attorney general, saying, "If it is a question of safety of the country, [or] the Constitution of the United States, why the Constitution is just a scrap of paper to me."

So it was. Over the next few days, General DeWitt kept pressing, saying that he believed Japanese spies on the mainland were in regular communication with Japanese submarines off the coast. For McCloy, this was a strong incentive. He now began to look for a way to remove Japanese citizens, in mass evacuations, from their homes and communities up and down the West Coast.

On February 11, at McCloy's urging, Secretary of War Stimson contacted Roosevelt about the evacuation plan. Stimson laid out his arguments, and Roosevelt readily agreed. As McCloy put it, "We have carte blanche to do what we want as far as the president is concerned."

Once more, there was a range of opinion. Not every military officer agreed. For one, General Mark Clark, the army's deputy chief of staff, strongly objected. Naval intelligence's leading specialist on Japan, Lieutenant Commander Kenneth D. Ringle, estimated that less than 3 percent (only about 3,500 individuals) actually represented a threat—and most of them were already in custody. And there were questions about whether Roosevelt had truly assented on his own to the evacuation scheme, or merely turned the decision over to Stimson. But what is clear is that the president, as commander in chief, left the final call up to the judgment of his War Department, and the military men and their civilian bosses had decided yes. Roosevelt signed Executive Order 9066 on February 19, without regret. "I do not think he was much concerned with the gravity or implications of this step," wrote Attorney General Francis Biddle.

Executive Order 9066 authorized the secretary of war to "prescribe military areas from which any and all persons might be excluded" and gave the War Department the power to determine the "right of any person to enter, remain, or leave" those areas. The next step to the round up the Japanese Americans. Forced from their homes, forced to sell their goods and their land, they lost over $400 million in property—well over $5 billion in today's dollars. The evacuations were based on location, but also on descent. Somewhat reminiscent of the early debate in Germany about the Jews, initially any Japanese American with as little as one sixteenth Japanese ancestry was to be subject to the evacuation orders, but that was later amended to exempt anyone with less than one half Japanese ancestry and a Caucasian background. Thus tens of thousands of Japanese Americans were now trapped at assembly centers; at one such center, the Santa Anita racetrack, they were housed in horse stables and surrounded by guard towers and searchlights.

By the end of 1942, over 100,000 Japanese had been formally interned across the west in tarpaper barracks, with schools, communal kitchens, churches, and recreation centers. The original man in charge of the project, Milton Eisenhower, General Dwight D. Eisenhower's younger brother, quit after three months. He told his successor to take the job, "if you can do it and sleep at night"; he himself could not. Yet McCloy remained dogged in his efforts to keep the West Coast Japanese Americans contained inside barbed wire; in a loose sense, what Long was to the Jews he was now to the Japanese Americans. And initially almost no one in Washington voiced any opposition.

For the Japanese Americans inside the camps, the conditions were often brutal. At Tule Lake, in California, half a dozen tanks patrolled the perimeter, a barbed-wire stockade surrounded the camp, and the armed guards were a full battalion strong, with machine guns. "No federal penitentiary so treats its adult prisoners," an indignant Chief Judge William

Denman of the Ninth Circuit Court of Appeals wrote later. "Here were the children and babies as well."

By late 1943, as concern about European Jewry mounted, there were renewed fears in official Washington about the continuing internment, and challenges to its constitutionality were making their way toward the Supreme Court. The debate mounted. Reviewing the overall issue, Attorney General Biddle insisted to Roosevelt that the "concentration camps" went against every tenet of democratic government. Henry Stimson also told Roosevelt, in May 1944, that there was no military reason for keeping faithful Japanese Americans prisoners. And Harold Ickes and Eleanor Roosevelt made their requests for release by early June. But Roosevelt, faced with a choice between reason and politics, chose politics: the 1944 election trumped all other concerns. And in the worst sort of pandering, the administration was afraid of losing the critical California vote if the Japanese were released. (Actually, the New York vote was far more important.) McCloy, for his part, was worried that if Roosevelt lost, Stalin would make a separate peace with the Germans, so he made it his job to keep the internment issue under wraps until the late fall.

The final order to release those remaining in the camps was made by the army on December 17, 1944, one day before the announcement by the Supreme Court that the War Relocation Authority had no right to detain citizens who were "concededly loyal"—a ruling that would require the release of all detainees who could not be proved to be disloyal.

But in June 1944 and beyond, the administration attitude of "wait and delay" would have profound and deadly consequences for hundreds of thousands of others besides Japanese Americans and their children. In large measure, this was because the man given the task of managing the Japanese internment, John J. McCloy, was about to become the point man for the War Department regarding what, if anything, was to be done to try to save the Jews trapped inside, or bound for, the Nazi death camp at Auschwitz.

~

In late May, the *New York Times* published another report, this time stating that the first group of Jews had been removed from the Hungarian countryside to "murder camps in Poland."

In mid-June, activists spearheaded a concerted effort to prod the American government into helping Hungary's Jews. Jacob Rosenheim of the Agudas Israel World Organization wrote a series of plaintive letters ("I beg to approach you") to high-ranking administration officials, asking them not just to utter strong words but to take concrete action. In the past, activists like Stephen Wise and Gerhart Riegner had often deferred to the government, but this time Rosenheim outlined specific policy suggestions. He asked that the Allies bomb the rail junctions at Presov and Kosice along the main railway route to Auschwitz. Such a measure, he argued, would "paralyze" the Nazis' extermination efforts. He noted that time was of the essence: "The bombing has to be made at once," he wrote, "because every day of delay means a very heavy responsibility for the human lives at stake."

Rosenheim's information was not speculative. He had had access to the Vrba-Wetzler report, which for the first time gave a specific name to the extermination camp—Auschwitz—and which in the course of thirty pages laid out in minute, chilling detail the inner-workings of the death camp, including the gas chambers themselves. After the report reached Budapest and the leadership of the Hungarian Jews in early May, it was relayed to Allen Dulles in Switzerland by mid-June—Dulles would later become the first civilian director of the Central Intelligence Agency—and then sent on to Roswell McClelland, the WRB's representative in Geneva. McClelland made a snap decision: Vrba and Wetzler's testimony was so gruesome and so strong, that McClelland decided to compose a longer cable outlining its implications. But knowing that haste mattered, on June 24 he dispatched an overview—a three-page cable to Pehle at the WRB in the capital.

With a heavy heart, he summarized: "There is little doubt that many of these Hungarian Jews are being sent to the extermination camps of Auschwitz (Oswiecim) and Birkenau (Rajska) in Western upper Silesia where according to recent reports, since early summer 1942 at least 1,500,000 Jews have been killed."

He added that a more detailed report would soon be cabled.

He also graphically described the circumstances of the deportations from Hungary: the grueling three-day journey to Poland, on which hundreds perished from lack of food and little air. And he passed on the request from the sources in Slovakia and Hungary that the railway lines, "especially bridges," be bombed as the only possible means of slowing down or stopping future deportations. Bureaucratically, McClelland understood that the WRB was not authorized to sanction military measures. Thus his memo stated that he could not "venture" an opinion on the utility of the proposed bombing. But the simple fact that he attached the proposal clearly signaled his own support for taking direct action against the transport routes to Auschwitz.

That same day, a worried Pehle sat down with McCloy in his spacious office at the War Department and discussed Rosenheim's suggestion. This was murky territory for Pehle, and he knew it. The WRB's initial mandate was to rescue Jews in imminent danger of death "consistent with the successful prosecution of the war." Did this mean the WRB could propose measures that entailed military force to rescue Jews? No and yes. In a sense, it came down to what the White House thought. Whatever Roosevelt's inclinations were, the president well knew that war had its own imperatives—and policies frequently gave way in response to change, improvisation, or duplication. "A little rivalry is stimulating, you know," he once said to Frances Perkins. "It keeps everybody going to prove he is a better fellow than the next man."

Still, Pehle intimated that he had "several doubts about the matter." He was reluctant to ask for military personnel, and he wondered aloud whether the rail lines would be incapacitated long enough to make a measurable difference to the functioning of the death camps. At this stage, Pehle was clearly feeling his way. Afterward he wrote a memo in which he made it "very clear" to McCloy that he was not specifically asking the War Department to take any action on the proposed bombing other than to "appropriately explore it." Yet he added one important proviso: "at this point at least." In other words, he was, at a minimum, hedging his bets, leaving the door open for a firmer request down the road.

McCloy, a master at working the system, told Pehle that he was taking this seriously and would "check into the matter." For his part, Pehle now sought to increase the pressure on McCloy. Within the week he sent McCloy a copy of McClelland's cable, underlining the injunction to bomb "vital sections" of the rail lines. Meanwhile, the machinery at the War Department was in motion, already generating a response to Rosenheim's original request. Here was institutional behavior reminiscent of the State Department. Absent further pressure from above, no actual study of the military feasibility of bombing the rail lines, or of any comparable measures to slow the deportations, was conducted. Instead, Lieutenant General John E. Hull, who had the onerous task of answering the cable, simply employed Roosevelt's public statements as well as the War Department's internal memorandums of February 1944. He gave the stock reply that "the most effective relief which can be given victims of enemy persecution is to ensure the speedy defeat of the axis."

When McCloy received Hull's response, he promptly signed off on it, and instructed Gerhardt, his personal aide, to "kill" the matter.

On July 3, 1944 Gerhardt wrote to McCloy. "I know you told me to 'kill' this but since those instructions, we have received the attached letter from Pehle. I suggest that the attached reply be sent."

As if everything had changed and nothing had changed, the response said: "The War Department is of the opinion that the suggested air operation is impracticable. It could be executed only by the diversion of considerable air support essential to the success of our forces now engaged in decisive operations and would in any case be of such very doubtful efficacy that [it would] not amount to a practical project." McCloy scarcely gave it a second thought, and signed Gerhardt's draft response.

This was cant, and Gerhardt must have known it. At the WRB, one of the staffers, Benjamin Akzin, was livid. He knew it was untrue that bombing the rail lines could be carried out only through the "diversion" of extensive air support. Since the spring, when the Allies had seized the Foggia air base in Italy, long-range American bombers had been consistently flying over the camp complex or nearby; also, the Allies' airpower had reduced Hitler's air force to a mere shell of itself. And as early as April 4 aerial reconnaissance photos had been taken of the Auschwitz camp—Vrba himself later vividly remembered the roar of the planes overhead—as well as of the neighboring IG Farben petrochemical plant. Photos were again taken on June 26, 1944, just a few days before McCloy informed Pehle that the bombing run was not possible.

In fact, the United States would conduct an intense air war against Germany's synthetic fuel plants in that same region in the weeks to come; frequently these attacks were close to the death camps themselves. So effective were the bombing raids that German production of synthetic oil fell from more than 1,000 tons a day on July 1 to only 417 tons on July 25; by all accounts, the Third Reich's military operations were being strangled by this loss of oil. In Germany itself, the minister of armaments, demoralized and desperate to ration fuel, requested that Hitler cease all air courier services, a measure that was once almost unthinkable. The same with passenger planes. The Allies had no such restrictions.

On August 7, a fleet of seventy-six bombers and sixty-four fighters of the U.S. Air Force set their sights on their targets and struck the refineries at Trzebinia, only thirteen miles northeast of Auschwitz. Then, at 10:32 p.m. on August 20, the Fifteenth U.S. Air Force bombed the Monowitz camp just three miles east of Auschwitz-Birkenau, causing "considerable damage." For twenty-eight earsplitting minutes, 127 Flying Fortresses, escorted by 100 Mustangs, dropped a total of 1,336 five-hundred-pound explosive bombs from an altitude of about twenty-seven thousand feet. The depleted German defenses were able to bring down only one plane. On the ground, there were casualties. Over three hundred slave laborers were injured; and although SS guards "ran away," scurrying into the bunkers, nonetheless a number of these guards themselves were also wounded. Monowitz, one of the subcamps of Auschwitz, produced synthetic oil and rubber.

The campaign continued. On August 27, 350 heavy bombers took to the skies and pounded Blechhammer, and two days later 218 bombers followed suit, assaulted Bohumín, again within range of Auschwitz.

United States planes flying reconnaissance above Auschwitz took aerial photographs of the camps on numerous other occasions in addition to April 4 and June 26, including August 9, 12, and 25. Had these images been carefully examined—they were not—the analysts could have pinpointed the gas chambers, the crematoriums, the railway sidings, the trains and the platforms, the huts in the women's camp, and even the specially landscaped gardens created to conceal the gas chambers. Taken in bright sunlight, the photographs of August 25 particularly stand out—hundreds of bomb craters are readily discernible, as are 151 different buildings including the camp housing for some thirty thousand Jews transferred from Birkenau to Auschwitz III. Also visible is something quite startling: a snaking line of Jews trudging on their way from a cattle car to a gas chamber. Moving across the frame, they are hauntingly visible.

As FOR THE HUNGARIANS arriving at Auschwitz by the hundreds of thousands, there was little doubt that most of them were fervently hoping for the Allies' bombers to come, even if it meant that they themselves perished in the raids. Watching the passage of Allied aircraft far overhead en route to their more distant targets, or hearing "the tremendous rumble" of bombers, deeply affected the inmates of Auschwitz. "We saw many times the silver trails in the sky," one prisoner, Erich Kulka, later recalled. "All the SS men would go into the bunkers but we came out of our huts, and prayed that a bomb will fall, or soldiers and weapons will be parachuted, but in vain." Hugo Gryn, a fifteen-year-old Hungarian boy, would later note that "one of the most painful aspects of being in the camp was a sensation of being totally abandoned." The Nobel Peace Prize winner and Auschwitz survivor, Elie Wiesel, would later explain, "We are no longer afraid of death, at any rate, not of that death." According to one of Edward Murrow's broadcasts, "At Buchenwald they spoke of the president just before he died." No doubt it was the same at Auschwitz. And Primo Levi, an Italian partisan imprisoned at Auschwitz, and future renowned novelist, wrote, "As for us, we were too destroyed to be really afraid. The few who could still judge and feel rightly, drew strength and hope from the bombardments."

But in Washington, Pehle himself was still nursing some doubts about the utility of bombing, cautiously navigating the bureaucratic maze. However, members of his own staff had no such hesitation. One of his aides, Benjamin Akzin, was so horrified by the graphic descriptions in the abbreviated Vrba-Wetzler report contained in Roswell McClelland's cable of June 24 that he sat down and wrote a memo unflinchingly arguing for bombing the gas chambers themselves. Presaging a debate that would continue until this very day, it laid waste to the notion that bombing the camps is simply a twenty-first-century concept based on twenty-first-century values. In any case, although it was written in the heat of the moment, it was a masterpiece of morality, strategy, and tactics.

Akzin pointed out that bombing the gas chambers would cause the "methodical German mind" to devote extensive time and resources to reconstructing them, or force it "to evolve" equally efficient procedures of mass slaughter; in any case, he rightly noted that German manpower and material resources were "gravely depleted" and that German authorities might no longer be in a position to devote themselves to the task of equipping "new large-scale extermination centres." Therefore, "some appreciable saving of lives" would be the outcome, "at least temporarily." Akzin also insisted to Pehle that this was a moral imperative, or what he called a "matter of principle." Marking the camp for destruction, he noted, would constitute the most tangible "evidence of the indignation aroused by the existence of these charnel houses."

Moreover, the bombings would, he contended, have sound military logic as well. For a start, they would cause many deaths among "the most ruthless and despicable of the Nazis." Akzin pointed out that the bombings would also be consistent with current military objectives, inasmuch as the Auschwitz complex was a crucial military target that contained "mining and manufacturing centres" playing an important part in the industrial armament of Germany. And he wrestled forthrightly with whether the Allies should be deterred by the fact that a large number of Jews would be killed by such a military operation. Resoundingly, he said no. Pointing out that these Jews were "doomed to death anyhow," he wrote that "refraining from bombing the extermination centres would be sheer misplaced sentimentality, far more cruel a decision than to destroy the centres." Actually, however, in the confusion created by the bombing some of the inmates might be able to hide and escape.

So here, finally, was a powerful, persuasive case for bombing Auschwitz. It was now clear to Akzin, as it was increasingly clear to much of the world, that some fifteen thousand Hungarian Jews were being shipped every twenty-four hours to Auschwitz. And as the days went by, evidence mounted that some twelve thousand Jews were being gassed each day in the camps, a figure that would rise in August to twenty-four thousand a day—a record even for the Nazis. Nevertheless, for the next couple of weeks Pehle remained unsure how to proceed. He was decisive on numerous issues facing the WRB, but when it came to bombing Auschwitz, he was in a box. Should he go to the War Department again? Enlist Morgenthau's aid? Approach the White House?

Instead, he waited in his office in the Treasury Department—and read the river of cables that came across his desk outlining the Auschwitz death machine in gut-wrenching detail. On July 1, his representative in Sweden, Iver Olsen, sent him a lengthy description of Auschwitz that left little question about the atrocities taking place—and the results of doing nothing. He read slowly, and would later comment that the news was "so terrible that it is hard to believe," adding, "There are no words to qualify its description." And the figures alone were equally unfathomable: some 600,000 Jews were now already dead or deported.

Olsen's account continued: "According to the evidence, these people are now being taken to a place across the Hungarian frontier in Poland where there is an establishment at which gas is being used for killing people. . . . These people of all ages, children, women, and men are transported to this isolated spot in boxcars packed in like sardines and . . . upon arrival many are already dead. Those who have survived the trip are stripped naked, given a small square object which resembles a piece of soap and told that at the bathhouse they must bathe themselves. The 'bathhouse' does in fact look like a big bathing establishment. . . . Into a large room with a total capacity of 2,000 packed together closely the victims are pushed. No regard is given to sex or age and all are completely naked. When the atmosphere of the hall has been heated by this mass of bodies a fine powder is let down over the whole area by opening a contraption in the ceiling. When the heated atmosphere comes in contact with this powder a poisonous gas is formed which kills all occupants of the room. Trucks then take out the bodies, and burning follows."

Interestingly, this cable was also later passed on to Winston Churchill, not by Franklin Roosevelt or the WRB but by Churchill's son, Randolph.

On July 8, Pehle received another cable from his representative in Switzerland, a lengthier eight-page summary of the Vrba-Wetzler report. It would still be some months before he would see the complete thirty-page text, but between the cable from Olsen and this one, he was shaken enough to again raise the issue of military action. This time he wrote a long report to the other members of the WRB and sent copies to the secretary of war, Henry Stimson, as well as to the assistant secretary, McCloy. Pehle proposed a number of audacious military actions, including bombing the camps, air-dropping weapons to the inmates of Auschwitz, and parachuting troops to help bring about the "escape of the unfortunate people."

Once more, McCloy did nothing. Did he believe that the mass extermination was being carried out on such a terrifying industrial scale? Probably. Did he comprehend it? This is unclear. But at the same time, it is clear that there was no follow-up from Roosevelt or the White House to force McCloy's hand or strengthen the WRB's. So, as he had thus far managed to do on the issue of the Japanese Americans' internment, McCloy was content to wait out Pehle. Still, as it happened, while the information was flooding into Washington, a summary of the Vrba-Wetzler report was reaching the Foreign Office in London, on July 4. Unlike the Americans, the British moved quickly and publicly. The next day Anthony Eden informed the House of Commons that the "barbarous deportations" had already begun and "many persons have been killed." And on a grim note he added that "unfortunately" there were no signs that the repeated declarations by the Allies had in any way mitigated "the fury" of the Nazis' death machine.

This, of course, was the challenge. The next day, Eden sat down with Churchill and raised the matter of bombing the death camps. Head bowed, eyebrows knitted, Churchill listened attentively. Eden explained that the idea had "already been considered" but said that he was now entirely in favor of it. As it turns out, so was the prime minister. In stark contrast to McCloy, the War Department, the State Department, and others in Washington, Churchill immediately grasped the significance of the reports about Auschwitz. He promptly gave his imprimatur for military action against the camps. On July 7, Churchill informed Eden: "You and I are in entire agreement. Get anything out of the Air Force you can, and invoke me if necessary." Then, in language that one might have expected from Roosevelt—though in truth, the president had remained totally silent on the matter—several days later Churchill eloquently told his foreign secretary: "There is no doubt that this is probably the greatest and most horrible crime ever committed in the whole history of the world, and it has been done by scientific machinery by nominally civilized men in the name of a great State and one of the leading races in Europe." He added that everyone connected with it "should be hunted down and put to death."

Suddenly, the idea of bombing was gaining support, at least in Britain. Eden wasted little time in following up on Churchill's declaration. He wrote to the British secretary of state about the "appalling persecution" of Hungary's Jews, and asked the Air Ministry's opinion about the "feasibility" of bombing Auschwitz itself. "I very much hope that it will be possible to do something," he told the secretary. "I have the authority of the Prime Minister to say that he agrees."

And if ever the case were to be made for bombing the camps, it occurred almost by happenstance. As the sun was setting in Budapest on July 4, Admiral Horthy informed the Nazi ambassador that throughout the day he was being "deluged" with angry calls protesting the deportations and telegrams asking him to halt the killings, including messages from the once silent Vatican and the once hesitant president of the International Red Cross; moreover, in good measure thanks to the WRB, he had received harsh criticism from the Swedish, Turkish, Swiss, and Spanish governments, all of which also added their voices to the fray.

However isolated Hungary may have felt, little of this gave the regime pause. In the blink of an eye, on its watch, nearly half a million Jews were now dead. But what did cause Horthy to think twice was a telegram that the Hungarians intercepted from the American representative in Bern. The cable proposed an Allied air attack on Budapest, and contained "exact and correct street and house numbers" of Hungarian and German institutions involved in the deportations; moreover, seventy individuals directly implicated in the deportations were explicitly named. Horthy may have allowed himself to be browbeaten by Hitler, but he had a strong instinct for self-preservation. More fearful of Allied reprisals than of Germany's retribution—in a telling coda to the skepticism about bombing Auschwitz, Budapest already had suffered an uncommonly fierce American bomber assault on its marshaling yards and even government buildings and private homes, on July 2—Horthy himself demanded that the deportations be suspended on July 7.

But even though the Hungarians' deportations ceased, the death trains still monotonously rolled in from other countries. And as the debate about whether to bomb Auschwitz continued, all those lives—some 300,000 more—hovered in limbo.

MEANWHILE, THE WRB HASTILY dispatched a thirty-one-year-old Swedish emissary Raoul Wallenberg, to Budapest under diplomatic cover; he immediately grasped at the first shafts of hope.

Working with another Swede, Iver Olsen, he arrived on July 9, carrying two knapsacks, a revolver ("to give me courage"), a windbreaker, and a sleeping bag. By this stage, the deportations from Hungary had been halted, but no one could say for how long, and the countryside had been cleared. Some 600,000 Jews had eerily vanished, literally within weeks. Wallenberg also knew that more than 300,000 Jews were still in peril. Employing a combination of heroics almost unequaled in the war, he became part diplomat and part spy, in his effort to rescue lives.

A linguist, a world traveler, and an architect, he was at once ingenious and relentless. His courtly manner was deceptive: when needed, he bluffed the Germans; when that didn't work, he blustered; and when other tactics were called for, he bribed the Germans, using funds funneled through the WRB. He did whatever it took to save lives. He was both meek and tough, petulant and sentimental, charming and emotional. But he was always cool, practical, and absolutely determined. He rented thirty buildings that became safe havens for Jewish refugees; the Spanish and Swiss legations followed his example. He devised an elaborate scheme to give tens of thousands of Jews forged passports or certificates of protection—particularly important for children under ten years of age who needed visas. The ruse worked.

He set up soup kitchens and smuggled food to Jews in the Hungarian ghetto. When armed patrols began seizing and slaughtering Jews, he directly confronted them. When the Arrow Cross, Hungary's much despised and dreaded pro-Nazi party, threatened to execute the ghetto's inhabitants, Wallenberg shouted at the SS commander and promised that he and his cohort would hang from lampposts if they carried out the mass executions. The Germans backed off. Wallenberg's efforts were not without considerable risk. Already Jane Haining—a Scottish missionary, a gentile, and head of a girls' home in Budapest run by the Church of Scotland—had been deported to Auschwitz, where she perished. Her crime? She had been charged with shedding tears while affixing yellow stars to the clothes of her Jewish girls.

Yet Wallenberg never flinched.

How many lives did Wallenberg save? Tens of thousands, perhaps as many as seventy-five thousand. But whatever the number, on the level of folklore he showed the world—and history—how to save lives. He gave new meaning to the concept of humanitarianism, and he proved that it was not merely a tarnished, fading virtue eclipsed by the fog of war. At his best, he, along with the WRB, provided Americans with an example of rescue that lasts to this day, so that the question lingers: what might have been possible if the WRB had been established by Roosevelt much earlier?

Wallenberg later disappeared mysteriously. It is believed he was killed by the Soviets.

THE DEBATE OVER BOMBING Auschwitz continued. Despite Churchill's wholehearted support, the British bureaucracy held back. The secretary of state told Anthony Eden that disrupting the railspurs to the death camps "is out of our power." As to bombing the camps, he maintained that "the distance" from British bases entirely ruled out "our doing anything of the kind." But, he suggested, the Americans might be able to carry out such raids in daylight, though these would be "costly and hazardous." Then he added with a touch of Orwellian doublespeak: "Even if the plant was destroyed, I am not clear that would really help the victims."

Back in Washington, this same hesitant attitude continued to prevail in the War Department. However, activists still pushed for the military option. In early August Leon Kubowitzki, head of the rescue department of the World Jewish Congress, sent McCloy an impassioned plea from a member of the Czech government in exile to bomb the camps and railways. Kubowitzki's entreaty carried special weight. Earlier in the summer, unable to stomach the fact that "the first victims would be the Jews," he, like others in the Jewish community, had had considerable reservations about bombing the camps. He instead proposed that the Soviets send in paratroopers to free the inmates, an idea that went nowhere. Now, as the situation changed—the Allies had made their spectacular landing in Normandy, and the shock of the earlier mass deportations in Hungary was still felt—he passed on the calls for the bombings because "so little time" was left. Once more, McCloy dismissed the request. Once more, he didn't even bother to contact air commanders in the European theater. Once more, he failed to thoroughly investigate the military options. Once more, he felt little need to talk with the WRB.

Repeating what he had said in the past, McCloy responded that the bombings would require the "diversion of considerable air support . . . engaged in decisive operations elsewhere." But this time he added a new wrinkle to the government response. While acknowledging the humanitarian motives behind the request, McCloy offered the mindnumbing notion that "such an effort, even if practicable, might provoke even more vindictive action by the Germans." Scratching their heads in despair, proponents of bombing wondered how any "more vindictive action" could be possible, while the inmates of Auschwitz couldn't have felt more differently from McCloy.

One young man, Shalom Lindenbaum, vividly recalled looking up as the Allied bombers appeared and then disappeared in the sky. "It will be difficult to describe our joy," he thought. "We prayed and hoped to be bombed by them, and so to escape the helpless death in the gas chambers. To be bombed meant the chance that also the Germans will be killed. Therefore we were deeply disappointed and sad when they passed over, not bombing."

And once more, the White House was silent on the matter.

ACTUALLY, COMPLICATED BOMBING RUNS were not impossible. On October 29, 1944, the *New York Times* published a report about Operation Jericho, a dazzling raid by the Royal Air Force that freed one hundred members of the French Resistance from Amiens prison in German-occupied France, where they were awaiting execution.

It was a daunting operation, the first of its kind in the war and extraordinary for its fearlessness and accuracy—more accuracy, in fact, than would be needed to attack Auschwitz. The airmen prepared by carefully examining a model of the prison, a crosslike building in a courtyard surrounded by an imposing wall twenty feet high and three feet thick. The task for the Royal Air Force seemed Herculean: the walls had to be breached and the German quarters destroyed, but with the least amount of explosives so that casualties would be minimal in the adjacent prison buildings.

A thick blanket of snow lay on the airfield—it was February 18, 1944, and the weather was dismal—as three squadrons of Mosquito bombers escorted by Spitfires took off, preparing to attack the prison in three successive waves. They carried eleven-second delayed-action bombs. Beforehand, Captain Percy Pickard had bellowed to his men: "It's a death or glory job, boys." En route, because of the foul weather, four Mosquitoes lost contact with the formation and had to return to their base. The rest continued.

At the northeast and northwest perimeter, the planes of the New Zealand squadron zoomed in first. It was one minute past noon when they reached the target. Their bombs fell, and the wall was ruptured. Minutes later came the second wave of bombers; they were the Australians, flying at an altitude of fifty feet. There were earsplitting sounds as the bombs hit the targets, pulverizing the guards' quarters on each end; they also "divided and slit open" the jail, and a direct hit on the guardhouse killed or disabled a number of the Germans. Smoke bellowed into the sky and fires broke out.

By then the job was done. So as to leave little to chance, elsewhere a diversionary attack was made on the local railway station.

One plane had a camera mounted on it, and made three runs over the prison. It brought back extraordinary film that showed Germans lying dead on the ground, bleeding into the snow; the camera also captured the exhilarating sight of prisoners rushing out through the smoldering holes in the walls and then disappearing across a snowy field outside the prison walls.

A number of the Frenchmen were cut down by the Nazis' machine-gun fire, and many were eventually recaptured. But a significant number made it to freedom, linking up with members of the underground who had been awaiting them in a nearby wooded area. Tragically, Captain Pickard was killed when the tail of his plane was severed by German flak. Nonetheless, the crewmen were ecstatic. One Australian pilot said,

"The feeling of the men in our squadron . . . was that this was a job where it did not matter if we were all killed." He added, "It was a sort of operation that gave you a feeling that if you did nothing else in this war, you had done something."

~

WHATEVER MAY HAVE BEEN the case with the Allies, in bits and pieces there were other stirring stories of those standing up to the Nazi killing machine and coming to the rescue of the Jews. In tiny Albania, which the Nazis had rolled into in September 1943, the seemingly fascist government pretended to collaborate with the Germans; it often did not. In little coastal towns and larger cities, in small mountain villages and even in the capital, ordinary citizens shuffled Jews from basement to basement, barn to barn, and hideout to hideout to help them elude capture. When the Nazi masters often asked for lists of Jews, the Albanian government insisted there were no Jews. A number of the rescues occurred in Nazi-occupied Kosovo, which had a sizable population of ethnic Albanians. False identification papers using Muslim names were issued to the Jews, allowing them to find safe haven in Albania. In one case in Albania itself, a grocer, Arsllan Rezniqi, transported 400 Jews from Macedonia to safety; he hid them in the back of a truck underneath fruits and vegetables.

Overall, Albania saved virtually all of its 200 native Jews, 400 Jewish refugees from Austria and Germany, and help ferry hundreds more through the treacherous Nazi-occupied territories of the Balkans. Remarkably, Albania had more Jews at the end of the war that at the beginning. Why did they do it? Because of a national creed that obligated its citizens to provide safe passage for those seeking protection—even at the risk of forfeiting their own lives.

~

THE WAR DEPARTMENT WAS against a coordinated bombing attack on Auschwitz. The military was against bombing the camp. And clearly so was the silent White House. Remarkably, it happened anyway.

On September 13, as part of the sustained Allied "oil war," the American air force made another run at the Monowitz oil plant, just five miles from the Auschwitz gas chambers. But this time a number of the bombs veered slightly off course, accidentally dropping on Auschwitz I. While air-raid sirens wailed, some of the SS barracks were destroyed, either flattened like paper bags or incinerated in a maelstrom of flame and smoke. Dashing for the shelters, or caught completely by surprise, fifteen SS men were killed; twenty-eight more were severely hit and left moaning and writhing. By happenstance, the clothing workshop was also struck. Twenty-three Jews perished, and sixty-five other inmates lay bleeding and badly hurt.

Significantly, in the same errant attack, American bombs fell for the first time on the nefarious Auschwitz-Birkenau itself—where the gas chambers were. Here was a measure of vengeance. Thirty civilian workers died when one bomb hurtled into the crematorium sidings. A second bomb plummeted down on the railway embankment leading into the camp. Still another bomb screamed into the SS bomb shelter. Suddenly, there was mayhem. Guard dogs barked wildly. The German soldiers frantically ran for the shelters. Sirens blared. But the Jews just stood there and watched. For a fleeting moment their own agonies subsided. Barely able to think, barely able to stand, they were nonetheless ecstatic. Never before had they seen the Nazis so vulnerable and so helpless. Never before had they seen the Nazis not in control.

"How beautiful was it to see squadron after squadron burst from the sky, drop bombs, destroy the buildings, and kill also members of the Herrenvolk," one inmate thought. "Those bombardments elevated our morale and, paradoxically, awakened . . . hopes of surviving, of escaping from this hell."

~

YET ON THE BATTLEFIELD, the boundaries of hell were being expanded.

The great Prussian strategist Carl von Clausewitz once pronounced his axiom on the friction of war: Little goes as planned, and tactics constantly change. As the Germans were being driven out of France and Greece and huge swaths of eastern Europe were being overrun by the Red Army, suddenly Warsaw was in revolt. Now, the War Department and Roosevelt were forced to reassess elements of their bombing strategy. It happened this way.

On August 1, the Polish Resistance Home Army began a massive assault against the Nazis in Warsaw. The revolt started as Soviet troops drew within twelve miles of the city, but then stopped. The expected plan was that the uprising, led by the Polish Home Army, would distract the Germans, allowing the Soviet forces to move on Warsaw. But they didn't advance.

Instead, for sixty-three days, thirty-seven thousand Polish resistance fighters battled the Germans alone. They traveled under the city, moving through the sewers. They had only around two thousand weapons, almost exclusively small arms and homemade gasoline bombs. In the early fighting, the Poles captured a number of buildings, including some governmental offices, and defiantly raised the Polish flag. In response, Himmler gave an order to the German forces to kill, rather than capture, the city's inhabitants, and to level Warsaw, to make an example of it. German tanks and air support were sent to the city, and twenty-one thousand Germans were eventually dispatched there. Meanwhile, gas was pumped into the sewers. The Luftwaffe dive-bombed the city.

Across the Vistula River, Soviet troops sat idle; their antiaircraft guns did not fire, and their planes remained on the ground. In London, a desperate Winston Churchill began pleading for help for the Polish rebels. Over time, the belief would grow that the Soviets, with Stalin in charge, had halted their offensive to allow the Polish rebels to be wiped out—or at least nearly wiped out—by the Germans, so that the postwar government would be firmly in the Soviet orbit. The Polish rebels had heard the Soviet guns and Moscow Radio had announced that "the hour of action has already arrived." But it hadn't. By August 7, German troops had conducted mass executions of more than sixty-five thousand civilians inside the city walls. Citizens were rounded up house by house and shot. But the Resistance continued fighting.

~

As THE WORLD WATCHED, the torment of Poland continued.

In London, Polish officials waged an intense campaign to persuade the British government to do something. They begged for resupply flights. Their Resistance fighters needed guns, food, and medical supplies. Yet John Slessor, the RAF commander in Italy, was hesitant. He warned that supply flights to Warsaw from Italy were a sideshow, which could not possibly affect the issue "of the war one way or another," and in any case, such runs would result in a "prohibitive" loss of airpower. That may have been the case, but Churchill, as with the proposal for bombing Auschwitz, wanted to keep faith with a devastated people. This time, he ordered the missions. During August and September, twenty-two night operations were carried out from Italy, employing 181 bombers all told. In Slessor's view, the effort achieved "practically nothing." But Churchill, never one to run away from a fight, let alone a cause, thought otherwise.

Meanwhile, the prime minister pressed Roosevelt to join the effort. Actually, the president needed little convincing: he quickly dispatched American bombers. His health was failing, though his mind was as much on the presidential campaign as on the war itself, and he could not ignore the Chicago ward bosses who reminded him that he needed the Polish vote. In the capital and on the campaign trail, notably Chicago, he had already told the Polish American Congress that he would protect the "integrity" of Poland. So in addition to sending the bombers, he joined Churchill—to no avail—in calling on Stalin to help the "patriot Poles of Warsaw."

He knew the situation was grim and the options were limited. A quarter of a million Warsaw Poles were dead; the majority of the city lay in waste, unrecognizable even to its inhabitants. Even the U.S. strategic air forces concluded that "the partisan fight was a losing one." Nevertheless, Roosevelt wrote that it was their duty to do the utmost to save as many of the "patriots there as possible."

Soon it was the American bombers' turn. Over four days, 107 Flying

Fortresses were loaded up with supplies and sat on runways in England, waiting for the right weather. And waiting. And waiting. Finally, on September 18, they were given the signal: go. And go they did. They dropped 1,284 containers of arms and supplies on Warsaw before making their way to airfields in the Soviet Union. For the Polish partisans, watching the crates float down from the skies, it was a minor miracle. But the effort remained largely futile, and Roosevelt knew it. Only 288 containers ever made it to the hands of the Polish Home Army. The others were seized by the Germans. The partisans would soon be butchered, and Poland itself would eventually be lost to the Soviets. When former envoy Arthur Bliss Lane asked the president to do more for Polish independence, Roosevelt tartly replied, "Do you want me to go to war with Russia?"

But a precedent had been set. The president, often accused of being hypocritical, nevertheless remained a practical man who could proceed boldly, and a romantic who could grasp the reins of political symbolism. And here, he was willing to divert considerable airpower when he concluded that the mission was "amply justified," as the director of intelligence for the U.S. Strategic Air Forces had said in summarizing the matter—even if the success of the mission was in grave doubt.

The director of intelligence went on to conclude, "Despite the tangible cost which far outweighed the tangible results achieved . . . one thing stands out, from the president down to the airmen who flew the planes. America wanted to, tried, and did help within her means and possibilities." And as Roosevelt and Churchill had said in their joint statement, "We are thinking of world opinion if the anti-Nazis in Warsaw are in effect abandoned."

ROOSEVELT, MORE THAN ANYONE else on the political scene, had masterfully led the Allies this far; of that there is no doubt. He knew that Hitler's cities were in ruins. In the summer of 1944 alone, Germany had suffered over 1 million dead, wounded, and missing; and earlier, 3 million had already been lost. Hitler may have been readying his last, desperate gamble in the west—the Germans' push in the Ardennes—but

Roosevelt, following the war on the wall charts in the map room, could glimpse the future.

There was no question: The war would soon be won, and if not in 1944, then 1945.

If there were moments when he felt victorious and congratulated himself, that would be understandable.

And at the end of 1944, his administration would have yet one more chance to put an end to the unspeakable cruelties taking place in the thick birch forests of Poland—or at least to make a statement to the world. One last time, his administration would have the chance to wrestle with whether events controlled strategy, or strategy controlled events.

AT THE TREASURY DEPARTMENT, in early November Pehle at last received the entire thirty-page text of the Vrba-Wetzler report, more than six months after the two escapees had first dictated it. Accompanying the document were two other, corroborative reports. Pehle was normally levelheaded, but as he read he grew angry and disgusted and sickened. He now realized that the time for bureaucratic excuses had long since passed. On November 8, once more he contacted McCloy. Appended to his cover note was a copy of the escapees' reports. "No report of Nazi atrocities received by the board has quite caught the gruesome brutality of what is taking place in these camps as have these sober, factual accounts of conditions in Auschwitz and Birkenau," he wrote. "I earnestly hope that you will read these reports."

In his own summary he noted that the destruction of so many victims was "not a simple process." In order to carry out such "murder on a mass production basis" the Nazis had to devote "considerable technological ingenuity and administrative know-how."

Then in perhaps one of the most poignant moments of decision in the war, he pointed out that despite pressures from many sources, he had been hesitant to urge the destruction of the camps by direct military action.

But he was hesitant no longer.

"I am convinced that the point has now been reached where such action is justifiable if it is deemed feasible by competent military authorities." That clause about military authorities was a pro forma statement; there was little doubt what he felt needed to be done. Moreover, to anticipate any hesitance by the military, he then made a strategic case for systematic bombing of the death camps. Krupp, Siemens, and Buna factories ("all within Auschwitz"), which manufactured hand grenade casings, would be destroyed in the operation, along with German barracks and guardhouses and even homes of the leadership. Echoing what Benjamin Akzin had already stressed to him, he wrote that the morale of the Polish underground, vital allies of the United States, would be "considerably strengthened." At the same time, an attack would destroy significant numbers of Nazi soldiers guarding the camp, among the worst of the worst. Last, many of the prisoners could escape in the chaos of battle—and, he added, in this regard there was both evidence and precedent. He appended the recent *New York Times* article on the British bombing of the Amiens prison camp where French Resistance fighters had slipped into the woods or escaped onto the roads.

As Pehle wrote his memo, the mass killings at Auschwitz were finally coming to an end. But in any case, once more McCloy dismissed Pehle's request. McCloy's arguments almost didn't matter; they simply proved the maxim that when the military or the White House didn't want to do something, they would find reasons not to. Nevertheless, the specifics merit scrutiny. On November 18 McCloy wrote that Auschwitz could be hit only by American heavy bombers based in Britain, and that this "would necessitate a hazardous round-trip flight unescorted of approximately 2,000 miles over enemy territory." In any case, he added that the target was "beyond the maximum range" of the Allied bombers and that the mission would entail "unacceptable . . . losses."

He of course made no reference to the Foggia air base in Italy, which reduced the distance by seven hundred miles. He ignored the fact that the round-trip had already been routinely carried out many times by U.S. planes bombing industrial targets throughout the Auschwitz region, and that for each raid a fighter escort had been provided and had proved effective. He of course failed to mention that P38 dive-bombers had made a longer run from their bases in Italy to destroy oil refineries at Ploiesti the previous June. He of course omitted the fact that the Allies had found a way to resupply the partisans of Warsaw.

And he of course made no note of the fact that Auschwitz-Birkenau had already been bombed inadvertently.

The War Department's conclusion, he told Pehle, was "a sound one."

~

In his reply to Pehle, McCloy enclosed the Vrba-Wetzler report without commenting on whether he had read it.

As his biographer Kai Bird notes, McCloy had showed great courage and initiative when dealing with other controversial issues, such as racial discrimination in the army and offering army commissions to veterans of the Lincoln Brigade—but this courage was missing when he dealt with the proposed military strikes against the death camps.

It is hard to imagine a decision weighted with more pathos. Had McCloy ushered the policy to bomb through in mid-August, some 100,000 Hungarian Jews almost certainly would have been given a reprieve from the gas chamber—about 30,000 more people than attended the 2013 Super Bowl, or slightly more than were serving in the Army of the Potomac at the time of the Battle of Gettysburg. If the decision had been made earlier—around July 7—50,000 more would have been spared. As it happened, nearly as many Hungarian Jews were slaughtered as the number of Allied troops that landed on the beaches of Normandy within the first two weeks.

~

Where was the president during all this? Earlier in September, Benjamin Akzin had told Pehle, "I am certain that the president, once acquainted with the facts, would realize the values involved and, cutting through the inertia-motivated objections of the War Department, would order the immediate bombing of the objectives suggested."

So what were the views of the era's most prominent symbol of humanitarianism when he was confronted with the globe's most compelling moral challenge? Here, history records a question mark. True, Roosevelt rarely put his private thoughts to paper and rarely confided his personal feelings to his aides. Yet, was there ever a spontaneous moment during this period when he put his head in his hands in remorse, as he did after the bombing of Pearl Harbor? Or, as the awful information about the ongoing slaughter filtered in, was there ever a time when he muttered under his breath in disgust and indignation? Did he ever pause to weigh the moral implications for history? Many years later McCloy told a journalist that Roosevelt's close adviser and good friend, Harry Hopkins, maintained that "the Boss was not disposed to" order the bombing of the death camp. Nonetheless, Hopkins himself had enjoined McCloy to solicit the advice of the War Department. McCloy indicated that the air force was against the idea of bombing the camps. Insisting that he had "never talked" to the president in person, McCloy said bluntly: "That was the end of that."

However, several years later McCloy, by then elderly and evidently conscience-stricken, gave a different version of what had happened. In an interview with Morgenthau's son, he indicated that he and Roosevelt had talked about whether to bomb Auschwitz. In this account, McCloy said the president felt that the bombing would amount to little except to make the United States seem complicit in the Final Solution, a view some Jews themselves held. Roosevelt then evidently told McCloy that the United States would be accused of "bombing these innocent people," and "we'll be accused of participating in this horrible business." Thus, the president himself denied the request, without offering any other imaginative alternatives.

Is either account true? Both have a ring of plausibility, yet ultimately the record remains unclear. What remains clear is the fact that no such coordinated bombing run took place. Not in June. Not in July. Not in August. Not in September. Not in October. Not in November. Not after the resupply of Warsaw. Not after word leaked out about the daring bombing and rescue of prisoners at the Amiens prison in occupied France. Not after the accidental bombing of Birkenau itself. Not to put an end to the most grisly death machine history had ever recorded, even after the president had all the details about it. Not in the early summer of 1944, when the mission would have been more difficult but would have had the greatest impact. Not in the middle of the summer, when the Allies had indelibly secured a beachhead in France, Paris was liberated, and Romania threw its lot in with the United States. Not after Johan J. Smertenko wrote to the president on July 24, 1944, a month after the Soviets had pounded the Germans on an eight-hundred-mile front in White Russia. Not in the fall, after D-Day, when the bombing operation could have been a far more straightforward affair, even if the operation of the gas chambers was winding down. Not to slow the death machine, as was entirely doable. Not to make a statement to the world that such heinous acts could not go unaddressed. Not as one victim after another victim after another victim after another took off his clothes, listened to the clink of the Zyklon B being activated, and heard the screaming and whimpering of the other victims. Not as the now lifeless bodies were incinerated in the crematoriums or in vast pits of fire.

There is little doubt that the refusal to directly bomb Auschwitz was the president's decision or at least reflected his wishes. He had access to as much information as anyone else in Washington but tragically chose never to the dwell on the issue—or make it his. Many years later, Congressman Emanuel Celler charged that the president failed to provide even a "spark of courageous leadership," and was "silent" and "indifferent." Yet it remains a fact that Roosevelt was absorbed in waging a global conflict, with countless issues tugging at his head and no doubt at his heart. Consumed by the awesome challenge of bringing the war to a close and establishing a structure for peace, in 1944 he seemed to be trapped in the twilight "between knowing and not knowing."

And more immediately, he was also consumed by something else: his rapidly dwindling health and his final race—a reelection campaign for a fourth term.

14

The Wind and the Silence

GERMANY HAD ITS LAST elections in 1938. But by then it was already a one-party state. The Nazis controlled the entire apparatus of government and attempted through that to control every mind as well. In 1938, 99 percent of the vote for the Reichstag went to the National Socialist German Workers Party. Opposition, where it existed, was dealt with swiftly and brutally. Lest anyone miss the point, six leading pamphleteers and graffiti artists of the White Rose, a nonviolent anti-Nazi protest movement, were summarily rounded up by the Gestapo and beheaded. Elsewhere, even Great Britain had postponed its parliamentary races because of the exigencies of wartime, and there had been no elections in Europe at all. In the United States, however, 1944 was a regular election year.

Indeed, since the United States entered the war, there had already been three congressional and hundreds of state elections. A presidential election in wartime had happened only once before—in 1864, during some of the bloodiest battles of the Civil War, including the ghastly Wilderness campaign. But the Constitution had no provision for suspending federal elections. Now, with an almost unparalleled belief in himself, Franklin Roosevelt, the American commander in chief, prepared to seek an unprecedented fourth term in office.

Roosevelt, however, announced none of this. His campaign was a phantom. In public, he said nothing; he did nothing; he barely acknowledged that it was an election year. He brushed off every question with quips such as "There is no news on that today," or "I am not going to talk about it now anymore than I did before." Otherwise, he was as silent as Calvin Coolidge. He became the nominee by consensus, for the most part enthusiastic, but not always. The first hurdle had been cleared in January, when a thundering political circus, the annual Southern Governors' Conference—all the members were Democrats, but nearly all very far to the right of Roosevelt—was held in Washington. At the closing, the governor of North Carolina emerged and noted bluntly, "We go into meetings and cuss him [Roosevelt] out, but we just can't figure out any other answer than Roosevelt in 1944."

The Democratic National Committee was far more eager. In January 1944, its members unanimously called on the president to serve another term as "the great world leader." But the convention was not until July. There were months for machinations to take place. Actually, some of the maneuvering was not on the Democratic side, where Roosevelt was completely unopposed, but among the Republicans. Their party had spent nearly twelve years out of the White House, and their anxiety was palpable. Candidates were trotted forward, starting with Wendell Willkie, who failed in the early competition for delegates. Then there was a wave of enthusiasm for the charismatic Pacific commander, General Douglas MacArthur. The plan was to keep him under wraps until he could be drafted at the convention. But that bubble burst when a Nebraska congressman published correspondence in which he had forcefully attacked the New Deal, and MacArthur had concurred, referring to "our present chaos and confusion." Shortly thereafter, MacArthur declared his lack of interest in the nomination saying that his place as a high-ranking officer was not in politics but in battle.

That left the Republicans with Thomas Dewey, now Governor of New York, as Roosevelt had been in 1932. Dewey was young, just forty-two and successful, and a captivating speaker. He had once thought of becoming a professional singer, and now he used his vocal skills in speeches, where each word seemed to glide mellifluously off his tongue. But he also had, in the words of James MacGregor Burns, "a reputation for being stiff, humorless, overbearing"; and Alice Roosevelt Longworth described him as looking like "the little man on the wedding cake." But Dewey had a plan of attack. In his convention speech, he chastised the Democrats for having grown "old and tired and stubborn and quarrelsome in office." And of course the chief Democrat, the face of the party, was President Franklin Roosevelt.

There is no doubt that Roosevelt liked being president. He liked the crowds, the outpouring of affection. He fed off the attention of the press corps, which frequently seemed to hang breathless on his every word. Being president meant that the world would come to him. There would always be witty dinner conversation, there would always be a line of callers outside the door of his Oval Office, there would always be a devoted self-sacrificing staff ready to do his bidding. But more than that, having been president at the start of World War II, Roosevelt was determined, even desperate, to see it through to its conclusion. He dreamed of succeeding where Woodrow Wilson had so grandly failed. He wanted to leave as his legacy an international organization that would eliminate the scourge of war, a new international order built on the foundation of a permanent peace. He did not want the war to end with the isolationists simply rearising, or with calls for America to once again exit from the world stage. He wanted to manage the war, but most of all he wanted to be the architect of the peace. That had been his mission since his early meetings with Churchill and his first meeting with Stalin. Now, in the summer of 1944, with D-Day complete and U.S. forces steadily moving across France, Roosevelt's goal at last seemed within reach.

He committed himself to the election as late as humanly possible, husbanding his failing energy and shrewdly limiting the time during which the Republicans could make him a target. After all, when he wasn't yet a candidate, all the chatter was focused on him and whether he would run. Any barbs that might have been thrown at him were at worst a sideshow. So he chose July 11, near the end of a press conference, throwing out a teaser: "I have got something else." The president began by reading a letter from the head of the Democratic National Committee, politely asking him to convey his intentions. In the middle, he asked for a cigarette, which his press secretary, Steve Early, dutifully lit. As the president held the letter, his hands trembled. Cigarette ash scattered across his desk. He began his reply: "If the convention should nominate me, I shall accept. If the people elect me, I will serve." He then slyly declared, "For myself, I do not want to run," but "as a good soldier, I repeat that I will accept and serve in this office."

The most important decision of the election was made not by Roosevelt or Dewey, but by a small group of Democratic bosses huddled in the second-floor study at the White House. These men were enjoined with finding a new vice presidential candidate to replace the current officeholder, Henry Wallace, who was deemed by his critics to be too intellectual, too liberal, and too impractical (Roosevelt did not much like him anyway). The bosses didn't quite know what man they wanted, but in light of Roosevelt's failing health, they knew that the vice president was likely to be the president sometime in the next four years, and perhaps sooner rather than later. They definitely did not want the possibility of President Wallace.

Actually, Roosevelt initially wanted Willkie, his former foe and more recently his ally, who would help him create a new political party. But that idea had quickly foundered. Then he proposed Justice William O. Douglas. That too foundered. The men eventually settled on Harry Truman, a senator from Missouri. Roosevelt had mixed emotions about Truman—he thought him too old—but he gave his tacit approval. True to form, however, he neglected to personally inform Wallace about this; it was Eisenhower and Marshall all over again. Also, he still supported one of the other potential nominees for vice president, Bill Douglas. It fell to the head of the Democratic National Committee to wrap things up in Chicago. Scurrying around on the presidential train, the DNC head got Roosevelt to at least place Truman's name before Douglas's in the letter to be delivered to the delegates. But for that switch, the man from Missouri might never have ascended to the ticket.

Truman himself was at first reluctant too—he was backing James Byrnes of South Carolina, who had resigned from the Supreme Court to head the Office of Economic Stabilization—but he signed on after some prodigious arm-twisting, including listening in on a call between Roosevelt and the DNC head, during which Roosevelt said that it would be Truman's "responsibility" if the Democratic Party was broken up "in the middle of a war." Once Truman assented, after a few more late-night phone calls, the convention was poised to nominate him for vice president. When a now sleepless Truman departed the room with his wife on his arm, ringed by a clutch of strangers, security men and gawkers alike, he was "scared to death." Bess Truman, horrified, asked, "Are we going to have to go through this for the rest of our lives?"

Roosevelt himself was not even at the convention. He was making his way by train to San Diego, and he would give his acceptance speech not in person but over the radio, from the observation car of his armor-plated train. The president did not have to worry about the convention-goers; they would back him all the way. His task now was to prove his vitality, his vigor, his command; to dispel all rumors of his failing health; and to remind the American public why they had loved and still loved FDR. His acceptance speech once again displayed his mastery of political theater; it was designed to make his most vulnerable point—his own stamina—into a strength, and to put his opponent squarely on the defensive. "I shall not campaign, in the usual sense, for the office," Roosevelt's voice said, over the loudspeakers. "In these days of tragic sorrow, I do not consider it fitting. And besides, in these days of global warfare, I shall not be able to find the time.

"What is the job before us in 1944?" he went on. "First, to win the war—to win the war fast, to win it overpoweringly. Second, to form worldwide international organizations, and to arrange to use the armed forces of the sovereign Nations of the world to make another war impossible within the foreseeable future. And third, to build an economy for our returning veterans and for all Americans—which will provide employment and provide decent standards of living." Roosevelt closed by quoting from Abraham Lincoln's eloquent second inaugural, speaking of binding up the nation's wounds, and of doing "all which may achieve and cherish a just and lasting peace among ourselves, and with all Nations."

Interestingly, Roosevelt had almost failed to deliver the speech.

Roosevelt had set out for California on what was to be a monthlong journey that would begin in San Diego and continue to Hawaii, where he was scheduled to meet with General Douglas MacArthur to discuss war strategy in the Pacific. The train moved, like all of Roosevelt's trains, slowly. There were leisurely meals, games of gin rummy; there was time to read, and also to do some work. Roosevelt reveled in the cocoon of company and conversation.

The train pulled into San Diego on July 20, 1944. Eleanor prepared to depart; Roosevelt was slated to watch a landing exercise in Oceanside the next day. That night, he would accept, for the fourth time, the Democratic nomination for president of the United States. Roosevelt was going to be joined by one of his sons, Jimmy, for the review. Jimmy was already on board the train as the commander in chief was preparing to depart.

Suddenly, much as had happened at Tehran, Roosevelt's face turned white. "His face took on an agonized look," Jimmy recalled.

"Jimmy, I don't know if I can make it," the president gasped. "I have horrible pains." Jimmy immediately wanted to race for the doctor, but Roosevelt refused. Instead, he insisted it was nothing more than stomach pains and instructed his son to help him from his bed and let him lie flat on the floor. For about ten minutes, the president of the United States lay on the floor of a railroad car. His eyes were closed, his face "drawn." Periodically his torso "convulsed as the waves of pain convulsed him." Jimmy was left to watch, alone, in excruciating silence.

As the minutes passed, the pallor disappeared and Roosevelt's body calmed itself. "Help me up now, Jimmy," he whispered. "I feel better." And as if nothing had happened, Roosevelt allowed himself to be transported to an open car, which headed to a high bluff where he would watch five thousand marines and three thousand navy men practice an invasion on a California beach. Within hours, Roosevelt was delivering his address to the Democratic faithful. The crowd cheered. However, as it happened, the aftermath was hardly cheerful.

After Roosevelt spoke, pool photographers were ushered in to take posed pictures of the president reading his speech. The photographers snapped closed-mouth shots and open-mouth shots; then the film was rushed to Los Angeles, where the AP could process it and transmit it to all the major outlets. The photo the AP editor picked off the roll of negatives showed an open-mouthed Roosevelt, speaking. But when the print was made, this shot showed much more. The president's eyes looked glassy; his face was haggard with exhaustion; his jaw was slack and he looked indescribably spent. Predictably, anti-Roosevelt newspapers used the image; and equally predictably Roosevelt's press secretary, Steve Early, erupted, expelling the photographer who had taken the shot from the remainder of the trip. But there was no returning the image to the darkroom. Thomas Dewey and his supporters would have ample ammunition to make Roosevelt's health an issue, if not the main issue, of the race. And they would be right to do so.

AS ROOSEVELT'S GAUNT IMAGE was being seen across the United States, Germany was concluding a frenzied manhunt. On July 20 a bomb had been detonated in the conference room at Hitler's retreat, Wolf's Lair, while the Führer was attending a briefing with his top military personnel. The thunderous explosion had shattered doors and windows. Glass sliced through the air. Blocks of wood were shredded into splinters, while scraps of paper and other debris rode on plumes of thick smoke. Flames rolled up the walls. Remarkably, the Führer emerged unharmed, suffering only superficial injuries, although his pants were briefly lit on fire and the back of his head was singed. He was one of only two occupants in the room to escape without a concussion.

This was not the first attempt on Hitler's life, but each previous time he had walked away unscathed. The first, rather feeble effort had been made as far back as 1939. It was followed by more elaborate plots. One was a bomb disguised as two bottles of cognac and was placed aboard Hitler's plane, but it inexplicably failed to detonate. Other earlier failed opportunities had included at least one at Wolf's Lair itself. However, the July 20 was to be the final, most definitive plot, carried out by an elegant, aristocratic colonel, Claus Schenk Graf von Stauffenberg. A former supporter of National Socialism, he had first begun to turn against the regime in 1938, over its drive toward war. The rising barbarity of the Nazi regime, particularly the reports of wholesale slaughter of Ukrainian Jews by the SS, intensified his opposition. A veteran of the North Africa campaign—there he had lost his right eye and right hand—Stauffenberg joined the July 20 conspirators initially as a plotter, and then, when a promotion gave him access to Hitler, became the designated assassin. His goal was to deliver Germany from the clutches of the Nazis. Of his own role, he said, "The man who has the courage to do something must do it in the knowledge that he will go down in German history as a traitor. If he does not do it, however, he will be a traitor to his own conscience."

He was right. But instead of Hitler's body being pulled from the wreckage, the lead conspirators were tracked down, rounded up, and shot by firing squad, illuminated by the headlights of parked cars—or hanged from giant meat hooks. The bodies were then dragged off to be buried. By the following morning, Himmler had issued orders to have the dead men exhumed and cremated. The last attempt to depose Hitler had literally gone up in a puff of ash.

One of Germany's greatest generals, the famed Desert Fox, Erwin Rommel, was implicated in the plot; the SS forced him to take poison.

Now the only way Hitler would be overthrown was when Allied tanks finally reached Berlin.

~

In San Diego, Roosevelt anxiously awaited details of the attempted assassination. And at midnight on July 21 he began his journey to Pearl Harbor to meet with General Douglas MacArthur. Under cover of darkness, a navy cruiser, the *Baltimore*, began evasive maneuvers, leaving the port and heading toward the open Pacific. Always a naval man at heart, Roosevelt was glad to be on the water, sailing toward a new destination.

At Pearl Harbor, the pier was mobbed. Hawaiians had turned out en masse, and sailors lined the rails of the ships, standing at attention. Cheers erupted when they spotted the dignitaries. Admiral Nimitz and others came up the gangplank to greet their commander in chief on the quarterdeck. Only one military man was absent—the head of the war in the Pacific, Douglas MacArthur. Imperious, overbearing, a riddle of a man, he had planned his own entrance. To the sound of police sirens, MacArthur arrived in a long, open-topped black car. A military driver was at the wheel, and MacArthur, in his trademark leather jacket, was seated in the back. There was a second round of mighty applause. But the commander in chief wasn't in the mood to be awed. "Hello, Doug," Roosevelt said. "What are you doing with that leather jacket on? It's a darn hot day."

MacArthur could only bluster, "Well, I've just landed from Australia. It's pretty cold there."

With the war winding down in Europe, Roosevelt now talked about strategy in the Pacific with his commanders—whether to attack the island of Formosa and the Chinese coast or to bypass Formosa and focus on liberating the Philippines (MacArthur's preference). He also made time to tour the island's military installations, including a military hospital with a ward for amputees. Once inside, Roosevelt requested a Secret Service agent to push him gingerly past the beds where, as Sam Rosenman observed, young men lay, missing one or both legs. Offering cheering smiles and a few words, the president said nothing in particular about his own withered, useless legs, but they were on full view. The message was clear: the president had once risen crippled from a bed and had embarked on a new life. So might they too. "I never saw Roosevelt with tears in his eyes," Rosenman recounted. "That day as he was wheeled out of the hospital, he was close to them."

The military issues were quickly resolved. One participant thought Roosevelt was "at his best." But privately, MacArthur reached a different, troubling conclusion. The general told his wife, "He is just a shell of the man I knew. In six months, he will be in his grave."

During the journey to Hawaii there had been inevitable rumors about the president's health. Talk had already spread across Washington: Roosevelt had had a clandestine operation for cancer while he had been at Hobcaw; others darkly hinted that he had had a stroke or a major heart attack. There was so much speculation that at one point Secret Service agent Mike Reilly had allowed reporters to watch Roosevelt from a distance in South Carolina, just to refute claims that the president was actually in a hospital in Boston or Chicago. Now, while Roosevelt was in Hawaii, Harry Hopkins wired to the president, saying that an FBI agent stationed on the island had told J. Edgar Hoover the Pacific trip had been scrubbed because Roosevelt was unwell. The president's next stop on his journey was the island of Adak, a U.S. military base off the western coast of Alaska. Then it was back to the mainland and Washington state for a final stop before the train ride home.

Whether it was because of the rumors about his health, or because of his own need to prove himself, or because his personality that fed on the adulation of a live crowd, the president did not want to start his train trip back to Washington, D.C., without first giving a large public address. He originally asked for a baseball stadium, but the Secret Service flinched. Harry Hopkins cabled, suggesting the deck of the destroyer that had taken him over the ocean, with the large guns as the backdrop for the speech. Roosevelt eagerly said yes. The audience was to be ten thousand dockyard workers at the Bremerton shipyard, plus a radio audience across the nation.

Roosevelt was determined to stand up as he spoke, but it was several months since he had last stood, and in the interval his legs had become more emaciated, with muscle wasting over the bone, so his braces no longer fit. He could barely keep his balance. There was a furious wind, and the deck rocked, so the president had to clutch his lectern and was barely able to turn the pages of his speech. His voice, usually sonorous, was in the words of biographer James MacGregor Burns, "tepid and halting," and the speech itself "rambling." Even more worrisome was what was happening to Roosevelt's body as he spoke. For the first fifteen minutes, a vise-like pain clenched his chest and diffused to both shoulders. The president was sweating profusely. Slowly, after many long minutes, these symptoms faded. It was an attack of angina—the only one he would ever suffer, but more than ever, his health was in a perilous state. When he left the deck, he returned to the captain's quarters and dropped almost motionless into a chair. Dr. Bruenn took a blood sample and ran an electrocardiograph. He found nothing to indicate permanent damage, but nevertheless prescribed rest for the entire journey home, and Roosevelt agreed.

Following the speech, the *Washington Post* offered, in effect, Roosevelt's political obituary, noting, "It looks like the old master has lost his touch," and adding that "his campaigning days must be over."

Five days after his return to Washington, Roosevelt was at Hyde Park. But the rest he sought was still elusive. The house was packed with guests. "The President still a little tense and nervous," Hassett observed, "not yet rested from his five weeks' trip into the Pacific area via land and sea. Too many visitors at mealtime—all ages, sexes, and previous conditions of servitude—hardly relaxing for a tired man." Even Eleanor noticed, recording, "Pa complains of feeling tired and I think he looks older. I can't help worrying about his heart."

But as the rumors about his health spread, Roosevelt's temper was up. He became incensed and energized. He would not be written off. Newsman David Brinkley would later note, "For months, he had seemed withdrawn and depressed, taking little interest in anything, unwilling to contribute more than a written statement now and then to his campaign. But for a moment in the fall of 1944 he regained his strength, driven by his hatred for Thomas E. Dewey."

EVENTS IN THE REST of the world were not waiting for either Franklin Roosevelt or the November 1944 election. Since early June, even though the German war machine was slowly and inexorably retreating from northern France, all across Europe trains had continued to chug north and east, past once glittering Vienna, past Kraków, pulling into the Auschwitz station. The script was the same. The disabled, the sick, the pregnant, children as well as old people, were still being gassed at the astounding rate of two thousand every thirty minutes—so that in a matter of hours more people were lost than in the entire first day's assault at Normandy. After a brief slowdown in July, the gas chambers were now working at full speed again.

On August 1, the conquered Poles defiantly rose up against the Germans in the city of Warsaw. Shortly thereafter, in Amsterdam, Gestapo agents were now coming, their boots pounding through the streets and up the stairs to the secret annex where the family of Otto Frank had been hiding. And awaiting them was Otto's daughter Anne. She, with the rest of her family, would board the last deportation train from the Netherlands to Auschwitz.

ON AUGUST 23, AS the Germans were bringing heavy mortars, incendiary rockets, and a remote-controlled vehicle mine into Warsaw in a further attempt to break the uprising, and Paris, the city of light, was being liberated by the Allies, Roosevelt was back for a brief stay in Washington, D.C. With Eleanor still in Hyde Park, Roosevelt spent an hour of the afternoon with Lucy Mercer Rutherfurd, along with her daughter and stepson, and Roosevelt's daughter Anna. They gathered on the South Portico and were served tea and biscuits. Returning to Hyde Park a week later, Roosevelt had his train take a different route and stopped at Lucy's estate in northern New Jersey. He even had her listen in as he spoke by phone with Churchill. The two heads of state were to meet, this time in Quebec, the following day, for their seventh summit. Churchill said he would be bringing his wife and Roosevelt replied that he would bring Eleanor. Afterward, the president asked the Secret Service if this New Jersey route could be used now and again to get to Hyde Park. After a study, the agents replied yes.

The Quebec summit of September 1944 was the start of a grueling fall season. At that time, the combined military chiefs were projecting that Germany would surrender within twelve weeks—by Christmas. Roosevelt apparently remained more skeptical, but he was still quite intent on establishing zones of occupation, and he was even willing to have the Americans take on the task of overseeing France. What to do about postwar Germany was more vexing. How, he wondered, to extract retribution and neutralize any future German threat, without sowing the seeds for another world war, as had happened after World War I?

From the Treasury Department, Henry Morgenthau again memorably offered his ideas: he wanted to see Germany divided into small states, then turned into a primarily agrarian, pastoral nation, devoid of heavy industry, with its coal mines closed and its factories dismantled, and in this way it would be incapable of waging future wars. Churchill was initially resistant, but by the second day he signed on, as did an enthusiastic Roosevelt. The president hotly told Stimson: "The German people as a whole must have it driven home to them that the whole nation has been engaged in a lawless campaign against the decency of modern civilization." Still, when news of the plan reached Washington after a series of press leaks, an uproar followed. Stimson at the War Department and Hull at the State Department were aghast. It was, Stimson said, "Semitism gone wild," and Hull thought it would guarantee resistance of the bitter-enders, those Germans who would fight to the last. Republicans jumped on the plan as a possible campaign attack, and Roosevelt promptly abandoned it. Within two weeks, he was stating that he had "no idea" how the plan could have been initiated.

Was this Roosevelt's masterly sleight of hand? Was he covering his tracks? Was it a further indication of his dwindling health? Churchill, who had himself just recovered from pneumonia, was so worried during the summit that he sought out Dr. McIntire to ask about the president. McIntire insisted Roosevelt was fine. But one of Churchill's aides, his physician Lord Moran, noted, "You could have put your fist between his neck and his collar—and I said to myself then that men at his time of life do not go thin all of a sudden just for nothing."

As the two leaders were leaving Quebec, there were new reports of mounting German resistance. The prediction that only twelve weeks remained until the war's end was now nothing more than an illusion.

After Quebec, there was a brief visit by the Churchills to Hyde Park. The prime minister kept his usual owlish hours and both leaders stayed up until 1 a.m. But when the Churchills had departed, Roosevelt took to his bed at 7 p.m. with strict instructions not to be awoken until the morning.

Meanwhile, Thomas Dewey was basing his campaign on his accusation that the U.S. government was being run by "tired old men." For many, it was hard to disagree with that assessment.

Roosevelt knew that he had to change the tenor and the direction of his own campaign. And he had less than eight weeks to do it.

THE NEW STATLER HOTEL was a popular destination during the last years of World War II. It was the place for conventions, ceremonial dinners, and speeches; the place where "plaques were awarded, backs were slapped and hands shaken." Located at 1001 Sixteenth Street, it was only a few blocks from the White House, and it had been specifically designed with the current occupant of 1600 Pennsylvania Avenue in mind. The Presidential Room had a spacious secure elevator to the mezzanine level, and a special entrance from the street to the massive elevator itself. Indeed, a presidential limousine could drive directly into the elevator and be "lifted" inside the hotel. Then, in complete privacy, the president could be carried from his car, transferred to his wheelchair, and whisked to a head table, out of sight from the watchful eyes of the press corps or anyone else. Not unsurprisingly, groups planning a dinner and expecting the president of the United States to attend went out of their way to reserve the Presidential Room at the Statler.

So it was that the Teamsters Union would hold a banquet at the Statler on September 23, 1944, and Franklin Roosevelt would be there to give the address.

After the nearly disastrous outing at Bremerton, the stakes for this speech were very high. The night before it, the president doggedly practiced using his braces—Sam Rosenman poignantly recalled, "He was literally trying to learn to walk again."—Roosevelt leaned against Dr. McIntire, but his emaciated limbs could barely support him, and it soon became clear that the only way Roosevelt could make the speech was sitting in his wheelchair.

The room was packed and the crowd was primed. As Roosevelt was introduced, his daughter, Anna, asked Rosenman in a hushed voice, "Do you think Pa will pull it over?" Throughout the hall, hundreds of burly unionists and Washington bureaucrats and activists slid back their seats "from their dinner tables" and waited. FDR began, slightly discordantly, but slowly warming to the speech with each word. "You know," he joked, drawing out the syllables for emphasis, "I am actually four years older, which is a fact that seems to an-noy some people." He continued, "In fact, in the mathematical field there are millions of Americans who are more" (another drawn-out word) "than eleven" (heavy emphasis) "years older than when we started to clear up the mess that was dumped into our laps in 1933." The room erupted, and Roosevelt, like a comedian after delivering a punch line, sat back.

It was a speech to the faithful, deriding Republicans who attacked labor for three and a half years and then embraced it in the few months before an election. He called his opponent "a fraud," and added, "We have all seen many marvelous stunts in the circus but no performing elephant could turn a hand-spring without falling flat on its back." And he noted, "If I were a Republican leader speaking to a mixed audience, the last word in the whole dictionary that I think I would use is that word 'depression.' " Roosevelt was in full swing and the crowd was transfixed. There were huzzahs, there was laughter, and one excited teamster began to beat a silver tray with a soup ladle. "The old master still had it," wrote a reporter for *Time* magazine. "He was like a veteran virtuoso playing a piece he had loved for years. . . . The President was playing what he loves to play—politics."

And the final barb was yet to come: Roosevelt powered through to the crescendo: "These Republican leaders have not been content with attacks—on me, or my wife, or on my sons. No, not content with that, they now attack my little dog, Fala. Well of course, I don't resent attacks, and my family doesn't resent attacks, but"—a brief pause—"Fala does resent them." Roosevelt added, "I think I have a right to resent, to object to libelous statements about my dog." That one evening was like magic, erasing months of speculation and returning the Roosevelt of old to the spotlight. But Dewey continued to press his case, and Roosevelt knew he needed to score an additional blow to have a real chance at a knockout. The blow would be a tour of New York City. The date was Saturday, October 21.

~

MEANWHILE, ON OCTOBER 2, the Polish underground army surrendered in Warsaw. About 200,000 Poles had died in the uprising; some wounded insurgents were burned alive in field hospitals by the advancing Germans. About 55,000 Poles were sent to concentration camps, and another 150,000 were transported to forced labor camps in Germany. The Germans reported 26,000 casualties: killed, wounded, or missing. In the following weeks, widespread looting began. As in the Soviet Union, the Nazis exacted vengeance. All raw materials, fine clothes, and even dining-room tables remaining in the embattled city were to be transported out; what was still left was to be leveled or demolished, either by fire or by specially placed German bombs.

~

THE SPECIAL PRESIDENTIAL TRAIN from Washington pulled into New York at 7 a.m. Roosevelt was slated to tour four boroughs—Brooklyn,

Queens, the Bronx, and, of course, Manhattan—in an open car with the top down. New York, however, was being drenched by the remnants of a hurricane. Streets were flooded; sidewalks and buildings were soaked. There was a cold, driving rain. Nevertheless, Roosevelt was determined not to change his plans. He began in Brooklyn with a stop at Ebbets Field, where, in his braces, he arduously made his way to a lectern behind second base, affirming his allegiance to the Dodgers and praising Senator Bob Wagner. The rain continued to fall in sheets as Roosevelt stood, his legs in the grip of his braces, his glasses fogged, and his hair matted to his head. Afterward, the soaked, shivering president got an improvised massage and warm clothes from a Coast Guard motor pool.

Then the tour continued, despite Dr. McIntire's strenuous pleas, with the car's top down. More than anyone else, Roosevelt knew what the crowds had come to see. They wanted a glimpse of a vibrant president, smiling even as his shirt was plastered to his outstretched arm by the pounding rain. It spilled off his fedora and ran in rivulets down his face. His suit was soaked. But the president, his adrenaline flowing, happily continued smiling and waving, and the people, gazing out from beneath their umbrellas, roared in reply. By mid-afternoon, the ride was over. A tired but ecstatic Roosevelt made his way to Eleanor's apartment on Washington Square, where Dr. McIntire suggested a shot of bourbon to warm up the shivering president. Roosevelt had three. It was his first visit to his wife's New York City home. She gave him a brief tour, pointing out that there were no stairs and that two rooms connected by a bath could be shut off from the rest of the apartment, in case he ever wanted to stay. In the afternoon, Roosevelt, finally dry, took a nap. Then he eased into a hot bath. That night, at the Waldorf Astoria, he was to address two thousand members of the Foreign Policy Association.

Roosevelt used the speech to once again muster support for a Council of the United Nations and to describe it as an organization that was central to his vision for a postwar world. After ad-libbing a story about how far U.S.-Soviet relations had advanced, he stated unequivocally that peacekeeping was to be a central tenet. "Peace, like war, can succeed only where there is a will to enforce it and where there is available power to enforce it," he insisted. The council "must have the power to act quickly and decisively to keep the peace by force, if necessary." Roosevelt then used one of his favorite techniques, the homespun analogy: "A policeman would not be a very effective policeman if, when he saw a felon break into a house, he had to go to the Town Hall and call a town meeting to issue a warrant before the felon could be arrested. So to my simple mind it is clear that, if the world organization is to have any reality at all, our American representative must be endowed in advance by the people themselves, by constitutional means through their representatives in the Congress, with authority to act." The crowd gave Roosevelt a standing ovation and overwhelming cheers. Below him, on a special track, his train was waiting to carry him to Hyde Park.

Roosevelt's aide, Hassett, noted that after the day with adoring crowds, "The President is in the pink of condition this morning. No trace of a cold, not even a sniffle," while Mayor Fiorello La Guardia had taken to his bed, and many of the Secret Service agents were sick. "Not so the Boss. He's madder than hell, his Dutch is up, and nothing will stop him now." Hassett added, "All my own fears and misgivings about the President's health . . . vanished like the morning dew."

Roosevelt made three more major stops: another ride in an open car through Philadelphia; a speech at Soldier Field in Chicago, with 100,000 people listening inside and another 100,000 outside, fighting against a cold lake wind; and Fenway Park in Boston. The speech at Fenway Park was to be his last major address, the concluding capstone of his political career. Four years earlier, he had promised America's mothers that he would keep their sons out of "foreign wars." Now he spoke of how Americans of all ethnicities and creeds were fighting together "all over the world." And he noted that "any real, red-blooded American" would have chosen to fight "when our own soil was made the object of a sneak attack." The crowd applauded, and Roosevelt basked in the campaign spotlight for a final time.

The next day, he would make the rounds near Hyde Park and deliver one more campaign radio address to the nation. Then there was nothing left to do but perform the usual ritual: sit at the dining table and tabulate the election results. Tally sheets were placed at the seats, pencils were arranged on tables, and cider and doughnuts were served. In staccato bursts, the big radio and the news tickers began to report. Neighbors came by to cheer the president at 11 p.m. and Roosevelt, sitting on the portico, greeted them as a photographer caught the moment for posterity. The president's voluminous cape was draped over the sides of his chair to cover the wheels. His trousers hung in deep folds from his crossed legs, and one ankle was clearly visible. The ankle was also clearly swollen, bulging out over his shoe, a sign of pooling blood and a failing heart. Beneath his fedora, his eyes were rimmed with gray, and the skin below them looked almost bruised; his weary face also looked pinched and hollow. But the jubilant crowd did not see what the photograph saw. And Roosevelt would not succumb, not that night. He waited up until after 3 a.m., when it was clear that the nation was going his way. He would be president of the United States for an unprecedented fourth term.

Dewey made his concession statement at 3:16, and Roosevelt readied himself for bed around four o'clock. Hassett strolled over to his boss to say good night, and the president gave his last pronouncement on the evening: "I still think he is a son-of-a-bitch."

WHILE HITLER WAS LEAVING his headquarters at Wolf's Lair for the last time and boarding a train for Berlin, in Washington, D.C., thirty thousand people waited outside Union Station under a torrential rain for Roosevelt to return, victorious, from Hyde Park. Here, as during that fateful campaign day in New York, the president insisted that his car top be down. His outgoing vice president, Henry Wallace, and his incoming vice president, Harry Truman, wedged themselves into the car along with him. Roosevelt's young grandson, Johnnie Boettiger, rode in the front. A band played; police motorcycles led the escort. Along the route to the White House, the crowds swelled to 300,000, including federal employees and schoolchildren who had been given the day off to welcome the president back. The electoral votes were decisive: 432 to

99 for Roosevelt—although the difference in the popular vote was only 3.6 million out of 48 million, the narrowest reelection since Woodrow Wilson's in 1916. Still, the president had a wealth of new allies in Congress, where leading conservatives and isolationists had been turned out of office. It was, for the president, as much a referendum on his sweeping vision of a postwar world governed by a United Nations as it was a victory for him personally.

But as buoyant as the day's spirit was, as much as Roosevelt felt free to laugh with the newsman who asked if he would run again in 1948, there was an undercurrent of unease. Although the president's blood pressure had actually dropped when he was on the campaign trail feeding off the adulation of the crowds, and although an exam two weeks after the vote found clear lungs, good heart sounds, and a blood pressure of 210/112, Roosevelt was tired. His appetite was withering, and his skin was chalkier and far grayer. And neither the war nor the peace was fully won.

FOR THE ALLIED ARMIES crossing France and the Low Countries, there was no blitzkrieg equivalent against the Germans. After the German Seventh Army was destroyed at Normandy, an SS panzer division in the south retaliated by massacring the entire town of Oradour-sur-Glâne. For now, Allied forces, despite having thirty-seven divisions, over 7,500 tanks, 6,000 bombers, 5,000 fighters, and 2,000 transport aircraft, lacked a major port. Nearly every bit of ammunition, every drop of fuel, every spare part, and every can of food had to be off-loaded in Normandy. This difficult supply line, combined with the continuing shafts of German resistance as Allied forces drew closer to the border, dashed hopes for an immediate end to the war; actually, interviews with young captured German officers revealed that they still fancifully believed in an eventual victory for the Nazis. Even in Italy, the Germans still clung on, holding two Allied armies at bay. And the Führer, when he wasn't directing fictional armies that didn't exist, had a plan for the

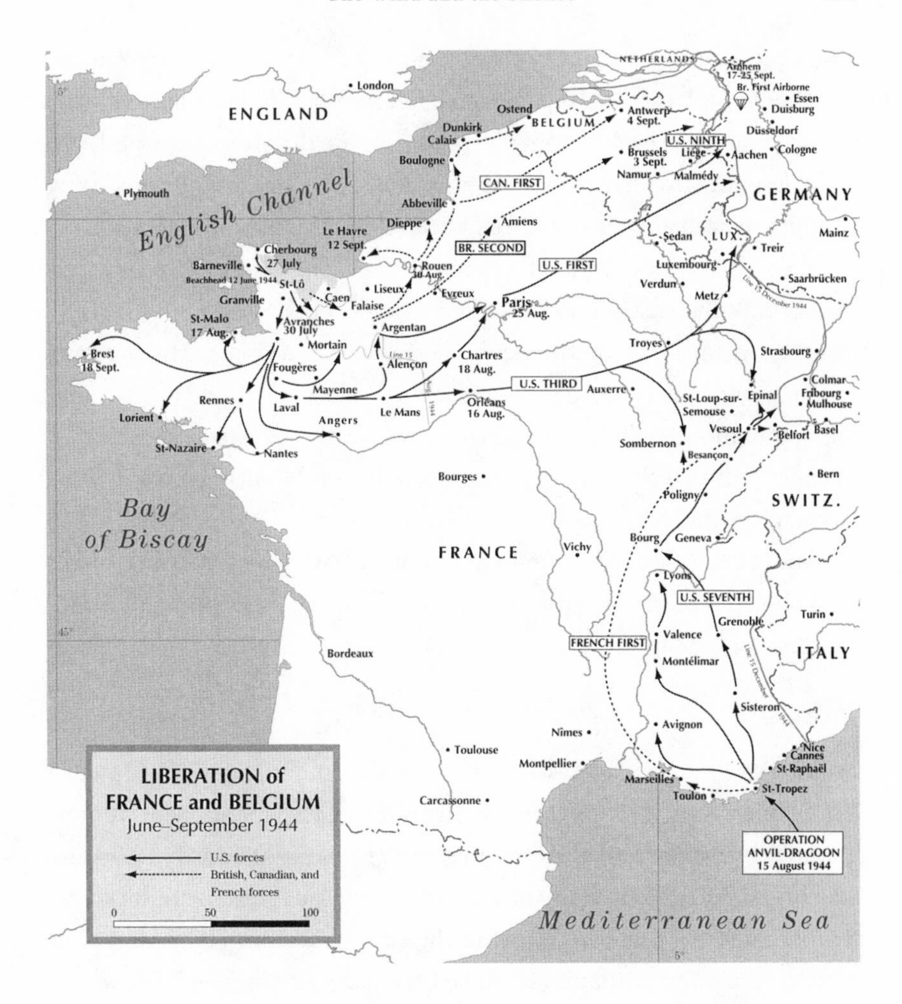

ones that did: wait until bad weather set in, lay a trap for the advancing enemy forces, and watch the U.S.-British alliance with Stalin crack.

It was a footling gesture. The desperate German commanders, whose troops now pathetically included boys from the Hitler Youth and old men, raced to reinforce towns, bridges, and ports and form defensive lines in the Allies' path, yet Germany's leadership was breaking down at the top. In early September, Hitler had repeatedly spoken of discomfort in his right eye, the legacy of von Stauffenberg's assassination attempt at Wolf's Lair. During the following weeks he had fluctuating blood pressure, tremors in his hands and legs, swollen ankles, dizziness, and then violent stomach spasms that left him bedridden. He developed jaundice, and by mid-October he was described by those around him as lifeless; he also had lost sixteen pounds. His heart was weakening and his tremors almost certainly indicated Parkinson's disease. Even his vocal cords were affected. His mood swings, phobias, and hysteria intensified. But as historian Ian Kershaw notes, Hitler "was not clinically insane." So was there pathology? There was—and not in Hitler alone; it was present in the broader leadership, "backed by much of a gullible population," which had undertaken to conquer and cleanse all of Europe. But now the Allied armies were inexorably driving toward the German borders.

And outside of his crumbling empire of war, his cherished other empire—his empire of death, the vast network of labor and death camps—was about to come under an assault. Finally.

AUSCHWITZ HAD NOT REALIZED its full potential until 1943, when the Belzec camp near the city of Lvov had been abandoned, and attempted uprisings had derailed the killing operations in Sobibór and Treblinka. After that Majdanek had been closed. Auschwitz-Birkenau then became the center of death in the eastern region. There were four new crematoriums, numbered II, III, IV, and V. Numbers IV and V, tucked away behind the camp's tall trees, became known as the "forest crematoriums." Their designers constantly sought modifications to make them more deadly, for example, by proposing heating systems that would warm the Zyklon B and thus speed the killing process. At peak capacity, the crematoriums could dispose of up to 4,756 corpses daily. Numbers II and III were the largest, each capable of reducing 1,440 bodies at a time to a gray blend of bone and ash. But even this capacity could not match the killing. Where the planners had expected two bodies, five would appear, lifted on hoists or carted in tubs, arms and legs sticking out at odd angles, hair shorn, teeth wrenched out for the gold fillings, fingers sliced to remove the rings. By the time the corpses reached the incinerators they were only remnants of humans.

As bodies were shoved in the ovens the chimneys repeatedly failed because of the massive overheating, so that the *Sonderkommando* were forced to burn the remains in vast open trenches. There, it took hours for the flames to eat their way through the corpses.

Life expectancy in the *Sonderkommando* was short; about eight months at most. Some of its members lived little more than a few weeks. When their usefulness was done, they were shot or gassed. Many took their own lives early on. The SS required hardy men for the *Sonderkommando*, and many of the members they recruited had once been part of the French Resistance and the Polish Communist underground. As early as the summer of 1943, the *Sonderkommando* members began forming secret units of their own. Nearly a year later, their plan was daring, even foolhardy, but certainly courageous: capture weapons, destroy the crematoriums, and organize a breakout; their strategy was written in a small notebook and buried underground in a jar.

They plotted—three girls smuggled explosives into Birkenau in a food tray with a false bottom—but it was the SS that ultimately chose the moment of confrontation. Discovering two hundred of the *Sonderkommando* after an attempted escape, the SS murdered them with cyanide in a storage room. Then others in the *Sonderkommando* were told to personally select three hundred more of their men for "evacuation"; October 7, 1944, was the day announced for transport to another camp, ostensibly to work there. But the men who loaded the ovens knew better. They knew this would be a day for death. And they knew they needed to act quickly.

It was either them or the SS.

At 1:30 in the afternoon, as a group of SS men were walking toward Crematorium IV, the *Sonderkommando*, shouting "Hurrah!" and armed with stones, axes, and iron bars, set upon them and threw one of the SS into the flames. While the SS men sought cover behind a barbed-wire fence, the insurgents torched hundreds of straw mattresses near

Crematorium IV, setting it ablaze. Then, with smuggled hand grenades, they blew up the building and its ovens. Nazi reinforcements quickly arrived on motorcycles, and the SS set up machine guns, firing into the crowd and driving fleeing prisoners into Crematorium IV. Near Crematorium II, some six hundred of the *Sonderkommando* cut the barbed wire and fled into the forest, through the fish hatcheries and the farmsteads along the Sola river. The alarm screeched and the SS surrounded the area. Nevertheless, some escapees made it. But when the SS found one group hiding in a barn, they locked it and set it on fire, roasting everyone inside alive—and shooting any who somehow ran out. The Jewish women who had smuggled the explosives from their work camp under their clothes and given them to the *Sonderkommando* were tortured—they never broke—and eventually hanged. At their execution, they betrayed no fear.

At least 425 of the *Sonderkommando* died in the insurrection. But the insurgents drew blood as well, killing three SS corporals and injuring twelve more.

And Crematorium IV was now gone. Remarkably, what the Allies had failed to do, the inmates themselves succeeded in accomplishing—in part. However, the remaining three crematoriums continued, sending ash and smoke into the sky. Two days after the revolt, four thousand Jewish women were gassed and burned, two thousand from an incoming transport along with another two thousand "specially" selected from those already confined at Birkenau. By the month's end, in just thirty-one days, more than thirty-three thousand Jews had been gassed, a pace not seen since the Hungarian transports.

IT DID NOT MATTER that the Führer was frequently bedridden; it did not matter that the U.S. Twelfth Army Group was pushing through the Ardennes forest in France, advancing on the Rhine; it did not matter that the Soviets were within reach of Warsaw; it did not matter that Franklin Roosevelt was riding through the streets of New York in an open car in the driving rain. Absent Allied actions, the way of Auschwitz remained unchanged, except that it began to slow down. And in Hungary, 200,000 Jews at most remained alive.

AS IN CONNECTING THE dots of a puzzle, the outlines and contours of Auschwitz were becoming visible as never before in the fall of 1944—not just to Washington, London, the Vatican, and New York, but to all the world. There had been the reports from Eduard Schulte the Polish government-in-exile as early as July 1942; then the Riegner Telegram; then the BBC reports in the fall of 1943; then Jan Karski's meeting with Roosevelt; then the Vrba-Wetzler report in the late spring and early summer of 1944, corroborated by two later escapees, Czeslaw Mordowicz and Arnost Rosin; then the articles, the radio reports, and the aerial photographs from the Allies' reconnaissance flights. The photographs taken in late June, while McCloy was refusing to bomb Auschwitz, were so detailed that it was possible to see the ramp lined with people walking toward the gas chambers and crematoriums.

By late July, the evidence was even more overwhelming. By then, the Soviets had liberated Majdanek, near Lublin, Poland, the origin of many of the transports to Auschwitz. There, they found gas chambers, innocuously labeled "Bath" and "Disinfection"; they found the crematoriums and the hastily covered-over mass graves. They found bodies along the road leading to and away from the camp. "They were not the bodies of soldiers felled in the heat of battle," recalled a Polish Jew who fought with the Soviet army. "They were the striped-cloth bodies of prisoners, of Jews, gunned down as they ran from the camp in the final hours before it fell. They were thin and hairless, and their clothes little more than rags. Some had died with their eyes open. Others had begun crawling after they were shot."

Inside the camp, inside the low single-story buildings beyond the double rows of electrified barbed wire, the Soviet army found piles of shoes, more than could be counted, "shoes piled like pieces of coal" or "rising in a high mound, like grain." Some shoes had worn-out soles and no laces; some had tumbled down off the high pile and had landed back on the floor. In one room, all the shoes were small, small enough to fit easily in a man's palm. They were baby and toddler shoes; many pairs were evidently the children's first shoes. Along with the shoes, there were piles of human teeth, piles of hair, and piles of eyeglasses with cracked lenses and bent or broken frames. Everywhere, there were piles of things. The Jewish soldier recalled, "When I closed my eyes, I saw those piles of small shoes," adding, "They took the children from their mothers, and they killed them. And they kept the shoes. Even when I slept, I saw the shoes. It was unrelenting." For his part, one *Time* magazine reporter wrote, suddenly everything became "real."

The secrets of Majdanek were gradually unearthed. On November 3, 1943, the Germans had held what they euphemistically called a "Harvest Festival": eighteen thousand people were machine-gunned in a single day in the woods (Vrba was there), while music blared to drown out the killing. But still, for all its horror, Majdanek was not Auschwitz.

Among camps, Auschwitz, where the dead were left with the wind and the silence, stood alone.

By September, members of the *Sonderkommando* had taken photographs inside Auschwitz. Through doorways, they captured fellow *Sonderkommando* prisoners standing alongside burning corpses in the open air. Another photo showed women removing their clothes outside before being herded into the gas chamber. The film was smuggled to the Polish Resistance movement in Kraków. The proof lay everywhere. But proof did not yet make policy. And regarding policy, almost nothing was clear.

ON OCTOBER 10, THE United States and Great Britain had broadcast a joint warning to the Germans, telling them that if mass executions were carried out at the concentration camps of Oswiecim and Brzezinka (Birkenau), all those "from the highest to the lowest" who were in any way involved would be held responsible, and no effort would be spared to bring the guilty to justice. The German telegraph service immediately responded that the reports were "false from beginning to end." The

British thought it "a satisfactory reaction," believing the declaration had made a difference. But in fact it had done little to stem the slaughter. Only the westward advance of the Soviet army at Auschwitz began to quell the fires.

Since the summer of 1944, trains and trucks had been carrying prisoners, piles of personal effects, building materials, and equipment from Poland into Germany and Austria. In effect, even as the Germans desperately sought to cover up their crimes, the process of death, albeit on a lesser scale, was simply being transferred closer to home, to Buchenwald, Flossenburg, Ravensbrück, Dachau, Mauthausen, Gross-Rosen, Bergen-Belsen, Natzweiler, Sachsenhausen, and Neuengamme. On November 26, a panicked Himmler, knowing of the rapid advances of the Allied armies, ordered the crematoriums at Auschwitz to be destroyed. Meanwhile, the motor of Crematorium II was to be crated up and transported to Mauthausen, as was its ventilation system. Its gas infrastructure was designated for Gross-Rosen. By November 29, aerial reconnaissance photos taken from a high altitude by U.S. planes showed Crematorium II being taken apart and also revealed that the Birkenau rail line was empty. No train was waiting to unload a human cargo.

Then came the methodical disposal of the evidence. As the prisoners continued to provide forced labor, the trenches where the corpses had been burned had to be filled in and leveled. On December 5, while snow was falling, fifty female Jewish prisoners were selected. Their orders: dig out every corpse that had been tossed into mass graves around Crematorium IV, the one that had been destroyed during the *Sonderkommando* revolt. Once the bodies were exhumed, they would be burned in open pits, despite the frigid temperatures and blanketing snowfall. Next, the cuts in the earth and the hollow places that had been repositories for human remains and broken-up skeletons had to be emptied, covered in turn, and masked with fresh plantings.

Crematorium I, its ovens taken apart, became an air-raid bunker. Its chimney, and the ceiling holes from which the gas settled, simply disappeared. The passageway between the gas chamber and the ovens was sealed and shut. As Benjamin Akzin had predicted, this process of destruction continued. By December 21, many of the guard towers and electrified fences around Birkenau had been taken down, as well as the fences around the crematoriums. Even the roof of one of the undressing rooms had been removed. But in a cruel twist of fate, what the gas chambers had not done, the cold and the deplorable conditions now slowly did: over two thousand women died during December in Auschwitz.

THIS METHODICAL DISMANTLING WAS begun just as the Nazi war machine was making a daring attack on Allied forces in the west. It came in the Ardennes and was to be known as the Battle of the Bulge. Again, this was a puzzle with the dots waiting to be connected. When refugees told the Allied forces that the Germans were massing tanks and armored vehicles, no one pursued the reports, which seem to have been discounted. Similarly, when German U-boats based in the Atlantic and Baltic sent large numbers of weather reports the intercepts were ignored, as were transmissions of the Germans' requests for aerial photos of the region around the Meuse. The prevailing view at the Allies' headquarters was that the Germans were using the Ardennes as a resting place, that they were going to pull back to the eastern front, and that they lacked enough fuel to mount any attack, let alone a winter assault. Great Britain's General Montgomery (not unlike Rommel, who went home with shoes for his wife on D-Day) planned a Christmas visit to England and had dispensed with his nightly situation conferences "until the war becomes more exciting."

The attack on the western front was Hitler's last ditch, desperate effort. It began at 6 a.m. on December 16 with an hour-long artillery barrage against the least defended section of the Allies' line, a section held by some of the greenest troops of the war. When the Waffen SS and the elite panzer armies appeared out of the frigid mist, "the result," according to one military historian, "was complete . . . panic, and shock." The Germans had taken advantage of a heavy forest and an impenetrable fog, and the attack was a total surprise. Within days, the key crossroad at the town of Bastogne was at risk. As if it were 1939, the Germans demanded that the 101st Airborne surrender; Brigadier General Anthony McAuliffe tersely replied: "Nuts!" He would not. Meanwhile, Eisenhower acted quickly. Like Robert E. Lee during the American Civil War, he split his forces, giving the divisions north of the German breakthrough over to General Montgomery. All those to the south would be under the command of an American, General Omar Bradley.

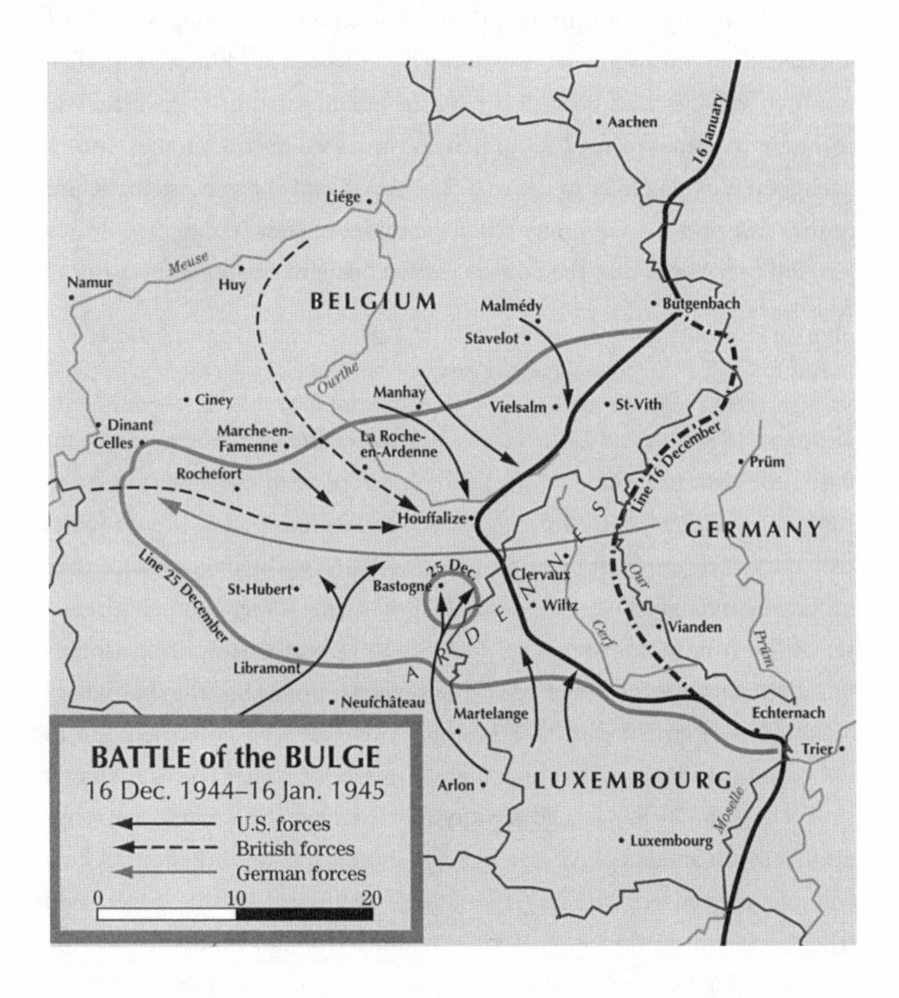

Both sides had to contend with the weather, especially the Americans, who had inadequate winter clothing. Roads turned to mud and the snowfall was so thick that tank drivers plunged ahead almost completely blind in the frosty white cloud. Bastogne, resupplied by air, did not fall to the Germans, and Eisenhower began a counterattack from the south, creating a pincer movement around the German forces. Then, on Christmas Eve, came a magnificent sight: the cloud cover broke and ten thousand planes rained hell on the Germans. This was the largest battle the U.S. Army had ever fought and by January 3, the Germans were driven back; Hitler's roll of the dice had foundered. The Germans were able to withdraw, but over thirty thousand of their men were dead, another forty thousand were wounded, and over six hundred of their armored vehicles had been destroyed or abandoned for lack of fuel. In response to pleas from Churchill, Stalin renewed his own forces' attack across the Vistula River in the east. The Allies had yet to cross the Rhine in the west or enter Germany from the east, but they would.

And every mile that the Soviets gained brought them a mile closer to Auschwitz.

By MID-JANUARY, WHEN SOVIET artillery fire could be heard echoing in the distance, there was nothing left to do but evacuate the death camp. Only the feeblest, those too weak or ill to move, and those too depleted to work were left behind: some 2,000 at Auschwitz and more than 6,000 at Birkenau. The rest—some 58,000 men, women, and children—set off on foot in enormous columns, with as many as 2,500 prisoners in a single group; the columns of Jews were so long that the war-weary SS could no longer keep track of them. Anyone who collapsed, fell to the ground, and could not immediately rise to his or her feet was simply shot. These inmates marched for days, not just from the main camps but also from the smaller slave labor camps in that section of Poland. As the columns poured into the larger cities, they were put into trains or open trucks and sent to the network of remaining German camps.

Elie Wiesel was one of the marchers. He was lucky: he was to be put on board a train where at least there was a roof to keep out the cold, or so he believed. He recalled how on the platform the prisoners tried to quench their thirst by eating the snow "off our neighbors' backs." They spent hours standing in the snow, staring down the tracks, waiting for the train to appear. "An infinitely long train, composed of roofless cattle cars. The SS shoved us inside, a hundred per car: we were so skinny!" When dawn came, the bodies inside were "crouching, piled one on top of the other, like a cemetery covered with snow." By now, there was "barely a difference" between the living and the dead. About fifteen thousand died along the way. Bodies that had been tossed out of the cars lined the train tracks. Inside one car, Wiesel watched as a son, his mind clouded by hunger and exhaustion, snapped and rained blows on his own father and snatched his morsel of bread. Then, as the son stuffed the bread into his own mouth, he was set on and killed.

Two dead bodies, side-by-side.

In the new camps, death stalked thousands more. In March 1945 alone, eighteen thousand perished from hunger, disease, and unspeakable filth.

And at Auschwitz, even with only the weakest left behind, the SS was taking no chances. Between January 20 and 23, the SS men shot hundreds in the sick bays. They set fire to the storage complex, "Canada"; the fire smoldered for six days. Only six of the thirty camp barracks were left standing. And then they completed the mission of blowing up the crematoriums and gas chambers, reducing their vaunted killing machines to rubble. They left Crematorium V standing long enough to burn the last corpses (of prisoners shot in the back of the neck), and then blew it up too. In the meantime, the Soviets were racing westward.

One and a half days later, at precisely 3 p.m. on a cloudy January 27, Soviet troops discovered Auschwitz.

THE WORLD HAD NEVER seen anything like it. There were just 7,000 survivors. Other numbers were far greater: 370,000 men's suits; 837,000 women's coats and dresses; 44,000 pairs of shoes; 14,000 carpets; and 7.7 tons of human hair, packed in neatly tied sacks and bundles, labeled, and ready for transport. And there were the uncounted suitcases that survived the destruction of "Canada"—piles of them, from all those who had arrived in transport after transport. In two and a half years, the Auschwitz system had killed nearly 1 million Jews from nearly every country in Europe that was occupied by the Germans or was Germany's ally. In addition, some 200,000 Soviet prisoners of war, Polish political prisoners, Gypsies, and other non-Jews from across Europe were deported to Auschwitz, and some 125,000 also died in the gas chambers and the camp. But whereas the Soviets had opened Majdanek for inspection and scrutiny. Auschwitz largely remained closed. There were reports from such outlets as the BBC, as well as rumors, but they were mostly fragmentary. The Soviet press itself said little. Not until April 27, after prodding by the British, did the Soviets respond with a perfunctory telegram: "It has been found from investigations from the Oswiecim group of concentration camps that more than 4,000,000 citizens of various European countries were destroyed by the Germans," adding, "No British were found among the survivors." The British considered the telegram "odd," and concluded, "The figure is certainly much exaggerated." It ultimately was too high—Rudolph Hoess himself later gave the figure of 3 million—but the actual figures were bad enough: 1.3 million deported and 1.1 million murdered, with the overwhelming number dying in just one year: 1944.

The year the Allies knew, beyond any doubt, that their war would be won.

ON SATURDAY, JANUARY 20, 1945, one week before the Soviets reached Auschwitz, Franklin Roosevelt was again sworn in as president of the United States. There was now yet another race, between his frail body and the Allied forces still pushing east.

Part Four

1945

Inmates wave a homemade flag when the U.S. Seventh Army liberates Allach concentration camp.

15

Reckoning

"THIS NEW YEAR OF 1945 can be the greatest year of achievement in human history," Franklin Roosevelt proclaimed to the American people in a January fireside chat. He held out the likelihood of the imminent fall of the Nazi "reign of terror" and the end of the "malignant power" of imperial Japan. But his fervent desire for 1945 was to see "the substantial beginnings of the organizations of world peace." With single-minded purpose, Roosevelt fixed his eyes on that goal. It had been his dream since early in the war, indeed since his first government service in the days of Woodrow Wilson. Now, the reality might at last be within his grasp.

But his grasp was an increasingly feeble one.

The day before his inauguration, Roosevelt gathered his cabinet. A shocked Secretary of Labor Frances Perkins, who had been with Roosevelt since the beginning of his administration, later noted not the discussion but the president leading it. While he could still muster ebullient cheer, his skin had turned unspeakably gray, his once lively eyes were dull, and his clothes hung upon him. By the meeting's end, he was supporting his head with his hand, as if its weight were too much for his neck and spine to bear. His lips had turned blue and there were tremors in his hands. He was even forgoing the ceremonial trip to the Capitol for the inauguration, husbanding every last ounce of strength.

Although his inaugural committee had pledged $25,000 for the celebration, Roosevelt countered that he thought he could do it for less than $2,000, without a parade and with a simple outdoor ceremony on the White House's South Portico. Thus, fewer than five thousand people—eight thousand had been invited—came to watch in the cold on a layer of dense, iced-over snow covering the South Lawn as a Marine band outfitted in gleaming red played. Roosevelt's son James and a Secret Service man offered him a cape—the bareheaded president turned it down—then hoisted him up from his seat so that he could reach the lectern. There, despite being "thoroughly chilled," and after having had "a stabbing pain" in his chest that morning, he took the oath of office and gave his speech.

"The great fact to remember," he said, "is that the trend of civilization itself is forever upward." As Roosevelt spoke, Japanese Americans were being released from internment camps across the west. Many were starting over with nothing; many would return home to find that strangers had moved into their homes or vanished with their property.

Balanced on his braces, gazing out from the South Portico, Roosevelt added, his voice quiet, "We have learned that we cannot live alone, at peace; that our own well-being is dependent on the well-being of other Nations, far away."

As Roosevelt spoke, the Nazis were preparing for the final evacuation from Auschwitz, marching prisoners west for travel in unheated trains and open trucks, without blankets, with nothing for warmth but the feeble parade of emaciated bodies next to them. The last SS men were still shooting the sickest prisoners who had been left behind.

Roosevelt continued, "We have learned that we must live as men and not as ostriches, nor as dogs in the manger."

Along the western front at the Bulge, the Allied forces staging a pincer movement had linked up four days earlier. But the Allied troops were still finding pockets of tenacious Germans, and the shooting and dying continued in the frigid cold. And as Roosevelt spoke, Hitler was frantically ordering his panzers out of the Ardennes forest.

Meanwhile, at Los Alamos, New Mexico, scientists were working feverishly to deliver by August 1, an atomic bomb with a force equivalent to ten thousand tons of TNT or, as one scientist put it, "brighter than a thousand suns"—one of Roosevelt's most momentous decisions. And nightly, the skies over Tokyo lit up with the blaze of American firebombs.

"We have learned," the president said to the crowd, "to be citizens of the world, members of the human community.

"We have learned the simple truth, as Emerson said"—and here Roosevelt, in his own paraphrase of Lincoln's second inaugural, slowed his words to add emphasis—" 'The only way to have a friend is to be one.' "

Two weeks later, Roosevelt would test the limits of his own wartime friendships at Yalta, when he met with Churchill and Stalin for what would prove to be the last time.

It was Winston Churchill's opinion that if the Allies had spent ten years on research, they could not have picked a worse place to meet than Yalta. In truth, Yalta itself was a casualty of war. Between the rugged mountains and the Black Sea, it was warmer than most of the surrounding region and had once been deliberately maintained as an unspoiled wilderness. There, Russian czars and the Russian gentry had come to relax, to enjoy its bright sun and warm sea breezes; its aura of health along the coastal waters and its emerald waters in the little harbor of the imperial estate; its groves of cypresses, orchards, and vineyards; and its flowering fruit trees, lilacs, and wisteria. There, Nicholas II had constructed an elaborate palace, Livadia, a gorgeous white limestone structure perched on the edge of a cliff overlooking the sea, with magnificent rose gardens in the front and views of snowcapped mountains in the back. But then came the Soviets, who converted the imperial estate into a tuberculosis sanatorium. When the vengeful Germans overran the Ukraine, they made a particular point of devastating Yalta and its environs. They had looted the palace, being as thorough there as at the death camps when they took the belongings of their victims. At Livadia, they meticulously removed not just furniture and art, but plumbing fixtures, doorknobs, and locks. It was surprising that they did not tear up the floorboards as well. In the large city of Sebastopol, nearby, the destruction was even more complete; every building appeared to have been shattered. The city's sports club was nothing more than a square of broken trees and old shell holes; a church was nothing more than a scarred shell.

Once the Germans retreated, rats and other local animals had free rein in the palaces and dachas of Yalta itself, infesting them with fleas and lice. It was hardly the most promising site for the Allied summit. So Soviet work crews had tenaciously scooped up the rubble and commandeered furnishings and decorations from dachas around Moscow to replace what the Germans had taken or destroyed. Staff had been brought in by train from three Moscow hotels. So appalling were the conditions that Stalin took the unusual step of letting U.S. Navy medical crews come in advance of the presidential party in order to clean the palace.

Churchill, who was just getting over a fever of 102 degrees, met briefly with Roosevelt in Malta before taking off by air for the Crimea. Churchill's daughter recalled having to hide her shock at the "terrible change" in the president since their last meeting in Tehran, only fourteen months before. Despite the president's charm and spirit, "It was quite obvious that he was a very sick man." Lord Moran, Churchill's physician, thought the president was suffering from advanced arterial sclerosis and gave him only six months to live. There was also a feeling that at this meeting, unlike previous gatherings, Roosevelt was very much cut off, increasingly surrounded and shielded by State Department aides. But that may have been due as much to Roosevelt's maneuverings with Stalin as to any additional protectiveness about the president's fragile health. As with the previous meeting of the Big Three, Stalin had dictated the location; and this time, with his armies quickly pushing westward, he held even more sway.

Once again, much like he had done on the final day at Tehran, Roosevelt mischievously sought to reach out to Stalin by excluding Churchill. Before the sessions got under way, Roosevelt met privately with Stalin and Molotov. The president expressed his utter horror at the devastation in the Crimea, adding that he felt even more cutthroat toward the Germans than he had earlier and that he hoped Stalin would repeat the toast to the "execution of fifty thousand German army officers"—the toast that had drawn such an indignant reaction from Churchill in Tehran. Stalin responded noncommitally that everyone was more bloodthirsty now than a year ago.

FDR then maneuvered the conversation toward France, and tantalizingly announced that he would tell Stalin something "indiscreet," because he would not wish to say it in front of Churchill. His tidbit was that for two years the British had artificially tried to build up France into a strong power, something anathema to the Russians who saw the French as collaborationists. The British, Roosevelt added insincerely, were a peculiar people, who wished to eat their cake and have it too. Stalin himself was happy to disparage the British as well, and Roosevelt left their little meeting believing that the old camaraderie of Tehran had been restored.

The Yalta conference ranged over eight days, and it was a sprawling affair. Ministers and military chiefs met in the morning, and the Big Three met at 4 p.m., but there were also discussions during lunch and dinner and private meetings between just two leaders. The Big Three would raise many issues, but rarely were any of them formally resolved. Instead, after some discussion, a question would be delegated to the participating foreign ministers or military chiefs or quietly dropped while another issue was taken up.

Roosevelt continued to believe in improvising solutions, but there were far more staff members at Yalta than had been present at Tehran, so there were fewer opportunities for freewheeling decision making. "As the conference progressed, it became obvious that Roosevelt had not studied [his briefing books] as much as he should have," noted the State Department adviser and Charles Bohlen, who was the president's interpreter.

Two items were not on the official agenda at Yalta. The first, understandably, was Roosevelt's health. Aside from a final evening toast by Stalin to the president's well-being, in which he saluted Roosevelt for Lend-Lease and the mobilization of the world against Hitler, that topic was out of bounds. In any case, Stalin could no doubt see that Roosevelt was clearly not well. Moreover, the Soviets' concealed recording devices, which included directional microphones that could capture a conversation two hundred yards away, probably picked up Dr. Bruenn's repeated blood pressure readings and electrocardiogram, and possibly detected that after the topic of postwar Poland was broached, the president's heartbeat was erratic. He recovered, but there were other worrying moments, including a rambling, less than coherent speech that Roosevelt delivered at the start of the second meeting: he went on about the Germany he had known as a boy in 1886, a Germany of thriving semiautonomous states that bore no resemblance to Hitler's creation. Centralization in Berlin was the cause of the world's current ills, the president concluded. The Soviets and the British did not respond. And, perhaps most tellingly, when Roosevelt hosted Stalin and Churchill for dinner, the president, for the first time, did not mix the cocktails.

The second item that did not come up for serious discussion in any of the official sessions was the fate of Europe's remaining Jews. True, Soviet troops had liberated Auschwitz a week before the start of the conference, yet there is no record that Stalin recounted, at any point, the horrors they had found. The only reference—a passing one—came at the final dinner meeting, when Stalin and Churchill began discussing the British parliamentary elections and an uneasy Stalin changed the subject by saying that the Jewish problem was complicated. The Russian leader noted that he had attempted to create a permanent home for the Jews within Birobidzhan, an agricultural zone in Russia, but after several years, the Jews had wandered away, scattering to the cities. "Only some small groups had been successful at farming," he added. At this point, Roosevelt joined the conversation, stating that he was a Zionist (indeed, both the Democratic and the Republican party platforms had a pro-Zionist plank), to which Stalin replied that he was one in theory, but there were considerable challenges. Roosevelt pushed slightly further, revealing that he would be meeting with the Saudi king to discuss the admission of Jews to Palestine. Stalin wondered if Roosevelt would be offering King Ibn Saud anything. The president retorted facetiously, "The six million Jews in the United States," using a number that in retrospect would turn out to be particularly ill-chosen. But Stalin in any case missed the awkward joke, instead pondering the literal implications of resettling American Jews, as he had tried to resettle Soviet Jews, and noting that Jews were "middlemen, profiteers, and parasites." Then in a moment of levity, Stalin quipped, "No Jew could live in Yaroslav"—a city that Bohlen, the interpreter, would explain was known for the shrewdness of its peddlers. Roosevelt offered no rejoinder—instead he simply smiled—and Stalin ultimately offered no objections to sending Jews to Palestine.

But otherwise, aside from a statement that all displaced civilians would be returned to their country of origin, the fate of Europe's Jews, both those who had been killed and those who clung to survival, was seemingly not a topic meriting consideration by the Big Three as they concluded their summit at Yalta.

Roosevelt was, despite his physical frailty, a towering figure still in command. He presided over each plenary session and made sure that the major topics were addressed. Now that the war against Hitler was all but won, a singular achievement in history, his primary concern was guaranteeing the entry of the Soviets into the Pacific war against the Japanese. He wanted to pocket that commitment and he did so, in a secret codicil to the official communiqué. Anticipating an extended fight to capture Tokyo, Roosevelt obtained Stalin's promise to enter the Pacific war no later than ninety days after the surrender of Germany, in exchange for control of parts of Manchuria after Japan surrendered. Second among the president's principal goals was securing an agreement for the establishment of the United Nations, which would be an international framework for peace. And there were the nagging post-war questions: What was to be done with Germany? Would the French have an occupation zone there? How would war reparations work? Would Germany be dismembered? And what was to become of Poland, home of Auschwitz, home of the Warsaw ghetto, home of the Warsaw revolt, and a symbol of the war? Would it be free and democratic? Or would it become a satellite of the Soviet Union? This was an issue that would dog Roosevelt's legacy for years to come.

The results were decidedly mixed, although most issues were seemingly resolved: the French would be included in the occupation of Germany, overseeing territory in the British and American zones, while Germany would pay reparations, with half the amount going to compensate the Soviet Union; and future governments of the buffer nations along the Soviet border would be "friendly" to Moscow. To the chagrin of many observers, the president gave too much on Poland. Poland's postwar government would include members of the Communist Party, which all but guaranteed that the Poles would be switched from one master, the Germans, to another, the Soviets. But in Roosevelt's defense, this was a fate virtually sealed by the axiom of geography, since Russian troops were already on the ground across Poland. Still, as a token, the official communiqué at least promised "free and unfettered elections," with universal suffrage and a secret ballot. And there was an agreement on the American plan for the United Nations Security Council: it would have five permanent members, and each would have a veto over any decisions the Council made. Other decisions on the UN were to be made later, at an inaugural meeting in San Francisco set for the end of April. Churchill had arguably lost the most; he had wanted a clearly democratic path for the countries in eastern Europe, which would not happen. But to some degree, Stalin had also compromised on the question of admitting France to the control commission in Germany. And Roosevelt clearly capitulated regarding Poland.

Yalta was initially hailed as a triumphant success and a signal that the Allies' collaboration would remain possible in the postwar world.

Roosevelt and the delegation left tired, but buoyed by thoughts of the future.

~

ON THE WAY HOME, the president stopped for a meeting with the kings of Egypt and Saudi Arabia and the emperor of Ethiopia. Wearing a flowing black cape, Roosevelt received each one on the gun deck of the USS *Quincy.* The Egyptian and the Ethiopian were the first to arrive for their consultations. Ibn Saud of Saudi Arabia came last, on the second day. An American destroyer, *Murphy*, had been sent to collect him, and it was, from the moment of its departure from Jeddah, a stunning sight—an "Arab Court in Miniature," wrote the *New York Times*. Thick carpets covered the destroyer's deck and a royal tent had been raised alongside the forward gun turret. When he came into view, the king was seated regally on a great gilt chair, surrounded by more carpets and guarded by barefoot Nubian soldiers, their sabers drawn. Along with the rugs, sheep, tents, charcoal cooking buckets, and holy water, Ibn Saud arrived with an entourage of relatives, guards, valets, and food tasters, as well as the royal astrologer and a ceremonial coffee server. In addition, there were "nine miscellaneous slaves, cooks, porters, and scullions." It was the first time that the Saudi king had left his desert homeland. Some of his traveling party had never seen the ocean, most had never been aboard a ship, and all balked at going belowdecks. The Saudis refused to eat anything from the ship's mess, instead slaughtering their own sheep, which were traveling in a specially built pen on the ship's fantail. Even more "eye-popping" to the ship's officers and crew was the sight of the Saudis brewing their coffee in braziers, which they had unknowingly set up next to the ready-ammunition hoist.

At seventy years old, Saud, like Roosevelt, was feeling his age. He walked slowly, with a limp, and relied on a stick for balance. The king took a plush seat next to Roosevelt on the breezy deck, and the two men sat elbow to elbow, King Saud's voluminous robes billowing along with Roosevelt's hefty cape. A low table for coffee had been set out, and in deference to the king, the deck of the *Quincy* was also covered in overlapping brightly woven rugs. Women were not permitted in the king's presence, so the president's daughter, Anna, who had accompanied him throughout the Yalta trip, had already been dispatched belowdecks.

After the initial pleasantries, gifts, and discussion of topics such as oil and reforestation, Roosevelt, having failed to deliver the Jews from Auschwitz, at least sought to help some of the survivors. His goal on behalf of a ravaged Jewry desperately in need of a homeland was not insignificant. He steered the conversation toward his main objective: asking Ibn Saud to permit ten thousand additional Jews to enter Palestine. Confident as always of his own charm and his own powers of persuasion, Roosevelt suggested that this number was a very small percentage of the total population of the Arab world. But what he received in return was an unequivocal no. Recalcitrant from the start, Ibn Saud then launched into a speech, denouncing Jews for using money from American and British capitalists to make the Arab countryside "bloom," accusing Jews of fighting Arabs rather than Germans (actually, the grand mufti sided with Hitler, and the Jews fought against the Germans), and vowing that the Arabs would take up arms themselves rather than give way to more Jewish emigration. "Arabs would choose to die rather than yield their land to Jews," was his tart reply. Roosevelt tried a couple of other tactics, downplaying pro-Zionist sentiment in the United States and adding that he, and not Congress, formed his own foreign policy. Still, as Roosevelt made each point, the king grew more adamant. Ibn Saud left the *Quincy* with the gift of an airplane, but without having given an inch on the question of Jewish refugees. Actually, Roosevelt's closest adviser, Harry Hopkins, was dismayed, worrying that the president, due to ill health, capitulated far too quickly on his pro-Zionist positions.

There was no other business to transact, except for a family lunch with Winston Churchill in the shadows of the fabled Egyptian city of Alexandria. Soon to be on his own deathbed, Harry Hopkins was there, and like Roosevelt ailing (Hopkins died in 1946). Meanwhile, the president's daughter joined Churchill and his children, Randolph and Sarah. Churchill later described Roosevelt as placid but frail, retaining only a slender contact with life. The American envoy to Saudi Arabia was even more blunt, describing Roosevelt's face as "ashen in color," and adding, "The lines were deep; the eyes would fade in helpless fatigue. He was living on nerve."

The trip turned stormy almost as soon as the *Quincy* steamed westward through the Mediterranean. The French general Charles de Gaulle, whom Roosevelt and Churchill had persuaded Stalin to include in the postwar architecture, disdainfully refused to meet with the president in Algiers, while a worn-out Harry Hopkins opted to fly home rather than spend more than a week at sea. Two days later, Roosevelt's longtime faithful aide, Pa Watson, died of congestive heart failure and a brain hemorrhage in the ship's surgery.

The president now stayed in bed in the mornings. He spent the afternoons on deck with his daughter, gazing off over the water, smoking, and from time to time flipping through the pages of whatever reading matter lay in front of him. Drinks and dinner brought back vestiges of the Roosevelt of old, although when the voyage concluded on February 27, Roosevelt wanted nothing else but to take the train straight to Washington. There, in two days, he would face Congress, for what would be the last time.

THROUGHOUT FEBRUARY AND INTO March, the removal of the Jews deeper into Germany continued. They walked for miles, in the biting cold. Those who heard the Soviets' artillery fire may have taken heart; however, they were likely to be put on trains that took them farther away from the front lines, and from liberation. Water was given every other day. Food barely at all. On one sealed train in March, of the thousand women who had left a Nazi camp east of Berlin in January, only two hundred remained alive.

The thousands who still walked—Jews who had survived the selections and evaded the gas chambers, starvation, and disease—were now being taken to notorious death mills in the heart of Germany and Austria. When they passed through German towns, the SS men told the residents not to offer them bits of food, saying, "It's Jews they are."

Children picked up stones from along the road and hurled them at the stumbling columns. Bergen-Belsen, Dachau, Buchenwald, Mauthausen, Sachsenhausen, and Ravensbrück and their sweeping tentacles of subcamps were the final repositories for the remnants of the Final Solution. The Nazis, more deluded than ever, believed that the Jews and the others from the evacuated camps would provide a fresh source of slave labor as the front lines drew closer to Berlin: In this warped vision, these prisoners would be the ones to repair roads, rail lines, and bridges; to set tank traps to blunt the Allies' advance; and to dig clusters of underground bunkers in the Sudeten mountains or the Alps, from where Hitler and the Wehrmacht could fancifully continue to direct the battle, an imaginary guerrilla war of attrition. The reality was very different.

At Bergen-Belsen, Jews lay on the floors, without blankets or food. As at Auschwitz, lice thrived, and typhus and cholera were rampant. Outside, the dead were left in piles that had begun slowly decomposing. Among those who had reached this camp was Anne Frank.

She and her sister, Margot, were two of the first to leave Auschwitz in October 1944 and be transported west. They had already proved themselves capable of heavy labor, moving rocks in Auschwitz. They were selected to be among the new workers sent west, while their father and mother stayed behind. One survivor remembers Anne at Bergen-Belsen, her round eyes and ready smile gone, poignantly begging for a bit of extra cereal. For the children and teenagers, starvation and typhus were common. Margot Frank was the first to fall ill. Her dreams of rescue dashed, Anne followed.

Meanwhile, the Allies, coming in their direction, were still miles away.

∾

PRESIDENTIAL ADDRESSES TO JOINT sessions of Congress are a tradition dating back to the days of George Washington, when the capital was first in New York and later in Philadelphia. In Washington, D.C., under the great dome, the legislators gathered to hear the chief executive in the chamber of the House of Representatives. The Senate occupies a more intimate space, with small mahogany desks on which members have carved their names and initials over the years. But the House chamber, dating from 1857, is a sprawling place, with rows of unassigned seats and a large, semicircular gallery. It was bustling on March 1 when Franklin Roosevelt arrived.

For the members of Congress, it was a jarring sight. The man who appeared before them now at the end of the war was very different from the one who had addressed them at its beginning. He did not walk confidently, wearing his braces and balancing on an aide's arm, as he had done for his address after Pearl Harbor. Instead, for the first time, he was gently wheeled into the chamber's well and transferred to a plush crimson velvet chair at a little table. Nevertheless, the reaction to his arrival was thunderous applause. Roosevelt began by making an unusual reference to the "ten pounds of steel" that he typically carried on his lower legs, and jokingly asked to be pardoned for sitting down. And much else about the speech was different too.

His partisans relished the speech, but most could not see the Roosevelt of old. As historians note, the president traced the text with his trembling finger, yet still he stammered over phrases and garbled his words. He ad-libbed; he wandered and digressed; his speech was halting and unmoored, the words drifting along. "I did not think it was a particularly good speech," Hassett confided to his diary: "Too long to begin with, and the President ad-libbed at length, a wretched practice which weakens even a better effort." Roosevelt mentioned in passing his meeting with Ibn Saud after Yalta, adding that he had learned much about the Muslim-Jewish problem from this meeting. Only occasionally did the president raise his voice for emphasis; mostly, the delivery was in a flat monotone. Dean Acheson, the famed future secretary of state, noted that it was the voice not of a commanding head of state, but of an invalid. And those assembled could not help noticing the president's hand quiver and tremble as he sipped his water.

Only at the end, after nearly an hour, when he spoke of his beloved United Nations and the coming meeting in San Francisco, did he display conviction. He spoke of how America had failed its fighting men at the end of World War I, adding, "We cannot fail them again, and expect the world to survive again." He said that Yalta, the Crimea Conference, had brought an end to centuries of unilateral action, exclusive alliances, spheres of influence, and balances of power—means that "have always failed." Instead, those outdated habits would give way to a universal organization "in which all peace-loving Nations will finally have a chance to join."

The president, having all but won the war and paved the way for the peace, left to another wild ovation. It was to be his final significant public appearance.

On March 3, Roosevelt left Washington for Hyde Park. He planned on returning to Hyde Park again in late March, before setting out for two weeks at Warm Springs. Then, on April 20, he was scheduled to depart on his train for the opening of the United Nations conference in San Francisco. In the White House there was a growing number of guests, including the Canadian prime minister, the king of Iraq, and members of the New York Democratic Committee, who overstayed their time, making the president late to lunch with Admiral Nimitz, commander of the Pacific fleet. Then, on March 17, the Roosevelts celebrated their fortieth wedding anniversary with friends and family. After cocktails in the Red Room, dinner, and a movie, the president went to bed and announced that he would sleep until noon. He had begun to lose the ability to taste his food.

Frequently at the White House, Charles Bohlen noted the persistent shaking in Roosevelt's hands, which made it difficult for him even to hold a telegram. The president could rouse himself for meetings with public figures and politicians, but to Bohlen it was clear that his "powers of concentration were slipping." Yet Bohlen added, "The thought did not occur to me that he was near death."

On March 30, Good Friday, Franklin Roosevelt arrived in Warm Springs to recuperate. He drove himself to his "Little White House," and then remained inside. William Hassett, who was traveling with the president, pulled the ever-vigilant Dr. Howard Bruenn aside and whispered, "He is slipping away from us and no earthly power can keep him here."

Hassett recorded that Bruenn at first "demurred," but as the exchange progressed, Bruenn conceded that Roosevelt had merely been maintaining a "bluff," adding, "I am convinced that there is no help for him." Hassett poured out his concerns: about Roosevelt's indifference before the start of the election; about how he had begun to stop chatting; about his weariness and his increasingly feeble signature—"the old boldness of stroke and liberal use of ink gone, signature often ending in a fade-out."

Bruenn, now attached to his patient more than ever, countered that Roosevelt's condition was precarious, but not hopeless. However, to Hassett, "this talk confirmed my conviction that the Boss is leaving us."

Uncharacteristically, Roosevelt confided to Hassett that he had lost twenty-five pounds. "Shocked at his appearance—worn, weary, exhausted . . . no strength, no appetite, tires so easily," Hassett jotted in his diary on the last day of March. It was now a question no longer of if, but of when.

IN EUROPE, THE AMERICAN armies, having miraculously crossed the bridge at Remagen, kept coming. Yet even as Nuremberg, the city where Hitler held his great Nazi rallies, lay in ruins, the Nazi death marches continued. Some of the captives had not only to walk but to pull heavy loads of the SS men's loot for miles. Other captives were put on trains; one woman, Aliza Besser, recalled the conditions after three days and nights in a sealed cattle car: "No water. They die of thirst. Lips are parched. . . . There are only a few cups in every truck, and everyone wants to drink. Commotion breaks out, and the German guards pour away the water in front of us all." Jewish prisoners who had been forced to repair Vienna's railway station were then marched away from the advancing Soviet forces. Their only food was what they could scavenge from the early spring fields. Those who moved too slowly were shot. Nearly half died on their way to Germany.

On April 3, the U.S. Seventh Army liberated six thousand Allied POWs, a day of indescribable joy. But April 4, though "a very quiet day all around" at Warm Springs, was an altogether different matter in

Germany. Under a bright sunny sky, American forces were advancing across the countryside. Suddenly, German mortar shells rained down. The road signs and maps indicated that the Americans were outside a town named Ohrdruf, best known as the place where Johann Sebastian Bach composed several of his works. It was almost by accident that a patrol from the 354th Infantry Regiment found a camp. Not unlike Robert E. Lee's army searching for shoes in an obscure place called Gettysburg, these men were simply exploring, looking for stray Germans, and happened to walk up a small rise in the land. On the other side, they saw a gate. And they began to walk down. An escaped prisoner may have led them, or they may have come to the place on their own.

The camp sat in the middle of a forest, framed by tall pine trees that filtered out the sun, and there was nothing about it to indicate that anything special had ever happened here. Stretching out from the swinging gate was a high barbed-wire fence, and above the entrance was a wooden sign strangely emblazoned with three words: "*Arbeit Macht Frei.*" The body of a lone guard lay motionless across the opening. Inside, however, nothing was at all ordinary. Behind the fences, some ten thousand prisoners had been crowded into the grounds and commanded to dig tunnels in a nearby mountain for a planned Nazi underground headquarters. At least four thousand inmates had died or been murdered since late 1944. The last several hundred had been shot just before the American forces arrived. The dead included Jews and also Polish and Russian prisoners of war. The fleeing Germans had left piles of dead, emaciated bodies behind. These victims were clad in striped uniforms, under which their bodies were all but fleshless, and bullet holes had pierced their skulls.

Charles Payne, a great-uncle of President Barack Obama, reached Ohrdruf on April 6. He remembered, "Almost a circle of people had been killed and were lying on the ground, holding their tin cups, as if they had been expecting food and were instead killed. You could see where the machine gun had been set up behind some bushes." They had apparently been too weak to begin the forced march to another camp, so they were gunned down where they stood.

"The smell was so horrible," recalled another American GI, twenty-year-old Bruce Nikols. He described an overwhelming odor of quicklime, dirty clothing, human feces, and urine. But the stench came from far more than the sixty or so bodies strewn about the parade ground.

Just off the open area, near the green-painted barracks, was a woodshed, which lay open on one side. Nikols recalled, "Bodies were stacked in alternate directions as one would stack cordwood." The shed had been used for punishment where inmates were beaten on their backs and heads with a shovel. There was also a gallows for hanging others. And there was a large pit for burning the remains.

A plea had gone out for all available medics, doctors, and nurses; but by now, getting such help was nearly an academic question: only a few survivors remained. Some of these fortunate ones had eluded their captors by hiding in their bunks. A few more had fled into the surrounding woods during the evacuation—incidentally, vindicating the WRB's contention that bombing the camps would have allowed prisoners to escape. The rest had been loaded onto trucks and driven deeper into Germany, to another camp. The weakest, too weak to move, were the ones who had been gunned down on the parade ground. "They didn't want them to be liberated," explained the American GI, "even at the end."

Ohrdruf was the first Nazi camp inside Germany to be liberated by the Allies.

So many upturned, unrecognizable faces. So much sorrow.

Three American generals, Eisenhower, Patton, and Bradley, heroes of D-Day, came to visit the camp on the morning of April 12, 1945. Patton would write in his diary about what lay on the other side of the door to the woodshed: "A pile of about 40 completely naked human bodies in the last stages of emaciation. These bodies were lightly sprinkled with lime, not for the purposes of destroying them, but for the purposes of removing the stench." Eisenhower himself recalled that Patton became physically ill—the famed general vomited after seeing all the dead—and could not bring himself to visit the punishment shed. Both generals did visit the pit where the bodies were burned. Patton described gazing on what he called a "mammoth griddle" consisting of railway tracks laid on brick foundations, where the Germans had attempted to burn the bodies of hundreds of the dead, pouring pitch on top of them and lighting fires below. "They were not very successful in their operations," he grimly noted, "because there was a pile of human bones, skulls, charred torsos on or under the griddle which must have accounted for many hundreds." Bradley, having seen more than his share of casualties, was dumbstruck. He said later, "The smell of death overwhelmed us even before we passed through the stockade. More than 3,200 naked, emaciated bodies had been flung into shallow graves. Lice crawled over the yellowed skin of their sharp, bony frames."

Among the things the generals saw as they walked through the camp was a butcher block where jaws had been smashed to remove gold fillings.

And Ohrdruf was only a satellite camp. It had no gas chamber, no crematorium. The main camp at Buchenwald, liberated on April 11, had far more horrors, including shrunken heads and ashtrays cut from human bone. When the first American troops arrived there, in tanks coming up a dirt road, they expected a firefight with the Germans. The tanks blasted through two layers of barbed-wire fences, felt the electric charge, and rolled toward a cluster of buildings on a hill. The first clear image nineteen-year-old Private First Class Harry Hedger had was of "a monster of a chimney." It was still smoking. "Black smoke was pouring out of it, and blowing away from us, but we could still smell it. An ugly horrible smell. A vicious smell." The tanks came to a halt and the men jumped off, ready to flatten themselves on the ground and start firing. Then they saw a group of ragged human beings starting "to creep out of and from between the buildings in front of us." Hedger remembered a uniform of "horribly coarse cloth," striped in alternating lines of dull gray and dark blue.

In weak, parched voices, some asked, "Are you American?"

Hedger was sent off to guard the fence line and told not to let anyone in or out. When Hedger's sergeant returned, he said in a very quiet tone that this was "what was called a 'concentration camp,' that we were about to see things we were in no way prepared for. He told us to look as long as our stomachs lasted, and then to get out of there for a walk in the woods." Hedger added, "I didn't understand, but I was about to learn." On the entrance gate was a heavy wooden beam, carved in German script with the three words "*Arbeit Macht Frei.*" Hedger and his fellow soldiers saw, stacked like matchsticks, bodies that had turned a dirty gray-green color. Nearby was a long two-story building. Inside, it was still warm.

They saw heavy metal trays pulled out of iron doors arranged row by row in a brick wall. And on the trays were partially burned bodies, three to a tray. "Three bodies to a tray, at least thirty trays—and the Germans still couldn't keep up."

Then they found the bunks inside buildings that looked like large barns, where hundreds of people were sleeping in one building. Living corpses wedged together stared at them aimlessly, lifelessly, out of sunken eyes. Hedger looked at the bunks and thought of the bodies and asked himself, "Where did the Germans get them all?"

FOR HIS PART, AT the liberation of Buchenwald, Elie Wiesel remembers throwing himself onto whatever food he could find. The prisoners were so beaten down by the Nazis that "that's all we thought about. No thought of revenge or of our parents. Only of bread."

AFTER HIS VISIT EISENHOWER sent around a memo asking for all nearby units not on the front lines to be taken to see Ohrdruf. A distraught Patton, after bellowing "See what these bastards did!," made his own inspection of Buchenwald; he then ordered the mayor of the nearby town of Weimar and every citizen who remained to go through Buchenwald and see what the German people were responsible for. None of the dead were to be buried until the townspeople had come. After visiting the camp, with Buchenwald's gates still visible behind them, some of the Germans began laughing. Bristling with anger, the American officer in charge made each of them turn around and go through the camp again, walking from building to building, much more slowly. This time it had an effect. "The next day," Hedger recalled, "we heard that after returning to their town, the mayor of Weimar and his wife both committed suicide."

Eisenhower ordered careful documentation of the atrocities perpetrated in the Nazi camps, then called Winston Churchill to describe what he had witnessed. Graphic photographs followed in a special dispatch to London. Churchill, who had long before just about anyone appreciated the monstrosity of the Nazi Holocaust, sent the images to each member of his cabinet.

But as night fell in Germany on April 12, the general could no longer cable his president to tell what he had seen.

ON APRIL 9, ROOSEVELT rode the eighty-five miles to Macon, Georgia, to see Lucy Mercer Rutherfurd, and she accompanied him back to Warm Springs. The next day, Dr. Bruenn reported that Roosevelt's color was "much better" and noted that his appetite was "very good," adding that the president requested "double helpings of food." But on April 11, when Henry Morgenthau dropped in for dinner, he was decidedly stunned by what he saw. He described Roosevelt as "very haggard," and noted how his hands shook so that he started to knock over the glasses. "I had to hold each glass," he added, "as he poured out the cocktail." Roosevelt's memory was clouded and he frequently confused names. And Morgenthau was particularly struck by how much difficulty the president had transferring himself from his wheelchair to a regular chair, writing, "I was in agony watching him."

The following morning, while Auschwitz overlord Adolf Eichmann was strutting about visiting Theresienstadt one last time, and American bombers were murderously strafing Schweinfurt at will, Roosevelt complained of a slight headache and some stiffness in his neck. Bruenn gave the president a light massage. A friend of Lucy Mercer's, a painter named Elizabeth Shoumatoff who had come to do a portrait of the president, noticed Roosevelt's high color, in contrast to his usual gray pallor, late that morning. The flush in his face was actually an ominous warning. At 1:15 in the afternoon of April 12, Franklin Roosevelt raised his hand to his head and said, "I have a terrific pain in the back of my head." He slumped over, never to awake again. "The heavy breathing which I heard as soon as I entered the cottage told the story," wrote Hassett shortly afterward. When he entered Roosevelt's bedroom, "His eyes were closed—mouth open—the awful breathing . . ." At just past 3:30, Roosevelt ceased to draw breath. Dr. Bruenn tried artificial respiration, a caffeine–sodium benzoate injection, and finally adrenaline injected directly into the heart, but to no effect. At 3:35, President Franklin Roosevelt was pronounced dead.

HOURS LATER, WHILE THE news flashed across telegraph wires, and a stunned Harry Truman prepared to take the oath of office, and Eleanor Roosevelt headed to Warm Springs to accompany her husband's body home, a trainload of 109 Jews left the Vienna station for the camp at Theresienstadt. It was to be the last official Nazi deportation by Eichmann's department. Days later, the Gestapo would hang twenty Jewish children in the basement of the Damn school in Hamburg.

On April 14, as hastily arranged funeral rites were being conducted in the East Room of the White House, American troops found a cremation pit for the dead inside another Nazi subcamp; its logs were still burning. And on April 15, the same day that Franklin Roosevelt was to be laid to rest in the rose garden at Hyde Park, American troops entered the Nordhausen camp, while a contingent of British entered the camp at Bergen-Belsen. Ten thousand exposed bodies awaited them. In the bunks, lying amid filth, the dead and the dying were nearly impossible to tell apart. A British colonel described how men and women collapsed "as they walked and fell dead." Inside the "verminous and stinking barracks," doctors "marked a red cross on the foreheads of those they thought had a chance of surviving." Three hundred died each day the first week. After that, for several weeks, some sixty or more died each day. American GIs, trying to be helpful, handed out chocolate bars to the emaciated survivors; but the chocolate was too rich for their systems, and many died as a result. The soldiers also gave away cigarettes. The inmates ate them rather than smoked them.

One Allied soldier, Peter Coombs, staring at open graves and a "carpet of dead bodies," wrote to his wife: "I saw their corpses lying near their hovels, for they crawl or totter out into the sunlight to die. I watched them make their last feeble journeys, and even as I watched, they died. . . . Their end is too inescapable, they are too far gone to be brought back to life. . . . Belsen is a living death . . . and if it is ever necessary, an undoubted answer to those who want to know what we have been fighting for."

What we have been fighting for. Those words must have echoed like an antiphon. Indeed, however ravenous the inmates were for food, they were equally ravenous for the Americans. Wherever the Americans arrived, the triumphant scenes were the same, scenes reminiscent of a moment forever frozen in time, Abraham Lincoln being deliriously surrounded by a flock of jubilant former slaves as he came into Richmond at the end of the Civil War in April 1865. J. D. Pletcher of the Seventy-first Division, who helped liberate Gunskirchen *Lager* (camp), said: "Just the sight of an American brought cheers, groans, and shrieks. People crowded around to touch an American, to touch the jeep, to kiss our arms—perhaps just to make sure that it was true. The people who couldn't walk crawled out toward our jeep. Those who couldn't even crawl propped themselves up on an elbow, and somehow, through all their pain and suffering, revealed through their eyes the gratitude, the joy they felt at the arrival of Americans."

The arrival of the Americans was on the lips of every inmate. As for the liberators themselves? Pletcher, like Coombs, observed, "I finally knew what I was fighting for, what the war was all about."

~

THE FUNERAL WREATHS HAD faded and been carried off. Eleanor had originally requested no flowers, but they arrived anyway, first at the

White House and then at Hyde Park. In the garden now, the grass was greening and the roses were leafing out. Within weeks, the first buds would swell, and one by one the blooms would open. Around it all was a high evergreen hedge, tempering the breeze. Franklin Roosevelt was finally to be at rest.

The outpouring of grief had been immediate. It came from Allies abroad and political opponents at home. Stock trading was stopped, baseball games were canceled, church bells rang. Across the fields of Europe, even battle-hardened soldiers wept. For many, too many to count, this was the saddest day of their lives. Hundreds of thousands stood, heads bowed, lining the tracks as the presidential train bearing Roosevelt's casket made the eight-hundred-mile journey from Warm Springs to Washington. Under the velvety sky, all along the route mourners gathered, watching in stunned silence. They watched, their eyes welling with tears. They watched, clasping hands and quiet. They watched from farms and planting fields and cities, standing mute and still, while bonfires were lit, and the train slowly glided by, like a ghost. Finally it entered Washington.

As the funeral procession crawled down Constitution Avenue to Eighteenth Street, eventually making its way to the White House, army air force airplanes flew overhead and throngs sobbed. There was a simple service in the East Room—it began with "Faith of our Fathers," a magnificent hymn the president had loved—and closed with his historic words, "The only thing we have to fear is fear itself." Then his body was taken to his beloved Hyde Park, where the sky was a radiant blue, where white lilacs were in bloom, and where the birds were singing. It was a moment of gallantry and reflection. Cannons boomed and army cadets fired three volleys into the air. Finally, the Reverend George Anthony intoned: "We commit his body to the ground. Earth to earth, dust to dust."

Once his body was laid to rest, however, the mourning in official Washington was brief. The Supreme Court justice Robert Jackson recalled riding back on the funeral train from Hyde Park on Sunday afternoon, following Roosevelt's interment. "There was much rushing about by those who had political axes to grind. The subdued tone of the train changed considerably on the return trip," he noted, adding an understatement: "The loyalties of politicians shift quickly." Harry Truman was now president, and abroad there was still a war to win.

It took five days of bitter fighting before Nuremberg eventually fell to Patton's troops on April 21. At this stage, Eisenhower remarked that the Germans had seen enough of the Allied explosives "to last them for a century." Then, by April 25, Berlin was cut off. Brazenly, for they were among the most despicable of the Nazis, Himmler and Göring both attempted to arrange an armistice with the western Allies. Hitler ordered both men stripped of their offices. German troops now began to calculate their field positions, hoping to be able to surrender to the Americans rather than to a Russian army thirsting for Nazi blood.

On April 28, the night sky was a fiery red from the bombardment in Berlin. Hitler's bunker came under direct assault from Soviet artillery. Shells rained down, and the walls and ceilings shuddered under the explosions. The next morning, the Führer ordered cyanide capsules to be distributed to his staff and administered to his beloved dog, Blondi. After shaking hands with each of his aides, reassuring them, he dictated a final political message appointing his successors and denouncing "Jewry" one last time. Then he hurriedly married Eva Braun. Now came word that there were no more Nazi tanks and the Germans were nearly out of bullets. At best, they could hold off the Soviets for twenty-four hours more.

Hitler's final action was, predictably, a suicide pact. By 3:30 in the afternoon on April 30, Eva Braun, sprawled on a sofa, swallowed poison and Adolf Hitler had bitten down on a cyanide capsule and simultaneously pulled the trigger of his pistol, shooting himself in the mouth. By coincidence, he died at nearly the same time of day as Roosevelt. And in a gruesome twist, upon the Führer's wishes, his and Eva's bodies were taken into the courtyard, doused with gasoline, and set aflame, the fire eating its way through their flesh and bone just as it had done to Hitler's millions of victims in crematoriums or open pits.

The following day, a German general who could speak Russian ventured out, holding a white flag. But he was not authorized to agree to unconditional surrender. Fighting continued until the ammunition was all but spent. Goebbels and his wife poisoned their children and then committed suicide as the Berlin garrison was handed over, unconditionally, to the Soviets. By this stage, as a lone Russian soldier waved the hammer-and-sickle flag over the roof of the Reichstag, the city lay largely in ruins. The Red Army had suffered 300,000 casualties. The civilians of Berlin had suffered 125,000 casualties. And those figures did not begin to capture all the losses.

When a group of Russian soldiers stumbled upon small, isolated handfuls of Jews surviving in Berlin, one soldier insisted that it "was not possible" that they were still alive. Staring through clouded eyes, these last few survivors, bedridden or on the verge of death, asked why not. In his awkward, fragmented German, the aghast Russian replied: "*Nichts Juden. Juden kaput*"—"You can't be Jews. The Jews are all dead."

The unconditional surrender of all German forces was finalized on May 7 and, to great fanfare, VE Day ("Victory in Europe") was formally announced the next day at a modest schoolhouse in Reims. Almost at once, the people of Moscow, whether in pajamas or fur coats, swarmed into Red Square, and the huge crowd roared, "Long live the great Americans!" The entire world was ecstatic: London, Paris, New York, Ankara, Brussels. And all across America, from Wall Street to Washington, Los Angeles to Chicago, confetti rained down, cannons boomed, and people poured into the streets, cheering and dancing and lingering deliriously for hours. Churchill pronounced the celebration "the greatest outburst of joy in the history of mankind." It was.

Here, then, were the fruits of 1944.

Yet it was not until May 15, 1945, in Yugoslavia, that the last of the German troops silenced their weapons. The war in the Pacific would not end until mid-August, with the dropping of the world-changing atomic weapons that Franklin Roosevelt had championed.

~

A WEARY ABRAHAM LINCOLN HAD lived to learn of the moving surrender at Appomattox. Franklin Roosevelt did not live to see the fall of Berlin or of Japan. Still, he knew each was coming. His eyes were fixed, as they had been almost since the first bombs fell and the first shots were fired, on the peace to follow. It was an extraordinary vision. Among his final words, an address he wrote for Jefferson Day that he would never give, he stated that "mere conquest of our enemies is not enough." He did not want just "an end to this war," he wanted "an end to the beginnings of all wars." With the body count of World War II amounting to an estimated 36 million—19 million of them civilians—Roosevelt's sentiment is understandable. Like many humanitarians before him, like many after, he wanted "an abiding peace."

Peace did come. True, war was hardly eradicated, and the world has remained a callous, dangerous place. And the United Nations, to which Roosevelt was so committed, has often been feckless and ineffectual, if not counterproductive. Yet in the seventy years since his death, there has been no mass world conflagration. The next global conflict was the Cold War, with tense standoffs, proxy conflicts, and ideological struggles, but it was not total war. And the modern-day specter of terrorism was something Roosevelt could probably not have foreseen. (Although he might have considered 9/11 analogous to Pearl Harbor.) That said, peace, at least on a large scale, as Roosevelt envisioned it, has in some ways been preserved.

However, there is a curious rhythm to Roosevelt's efforts, one laden with a measure of pathos and tragedy. By making the war about its end, Franklin Roosevelt accomplished the historic goal of defending democracy and the western way of life, but nonetheless may have missed his own "Emancipation Proclamation moment." The Civil War, a cataclysmic conflict in its own right, began as a war about secession, but it ended up becoming a war about slavery and human freedom. Abraham Lincoln, fresh off his stunning victory at Antietam, made it that, with his words and his deeds. When he issued the Emancipation Proclamation, the war was no longer simply about federalism and states' rights or even about preserving the Union; it was about freedom—and ending the scourge of human bondage. He did this even though the country never countenanced a war on behalf of the blacks, and despite considerable opposition in the north and even within his own party. Still, Lincoln boldly led the way, and once he took that step, there was no turning back. Meanwhile, Roosevelt spoke many fine words and much soaring praise for democracy and human dignity—here, the *New York Times* was surely right when it wrote that his leadership "inspired freemen in every part of the world to fight with greater hope and courage"—yet there was no moment when he unequivocally made World War II about the vast human tragedy occurring in Nazi-controlled Europe, about the calculated efforts to wipe an entire people from the earth. Unlike the Civil War, World War II was ultimately always about winning and not about something bigger, at least not until the fighting had all but ceased. Then, General Eisenhower, who had just glimpsed the Final Solution for the first time at the Nazi camp at Ohrdruf in April 1945, poignantly wrote, "We are told the American soldier does not know what he is fighting for. Now, at least, he will know what he is fighting against."

That Roosevelt had no Emancipation Proclamation moment is tragic because, unique among most public figures in history, Roosevelt both embodied and embraced humanity and had an immense capacity to inspire others. Justice Jackson, who would take a leave from the Supreme Court to serve as the chief prosecutor of the surviving Nazi high command in the international war crimes trials at Nuremberg, wrote of the man he admired, "How much his passing affects the destinies of mankind, we can never estimate." For Jackson, as for so many, Roosevelt had a "personality so appealing, a mind so richly endowed and informed, a heart so warm and understanding, a spirit so unconquerable." For his part, Republican Robert Taft expressed what many felt, calling Roosevelt "the greatest figure of our time."

On the homefront, the war presented Roosevelt with the thorny challenge of uniting the nation. In the main, he succeeded. "Businessmen who had been the sworn enemies of the President enlisted under him in various posts. People who had distrusted him became his followers. The opposition pretty much melted out," added Jackson. And Isaiah Berlin rightfully observed, "He was one of the few statesmen in the 20th century, or any century, who seemed to have no fear of the future."

It would be hard to disagree. As clearly as anyone else, save for perhaps Churchill, Roosevelt saw the threat of a rising Nazi Germany. As time went on, he deftly managed to navigate through the shoals of isolationist sentiment, while inching the nation ever closer to conflict. His Lend-Lease concept was a brilliant masterstroke, a lifeline for Britain and then the Soviet Union that also bought the United States vital time to turn its production and human capabilities toward war. Once the conflict came, he built a vast, unconquerable arsenal of democracy, and increasingly hurled his military resources against the Nazi regime. Statesman, strategist, commander in chief, he dominated the summits with the Allied leaders, no small feat given that his outsized partners were Churchill and Stalin. He mobilized the war industry on a scale difficult to fathom: during the conflict, the United States produced 2 million trucks; 300,000 warplanes; more than 100,000 tanks; 87,000 warships; 5,000 cargo ships; over 20 million rifles, machine guns, and pistols; and 44 million rounds of ammunition—the equivalent of building two Panama Canals every month. He personally made the difficult decision to invade North Africa, then kept the matériel flowing to the eastern front. He gave Churchill the Italian campaign; and even as his health was failing, he oversaw D-Day and persevered when the success of Overlord seemed to be in doubt. And he did it all so persuasively and with such unmatchable instinct that the American people followed him almost without reservation.

They listened to his fireside chats and felt as if he were speaking personally with each one of them. Huddled around the radio, they were touched by his sparkling personality and thought of him as a personal friend. And they never lost faith in the war, because he never lost faith. Unable to easily wade into a crowd and reach for hand after hand, Roosevelt reached out instead with his voice. He discovered how to use words. Not since Lincoln had a president so been able to move the nation.

And the feeling for Roosevelt extended far beyond America. State Department adviser Charles Bohlen, who was hardly a fanatical admirer of Roosevelt, noted that the president almost always had the upper hand in dealing with foreign leaders, owing in large measure to "his enormous popularity throughout the world, even in countries he had never been in." At home, he was far more beloved than his major wartime predecessors, Abraham Lincoln, Woodrow Wilson, and John Adams. And unlike Lincoln, he did not need to die to receive an outpouring of public affection. Even the passage of time has done little to dim his greatness in the public mind and in the minds of historians, and justly so. His overall stewardship of the war was nothing if not a monumental achievement.

And albeit late, Roosevelt did with his War Refugee Board bring about the rescue of several hundred thousand who might otherwise have perished at the Nazis' hands. Britain took in some refugees, and the Soviet Union absorbed eastern European Jews who fled, but neither made a conscious effort at wide-scale rescue.

Roosevelt was larger than life and endowed with exquisite timing; nothing seemed to be beyond his reach, or his ability to solve, or his imagination. Except one thing: a Holocaust increasingly unfolding in plain sight. He could never quite see beyond the exigencies of winning the war and crafting the postwar structure of peace.

Given the depth of public admiration for him, had Roosevelt at some point desired to make this a war for human liberation—a war against the Final Solution, a war to end the unimaginable Nazi cruelties, a war to save hundreds of thousands if not millions of innocent lives—he could no doubt have roused the American public to follow him. In 1944 he had his chances. His choice not to take more sustained action was among his most fateful decisions, every bit as much as were his greatest military initiatives. And herein lay not just the grandeur of the war, but its tragic irony: when the guns finally fell silent and the city lights were finally turned on, when the victory parades eventually ended and national flags again snapped triumphantly in the breeze, and when the dancing ceased in the streets, the full magnitude of the Holocaust became evident.

Sometimes in a hush, sometimes in a shout, to this day the millions of deaths have left a gaping, tormenting echo in history.

The other fruit of 1944.

~

THE WAR WAS WON and the peace was made, both singular achievements. But the larger, ambiguous humanitarian questions have haunted not just history or Roosevelt's own legacy, but his successors as well. We can see them looming over the Prague spring and the Hungarian uprising, when presidents hesitated to act. These same questions must be asked about the other successors to the Holocaust, the times when America shrugged its shoulders and stood idly on the sidelines: Pol Pot's horrific genocide in Cambodia, to which the world turned a blind eye; the tragedy of Rwanda, among the fastest of killing sprees in the century; the blatant ethnic cleansing in the former Yugoslavia; the rise of the brutal Taliban in pre-9/11 Afghanistan; the intermittent attention paid to Darfur in the Sudan; and internecine carnage in the Middle East. Why does a beheading, a famine, or wholesale slaughter in one nation draw our attention and intervention, while we avert our gaze from another nation? One has to wonder. How much can be traced to our ambivalence in World War II? Could it be that our halting, tentative measures then have left later presidents feeling conflicted and uncertain? It is one of history's interminable conundrums.

At the war's end, a somber Edward Murrow, broadcasting from Buchenwald, said, "They spoke of the president just before he died." As for Auschwitz? "Sometimes I am asked if I know the response to Auschwitz," Elie Wiesel has written. "I answer that not only do I not know it, but that I don't even know if a tragedy of this magnitude has a response. What I do know is that . . . when we speak of this era of evil and darkness, so close and yet so distant, 'responsibility' is the key word." Or as Abraham Lincoln himself once memorably said to Congress, "We must think anew, and act anew. . . . Fellow citizens, we cannot escape history. We—even we here—hold the power, and bear the responsibility."

Seventy years later, around the globe, we are still struggling to answer the question whispered through the Nazi camps: When will the Allies come? When will the Americans come?

ACKNOWLEDGMENTS

One night some years back in a New York hotel, I was invited to a little dinner with Martha Stewart, Mike Wallace, Frank McCourt, our hosts Wayne and Catherine Reynolds, and Elie Wiesel. It was a far-ranging, eclectic discussion. At one point I looked over to Elie, who remains the paragon of moral authority on the Holocaust, and asked if Franklin Roosevelt did the right thing with Auschwitz. He looked over to me with a sideways glance and exclaimed in a soft voice, "This is too important to discuss now." He gave me much to think about as I constructed *1944*.

Another evening, a little group of historians gathered for a meal at the British ambassador's in Washington to talk about World War II. The group included historian Andrew Roberts, Chris Buckley, Christopher Hitchens, Michael Beschloss, Rick Atkinson, and me. Once again, I came away with much to think about concerning the diplomatic and military side of World War II, which came into play also in writing *1944*.

As with my previous books, my first debt goes to the outstanding list of distinguished scholars and peerless historians, too extensive to name here, whose work has at once inspired and educated me. I also want to thank the staffs of the Franklin D. Roosevelt Presidential Library in Hyde Park, which helped me enormously, particularly Matthew Hanson; the Dwight D. Eisenhower Presidential Library, particularly Kathy Struss; the United States Holocaust Memorial Museum, particularly Judith Cohen and Michael Abramowitz; the U.S. Army Center of Military History at Fort McNair in Washington, D.C.; and the U.S. Army Military History Institute.

I have written about the Civil War, Abraham Lincoln, and his era; the founding period, George Washington, and his tumultuous era; and now I've turned my attention to World War II, Franklin Roosevelt, and his era. It is a rare privilege to have lived in the world of America's three greatest presidents. Once more, my work is a narrative and my orientation is to weave together disparate pieces of scholarship in history in order to re-create events faithfully as they happened. Having dealt with the other presidential giants and the other towering epochs in American history has, I believe, provided me with considerable insights for World War II and presidential leadership. And I have immeasurably benefited from great scholars of these earlier time frames, people whom I enormously admire, like my good friend, Gordon Wood, and James McPherson.

As in the past, I have been fortunate to be supported by a number of fellow authors and supporters of the humanities, who provided help and good cheer throughout the writing of this book. I want to thank my friends Chris Buckley, P. J. O'Rourke, Wayne and Catherine Reynolds, Mark Penn and Nancy Jacobson, and James Guerra. Also Howard Owens, formerly the president of National Geographic Channels, with whom I had such a wonderful collaboration; Evan Thomas; Ron Chernow; Max Boot; David Ignatius; Chris Wallace; Bret Baier; James Rosen; my fellow board members and colleagues at Ford's Theatre, including Eric Spiegel, and Paul Tetreault; and the distinguished scholar Richard Breitman, who carefully read chapter 9 about Eduard Schulte (he literally wrote the book about him) and made countless helpful comments. Lyric Winik assisted with editing. Then there are some of the nation's top policymakers with whom I've been fortunate to discuss this book, including the fateful decision over whether to bomb Auschwitz: President Bill Clinton; President George W. Bush, over a private lunch at the White House; Secretary of State Condoleezza Rice, during a private dinner at the State Department; Homeland Security Secretary Michael Chertoff; former White House Chief of Staff Josh Bolten; General Dave Petraeus, who gave me much to think about concerning the military side of things; former Defense Secretary Bill Cohen; and Judge Larry Silberman, who has a vast reservoir of knowledge about World War II as well as FDR, and who challenged and reminded me of more things than I care to mention. His wonderful wife, Tricia, made sure I was well fed.

John Fahey of the National Geographic Society provided encouragement. Also: Speaker Nancy Pelosi, John Roberts, Stephen Breyer, Antonin Scalia, and Sam Alito. Rick Atkinson, an inspiration; as well as Doris Kearns Goodwin, who has set the standard. Former Congressman Steve Solarz, before he passed away, suggested an idea to me for a book—a variation of what I ended up writing about.

Special thanks to Ed Grosvenor, publisher of the marvelous *American Heritage* magazine, who generously made some of the maps from the outstanding *AH* collection available to me.

For further encouragement, Roy and Abby Blunt, Janet Cohen, Chuck Robb,

Wayne and Lea Berman, and Meryl Chertoff. Also Rusty Powell; Ken Weinstein and Amy Kauffman; Carol Watson of the National Endowment for the Humanities; the former NEH chairmen, Jim Leach and Bruce Cole, and now especially William "Bro" Adams, the current NEH chairman; Marvin Krislov; John Gaddis; former British ambassador Sir Nigel Sheinwald, whose historian dinners at the embassy always challenged me; Sir Peter Westmacott; and former Senate Majority Leaders Harry Reid and Tom Daschle along with Mitch McConnell and Rose Styron.

With Steve Gillon and Anthony Giacchino at the History Channel, I participated in a marvelous documentary special about Pearl Harbor and FDR, which did much to stimulate my thinking.

Throughout some ups and downs in the course of writing *1944*, I was fortunate to have dear friends in my corner, Burnie Bond and Mark Werksman. Also Rick Kahlenberg, the wonderful Mari Will, Mark and Margot Bisnow, Victoria and Chris Knopes, Eleni Rossides, Clint Stinchcomb, Jim Denton, Alice Kelly, Adam Lovinger, Rick and Susie Leach, Nina Solarz, tennis pal David Cody, and Stewart Patrick. I need to give a special shout out to my brother and sister-in-law, Gary and Trish Winik. Also to Larry Goldstein. My faithful computer guru, Roy Hewitt, was always there, as was my other savvy computer guru, Ari Goldberg. Thomas Simpson helped with research as did Nicholas Cravatta. Rachel Dillan was fabulous in collecting original documents and other mounds of research for me.

I owe special gratitude to Simon & Schuster, which brought the book to publication as only Simon & Schuster can. Thanks go to my incomparable publisher, Jonathan Karp, who is an old friend and the very best in the business. My first editor, Thomas LeBien, worked passionately with me to help shape the book and sharpen my ideas and concepts. Priscilla Painton, who took over from him, deftly and energetically shepherded the manuscript to publication, with help from her talented assistant, Sophia Jimenez. Richard Rhorer and Dana Trocker helped with marketing. Anne Tate Pearce was a valued partner for publicity. I turned over my sources to Andrea Sachs, formerly the senior reporter for publishing for *Time* magazine, who checked to ensure the originality of my prose against the sources and helped in countless other ways, including key facts and fact checking. She was a joy to work with. As in the past, I was represented by my literary agent, Michael Carlisle of Inkwell Management.

And then there are family members. My mother, Lynn Abrams, lost a protracted battle with cancer during the writing of this book. She loved my writing and loved books. We spoke almost every day. I miss her terribly. I know this is a book that would speak to her. My stepfather, Steve Abrams, was always good about checking in on me, so we both could talk about my mother. My marvelous cousins Peter and Sylvia Winik were always there as well, above and beyond the call of duty.

And most of all, there are my two precious boys, Nathaniel, thirteen, and BC, eleven, who are the greatest blessing in my life. When we are not talking tennis, which is often, we're talking history. Both became intimately familiar with 1944. Both know about FDR, D-Day, and the Holocaust. BC is a talented military historian. His brother Nathaniel, an academic superstar, has already read all of his "daddy's books." He balances his love of history and biography (he can already debate the issues of World War II with his little brother) with a penchant for science fiction (history in the future). They are my two special treasures, and with as much love as I can muster, this book is dedicated to them.

NOTES

In my previous works, I was fortunate enough to live in the world of Abraham Lincoln and the Civil War, and then the world of George Washington and the founders in the 1790s, both extraordinarily rich, important, and fascinating periods, among the most important in modern world history. Now, I've cast my net on Franklin Roosevelt and World War II, a time no less important, no less fascinating, no less filled with giants and giant issues on the world stage. As in the past, my orientation and goal are to offer a comparative story that draws on a broad and often disparate set of history and scholarship, in this case, melding works about Roosevelt, World War II, and the Holocaust, as well as seeking to provide perspectives and biography from the German side. My first debt goes to the remarkable network of distinguished public historians and dedicated scholars who have inspired me and taught me. These gifted historians, on whose shoulders I've sought to stand, too numerous to name, have made this book possible. Other historians, whose distinguished works I've drawn heavily on, do warrant mention here: Elie Wiesel, James MacGregor Burns, Ian Kershaw, Martin Gilbert, William Shirer, Doris Kearns Goodwin, Bill Brands, Jon Meacham, Jean Edward Smith, Richard Breitman, David S. Wyman, Arthur Schlesinger Jr., Rick Atkinson, Stephen Ambrose, Geoffrey C. Ward, Michael Beschloss, Michael Neufeld and Michael Berenbaum, Sam Rosenman, William Hassett, Kai Bird, Robert H. Abzug, and Douglas Brinkley. And of course I have also drawn on the Franklin D. Roosevelt Presidential Library (FDRL).

To avoid an unwieldy notes section, which could otherwise stretch for hundreds of pages, I have followed the widespread practice of using collective references rather than individual numbered citations. As there is a common "body" or "text" of literature, I have resisted the temptation to cite every single source I consulted or to offer a note for every quotation and point. Rather, I have listed works, primary and secondary, that interested readers may consult for further information or that provided useful background for me. From time to time, I've listed books, papers, diaries, newspapers, and journal articles that were influential in molding my interpretations and writing. Also from time to time, I have offered a brief discussion of sources, or an amplification of a salient point. Having said this, I should add that reading the original memos—often urgent or impassioned—of the participants, or sifting through newspapers or periodicals of the time, is an extraordinary experience and a treat for any scholar.

Since public and private collections alike are now widely available online, for Internet sources, I frequently simply state where researchers and readers should go to find crucial information. Increasingly, the Internet is providing a gold mine for scholars, at their fingertips.

One significant fact is that before I took up writing, my background was in government and international affairs, where I dealt with issues of war, diplomacy, leadership, and policy making; the nature of bureaucratic decision making; and—perhaps most important for this book, the stain of genocide, in my case the killing fields of Cambodia. Along the way I advised two secretaries of defense. As a result of this experience, I've been fortunate to develop instincts as well as what I believe are invaluable insights about the policy process and leaders, which I trust can do much to enhance our understanding of events. Ultimately, however, my vantage point is that of a historian seeking to re-create the crucial events as faithfully as I could, re-creating the world as the actors themselves saw it, of living in their heads and their hearts and listening to their disparate voices; and of measuring their fears, concerns, hopes, and dreams.

Finally, there remains the question of what type of a story the pivotal year 1944 is. An exhilarating war story about the unvarnished triumph of democracy over a monstrous dictatorial system? To be sure. A story of an uncommon president who roused the American people and the western world to victory, an uncommon triumph in every sense of the word? Also to be sure. But then: is it also a bittersweet story? Is it a story of vanquishing Nazism, one of the worst regimes ever known to humankind, but also a story of missed opportunities, of countless innocent lives that could have been saved, of a statement for humanity that was never fully or adequately made?

History, 1944 being no exception, is rarely tidy or simple. I leave this for the reader to judge.

PRELUDE: THE SPHINX

1 **Stretching to the horizon . . . entire war:** Sarah Churchill, *A Thread in the Tapestry* (Sphere, 1968), 62–63; Rick Atkinson, *An Army at Dawn: The War*

in North Africa, 1942–1943 (Holt, 2007). For Churchill/FDR Cairo meeting: Notes from FDR library, official log of the president's trip, November 23; FDR pocket diary longhand notes; FDR letter to Grace Tully, in Jon Meacham, *Franklin and Winston: An Intimate Portrait of an Epic Friendship* (Random House, 2004), 246–49. See also *New York Times*, Cairo dateline, December 5; James MacGregor Burns, *Roosevelt: The Soldier of Freedom: 1940–1945* (Open Road Media, 2012), 404–16, especially 415–16. For background on Egypt, see Stacy Schiff, *Cleopatra: A Life* (Random House, 2010), 1–2, 76; see also the outstanding work by Desmond Stewart, *The Pyramids and Sphinx* (*Newsweek*, 1979).

5 **That same late-November sun . . . Churchill had in mind:** See Stephen Ambrose, *D-Day: June 6, 1944: The Battle for the Normandy Beaches* (Pocket Books, 2002), 41. For discussion of the bombing of Berlin on November 22–23, 1943, see Donald Miller, *Masters of the Air: America's Bomber Boys Who Fought the Air War Against Nazi Germany* (Simon & Schuster, 2007); A. C. Grayling, *Among the Dead Cities* (Bloomsbury, 2006); Alan W. Cooper, *Bombers over Berlin: The RAF Offensive November 1943–March 1944* (Pen and Sword, 2013); Robin Neillands, *The Bomber War: The Allied Air Offensive Against Nazi Germany* (Barnes and Noble, 2005); Robert F. Dorr, *Mission to Berlin: The American Airmen Who Struck at the Heart of Hitler's Reich* (Zenith, 2011). Here, the bombing of Berlin relies mainly on Martin Middlebrook, *The Berlin Raids: R.A.F. Bomber Command Winter 1943–1944* (Viking, 1988), 104–23; and the superb work by Roger Moorhouse, *Berlin at War* (Basic Books, 2010), 307–35. For "sea of flames": Moorhouse, 318. Urinated: the temperature often reached fifty below for the airmen. "Everywhere it is still burning" and "remnants of walls and debris": Moorhouse, 321–22; for further details see Louis Lochner, ed, *The Goebbels Diaries, 1942–1943* (Doubleday, 1948), 432–33. "Everywhere, . . . glass fragments": Moorhouse, 309. For list of ruins, see eyewitness testimony, Moorhouse, 321. Shrunken to the size of small children: Moorhouse, 328. "You see nothing but remnants": Moorhouse, 322. An American general boasted; Stephen Ambrose, *The Wild Blue: The Men and Boys Who Flew the B-24s over Germany, 1944–1945* (Simon & Schuster, 2002), 108. The general was Hap Arnold. Regarding the bomber offensive, it is of note that the British were hoping it would crush the morale of the Germans, while the Americans' strategy was to hit precise targets crucial to winning the war. For more see Jorg Friedrich, *The Fire: The Bombing of Germany 1940–1945* (Columbia University Press, 2008), especially 350–51; see also the detailed work in Daniel Oakman, "The Battle of Berlin," *Wartime*, Issue 25 (2004). Oakman quotes Goebbels as lamenting that "hell itself seems to have broken loose over us." Yet German propaganda at the same time sternly referred to the bombing as

the work of "Anglo-American terror plots." For more, see Helga Schneider, *The Bonfire of Berlin: A Lost Childhood in Wartime Germany* (Random House, 2006), p. 65. This book powerfully captures the reality of wartime Berlin under siege. Schneider's father was fighting on the Eastern front; her mother actually left Berlin to work as a guard in Auschwitz-Birkenau.

10 **Yet there were . . . at Tehran:** For the fruit trees, see the chilling memoirs of Rudolf Hoess, who calmly writes of people walking beneath the budding fruit trees of the farm into the gas chamber: Rudolph Hoess, *Death Dealer: The Memoirs of the SS Kommandant at Auschwitz* (De Capo, 1996), 159. For this episode see the magisterial work by Martin Gilbert, *The Holocaust—A History of the Jews, 1933–1945: The Years of Extermination* (Norton, 2012), 633. See also Jadwiga Bezwinska, Danuta Czech, and Krystyna Michalik, *Amidst a Nightmare of Crime: Manuscripts of Prisoners in Crematorium Squads Found at Auschwitz* (Howard Fertig, 2013), 118–19, hereafter cited as *Amidst a Nightmare.* Written in black ink on twenty-one pages, in Yiddish, this manuscript was discovered in 1952 at the site of Crematorium III. The author's name is unknown. "The German nation": Gilbert, *The Holocaust*, 636–37.

CHAPTER 1

16 **"I have just":** For this paragraph and indeed the entire conference (as well as visit to Sphinx, 419), see this seminal memoir: Winston Churchill, *Closing the Ring* (Rosetta, 2010), 306–18, 325–418. See also these outstanding works: Jon Meacham, *Franklin and Winston: An Intimate Portrait of an Epic Friendship* (Random House, 2004), 248; Charles Bohlen, *Witness to History: 1929–1969* (Norton, 1973), 132; James MacGregor Burns, *The Soldier of Freedom: 1940–1945* (Open Road Media, 2012), 402; Doris Kearns Goodwin, *No Ordinary Time: Franklin and Eleanor Roosevelt—The Home Front in World War II* (Simon & Schuster, 1994), 473; and H. W. Brands, *Traitor to His Class* (Doubleday, 2008), 727–28.

16 **"The difficulties of the":** Churchill, *Closing the Ring*, 341.

17 **The first official presidential airplane:** See White House Museum, Air Force One.

17 **which Roosevelt dreaded:** Roosevelt's childhood had been marred by his fear of fire; a favorite aunt of his had burned to death. See Geoffrey Ward, *Before the Trumpet: Young Franklin Roosevelt, 1882–1905* (Harper and Row, 1985), 117–19.

18 **The clipper planes, although:** See Von Hardesty and Bob Schiefferr, *Air Force One: The Aircraft That Shaped the Modern Presidency* (Creative Publishing International, 2005), 36–41.

18 **"You can have your clouds":** For more on trips and Roosevelt's distaste for flying, see, for instance, Meacham, *Franklin and Winston,* 204.

18 **The 1,300-mile journey:** FDR to ER, November 18, 1943, box 12, Roosevelt Family Papers, FDRL, Franklin D. Roosevelt Library; also very good are MacGregor Burns, *Soldier of Freedom*, 406; Goodwin, *No Ordinary Time*, 473. By any definition, the image of Roosevelt peering out his window to see Lend-Lease matériel is fascinating, particularly because he had just flown over Jerusalem, the ancient homeland of the Jewish people.

19 **suite of private rooms:** Jean Edward Smith, *FDR* (Random House, 2008), 630; David Reynolds, *In Command of History: Churchill Fighting and Writing the Second World War* (Allen Lane, 2004), 326; Warren F. Kimball, *A Different Take on FDR at Teheran* (Center for the Study of Intelligence, 2007), http://www.cia.gov/library/center-for-the-study-of-intelligence/csi-publications/csi-studies/studies/vol49no3/html_files/FDR_Teheran_12.htm.

19 **Tehran in late November 1943:** See, for example, Philip Mattar, *Encyclopedia of the Modern Middle East and Africa*, 2004 (Macmillan Library Reference, 2004); Elliott Roosevelt, *A Rendezvous with Destiny: The Roosevelts of the White House* (Putnam, 1975); and Michael F. Reilly, *Reilly of the White House*, 173–74. On the young Washington, D.C. see Jay Winik, *The Great Upheaval* (Harper, 2007), chap. 11.

20 **The drive from the airfield . . . went directly to bed:** See Sarah Churchill, *A Thread in the Tapestry* (Sphere, 1968), 64–65; Churchill, *Closing the Ring*, 342–43; and Bohlen, *Witness to History*, 135. Sarah was a keen observer of events. She also notes that the traffic blockage was due to the fact that the shah of Iran was also driving through the city at the same time; nobody had mentioned this to the Allied delegation in advance.

21 **he moved his personal staff:** See, for instance, Bohlen, *Witness to History*, 135; and Churchill, *Closing the Ring*, 343–44. Bohlen was skeptical about the threats to the American delegation. I concur with him.

21 **"cops and robbers stuff":** For this and the protection detail see Reilly, *Reilly of the White House*, 178–79.

21 **"Everywhere you went":** Ibid., 179. For more on Soviet security, which was present as much to spy on the American delegation as to protect it, see also Brands, *Traitor to His Class*, 732; MacGregor Burns, *Soldier of Freedom*, 406; Meacham, *Franklin and Winston*, 249.

22 **conference was vintage FDR:** Bohlen was nervous about being Roosevelt's sole interpreter and about the freewheeling nature of Roosevelt's ideas for how to structure everything. See Bohlen, *Witness to History*, 136.

22 **to work his legendary, Prospero-like magic on Stalin:** Forrest Davis, "What Really Happened in Tehran," *Saturday Evening Post*, May 13 and 20, 1944; Goodwin, *No Ordinary Time*, 474–75; Brands, *Traitor to His Class*, 737–39; Meacham, *Franklin and Winston*, 253–54.

24 **"my little man":** For this section on the young Roosevelt, see in particular Smith, *FDR*, especially for Grover Cleveland, 23 and 17–22, which I draw upon extensively for this section.

25 **entered Groton:** For this and the powerful influence of Endicott Peabody, ibid., especially 28; see also H. W. Brands, *Traitor to His Class*, 24–27. Smith makes the point that Roosevelt found solace in his religious faith after his father's death. Roosevelt was so taken by Peabody's reading of *A Christmas Carol* that on every Christmas Eve he gathered his own family to listen to a reading of a condensed version, which included Tiny Tim's words, "God bless us every one." See Rexford G. Tugwell, *The Democratic Roosevelt* (Doubleday, 1957), 510; also James Roosevelt and Sydney Shalett, *Affectionately, FDR: A Son's Story of a Lonely Man* (Harcourt, Brace, 1959), 57. On becoming president FDR did write to Peabody, thanking him for his "inspiring example."

26 **When Porcellian . . . turned him down:** For Roosevelt's time at Groton, his rejection from Porcellian, and his curriculum I've drawn heavily on Smith, *FDR*, 30; Brands, *Traitor to His Class*, 32–33; Geoffrey Ward, *First-Class Temperament: The Emergence of Franklin Roosevelt* (Harper and Row, 1989), 31, 34, 41. "Everything I was taught was wrong": This observation would guide Roosevelt when he was president. An empiricist by nature and temperament, he was never quite the rigid ideologue that his critics depicted. Roosevelt would later comment that the most useful preparation he had in college for public service "was on the *Harvard Crimson*": quoted in Nathan Miller, *FDR: An Intimate History* (Doubleday, 1983), 39.

27 **"One of the most":** For this and the trip to Washington and meeting with Theodore Roosevelt see especially Smith, *FDR*, 32.

28 **"I did not wish to be a cow":** "Dearest Cousin Sally," ER to Sara Roosevelt, December 2, 1903. See also "Dearest Mama" to Sara Roosevelt, December 4, 1903; Smith, *FDR*, 36; Ward, *First-Class Temperament*, 16–17; Brands, *A Traitor to His Class*, 36, 38–41. Ward in particular conducted original research on this subject, especially FDR's relationship with Alice Sohier, about whom he once remarked that of all the debutantes "she was the loveliest." See (Franklin D. Roosevelt Library hereafter FDRL), March 21, 1934, FDR to Colonel Sohier. See also Ward, *Before the Trumpet*, 253–55. I draw heavily on all these accounts.

29 **Eleanor's world:** On Eleanor's youth and Progressive tendencies see Smith, *FDR*, 46.

30 **"boy darling":** For the quotations and FDR and Eleanor's early relationship see ER to FDR, January 4, 1904, FDRL; Blanche Wiesen Cook, *Eleanor Roosevelt, 1884–1933* (Viking, 1992); Crystal Eastman, *On Women and Revolution* (Oxford University Press, 1978); Smith, *FDR*, 47; Meacham, *Franklin and Winston*, 16, 22.

30 **"under his roof,"** Smith, *FDR*, 49. Though his father and grandfather were Democrats, FDR made a point of noting that he voted for Theodore for president.

31 **Vaguely bored . . . "made no effort":** Smith, *FDR*, 50.

31 **adjoin a second home:** For instance, ibid., 54. The town houses were connected by internal sliding doors. For more on FDR's relationship with his mother until his college years see Meacham, *Franklin and Winston*, 14–16, 20–22. Meacham stresses that Sara meant to dominate FDR's married life the way she did his youth, 22.

31 **"I think he always thought":** Smith, *FDR*, 55. For the rest of his life, including as president, Roosevelt clung to the notion that he could ignore matters and that they would resolve themselves.

32 **"Father was fun":** Ibid., 57. He also had an insatiable desire to please, and in Goodwin's words, could be evasive, devious, and lacking in candor. He also mastered the art of masking his true feelings. For a concise and elegant background treatment of Roosevelt, see Goodwin, *No Ordinary Time*, 76–80.

32 **to run for the state senate:** See especially Ward, *First-Class Temperament*, 122; see also Brands, *Traitor to His Class*, 69.

33 **"Franklin finds it hard to relax":** See Ward, *First-Class Temperament*, 138–39. There is considerable debate about whether this is true. Some, like Daniel O'Connell, the veteran boss at Albany County, who would work closely with FDR, thought Roosevelt was a bigot or didn't like poor people or was tinged with anti-Catholicism. Certainly this changed over time, if it was ever true. What is definitely true is that he was a product of his upbringing early on—of a life that was rigorously scheduled, in which he saw men and women only of his class, many of whom were distant members of his own extended family, and in which he had little access to a more diverse set of people. Ward makes the point, a good one, that Roosevelt learned tolerance as he went along, "dictated by the realities of power," 138.

33 **less than temperate observations about Jews:** It goes without saying that Eleanor later changed her views considerably. See Goodwin, *No Ordinary Time*, 102; Smith, *FDR*, 148. I would argue that she changed considerably more than Roosevelt himself. In fact, she, as much as anyone in the administration, would become a passionate supporter of the Jews in their time of need.

34 **"I was an awfully mean":** Ward, *First-Class Temperament*, 159; Frances Perkins, *The Roosevelt I knew* (Penguin Classics, 2011), 9; Brands, *Traitor to His Class*, 54–55. This was a rare moment of introspection on Roosevelt's part.

34 **self-interest most of all:** Even here one can discern Roosevelt's pragmatic roots, that he was as much a politician as a committed ideologue. Ward, *First-Class Temperament*, 162.

34 **Roosevelt fell seriously ill:** Of note, Eleanor fell ill as well. Ward, *First-Class Temperament*, 188. Eleanor blamed this on dirty water that she and Franklin used to brush their teeth while coming back from Campobello. Tellingly, she recuperated very quickly; in an omen of things to come, he did not.

34 **by contacting Louis Howe:** See Ward, *First-Class Temperament*, 196–99. Howe once remarked, "I am hated by everybody. . . . And I want to be hated by everybody." The only thing that mattered to him was the sickly candidate who wanted his help, 196. For more on Louis Howe, who was a pivotal and fascinating figure in Roosevelt's life, see Goodwin, *No Ordinary Time*, 20, 90–91, 588–89; Brands, *Traitor to His Class*, 69–71; Meacham, *Franklin and Winston*, 26, 29. Howe, this ugly little man, riddled with quirks and eccentricity, was a genius as well, in some ways a forerunner of James Carville. Howe would be inseparable from Roosevelt for the next twenty-three years. For more, see James MacGregor Burns, *The Lion and the Fox* (Harcourt, Brace, 1956), 45.

35 **In the Navy Department:** *Walton Chronicle*, September 23, 1914; FDR to Langdon P. Marvin, October 19, 1914; see also Smith, *FDR*, 123–25, from which I've extensively drawn this paragraph.

35 **his fire hose analogy:** See FDR to Navy League Convention, April 13, 1916; see also Smith, *FDR*, 132–34.

37 **"Your hands were on the wheel":** For quotation and Lucy Mercer see Michael Teague, *Mrs. L: Conversations with Alice Roosevelt Longworth* (Doubleday, 1981), 157–58; see also Smith, *FDR*, 153. Elliott Roosevelt, *An Untold Story*, 82, described "a hint of fire" in Lucy's eyes. Teague describes it as "lonely boy meets girl."

38 **"As Roosevelt retold":** Smith, *FDR*, 158. It is worth noting that at age thirty-one, Roosevelt was the youngest assistant secretary since 1860.

38 **"perfect of their kind":** For this and Roosevelt's itinerary, Smith, *FDR*, 158.

38 **"dull boom"** and **"rain-stained love letters":** Ward, *First-Class Temperament*, 392–93, 401–2; Smith, *FDR*, 158–59.

39 **"the bottom dropped":** ER to Joseph Lasch, October 25, 1943, quoted in Lasch, *Eleanor and Franklin: The Story of Their Relationship* (Norton, 1971), 220. For a particularly vivid account of Roosevelt's contracting pneumonia, see Ward, who is outstanding on FDR's health issues, *First-Class Temperament*, 408, 410–412. See also Smith, *FDR*, 159–60.

39 **the 1920 campaign would begin:** I particularly draw heavily on Smith, *FDR* 165–87; Ward, *First-Class Temperament*, 417–23; Goodwin, *No Ordinary Time*, 16, 20. FDR did remark about TR, "I do not profess to know what Theodore Roosevelt would say if he were alive today, but I cannot help think that the man who invented the word 'pussy footer' could not resist the temptation to apply it to Mister Harding": FDR speech at Waukegan, Illinois, August 12, 1920, FDRL. As to Roosevelt's speaking style, it was not yet

legendary or polished. Eleanor remarked, "It is becoming almost impossible to stop F. when he begins to speak. 10 minutes is always 20, 30 is always 45, and the evening speeches are now about two hours!" ER to SDR, October 19, 1920, FDRL.

40 **It began as a vague . . . "I believe":** I rely upon Smith, *FDR*, 188–98; Goodwin, *No Ordinary Time*, 16–17; Brands, *Traitor to His Class*, 69–71; Goodwin's account is quite poignant. The most thorough and compelling account is Ward, *First-Class Temperament*, 584–98. Anna actually hid in the closet to listen to Doctor Lovett's pronouncements and thereby learned what was wrong with her father before he himself knew: John W. Boettiger, *A Love in Shadow* (Norton, 1978), 88. In later years, several of the children would remember that they had the sniffles as well as Franklin and they couldn't shake the thought that they too had been struck with polio, but in its mildest form. Ward, *First-Class Temperament*, 590, suggests that Grace Howe may have been moderately afflicted. Drastic measures were also contemplated. Doctor Samuel A. Levine from Boston believed that a lumbar puncture had to be done within twenty-four hours to relieve the pressure on the spine. This procedure would have immediately produced fever; in the end it was never carried out.

41 **"If you can't use your legs":** See Smith, *FDR*, 210–27, from which I draw this paragraph.

42 **The Great Depression was horrific:** I have drawn on PBS, *The American Experience*, "The Bonus March," www.history.com/topics/newdeal. For a brilliant treatment of the Depression see David Kennedy, *Freedom from Fear: The American People in Depression and War, 1929–1941* (Oxford University Press, 2001). See also Robert S. McElvaine, *The Great Depression: America 1929–1941* (Times Books, 1993); and T. H. Watkins, *The Great Depression: America in the 1930s* (Little, Brown, 1993).

43 **In his race against Hoover:** On Roosevelt's election, I have drawn upon Smith, *FDR*, 249–87. For more on Roosevelt's stunning election see Goodwin, *No Ordinary Time*, 100, 110, 115; Brands, *Traitor to His Class*, 264–65.

43 **"He has been all but":** Arthur Schlesinger, *The Politics of Upheaval: 1935–1936*, Volume 3, *The Age of Roosevelt* (Mariner, 2003), 3.

44 **"had more serenity":** Goodwin, *No Ordinary Time*, 204.

45 **"cut his throat":** Brands, *Traitor to His Class*, 561–62. As regards Roosevelt's working of the press corps, in his first term he held 337 press conferences, usually at 10 a.m. on Wednesdays and 4 p.m. on Fridays. Editors were able to see the president separately. See Frank Freidel, *Franklin D. Roosevelt: Launching the New Deal* (Little, Brown, 1973), 224n.

45 **"bunch of incompetent":** Bohlen, *Witness to History*, 210n. Bohlen goes on to say that Roosevelt felt the only way to get anything done with the Senate was to bypass it altogether. Moreover, he asserts correctly that Roosevelt

despised protocol. One surprising observation he makes is that Roosevelt was not "a likable man." Instead he was likable by virtue of his position, Bohlen contends. Finally, Bohlen suggests that he did his job only "moderately well" in foreign affairs.

45 **"we are fighting to save":** Schlesinger, *The Politics of Upheaval*, 67. Roosevelt's intuitive grasp of the enormity of Hitler's threat comes through in his eloquence here.

46 **"It's more than a New Deal":** Ray Tucker, "Ickes—and No Fooling," *Collier's*, September 30, 1933; Smith, *FDR*, 332. See also Jonathan Alter, *The Defining Moment: FDR's Hundred Days and the Triumph of Hope* (Simon & Schuster, 2006).

46 **"Well, Bill, it has come":** For this seminal episode, see Smith, *FDR*, 434.

46 **"I've said this before":** Radio Address to *New York Herald Tribune* Forum, October 26, 1939; also Smith, *FDR*, 440. To be sure, Roosevelt was shameless in saying there would be no boys going to the battlefields of Europe.

47 **"The government had to choose":** Joachim C. Fest, *Hitler* (Harcourt Brace Jovanovich, 1974), 567, 572. For Mussolini deriding democracy at the same time, and for Chamberlain, see Smith, *FDR*, 425.

47 **"would drop into the basket"** Transcript, Conference with the Senate Military Affairs Committee, January 31, 1939, Item 1565, 8; *Franklin D. Roosevelt on Foreign Affairs*, Donald B. Schewe, ed. (New York: Garland, 1979). See also Smith, *FDR*, 431. Roosevelt's words were met by enthusiastic applause by the senators present.

47 **"This nation will remain":** From 8 *Public Papers and Addresses* (Random House, Macmillan, Harper and Brothers, 1933–58), 460–64. It can also be found in Smith, *FDR*, 436. Cordell Hull strongly objected to the statement, which also proved to be a tacit rebuttal to Woodrow Wilson's contention about the nation remaining "neutral in fact as well as in name."

47 **"Our acts must be guided":** Message to Congress, September 21, 1939, 8 *Public Papers and Addresses*, 512–22. See also Joseph Alsop and Robert Kintner, *American White Paper* (New York: Simon & Schuster, 1940), 73ff; Smith, *FDR*, 438.

48 **"I'm almost literally walking":** FDR to Lord Tweedsmuir, October 5, 1939, 2 *FDR: His Personal Letters* 934, Elliott Roosevelt, ed., 4 Vols (Ovoll, Sloan & Pearce, 1947–50), Smith, *FDR*, 439.

48 **Admiral Ross McIntire:** Smith, *FDR*, 445–46. McIntire became a stern monitor of Roosevelt's health for the duration of the war. Here again we see the private eloquence of Roosevelt, though he remained reluctant to speak out publicly or expend too much political capital.

49 **Churchill proposed laying poison gas:** Churchill was always a whirlwind of ideas, some eminently practicable, some not. See Meacham, *Franklin and*

Winston, 10–12. For two marvelous biographies, see Martin Gilbert, *Churchill: A Life* (Holt, 1992), and William Manchester, *Winston Spencer Churchill: Alone* (Delta, 2008), 3–36; BBC Dunkirk fact page, http://www.bbc.co.uk/history/ww2peopleswar/timeline/factfiles/nonflash/a1057312.shtml.

49 **German forces prepared:** For the German side of the picture, especially after Dunkirk, see the magisterial work by Ian Kershaw, *Hitler: A Biography* (Norton, 2010), 557–59, hereafter cited as Kershaw, *Hitler*; Smith, *FDR*, 444–48. Of interest, the late historian Stephen Ambrose made the interesting point that Roosevelt should have intervened much more forcefully earlier on. This is a debate that still properly rages.

51 **militarily Roosevelt was hamstrung:** On America's lack of preparedness, and the inadequacy of American troops, see Goodwin, *No Ordinary Time*, 143; Smith, *FDR*, 428. Actually, Roosevelt feared the Western Hemisphere was in danger.

52 **slapped his thighs:** For this eerie scene, see especially Kershaw, *Hitler*, 561. The reader may also go to YouTube, which has clips of the Nazis marching through Paris and of a jubilant Hitler.

52 **"the greatest warlord":** Kershaw, *Hitler*, 562. The general was Wilhelm Keitel. It is hard to overstate the degree to which a number of Hitler's generals were transfixed by him.

52 **showdown with the Soviet Union:** I have heavily used Kershaw, *Hitler*, 566, 569.

52 **smash Great Britain from the air:** For an overview, I've drawn extensively from Stephen Ambrose and C. L. Sulzberger, *The American Heritage New History of WWII* (Viking Adult Press, 1997), 84, 87, 94–95, hereafter cited as Ambrose, *American Heritage*. For more on the Battle of Britain, see Miller, *Masters of the Air*, especially 1–24 on the heroics of the airmen.

54 **"How much they can stand":** From Murrow's broadcasts during the blitz, reprinted in Ambrose, *American Heritage*, 94.

54 **not everyone loved:** On the criticism of Roosevelt, I have closely followed MacGregor Burns, *Soldier of Freedom*, 388; I think he gets it just about right.

55 **mounting problems at home:** Ibid., 335, 388. This paragraph follows MacGregor Burns closely; he notes that in 1943, every week brought a new crisis at home—walkouts in railroads, wildcat strikes, miners' strikes, etc. See also Goodwin, *No Ordinary Time*, which recounts the same incidents: Goodwin is particularly deft at pointing out the domestic obstacles that Roosevelt faced.

55 **"We, who hate":** This vivid quote is from the Kansas Republican William Allen White, quoted in MacGregor Burns, *Soldier of Freedom*, 331.

56 **"He wants to":** For a treatment of Roosevelt's style of governance, see Robert Dallek, *Franklin D. Roosevelt and American Foreign Policy, 1932–1945* (Oxford University Press, 1979); MacGregor Burns, *Soldier of Freedom*, 351.

57 **"hesitant and confused":** Schlesinger, *Politics of Upheaval*, 8, 91. Schlesinger's treatment of Roosevelt remains necessary reading to this day. To be sure, Walter Lippmann, however distinguished, was often erratic.

58 **"The amusing thing":** MacGregor Burns, *Soldier of Freedom*, 249, and for the dedication of the Jefferson Memorial, 356–57.

58 **Isaiah Berlin said of Roosevelt:** Robert Rosen, *Saving the Jews: Franklin D. Roosevelt and the Holocaust* (Basic Books, 2007), 434–35.

58 **weekends at Shangri-La:** I relied on MacGregor Burns, *Soldier of Freedom*, 254. On Camp David, see especially Goodwin, *No Ordinary Time*, 385–86, which I drew on.

59 **"a law unto himself"** and **"unanimous in their hate":** Schlesinger, *The Politics of Upheaval*, 8, 637. The Madison Square Garden speech may also be viewed on YouTube.

59 **"Hell, a balanced budget":** Schlesinger, *The Politics of Upheaval*, 511, 553, 650. This comment, of course, represents a debate that remains unresolved.

60 **In Tehran Roosevelt:** Bohlen, *Witness to History*, 138–42. For more on this conference, see Dallek, *Roosevelt and American Foreign Policy*, 429–42; Brands, *Traitor to His Class* 546–56; Goodwin, *No Ordinary Time*, 471–78; Meacham, *Franklin and Winston*, 248–66. For "any kind of personal," see Brands, 552. The intensity of the meeting is suggested by Bohlen's observation that at this summit he worked harder than at any other time in his career. Brands, 552, makes the point about the lack of progress cementing a personal connection between the two leaders.

62 **The leaders and their staffs:** Churchill, *Closing the Ring*, 347; Bohlen, *Witness to History*, 141–42; Brands, *Traitor to His Class*, 549. Bohlen found Stalin surprisingly soft-spoken and very fluent in choosing just the right words.

63 **"The Channel is such":** and this episode, see, for instance, Averell Harriman and Elie Abel, *Special Envoy to Churchill and Stalin, 1941–1946* (Random House, 1975), 267; Brands, *Traitor to His Class*, 549; and Meacham, *Franklin and Winston*, 251.

65 **the president's Filipino cooks:** Reilly, *Reilly of the White House*, 150, 180.

65 **mixing cocktails:** Ibid., 180; Bohlen, *Witness to History*, 143; Meacham, *Franklin and Winston*, 145.

66 **more crucial issue of Germany:** Bohlen, *Witness to History*, 143; Meacham, *Franklin and Winston*, 252–54; Brands, *Traitor to His Class*, 551. Regarding "access to the Baltic Sea": Stalin, because of a mistaken interpretation, thought Roosevelt was talking about the Baltic states, not the Baltic Sea.

66 **no words came out:** Roosevelt's health incident is found in Bohlen, *Witness to History*, 143–44; and Meacham, *Franklin and Winston*, 254, both of which I draw heavily upon.

67 **his vision of a postwar world:** See Bohlen, *Witness to History*, 144–45.

67 **increasingly thorny issue:** One can see here the three leaders jockeying more than ever for influence. Churchill, *Closing the Ring*, 363–65. On the monumental choice of Eisenhower, seemingly made at the last second, see also Michael Korda, "An Interview with George C. Marshall," Forrest C. Pogue, October 5, 1956 (Marshall files, George C. Marshall Research Library, Virginia Military Institute, Lexington); and Mark Perry, *Partners in Command* (Penguin, 2007), 238–40. Roosevelt did say that Marshall was "entitled to have his place in history": Robert Sherwood, *Roosevelt and Hopkins: An Intimate History* (Enigma, 2008), 770. Ultimately, Marshall was a victim of complicated politics within the military command structure, at home as well as with the Allies. As Perry points out, Roosevelt was slowly tilted away from Marshall's candidacy. Roosevelt was hoping that Marshall himself, ever the good soldier, would make the decision to bow out. But Marshall, who very much wanted the command, hemmed and hawed, forcing Roosevelt to make the decision, in what was surely one of the most "uncomfortable meetings" (Perry, 240) in the history of American civil-military relations. These are Perry's words, 240.

68 **Now it was Stalin's turn:** Bohlen, *Witness to History*, 146; Churchill, *Closing the Ring*, 371–73.

68 **He alternately "teased":** Reilly, *Reilly of the White House*, 181; Bohlen, *Witness to History*, 146–47; Churchill, *Closing the Ring*, 373.

69 **"never tolerate mass executions":** Discussion and quotation are from Bohlen, *Witness to History*, 146–57; Churchill, *Closing the Ring*, 373–74; Brands, *Traitor to His Class*, 553; Meacham, *Franklin and Winston*, 258–61.

70 **But it was Stalin who rose:** For this charming vignette see Sarah Churchill, *A Thread in the Tapestry*, 66.

71 **chose an opposite course:** Roosevelt's efforts to woo Stalin may be found in two sources that I draw heavily on, Meacham, *Franklin and Winston*, 264–65, 258; and Brands, *Traitor to His Class*, 552–53. "He always enjoyed other people's discomfort": MacGregor Burns makes this point as well, in *Soldier of Freedom*.

74 **first time in eleven years:** Brands, *Traitor to His Class*, 580.

CHAPTER 2

75 **"we have got"** Antony Shaw, *World War II: Day by Day* (Chartwell, 2010), 133; *The Suction Pump*, March 8, 1944, PPA 1944–1945, 99–100. See also MacGregor Burns, *Roosevelt: The Soldier of Freedom* (Harcourt, 1970), 438. Around this time, Churchill was recovering from pneumonia, for which he was prescribed antibiotics and digitalis.

76 **"The name 'Roosevelt' was a symbol":** and paragraph from Edward R. Murrow, *In Search of Light: The Broadcasts of Edward R. Murrow 1938–1961*,

Edward Bliss Jr., ed. (Knopf, 1967), 90–95. This is from his haunting broadcast of April 15, 1945, from Buchenwald, also reprinted in Robert Abzug, *American Views of the Holocaust, 1933–1945: A Brief Documentary History* (St. Martin's, 1999), 202.

76 **mired in the invasion of Italy:** See especially MacGregor Burns, *Soldier of Freedom*, 438–39, from which I borrowed the phrase "soldier's hell"; W. G. F. Jackson, *The Battle for Italy* (Harper, 1967), 182–201; Ambrose, *American Heritage*, 359. Rick Atkinson, *The Day of Battle: The War in Sicily and Italy, 1943–1944* (Holt, 2008), provides a superb account of the obstacles confronting the GIs and getting bogged down in the Italian campaign. See also Mark Perry, *Partners in Command* (Penguin, 2007), 272–378.

78 **"the Purple Heart Valley":** Ambrose, *American Heritage*, 365.

78 **largest amphibious invasion in history:** Material on the background of the invasion is voluminous, and I've drawn extensively from it. See, for example, Perry, *Partners in Command*, 268–72, 277–98; Roland Ruppenthal, *Logistical Support of the Armies*, Volume 1, *The European Theatre of Operations* (Office of the Chief of Military History, 1953); Forrest Pogue, *D-Day: The Normandy Invasion in Retrospect* (University of Kansas Press, 1971); B. H. Liddell Hart, *The Rommel Papers* (Harcourt, Brace, 1953), 465; Cornelius Ryan, *The Longest Day* (Simon & Schuster, 1959); Samuel Eliot Morison, *The Invasion of France and Germany 1944–1945* (Little, Brown, 1959); MacGregor Burns, *Soldier of Freedom*, 473. Stephen Ambrose, *The Supreme Commander: The War Years of Dwight Eisenhower* (Anchor, 2012), provides a condensed overview, along with Ambrose, *American Heritage*, both of which I heavily relied on. For more on the vast preparations, see, for example, Ambrose, *Supreme Commander* 412–13; see also Max Hastings, *Overlord and the Battle for Normandy* (Vintage, 2006), chap. 17. In Great Britain there was a joke that the Americans were sending over so many men and so much matériel that were it not for the barrage balloons, the island would sink into the sea.

81 **GIs . . . crossed themselves:** Ambrose, *American Heritage*, 413, 465.

81 **presence of a red telephone:** For the delicious details of red and green phones, see MacGregor Burns, *Soldier of Freedom*, 474.

81 **"We cannot afford":** Ambrose, *The Supreme Commander*, 431; see also Stephen Ambrose, *D-Day: June 6, 1944—The Battle for Normandy Beaches* (Pocket Books, 2002), 68.

81 **one of Hitler's shrewdest:** Erwin Rommel, The *Rommel Papers*, B. H. Liddell Hart, ed. (Harcourt, Brace, 1953); Ambrose, *D-Day*, 41, 588; Morison, *The Invasion*, 152–53. For a discussion of landing craft, see Gordon Harrison, *Cross Channel Attack* (Department of the Army, 1951), 59–63.

82 **erected a formidable web:** Hitler's subsequent failure to use the panzer tanks would be among his worst decisions of the war, right up there with opening

a second front against the Soviet Union and declaring war on the United States. In this paragraph I draw heavily on Ambrose, *American Heritage*, 465. For more on the Atlantic Wall, see J. E. Kaufmann and H. W. Kaufmann, *Fortress Third Reich: German Fortifications and Defense Systems in World War II* (Da Capo, 2007), 194–223; and Alan Wilt, *The Atlantic Wall: Hitler's Defenses in the West, 1941–1944* (Enigma, 2004).

83 **"The war will be won":** I draw particularly on Ambrose, *American Heritage*, 461–66.

83 **all but a dying man:** *Time*, May 29, 1944, 18; Tully, *FDR, My Boss*, 274; William Hassett, *Off the Record with FDR* (Rutgers University Press, 1958), 239, hereafter cited as Hassett, *Off the Record*. For an outstanding overview, see Goodwin, *No Ordinary Time*, 491–92; Brands, *Traitor to His Class*, 581–84. In a marvelous documentary by David Grubin, *FDR*, on American Experience, PBS, 1994, we hear about Roosevelt falling out of his chair.

84 **"tired and worn":** *New York Times*, March 26, 1944, 35; Hassett, *Off the Record*, 239; Goodwin, *No Ordinary Time*, 492; Brands, *Traitor to His Class*, 579; Atkinson, *The Day of Battle*, 20.

85 **"One trouble followed":** It is difficult to overstate the degree to which Roosevelt's health was impaired during this period. Too often this has been overlooked or underplayed by historians. Yet there were some contemporary accounts questioning his health, and now there is some critical literature. See Stephen Lomazow, MD, and Eric Fettmann, *FDR's Deadly Secret* (Public Affairs, 2009). For additional details about Roosevelt's health, see James MacGregor Burns, "FDR: The Untold Story of His Last Year," *Saturday Review*, April 11, 1970; "Did the US Elect a Dying President? The Inside Facts of the Final Weeks of FDR," *U.S. News and World Report*, March 23, 1951; George Creel, "The President's Health," *Collier's*, March 3, 1945; Karl C. Wold, "The Truth About FDR's Health," *Look*, February 15, 1949; Noah Frapericant, "Franklin D. Roosevelt's Nose and Throat Ailments," *Eye, Ear, Nose and Throat Monthly*, February 1957, 103–6; Rudolph Marx, "FDR: A Medical History," *Today's Health*, April 1961, 54; Richard Norton Smith, " 'The President Is Fine' and Other Historical Lies," *Columbia Journalism Review*, September–October 2001.

86 **"I feel like hell":** See Jim Bishop, *FDR's Last Year* (Morrow, 1974), 4; Smith, *FDR*, 603. Very good on this is the White House aide Hassett, *Off the Record*, 231, 233, 239–41. Significantly, as a sign of Roosevelt's declining health, in July 1935, Roosevelt's blood pressure was 136/75; on March 27, 1944, it was 186/108.

86 **"very gray":** For this and the next two paragraphs, Goodwin, *No Ordinary Time*, 494–95, drawn from her interview with Bruenn. For more on McIntire, who plays a central role in the drama of Roosevelt's health and who

frequently clashed with Dr. Bruenn, see Robert H. Farrell, *The Dying President: Franklin Roosevelt* (Missouri, 1978). "It was worse than I feared": For more, see Howard Bruenn, "Examination Revealed," *Annals of Internal Medicine* (April 1970), 580–81.

88 **"The president's color":** Goodwin, *No Ordinary Time*, 494; Smith, *FDR*, 604; Lomazow and Fettman, *FDR's Deadly Secret*, 101.

88 **visibly suffering:** Brands, *Traitor to His Class*, 581.

88 **"The president can't":** For this and following paragraphs, see Atkinson, *The Day of Battle*, 308; Goodwin, *No Ordinary Time*, 495, 496; Smith, *FDR*, 603. Of note, Goodwin interviewed Bruenn on digitalis, which was considered by some a miracle drug but which could have serious side effects. By way of comparison, when Churchill had pneumonia he took a course of it as well. Lomazow and Fettman discuss the president's wen at great length, as well as the fact that he had a prostate exam and that digitalis was used for congestive heart failure, in *FDR's Deadly Secret*, 103–4. Bruenn had little advance notice that he would actually be treating Roosevelt, and at the outset was not provided with the president's medical file.

89 **"some sunshine and":** Smith, *FDR*, 603–5; Goodwin, *No Ordinary Time*, 497. Smith and Goodwin provide two different dates. April 3 is the correct date.

89 **completely in the dark:** See Brands, *Traitor to His Class*, 581; Dallek, *Roosevelt and American Foreign Policy*, 442. However, Lomazow and Fettman believe that Roosevelt was fully apprised of his condition, and that privately he was worried about it: *FDR's Deadly Secret*, 104–5.

90 **find ways to overcome obstacles:** In *April 1865*, I make this point about leaders having to find a way during the Civil War. See also Atkinson, *Day of Battle*, 22.

91 **Roosevelt stayed for a month:** See especially "President Returns from Month's Rest on Baruch Estate," *New York Times*, May 8, 1944, A1. See also Lee Brockington, *Plantation Between the Waters: A Brief History of Hobcaw Barony* (History Press, 2006), 95; Bernard Baruch, *Baruch: The Public Years* (Pocket Books, 1962) 335–37; and Goodwin, *No Ordinary Time*, 497.

92 **On any map:** My discussion of Auschwitz—the town and its history—closely follows the excellent background in Sybille Steinbacher, *Auschwitz: A History* (Harper Perennial, 2005), 5–22, 22–23, 27, 89, 95, hereafter cited as Steinbacher, *Auschwitz*. An invaluable trip for any reader is to go to Auschwitz itself, to the U.S. Holocaust Museum in Washington, DC, or to Yad Vashem in Israel.

94 **"How old?":** The literature on the notorious selection process is vast. The reader may want to consult Elie Wiesel, *Night* (Hill and Wang, 2006), I; Wiesel vividly describes the process from his own personal experience. I've also

used Primo Levi, *Survival in Auschwitz* (Touchstone, 1996), 18–22 and, for the train ride to Auschwitz, 16–19 (which includes "Luggage afterwards").

95 **After the selections:** The discussion on Auschwitz here comes from extensive material on which I've heavily drawn. See Peter Hellman, *The Auschwitz Album: A Book Based upon an Album Discovered by a Concentration Camp Survivor, Lili Meier* (Random House, 1981), 166. See also Steinbacher, *Auschwitz* (for plunder specifically, 104–5); Deborah Dwork and Robert Jan Van Pelt, *Auschwitz* (Norton, 2002); Otto Friedrich, *The Kingdom of Auschwitz, 1940–1945* (Harper Perennial, 1994); Yisrael Gutman and Michael Berenbaum, *Anatomy of the Auschwitz Death Camp* (Indiana University Press, 1998); Rudolf Hoess, *Death Dealer: The Memoirs of the SS Kommandant at Auschwitz* (Da Capo, 1996); Primo Levi, *Auschwitz Report* (Verso, 2006); Laurance Rees, *Auschwitz: A New History* (Public Affairs, 2006). For the chilling world of the *Sonderkommando*, whose members were slaves twice over and forced to collaborate with the Nazis in the most horrific ways, or face immediate death, see Shlomo Venezia, *Inside the Gas Chambers: Eight Months in the Sonderkommando of Auschwitz* (Polity, 2011); Rudolf Vrba, *I Escaped from Auschwitz* (Barricade, 2007). "The door was thick": Lyric Winik interview with Hans Munch, *Moment Magazine*, October 1998, 60–61, 75–78.

CHAPTER 3

103 **South Carolina was hardly:** Elliott Roosevelt, *As He Saw It* (Duell, Sloane and Pierce, 1946), 370; Robert Dallek, *Franklin D. Roosevelt and American Foreign Policy*, 1932–1945 (Oxford University Press, 1979), 442.

103 **to rejuvenate themselves:** This section closely tracks and benefits enormously from the small, original photographs of the Nazis, too often overlooked, that are lodged in the Holocaust Museum in Washington, D.C. They are a veritable treasure trove. Originally belonging to Karl Hoeker, an aide to Richard Baer, one of the commandants of Auschwitz, this album containing 116 photos is one of the great finds in studies on the Holocaust and of importance for understanding the mind-set of the Nazi high command at Auschwitz. This section also closely follows Jennifer Geddes, "Blueberries, Accordions, and Auschwitz," in *Culture* (Institute for Advanced Studies in Culture, 2008), 2–5.

104 **eight days of vacation:** The photographs of these vacationing Nazis are chilling because they portray these Germans as loving, normal, people, as if they were our next-door neighbors.

106 **funeral in the snow:** The German notations accompanying these photographs refer to the Allies who caused Nazis' deaths as "terrorists."

107 **Every day, they were awakened:** For the horrific conditions at Auschwitz and the other camps, see Jan Karski, "Polish Death Camps," *Collier's*

(October 14, 1944), 18–19, 60–61; Robert Abzug, *America Views the Holocaust, 1933–1945: A Brief Documentary History* (St. Martin's, 1999); Yisrael Gutman and Michael Berenbaum, *Anatomy of the Auschwitz Death Camp* (Indian University Press, 1998); Deborah Dwork and Robert Jan Van Pelt, *Auschwitz* (Norton, 2002); Christopher Browning, *Remembering Survival: Inside a Nazi Slave Labor Camp* (Norton, 2011); Otto Friedrich, *The Kingdom of Auschwitz, 1940–1945* (Harper Perennial, 1994); Olga Lengyel, *Five Chimneys: The Story of Auschwitz* (Chicago Review Press, 1995); Flip Mueller, *Eyewitness Auschwitz: Three Years in the Gas Chambers* (Ivan R. Dee, 1999); Steve Hochstadt, *Sources of the Holocaust: Documents in History* (Palgrave Macmillan, 2004). Karski's observations are particularly trenchant, because he was an eyewitness at one of the camps.

109 **the dreaded "cat":** The basis for this chapter is the remarkable memoir by Rudolf Vrba, *I Escaped from Auschwitz* (Barricade, 2002). For the sake of authenticity, I have sought to preserve his wording and voice. It was Vrba who called the whip used to lash prisoners the "cat." See also Steinbacher, *Auschwitz.*

110 **"the way of Auschwitz":** Interview with Hans Munch, *Moment Magazine*, October, 1998.

113 **New Year's celebration:** For this New Year's Eve festival at Auschwitz and the dinner menu, as well as the other entertainments and beautification efforts, see Steinbacher, *Auschwitz*, 73–75, also 42, on which I've extensively drawn.

114 **master potter Josiah Wedgwood:** See Jay Winik, *The Great Upheaval* (Harper Perennial, 2008), especially 177.

114 **In Hitler's . . . worldview:** Kershaw, *Hitler*, 716–17. Of course like so many other Nazi prophecies this one proved to be false; it demonstrated the megalomania, delusions, and hubris of Hitler and the Nazi high command. They believed history would vindicate them. See also Michael Kimmelman, "50 Years After Trial Eichmann Secrets Live On," *New York Times*, May 9, 2011.

114 **No man appeared less suited:** For background see Vrba, *I Escaped from Auschwitz*, 14–17. Vrba was a remarkably intelligent man, despite his limited education.

115 **Ghettos sprang up:** Ibid., 15.

117 **"neatness and order":** Ibid., 75.

118 **dream of escaping:** Ibid., 121.

118 **became a courier:** Ibid., 182–85.

119 **nibble on a piece of chocolate:** Ibid., 137.

120 **"six months quarantine with special treatment":** Ibid., 189.

120 **a distorted fantasy:** This section on the Jews from Theresienstadt closely follows Martin Gilbert's harrowing account, *Auschwitz and the Allies* (Holt,

1981), 192–95, see also 178. On July 30, 1980, Vrba gave further information in a letter to Gilbert.

121 **to sing . . . Czechoslovak national anthem:** See O. Kraus and E. Kulka, *The Death Factory* (Oxford University Press, 1966), 172–74; Erich Kulka, *Utek z tabora smrti* (Howard Fertig, 2013), 69–71; Yuri Suhl, *They Fought Back: The Story of Jewish Resistance in Nazi Europe* (London, 1968), 244; Jadwiga Danuta, *Amidst a Nightmare*, 118–19. This twenty-one-page Yiddish manuscript (cited above), written in black ink, was discovered on the site of Crematorium III in 1952. The author is unknown and the final entry is dated November 26, 1944.

122 **"an army one million strong":** Vrba, *I Escaped from Auschwitz*, 207.

123 **the would-be escapees:** Ibid., 210.

124 **"It was clear":** Ibid., 211.

124 **with salt and potatoes:** Ibid., 214.

125 **Their bodies, mutilated:** Ibid., 218.

125 **devised an audacious scheme:** Ibid., 219–21.

129 **first known photographs of Auschwitz:** tragically, the intelligence personnel didn't realize the significance of the photographs. I have drawn heavily upon "Interpretation Report D:377A," April 18, 1944, "Locality Oswiecim (Auschwitz): Synthetic Rubber and Synthetic Oil Plant," *United State Strategic Bombing Survey*, Record Group 243; on the dramatic writeup in Gilbert, *Auschwitz and the Allies*, 190–91; and on Vrba, *I Escaped from Auschwitz*, 242.

131 **"They're toying":** Vrba, *I Escaped from Auschwitz*, 242.

132 **"to tear a man":** On patrol dogs, see Himmler's letter, February 8, 1943, in Raul Hilberg, *The Destruction of the European Jews* (Harper Colophon, 1979), 584. They could also hear the chilling "monotonous sounds" of Jews being gassed and cremated.

133 **they were hiding right near:** Vrba, *I Escaped from Auschwitz*, 245.

134 **housed in the Majdanek concentration camp:** On this episode at Majdanek, see especially Gilbert, *Auschwitz and the Allies*, 201.

135 **humming in the sky:** Ibid., 245–46. This dramatic episode of listening to the planes obviously plays into the debate about whether Auschwitz should have been bombed.

136 **"full report":** Ibid., 246. For this episode, see Gilbert, *Auschwitz and the Allies*, 196.

137 **They never looked back:** See Vrba, *I Escaped from Auschwitz*, 247–48.

CHAPTER 4

139 **depart for Hobcaw Barony:** See Bernard Baruch, *Baruch: The Public Years* (Holt, Rinehart and Winston, 1960), 335–37; Lee Brockington, *Plantation*

Between the Waters: A Brief History of Hobcaw Barony (History Press, 2006); Belle W. Baruch Foundation website; Mary Miller, *Baroness of Hobcaw: The Life of Belle W. Baruch* (University of South Carolina Press, 2010).

140 **the Secret Service detail was busy:** Michael F. Reilly, *Reilly of the White House* (Simon & Schuster, 1947), 16. Also see A. Merriman Smith, *Thank You, Mister President: A White House Notebook* (Harper, 1946), 139. Roosevelt's well-known fear of fire from his paralysis as well as from childhood experience.

140 **kept to a simple routine:** FDRL video 135, a silent film of Roosevelt's stay at Hobcaw Barony, may be seen on YouTube. This video shows Roosevelt's attendants, the magnificent estate of Hobcaw, the American flag flapping in the wind, Fala galloping with a black cat, and near the end Roosevelt fishing from Bernard Baruch's boat.

141 **"master raconteur":** From Doris Kearns Goodwin's interview with Dr. Bruenn, in *No Ordinary Time* (Simon & Schuster, 1994). One can wonder whether McIntire was lax in not discussing more with Roosevelt. Roosevelt was surely content to hear as little as possible, but should McIntire have said more? It is of note that Dr. Hugh E. Evans points out that illness was not typically "discussed with patients." He adds "presidential health matters were assumed to be private, rarely reported frankly or with clinical detail." *The Hidden Campaign: FDR's Health in the 1944 Elections* (M. E. Sharp, 2002), 61.

143 **"Attention! This is Auschwitz":** Rudolf Vrba, *I Escaped from Auschwitz* (Barricade, 2002), 248.

144 **Copies of the telegram:** For the text of the telegram, see Erich Kulka, "Five Escapes from Auschwitz," in Yuri Suhl, ed., *They Fought Back: The Story of Jewish Resistance in Nazi Europe* (Crown, 1968), 232. This paragraph closely follows Martin Gilbert, *Auschwitz and the Allies* (Holt, 1981), 196.

145 **told to shoot Jews:** Vrba, *I Escaped from Auschwitz*, 250.

146 **Suddenly, two children:** Ibid., 248–51.

147 **Bielsko was exactly:** Ibid., 251–54.

149 **en route to Slovakia:** Ibid., 254–59.

155 **the British and the Americans as well:** Roosevelt, of course, had considerable information about the impending slaughter, though not as detailed nor as authoritative as what Vrba and Wetzler could provide. Vrba and Wetzler had no way of knowing this. Ibid., 258–59. See also Vrba's detailed letter in Gilbert, *Auschwitz and the Allies*, 203; more can be found in Kulka, "Five Escapes from Auschwitz," 233.

155 **Oskar Krasnansky, a chemical engineer:** Krasnansky was extremely impressed by Vrba's and Wetzler's extraordinary "memory" as he cross-examined them for two straight days on the specifics of Auschwitz. His note expressing his

belief in the two escapees was first published by the War Refugee Board in Washington on November 26, 1944, as part of the overall official publication of the Vrba-Wetzler report. Yet to this very day, the details of how the Vrba-Wetzler memorandums got derailed remain clouded by the Nazis' deceptiveness, the "blood for goods" proposal, and self-deception on the part of some prominent Jews. The story is worthy of a spy thriller. See, for instance, Vrba, *I Escaped from Auschwitz*, 262–65.

156 **His old love:** For more on Lucy Mercer see Jean Edward Smith, *FDR* (Random House, 2008), 160–64; James MacGregor Burns with Susan Dunn, *The Three Roosevelts: Patrician Leaders Who Transformed America* (Grove, 2001), 155–56; Joseph P. Lash, *Eleanor and Franklin: The Story of Their Relationship* (Norton, 1971), 220; Elliott Roosevelt, *An Untold Story: The Roosevelts of Hyde Park* (Putnam, 1973); David D. Roosevelt, *Grandmere: A Personal History of Eleanor Roosevelt* (Warner, 2002), for example, 112.

156 **had his own scare:** see Howard Bruenn, "Clinical Notes," *Annals of Internal Medicine*, April 1970, 548. Nevertheless Merriman Smith observed that Roosevelt was "in good spirits." See Smith, *Thank You*, 140–1. See also Goodwin, *No Ordinary Time*, 500; Eleanor Roosevelt, *This I Remember* (Harper, 1949), 371.

157 **Allied assault forces:** Stephen Ambrose, *D-Day* (Pocket Books, 2002), 170. For a thorough treatment of the Slapton Sands episode, see Ken Small, *The Forgotten Dead* (Bloomsbury, 1988).

161 **"colored troops":** See Craig Smith, January 24, 2005, BBC printout on Slapton Sands; Small, *Forgotten Dead*, for example 44–48. Small's account includes this description (48): "There were men shouting, screaming, praying and dying. . . . But the crying and yelling and screaming and praying had tapered off. The men were falling asleep, and letting go of the rafts—and dying." See also Alex Kershaw, *The Bedford Boys: One American Town's Ultimate D-Day Sacrifice* (Da Capo, 2003), 89, 90; Tom Sollosi, *Valley Independent*, June 3, 2004. Kershaw writes that some officers were so shocked by the "botch-up" at Slapton Sands that they began to question their role in Overlord.

162 **"the absence of toughness":** See Harry Butcher, *My Three Years with Eisenhower* (Simon & Schuster, 1946), 531; Kershaw, *Bedford Boys*, 91. Kershaw notes (92) that secrecy about the disaster was imperative because if it became widely known it would alert the Germans to Overlord. See also Ralph Ingersoll, *Top-Secret* (Harcourt, Brace, 1946), 105. Over time, the bodies of all the intelligence officers were found; this was deemed a minor miracle.

162 **"The Bible says":** And rest of paragraph, see Rick Atkinson, *The Day of Battle* (Holt, 2007), 311.

163 **"brown as a berry":** *New York Times*, May 8, 1944. For "He is thin," see Goodwin, *No Ordinary Time*, 501–2; Hassett, *Off the Record*, 241.

163 **"let the world go hang":** See, for example, H. W. Brands, *Traitor to His Class* (Doubleday, 2008), 583.

CHAPTER 5

165 **Roosevelt was sixty-two:** Eleanor Roosevelt, *This I Remember* (New York, Harper, 1949), 372.

166 **"We must constantly":** Morton Mintz, *Washington Post*, April 17, 1983.

167 **dispatched Joel Brand:** For more on the tangled, mysterious episode known as the "Brand affair," see Yehuda Bauer, *Flight and Rescue* (Magnes Press, 1981), 345. Also see Kai Bird, *The Chairman* (Simon & Schuster, 1992), 218. A young diplomat with the War Refugee Board, Ira Hirschmann, also wrote a detailed memo about the affair. For this, see especially Bird, 690, and Robert Rosen, *Saving the Jews: Franklin D. Roosevelt and the Holocaust* (Thunder's Mouth, 2006), 392–94. In the beginning, Roosevelt enjoined Hirschmann to "keep talking." While Hirschmann talked, FDR felt "these people [would] still have a chance to live."

167 **"incredible Nazi black maneuver":** Eichmann smoothly told Brand, "I want goods for blood." Martin Gilbert, *Auschwitz and the Allies* (Holt, 1981), 202. See also Bauer, *Flight and Rescue*, 144–49. Predictably, the whole affair eventually fell apart.

168 **last remnant of European Jewry:** For a powerful account, see especially Elie Wiesel, *Night* (Hill and Wang, 1958), 3; Rudolf Vrba, *I Escaped from Auschwitz* (Barricade, 2002), 266; and Gilbert, *Auschwitz and the Allies*, especially 182–210. The crematoriums were "littered with amorphous heads of corpses": Yehuda Bauer, *A History of the Holocaust* (Franklin Watts, 2001), 344.

168 **headed into cattle cars:** Primo Levi, the distinguished writer and Holocaust survivor, is particularly strong on this. See *Survival in Auschwitz* (Touchstone, 1996), especially 13–19. See also Vrba, *I Escaped from Auschwitz*, 40–55.

168 **hunted down:** Bauer, *History of the Holocaust*, 344–45. See also Kershaw, *Hitler*, 760–65, 868.

169 **their finest clothes:** Bauer, *History of the Holocaust*, 344. Wiesel, *Night*, for one, also documents the illusions many of the fearful Jews harbored.

170 **roundups were repeated:** Bauer, *History of the Holocaust*, 344. Gilbert, *Auschwitz and the Allies*, also underscores how the roundups continued.

170 **four thousand frightened children:** BBC interviews with survivors. These transports were among the most poignant. Survivors remembered the children before they boarded the trains.

170 **Each train made its way:** For conditions within cattle cars, see Levi, *Survival*, 17; Gilbert, *Auschwitz and the Allies*, 437.

171 **Few said a word:** I have taken this directly from Levi, *Survival*, 17: I think Levi captures these tense moments as well as anyone. See also *The Last Days*, a documentary about five Hungarian Jews, directed by James Moll, executive producer Steven Spielberg.

172 **"Will there be playgrounds":** See, for instance, Gilbert, *Auschwitz and the Allies*; Levi, *Survival*, 18–19; Vrba, *I Escaped from Auschwitz*, 49; Deborah Dwork and Robert Jan van Pelt, *Holocaust: A History* (Norton, 2002), especially 239–84.

173 **deaf ears:** I'm basing this assessment on the interpretation of David Wyman, *The Abandonment of the Jews: America and the Holocaust, 1944–1945* (New Press, 2007), 291.

173 **"I'll see you":** Stephen Ambrose, *D-Day: June 6, 1944* (Pocket Books, 2002), 166–69, quote from 168. I have drawn extensively on Ambrose for this paragraph; the English towns are from 116.

174 **Allied heavy bombers:** See Gilbert, *Auschwitz and the Allies*, 190. For more on the Italian campaign see Carlo D'Este, *Fateful Decision: Anzio and the Battle for Rome* (Harper Perennial, 1992); see also John Keegan, ed., *The Times Atlas of the Second World War* (HarperCollins, 1989).

174 **"a disgraced president":** Rarely did Roosevelt indulge in such distraught thinking, but this was one such moment. See interview with Jay Winik in the documentary *Pearl Harbor: 24 Hours After*, History Channel, Anthony Giachinno, director, 2010; see also the American Experience PBS documentary *FDR*, David Grubin, director. For more, see Doris Kearns Goodwin, *No Ordinary Time* (Simon & Schuster, 1994), especially 506–7 on Roosevelt wishing to be in London.

175 **"Flash. Eisenhower headquarters announces":** *New York Times*, June 4, 1944.

175 **The weather, the waiting:** Here I draw extensively on Goodwin, *No Ordinary Time*, 507; Ambrose, *D-Day*, 182–85; and *American Heritage: New History of World War II*, revised and updated by Stephen Ambrose (Penguin, 1997), 470–71. For more on the thoughts, concerns, and fears of the troops, see the magisterial Max Hastings, *Overlord: D-Day and the Battle for Normandy* (Vintage, 2006); see also *D-Day: The Normandy Landings in the Words of Those Who Took Part*, Jon E. Lewis, ed. (Magpie, 2010). There was a stark difference between the Germans' and the Allies' forecasting. The Germans were impeded by the loss of their outlying weather stations, and this situation would contribute to their lack of preparedness. Whereas Captain Stagg predicted a "window" of reasonable weather after the poor conditions, on June 5, the Germans did not. This was a fatal error for them. See also Russell Weigley,

Eisenhower's Lieutenants (Indiana University Press, 1980); and Omar Bradley, *A Soldier's Story* (Vintage, 1964). Stephen Ambrose, *The Supreme Commander* (Doubleday, 1970), is also quite good, and for the decision to initiate D-Day, I draw extensively on 414–18, which provides the most comprehensive treatment. An especially important resource is Captain Harry C. Butcher, *My Three Years with Eisenhower* (Simon & Schuster, 1946). These sources, on which I draw heavily, are the basis for my scene about the decision to go and the beginning of D-Day. Hastings's and Ambrose's accounts are particularly strong and vivid, and were crucial to my vignettes in these pages.

176 **tremendous fleet of vessels:** For these passages I have relied on (among other sources) James MacGregor Burns, *Roosevelt: The Soldier of Freedom* (Harcourt, 1970), 475–76. On Eisenhower's decision to commence the Overlord invasion, see, for example, Mark Perry, *Partners in Command* (Penguin, 2007), 296–99. Some historians have Eisenhower saying, "Let's go." Perry gives the version, "We'll go!" See also Ambrose, *D-Day*, 188–89; I follow Ambrose's timing of the decision. Here, see Carlo D'Este, *Eisenhower: A Soldier's Life* (Holt, 2002), 525. "You know I'm a juggler": This is one of Roosevelt's most revealing statements.

180 **When the planes emerged:** For these pages detailing casualties and mishaps; see in particular Ambrose: *D-Day*, 312–14; and MacGregor Burns, *Soldier of Freedom*, 476–77, on which I've drawn extensively. It was expected that the gliders would encounter problems and even crashes. Communication mishaps, however, such as those with battlefield radios, were not anticipated. Here of course is what the master strategist Carl von Clausewitz called the "fog of war."

183 **"We are staying here":** This material is from Ambrose, *D-Day*, 313; and Hastings, *Overlord*. For Hitler sleeping, see Kershaw, *Hitler*, 804–6; Walter Warlimont, *Inside Hitler's Headquarters* (Presidio Press, 1962), 403–6.

184 **"We could not see":** Ambrose, *D-Day*, 264.

184 **"Most of us":** Ambrose, *D-Day* (from which I've drawn extensively for this section), 263; for list of ships, see 235.

184 **"crescendo of a great symphony":** Ibid., 271. Goodwin, *No Ordinary Time*, is very good on the mishaps at Omaha Beach.

185 **And along Omaha beach:** For more on the mishaps at Omaha, I have heavily tapped into the descriptions provided by Ambrose, *American Heritage*, 467. For more on the Bedford boys, see Alex Kershaw, *The Bedford Boys: One American Town's Ultimate D-Day Sacrifice* (Da Capo, 2003). Bedford, Virginia, was a small blue-collar town of some three thousand people. No town in America endured such a great loss on a single day, and Kershaw's vignettes—for example, of mothers and wives being notified by Western Union telegrams—are deeply moving. Many were devastated by the loss.

188 **"I became . . . a visitor":** Ambrose: *D-Day*, 331; the next two paragraphs closely follow 331–35. For further tribulations encountered by the Americans, see especially 337–38; for "Mother, Mom," 337.

188 **retreat was not a feasible strategy:** Max Hastings, *Overlord* (Simon & Schuster, 1984), 92; Ambrose, *D-Day*, 435. For a while, Bradley was close to despair; see Omar Bradley and Clay Blair, *A General's Life: An Autobiography* (Simon & Schuster, 1983), 249. One German observed, "Here they had to fight savagely for every inch," Lewis, *D-Day*, 148.

188 **the Allies kept coming:** As one soldier put it, "Now it was open country and we had broken through the 'Atlantic Wall,' " Lewis, *D-Day*, 135. Nonetheless, as one lieutenant pointed out, "the bombs were bursting literally everywhere all the time," Lewis, *D-Day*, 134. See also Ambrose, *D-Day*, 340.

189 **"run us right back . . .":** Ambrose, *D-Day*, 381, 340–42. And as Kershaw, *Hitler*, points out, almost pathetically, Hitler was still sleeping.

190 **word about the invasion:** Details of the giddy reactions to the Allies' successes closely follow *New York Times*, June 6 and June 7, 1944; Michael Korda, *Ike* (Harper Perennial, 2007), 479–81; Ambrose, *D-Day*, 486–508, especially 489–90.

192 **"Here is something material":** This vignette is from my *April 1865: The Month That Saved America* (HarperCollins, 2001). International and national reaction in *New Yorker*, June 10, 1944; *Wall Street Journal*, June 7, 1944; *Milwaukee Journal*, June 7, 1944; *New Orleans Times Picayune*, June 7, 1944; *New York Times*, June 7, 1944; David Lang, "Letter from Rome," *New Yorker*, June 17, 1944; *Times* (London), June 7, 1944; Alexander Werth, *Russia at War, 1941–1945* (New York: Dutton, 1964), 853–55; *Atlanta Constitution*, June 7, 1944; *Bedford Bulletin*, June 8, July 6, 1944. For an overall compilation, see also Ambrose, *D-Day*, 494.

CHAPTER 6

197 **the bloody North African campaign:** See the magisterial work by Rick Atkinson, *The Day of Battle: The War in Sicily and Italy, 1943–1944* (Holt, 2007), 269.

197 **As he rode with Eisenhower:** Ibid. for these three paragraphs.

198 **Rommel wasn't even at the front:** See Michael Korda, *Ike* (Harper Perennial, 2007), 479, for this and "Faster."

199 **"We waited":** *D-Day*, Jon E. Lewis, ed. (Magpie, 2010), 92.

199 **"The sun is shining":** See Stephen Ambrose, *D-Day* (Pocket Books, 2002), 483. So stunning was the Allies' offensive on D-Day that Rommel told an aide on his ride back from Germany, "If I was commander of the Allied forces right now, I could finish off the war in 14 days": from Korda, *Ike*, 483.

200 **"Hitler must have been mad":** Ambrose, *American Heritage*, 476. The pilot saw the action from his P47. For these paragraphs, see also Korda, *Ike*, 477–83; James MacGregor Burns, *Roosevelt: The Soldier of Freedom* (Harcourt, 1970), 476–77; and Ambrose, *D-Day*, 530, 548, 576–77. Later there was a Wehrmacht joke—"If the plane in the sky was silver it was American, if it was blue it was British, if it was invisible it was ours": see Ambrose, *D-Day*, 578.

201 **"Wetzler and I saw":** Martin Gilbert, *Auschwitz and the Allies* (Holt, 1981), 231–32; for the two additional escapees, 222.

201 **Otto Frank:** For the Franks, including Otto, once the owner of a successful spice company, following the progress of the war became an emotional lifeline. For more on this, see the excellent website of the Anne Frank House and Museum, which takes the viewer to the secret annex behind the bookcase, where by day the eight people in hiding had to be completely silent and had to subdue every move, every action, and every cough.

202 **"the whole globe":** Anne Frank, *The Diary of a Young Girl* (Longman, 1993), 55, 53, 65. The diary, actually an autograph book that she was using, ranks as one of the great works of literature. Of the million children who died in the Holocaust, Anne is surely the most famous.

202 **"from one room to another":** For these quotes, ibid., 55, 67.

206 **his terrible secret:** I have drawn heavily on Kershaw, *Hitler*, 691, 698, in these paragraphs. Kershaw underscores the seeming paradox of Hitler's secrecy regarding the destruction of the Jews. For various quotes, including "the unity of the European states," see 677, 691.

CHAPTER 7

210 **"I have very often in my lifetime":** Kershaw, *Hitler*, 469. In retrospect, this was surely one of Hitler's most significant speeches, even if it was not recognized as such at the time.

211 **"lice," "vermin":** Ibid., 468. See also Martin Gilbert, *Auschwitz and the Allies* (Holt, 1981), 13.

211 **"If only the anger":** Kershaw, *Hitler*, 456. See also Walter Laqueur and Richard Breitman, *Breaking the Silence: The German Who Exposed the Final Solution* (Brandeis University Press, 1994), 56. For more on the "night of broken glass," see Martin Gilbert, *The Holocaust: A History of the Jews of Europe During the Second World War* (Holt, 1985), 69–75; this book is a remarkable resource, filled with a compendium of the voices of Jews throughout the war and in the Holocaust itself. The reader may also consult two excellent works: Yehuda Bauer, *A History of the Holocaust* (Franklin Watts, 2001), 116–17; and Jean Edward Smith, *FDR* (Random House, 2008), 426. Three weeks earlier, in Berlin, famed aviator Charles Lindbergh was

decorated by Hermann Göring with the Service Cross. See William Shirer, *The Nightmare Years 1930–1940* (Birlinn, 1984), 238. The "night of broken glass" caused mass panic among the Jews, who were forced to pay a staggering 1 billion reichsmarks for the destroyed property. For more see Lucy S. Dawidowicz, *The War Against the Jews* (Bantam, 1986), Hitler's Reichstag speech, 142.

212 **"Bravo":** Kershaw, *Hitler*, 458. Kershaw makes significant copious use of Goebbels's diaries.

213 **"How can this barbarity":** from the marvelous story by Diane Ackerman, *The Zookeeper's Wife: A War Story* (Norton, 2007), 103. For "I myself could scarcely," see Smith, *FDR*, 426. For "I ask nothing," see Ackerman, *Zookeeper's Wife*, 104.

214 **economic solution:** Here I draw upon Kershaw, *Hitler*, 459–61. Kershaw makes this astute observation: Consider the titles of the German laws themselves. For instance, there was the Law for the Protection of German Blood and German Honor. While severely circumscribing the ability of Jews to participate in civic life, it stated almost ludicrously that the right of Jews "to display the Jewish colors" enjoyed "the protection of the state." See Bauer, *History of the Holocaust*, 111 and for texts of the laws, 108–112.

214 **convened the Évian Conference:** On Roosevelt and immigration, see, for example, Smith, *FDR*, 427. When Roosevelt was given political latitude, Smith points out, he sought to do what he could. After Kristallnacht, he suggested that German citizens in the United States on visitor permits be allowed to stay longer. "I don't know, from the point of humanity, that we have a right to put them on a ship and send them back to Germany," he said (428). Yet a key point would be that Roosevelt was unwilling to expend too much political capital.

215 **"It is a shameful spectacle":** For quotes from session 9, see Morris Wortman, MD, *The Holocaust: From Poland to Barbarossa* (1939, online).

216 **the luxury liner *St. Louis*:** I have relied on Doris Kearns Goodwin, *No Ordinary Time: Franklin and Eleanor Roosevelt—The Home Front in World War II* (Simon & Schuster, 1994), 102. For more on the Évian conference and the *St. Louis* episode, see "Topics of the Times: Refugee Ship," *New York Times*, June 8, 1939; the *Times* put it well when it wrote, "Germany, with all the hospitality of its concentration camps, will welcome these unfortunates home." See also David S. Wyman, *The Abandonment of the Jews: America and the Holocaust, 1941–1945* (New Press, 1984); Arthur Morse, *While Six Million Died: A Chronicle of American Apathy* (Overlook, 1967), 270–88. In their careful study, Richard Breitman and Allan Lichtman, *FDR and the Jews* (Belknap Press of Harvard University Press, 2013), 136–39, give a very different interpretation of the *St. Louis* affair, stating that only

254 of the passengers eventually died either in the camps or seeking to evade the Nazis. They also detail the Coast Guard was not seeking to prevent any passengers from reaching American shores—rather, it was simply trying to maintain a chance to find a solution. See also Sarah Ogilvie and Scott Miller, *Refuge Denied: The* St. Louis *Passengers and the Holocaust* (University of Wisconsin Press, 2010); and Gordon Thomas and Max Morgan-Writt, *Voyage of the Damned: A Shocking True Story of Hope, Betrayal and Nazi Terror* (Skyhorse, 2010). For "what I am interested in," see Geoffrey Ward, *A First-Class Temperament: The Emergence of Franklin Roosevelt* (Harper and Row, 1989), 254.

219 **"The children are not":** *New York Times*, July 7, 1940, A5; see also Goodwin, *No Ordinary Time*, 100.

219 **The British refugee children:** See the excellent and nuanced discussion in Goodwin, *No Ordinary Time*, 101.

220 **The Roper polls consistently found:** Daniel Yankelovich, "German Behavior, American Attitudes," talk given in May 1988 at a conference at Harvard on the Holocaust and the media. See also Goodwin, *No Ordinary Time*, 102.

220 **"treacherous use of the fifth column":** David S. Wyman, *Paper Walls: America and the Refugee Crisis, 1938–1941* (Pantheon, 1985), 188–91; see also Henry Feingold, *The Politics of Rescue: The Roosevelt Administration and the Holocaust, 1938–1945* (Rutgers University Press, 1970), 128–31; Goodwin, *No Ordinary Time*, 103; and clips of Roosevelt's speech on YouTube and on American Experience, *FDR*, PBS documentary by David Gruban.

221 **responsibility of one man:** *Nation*, December 28, 1940, 649. For more on the critical figure, Breckinridge Long, see Feingold, *Politics of Rescue*, 131–35. For "an enormous psychosis" see Breckinridge Long, *The War Diaries of Breckinridge Long: Selections from the Years 1939–1944*, Fred L. Israel, ed. (University of Nebraska Press, 1966), 108.

225 **secret intradepartmental memo:** *New York Times*, December 11, 1943, A1. This memo by Breckinridge Long about delaying and effectively stopping immigration ranks among the ugliest in State Department history.

226 **"There does seem":** Goodwin, *No Ordinary Time*, 173.

226 **the president met with Long:** *Nation*, December 28, 1940, 648.

227 **Roosevelt met with James G. McDonald:** Ibid., 649. *The Nation* proved to be one of the most eloquent voices on behalf of the embattled Jews and on the immigration issue. For more on McDonald, see James McDonald, *Refugees and Rescue: The Diaries and Papers of James G. McDonald, 1935–1945*, Richard Breitman, Barbara McDonald Stewart, and Severin Hochburg, eds. (Indiana University Press), 2009.

227 **"pull any sob stuff":** Wyman, *Paper Walls*, 147; Goodwin, *No Ordinary Time*, 174.

228 **SS *Quanza*:** For this episode, see the detailed article in the *New York Times*, August 19, 1940, A5. For extensive details, see YouTube video by Greg Hansard of Virginia Historical Society.

228 **"Mrs. Roosevelt saved my life":** Stella Hershan, *A Woman of Quality* (Crown, 1970), 41; Goodwin, *No Ordinary Time*, 174.

229 **"deepest regret":** From Eleanor's interview with James Roosevelt; for more, see Goodwin, *No Ordinary Time*, 174–76. Eleanor's contention that Long was a Fascist comes from Justine Polier, oral history in FDRL.

229 **Baffled observers wondered:** Churchill's biographer William Manchester, a fan of Roosevelt's, makes this point about Roosevelt's reticence in *Winston Spencer Churchill: The Last Lion* (Delta 1988), 465. "The record is one": For these eloquent words, see the *Nation*, December 28, 1940, 649.

230 **find another route for help:** Wyman, *Abandonment*, 15.

231 **sitting this one out:** See James MacGregor Burns, *Roosevelt: The Soldier of Freedom: 1940–1945* (Harcourt, 1970), 11; Smith, *FDR*, 447.

231 **"Full speed ahead!":** And other quotes, see, for example, Smith, *FDR*, 448–49. By any measure, this was a deeply expressive speech, making it clear where Roosevelt's heart was in this war.

231 **Churchill huddled by the radio:** *New York Times*, December 18, 1940, 1, 10. For Churchill's jubilation, and critics of Roosevelt, see Smith, *FDR*, 449, 436. As a result of what came to be known as the "stab in the back speech" (Italy declaring war on France), Smith makes the point that Roosevelt was now standing shoulder to shoulder with France and England.

232 **a Gallup poll found:** See, for instance, Smith, *FDR*, 464.

233 **Yet bit by bit:** Goodwin, *No Ordinary Time*, 194. For more on the America First committee, see Wayne S. Cole, *America First: The Battle Against Intervention, 1940–1941* (University of Wisconsin Press, 1953), 14.

233 **Roosevelt was reelected:** MacGregor Burns, *Soldier of Freedom*, 4. Stephen Ambrose, the noted historian, had in the past been critical of Roosevelt's timidity about getting into the war.

234 **"The more I sleep":** Smith, *FDR*, 481; Goodwin, *No Ordinary Time*, 191.

234 **"with great respect":** Smith, *FDR*, 467; Ambrose, *American Heritage*, 113. This is among Churchill's most famous lines in the entire war.

235 **"the most important action":** This paragraph from *No Ordinary Time*, Goodwin, 142; Smith, *FDR*, 472. See also Winston S. Churchill, *The Second World War*, Volume 2, *Their Finest Hour* (Houghton Mifflin, 1949), 358.

235 **"America's first dictator":** MacGregor Burns, *Soldier of Freedom*, 441; Goodwin, *No Ordinary Time*, 148.

236 **how to help a beleaguered Britain:** See, for instance, Smith, *FDR*, 483; I've drawn extensively on this in-depth discussion.

236 **"most important":** For Churchill's crucial 4,000 word letter see Smith, *FDR*, 484; Ambrose, *American Heritage*, 114; Goodwin, *No Ordinary Time*, 192–93; MacGregor Burns, *Soldier of Freedom*, 12, 13.

238 **question of Britain's troubled finances:** There are many fine accounts. I have used Smith, *FDR*, 484.

238 **dubbed Lend-Lease:** This was vintage Roosevelt. See, for starters, the outstanding portrait by Jon Meacham, *Franklin and Winston: An Intimate Portrait of an Epic Friendship* (Random House, 2003), 78–81; MacGregor Burns, *Soldier of Freedom*, 25; Smith, *FDR*, 485.

238 **numerous meetings:** MacGregor Burns, *Soldier of Freedom*, 26.

239 **"eliminate the dollar sign":** MacGregor Burns, *Soldier of Freedom*, 26. These paragraphs draw extensively from Burns's detailed recounting of Roosevelt's speech. See also Smith, *FDR*, 485.

239 **"most unsordid act."** Which was not an understatement. See Smith, *FDR*; MacGregor Burns, *Soldier of Freedom*, 27.

241 **"Arsenal of Democracy":** For this speech, I've chosen Smith, *FDR*, 486.

242 **ended with an equally eloquent:** Meacham, Franklin and Winston, 79. The Miller Center for Public Affairs at the University of Virginia has put Fireside Chat 16 on YouTube, with photos. This speech was one of Roosevelt's most stunning efforts; his voice is clear, resonant, and authoritative. For quotes, see also MacGregor Burns, Soldier of Freedom, 27–29. Roosevelt himself emphasized that this was not "an ordinary" fireside chat.

244 **"We are strong enough":** See Smith, *FDR*, 489–90; Meacham, *Franklin and Winston*, 81. In the actual defense supplemental, Congress authorized 900,000 feet of fire hose. Notably, Wendell Willkie broke with his party's leadership and publicly endorsed Lend-Lease.

244 **public was with the president:** MacGregor Burns, *Soldier of Freedom*, 44–48. Roosevelt, at the White House Correspondents' Association, memorably said that the decisions of democracy may be slowly arrived at, but that they are proclaimed "not with the voice of one man but with the voice of 130 million."

245 **a lightning assault on Yugoslavia and Greece:** This passage closely follows Ambrose, *American Heritage*, 114.

247 **Churchill, his head sunk in despair:** See *New York Herald Tribune*, April 6, 1941, A1; Ambrose *American Heritage*, 98.

247 **preparing to quietly meet:** See, for example, Smith, *FDR*, 492.

248 **"I am waiting":** Ibid., 493; see also MacGregor Burns, *Soldier of Freedom*, 66.

248 **remaining noncommittal:** On Roosevelt's strategy, and "I am waiting to be pushed," see, for instance, MacGregor Burns, *Soldier of Freedom*, 91–92; Smith, *FDR*, 492. In a sense, this is what Abraham Lincoln did in the Civil

War, insisting that it be the Confederates who would fire first on Fort Sumter and be regarded as the belligerents. That said, there are of course profound differences between World War II and the American Civil War.

CHAPTER 8

251 **"they sat there":** James MacGregor Burns, *Roosevelt: The Soldier of Freedom, 1940–1945* (Harcourt, 1970), 72.

251 **"We have only to kick":** Ibid. For other quotes, Kershaw, *Hitler*, 620. I have relied extensively on Kershaw's book, which could well be the finest one-volume modern work on Hitler. For more on Hitler's relations with his generals, which are crucial to the story, see *Hitler's Secret Conversations* (Farrar Straus and Young, 1953), especially the introduction by Hugh Trevor-Roper; Hugh Trevor-Roper, ed., *Blitzkrieg to Defeat: Hitler's War Directives, 1939–1945* (Holt, Rinehart and Winston, 1965); Walter Warlimont, *Inside Hitler's Headquarters* (Praeger, 1964); Barton Whaley, *Codeword Barbarossa* (MIT Press, 1973); Hugh Trevor-Roper, *Hitler's Tabletalk, 1941–1944*, (Enigma Books, 2007); Telford Taylor, *Sword and Swastika* (Simon & Schuster, 1952).

252 **"to intervene":** MacGregor Burns, *Soldier of Freedom*, 68–70. For this paragraph, see Kershaw, 587, on which I've relied.

253 **code name was Barbarossa:** This paragraph relies principally on MacGregor Burns, *Soldier of Freedom*, 68; and Kershaw, *Hitler*, 619. Operation Barbarossa was Hitler's most significant strategic military decision, all but ensuring his eventual defeat.

254 **the tense Molotov responded:** This dramatic episode with Molotov is derived from MacGregor Burns, *Soldier of Freedom*, 95. It highlights how even at the highest levels of government the stress on the leaders was unremitting. The reader may recall that Roosevelt privately panicked after the bombing of Pearl Harbor; further, Stalin himself collapsed when Hitler attacked on the Eastern Front.

254 **the Germans' assault took place:** For the initial assault and details, Doris Kearns Goodwin, *No Ordinary Time* (Simon & Schuster, 1994), 253; Kershaw, *Hitler*, 621–22; MacGregor Burns, *Soldier of Freedom*, 96.

255 **the German march:** Kershaw, *Hitler*, 622. For more on Hitler's mastery of Europe, and comparisons with other leaders, see for example my treatment of Napoleon seeking to swallow the Middle East: Jay Winik, *The Great Upheaval* (Harper, 2006). Napoleon of course made comparable mistakes in lunging into the vastness of Russia.

256 **conceived as a territorial:** Kershaw, *Hitler*, 669.

256 **reality was far different:** Ibid., 670. Kershaw's point, too rarely appreciated, is that the initial instructions were ad hoc, often confusing, and anything but systematic; I've leaned heavily on his greater explication.

257 **"Vengeance" he wrote:** Kershaw, 671.

257 **Lithuanian town of Kovno:** There are tapes, or movie reels, of this chilling, seminal episode in Lithuania.

258 **were "vile," they were "lice":** Kershaw, *Hitler*, 671–77, on which I have also relied for the lapse in professionalism among the German generals in the conquered territories.

258 **Babi Yar:** wrenching account in Martin Gilbert, *The Holocaust* (Holt, 1985), 202–3; Anatoly Kuznetsov, *Babi Yar* (Dell, 1970).

260 **"scramble over the ledge":** Gilbert, *Holocaust*, 204–5.

260 **"like ghosts":** Ibid., 212–17, from which I have drawn extensively.

261 **"None has suffered more":** *Jewish Chronicle*, November 14, 1941; Gilbert, *Holocaust*, 232–33. Churchill's "the mills of God" is from Friedrich von Logau's poem "Retribution," translated by Henry Wadsworth Longfellow.

262 **"whether to Siberia":** Kershaw, *Hitler*, 677.

263 **"As far as Jews":** For this and related quotes, as well as discussion of the Final Solution, see Kershaw, *Hitler*, 678, 686; Gilbert, *Holocaust*, 213; and the very fine work by Anthony Read, *The Devil's Disciples: Hitler's Inner Circle* (Norton, 2004), especially 751.

263 **took a toll on the killers:** Letter to Walther Rauff, May 16, 1942, Report of October 30, 1941, to the Commissioner General, Minsk; see also Gilbert, *Holocaust*, 222. It is a cruel irony that the Nazis wanted clean hands in carrying out their butchery.

264 **"death comes faster":** Letter to Walther Rauff, May 16, 1942.

265 **Chelmno woods:** Gilbert, *Holocaust*, 239, 245; Read, *Devil's Disciples* 753. I have leaned on both.

265 **first days of the "final solution":** This episode, helping to inaugurate the final solution, is rendered in detail in Gilbert, *Holocaust*, 240.

265 **"Do you think":** Gilbert, *Holocaust*, 245–47.

266 **Wannsee conference:** See especially Raul Hilberg, *The Destruction of the European Jews*, 1967, 262–64; Raul Hilberg, ed., *Documents of Destruction: Germany and Jewry, 1933–1945* (W.H. Allen, 1972), 88–99; also Gilbert, *Holocaust*, 284. On qualms about killing valuable workers, see Read, *Devil's Disciples*, 751. The Holocaust History Project also has a very useful discussion. Online, the reader may also see the villa in which the meeting took place; and BBC/HBO dramatized the conference in the compelling movie *Conspiracy* (2001), which may be watched on YouTube on demand. It strikes me as a largely accurate rendition, at least in the broad brush strokes. At the conference itself, the word "extermination" was never mentioned; instead, taking a cue from Hitler, participants talked of being "firm" and "severe." Nonetheless, their intentions were unmistakable. The participants spoke with the clinical detachment of doctors.

268 **numbers of all the Jews:** See Gilbert, *Holocaust*, 281.

268 **"bit by bit":** Ibid., 282.

269 **They sipped brandy:** Ibid., 283.

269 **"The hour will come":** Text for Hitler's fateful speech: from Foreign Broadcast Monitoring Service, January 30, 1942, Federal Communications Commission; see also, Gilbert, *Holocaust*, 285.

270 **new death camps:** See Read, *Devil's Disciples*, 755; Gilbert, *Holocaust*, 285–87.

272 **"We've got to go":** For this and further quotes, and for Marshall's and Eisenhower's strategic thinking, see Goodwin, *No Ordinary Time*, 342; Mark Perry, *Partners in Command: George Marshall and Dwight Eisenhower in War and Peace* (Penguin, 2007), 76.

272 **peripheral attack:** On Churchill's thinking, see Goodwin, *No Ordinary Time*, 345. After the war, Churchill repudiated with great fervor the belief that he had been against an all-out assault against Europe: Winston S. Churchill, *The Grand Alliance* (Houghton Mifflin, 1950), 581–82.

272 **plans for the great cross-Channel assault:** See Goodwin, *No Ordinary Time*, 342, on which I've relied heavily here.

273 **"What Harry and George":** Ibid., 343. I've also especially drawn from Perry, *Partners in Command*, 77–79, which is very strong on the strategic interaction of the generals. See also Forrest C. Pogue, *George C. Marshall: Education of a General* (Viking, 1963). What comes across is that the American generals, as befitting the democratic process, were far more outspoken than the cowardly Nazi generals. This is an important resource because from August 1956 to April 1957 Pogue conducted a series of five extensive interviews with Marshall; these provide the best and most comprehensive account of Marshall's outlook. The interviews were taped and involved prearranged questions. It's important to note that Marshall and Eisenhower had similarities as well as differences; see Forrest C. Pogue, "The Supreme Command," in *US Army in World War II: European Theater of Operations* (U.S. Army Center of Military History, 1996), 33–35. See also Dwight D. Eisenhower, *Crusade in Europe* (Doubleday, 1948), 17; Carlo D'Este, *Eisenhower: A Soldier's Life* (Holt, 2002); Ed Cray, *General of the Army: George C. Marshall, Soldier and Statesman* (Rowman and Littlefield, 1990).

273 **Molotov arrived at the White House:** Goodwin, *No Ordinary Time*, 344; Forrest C. Pogue, *George C. Marshall: Ordeal and Hope* (Viking, 1966), 328.

274 **Machination now followed:** I've drawn upon Perry, *Partners in Command*, 97.

274 **Roosevelt and Churchill . . . at Hyde Park:** See Pogue, *George C. Marshall: Ordeal and Hope*, 323; Perry, *Partners in Command*, 99, on which I've relied.

275 **Tobruk . . . had fallen:** For this fascinating episode, when Churchill was despondent—not unlike Roosevelt in private after Pearl Harbor—see Perry, *Partners in Command*, 100; Goodwin, *No Ordinary Time*, 347; Jon Meacham, *Franklin and Winston* (Random House, 2003); Winston S. Churchill, *The Hinge of Fate* (Houghton Mifflin, 1950), 280–88, 343.

275 **"What can we do to help?":** Roosevelt's reaction was no doubt instinctive; see Goodwin, *No Ordinary Time*, 347–48; Consult also Hadley Cantril, "Evaluating the Probable Reactions to the Landing in North Africa in 1942: A Case Study," *Public Opinion Quarterly*, Fall 1965, 400–10.

275 **A jubilant Churchill:** "Here is the true" and other quotes. Goodwin, *No Ordinary Time*, 348. For Stalin's misgivings on political aspects of Torch, see Robert E. Sherwood, *Roosevelt and Hopkins* (Harper, 1948), 618.

276 **"the blackest day":** Captain Harry Butcher, *My Three Years with Eisenhower: The Personal Diary of Captain Harry C. Butcher, 1942–1945* (Simon & Schuster, 1946), 29.

276 **"we had only weeks":** Dwight D. Eisenhower, *Crusade in Europe* (Doubleday, 1948), 72.

277 **"secret baby":** See Henry Stimson's diary, June 21, 1942, Yale University. "We failed to see": Eric Larrabee, *Chief Franklin Delano Roosevelt, His Lieutenants, and Their War* (Harper and Row, 1987), 9; MacGregor Burns, *Soldier of Freedom*, 288–89; Goodwin, *No Ordinary Time*, 349. For more on the background of the invasion, see William L. Langer, *Our Vichy Gamble* (Knopf, 1947).

277 **"I feel very strongly":** MacGregor Burns, *Soldier of Freedom*, 289–90. On this issue in 1942, Roosevelt was far ahead of his advisers, who didn't appreciate the importance of the morale of the American public. Roosevelt knew U.S. troops had to be in the fight. See Goodwin, 349–49. For more on the Churchill-Roosevelt exchange in the planning of Torch, see Churchill, *Hinge of Fate*, 530–43.

278 **"in the night, all cats are gray":** MacGregor Burns, *Soldier of Freedom*, 289–90.

CHAPTER 9

279 **Eduard Schulte was German:** This chapter draws very heavily upon the extremely important but often overlooked book about Eduard Schulte by two extremely important Holocaust scholars: Walter Laqueur and Richard Breitman, *Breaking the Silence: The German Who Exposed the Final Solution* (Brandeis University Press, 1994), hereafter cited as *Breaking the Silence*. These authors have gone to great lengths to reconstruct Schulte's life under the Nazi regime and have produced an outstanding work of scholarship. Biographical material here is from *Breaking the Silence*, 18–37. There is also

a significant article, James M. Markham, "An Unsung Good German: 'Fame' Comes at Last," *New York Times*, November 9, 1983. Breitman generously read chapter 9 and made detailed comments, for which I am grateful.

284 **alarms were everywhere:** *Breaking the Silence*, 41, for Schulte's personal views, which provide a rare insight into the thoughts of an opponent of the Nazi regime. For more on the Night of the Long Knives, see Anthony Read, *The Devil's Disciples* (Norton, 2004), 345–74; and Kershaw, *Hitler*, 309–16. For background on Schulte, religion, family life, marriage, early reaction to Hitler, see *Breaking the Silence*, 18–37.

285 **"gangsters":** *Breaking the Silence*, 37–51. On Hitler's foreign policy, to which Schulte was also reacting, see Gerard Weinberg, *The Foreign Policy of Hitler's Germany: Starting World War II, 1937–1939* (University of Chicago Press, 1980), 313–27. For the German military's surprising attitude toward Hitler in the 1930s, see Peter Hoffman, *The History of the German Resistance, 1933–1945* (McGill-Queens University Press, 1996).

286 **invited to . . . an extraordinary meeting:** For Schulte's perspective, see *Breaking the Silence*, 41. Details of this meeting between Hitler and the industrialists can also be found in William Manchester, *Winston Spencer Churchill: The Last Lion, Alone, 1932–1944* (Delta, 1988), 62–65.

287 **with Julius Schloss, an old friend:** Here I have relied extensively on *Breaking the Silence*, 55.

288 **Otto Fitzner:** Ibid., 68–69.

289 **talk was still a common currency:** For example, ibid., 59, 104.

290 **riffling through a newspaper:** Ibid., 12.

290 **visiting "Auschwitz":** For background on Himmler and on Auschwitz, see Read, *Devil's Disciples*, 86, 757; also Sybille Steinbacher, *Auschwitz: A History* (Harper Perennial, 2005), 11.

293 **"be proud of":** See Read, *Devil's Disciples*, 179–80.

293 **"hereditary health":** Ibid., 179. See also Martin Gilbert, *The Holocaust* (Holt, 1985), 387, for Himmler's July 19 directive to resettle the Jews.

294 **For Himmler, in the early weeks:** Gilbert, *Holocaust*, 373.

294 **Treated like a visiting head of state:** The best treatment of Himmler coming to Auschwitz can be found in Rudolf Vrba, *I Escaped from Auschwitz* (Barricade, 2002), 3, 5.

294 **watched the complete process of gassing:** Ibid., 6; for this paragraph I have also relied heavily on Read, *Devil's Disciples*, 757–59.

296 **"best sparkling form":** Read, *Devil's Disciples*, 758. See also *Breaking the Silence.*

297 **boarded the train at Breslau:** Schulte's harrowing train ride into Switzerland. For these exquisite details I've drawn extensively from *Breaking the Silence*, 117–18.

299 **"there were problems":** Ibid., 123.

300 **"life and death":** Ibid., 122–24. Here, in miniature, one can see even Jews wrestling with the dimensions and ghastly details of the Final Solution. Schulte's contact was Isidor Koppelmann, the right-hand man of a close business associate of Schulte's. For more on Sagalowitz, his papers are at Yad Vashem in Jerusalem.

300 **"I've received information":** *Breaking the Silence*, 129.

301 **"May I quote him":** Ibid.

301 **Was this just propaganda:** Ibid., 131. Many people were seduced by the notion that the atrocities were figments of the imagination or wild propaganda, akin to the stories that had been rampant during World War I; see Walter Laqueur, *The Terrible Secret: Suppression of the Truth About Hitler's "Final Solution"* (Holt, 1988), especially 171–83.

303 **talked for five hours over lunch:** These exquisite details of the extended lunch in *Breaking the Silence*, 137, on which I've heavily relied.

306 **he decided to approach:** Ibid., 139.

306 **met with the vice consul:** Martin Gilbert, *Auschwitz and the Allies* (Holt, 1981), 57; Gilbert, like Breitman, had the benefit of directly interviewing Riegner. Details about Schulte in Breslau are found in *Breaking the Silence*.

306 **"great agitation":** Quotations from Elting's summary of the meeting, in David S. Wyman, *The Abandonment of the Jews: America and the Holocaust, 1941–1945* (New Press, 1984), 43. Wyman's book, one of the most significant works on this subject, is deeply critical of Roosevelt. Notably, Wyman himself is not Jewish, and no study of the subject can discount the rigor of his scholarship.

306 **"personal opinion":** *Breaking the Silence*, 148.

307 **"war rumors inspired by fear":** Ibid., 149.

307 **Riegner's telegram wound up:** I have drawn from the assessment in Wyman, *Abandonment*, 44.

CHAPTER 10

309 **"if the Rabbi":** From David S. Wyman, *The Abandonment of the Jews* (New Press, 1984), 43–44. For more on this pivotal figure, see Stephen Wise, *Challenging Years: The Autobiography of Stephen Wise* (East and West Library, 1949); Carl Herman Voss, ed., *Stephen S. Wise: Servant of the People* (Jewish Society, 1969); Melvin Urofsky, *A Voice That Spoke for Justice: The Life and Times of Stephen S. Wise* (State University of New York Press, 1982).

309 **"to third parties":** Martin Gilbert, *Auschwitz and the Allies* (Holt, 1981), 58–59. Beyond ideology and sentiments about the Middle East and Jews, one benign explanation of the State Department's behavior is bureaucratic politics; see the classic work on the bureaucracy in action, Graham Allison,

Essence of Decision: Explaining the Cuban Missile Crisis (Pearson, 1999). Another possible explanation is groupthink; see Irving Janis, *Groupthink: Psychological Studies of Foreign-Policy Decisions and Fiascoes* (Houghton Mifflin, 1983).

312 **"He re-won my":** Wyman, 69, *Abandonment*, for quotations, Wise's background and trust in Roosevelt.

313 **Charlie Chaplin:** This paragraph benefits from William Manchester, *Winston Spencer Churchill: The Last Lion* (Delta, 1988), 63.

316 **deemed Riegner a scholar of "entire reliability":** From Wyman, *Abandonment*, 45, on which I lean heavily here. See also Benjamin Wells, *Sumner Welles: FDR's Global Strategist* (St. Martin's 1997).

316 **than from Cordell Hull:** For more see Cordell Hull, *The Memoirs of Cordell Hull* (Macmillan 1948); Harold Hinton, *Cordell Hull: A Biography* (Doubleday, 2008); For their interaction, see Irwin F. Gelman, *Secret Affairs: FDR, Cordell Hull and Sumner Welles* (Enigma, 2003); Walter Isaacson and Evan Thomas, *The Wise Men: Six Friends and the World They Made* (Simon & Schuster), 1986.

317 **"great uneasiness and apprehension":** Manchester, *The Last Lion*, 87.

317 **That same year:** This paragraph is drawn from the remarkable story by Erik Larsen, *In the Garden of Beasts: Love, Terror, and an American Family in Hitler's Berlin* (Crown, 2012), 241, 32, 17.

318 **Fatefully, Wise relented:** See *Breaking the Silence*, 153 for this and the quotation from the State Department.

319 **"I am almost demented":** Voss, *Stephen S. Wise: Servant of the People*, 248–50; Justine Polier and James W. Wise, eds., *The Personal Letters of Stephen Wise: 1933–1949* (Beacon Press 1956), 260–1. This passage also follows Wyman, *Abandonment*, 45–46. It's important to emphasize that by this stage virtually all the Jewish leaders in America understood that the extermination of the Jews was under way, a point Wyman makes. By contrast, Walter Laqueur, in *The Terrible Secret* (Holt, 1988), suggests that American Jewish leaders were very slow to believe systematic extermination was taking place. Both explanations have elements of truth to them, but Wyman is more compelling.

319 **"Only energetical steps":** From *Breaking the Silence*, 46. It's important to note, and not underestimate, the degree to which prominent Jews of this day were fearful of seeming too Jewish, or more Jewish than American. Frankfurter fits the bill here.

319 **The dimensions of the threat:** Ibid., 155.

320 **Wise had a full schedule:** Ibid., 154–55, for these paragraphs; also Wyman, *Abandonment*, 48.

321 **"fearful retribution":** See Robert N. Rosen, *Saving the Jews: Franklin D. Roosevelt and the Holocaust* (Thunder's Mouth, 2006), 237–38.

321 **The killing and dying continued:** For quotations and the meeting with Harrison, see Wyman, *Abandonment*, 47; *Breaking the Silence*, 157.

322 **handed Harrison a sealed envelope:** The contents of the understated yet traumatic note can be found in *Breaking the Silence*, 158.

322 **Where were all the Jews:** *National Jewish Monthly*, October 1942, 36–37. See also Wyman, *Abandonment*, and 48–49; *New York Times*, October 30, 1942. Clearly, by this stage the pieces of the puzzle about the disappearing Jews and the Holocaust were falling into place.

325 **"My comrades":** From text of the September 30, 1942, Winter Relief Campaign speech. Details on Hitler's routine can be found throughout Kershaw, *Hitler*.

326 **"special camps":** Wyman, *Abandonment*, 52, on which I extensively draw.

326 **"to great crematoriums":** *New York Times*, November 25, 1942, A10. It is said that nothing was known about Auschwitz, but this dispatch from Jerusalem specifically mentioned it, using the name "Oswiecim." Government officials had only to read the newspaper. For statistics of Jews killed in the previous twelve months, see Martin Gilbert, *The Second World War* (Holt Paperbacks, 2004), 386; see also Gerard Weinberg, *Germany, Hitler and World War II* (Cambridge University, 1966), 218.

326 **"Himmler Program Kills":** *New York Times*, November 25, 1942, A10.

327 **On December 2:** Details from *New York Herald Tribune*, November 25, 1942, 1. For more on the Day of Mourning and Prayer, see Doris Kearns Goodwin, *No Ordinary Time* (Simon & Schuster, 1994), 396; and Wyman, *Abandonment*, 71.

328 **"The question of":** Willi A. Boelcki, ed., *Secret Conferences of Doctor Joseph Goebbels: The Nazi Propaganda War, 1939–1943* (Dutton, 1970), 240; see also Goodwin, *No Ordinary Time*, 397.

328 **"Dear Boss":** From Adolph Held, Jewish Labor Committee Archives, December 8, 1942; the quotations may also be found in Wyman, *Abandonment*, 71–72, which presents this episode in detail.

329 **"Do all in":** The meeting with Roosevelt is drawn heavily from *Breaking the Silence*, 162; and Rosen, *Saving the Jews*, 244. See also Deborah Lipstadt, *Beyond Belief: The American Press and the Coming of the Holocaust, 1933–1945* (Free Press, 1986), 1984–85; Richard Breitman, *Official Secrets: What the Nazis Planned, What the British and Americans Knew* (Hill and Wang, 1998), chap. 9 (this is a fascinating book); and Arthur Morse, *While 6 Million Died: A Chronicle of American Apathy* (Random House, 1968), 28.

329 **"an insane man":** Wyman, *Abandonment*, 73.

330 **"Gentlemen" and "We shall do":** Ibid.

330 **"Don't bother going":** James MacGregor Burns, *Roosevelt: The Soldier of Freedom, 1940–1945* (Harcourt, 1970), 286–87. Here we see vintage Roosevelt circumventing the bureaucracy when it suited his purposes.

330 **Once more, Wise convened:** *Palcor Bulletin*, December 17, 1942, for these paragraphs; see also Martin Gilbert, *Auschwitz and the Allies* (Holt, 1981), 103–4, for a moving account of this episode.

331 **"grave doubts":** Wyman, *Abandonment*, 74.

331 **"beyond doubt"** and views of the ***Christian Century*****:** See Wyman, *Abandonment*, 65–66.

332 **"The ugly truth":** Goodwin, *No Ordinary Time*, 397.

332 **"The most tragic":** *New York Times*, December 18, 1942, 46; quotations are also found in Wyman, *Abandonment*, 76.

333 **"How horrible, fantastic":** William Manchester, *Winston Spencer Churchill: The Last Lion* (Delta, 1988), 345.

333 **On the domestic front:** This paragraph is drawn heavily from the *New York Times*, April 23, 1942, 1, 16; and August 16, 1942, section 7, 5. For related information, see *New Republic*, September 21, 1942, 336; *Fortune*, November 1942, 227; *Time*, May 25, 1942, 16. For an overview see Goodwin, *No Ordinary Time*, 356–59.

338 **"We are standing":** Forrest Pogue, *George C. Marshall* (Viking, 1963), 123, 402; and Mark Perry *Partners in Command* (Penguin, 2007), 127.

338 **not only was their training inadequate:** Perry, *Partners in Command*, 166, 175. For equipment see Goodwin, *No Ordinary Time*, 387.

339 **Roosevelt had instructed:** Roosevelt's instruction to Robert Murphy is in Charles Murphy, "The Unknown Battle," *Life*, October 16, 1944, 102, 106.

340 **"My friends":** MacGregor Burns, *Soldier of Freedom*, 292.

341 ***Newsweek* wrote:** Goodwin, *No Ordinary Time*, 388.

342 **"every bullet we":** Perry, *Partners in Command*, 139.

342 **"We are attacked"** and **Darlan deal:** Major General Richard W. Stephens, "Northwest Africa: Seizing the Initiative in the West," in *US Army in World War II, Mediterranean Theater of Operations* (Government Printing Office, 1956), 260–65. See also the excellent writeup in Burns, *Soldier of Freedom*, 296, which includes the quotes in these paragraphs. I have relied heavily on Rick Atkinson, *An Army at Dawn* (Holt, 2007), 121–22; and Jean Edward Smith, FDR (Random House, 2008) 562–64.

343 **"opposed to Frenchmen":** MacGregor Burns, *Soldier of Freedom*, 297. The Vichy government in North Africa feared (correctly) that it would be under threat from the Germans. Complicating matters, the Allies had to deal with two sets of French leaders.

343 **"walk with the devil":** Ibid. For Marshall's and Eisenhower's defense of the "Darlan deal," see Conference with Marshall, November 15, 1942, Clapper Papers, Library of Congress. For more on the military and politics, see Harry Butcher, *My Three Years with Eisenhower* (Simon & Schuster, 1946), 165.

344 **"I'm happy today":** MacGregor Burns, *Soldier of Freedom*, 300.

345 **"in a department store":** Ibid.

345 **"Now, this is not":** Robert E. Sherwood, *Roosevelt and Hopkins* (Harper, 1948), 656; see also Goodwin, *No Ordinary Time*, 389. What comes across here is that Roosevelt could clearly envision the successful end of the war. Similarly, in the Civil War, when Ulysses Grant squared off against Robert E. Lee, Grant's triumph, despite appalling losses, especially in the Wilderness Campaign, became a matter of military mathematics and time.

345 **"This . . . is London":** See Kai Bird, *The Chairman, John J. McCloy: The Making of the Establishment* (Simon & Schuster, 1992), 202; this is an outstanding work.

345 **New Year's Eve:** See Sherwood, *Roosevelt and Hopkins*, 665; Samuel Rosenman, *Working with Roosevelt* (Harper, 1952), 365; MacGregor Burns, *Soldier of Freedom*, 302.

CHAPTER 11

348 **"We can become":** Roger Moorhouse, *Berlin at War* (Basic Books, 2010), 336–40. The text of Goebbels's speech may be found online in German and in English. See also William Shirer, *The Rise and Fall of the Third Reich* (Simon & Schuster, 1960).

349 **issued a gas mask:** For Washington, D.C., during wartime, I have relied extensively on a marvelous little book, brimming with keen observations, by the veteran journalist David Brinkley, *Washington Goes to War: The Extraordinary Story of the Transformation of the City and a Nation* (Random House, 1999), 23, 73, 74–75, 83, 95–96. The reader can also consult Paul K. Williams, *Washington DC: The World War II Years* (Arcadia, 2014). Taken together, these two books are reminiscent of Margaret Leech's Pulitzer prize–winning study, *Reveille*, about the capital during the Civil War.

350 **"Last year":** James MacGregor Burns, *Roosevelt: The Soldier of Freedom, 1940–1945* (Harcourt, 1970), 305–6; for text of speech, Samuel Rosenman, ed. *The Public Papers and Addresses of Franklin D. Roosevelt*, Volumes 1941–1945 (Harper, 1950), 21–34; for Roosevelt preparing the message for Congress, see Samuel Rosenman, *Working with Roosevelt* (Harper, 1952), 366. The text may also be found online.

351 **in liberated Casablanca:** Michael Reilly, *Reilly of the White House* (Simon & Schuster, 1947), 150, 180.

351 **Elliott Roosevelt, who had been summoned:** Elliott Roosevelt, *As He Saw It* (Duell, Sloane and Pierce, 1946), 324–25.

352 **Much of the talk was speculation:** For discussions and strategy at Casablanca see H. W. Brands, *Traitor to His Class: The Privileged Life and Radical Presidency of Franklin Delano Roosevelt* (Doubleday, 2008), 695–708,

521–22; Jean Edward Smith, *FDR* (Random House, 2008), 565–66. It's important to remember that as a backdrop to these discussions, Rommel's panzers drubbed the U.S. II Corps at Kasserine Pass in mid-February 1943; see Dwight D. Eisenhower, *Crusade in Europe* (Doubleday, 1948), 163.

353 **Churchill "used humor":** These two paragraphs rely heavily upon Jon Meacham, *Franklin and Winston* (Random House, 2004), 204, 207, and the marvelous photograph of Churchill having his way, 205; see also Elliott Roosevelt, *As He Saw It*, 329.

353 **"Once in a jeep":** For these paragraphs, including unconditional surrender, Meacham, *Franklin and Winston*, 208, 209; Doris Kearns Goodwin, *No Ordinary Time* (Simon & Schuster, 1994), 409–10; Smith, *FDR*, 567–68. Smith makes the point that unconditional surrender had been thoroughly discussed and that Roosevelt was not shooting from the hip. The debate has continued to this day.

357 **"I congratulate you":** From MacGregor Burns, *Soldier of Freedom*, 330. Burns's account of Hitler during this period is very strong, and I rely heavily on his interpretations.

357 **"would inevitably have led":** Ibid.

357 **Hitler's foul moods:** For Hitler's deterioration, pill taking, and symptoms, see Kershaw, 752–54, on which I extensively draw in these paragraphs. See also MacGregor Burns, *Soldier of Freedom*, 331 and for the list of those Hitler hated, 309–10 (I have made some additions to this).

360 **"I had honored my father":** Kershaw, *Hitler*, 5–20; it is hard to overstate the impact of the early death of his mother on Hitler. My biography of Hitler is extensively drawn from Kershaw. Other works I've consulted are Adolf Hitler, *Mein Kampf* (Houghton Mifflin, 1998); Albert Speer, *Inside the Third Reich* (Simon & Schuster, 1997); Alan Bullock, *Hitler: A Study in Tyranny* (Harper Perennial, 1991); Ron Rosenbaum, *Hitler: The Search for the Origins of His Evil* (HarperCollins, 1998); William Shirer, *The Rise and Fall of the Third Reich* (Rosetta, 2011); Daniel Goldhagen, *Hitler's Willing Executioners* (Vintage, 2011); *Adolf Hitler: A Concise Biography* (Berkeley, 2000). Burns's *Soldier of Freedom* also has fascinating insights into the Führer. For more on the crucial relationship of Hitler and his generals, see Corelli Barnett, *Hitler's Generals* (Grove Weidenfeld, 1989).

361 **Hitler dropped out of school:** For these paragraphs, see Kershaw, *Hitler*, 9–11. Kershaw makes a powerful case that Hitler was early on a dreamer and a dilettante beset by delusions and phobias.

361 **The dream soon ended:** Ibid., 15, 22–24, 33, for this material.

362 **"Ohm Paul Kruger":** Ibid., 31.

362 **his cherished Wagner:** Ibid., 21.

363 **Hitler himself was a deviant:** Ibid., 27–37, which includes his burgeoning worldview and "the greatest German mayor." It is important to note that Hitler was imbibing the anti-Semitism of the time.

364 **For the first time he had a sense of belonging:** For instance, ibid., 50–59. World War I is crucial for understanding Hitler.

366 **"stumbled across his greatest talent":** Ibid., 63–75.

366 **"Goodness he's got":** Ibid., 75.

367 **"beer hall":** Ibid., 128–48. See also *Mein Kampf*. It is remarkable in hindsight to think about what an extraordinary bestseller *Mein Kampf* was; it is equally remarkable to think of how Hitler was treated as a celebrity in jail. It calls to mind Harriet Beecher Stowe and her extraordinary book *Uncle Tom's Cabin*, which propelled her to international celebrity and bolstered the antislavery movement, prompting Abraham Lincoln to say to her, "So you are the little lady who started this great war." The profound difference, of course, is that Hitler was laying the groundwork for the Holocaust and the evisceration of morality, while Stowe was appealing to national and international morality with her tract.

369 **In 1932, the Nazis received . . . 18.3 percent:** Kershaw, *Hitler*, 204–5.

369 **Yet he did not come to power:** The delusions of the moderates regarding Hitler were endless. On this, and for quotes, ibid., 291; and William Manchester, *Winston Spencer Churchill: The Last Lion* (Delta, 1988), 63.

370 **"Hitler is Reich Chancellor":** For this and Walter Lippmann's observations, Kershaw, *Hitler*, 256; Manchester, *The Last Lion*, 81. Lippmann was considered one of America's greatest journalists, yet he was always ambivalent about his own Jewishness, and this ambivalence at times clouded his judgment: see Ronald Steel, *Walter Lippmann and the American Century* (Little, Brown, 1980).

370 **Upon coming to power:** For these paragraphs about the consolidation of Hitler's power I draw heavily on Kershaw, *Hitler*, 256; Manchester, *The Last Lion*, 79–81; and Erik Larsen, *In the Garden of Beasts* (Crown, 2012), 19.

373 **Hitler was a born thespian:** See Manchester, *The Last Lion*, 117; Kershaw, *Hitler*, 174.

375 **In late February 1943:** On the critical Senate vote, see David S. Wyman, *The Abandonment of the Jews* (New Press, 1984), 95.

376 **"The Jews are being slaughtered":** Ibid. 105; and *New York Times*, December 13, 1942.

376 **"In this country":** *Nation*, March 13, 1943, 366–67; and Wyman, *Abandonment*, 89–90. The *Nation* remained among the most eloquent voices of the time.

376 **"We Will Never Die":** At the United States Holocaust Memorial Museum and at its website, the reader may see film footage from the pageant. The American Experience website and PBS, which produced *America and the*

Holocaust, have more information. See also Wyman, *Abandonment*, 91, on which my account draws heavily.

377 **"one of the most impressive":** See Wyman, *Abandonment*, 91.

378 **"Romania Proposes":** *New York Times*, February 13, 1943.

379 **"For Sale to Humanity":** *New York Times*, February 16, 1943. See also Wyman, *Abandonment*, 86–88, on which I draw heavily, for Wise's efforts to galvanize the administration and Congress.

380 **the administration was now feeling the political pressure:** See Wyman, *Abandonment*, 89.

381 **President Roosevelt met in Washington:** See minutes of the Meeting of the Joint Committee, March 29, 1943, in Wyman, *Abandonment*, 382; see also 97.

382 **"There is always the danger":** For this material, Wyman, *Abandonment*, 99; see also, for Sir Thomas Moore, Manchester, *The Last Lion*, 101.

383 **diplomats convening in Bermuda:** On the splendor of the conference, see *London Observer*, April 20, 1943; and *New York Times*, April 20, 1943. On the setup for the Bermuda conference, see especially Wyman, *Abandonment*, 109–10.

384 **Once the conference began:** On the sidestepping of the main issues, see dispatches in *Manchester Guardian*, April 20–24, 1943. See also Arthur Morse, *Apathy* (Ace Publishing, 1968), 54, 60.

384 **"with wooden legs":** MacGregor Burns, *Soldier of Freedom*, 396.

385 **"send a large number of picked":** See Wyman, *Abandonment*, 113–15, 396. I draw heavily on Wyman for the unfolding of the conference.

385 **was more complicated:** On the back-and-forth that went nowhere, ibid., 221.

385 **Dodds, the chair:** *Foreign Relations of the U.S.* Volume 1, 1943, 134.

386 **"subject to military"** and paragraph: Readers may consult Wyman, *Abandonment*, 117, for this interpretation.

386 **no serious dissenting voices:** See Meacham, *Franklin and Winston*, 227.

386 **"shocked by the":** For this and other quotes, Wyman, *Abandonment*, 119; for the candid discussion among the American delegates on Easter, when they finally started seeing this as what Wyman calls a people problem, see his Appendix A, 356. The German comes from Manchester, *The Last Lion*, 121. See also Meacham, *Franklin and Winston*, 227, for discussion of the administration's view on the Bermuda conference. Meacham notes that this is one of the few times when Roosevelt and Churchill actively discussed the Holocaust in May, though they reached no decision. Churchill wrote to Roosevelt on June 30, 1943, "Our immediate facilities for helping the victims of Hitler's anti-Jewish drive are so limited at present that the opening of the small camp proposed for the purpose of removing some of them to safety seems all the more incumbent on us."

387 **"destroyed every hope":** See Wyman, *Abandonment*, 120–22, 143.

388 **Polish city of Warsaw:** This discussion follows Martin Gilbert, *The Holocaust* (Holt, 1985), 461. Also see Dan Kurzman, *The Bravest Battle: The 28 Days of the Warsaw Ghetto Uprising* (Da Capo, 1993); Israel Gutman, *Resistance: The Warsaw Ghetto Uprising* (Mariner, 1998); Kazik, *Memoirs of a Warsaw Ghetto Fighter* (Yale University Press, 2002); Emmanuel Ringleblum, *Notes from the Warsaw Ghetto* (iBooks, 2006).

390 **"We fight like animals":** This and preceding two paragraphs from Gilbert, *Holocaust*, 557–64.

390 **a few Jews inside:** Ibid., 564–67. The two words "save us," would heroically echo through the ranks of Jews everywhere who heard them.

392 **the renowned poet:** I am indebted to MacGregor Burns for Roosevelt's exchange with Archibald MacLeish recording the history of the war. This paragraph follows MacGregor Burns, *Soldier of Freedom*, 389–92.

392 **For two weeks:** On the Trident conference and the discussion about Italy, see for example Goodwin, *No Ordinary Time*, 439. Smith, *FDR*, 572–76; Meacham, *Franklin and Winston*, 223–26.

394 **"Gambia fever"** See MacGregor Burns, *Soldier of Freedom*, 390; Meacham, *Franklin and Winston*, 214; Goodwin, *No Ordinary Time*, 419.

397 **"I don't care":** Smith, *FDR*, 576, for this and other quotes.

CHAPTER 12

399 **"I get so many conflicting":** Harold D. Smith diary, FDRL, Roosevelt memorandum on September 14, 1942; also may be found in MacGregor Burns, *Roosevelt: The Soldier of Freedom, 1940–1945* (Harcourt, 1970), 343. For Roosevelt as chief executive, see Barry Dean Karl, *Executive Reorganization and Reform in the New Deal* (Harvard University Press, 1963); see also a fine study by Richard E. Neustadt, *Presidential Power* (Wiley, 1960), especially 214–15, which sheds light on Roosevelt's leadership. Henry Stimson also had keen observations on Roosevelt as an administrator: see his diary entries, January 23, 1943, February 3, 1943, and March 28, 1943, Stimson Papers, box 400, Library of Congress.

401 **"vague" and "noncommittal":** in Doris Kearns Goodwin, *No Ordinary Time* (Simon & Schuster, 1994), 453. For more on the emergency conference, see David S. Wyman, *The Abandonment of the Jews* (New Press, 1984) 146. I draw on both Goodwin and Wyman.

401 **"in any way":** Quotes from Goodwin, *No Ordinary Time*, 454.

402 **"I do not think":** Wyman, *Abandonment* 148.

403 **"there was hardly a square yard":** These paragraphs are drawn extensively from Jan Karski, *Collier's*, October 14, 1944, 18–19, 60–61. Karski went to great lengths to document everything he saw and experienced. Karski's article is haunting. See also Goodwin, *No Ordinary Time*, 454.

405 **"You have a *friend*":** See American Experience PBS documentary, *America and the Holocaust*; Henry Morgenthau Diary FDRL; Robert N. Rosen, *Saving the Jews* (Thunder's Mouth, 2006), 297, 347. For more, see E. Thomas Wood and Stanislas Jankowski, *Karski: How One Man Tried to Stop the Holocaust* (Wiley, 1996). It is worth recalling that Karski's original mission was to lobby for a free Poland and to warn Roosevelt about the Soviet Union, but Karski had an awakening because of what he saw in the death camp. In addition to Cordell Hull, it was John Pehle who asserted that Roosevelt was "stunned" by Karski's account.

406 **"What I think I will do":** MacGregor Burns, *Soldier of Freedom*, 397. Allis Radosh and Ronald Radosh, *A Safe Haven: Harry S. Truman and the Founding of Israel* (Harper Perennial, 2009), 18–22. Roosevelt said the problem of Jews in Palestine could be settled by putting a barbed-wire fence around it. Sam Rosenman told Roosevelt in turn, yes, if it "keeps Jews in and Arabs out," 20. On colonization of the Jews: For Lincoln, I discussed this in *April 1865*. It also turns out that the principal author of the Constitution, James Madison, had comparable ideas about slaves and blacks colonizing Liberia. On the shifting sands of the Middle East: My discussion here closely follows MacGregor Burns's observation that the success in Italy opened up countless possibilities in the Middle East; for more, see Morgenthau Diary, December 3, 1942, FDRL.

407 **"Will any of these Jews survive":** From Wyman, *Abandonment*, 150.

408 **"Stephen, why don't you":** Rosen, *Saving the Jews*, 289, 391. On Romanian Jews: Wyman, *Abandonment*, 82–84.

409 **"Hitler . . . started boasting":** From Franklin Delano Roosevelt, Message to Congress, September 17, 1943, 106, online (see American Presidency Project). Rosen, *Saving the Jews*, 290, has the Goebbels quote.

411 **"alchemists of former days":** MacGregor Burns, *Soldier of Freedom*, 250.

412 **"Three months' delay":** My discussion of the technology of war here draws extensively on Irvin Stewart, *Organizing Scientific Research for War* (Little, Brown, 1948), 5–7; as well as Jean Edward Smith, *FDR* (Random House, 2008), 578–81; and MacGregor Burns, *Soldier of Freedom*, 249–52, a section written with Douglas Rose and Stuart Burns, especially 252. My list of conventional weapons comes from MacGregor Burns and Rick Atkinson. On NDRC and civilian military cooperation and American-British scientific exchange, see James P. Baxter, *Scientists Against Time* (Little, Brown, 1946), 14–16, 119–23, 129. On the development of the atomic bomb and the fear that Hitler could get it first, there are a number of fine books. See Richard Rhodes, *The Making of the Atomic Bomb* (Simon & Schuster), 2012; Richard Rhodes, *Arsenals of Folly: The Making of the Nuclear Arms Race* (Vintage, 2008); Robert Jungk, *Brighter Than a Thousand Suns: A Personal History of the Atomic Scientists* (Mariner, 1970); and the outstanding work

by Kai Bird and Martin Sherwin, *American Prometheus: The Triumph and Tragedy of J. Robert Oppenheimer* (Vintage, 2006).

413 **"the relatively simple matter":** This discussion follows Wyman, *Abandonment*, 182–89. Morgenthau's "satanic combination" is surely one of the bluntest lines coming from a cabinet member in American history; it has also become legendary for its incisiveness. By this stage, one sees, Morgenthau was at his wit's end.

413 **"When you get through with it":** Wyman, *Abandonment*, 183. Time has dimmed the intensity of the Treasury Department's feelings about the government unwittingly collaborating with Hitler in the destruction of the Jews, about as harsh a criticism as could be leveled. These quotations, almost mocking in tone, evidently said with a sneer, capture some of the concern of Morgenthau and the people around him.

414 **tough-minded Oscar Cox:** See the excellent work by Richard Brightman and Allan Lichtman, *FDR and the Jews* (Belknap Press of Harvard University Press, 2013), 229. By this stage, things were moving very fast politically. In hindsight, the question has to be raised: did politics trump morality?

414 **"haunted by the suffering":** This paragraph is from Rosen, *Saving the Jews*, 342; Wyman, *Abandonment*, 183.

414 **"The trouble is":** Material from Wyman, *Abandonment*, 186. That Morgenthau accused Long of being anti-Semitic indicated he was holding nothing back. That Cordell Hull sought to blame bureaucratic politics was, in the end, a flimsy explanation and an abdication of leadership.

416 **"You have to figure":** Wyman, *Abandonment*, 194–203.

416 **"I personally agree":** This and next three paragraphs are drawn from the text of the House Foreign Affairs Committee Meeting, November 26, 1943 (Government Printing Office), 32. The entire text—"Rescue of the Jewish and Other Peoples in Nazi Occupied Territory, Hearings Before the Committee on Foreign Affairs, 78th Congress, First Session on H. Res. 350 and H. Res 352, Resolutions Providing for the Establishment by the Executive of a Commission to Effectuate the Rescue of the Jewish People of Europe"—is fascinating, and wrenching, reading.

417 **"580,000 Refugees Admitted":** *New York Times*, December 12, 1943; see also Wyman, *Abandonment*, 198–203. The *New York Times* and other major newspapers largely followed the administration line in their reporting.

418 **"boiling pot":** Wyman, *Abandonment*, 203.

419 **"Report to the Secretary on the Acquiescence of This Government in the Murder of the Jews":** Quotes are taken from the actual report. The report may be found online at the website of the Jewish Virtual Library. There has probably never been as hard-hitting a memo about the government, and this is required reading in its entirety.

420 **Morgenthau Jr. was a product:** Here I benefited extensively from Michael Beschloss, *The Conquerors: Roosevelt, Truman and the Destruction of Hitler's Germany, 1941–1945* (Simon & Schuster, 2002), especially 44–55. Other valuable sources include John Morton Blum, *Roosevelt and Morgenthau* (Houghton Mifflin, 1970); John Morton Blum, ed., *From the Morgenthau Diaries*, 3 vols. (Houghton Mifflin, 1959, 1965, 1967); and Henry Morgenthau III, *Mostly Morgenthaus: A Family History* (Ticknor and Fields, 1991). For specific quotations and details see Blum, *Morgenthau Diaries*, xvi, 12–15, 193–94, 206–8, 211, 245–65; *Mostly Morgenthaus*, xiii. On Fishkill Farms, see *Time*, January 25, 1943; Henry Morgenthau III writes that Henry Sr. bought the farm for his son (Blum, *Roosevelt and Morgenthau*, 218), then Morgenthau himself insisted to journalists that he bought the farm, using profits made from his investments of family money. On Morgenthau and his changing relationship with Judaism, see *Mostly Morgenthaus*, xiii. On the Morgenthau relationship with Zionism, see *Diaries*, 193–94, 206–8. See also Geoffrey Ward, *First-Class Temperament* (Harper and Row, 1989), 253.

423 **"From one of":** Beschloss, *The Conquerors*, 48. Original signed photo is at FDRL.

423 **"put it on the line":** See *Mostly Morgenthaus*, 267–68, 271–72; Beschloss, *The Conquerors*, 49; Blum, *Morgenthau Diaries*, Volume 1, 77.

423 **"stupidity and Hebraic arrogance,":** This stunning quote from Kai Bird, *The Chairman* (Simon & Schuster, 1992), 100; other quotes from Beschloss, *The Conquerors*, 48–52. It is interesting to note that Morgenthau never attended a Passover seder until after the war by which time he had an awakening about his Jewishness.

424 **"You and I will run":** This paragraph is extensively drawn from Beschloss, *The Conquerors*, 50–51; and Kai Bird, *The Chairman*, 224.

424 **"depression within a depression":** This is among Morgenthau's most prominent observations. "If we don't stop": On Morgenthau and pre–World War II preparedness, see Blum, *Morgenthau Diaries*, Volume 2, 86–93; *Mostly Morgenthaus*, 318–20. For "war loving race," see Beschloss, *The Conquerors*, 71 and Bird.

424 **"get rid of him":** This paragraph is drawn from Beschloss, *The Conquerors*, 51–54. For "very dangerous advisor," "biased by his Semitic," see Bird, *The Chairman*, (Simon & Schuster), 225–26. For "were a member of the cabinet in Germany" see Irwin Gellman, *Secret Affairs: Franklin Roosevelt, Cordell Hull and Sumner Welles* (Johns Hopkins University Press, 1995), 25–26, 97–99, 209, and 286; and Beschloss, *The Conquerors*, 54.

425 **"Roosevelt was not the greatest":** see Josiah Dubois interview, Henry Morgenthau III, Private Archive, Cambridge, Massachusetts, HMPA; see also

Beschloss, *The Conquerors*, 54. For Jews around Roosevelt, see Ward, *First-Class Temperament*, 253–55; *Mostly Morgenthaus*, 321–22.

426 **"What I want is his intelligence and courage":** See Samuel Rosenman, *Working with Roosevelt* (Harper, 1952), 340; *Morgenthau Diaries*, 693, 196, 202–10; Wyman, *Abandonment*, 181–83; Rosen, *Saving the Jews*, 340–47; and Richard Breitman and Alan Kraut, *American Refugee Policy* (Indiana University Press, 1988), 189. Significantly, Morgenthau would compare his activism for the Jews to his father's efforts on behalf of the Armenians: Blum, *Roosevelt and Morgenthau*, 8.

426 **if the facts were properly laid before the president:** See, for instance, Rosen, *Saving the Jews*, 341.

427 **where Roosevelt greeted them:** Blum, *Roosevelt and Morgenthau*, 531–32; Josiah DuBois interview, HMPA; "FDR Day by Day—The Pare Lorentz Chronology," January 16, 1944, FDRL. For simplicity, one may consult the account in Beschloss, *The Conquerors*, 56.

428 **"those terrible eighteen months":** For this paragraph see Blum, *Roosevelt and Morgenthau*, table of contents; Beschloss, *The Conquerors*, 58; MacGregor Burns, *Soldier of Freedom*, 346–48 (including "You punch it"). Other scholars, such as Wyman, have described the period of inactivity as fourteen months. The War Refugee Board estimates that it saved 200,000 Jews; see *Mostly Morgenthaus*, 335. Others put the figure at tens of thousands; see Henry Feingold, *The Politics of Rescue*, 307; see also Wyman, *Abandonment*, 331.

CHAPTER 13

433 **The rolls of the death camps:** I am indebted to Rachel Dillan for helping me compile this list of American Jews who could have perished in the Holocaust; for more about them, see Biography.com.

435 **"The Nazis entered":** see the outstanding work by Donald L. Miller, *Masters of the Air: America's Bomber Boys Who Fought the Air War Against Nazi Germany* (Simon & Schuster, 2006), 255–57; 260–66; Walter S. Moody, "Big Week: Gaining Air Superiority over the Luftwaffe," *Air Power History* 41, no. 2 (Summer 1994); Robert N. Rosen, *Saving the Jews* (Thunder's Mouth, 2006), 366; Charles Murphy, "The Unknown Battle," *Life*, October 16, 1944, 104; Bernard Lawrence Boylan, "The Development of the American Long-Range Escort Fighter," PhD dissertation, University of Missouri, 1955, 218–19.

435 **"We are over there":** This paragraph is drawn heavily from Rosen, *Saving the Jews*, 348; see also David S. Wyman, *The Abandonment of the Jews* (New Press, 1984), 219–29; "History of the WRB," FDRL, 289.

435 **WRB scoured Europe:** For efforts by WRB, see Wyman, *Abandonment*, 209–20.

436 **"all oppressed peoples":** For establishment of an American haven for Jews, ibid., 268–72; Rosen, *Saving the Jews*, 362; Harvey Strum, "Fort Ontario Refugee Shelter, 1944–1946," *American Jewish History* 63 (September 1983–June 1984), 404; Richard Breitman and Alan Kraut, *American Refugee Policy and European Jewry, 1933–1945* (Indiana University Press, 1988), 197–99.

437 **Hungary:** For the takeover of Hungry, I draw on Kershaw, *Hitler*, 795.

438 **"enlarged also to":** William Hassett, *Off the Record with FDR* (Rutgers University Press, 1958), 239. "In one of the blackest crimes": Michael Beschloss, *The Conquerors* (Simon & Schuster, 2002), 59; Wyman, *Abandonment*, 237; complete text is online. Actually, Roosevelt's original statement drafted by the WRB was stronger, but Sam Rosenman watered it down, saying its explicit and sole mention of the Jews would weaken it. Nonetheless the statement—about Hitler's "insane criminal desires," among other things—was a departure from the past and electrifying. Roosevelt also had cleared it with Stalin and Churchill in advance.

439 **"Roosevelt Warns Germans":** *New York Times*, March 26, 1944; Rosen, *Saving the Jews*, 358, 356.

440 **"Germans!":** Eisenhower's statement may be found, among other places, in Rosen, *Saving the Jews*, 356–57, or online.

441 **"Jews in Hungary":** *New York Times*, May 10, 1944, A1, for these paragraphs.

443 **1944 was an election year:** On the Japanese American question, Kai Bird, *The Chairman* (Simon & Schuster, 1942), 171, makes the point that politics proved to be a strong motivator. McCloy also early on talked about the Constitution as if it were a scrap of paper when weighed against security concerns; see Jean Edward Smith, *FDR* (Random House, 2008), 551.

443 **John Jay McCloy:** I rely strongly on Bird, *Chairman*, a Pulitzer prize–winning biography; on McCloy's mother and his early years, see 27–28.

444 **When McCloy was twelve:** For these paragraphs, ibid., 28–46, 50–53.

444 **German secret agents:** Ibid., 77.

445 **"obsessed":** Ibid., 126, 138.

445 **"an enemy fleet":** Ibid., 142–43 and 147–49, from which this paragraph is drawn.

446 **"hysteria and lack of judgment":** Smith, *FDR*, 549–50. By this stage, J. Edgar Hoover was in his twentieth year. He also called the evacuation "utterly unwarranted." For other material here, see Bird, *Chairman*, 148–49.

446 **"Constitution is just a scrap of paper":** Significantly, the Fourteenth Amendment to the Constitution provided American citizenship to all those born in the United States regardless of ethnic heritage or their parents' status. For this reason, Smith, *FDR*, rightly describes the whole incident as "shabby." For other material, see Bird, *Chairman*, 148–49.

446 **As McCloy put it:** From Bird, *Chairman*, 151–52. For a significantly different picture of Roosevelt's and McCloy's actions, see H. W. Brands, *Traitor to His Class* (Doubleday, 2008), 489–92. Brands makes the points that Roosevelt was following a historical practice of focusing on enemy aliens during wartime; that Roosevelt did not deport the Japanese Americans but instead detained them; and that Roosevelt was unwilling to risk another Pearl Harbor. For her part, Doris Kearns Goodwin, *No Ordinary Time* (Simon & Schuster, 1994), describes this decision as "tragic," quotes the American Civil Liberties Union as saying that it was "the worst single wholesale violation of civil rights of American citizens in our history," and adds that the claim of military necessity was fueled by "racism," 321–22, especially 321. Regarding the influence of McCloy on national security matters, Bird writes that McCloy "became the country's first national security manager, a sort of 'political commissar' who quietly brokered any issue where civilian political interests threatened to interfere with the military's effort to win the war," *Chairman*, 175. For a short biography of McCloy, see Alan Brinkley, "Minister Without Portfolio," *Harper's*, February 1983, 31–46.

446 **"We have carte blanche":** See Bird, *Chairman*, 149–50. For more on the evacuation of Japanese Americans, see the work by Robert Dallek, *Franklin D. Roosevelt and American Foreign Policy 1932–1945* (Oxford University Press, 1979), 334–37. Dallek makes the point that Roosevelt was rarely theoretical and pursued "military necessity" above all else. Roosevelt even joked to Hoover, "Have you pretty well cleaned out the alien waiters in the principal Washington hotels?" Dallek says that Roosevelt's hypocrisy on these matters is "striking," 336. He points out that at the time when the president was railing against Nazi "barbarism" and speaking about "the great upsurge of human liberty" in America, he was egregiously violating the constitutional guarantees of Japanese Americans.

447 **inside the camps:** For more details on the internment, see Bird, *Chairman*, 153–55, 160–61; and Smith, *FDR*, 551–53. "No federal penitentiary": Michi Nishigiura Wegyln, *Years of Infamy: The Untold Story of America's Concentration Camps* (University of Washington Press, 1995), 156.

448 **about the continuing internment, and challenges:** James MacGregor Burns, *Roosevelt: The Soldier of Freedom, 1940–1945* (Harcourt, 1970), 463.

449 **"The bombing has to be made":** For this and Jacob Rosenheim's efforts, I've drawn from Bird, *Chairman*, 211; Michael Gilbert, *Auschwitz and the Allies* (Holt, 1981), 237; Wyman, *Abandonment*, 290–91.

449 **"There is little doubt":** On McClelland's efforts, see Harrison Gerhardt (McClelland) to Secretary of State for War Refugee Board, 6/24/44, ASW,

400, 38, Jews, box 44, RG 107, NA; see also Bird, *Chairman*, 212, a summary that I employ. Clearly McClelland was going out on a limb, and this underscores how the evidence about the slaughter of the Jews was becoming increasingly horrifying.

450 **"A little rivalry":** See MacGregor Burns, *Soldier of Freedom*, 343, on Roosevelt's management style.

450 **"several doubts about":** Quotes can be found in Bird, *Chairman*, 213, as can the original memo, a copy of which the author has. See also Dino Brugioni and Robert Poirier, *The Holocaust Revisited: A Retrospective Analysis of the Auschwitz Birkenau Extermination Complex* (Central Intelligence Agency, 1979), 5.

451 **Benjamin Akzin, was livid:** For the bombing debate and the military's reluctance, see the excellent work *The Bombing of Auschwitz: Should the Allies Have Attempted It*?, Michael Neufeld and Michael Berenbaum, eds. (University Press of Kansas with United States Holocaust Memorial Museum, 2003), especially 276. For a number of provocative and fascinating essays on whether or not to bomb Auschwitz, 80–181. See also the essay by Gerhart Riegner, who was of course a key actor in the drama; he feels betrayed by the Allies who failed to act when given the information. The criticized essay by Tammy Biddle is a good overview. The editors also helpfully put together all the principal documents, making their book an invaluable resource; see 240–81. For my purposes, I have used copies of originals in the WRB files. See also Bird, *Chairman*, 213–14, for a summary.

452 **So effective were the bombing raids:** See Richard Davis, *Carl Spaatz and the Air War in Europe* (Smithsonian Institution Press for Center for Air Force History, 1993); Wesley Frank Craven and James Lea Cate, *The Army Air Forces in World War II*, 7 vols. (University of Chicago Press, 1948–1958). See also Gilbert, *Auschwitz and the Allies*, 283, 301–8, especially 307.

453 **On August 27:** See Gilbert, *Auschwitz and the Allies*, 311.

453 **took aerial photographs:** Ibid., 309–10; Gilbert is superb on this, and I draw on him. I also rely on Dino Brugioni, "The Aerial Photos of the Auschwitz Birkenau Extermination Complex," in Neufeld and Berenbaum ed., *The Bombing of Auschwitz* (Kansas Press, 2000), 52–58. Brugioni points out that the Birkenau complex was photographed at least thirty times. He carries special authority on this issue, as he was a member of a bomber crew during World War II and then, after being hired by the Central Intelligence Agency in 1948, became a founder of the National Photographic Interpretation Center. Reexamining the photos later in time, he was surprised to find that they did indeed show considerable activity relating to the Holocaust at both Auschwitz and Birkenau—evidence that was completely overlooked after 1944 and early 1945. Among other images, people could be clearly

seen being marched to their deaths or being processed for slave labor. Walter Laqueur, *The Terrible Secret: Suppression of the Truth About Hitler's "Final Solution"* (Little, Brown, 1980), 84–86, asserts that the intelligence services, such as British cryptologists who were able to track large numbers of trains carrying Jews to the Silesian death camps, suppressed the information. It is also possible that Churchill saw other evidence of the death camps. See also Peter Calvocorressi, *Top-Secret Ultra* (Ballantine, 1981), 16. In this memoir, Calvocorressi, a British veteran of Bletchley Park, maintains that fellow cryptologists began intercepting the daily statistics radioed to Berlin from each concentration camp. Strikingly, he says the intercepts detailed the number of new arrivals, the number of inmates in each camp, and the number killed. If so, Bletchley Park would have been expected to inform the British policy makers.

453 **"the tremendous rumble":** Gilbert, *Auschwitz and the Allies*, 301, 308.

453 **"We are no longer":** Robert L. Beir with Brian Josepher, *Roosevelt and the Holocaust: A Rooseveltian Examines the Policies and Remembers the Times* (Barricade, 2006), 254; Elie Wiesel, *Night* (Avon, 1958); Primo Levi, *Survival in Auschwitz* (Summit, 1986), 388; see also Bird, *Chairman*, 214.

454 **"methodical German mind":** I have taken these quotes from the original documents; they may also be found in Bird, *Chairman*, 214–15. One of the strongest arguments against bombing has been that it applies twenty-first-century morals to World War II. Akzin's devastating memo shreds this notion.

455 **"so terrible that it is hard":** Quotes and emerging details of the death camps are taken from Bird, *Chairman*, 214–16. See also Neufeld and Berenbaum, *The Bombing of Auschwitz*, 274–79, for reproductions of the relevant memos.

457 **Eden sat down with Churchill:** See Gilbert, *Auschwitz and the Allies*, 276–77; Bird, *Chairman*, 217. Churchill also roared that he was entirely in accord with making "the biggest outcry possible," Gilbert, *Auschwitz and the Allies*, 276. There is no doubt that Churchill's eloquence was unequivocal and heartfelt.

458 **he had received harsh criticism:** For the pressure on the regime in Hungary, see Gilbert, *Auschwitz and the Allies*, 266, on which I heavily leaned; on the decision to cease the deportations, see, 292, 302. Significantly, the bombing of Budapest also hit government buildings and private homes, further increasing the pressure.

458 **death trains still . . . rolled in:** Bird, *Chairman*, 217.

458 **Raoul Wallenberg:** See Wyman, *Abandonment*, 240–43. Rosen, *Saving the Jews*, 464–65, presents a more skeptical view, referring to Wallenberg as an American agent.

459 **yellow stars to the clothes:** Gilbert, *Auschwitz and the Allies*, 293.

460 **"is out of our power":** For these quotes, Bird, *Chairman*, 214.

460 **In early August:** See the extraordinary exchange of letters between McCloy and Kubowitzki, August 9 and August 14, reproduced in Neufeld and Berenbaum, *The Bombing of Auschwitz*, 273–74.

461 **"It will be difficult":** Gilbert, *Auschwitz and the Allies*, 311.

463 **"It was a sort of operation":** *New York Times*, October 29, 1943, 7. Advocates of bombing Auschwitz were in general aware of this remarkable operation.

463 **In tiny Albania:** *New York Times*, November 19, 2013, A9.

464 **"How beautiful was it":** Gilbert, *Auschwitz and the Allies*, 315.

465 **assault against the Nazis in Warsaw:** I extensively used Kershaw, *Hitler*, 868; online sources, such as www.warsawuprising.com; Gordon Corrigan, *The Second World War: A Military History* (Thomas Dunne, 2011), 476–77; Neil Orpen, *Airlift to Warsaw: The Rising of 1944* (University of Oklahoma Press, 1984). On the Warsaw ghetto itself, read the rare wartime firsthand account by an escapee, Tosha Bialer, "Behind the Wall (Life—and Death—in Warsaw's Ghetto)," *Collier's*, February 20, 1943, 17–18, 66–67; February 27, 1943, 29–33. This powerful story reached millions of Americans only two months after the Allies confirmed a mass killing of European Jews; it included haunting photographs of children with legs like toothpicks sleeping in abandoned newsstands. See also Robert H. Abzug, *America Views the Holocaust 1933–1945: A Documentary History* (St. Martin's, 1999). For Slessor's account of the Warsaw uprising, see *The Central Blue: The Autobiography of Sir John Slessor, RAF* (Praeger, 1957), 611–21.

466 **begged for resupply:** For the complex politics of resupplying the Polish Resistance, and quotes ("Do you want me"), I draw on Slessor, *Central Blue*, 620; MacGregor Burns, *Soldier of Freedom*, 534–37; Dallek, *Franklin D. Roosevelt and American Foreign Policy*, 517–21; and Smith, *FDR*, 630–31.

467 **willing to divert considerable airpower:** See Wyman, *Abandonment*, 306; Slessor, *Central Blue*, 620.

467 **"Despite the tangible cost":** Wyman, *Abandonment*, 306.

468 **The war would . . . be won:** Goodwin, *No Ordinary Time*, 520; American Heritage, *New History of World War II* (Ambrose), 488–503; MacGregor Burns, *Soldier of Freedom*, 553.

468 **he contacted McCloy:** See the exchange of memos between John Pehle and John J. McCloy, November 8 and November 18, 1944, in Neufeld and Berenbaum, *The Bombing of Auschwitz*, 278–80. The contemporary literature about bombing Auschwitz is extensive, highly detailed, at times confusing or misleading, and often fascinating. The leading proponent of bombing is Wyman, in *Abandonment*; two of his principal critics are James H. Kitchens III and Richard H. Levy, who marshal facts about the availability and

accuracy of bombers: German defenses; and the distance and placement of targets. Their central point is that it was not militarily practicable or feasible to bomb Auschwitz. However, Stuart G. Erdheim all but demolishes their arguments in a highly detailed rebuttal. Erdheim methodically points out that the failure to bomb resulted not from operational impracticability but from the Allies' mind-set and Roosevelt's policies. He points out that the logic of the critics would have led to aborting countless other World War II bombing missions. In his rigorous argument, Erdheim takes into account Luftwaffe fighter defenses, the status of German air defenses, the accuracy of bombing, weather, and other factors. There is little doubt, from what he writes, that P38 or Mosquito fighters using low-level precision bombing could have attacked Auschwitz. So could heavy bombers, though the casualties would have been greater. Erdheim's reasoning is buttressed independently by the Air Force historian Rondall R. Rice, who points out that the Fifteenth Air Force, with B17s and B24s, had both the technical means and a window of opportunity to bomb Auschwitz with a "high probability of success"; the only reason it did not do so was a lack of political will. The distinguished military historian Williamson Murray insists that the military was preoccupied with the invasion of France and was working around the clock; but another military historian, Richard G. Davis, takes issue with that. Richard Breitman, for one, points out that on the basis of intelligence reports received in 1943, a raid could have been planned for early 1944, if there were the political will. There is also a hypothetical scenario: if Roosevelt had ordered an attack at the time of his March 24, 1944, speech, and it took place just as the Hungarian deportations were about to commence, the Nazis' killing process would have been severely impeded. It took eight months to build the complex industrial killing machines when Nazi Germany was at the zenith of its strength; in the spring of 1944, for a depleted Third Reich, rebuilding would have been very difficult. As to the contention that bombing Auschwitz is an ahistorical debate, reflecting our values in the twenty-first century, Benjamin Akzin's memorandum completely undermines that claim. Levy suggests that the Jewish community was considerably divided; by way of comparison, so was the Union during the Civil War, but this didn't stop Abraham Lincoln from issuing the Emancipation Proclamation or from forming Negro fighting units in the army. For the back-and-forth in these articles and more, see the individual essays in Neufeld and Berenbaum, *The Bombing of Auschwitz.* For discussions of accuracy and comparisons between the American and British bombing forces, see W. Hays Parks, " 'Precision' and 'Area' Bombing: Who Did Which, and When?" *Journal of Strategic Studies* 18 (March 1995): 145–74. For general discussions, see Richard G. Davis, "German Railyards and Cities: US Bombing Policy, 1944–1945," *Air*

Power History 42 (Summer 1995): 47–63; and Tammy Davis Biddle, "Air War," in Michael Howard, George Andreopoulos, and Mark Shulman, eds., *The Laws of War* (Yale University Press, 1994). On the degradation of Germany from the air assault by the Allies, see especially Alfred C. Mierzejewski, *The Collapse of the German War Economy, 1944–1945* (University of North Carolina Press, 1988). Around this time the Germans were seeking to divert the Allies with their "blood for goods" proposal: See Yehuda Bauer, *Jews for Sale? Nazi-Jewish Negotiations, 1933–1945* (Yale University Press, 1944); and Richard Breitman and Shlomo Aronson, "The End of the 'Final Solution'? Nazi Plans to Ransom Jews in 1944," *Central European History* 25 (1992); 177–203. For general discussions, see Verne Newton, ed., *FDR and the Holocaust* (St. Martin's, 1996).

470 **"I am certain that":** Rosen, *Saving the Jews*, 398.

471 **history records a question mark:** See the discussion in Brands, *Traitor to His Class*, 570. Brands sees the issue very differently from Goodwin in *No Ordinary Time* or Smith in *FDR*, for example. Both Goodwin and Smith see Roosevelt's failure to take stronger action as a considerable moral and political lapse, even a stain, on his otherwise stellar leadership during World War II. In hindsight, although Roosevelt left few fingerprints on the issue, there are subtle clues that he realized history might not judge inaction regarding the Jews very well. If one reads Henry Morgenthau's diary entry of December 3, 1942, one sees Roosevelt grasping for some solution that would at least save the living Jews who had escaped Hitler's clutches by providing them with a sustainable homeland in Palestine. He had ideas for Jews outside Europe as well as those in "the heart of Europe." The president told Morgenthau, "I am studying many other places in the world where the refugees from Europe can be moved." Morgenthau was surprised "that the president was studying this thing with so much interest and had gone as far as he had in making up his mind on what he wants to do. It was most encouraging to me and most heartening." See "Concerning Placing Jewish Refugees," Morgenthau Diary, December 3, 1942, in *America and the Holocaust: Responsibility for America's Failure*, Volume 13, David S. Wyman, ed. (Garland, 1991), 8–9. See also Abzug, *America Views the Holocaust*, 134–35.

472 **"spark of courageous leadership":** See Wyman, *Abandonment*, 313. For "between knowing and not knowing," it comes from the Protestant theologian W. A. Visser't Hooft. I found this beautiful quote in Bird, *Chairman*, 222.

CHAPTER 14

474 **"There is no news":** David Brinkley, *Washington Goes to War* (Random House, 1999), 255.

474 **"our present chaos":** Ibid.; and James MacGregor Burns, *Roosevelt: The Soldier of Freedom, 1940–1945* (Harcourt, 1970), 499–501.

475 **"a reputation for":** MacGregor Burns, *Soldier of Freedom*, 502–3; Brinkley, *Washington*, 260.

476 **"I have got something else":** See Brinkley, *Washington*, 257–58. We can still see how Roosevelt came alive in the campaign. He loved nothing more than to be coy and then surprise his opponents.

476 **finding a new vice presidential candidate:** Ibid., 259–60; MacGregor Burns, *Soldier of Freedom*, 504–5. I have drawn on both for these two paragraphs.

477 **"I shall not campaign":** See MacGregor Burns, *Soldier of Freedom*, 506: Roosevelt's acceptance speech is also online.

477 **"What is the job":** MacGregor Burns, *Soldier of Freedom*, 507. For more on Lincoln's second inaugural address, which remains the finest presidential speech in history, see Jay Winik, *April 1865* (HarperCollins, 2001), 34–36.

478 **"His face took on":** See Doris Kearns Goodwin, *No Ordinary Time* (Simon & Schuster, 1994), 529. It is interesting that even now Roosevelt was bubbling with ideas, such as irrigating the Sahara Desert. At his core, even while he was a realist, he always remained a palpable idealist.

479 **The photo the AP editor picked:** See Goodwin, *No Ordinary Time*, 529–30; Samuel Rosenman, *Working with Roosevelt* (Harper, 1952), 453; Brinkley, *Washington*; MacGregor Burns, *Soldier of Freedom*, 508. Dick Strobel, who took the photo, said "all hell broke loose" when it appeared; not unlike presidential staffers today, Roosevelt's people were furious with the AP. For these delicious details, Goodwin interviewed Strobel. According to MacGregor Burns, the intense concern about Roosevelt's health gave rise to a rumor that he had had a secret operation at Hobcaw Barony in May.

480 **"The man who":** See Kershaw, *Hitler*, 816–841, for a detailed account of the assassination attempt; quotation, 818.

481 **"Hello, Doug":** Jean Edward Smith, *FDR* (Random House, 2008), 620; Goodwin, *No Ordinary Time*, 530–31.

481 **including a military hospital:** On the extraordinary scene in the military hospital, where Roosevelt for the first time let his guard down, see Rosenman, *Working with Roosevelt*, 458; Smith, *FDR*, 621; Goodwin, *No Ordinary Time*, 532.

482 **"He is just a shell":** Smith, *FDR*, 622; William Manchester, *American Caesar, 1880–1964* (Little, Brown, 1978), 369. MacArthur was of course prescient; Of note, he did think Roosevelt was a man of "great vision" once he had all the facts.

483 **"tepid and halting":** MacGregor Burns, *Soldier of Freedom*, 507–9; on Bruenn's observations, see Goodwin, *No Ordinary Time*, 537. By way of comparison, during the Civil War, Robert E. Lee suffered from angina, which

prematurely aged him. For the speech in Bremerton, see Rosenman, *Working with Roosevelt*, 461–62. For more on FDR's collapse, see Elliott Roosevelt and James Brough, *A Rendezvous with Destiny: The Roosevelts of the White House* (Putnam, 1975), 378.

483 **"It looks like":** See Rosenman, *Working with Roosevelt*, 462; Smith, *FDR*, 623.

483 **Five days after:** See William Hassett, *Off the Record with FDR* (Rutgers University Press, 1958), 266–67.

483 **"For months, he had":** Brinkley, *Washington*, 262. This blunt observation was typical of Brinkley, who would later become the dean of the Washington press corps.

485 **estate in northern New Jersey:** Goodwin, *No Ordinary Time*, 541–42. This time Roosevelt managed to see Lucy again at Tranquility Farms. During this period, Churchill was recovering from a bout with pneumonia.

485 **Quebec summit:** For the following paragraphs, I drew heavily on Lord Moran, *Churchill: Taken from the Diaries of Lord Moran—The Struggle for Survival, 1940–1965* (Houghton Mifflin, 1966), 192; Smith, *FDR*, 623–24; Cordell Hull, *The Memoirs of Cordell Hull*, 2 vols. (Macmillan, 1948), 1613–21; MacGregor Burns, *Soldier of Freedom*, 519–21. Anthony Eden and Churchill exchanged sharp words about the Morgenthau plan, with Eden insisting that Churchill could not support it; in the end, Eden had his way.

485 **"The German people":** See Robert Dallek, *Franklin D. Roosevelt and American Foreign Policy, 1932–1945* (Oxford University Press, 1979), 473.

486 **"tired old men":** See Goodwin, *No Ordinary Time*, 546–47. This phrase is actually Goodwin's, indicating the spirit of Dewey's campaign. Rosenman makes the point that Roosevelt had to learn to walk with his braces all over again. See Rosenman, *Working with Roosevelt*, 474.

486 **The new Statler Hotel:** Brinkley, *Washington*, 253–54.

487 **"He was literally trying":** Rosenman, *Working with Roosevelt*, 474.

487 **The room was packed:** Ibid., 478; for these two paragraphs, and quotes, I drew extensively on Rosenman, "The old master": *Time*, October 2, 1944, 21. See also MacGregor Burns, *Soldier of Freedom*, 521–23; Goodwin, *No Ordinary Time* 547–48. On the joke about Fala, see Franklin D. Roosevelt, *Public Papers and Addresses, 1944–45* (Harper, 1950), 290, also online.

488 **surrendered in Warsaw:** See especially Kershaw, *Hitler*, 868. In an act of continuing spite, Hitler turned the city over, not to the Wehrmacht, but instead to Himmler and the SS for destruction.

488 **pulled into New York:** For Roosevelt's campaign in New York, I rely on the excellent accounts in Goodwin, *No Ordinary Time*, 549–51; and MacGregor Burns, *Soldier of Freedom*, 525–26—the latter calls the day in New

York a double triumph. For the apartment, Eleanor Roosevelt, *This I Remember* (Harper, 1949), 337. For "Peace, like war," Franklin D. Roosevelt, *Public Papers, 1944*, 350.

490 **"The President is in the pink":** Hassett, *Off the Record*, 282. Hassett could not have been more wrong; Roosevelt would not bury his detractors. For the following three paragraphs, and election results, see Harold Gosnell, *Champion Campaigner: Franklin D. Roosevelt*, (Macmillan, 1952), 211–12.

491 **"son-of-a-bitch":** (Roosevelt's quip) Hassett, *Off the Record*, 294.

492 **had a plan:** On Hitler and his desperate efforts at this time, Gordon Corrigan, *The Second World War: A Military History* (Thomas Dunne, 2011), 457, 485–88.

494 **"not clinically insane":** For Hitler's diminishing health and his phobias, ibid., 488; and Kershaw, *Hitler*, 869–71. The phrase "gullible population" is Kershaw's. Kershaw does note that aided and abetted by his quack doctor, Theodore Morrell, Hitler almost certainly did suffer from psychiatric and personality disorders.

495 **so that the *Sonderkommando*:** For handy reference, see Sybelle Steinbacher, *Auschwitz: A History* (Harper Perennial, 2005), 96–104, 119–21; Martin Gilbert, *Auschwitz and the Allies* (Holt, 1981), 324–26 naming other places.

497 **had liberated Majdanek:** See Richard Lauterbach, "Murder, Inc.," *Time*, September 11, 1944, 36. The Soviets saw the showers, the gas chambers, the double rows of electrically charged barbed wire, the "road of death," the room full of passports and documents—and the "sea of shoes, 820,000 pairs, piled, like pieces of coal," of which the correspondent wrote movingly: "Majdenek suddenly became real. It was no longer a half remembered sequence from an old movie or a clipping from Pravda or chapters from a book by a German refugee." He also wrote of German food production: "Kill people; fertilize cabbages," after cutting bodies up scientifically before sliding them into coke-fed ovens. Remarkably, *Christian Century* wrote about this account as little more than exaggerations and fabrications: see "Biggest Atrocity Story Breaks in Poland," *Christian Century*, September 13, 1944, 1045. See also Robert H. Abzug, *America Views the Holocaust* (St. Martin's, 1999), 179–82.

498 **"Harvest Festival":** Martin Gilbert, *The Holocaust* (Holt, 1985), 627–32; on Majdanek, its liberation, and the Allies' advance, 706–11. Gilbert makes the point that "liberation and enslavement were taking place" at the same time on July 18, 1944. Photographs were published of charred human remains, arousing widespread horror. One SS brigadier fumed about the "slovenly . . . rabble" who did not "erase the traces" in time. See also accounts in Steinbacher, *Auschwitz*, 121; Gilbert, *The Holocaust*, 706–30; and Corrigan, *Second World War*, 474.

500 **Battle of the Bulge:** See Corrigan, *Second World War*, 535–38; Martin Gilbert, *The Second World War: A Complete History* (Owl, 1989), 626. For details, see the masterly account by Pulitzer Prize–winner Rick Atkinson, *The Guns at Last Light: The War in Western Europe, 1944–1945* (Holt, 2013), 412–92. For the battle, the demand for surrender, and my casualty figures, I have also drawn on Ambrose, *American Heritage*, 502–3.

502 **"off our neighbors' backs":** Elie Wiesel, *Night* (Hill and Wang, 2006), 96, 101–2; Gilbert, *Auschwitz and the Allies*, 333–38; Steinbacher, *Auschwitz*, 127–35; and U.S. Holocaust Memorial Museum, "Auschwitz," for the opening of Auschwitz. The reader may also go to YouTube for uncensored clips of the liberation of the camp and its aftermath. A related YouTube video of the liberation of Ohrdruf is particularly powerful, as local Nazis are forced to watch the results of their handiwork in the death camp itself; Gilbert has an account of this in *The Holocaust*, 790.

CHAPTER 15

507 **The day before his inauguration:** For these paragraphs see Franklin D. Roosevelt, *Public Papers and Addresses of Franklin D. Roosevelt, 1944–45* (Harper, 1950), 523; Samuel Rosenman, *Working with Roosevelt* (Harper, 1952), 516; and James MacGregor Burns, *Roosevelt: The Soldier of Freedom, 1940–1945* (Harcourt, 1970), 558–63, from which this account is drawn. Interestingly, after the ceremony Roosevelt held the largest luncheon of his twelve years in the White House: two thousand guests. For "a stabbing pain" and "thoroughly chilled" (a symbolic omen of what was to come), see James Roosevelt and Sydney Schalett, *Affectionately FDR* (Harcourt Brace, 1959), 355; and Doris Kearns Goodwin, *No Ordinary Time* (Simon & Schuster, 1994), 572–73. On the large luncheon, Bess Furman, *Washington By-Line* (Knopf, 1949), 3. On Japanese Americans' internment, Roger Daniels, *Concentration Camps USA: Japanese-Americans and World War II* (Holt, Rinehart and Winston, 1970); Allen Bosworth, *America's Concentration Camps* (Norton, 1967); Gordon Corrigan, *The Second World War: A Military History* (Thomas Dunne, 2011) 538; Allis Radosh and Ronald Radosh, *A Safe Haven: Harry S. Truman and the Founding of Israel* (Harper Perennial, 2010), 1. See also Bertram Hulen, "Shivering Thousands Stamp in Snow at Inauguration," *New York Times*, January 21, 1945, 1.

509 **worse place to meet than Yalta:** On the preparations for Yalta and opening of the summit, see H. W. Brands, *Traitor to His Class* (Doubleday, 2008), 592; Sara Churchill, *A Thread in the Tapestry* (Dodd, Mead, 1967), 76, 79–80; Charles Bohlen, *Witness to History, 1929–1969* (Norton, 1973), 174; Jean Edward Smith, 629–30; Robert Dallek, *Franklin D. Roosevelt and American*

Foreign Policy (Oxford University Press, 1998), *FDR* (Random House, 2008), 507–21.

510 **"terrible change":** On Roosevelt's declining health, Frances Perkins found him "looking very badly," although Bohlen insisted that "our leader was ill, but he was effective." See Bohlen, *Witness*, 177–84; Smith, *FDR*, 630–31; Dallek, *Franklin D. Roosevelt and American Foreign Policy*, 519.

510 **Roosevelt's maneuverings with Stalin:** He mentioned that de Gaulle compared himself to Joan of Arc; MacGregor Burns, *Soldier of Freedom*, 566.

513 **he was a Zionist:** Ibid., 577–78; Bohlen, *Witness*, 203; Radosh and Radosh, *Safe Haven*, 11, 25, Richard Breitman and Allan J. Lichtman, *FDR and the Jews* (Belknap Press, 2013), 301; Bohlen, 203.

514 **what was to become of Poland:** Supporters insist Roosevelt did all that could be done, while critics assert that he sold the Poles out; see Dallek, *Franklin D. Roosevelt and American Foreign Policy*, 514–15. For a very incisive account that is harshly critical of Roosevelt, see Amos Perlmutter, *FDR and Stalin: A Not So Grand Alliance, 1943–1945* (University of Missouri Press, 1993); see also Jonathan Fenby, *Alliance: The Inside Story of How Roosevelt, Stalin and Churchill Won One War and Began Another* (MacAdam/Cage, 2007). Goodwin, *No Ordinary Time*, 597, notes that after Yalta, relations between Stalin and Roosevelt reached a "point of crisis" because of the deteriorating situation in Poland. Stalin promptly violated his solemn promise that the Communist regime in Warsaw would hold free elections as well as broaden its base; instead, the Communists held on to power and took over, laying the groundwork for the Cold War.

515 **Ibn Saud of Saudi Arabia:** For details of the meeting, see especially "U.S. Warship Becomes Arab Court in Miniature for Ibn Saud's Voyage," *New York Times*, February 21, 1945, 1; "White House Announcement of New Talks," *New York Times*, February 21, 1945; William Eddy, *FDR Meets Ibn Saud* (American Friends of the Middle East, 1954), 31–32; Bohlen, *Witness*, 203–4, who basically recounts the meeting word-by-word, which stands as the basis for all other accounts; Breitmann and Lichtman, 302; MacGregor Burns, *Soldier of Freedom* 578–79; Radosh and Radosh, *Safe Haven*, 19, 26–27. Harry Hopkins, the president's adviser, was unwell, but nonetheless would later write that he felt the president had not fully comprehended what Ibn Saud was saying, particularly the fact that the Arabs would take up arms against the Jews almost no matter what.

518 **At Bergen-Belsen:** For Bergen-Belsen and the Frank family, see, for instance, Martin Gilbert, *The Holocaust* (Norton, 2012), 784–92; and Anne Frank, *The Diary of a Young Girl* (Longman, 1993).

520 **"We cannot fail them again":** For the joint session, MacGregor Burns, *Soldier of Freedom*, 581–82; Smith, *FDR*, 632–33; and the candid observations

of William Hassett, *Off the Record with FDR* (Rutgers University Press, 1998), 318.

520 **"powers of concentration":** On Roosevelt's sharp decline, see especially Hassett, *Off the Record*, 319–29; and Bohlen, *Witness*, 206.

522 **Ohrdruf:** On the liberation of Ohrdruf, a subcamp at Buchenwald, see, for instance, the first-person account by David Cohen, Jewish Virtual Library, online; and American Centuries, University of Massachusetts, oral history. Cohen was a radio operator with the Fourth Armored Division. Meanwhile, General Eisenhower, not prone to overstatement, called "the barbarous" treatment of the Jews "unbelievable." And he summoned members of Congress to become spokesmen to the world for the horror rendered by the Nazis. For his part, General Patton screamed, "See what these bastards did!" See also War History Online, Liberation of Ohrdruf; Gilbert, *The Holocaust*, 790–92.

525 **"that's all we thought about":** Elie Wiesel, *Night* (Hill and Wang, 2006), 115.

526 **"much better":** For Roosevelt's death, Smith, *FDR*, 635–36; Brands, *Traitor to His Class* 605–7; Goodwin, 602–3; Hassett, *Off the Record*, 332–37. Hassett was quite poetic about Roosevelt's passing, essentially making the point that everyone saw it coming, but nobody was really ready for it.

527 **collapsed "as they walked"** and **"I saw their corpses":** Gilbert, *The Holocaust*, 790–96.

528 **"Just the sight":** J. D. Pletcher, "The Americans Have Come—at Last!" in *The 71st Came . . . to Gunskirchen*, Witness to the Holocaust Publication Series, no. 1 (Emory University, 1979), 4–11; and reprint in Robert H. Abzug, *America Views the Holocaust* (St. Martin's, 1999), especially 195–96.

528 **funeral wreaths:** Goodwin, *No Ordinary Time*, especially 613–15, is particularly moving; for her assessment of Roosevelt, see 606–11. For "There was much rushing," see Robert Jackson, *The Man: An Insider's Portrait of Franklin Roosevelt* (Oxford University Press, 2003), 167.

531 **"You can't be Jews":** For this marvelous quote, originally in German, see Roger Moorhouse, *Berlin at War* (Basic Books, 2010), 306.

531 **A weary Abraham Lincoln:** For comparison with Lincoln, see Jay Winik, *April 1865* (Harper Collins, 2001), 247–49; Alan Guelzo, *Lincoln's Emancipation Proclamation: The End of Slavery in America* (Simon & Schuster, 2006).

532 **Estimates of war dead:** Allis Radosh and Ronald Radosh, *A Safe Haven* (Harper Perennial, 2009), 2; Tony Judt, *Postwar: A History of Europe Since 1945* (Penguin Press, 2005, 17–18.

533 **"How much his passing":** Jackson, *The Man*, 169, 158.

533 **"He was one":** Isaiah Berlin, *Personal Safe Impressions*, Henry Handy, ed. (Viking, 1981), 26. For other assessments of Roosevelt, see the following.

New York Times, April 13, 1945, 18: "It was his leadership which inspired freemen in every part of the world to fight with greater hope and courage." Brands, *Traitor to His Class*, 613–14. Eric Larrabee, *Commander-in-Chief: Franklin Delano Roosevelt, His Lieutenants, and Their War* (Harper and Row, 1987), 644; Larrabee writes that Roosevelt's conduct as commander in chief "bears the mark of greatness." William Leuchtenberg, *Franklin D. Roosevelt and the New Deal* (Harper and Row, 1963), 327; Leuchtenberg writes that under Roosevelt "the White House became the focus of all government—the Fountainhead of ideas, the initiator of action, the representative of the national interest. [He] re-created the modern presidency." Roosevelt himself once said, "I am like a cat. I make a quick stroke and then I relax"; here, perhaps, was one secret of his greatness. See also James MacGregor Burns, *Leadership* (Harper and Row, 1978), 281.

534 **"his enormous popularity":** Bohlen, *Witness*, 210.

INDEX

Page numbers in *italics* refer to illustrations.

ABOUT THE AUTHOR

The author of the *New York Times* and #1 bestselling *April 1865* and the *New York Times* bestseller *The Great Upheaval*, Jay Winik is renowned for his creative approaches to history. The *Baltimore Sun* called him "one of our nation's leading public historians." He is a popular public speaker and a frequent television and radio guest. He has been a regular contributor to the *Wall Street Journal* book review section as well as to the *New York Times*. His many national media appearances include the *Today* show, *Good Morning America, World News Tonight,* and NPR, and he covered both of Obama's historic inaugurations as a FOX News presidential historian. He is a former board member of the National Endowment for the Humanities and was a historical advisor to National Geographic Networks.